Joanne CREAN

P. 584 . Competence .

HEALTH AND SAFETY
LAW AND PRACTICE
(Second Edition)

UNITED KINGDOM
Sweet & Maxwell Ltd
London

AUSTRALIA
Law Book Co.
Sydney

CANADA and USA
Carswell
Toronto

NEW ZEALAND
Brookers
Wellington

SINGAPORE AND MALAYSIA
Sweet & Maxwell
Singapore and Kuala Lumpur

Health and Safety
Law and Practice
(Second Edition)

GEOFFREY SHANNON

B.Comm., LL.B., LL.M.

DUBLIN
ROUND HALL LTD
2007

Published in 2007 by
Round Hall Ltd
43 Fitzwilliam Place
Dublin 2
Ireland

Typeset by
Datapage International Limited
Dublin

Printed by
MPG Books, Cornwall

A CIP catalogue record for this book is available
from the British Library

ISBN 978-1-85800-439-6

FOREWORD

The First Edition of this work published in 2002 has proved invaluable to practitioners, students and safety, health and welfare professionals. The necessity for a Second Edition reflects the rapid changes which have taken place in this area of the law in just four short years. The Author deals comprehensively with the Safety, Health and Welfare at Work Act 2005 and Regulations made under the same, including the Safety, Health and Welfare at Work (General Application) Regulations 2007 and the Safety, Health and Welfare at Work (Construction) Regulations 2006. A separate chapter has been devoted to each of these Regulations. However, the scope of the work extends well beyond the 2005 Act and Regulations under the same. Each problem area is considered in terms of the common law as well as statutory intervention. The chapter on bullying, harassment and stress as health and safety issues is particularly impressive considering these problems in light of the common law in terms of torts and wrongful dismissal, the Unfair Dismissal Acts, the Employment Equality Acts and drawing on authorities from within and without this jurisdiction. Equally impressive is the manner in which the Author deals with occupiers' liability, issues relating to pregnancy, smoking in the workplace and young persons. It will be abundantly clear from the foregoing that the issues covered in the book extend far beyond those of interest only to specialists in employment and health and safety law. Within these covers will be found answers to problems which will be presented to specialists and non-specialists alike. I recommend to barristers and solicitors that they should find space for it on their book shelves.

I congratulate the Author on the success of the First Edition of his book, on his industry in preparing this Second Edition and thank him for the benefit which his labours will confer on his fellow practitioners and all those who are concerned with the areas of the law of which he treats.

The Hon. Mr. Justice Joseph Finnegan
The Supreme Court

PREFACE

There have been many changes in health and safety law since the first edition of this book was published in 2002. The second edition of *Health and Safety: Law and Practice* attempts to describe the main elements of the legal developments introduced since 2002. It is hoped that this second edition will act as a guide to the new and emerging workplace health and safety issues.

Part I of this book sets out the principal elements of the law on safety and health at work. Part II provides some useful precedent documentation and guidance material. Parts III and IV consist primarily of relevant Acts and Regulations on Safety and Health, together with authoritative Guidelines published by the Health and Safety Authority on the most significant risks that arise in the workplace.

The Safety, Health and Welfare at Work Act 2005 (hereafter "the 2005 Act") has now largely replaced the Safety, Health and Welfare at Work Act 1989. The 2005 Act, discussed in chapter 3, places increased emphasis on deterrence by the strengthening of the enforcement provisions. In many ways, the 2005 Act reflects and accommodates the radical changes that have taken place in the nature of work in Ireland since the 1989 Act was introduced.

The 2005 Act imposes new obligations on every employer in the prevention of harassment, bullying and stress-related injuries in the workplace. Chapter 4 considers these issues in terms of minimising liability and managing risks. The Regulations implemented under the 2005 Act are considered in chapters 5, 6 and 7.

Chemical agents and dangerous substances are examined in chapter 8. This chapter also considers REACH, the new omnibus Regulation which entered into force on June 1, 2007. It significantly alters the manner in which industry registers, evaluates, authorises and restricts chemical products throughout the EU.

The ban on smoking in the workplace is evaluated in chapter 9. The smoking ban has enjoyed a high level of compliance in Ireland which indicates a sea change in Irish society's attitude to smoking.

Chapters 18 and 19 examine the sanctions provided under the 2005 Act. They are significantly greater than those provided under the 1989 Act. Both individuals and corporate bodies may be prosecuted. The 2005 Act introduces new offences for directors, employers, officers and senior managers who, for the first time, could be personally liable for breaches of health and safety legislation. The "guilty until proven innocent" provision in the 2005 Act is likely to be very useful to the Health and Safety Authority and the DPP in initiating prosecutions under the 2005 Act. It should be stated, however, that the success of health and safety legislation is not merely dependent on ensuring compliance with statutory provisions but also depends on changing mindsets. The second edition of this book concludes by considering the duty of care likely to be imposed on employers in the future.

Given the volume of legislation to be considered in the health and safety area at present, it seems appropriate to recall a portion of US President Abraham Lincoln's first State of the Union address in 1861:

> "The statute laws should be made as plain and intelligible as possible, and be reduced to as small a compass as may consist with the fullness and precision of the will of the legislature and the perspicuity of its language".

It is hoped that the newly consolidated 2007 General Application Regulations will assist, to a significant extent, in achieving what Lincoln propounded by making our way through the myriad of regulatory laws in the health and safety area much easier.

I would like to thank Thomson Round Hall for publishing the second edition of this book. In addition, I would like to acknowledge the assistance of Roberta Guiry and Catherine Dolan of Thomson Round Hall in bringing this book to completion. Thanks also to the library staff in the Law Society for all their help.

While every effort has been made to cover the law on the basis of materials available to me in September 2007, I accept no responsibility for any errors or omissions.

Geoffrey Shannon
September 2007

CONTENTS

PART II

PART III

PART IV

TABLE OF CASES

IRISH CASES

EMPLOYMENT APPEALS TRIBUNAL DECISIONS

LABOUR COURT DECISIONS

ENGLISH CASES

NORTHERN IRISH CASES

SCOTTISH CASES

UNITED STATES OF AMERICA CASES

AUSTRALIAN CASES

EUROPEAN COURT OF JUSTICE CASES

EUROPEAN COURT OF HUMAN RIGHTS CASES

TABLE OF LEGISLATION

IRISH STATUTES

IRISH STATUTORY INSTRUMENTS

EUROPEAN REGULATIONS

EUROPEAN DIRECTIVES

ENGLISH STATUTES

ENGLISH STATUTORY INSTRUMENTS

NORTHERN IRISH STATUTES

TREATY OF THE EUROPEAN UNION

THE IRISH CONSTITUTION

EUROPEAN CONVENTION ON HUMAN RIGHTS

CANADIAN STATUTES

PART I

CHAPTER 1

INTRODUCTION

1–01 The focus of this book is on the legislative and common law positions relating to health and safety and the consequent implications for employers and employees. It reviews in particular the Safety, Health and Welfare at Work Act 2005 and the Regulations implemented under the Safety, Health and Welfare at Work Act 2005. It also considers the duty of care likely to be imposed on employers in the future.

1–02 The burden or liability placed upon employers has significantly altered in the past 200 years. It is clear from any examination of this area that the process must be viewed as a continuum, with virtually all developments broadly moving in one direction, generally favouring employees. The regime of protection established may be classified under two general headings: obligations imposed by the legislature, and obligations imposed by the judiciary under the common law.

1–03 Until the nineteenth century there was little or no statutory intervention by the legislature, which was composed, in the main, of property owners and employers, to afford protection to employees. However, in the early nineteenth century, specific limited intervention was demanded to remedy glaring injustices. One of the earliest examples of legislative intervention to stem from this clamour for reform was the Act of 1802 entitled "An Act for the Preservation of the Health and Morals of Apprentices and Others Employed in Cotton and Other Mills and Cotton and Other Factories".[1] This first Act to regulate the operation of factories provided, *inter alia*, that the rooms in mills or factories to which the Act applied should be washed with quicklime and water twice a year and that care should be taken to admit fresh air. It also provided that no apprentice should be employed or compelled to work for more than 12 hours (excluding meal times) in any one day, as well as requiring that no more than two apprentices should sleep in the one bed. Progress continued apace, however reluctantly granted, with further reforming legislation which, in the main, sought to improve the safety and working conditions of employees.

1–04 Major reform, so far as factories were concerned, was introduced in the Factories and Workshop Act 1878. This Act consolidated and amended all earlier statute law governing factories and introduced additional sanitary and

---

[1] 42 Geo. III c. 73.

safety provisions. It limited the hours that might be worked by children, young persons and women, and it prohibited children under the age of 10 years from being employed in a factory or workshop.[2] This Act and subsequent amending measures were repealed by the Factories and Workshop Act 1901. Following the now established practice, the Act brought all previous legislation in the area within the ambit of the one enactment. Further, it expanded both in substance and application the provisions relating to health and safety. It still, however, continued only to apply to factories and workshops. Importantly, s.79 of the 1901 Act provided the Secretary of State with the power to make special Regulations for health and safety in respect of factories, workshops, building operations, operations at docks, quays and warehouses. The importance of this procedure will be evidenced later as it is under this procedure that all modern Regulations are introduced.

1–05   The next significant enactment was the Factories Act 1955. This Act repealed and replaced the 1901 Act in Ireland. Unlike previous legislation it did not seek to ameliorate or eliminate specific hazards. Rather, it provided a code to ensure the safety, health and welfare of factory employees. Section 3(1) of the Factories Act 1955 provided a primary definition of the term "factory":

> "Subject to the provisions of this section, in this Act 'factory' means any premises in which, or within the close or curtilage or precincts of which, persons are employed in manual labour in any process for or incidental to any of the following purposes:
>
> (a)   the making of any article or part of any article;
> (b)   the altering, repairing, ornamenting, finishing, washing, or the breaking up or demolition, of any article;
> (c)   the adapting for sale of any article,
>
> being premises in which, or within the close or curtilage or precincts of which, the work is carried on by way of trade or for purposes of gain and to or over which the employer of the persons employed therein has the right of access or control ..."

1–06   If a place of work fell within the ambit of the primary definition, then it was deemed a "factory" within the meaning of the Act. In addition, the Act contained the proviso that its provisions would also apply to places not otherwise falling within s.3(1). These "notional factories" included, *inter alia*, docks, warehouses, building operations and electrical stations.

1–07   There were further Acts, including the Office Premises Act 1958, the Mines and Quarries Act 1965, the Safety in Industry Act 1980 and the Safety, Health and Welfare at Work (Offshore Installations) Act 1987, as well as various Regulations made under these Acts. All these legislative interventions went a long way towards improving the safety, health and welfare of employees. However, three major difficulties remained. First, the piecemeal approach to

---

[2]   Section 20 of the Factories and Workshop Act 1878.

legislation, with each new Act superseding and amending prior legislation, rendered the law both inaccessible and confusing. Secondly, despite the volume of legislation, many premises and places of work were entirely excluded from regulation. Consequently, those employees were deprived of protection granted as a matter of course to others. Finally, the myriad of statutory provisions had entirely failed in the preceding years to reduce the level of accidents. Allied to the realisation of the foregoing considerations was the requirement to introduce into domestic law the terms of the 1989 Framework Directive on Safety and Health.[3] A central feature of this Directive was the setting down of a minimum level of protection for all employees throughout the Member States of the European Community. It established general rules on occupational health and safety that employers were required to conform to, and set out employee obligations and responsibilities. The Framework Directive was followed by six further Directives, all of which were required to be implemented by January 1, 1993.

---

[3] 89/391/EEC.

CHAPTER 2

COMMON LAW

2–01 As well as obligations under statute law, employers have a common law duty of care to their employees. For example, employers owe a specific duty to their employees to provide them with safe premises, independently of any duty they may owe to them under the health and safety legislation. The common law rules are laws extracted from several hundred years of judicial experience and decisions. Over the centuries, remedies and, more importantly, compensation were available to an injured employee. However, the grounds for recovery in the eighteenth and nineteenth centuries were extremely circumscribed. In the nineteenth century, "fault" or negligence fell to be the main basis upon which liability was to be decided. To recover against an employer, an injured employee had to prove that his employer failed to act in the same manner as a reasonable employer would have acted in the circumstances. He also had to demonstrate that this failure caused the loss or damage of which he complained. Further, even were he to so demonstrate, he still had to surmount the infamous triumvirate of defences created by the judiciary and relied upon by employers: *volenti non fit injuria* (voluntary assumption of risk), the doctrine of common employment and the preclusion from recovery of a finding of contributory negligence on the part of the employee. These defences have now been considerably relaxed as a result of legislative intervention.

Volenti non fit injuria

2–02 The defence of *volenti non fit injuria* equated knowledge on the part of the employee of the risk of harm with the consent of the employee to accept that risk. As Hawkins J. in *Thrausser v Handyside*[1] commented, the employee's "poverty, not his will, consented to incur the danger". This defence was only finally emasculated in this jurisdiction by virtue of s.34(1)(b) of the Civil Liability Act 1961. It is important to note, however, that this defence was never accepted in actions for breach of statutory duty. This obviously increased the importance of statutory duties being imposed on employers.

McMahon and Binchy in their seminal work, the Irish Law of Torts,[2] summarise the weight likely to be given to the defence of voluntary assumption of risk as follows:-

---

[1] [1880] 20 Q.B.D. 359, at 364.
[2] McMahon and Binchy, *Law of Torts*, (3rd ed., Butterworths, Dublin, 2000).

"Formerly the defence of voluntary assumption of risk was fairly readily accepted in cases dealing with employer's liability. In recent years however, the defence 'has virtually disappeared in such cases which turn on common law negligence'[3] ... Today only a communicated waiver of a right of action will constitute a voluntary assumption of the risk; an uncommunicated determination will not suffice. The employee may, however, still be defeated by holding that, having regard to the risks inherent in a particular business, the employer was not in breach of his duty of care to the employee".

Doctrine of common employment

2–03 The doctrine of common employment operated to oust the doctrine of vicarious liability in circumstances where an employee was injured through the negligence of a fellow employee.[4] Vicarious liability arises where an employer is liable for the wrongs of his employees. In summary, the doctrine of common employment provided that where one employee was injured through the negligence or wrongdoing of another employee, and where both employees were employed by the same employer, the employer could not be held liable for that wrong. This doctrine was curtailed over the years, surviving, albeit in a limited form, until the enactment of the Law Reform Personal Injuries Act 1958.

Contributory negligence

2–04 Until the enactment of the Civil Liability Act 1961, contributory negligence was a complete bar to recovery. Section 34 of the 1961 Act provided that contributory negligence could only operate to reduce the amount of damages awarded, having regard to the respective degrees of fault of both the plaintiff and defendant.

The evolution of the modern duty of care owed by an employer to an employee

2–05 It was not until 1937, with the decision of the House of Lords in England in *Wilson and Clyde Coal Company Ltd v English,*[5] that the modern duty of care owed by an employer to an employee was established. In summary, an employer was deemed to owe a duty of care to his employees, which was personal to the employer and was not capable of being discharged merely by delegating its performance to another apparently competent person. This duty included the provision of a safe place of work, a safe system of work, competent staff and proper equipment. These particular duties, in expanded form, were finally enacted into legislation in Part II of the Safety, Health and Welfare at Work Act 1989.

---

[3] *William O'Hanlon v Electricity Supply Board* [1969] I.R. 75.
[4] *Priestly v Fowler* [1837] 3 M. & W. 1.
[5] [1937] 3 All E.R. 628.

2–06   In the case of *Dalton v Frendo*,[6] O'Higgins C.J. stated that "the duty of an employer towards a servant is to take reasonable care for the servant's safety in all the circumstances of the case".

2–07   Henchy J. considered the standard of care owed by an employer to an employee in respect of safety in the leading case of *Bradley v CIE*.[7] The learned judge stated:

> "The law does not require an employer to ensure in all circumstances the safety of his workmen. He will have discharged his duty of care if he does what a reasonable and prudent employer would have done in the circumstances".[8]

In *Kennedy v Hughes Dairy Ltd*,[9] McCarthy J. held that "the essential question in all actions of negligence is whether or not the party charged has failed to take reasonable care whether by act or omission". Barron J. in *Dunne v Honeywell Control Systems Ltd* considered the employer's duty of care with regard to the safety of the premises of third parties. The learned judge stated:

> "An employer has a duty to take reasonable care for the safety of his employees. Where an employee is working on premises other than that of his employer the duty of the employer to use reasonable care for his safety does not in any way diminish. Nevertheless what might be reasonable for an employer to do for the safety of his employee on his premises may no longer be reasonable where the employee is working elsewhere."[10]

2–08   McGuinness J. considered the modern duty of care in *Ian Barclay v An Post and Martin Murray*.[11] The case concerned an employee of the defendant company, who sustained back injury while delivering letters to low level letterboxes in June 1993. He reported the matter to his supervisor and subsequently attended the company doctor. The injury resulted in an absence of two months by the plaintiff from the defendant's employment. His injury and consequent vulnerability were well known to his employers, yet, in October 1993, he was dispatched on non-emergency overtime to deliver mail to a development where some 350 houses had low level letterboxes. During the course of this delivery the plaintiff again suffered back injury. McGuinness J. held that the defendant company's duty of care towards the plaintiff included a duty to ensure that, at least in the short term after his illness, he did not assume duties which would place undue and extraordinary strain on his back. Consequently, the defendant company was held liable as it did not properly discharge the employer's duty of care in the case of the plaintiff's second injury.[12]

---

[6]   Unreported, Supreme Court, December 15, 1972.
[7]   [1976] I.R. 217.
[8]   *ibid.* at p.223.
[9]   [1989] I.L.R.M. 117 at p.123.
[10] [1991] I.L.R.M. 595 at p.600.
[11] [1998] 2 I.L.R.M. 385.
[12] It should be noted that the Building Regulations (Amendment) (No. 2) Regulations 2000 (S.I. No. 249 of 2000) now control the level of letterboxes above standing level and are consequently aimed at reducing the risk of injuries to postmen. These Regulations complement the existing health and safety provisions aimed at preventing musculoskeletal disorders. See paras 6–18 to 6–24 of this book. The Regulations provide that letterboxes in new buildings need to be at a height that will not require a person to stoop to deliver the post.

2–09 McGuinness J's approach to the employer's duty of care is consistent with the approach adopted in previous cases. These cases, discussed above, decided that an employer discharges his duty of care "if he does what a reasonable or prudent employer would have done in the circumstances". The employer's duty is therefore not an unlimited one and varies according to the employee's circumstances. This can be seen from *Clabby v Global Windows Limited and An Post*.[13] This case presents facts quite similar but distinct to those in *Barclay*. Here there was no prior injury and it was accepted that the training the plaintiff received for adequate delivery to low letter boxes was appropriate.

---

[13] Unreported, High Court, Finnegan P., January 21, 2003.

CHAPTER 3

THE SAFETY, HEALTH AND WELFARE AT WORK ACT 2005

3–01   The Safety, Health and Welfare at Work Act 1989 ("the 1989 Act") was a groundbreaking piece of legislation. For the first time, all places of work within the State were afforded protection under the umbrella of one statute. All persons involved with or connected to places of employment, including employers, employees, designers, builders and manufacturers were covered by the Act. Unlike previous Acts, which were aimed at defining the circumstances whereby liability was imposed, this Act was proactive in seeking to prevent accidents by obliging employers to assess and address potential risks in their place of work and by establishing a regulatory body with enforcement powers. Generally, the 1989 Act provided only for criminal liability for breaches of its provisions. That said, s.28 of the Act allowed for the making of Regulations that attracted civil liability.

3–02   The Safety, Health and Welfare at Work Act 2005 ("the 2005 Act") repeals and replaces the 1989 Act as the statutory framework for securing the safety, health and welfare of persons at work. It came into force on September 1, 2005.[1] The 2005 Act re-enacts an expanded version of many of the provisions contained in the 1989 Act, with some significant additions. It is organised in eight parts and seven schedules. In introducing the Bill at Second Stage in the Oireachtas, the Minister of State at the Department of Enterprise, Trade and Employment, Tony Killeen, T.D., stated that it represented:

> "… a modernisation of our occupational health and safety laws. It is significant social legislation which affirms the Government's interest in ensuring that labour law is kept up to date and relevant".[2]

---

[1]   See Safety, Health and Welfare at Work Act 2005 (Commencement Order) (S.I. No. 328 of 2005) which brought into force many of the provisions of the 2005 Act except, for example, the provision that repeals the Safety, Health and Welfare at Work (General Application) Regulations, 1993 and 2003. The 1993 Regulations therefore generally remain in place until November 1, 2007, save for arts 5–15 (see S.I. No. 392 of 2005) which are now incorporated into ss.8–12 of the 2005 Act. See also Safety, Health and Welfare at Work (General Application) (Revocation) Regulations 2005 (S.I. No. 392 of 2005) operative since August 31, 2005 and Safety, Health and Welfare at Work Act 2005 (Repeals) (Commencement) Order 2007 (S.I. No. 300 of 2007), operative from November 1, 2007.

[2]   Dáil Debates, October 14, 2004, p.600.

3–03   The 2005 Act is framework in nature and focuses on broad general duties and the organisational arrangements necessary to achieve better safety and health. It sets out the duties of employers, employees and other parties such as the designers of workplaces and work equipment and the suppliers of goods for use in the workplace. As with its predecessor, the general ethos of the Act is that of prevention of accidents and illnesses. It places an increased emphasis on the management of health and safety and integrates disputes regarding safety and health issues into mainstream employment law dispute resolution. The failure to observe the new more onerous responsibilities is therefore likely to be pleaded in personal injuries actions taken in the courts. There is increased emphasis on deterrence by the strengthening of the enforce-ment provisions. The 2005 Act reflects and accommodates many of the radical changes that have occurred since the 1989 Act was introduced. In particular, these changes have taken place in the nature of the work occurring in Ireland and how and where that work is carried out. The 2005 Act has also taken account of the increasing ethnic and cultural diversity of the Irish workforce.

3–04   While the 2005 Act could not be described as a radical departure from its predecessor, some of the more striking features in the Act include:

– a definition of "competent person" and "reasonably practicable";
– an increase in the explicit duties and responsibilities of both employees and employers;
– provision for testing employees for intoxicants;
– specific provision regarding the responsibilities of designers, manufactur-ers and importers;
– new duties for persons who commission, procure, design or construct places of work;
– a reduction in the onus on small business and the farming sector regarding safety statements;
– joint safety and health agreements;
– a new dispute resolution mechanism for dealing with disputes between employers and employees concerning health and safety matters;
– expanded provisions concerning responsibilities of directors and managers;
– evidentiary changes for the prosecution of directors and persons signifi-cantly influencing the management of a company; and
– a strengthening of the enforcement powers for non-compliance (increased penalties and also on-the-spot fines).

3–05   Although the 2005 Act largely retains the same structure as the 1989 Act, it clarifies certain matters with an expanded list of definitions in Part 1 of the Act, which deals with preliminary and general matters.

Definitions

3–06   There are a number of new definitions in the 2005 Act worthy of comment.

3–07 A "competent person" is a concept or term used throughout the 2005 Act. Section 2(2)(a) of the 2005 Act introduces a definition of "competent person" and places on a statutory basis an expanded definition of "competent person" previously contained in the Safety, Health and Welfare at Work (General Application) (Amendment No. 2) Regulations 2003. It states:

> "For the purposes of the relevant statutory provisions, a person is deemed to be a competent person where, having regard to the task he or she is required to perform and taking account of the size or hazards (or both of them) of the undertaking or establishment in which he or she undertakes work, the person possesses sufficient training, experience and knowledge appropriate to the nature of the work to be undertaken."

3–08 Section 2(2)(b) of the 2005 Act should be noted in that it makes specific reference to the "framework of qualifications referred to in the Qualifications (Education and Training) Act 1999". This is a significant provision and is likely to lead to a requirement that those persons with responsibilities for health and safety undergo accredited health and safety courses.

3–09 Regulation 59 and the twelfth schedule to the 1993 Regulations provides that a dangerous occurrence had to be reported to the Authority. "Dangerous occurrence" is now defined in s.2(1) of the 2005 Act as:

> "an occurrence arising from work activities in a place of work that causes or results in–
> (a) the collapse, overturning, failure, explosion, bursting, electrical short circuit discharge or overload, or malfunction of any work equipment,
> (b) the collapse or partial collapse of any building or structure under construction or in use as a place of work,
> (c) the uncontrolled or accidental release, the escape or the ignition of any substance,
> (d) a fire involving any substance, or
> (e) any unintentional ignition or explosion of explosives,
> as may be prescribed; …".

3–10 "Director" is defined broadly and includes a shadow director. Section (2)(1) of the 2005 Act defines a director to include:

> "a person in accordance with whose directions or instructions the directors of the undertaking concerned are accustomed to act but does not include such a person if the directors are accustomed to so act by reason only that they do so on advice given by the person in a professional capacity; …"

3–11 As in the 1989 Act, "place of work" is broadly defined but now includes "any, or any part of any, place (whether or not within or forming part of a building or structure)". The reference to a "trailer" in subs.(b) is new and was not included in subs.(c) of the 1989 Act definition. A "place of work" is therefore now defined in the 2005 Act to include:

> "any, or any part of any, place (whether or not within or forming part of a building or structure), land or other location at, in, upon or near which, work is carried on whether occasionally or otherwise and in particular includes–

(a) in relation to any extractive industry including exploration activity, the whole area intended to house workstations to which employees have access for the purpose of their work relating to the immediate and ancillary activities and installations of, as appropriate–

    (i) the surface or, as the case may be, underground extractive industry, including overburden dumps and other tips and any accommodation that is provided and, in the case of the underground extractive industry, any working area,

    (ii) the extractive industry through drilling onshore including any accommodation that is provided, and

    (iii) the extractive industry through drilling offshore, including any accommodation that is provided,

(b) a tent, trailer, temporary structure or movable structure, and

(c) a vehicle, vessel or aircraft; …".

3–12 The 2005 Act contains the first ever statutory definition of the words "reasonably practicable". Section 2(6) of the 2005 Act states:

> "For the purposes of the relevant statutory provisions, "reasonably practicable", in relation to the duties of an employer, means that an employer has exercised all due care by putting in place the necessary protective and preventive measures, having identified the hazards and assessed the risks to safety and health likely to result in accidents or injury to health at the place of work concerned and where the putting in place of any further measures is grossly disproportionate having regard to the unusual, unforeseeable and exceptional nature of any circumstance or occurrence that may result in an accident at work or injury to health at that place of work."

The foregoing definition establishes a strict liability test and clearly imposes a high standard on employers by obliging them to show that they have taken all reasonably foreseeable steps against risk. That said, this definition appears to apply only to "the duties of an employer" and self-employed persons. What then do the words "reasonably practicable" mean and how are the courts likely to interpret the new statutory definition accorded to such words? Section 2(6) of the 2005 Act attempts to incorporate the terms of Art.5(1) of the Framework Directive, which imposes an absolute duty on employers "to ensure the safety and health of workers in every aspect related to work". Article 5(4) of the Framework Directive, which is also reflected in the statutory definition, states:

> "The Directive shall not restrict the option of a Member State to provide for the exclusion or the limitation of the employers' responsibility where occurrences are due to unusual and unforeseeable circumstances beyond the employers' control, or to exceptional events, the consequences of which could not have been avoided despite the exercise of all due care".

The Framework Directive exception to the general duty alludes "to unusual and unforeseeable circumstances beyond the employers' control, or to exceptional events", while s.2(6) of the 2005 Act refers "to the unusual, unforeseeable and exceptional nature of any circumstance or occurrence".[3]

---

[3] See *Commission of the European Communities v United Kingdom of Great Britain and Northern Ireland*, Case C-127/05, June 14, 2007.

3–13　It is important to distinguish the concept of negligence from the statutory definition of what is "reasonably practicable". A defendant may avoid liability in negligence for failing to fulfil certain duties merely by demonstrating that the burden imposed upon him/her (time and/or cost) by taking those precautions outweighs the scale of the loss, taking into account the chance of that loss occurring. It is clear from s.2(6) of the 2005 Act that reasonable practicability is an altogether different creature. For reasonable practicability there must be a gross disproportion. An employer must be in a position to establish that any further measures would have been "grossly disproportionate having regard to the unusual, unforeseeable and exceptional nature of any circumstance or occurrence that may result in an accident at work or injury to health at that place of work". It is evident from the foregoing that the burden imposed by what is "reasonably practicable" in s.2(6) of the 2005 Act is set at a higher standard than that imposed by the general principle of negligence. It would appear, therefore, that in monetary terms the monies required to be expended would have to be very significant before it would not be "reasonably practicable" to take the precautions. That said, it would seem that what could be construed as being "reasonably practicable" for a multinational corporation might not necessarily pertain in a small corner shop.

3–14　For other duty holders under the 2005 Act, such as manufacturers, suppliers and designers, the common law definition is likely to continue to apply. The 2005 Act lacks clarity on this issue in that the interpretation section of the Act[4] does not expressly confine the statutory definition to the duties of an employer and states:

> "reasonably practicable has the meaning assigned by *subsection (6)*".

If a court were to apply the statutory definition of "reasonably practicable" in s.2(6) of the 2005 Act to other duty holders, a higher standard would apply than if the common law definition were to be followed.

　　The common law definition of "reasonably practicable" has been elaborated upon in a number of cases. Asquith L.J. classically defined the "reasonably practicable" standard in *Edwards v National Coal Board*,[5] in the following manner:

> "'[R]easonably practicable' is a narrower term than 'physically possible' and seems to me to imply that a computation must be made by the owner in which the quantum of risk is placed on one scale and the sacrifice involved in the measures necessary for averting the risk (whether in money, time or trouble) is placed in the other, and that, if it be shown that there is a gross disproportion between them – the risk being insignificant in relation to the sacrifice – the defendants discharge the onus on them. Moreover, this computation falls to be made by the owner at a point of time anterior to the accident ...".

In *Margaret Daly v Avonmore Creameries Ltd*, McCarthy J. in the Supreme Court considered "reasonably practicable" at p.131:

---

[4]　See s.2(1) of the 2005 Act.
[5]　[1949] 1 All E.R. 743 (C.A.).

"I am not to be taken as supporting a view that, where lives are at stake, consid-erations of expense are any more than vaguely material …".[6]

The Supreme Court reinforced this view in *Boyle v Marathon Petroleum (Ireland) Ltd.*[7] In that case, O'Flaherty J. made reference to what "reasonably practicable" meant. He stated:

"I am … of the opinion that this duty is more extensive than the common law duty which devolves on employers to exercise reasonable care in various aspects as regards their employees. It is an obligation to take all practical steps. That seems to me to involve more than that they should respond that they, as employ-ers, did all that was reasonably to be expected of them in a particular situation. An employer might sometimes be able to say that what he did by way of exer-cising reasonable care was done in the 'agony of the moment', for example, but that might not be enough to discharge his statutory duty under the section in question."[8]

3–15 It is a matter for each individual employer to determine, however, what is "reasonably practicable" as pursuant to s.81 of the 2005 Act, in any prose-cution for an offence consisting of a failure to comply with a duty to do some-thing, so far as it was practicable or "reasonably practicable", it is for the accused to prove that it was not practicable or was not "reasonably practicable" to do more than was in fact done to satisfy this duty or requirement.

3–16 "Undertaking" is defined for the first time and need not be "for gain". It includes:

"an individual, a body corporate or an unincorporated body of persons engaged in the production, supply or distribution of goods or the provision of a service (whether carried on by him or her for profit or not);…".[9]

3–17 The 2005 Act does not define the words "health", "safety" or "welfare" but rather leaves these words for the Irish Courts to interpret. That said, the European Court of Justice (ECJ) in *United Kingdom v Council* provides some guidance on the approach likely to be adopted by the Irish courts in interpreting these words. The ECJ stated:

"There is nothing in the wording of Article 118a [new numbering Article 137] to indicate that the concepts of … 'safety' and 'health' as used in that provision should, in the absence of other indications, be interpreted restrictively, and not as embracing all factors, physical or otherwise, capable of affecting the health and safety of the worker in his working environment … On the contrary, the words 'especially in the working environment' militate in favour of a broad interpretation of the powers which Article [137] confers upon the Council for the protection of the health and safety of workers. Moreover, such an interpretation of the words 'safety' and 'health' derives support in particular from the preamble

---

6   [1984] I.R. 131.
7   [1999] 2 I.R. 640.
8   See also the Scottish case of *Mains v Uniroyal* ([1995] I.R.L.R. 544), heard in the Court of Session before Lords Wylie, Sutherland and Johnston.
9   Section 2(1) of the 2005 Act.

to the Constitution of the World Health Organisation to which all Member States belong. Health is there defined as a state of complete physical, mental and social well-being that does not consist only in the absence of illness or infirmity."[10]

Self-employed persons

3–18   Section 7 of the 2005 Act provides that the provisions of the 2005 Act are to apply, "where appropriate", to a self-employed person as if that self-employed person was an employer and his or her own employee.

GENERAL DUTIES

3–19   Part 2 of the 2005 Act sets out a number of general duties owed by various stakeholders under the Act. Each of these duties will be considered in turn.

3–20   Chapter 1 of Part 2 of the 2005 Act sets out a range of general duties of employers. The overriding duty of an employer is to ensure, so far as is reasonably practicable, the safety, health and welfare at work of his or her employees. Many of the duties provided for in the 1989 Act and the Safety, Health and Welfare at Work (General Application) Regulations 1993 and 2003 ("the 1993 Regulations") are reiterated in the 2005 Act. The significance of the 2005 Act arises from the fact that many of the employer's obligations contained in the 1993 Regulations are now placed on a statutory footing. The ease of assessing rights that are now consolidated in one statute is significant. There are some additional obligations on the employer, which are set out below.

3–21   Section 8(1) of the 2005 Act addresses the general duty on employers and provides that it shall be the duty of every employer to do everything he or she can, as far as is reasonably practicable, to ensure the safety, health and welfare of his or her employees.[11]

3–22   Twelve specific matters, which an employer must consider when fulfilling the duty imposed by s.8(1) of the 2005 Act, are referred to in s.8(2). It is important to note that this list is not exhaustive and is merely an expanded statement of the existing common law position.[12] Further, the duties imposed under the 2005 Act cannot be taken by employers as granting them a licence to implement draconian measures under the guise of purported compliance with the 2005 Act. The actions of the employer in each particular case must be reasonable in the circumstances. In the case of *Donegal County Council v Porter, McLaughlin, McGonigal and Bredin*,[13] the County Council sought to implement a December 1985 Department of Environment circular which recommended, *inter alia*, the

---

[10]   [1996] ECR I-5755, para.15.

[11]   Section 8(1) of the 2005 Act provides:
  "(1) Every employer shall ensure, so far as is reasonably practicable, the safety, health and welfare at work of his or her employees."

[12]   The common law duty owed by employers to employees is broadly stated so as to provide a safe place of work, a safe system of work, proper equipment and competent staff.

[13]   [1993] E.L.R. 101.

introduction of a retirement age of 55 for all fire fighters and a compulsory annual medical examination "on a uniform basis for all operational personnel". Porter and the other respondents refused to undergo a medical examination requested by the Council due to an industrial dispute. They were dismissed after refusing to undergo the medical examination for three years.

3–23　　The Council relied for its defence, in part, on *Maureen Heeney v Dublin Corporation*.[14] In this case, the widow of a fire officer successfully sued Dublin Corporation for damages in negligence arising from her husband's death on October 12, 1985. Mr Heeney, a fire fighter, collapsed and died from a heart attack after entering a burning building on a number of occasions without breathing apparatus. On March 12, 1985, the Labour Court had recommended the retirement of fire fighters for ill health at the age of 55, as well as annual medical examinations for all fire fighters over the age of 55. No such medical examinations were in place at the time of Mr Heeney's death. Mr Heeney suffered from hypertension and was aged in excess of 55 at the time of his death.

3–24　　Donegal County Council, in its case against Porter and others, claimed that the *Heeney* case demonstrated a clear risk to the safety, health and welfare of Porter and his fellow respondents that the Council was seeking to avoid by requiring a medical examination. The Council, relying on s.6 of the Safety, Health and Welfare at Work Act 1989,[15] in furtherance of complying with its duty to ensure the safety, health and welfare of the respondents, so far as it was reasonably practicable, argued that their dismissal was permitted under the Unfair Dismissals Acts 1977–2001. Flood J., however, held that the respondents' dismissal was unfair:

> "[D]ismissal, as I see it, would be a blanket performance [of] the statutory duty under section 6 of the Safety, Health and Welfare at Work Act, 1989 [Section 8 of the Safety, Health and Welfare at Work Act 2005]. In my view there is undoubtedly a statutory duty to observe. The council can observe it by a much less draconian measure than dismissal at the age of 55 and one which does not involve a blatant disregard for the council's contractual obligations to the respondents and others in their category."

It is clear, therefore, that an employer, in endeavouring to comply with the general duty imposed upon him by virtue of s.8(1) of the 2005 Act, must take into account all the circumstances of each case and act accordingly.[16] If an employee's conditions and terms of employment are to be affected, only the minimum intrusion possible will be countenanced.[17]

---

[14]　Unreported, High Court, Barron J., May 16, 1991.
[15]　Section 6 of the 1989 Act mirrors s.8 of the 2005 Act.
[16]　See also *Scally v Westmeath County Council* [1996] E.L.R. 96.
[17]　See *Deborah Timmons v Oglesby & Butler Ltd* [1999] E.L.R. 119 and *Ó Ceallaigh v An Bord Altranais* [2000] 4 I.R. 54. Also *Catherine McNamara v South Western Area Health Board* [2001] E.L.R. 317, wherein Kearns J. held that the suspension of a senior consultant without pay was a breach of fair procedures in that it was "open ended" and "non-specific in duration".

3–25   Section 8(2) of the 2005 Act contains an expanded list of specific matters, which an employer must consider in order to discharge his or her duty to
ensure, so far as is reasonably practicable, the safety, health and welfare at
work of all his or her employees. Some of the new duties identified in s.8(2) of
the 2005 Act include:

> "(a) managing and conducting work activities in such a way as to ensure, so far
>   as is reasonably practicable, the safety, health and welfare at work of his or
>   her employees;[18]
> (b) managing and conducting work activities in such a way as to prevent, so far
>   as is reasonably practicable, any improper conduct or behaviour likely to
>   put the safety, health or welfare at work of his or her employees at risk.[19]"

The foregoing provisions require employers to manage and conduct work
activities:

i.   in such a way as to ensure, so far as is reasonably practicable, the safety,
     health and welfare at work of his or her employees; and
ii. in such a way as to prevent, so far as is reasonably practicable, any
     improper conduct likely to put the safety, health or welfare at work of his
     or her employees at risk.

Section 8(2)(a) has a particular relevance to contractor selection in that it
requires an employer to manage and conduct his or her work activities to
ensure the health and safety of his or her employees. An employer must therefore be in a position to demonstrate that he/she has checked the suitability of a
contractor to undertake the task in question. This should involve, for example,
making reasonable enquiries as to the contractor's competence.

Section 8(2)(b) is of particular note and imposes an obligation on employers
to outline in their human resources policies behaviour which will not be
acceptable. Any such policies should also specify the action to be taken where
employee behaviour poses a threat to the health and safety of other employees.

These new provisions also underline the importance of an employer having
an integrated safety management system and are particularly relevant when
addressing the identification of bullying,[20] harassment and stress in the workplace. The enforcement mechanisms available under the 2005 Act could be
invoked, for example, where the Authority considered that an employer was
exposing his or her employees to unacceptable levels of stress. In such circumstances, the Authority could issue directions for an improvement plan.

3–26   Section 8(2)(b) makes reference to "improper conduct", which is not
defined in the 2005 Act. It is, however, likely to cover "horse play", which did
not, as such, come within the scope of the 1989 Act. In addition, it might cover
the inappropriate use of work equipment or unsafe work practices.

---

[18] See s.8(2)(a) of the 2005 Act.
[19] See s.8(2)(b) of the 2005 Act.
[20] See *Code of Practice for Employers and Employees on the Prevention and Resolution of
      Bullying at Work* (Health and Safety Authority, 2007). This Code is in operation since
      May 1, 2007.

3–27   Section 8(2) of the 2005 Act amends or reiterates many of the duties prescribed by the 1989 Act and the 1993 Regulations. Some of these duties are dealt with below:

1.   The employer's duty has been extended, under s.6(2)(h) of the 1989 Act, to ensure safety and the prevention of risk to health at work in connection with the use of any substance or article. The corresponding provision in the 2005 Act has particular relevance to the construction industry and includes a duty to protect employees against exposure to noise, vibration or ionising or other radiations or any other physical agent.[21]

2.   Section 8(2)(e) of the 2005 Act expands the duty to provide safe systems of work by obliging the employer to revise and update them as appropriate. The use of the word revise indicates that the provision of a safe system of work is not a static, once-off requirement.

3.   Section 8(2)(f) of the 2005 Act requires an employer to provide and maintain "facilities and arrangements for the welfare of his or her employees at work". This provision should be considered alongside s.22(1) of the 2005 Act, which imposes a statutory obligation on an employer in respect of health surveillance.

4.   Section 8(2)(h) of the 2005 Act is a broad new provision which may impose new obligations on employers to address stress in the workplace. It requires the employer to determine and implement the safety measures necessary for the protection of the safety, health and welfare of his or her employees when identifying hazards and carrying out a risk assessment under s.19 of the 2005 Act, or when preparing a safety statement under s.20 of the 2005 Act. These safety measures must have regard to the general principles of prevention contained in Sch.3 of the 2005 Act.[22] Broadly, these relate to the evaluation and avoidance of risk, the adaptation of the workplace, system of work and the provision of safe equipment to the employee. This subsection emphasises that the duty of an employer is not merely confined to formulating health and safety procedures but also extends to implementing such procedures.[23]

5.   Section 8(2)(i) of the 2005 Act consolidates into one provision the employer's duty to provide protective clothing or equipment, where risks cannot be eliminated or adequately controlled as per s.6(2)(f) of the 1989 Act, and contains a precondition that an employer evaluate a risk as one not avoidable by other means before the use of protective equipment as per art.62 of the 2007 General Application Regulations[24].

6.   The employer's duty under s.6(2)(g) of the 1989 Act to prepare and revise plans as necessary to be followed in an emergency situation has been extended by s.8(2)(j) of the 2005 Act. The 2005 Act now obliges preparation and revision, as appropriate, of adequate plans and procedures to be followed in emergencies and in cases of serious and imminent danger. The 2005 Act obliges employers to implement plans and procedures for

---

[21]   Section 8(2)(d) of the 2005 Act.

[22]   The general principles are also set out in Sch.1 of the 1993 Regulations.

[23]   See the Circuit Court case of *DPP v PJ Carey*.

[24]   S.I. No. 299 of 2007.

emergencies as appropriate (not "as necessary") and extends the duty to cases of serious and imminent danger. The inclusion of "procedures" in the section requires the employer to set down the procedures for carrying out any emergency plans. The addition of "circumstances of imminent danger" suggests that plans and procedures must be in place not only in respect of the case of an actual emergency but also in respect of a situation where there is an immediate threat of an emergency. Furthermore, the 1989 Act required that plans be revised "as necessary", whereas the 2005 Act provides that the revision of such plans and procedures must take place "as appropriate".

7.   The duty to obtain, as necessary, the services of a competent person[25] as per s.6(2)(j) of the 1989 Act mirrors s.8(2)(l) of the 2005 Act.

8.   The duty on employers to report accidents and dangerous occurrences,[26] as may be prescribed, to the Health and Safety Authority ("the Authority") is now contained in s.8 of the 2005 Act.[27] It should be noted that a late addition to the 2005 Act was the expansion of the definition of "dangerous occurrence" to include "the collapse or partial collapse of any building or structure under construction or in use as a place of work", "a fire involving any substance" and "any unintentional ignition or explosion of explosives". Accidents and incidents that must be reported to the Authority arise in three situations: a "dangerous occurrence", a fatal accident or any accident at a place of work preventing a person from performing his normal work for more than three consecutive days.

3–28   Section 8(2)(c) of the 2005 Act provides that an employer's duty extends, as regards the place of work concerned, to ensuring, so far as is reasonably practicable:–

"(i)   the design, provision and maintenance of it in a condition that is safe and without risk to health,

(ii)   the design, provision and maintenance of safe means of access to and egress from it, and

(iii)   the design, provision and maintenance of plant and machinery or any other articles that are safe and without risk to health; …".

While the foregoing duties correspond to the duties previously contained in subss.6(2)(a) to (c) of the 1989 Act, they only applied to "any place of work" which was "under the employer's control".[28] Significantly, these words have been deleted from the 2005 Act so that an employer is now required to ensure, so far as is reasonably practicable, compliance with the duties detailed in s.8(2)(c) of the 2005 Act, even if the place of work is not under his or her control. This subsection imposes an increased burden on an employer with respect to employees who carry out their work otherwise than at the employer's place of work, *e.g.* an electrician or haulier.

---

[25]   The definition of competent person is now set down in s.2 of the 2005 Act.

[26]   The definitions of "accident" and "dangerous occurrence" are set out in s.2 of the 2005 Act.

[27]   This duty is also provided for in Pt. X of the 1993 Regulations, which will continue to apply after November 1, 2007.

[28]   See s.6(2)(a) of the 1989 Act.

3–29   Section 8(3) of the 2005 Act specifically extends the duties of the employer to temporary or fixed-term employees[29].[30] Section 8(4) obliges the employer to ensure that the working conditions for the duration of an assignment of any fixed-term or temporary employee will protect the safety, health and welfare of such an employee.[31] In considering the concept of employee, s.2(1) of the 2005 Act should also be noted in that it defines an employer in relation to an employee as:

(a)   the employer under the terms of a contract of employment;
(b)   a person (other than an employee of that person) under whose control and direction an employee works; and
(c)   the successor of the employer or an associated employer of the employer, where appropriate.

It is clear from the foregoing that where an employer uses employees from another business/company for temporary purposes, that employer bears the responsibility for ensuring the place of work is safe as he or she is in control of the working environment. This position obtains regardless of whether he or she is the true employer of the worker/employee.

In summary, an employer/employee relationship, for the purposes of the 2005 Act, arises where an employee is working in the capacity of an employee (regardless of whose employee he or she is) and is under an employer's direction and control.

3–30   Section 8(5) of the 2005 Act mirrors art.7 of the 1993 Regulations. This section obliges an employer to ensure that any measures taken by him or her in relation to the safety, health and welfare at work do not involve financial cost to his or her employees.

3–31   Any breach of s.8 of the 2005 Act attracts criminal liability.[32]

Information for employees

3–32   Section 9 of the 2005 Act broadly mirrors art.11 of the 1993 Regulations and Art.10 of the 1989 EC Framework Directive on health and

---

[29]   Section 2(1) of the 2005 Act defines a "temporary employee" as being an employee who is assigned by a temporary employment business to work for and under the control of another undertaking availing of the employee's services. The aforementioned s.2(1) defines "fixed-term employee" as an employee "whose employment is governed by a contract of employment for a fixed-term or for a specified purpose".

[30]   Section 8(3) provides:
"Any duty imposed on an employer under the relevant statutory provisions in respect of any of his or her employees shall also apply in respect of the use by him or her of the services of a fixed term employee or a temporary employee."

[31]   Section 6(3) of the 1989 Act provided that persons carrying on work experience or training were deemed to be employees for the purposes of the 1989 Act. Section 2 of the 2005 Act provides that apprentices are employees for the purposes of the Act other than when present at a course of study in a university, college or school. See the definition of "contract of employment" and "employee" in s.2 of the 2005 Act.

[32]   See s.77(2)(a) of the 2005 Act.

safety.[33] This section imposes a duty on an employer regarding information to his or her employees. Section 9(1) of the 2005 Act includes an additional requirement that the employer, when furnishing information to employees, regarding health and safety matters, does so in a manner, form and, as appropriate, language that is reasonably likely to be understood by his or her employees.[34] This section goes some way to address the needs of non-English speaking employees,[35] although it does not, as such, require an employer to ensure an employee has understood the relevant information. The obligation to translate information into a foreign language is qualified by the phrase "as appropriate". That said, s.9(1) requires employers to provide information "on matters relating to" employees' safety, health and welfare "that is reasonably likely to be understood by the employees concerned". Section 9(1)(b) of the 2005 Act sets out the information that every employer should give to his or her employees. It requires that the information provided should include information on:

> "(i)   the hazards to safety, health and welfare at work and the risks identified by the risk assessment,
> (ii) the protective and preventive measures to be taken concerning safety, health and welfare at work under the relevant statutory provisions in respect of the place of work and each specific task to be performed at the place of work, and
> (iii) the names of persons designated under *section 11* [*i.e.* persons to contact in an emergency situation] and of safety representatives selected under *section 25,* if any."

The Authority has stated that s.9(1) of the 2005 Act may also impact on how information is imparted to employees with reading or literacy difficulties.[36]

3–33   Section 9(2) of the 2005 Act should be noted in that it requires an employer who has an employee of another undertaking engaged in work activities at his or her place of work, to ensure that his or her employee's employer receives "adequate information" in respect of safety management systems at his or her place of work. Therefore, while the duty is on the main contractor to give the information on safety and health requirements to the subcontractor, it is the

---

[33]   89/391/EEC.

[34]   Section 9(1) states:

> "Without prejudice to the generality of *section 8*, every employer shall, when providing information to his or her employees under that section on matters relating to their safety, health and welfare at work ensure that the information—
>
> (*a*) is given in a form, manner and, as appropriate, language that is reasonably likely to be understood by the employees concerned, ..."

The Authority's Safe System of Work Plan for Construction demonstrates the practical application of s.9(1) in that it uses simple diagrams to convey hazards and outlines the appropriate controls, which need to be put in place.

[35]   Between January and December 2005 there were 74 deaths in the workplace. This represented an increase of over 20 per cent in the fatality rate on 2004. Over ten per cent of those killed were non-nationals. In 2006, there were 50 work-related fatalities. The death rate of workplace accidents for non-national workers was 3.2 per 100,000, compared to 2.0 per 100,000 for Irish workers.

[36]   See also the Authority's Guidelines to the Safety, Health and Welfare at Work Act, 2005, p.17.

subcontractor who is required to ensure that his or her own workers/employees on the site have the requisite information. In effect, the subcontractor, as the direct employer, has the duty towards his or her own employees.

3–34 It appears that the obligation to inform is related to the employees at a place of work and not merely to a particular undertaking. Therefore, an employer, such as the Health Service Executive (HSE), with multiple places of work, is required to provide information on health and safety matters at each place of work.

3–35 The Safe System of Work Plan, launched by the Authority on January 19, 2005, enables employees to carry out their own risk assessments and was devised to help, in particular, non-nationals and workers with literacy problems. The initiative involves the use of booklets with pictograms outlining potential hazards and the steps needed to address them. The focus on pictograms rather than words is designed to make the booklets accessible to employees with English language or literacy problems. In 2004, more than 1,200 work permits were granted to construction workers from 39 countries, including 411 workers from Turkey, 255 from Poland and 120 from Romania.

3–36 Any breach of s.9 of the 2005 Act attracts criminal liability.[37]

Instruction, training and supervision of employees

3–37 Section 10 of the 2005 Act mirrors many of the provisions in art.13 of the 1993 Regulations in respect of providing appropriate training, instruction and supervision of employees. Section 10(1)(a) of the 2005 Act requires an employer, when furnishing instruction, training and supervision to employees regarding health and safety matters, to do so in a manner, form and, as appropriate, language that is reasonably likely to be understood by his or her employees. The observations made in respect of s.9(1) of the 2005 Act are equally applicable to this section of the 2005 Act.

3–38 Section 10(1)(b) of the 2005 Act[38] imposes an additional obligation on employers to give employees time off work with no loss of pay to receive instruction on emergency measures. This section broadly mirrors art.13(1)(a) of the 1993 Regulations. The phrase "where appropriate", however, has been added, which arguably qualifies the duty on employers to comply with this obligation.

---

[37] See s.77(2)(a) of the 2005 Act.
[38] Section 10(1)(b) of the 2005 Act states:
"employees receive, during time off from their work, where appropriate, and without loss of remuneration, adequate safety, health and welfare training, including, in particular, information and instructions relating to the specific task to be performed by the employee and the measures to be taken in an emergency, …".

3–39   Article 13(b) and (c) of the 1993 Regulations imposes a general duty on employers to assess an employee's capabilities in assigning work to be carried out. This article requires an employer, in particular, to take account of workers' capabilities in relation to the manual handling of loads, having regard to the individual risk factors set out in the Ninth Schedule to the 1993 Regulations. Section 10(1)(c) of the 2005 Act mirrors the aforementioned general duty in the 1993 Regulations and requires that the employee's capabilities are taken into account in relation to any specific task assigned to an employee. This subsection is of particular importance where an employee has a pre-existing condition but should be applied having regard to the reasonable accommodation requirement under the Employment Equality Acts.

Section 10(2) of the 2005 Act states:

> "Training ... shall be adapted to take account of new or changed risks to safety, health and welfare at work and shall, as appropriate, be repeated periodically."

This section requires training to be adapted periodically to respond to new or changed risks to safety.

3–40   Section 10(4) of the 2005 Act[39] imposes a further obligation on an employer, if an employee requires competency for a certain task, to release an employee from work, without loss of pay, where appropriate, so to allow for the training of the employee in safety and health matters regarding that activity. As stated earlier the phrase "where appropriate" qualifies the obligation under this section.

3–41   Any breach of s.10 of the 2005 Act attracts criminal liability.[40]

Emergencies and serious imminent dangers

3–42   Section 11 of the 2005 Act mirrors reg.9 of the 1993 General Application Regulations and should be considered alongside s.8(2)(j) of the 2005 Act. In summary, this section sets down an employer's duty in the case of an emergency or serious and imminent danger. It imposes an obligation on an employer to prepare and revise, as necessary, plans and procedures to be followed and measures to be taken in the case of an emergency or serious and imminent danger. In particular, s.11 requires an employer to make provision and take measures that cover first aid, fire fighting and the evacuation of employees and any other individual present in the workplace in the case of an emergency or serious and imminent danger.[41] It also imposes an obligation on an employer to arrange any necessary contacts with the emergency services. An employer must consult with employees in the designation of employees

---

[39]   Section 10(4) of the 2005 Act provides:
   "Where, in respect of any particular work, competency requirements are prescribed, the employer shall provide for the release of employees, during working hours, where appropriate, and without loss of remuneration, for the purpose of attending training in matters relating to safety, health and welfare at work as regards the particular work."
[40]   See s.77(2)(a) of the 2005 Act.
[41]   See further Chap.10, Fire and Emergencies.

(under this section) required to implement emergency plans in the case of emergencies or serious and imminent dangers.[42]

3–43 Any breach of subss.11(1)–11(4) of the 2005 Act attracts criminal liability.[43]

Persons other than employees

3–44 Section 12 of the 2005 Act concerns risks posed to third parties. These risks were formerly dealt with in s.7 of the 1989 Act which provided that:

> "(1) It shall be the duty of every employer to conduct his undertaking in such a way as to ensure, so far as is reasonably practicable, that persons not in his employment who may be affected thereby are not exposed to risks to their safety or health.[44]
> (2) It shall be the duty of every self-employed person to conduct his undertaking in such a way as to ensure, so far as is reasonably practicable, that he and other persons (not being his employees) who may be affected thereby are not exposed to risks to their safety or health.
> (3) In such cases as may be prescribed, it shall be the duty of every employer and self-employed person, in the prescribed circumstances, and in the prescribed manner to give to persons (not being his employees) who may be affected by the way in which he conducts his undertaking the prescribed information about such aspects of the way he conducts his undertaking as might affect their safety or health."

This provision was broadly drawn in that there was no limit, as such, on the duty of an employer provided that an injured party could demonstrate that he or she was affected by the "conduct" of an "undertaking".

3–45 Section 12 of the 2005 Act now provides that every employer must manage and conduct his or her undertaking in such a way as to ensure, so far as is reasonably practicable, that in the course of work being carried on, others at the place of work, not being employees, are not exposed to risks to their safety, health or welfare. This provision imposes a duty on employers to members of the public. It clearly applies, for example, to school pupils and their parents. The use of the words "manage and conduct his or her undertaking" in s.12 of the 2005 Act is significant in that it underlines the new emphasis in the 2005 Act on safety management. This section applies to members of the public that have access to a place of work, while work is in progress.[45] For example, this section applies to invitees, visitors or, possibly, trespassers entering a business. The reference to "in the course of the work being carried on" seems to limit the

---

[42] See s.26 of the 2005 Act.
[43] See s.77(2)(a) of the 2005 Act.
[44] This provision has its genesis in s.3 of the English Health and Safety at Work Act, 1974 which provided that:
> "It shall be the duty of every employer to conduct his undertaking in such a way as to ensure, so far as is reasonably practicable, that persons not in his employment who may be affected thereby, are not thereby exposed to risks to their health or safety."
[45] See also the Authority's Guidelines to the Safety, Health and Welfare at Work Act, 2005, p.19.

liability of an employer in respect of injuries suffered by members of the public at his or her place of work. The definition of "place of work" in s.2 of the 2005 Act should, however, be noted in interpreting s.12 of the 2005 Act in that it refers to "a place of work" as being "a location at, in, upon or near which work is carried on". Therefore, the duty owed by employers to members of the public is not as geographically restrictive as might appear from a first reading of s.12 of the 2005 Act[46] and will, of course, depend on the nature of the hazard under consideration. A new addition to s.12 of the 2005 Act is the protection of the "welfare" of persons other than employees.

3–46   Any breach of s.12 of the 2005 Act will attract criminal liability.[47]

General duties of employees and persons in control of places of work

3–47   Chapter 2 of Part 2 imposes a number of general duties on employees and persons in control of places of work such as landlords.

3–48   Section 13 of the 2005 Act sets down the duties owed by all employees while at work. Many of these duties extend to "any other person". Consequently, school pupils, for example, are owed a range of duties under this section which may lead to the imposition of vicarious liability on schools.[48] Under s.13 employees have duties as well as rights. The employees' primary duty is to take reasonable care for their own and others' safety, health and welfare. There is also a duty on an employee to co-operate with his or her employer, to use the protective equipment and clothing provided to him or her and to report dangerous risks of which he or she becomes aware. The section is of some use in defending claims, as it enables an employer possibly to reduce his or her liability by claiming that an employee failed to comply with the obligations imposed upon him or her under this section, and was thus guilty of contributory negligence. Therefore, the section offers considerable assistance to employers, particularly in so far as discipline is concerned. This section would also appear to strengthen the position of employers defending cases before the Employment Appeals Tribunal (EAT) in the instances of employees dismissed for serious breaches of safety rules. In the case of *Michael Kellegher v Power Supermarkets Ltd*[49] the dismissed employee lifted the forks on a forklift some 17 to 20 feet in the air, while another employee was perched on them. He then drove back and forth, stopping quickly, thereby causing the forks to rattle. The nightcrew manager, Declan Doyle, observed the claimant's actions and he was dismissed. Subsequently the EAT unanimously held the applicant's dismissal for a breach of the safety procedure to have been justified in the circumstances. Mr Eamon Leahy, Chairman of the EAT, summarised the position in the following terms:

---

[46]   See, for example, *Sterling Winthrop Group v Allan* [1987] SCCR 25.
[47]   See s.77(2)(a) of the 2005 Act.
[48]   See *Magrowski v Guy's & St. Thomas's NHS Trust* [2005] E.W.C.A. Civ. 251.
[49]   M 2276, U.D, 720/89.

"[H]aving regard to the seriousness of the incident which brought about the dismissal, it is the unanimous view of the Tribunal that the respondent acted reasonably in dismissing the Appellant."

Duties of employees

3–49 Many of the duties of employees provided for in s.9 of the 1989 Act and art.14 of the 1993 Regulations are re-enacted in the 2005 Act. A number of new employee obligations are created in s.13 of the 2005 Act. These include an obligation:

- to comply with the relevant statutory provisions, as appropriate[50];
- not to be under the influence of an intoxicant at the place of work to the extent that the state he or she is in, is likely to endanger his or her own safety, health or welfare at work or that of any other person[51];
- if reasonably required by his or her employer, to submit to any appropriate, reasonable and proportionate tests for intoxicants by, or under the supervision of, a registered medical practitioner who is a competent person, as may be prescribed[52];
- not to engage in improper conduct[53] or behaviour that is likely to endanger his or her own safety or that of any other person[54];
- to attend such training and, as appropriate, undergo such assessment as may reasonably be required by his or her employer or as may be prescribed relating to safety, health and welfare at work or relating to the work carried out by the employee[55];
- to report to his or her employer or any other appropriate person as soon as practicable any work being carried on, or likely to be carried on, in a manner which may endanger the safety, health or welfare at work of an employee or that of any other person, of which he or she is aware[56];
- to report to his or her employer or any other appropriate person[57] as soon as practicable any contravention of the relevant statutory provisions which may endanger the safety, health and welfare at work of the employee or that of any other person, of which he or she is aware[58]; and
- not, on entering into a contract of employment, to misrepresent himself or herself to an employer with regard to the level of training he or she may have.[59]

---

[50] Section 13(1)(a) of the 2005 Act.
[51] Section 13(1)(b) of the 2005 Act.
[52] Section 13(1)(c) of the 2005 Act.
[53] The 2005 Act does not define "improper conduct", which will fall to be determined by the courts on a case by case basis.
[54] Section 13(1)(e) of the 2005 Act. This subsection is relevant to the area of workplace bullying. See *Code of Practice for Employers and Employees on the Prevention and Resolution of Bullying at Work* (Health and Safety Authority, 2007).
[55] Section 13(1)(f) of the 2005 Act.
[56] Section 13(1)(h)(i) of the 2005 Act.
[57] It is likely that "any other appropriate person" includes the Authority, though this is not clear from the wording of this subsection.
[58] Section 13(1)(h)(iii) of the 2005 Act.
[59] Section 13(2) of the 2005 Act.

3–50   One of the most significant additions to the duties of employees is to submit to any appropriate testing for intoxicants. Concerns have been expressed regarding this broad and far-reaching provision.[60] Regulations will be introduced detailing the circumstances and sectors to which the provision will apply. While the overarching objective of this provision is to ensure optimum safety, it does raise civil liberty issues. Employers must therefore be careful to ensure that in applying this provision in the pursuit of safety, they are not trespassing on the rights of employees. The difficulty with this provision from the employer's perspective is that it may provide an employee with a cause of action for unfair dismissal or victimisation.

An "intoxicant" is defined in s.2(1) of the 2005 Act as "alcohol and drugs and any combination of drugs or of drugs and alcohol". This definition does not discriminate between prescription and non-prescription drugs and provides no guidance on what is an acceptable quantity of drugs or alcohol. The testing must be carried out by a registered medical practitioner. It would appear that the requirement to submit to tests for intoxicants in s.13(1)(c) of the 2005 Act is not limited to health and safety requirements as it is not made subject to s.13(1)(b). This provision will be interesting to watch in that the benefits of random drug and alcohol testing as a deterrent have never been conclusively proven.

The provision for testing employees for intoxicants is short on detail, although it will not come into force in the absence of Regulations, which are expected to be introduced in late 2007. For example, no mention is made of the specific forms of testing. The uncertainty continues in that the provision makes no reference to the levels or degree of the intoxicant. For example, what amount of alcohol or other drug will be accepted within an employee's system? Further, s.13(1)(c) does not specify whether the employee may be subject to random testing[61] or merely when the employer suspects that the employee is under the influence of an intoxicant.

Section 13(1)(c) of the 2005 Act prescribes three preconditions that must be satisfied before such testing may be carried out. These preconditions are that the test must be:

(1)   appropriate;
(2)   reasonable; and
(3)   proportionate.

In light of the possible violation of an employee's constitutional right to liberty,[62] the above preconditions must be strictly construed. Whether a test for intoxicants is reasonably required will depend on the individual circumstances and the nature of the work activity. Regard should be had, for example, as to whether the employee, if intoxicated, would be likely to cause harm to himself, herself or others. The work activities of an employee will be relevant: an office worker might not pose the same risk to himself, herself or indeed others as a

---

[60]   Section 13(1)(c) of the 2005 Act.
[61]   On random testing, see random breath testing provision in the Road Traffic Act 2006.
[62]   Article 40.1.4° of the Constitution. The enactment of the European Convention on Human Rights Act 2003 is also relevant as it arguably gives added impetus to Art.40.1.4° of the Constitution.

bus driver or a person operating machinery. It is likely that an employer must be satisfied that the employee is under the influence of intoxicants, before requiring that the employee submit to tests. To satisfy the test of proportionality, it is likely that the employer will have to show that the test was necessary to prevent the employee endangering his or her own safety or the safety of others and that it was the least restrictive means to achieving that objective.[63]

An issue likely to arise is the entitlement of an employer to dismiss an employee for refusing to submit to tests.[64] Would such a dismissal be presumed unfair under the Unfair Dismissal Acts? As there is no specific guidance on this issue in the 2005 Act, it is likely that the presumption of unfairness will prevail. In any event, it would appear that a request to an employee to submit to such a test will have to be done in accordance with the three conditions prescribed. It is clear from s.13(1)(c) that these three conditions will have to be strictly adhered to.

Where employees are engaged in safety critical work, it is imperative that the employer has a drug and alcohol policy. Such a policy must be clearly understood by all employees and should be applied equally to all staff.

3–51 Section 14(a) of the 2005 Act mirrors s.9(2) of the 1989 Act. It imposes a duty on a person (whether an employee or not) not to interfere with, damage or misuse any items provided for securing safety, welfare or health at work. Section 14(b) introduces an additional duty which requires a person (whether an employee or not) not to endanger other persons in connection with his or her work activities.

3–52 A breach of any of the duties prescribed in ss.13 or 14 of the 2005 Act attracts criminal liability.[65] Pursuant to s.48(1) of the 1989 Act, only a breach of s.9(1) of the 1989 Act (the duty of an employee to take reasonable care for himself or herself) attracted criminal liability.

General duties of persons in control of places of work

3–53 The duties of persons in control of "places of work" are set out in s.15 of the 2005 Act. This section broadens the general duties of an employer to persons other than employees contained in s.8 of the 1989 Act. It requires a person who has control "to any extent" of a workplace, or the means of access to or egress from that place of work, or any article or substance used in that place of work, to ensure, so far as is reasonably practicable, that these are safe and without risk to health. A significant difference between s.15 of the 2005 Act and the corresponding provision in the 1989 Act is in the improved clarity of expression and simplicity of layout. The reference to

---

[63] For a more detailed exploration of the principle of proportionality, see *Heaney v Ireland* ([1994] 3 I.R. 593); *R v The Intervention Board, ex parte E.D. & Man (Sugar) Ltd* ([1985] E.C.R. 2889); and *Haur v Land Rheinland-Pfalz* ([1997] E.C.R. 3727).

[64] See also *Trevor Kennedy v Veolia Transport Ireland Limited*, Employment Appeals Tribunal (EAT) Decision of October 20, 2006. In that case the EAT upheld the decision to dismiss the claimant who had registered a positive result following a test for alcohol.

[65] See s.77(2)(a) of the 2005 Act.

"a non-domestic place of work" in s.15(1)(a) of the 2005 Act is probably intended to exclude building contractors working on a person's home from the terms of this provision. Section 15 expressly includes landlords and tenants, and licensors and licensees.

3–54   A breach of s.15 of the 2005 Act attracts criminal liability.[66]

General duties of other persons

3–55   Chapter 3 of Part 2 of the 2005 Act sets out a range of duties of several other stakeholders.

Designers, manufacturers, importers and suppliers

3–56   Section 10 of the 1989 Act imposed duties on designers, manufacturers, importers and suppliers of articles and substances. Section 16 of the 2005 Act is the corresponding new provision. It is preventative in nature, in that it attempts to ensure that all articles and substances used in the workplace are properly designed, constructed and tested, prior to supply and use. This section imposes onerous duties on persons who commission, procure, design and construct places of work to ensure, so far as is reasonably practicable, that any such place of work, is designed and capable of being constructed in a safe manner or without risk to health. In particular, s.16(1)(a) provides that it is the duty of "a person who designs, manufactures, imports or supplies any article for use at work" to ensure, so far as is reasonably practicable, that the article is designed and constructed so as–

> "(i) to be safe and without risk to health when properly used by a person at a place of work, and
> (ii) to comply with the relevant statutory provisions and with the provisions of any relevant enactment implementing any relevant directive of the European Communities, …".[67]

Significantly, this section places on a statutory basis the obligations on designers, manufacturers, importers and suppliers of articles and substances to comply with any relevant legislation implementing an E.U. directive. The expanded definition of "article" in s.2 of the 2005 Act should also be noted. The definition of "article" now includes machine, appliance and tool, any article designed for use as a component part of or to control any such plant, machine, machinery, and appliance or any other product used by a person at work. The 2005 Act does not amend the definition of "substance". Of particular importance is s.16(1)(b) of the 2005 Act, which obliges designers, manufacturers, importers and suppliers of articles and substances to conduct research in order to remove or minimise any risk to the safety and health of any future users.

3–57   Section 16(1)(c) of the 2005 Act imposes a duty on a person who designs, manufactures, imports or supplies any article to provide adequate

---

[66] See s.77(2)(a) of the 2005 Act.
[67] See s.16(1) of the 2005 Act.

information about any such article to the persons to whom it is supplied to ensure that it is used safely. A new provision worthy of note is s.16(1)(d), which requires the supplier to provide persons to whom the article is supplied with any revisions of the information provided under s.16(1)(c) as are necessary "by reason of it becoming known that anything relating to the article gives rise to a serious risk to safety or health". Significantly, no time limit is placed on the provision of such information. Some guidance as to what amounts to "adequate information" concerning articles is to be found in s.16(2) which provides that adequate information includes information relating to:

> "(a) the use for which the article has been designed, manufactured or tested, as the case may be, and
> (b) any conditions necessary to ensure its safe installation, use, maintenance, cleaning, dismantling or disposal without risk to safety or health."

The duty imposed on manufacturers, importers or suppliers of any substance to provide adequate information on a substance to the person to whom it is supplied is an onerous one.[68] Such information is to include any risk to safety or health "associated with its inherent properties".[69] This is the case not only for manufacturers but also for providers or suppliers of a substance.

3–58   Section 16(4) provides that a person who erects, assembles or installs any article in the place of work must ensure that it is not unsafe or a risk to health when operated in the place of work.

3–59   Any breach of s.16 of the 2005 Act attracts criminal liability.[70]

Construction work

3–60   Section 17 of the 2005 Act combines duties imposed on designers under the 1989 Act and the duties imposed on clients, designers, contractors, project supervisors for the design stage and project supervisors for the construction stage under the Safety, Health and Welfare at Work (Construction) Regulations 2001 and 2003 ("Construction Regulations"). It is a framework section setting out general obligations and applies to the following:

- someone who commissions or procures a project[71];
- someone who designs a project[72]; and
- someone who carries out construction work.[73]

Section 17 of the 2005 Act should be considered alongside the Safety, Health and Welfare of Work (Construction) Regulations 2006[74].

---

[68] See s.16(6) of the 2005 Act.
[69] See s.16(6)(b) of the 2005 Act.
[70] See s.77(2)(a) of the 2005 Act.
[71] Section 17(1) of the 2005 Act.
[72] Section 17(2) of the 2005 Act.
[73] Section 17(3) of the 2005 Act.
[74] S.I. No. 504 of 2006 and Chap. 7.

3–61   Section 17(1) creates new obligations for persons who commission or procure[75] a project for construction work,[76] which include the appointment of a competent person or persons to *ensure*, so far as is reasonably practicable, that the project:

- is designed and is capable of being constructed to be safe and without risk to health[77];
- is constructed to be safe and without risk to health[78];
- can be maintained safely and without risk to health during subsequent use[79]; and
- complies in all respects, as appropriate, with all the relevant statutory provisions.[80]

The appointment of a competent person or persons must be "in writing".[81]

3–62   Section 17(2) of the 2005 Act expands the duties of a person who designs a project for construction work. Pursuant to the 2005 Act, such a person must ensure, so far as is reasonably practicable, that it is designed and is capable of being constructed without risk to safety and health, that it can be maintained safely and that it complies in all respects with the relevant legislation.[82]

3–63   Section 17(3) sets out duties in respect of persons who carry out construction work and is similarly phrased to its counterpart in the 1989 Act.[83] It provides that a contractor "shall ensure, so far as is reasonably practicable, that [any construction work is] safe and without risk to health and that it complies in all respects, as appropriate, with the relevant statutory provisions". Section 17(4) of the 2005 Act defines "project" for the purposes of the section. It states:

> "For the purposes of this section, 'project' means any development which includes or is intended to include construction work."

3–64   Section 17 of the 2005 Act increases considerably the standard of care to be exercised by all involved in the construction process, and, in particular, clients and consultants. The use of the word "ensuring" in s.17 of the 2005 Act has increased the duties of clients, designers, contractors and project supervisors.

3–65   Detailed regulations have been introduced expanding on the general obligations set out in s.17. It is interesting to note that the new Safety, Health and

---

[75]   The 2005 Act does not define either "commission" or "procure". There is no guidance, as such, as to when a project is commissioned or procured. Does this occur when you buy the site, when you apply for planning permission or when you commence building?

[76]   "Construction work" is defined in the 2005 Act as "the carrying out of any building, civil engineering or engineering construction work" as may be prescribed by regulations to be made under the 2005 Act.

[77]   Section 17(1)(a) of the 2005 Act.

[78]   Section 17(1)(b) of the 2005 Act.

[79]   Section 17(1)(c) of the 2005 Act.

[80]   Section 17(1)(d) of the 2005 Act.

[81]   Section 17(1) of the 2005 Act.

[82]   Formerly s.11(1) of the 1989 Act.

[83]   See s.11(2) of the 1989 Act.

Welfare at Work (Construction) Regulations require employers to provide employees with site specific safety induction before commencing work on a construction site. These regulations, discussed in Chapter 7, came into force on November 6, 2006.

3–66 Any breach of s.17 of the 2005 Act by those with health and safety responsibilities (*i.e.* a client, project supervisor for the design process or designer) attracts criminal liability.[84]

PROTECTIVE AND PREVENTIVE MEASURES

3–67 Part 3 of the 2005 Act focuses on protective and preventive measures and identifies the approach to be adopted to eliminate or reduce accidents and ill health at work.

Competent person

3–68 An employer is obliged to engage one or more competent persons to enable him or her to perform functions to be specified by the employer in order to ensure the prevention of risks to safety, health and welfare at work. Unlike the 1989 Act, s.18 of the 2005 Act requires an employer to appoint a "competent person" as the organisation's safety officer. Section 18(4) should be noted in that it permits an employer to appoint a person as the competent person in the area of compliance in circumstances where such a person is available in the workforce. Moreover, such a person is to be preferred over external competent persons not in the "employer's employment". Section 2(2)(a) of the 2005 Act defines "competent person".[85] Significantly, s.2(2)(b) provides as follows:

> "Account shall be taken, as appropriate, for the purposes of *paragraph(a)* of the framework of qualifications referred to in the Qualifications (Education and Training) Act 1999."

It is clear from the foregoing that FETAC recognised qualifications shall be taken into account in assessing competence.

Risk assessment

3–69 Section 19 of the 2005 Act incorporates many of the provisions in the 1993 Regulations including the requirement in reg.10 that risk assessments must be in writing and periodically reviewed. It provides that every employer and every person controlling a workplace must identify the hazards at the place of work, assess the risks presented by those hazards and have a written assessment of the risks as they apply to his or her employees, including any single employee and group (or groups) of employees who may be exposed. The words "hazards" and "risks" are not defined in the 2005 Act. That said, the Authority has produced useful guidance on these terms. A "hazard" refers to the potential to cause harm and could be a machine or a chemical substance.

---

[84] See s.77(2)(a) of the 2005 Act. Also ss.80(1) and 80(2) of the 2005 Act.
[85] See para.3–07.

"Risk" denotes the chance of the aforementioned harm taking place, the consequences of the harm should it take place and the number of persons who might be exposed to the hazard.

3–70   Section 19(2) of the 2005 Act is a new section. It provides that in carrying out the risk assessment the employer must have regard to the duties imposed by health and safety legislation. Section 19(4) of the 2005 Act requires an employer to implement any improvements considered necessary in respect of the safety, health and welfare at work of his or her employees arising from the most recent risk assessment.

3–71   Section 19(3) of the 2005 Act states that the risk assessment must be reviewed where there has been a significant change in the matters to which it relates, or where there is another reason for believing it is no longer valid. In an earlier text of the legislation an employer was obliged to review the risk assessment annually, regardless of whether there had been any changes or not. The removal of the requirement for an annual risks assessment was unfortunate, as it would have ensured greater vigilance in the maintenance of a low-risk health and safety environment.

3–72   Section 19(4) of the 2005 Act mirrors reg.5(c) of the 1993 General Application Regulations in that it requires an employer to take steps to implement any improvement considered necessary following a risk assessment.

Safety statement

3–73   Section 20 is probably the most important provision in the 2005 Act in terms of the implementation and application of health and safety measures. Under s.20 every employer must prepare or cause to be prepared a statement in writing which is known as a safety statement. This statement is to be based on the hazards identified and the risk assessment carried out under s.19 of the 2005 Act. It must set out how the safety, health and welfare of employees is to be secured and managed in the workplace.

3–74   The safety statement should contain a summary of the organisation's safety and health goals and objectives, assignment of responsibilities and the means of achieving the stated aims and objectives. The safety statement should demonstrate how the employer intends to comply with s.8(2) of the Safety, Health and Welfare at Work Act 2005, which details the key duties of an employer.[86] The purpose of the safety statement is to require employers to assess the workplace over which they have control and to identify the hazards to safety, health and welfare at that place of work.

The safety statement therefore must be based on a systematic and comprehensive identification of hazards. Risk assessment must be followed by the implementation of risk reduction measures.

---

[86] See paras 3–20 to 3–31.

3–75 The risk assessments undertaken in the preparation of a safety statement take the form of a systematic informed evaluation of the risk or danger associated with work tasks. They are a vital planning and management tool to which the phrase *premonitus premunitus* (forewarned is forearmed) is directly applicable. Thus, the emphasis that the enforcement authorities will place on such assessments cannot be overestimated. Visiting inspectors often take as their starting point a review of the risk assessments; this is evidence that the organisation is taking responsibility for the health and safety of its employees and is up-to-date with current legal requirements. (Frequently asked questions include: "Where is the safety statement? Where is the risk assessment for the fork lift truck?") Risk assessments are a key mechanism for achieving and maintaining safety in the workplace.

3–76 A relevant and instructive case is *Miles v Parsons*.[87] This case concerned a 14-year-old newspaper delivery girl who was injured in a road traffic accident when a vehicle hit her as she was crossing a busy road on her bicycle. It was held that the third named defendant had failed to assess the route, traffic conditions or general safety implications of the paper round at any time prior to the accident. The court stated that the newsagent should have devised an order of delivery that effectively minimised crossing of the road. It further held that he should have outlined to the claimant the manner in which the round had been devised so as to minimise the crossing of the road. The court held that the third named defendant's breach of his duty of care had caused the accident. On the evidence, the court noted that the driver had been aware of the claimant when she was at least 100 yards away. On that basis, the court found that he had moved to the centre of the road to give the claimant a wide enough berth, but had only moved at the last minute to avoid a collision and was travelling at too great a speed to overtake safely. The court accordingly attributed 20 per cent negligence to both the driver and claimant. The third named defendant was held to be 60 per cent negligent due to the absence of a risk assessment.

3–77 Section 20(2) of the 2005 Act identifies the essential components of a safety statement, and provides that every employer must ensure that a safety statement specifies–

"(a) the hazards identified and the risks assessed,
  (b) the protective and preventive measures taken and the resources provided for protecting safety, health and welfare at the place of work to which the safety statement relates,
  (c) the plans and procedures to be followed and the measures to be taken in the event of an emergency or serious and imminent danger, in compliance with *sections 8* and *11* [of the 2005 Act],
  (d) the duties of his or her employees regarding safety, health and welfare at work, including co-operation with the employer and any persons who have responsibility under the relevant statutory provisions in matters relating to safety, health and welfare at work,

---

[87] Unreported, Q.B.D., February 10, 2000.

(e)   the names and, where applicable, the job title or position held of each person responsible for performing tasks assigned to him or her pursuant to the safety statement,
and

(f)   the arrangements made regarding the appointment of safety representatives and consultation with, and participation by, employees and safety representatives, in compliance with *sections 25* and *26* [of the 2005 Act], including the names of the safety representative and the members of the safety committee, if appointed."

The safety statement must now specify the risks assessed and identify the hazards to safety, health and welfare at the place of work, which is a new requirement introduced under s.20(2)(a) of the 2005 Act. It must also set out the protective and preventive measures taken and the resources provided for safeguarding safety, health and welfare at the place of work to which the safety statement relates. The safety statement must specify the plans and procedures to be followed and the measures to be taken in the event of an emergency or serious and imminent danger. In addition, a safety statement must identify the co-operation required from employees and include the names and job titles of persons responsible for the safety tasks assigned to them under the 2005 Act and under the safety statement. Another new provision in s.20(2)(f) of the 2005 Act is that a safety statement must specify the arrangements made regarding the appointment of safety representatives and safety consultation in the place of work. The names of the safety representatives and the members of the safety committee, if appointed, must also be included in the safety statement pursuant to subs.(2)(f).

3–78   Section 20(3) of the 2005 Act provides that the employer must bring the terms of the safety statement to the attention of employees annually or following any amendment of it. Employers must also bring the safety statement to the attention of new employees upon commencement of employment and other persons at the place of work who may be exposed to any specific risk to which the safety statement refers. This must be done in a form, manner and, as appropriate, in language that is reasonably likely to be understood by the employees. This requirement should prompt employers to examine the profile of their workforce in order to decide whether the safety statement should be made available in one or more languages. A similar requirement applies in respect of a Safety Plan.[88]

3–79   Where specific jobs being performed at the place of work pose serious risks to safety, health or welfare, the employer must bring to the attention of those affected by the risks the relevant extracts of the safety statement covering the risk identified, the risk assessment and the protective and preventive measures taken.[89] Section 20(4) of the 2005 Act is, however, silent on what amounts to a "serious risk". A serious risk is presumably equivalent to a high risk.

3–80   The obligation to review annually the safety statement has been removed. Section 20(5) of the 2005 Act now requires an employer to review

---

[88]   See Chap.7.
[89]   Section 20(4) of the 2005 Act.

the safety statement where there has been a significant change in the matters to which a safety statement refers or when there is reason to believe that the safety statement is no longer valid. This section also empowers an inspector to require that a safety statement be amended.

3–81 Employers conducting activities as may be prescribed in regulations or rules and who contract for services with another employer must check that the service supplier has an up-to-date safety statement. This provision adopts a holistic and joined up approach to the management of safety and health. In particular, s.20(6) of the 2005 Act attempts to target large organisations, including those in the public sector, which buy in services extensively. It will require all employers who engage sub-contractors to ensure that the sub-contractor has an up-to-date safety statement.[90]

3–82 A copy of a safety statement or relevant extract must be kept available for inspection in or near every place of work to which it relates while work is being carried out there.[91] This provision attempts to ensure that the safety statement is a living document to be used as necessary.

3–83 The 2005 Act introduces a significant change to the requirement that every employer have a safety statement where the employer has three or fewer employees. In particular, s.20(8) of the 2005 Act adopts a more streamlined approach to complying with the requirement to prepare a safety statement by removing the requirement on an employer with three or fewer employees to have an up-to-date safety statement. It provides that such an employer can satisfy the safety statement requirement by observing the terms of a special Code of Practice,[92] if any, to be developed by the Authority for a number of industries and sectors. The farming sector and small businesses in the maintenance and service sectors are the likely beneficiaries of the relief available under this provision. In fact, the Authority is currently working on the drafting of three codes of practice, one of which has been completed and is in relation to agriculture[93].[94] If there is no code of practice covering the type of work activity carried on by the employer, what duty arises for such an employer in respect of the preparation of a safety statement? The Act is silent on this point, though prudence would dictate that such an employer should prepare a safety statement. Regulations on this issue are expected in late 2007.

3–84 Section 20(9) of the 2005 Act should be noted in that it imposes an obligation on an employer in preparing a safety statement to take account of his or her duties to persons other than employees.[95]

---

[90] Section 20(6) of the 2005 Act.
[91] Section 20(7) of the 2005 Act.
[92] A Code of Practice prepared and published by the Authority under s.60 of the 2005 Act.
[93] This Code of Practice consists of three distinct documents for use by farmers and was published in September 2006. The code of practice pack contains the actual code of practice itself, a risk assessment document, the safe system of work plan for agriculture and the farm safe DVD.
[94] The other codes of practice in preparation are in the areas of quarrying and construction.
[95] See ss.12 and 15 of the 2005 Act. Also s.19(5) of the 2005 Act.

3–85 It should be noted that s.12(6) of the 1989 Act, which required the annual report of a company to include an evaluation of the extent to which the policy set out in the safety statement was fulfilled during the period of time covered by the report, has been omitted from the 2005 Act. That said, it is good practice to include such an evaluation in the annual report, even though it is no longer required under statute.

3–86 The Health and Safety Authority have published excellent guidance on the drafting of a safety statement.[96]

3–87 Where there has been loss or damage suffered by an employee, the mere failure of an employer to prepare a safety statement does not automatically impose liability on the employer for that loss or damage. In *Matthews v The Irish Society of Autism*[97] it was held that the defendant's failure to prepare a safety statement was irrelevant in that case, as the risk in question was not one that would have been adverted to in the safety statement, had one been prepared.[98]

3–88 In a ruling of the Master of the High Court in the context of an application for discovery the following statement appears:

> "In a factory accident context, the failure of the defendant to comply with his statutory obligation to prepare a safety statement is ... a 'surplus' fact. I always consider most carefully requests for discovery of safety statements before rejecting them. The non-existence of such a statement is directly probative of nothing except failure to compile same and though if indirectly probative of the defendant's attitude to safety issues, this attitude is rarely material. The contents of same if one exists is not probative of the standard of care actually implemented. And though undoubtedly probative of the defendant's knowledge of the existence of a risk, if the risk is referred to therein, the defendant's state of knowledge is hardly ever a material fact in such a case ... Since it is not probative of any disputed material fact, it is neither 'genuinely necessary' nor 'really needed'."[99]

Shared places of work

3–89 Section 21 of the 2005 Act mirrors reg.6 of the 1993 General Application Regulations and provides that, in addition to the general duties arising under the 2005 Act, employers who share a place of work must, having regard to the nature of the work carried on at the place of work, co-operate, coordinate and exchange information with "their respective employees and safety representatives (if any) of any risks to their safety, health and welfare arising from the work activity". This

---

[96] See "New Safety Statement Guidelines" (Health and Safety Authority, 2006) and Part IV of this book.

[97] Unreported, High Court, Laffoy J., April 18, 1997. Also *McLoughlin v Carr* unreported, High Court, Peart J., November 4, 2005.

[98] See Part IV of this book for guidelines on the preparation of a safety statement.

[99] *Michael Linsley v Cadbury Schweppes International Beverages Limited*, decision of Master Edmund Honohon of the High Court, February 19, 2004.

may take the form of exchanging safety statements or relevant extracts therefrom relating to hazards and risks to employees.

Health surveillance and medical fitness to work

3–90 Section 22 of the 2005 Act mirrors reg.15 of the 1993 General Application Regulations.[100] It imposes specific duties in respect of health surveillance on every employer. Health surveillance is defined in s.2(1) of the 2005 Act as follows:

> "'health surveillance' means the periodic review, for the purpose of protecting health and preventing occupationally related disease, of the health of employees, so that any adverse variations in their health that may be related to working conditions are identified as early as possible."

3–91 Section 22(1) provides that "[e]very employer shall ensure that health surveillance appropriate to the risks to safety, health and welfare that may be incurred at the place of work identified by the risk assessment ... is made available to his or her employees". This duty could be construed as requiring an employer to make available a counselling service or an employee assistance programme. It should be noted that in *Hatton v Sutherland*[101] the Court of Appeal held that an employer who offers a confidential advice service, "with referral to appropriate counselling or treatment services", was unlikely to be found in breach of his or her duty to employees. Hale L.J. stated:

> "The key is to offer help on a completely confidential basis. The employee can then be encouraged to recognise the signs and seek that help without fearing its effects upon his job or prospects; the employer need not make intrusive inquiries or over-react to such problems as he does detect; responsibility for accessing the service can be left with the people who are best equipped to know what the problems are, the employee, his family and friends; and if reasonable help is offered either directly or through referral to other services, then all that reasonably could be done has been done. Obviously, not all employers have the resources to put such systems in place, but an employer who does have a system along those lines is unlikely to be found in breach of his duty of care towards his employees ... except where he has been placing totally unreasonable demands upon an individual in circumstances where the risk of harm was clear."

In *Michael Maher v Jabil Global Services Limited*, Clarke J. adopted a similar approach, although he noted *obiter* that the benefit of providing counselling to avoid a finding of liability would be subject "to a caveat that if the court was satisfied that notwithstanding the provision of such a service the truth was that an employer was intent on removing an employee the availability of such a service might be regarded as being more a matter of form than substance".[102]

3–92 Section 23 of the 2005 Act is a new provision. It provides that where an employee is working in a safety critical situation, he or she, subject to such

---

[100] Article 15 of the 1993 Regulations was the provision which dealt with health surveillance in the 1993 Regulations.
[101] [2002] 2 All E.R. 1.
[102] Unreported, High Court, May 12, 2005 at pp. 21–22. See also Chap.4.

regulations as may be prescribed (*i.e.* in accordance with the regulations that have yet to be introduced by the Minister), may be required to undergo a periodic medical assessment of fitness for work to be carried out "by a registered medical practitioner, nominated by" his or her employer.[103] Section 23(2) provides:

> "An employer shall ensure that employees undergo assessment by a registered medical practitioner of their fitness to perform work activities, as may be prescribed, which, when performed, give rise to serious risks to the safety, health and welfare of persons at work."

The work activities likely to be prescribed are, for example, those involving construction work. This section of the 2005 Act is short on detail in that no guidance is provided as to what is meant by "serious risks".

If, following an assessment, the registered medical practitioner is of the opinion that the employee is unfit for the work activity concerned, he or she must inform the employer, "by the quickest practicable means", of that opinion, giving reasons for it "and the likelihood of early resumption of work for rehabilitative purposes". The registered medical practitioner must also inform the employee of his or her opinion and the reasons for it.

Should an employee become aware that he or she is suffering from any disease, or physical or mental impairment, which if he or she were to perform the safety critical activity concerned would be likely to cause him or her to expose himself or herself or another person to danger, then the employee is under a duty to "immediately notify the employer concerned or a registered medical practitioner nominated by that employer who shall in turn notify the employer".[104]

Section 23(5) of the 2005 Act provides that where an employer receives a notification either by a registered medical practitioner or by the employee "he or she shall immediately take appropriate action" to manage the situation so as "to comply with his or her general duties" under the 2005 Act.

Joint safety and health agreements

3–93 Section 24 of the 2005 Act includes an innovative new provision which has its origins in a number of the northern member states of the European Union. In summary, it enables the social partners (i.e. trade unions and bodies representing employers) to enter into agreements setting out practical guidance on safety, health and welfare, and the requirements of health and safety laws. Such an agreement is known as a "joint safety and health agreement". The parties can apply to the Authority for approval of a joint safety and health agreement or of its variation. The Authority can approve such an agreement where it is satisfied that:

> "(a) the parties concerned consent to the approval sought,
> (b) the agreement is expressed to apply to all employees of a particular class and their employers and the Authority is satisfied that it is normal and desirable that it should so apply,

---

[103] See s.23(1) of the 2005 Act.
[104] See s.23(4) of the 2005 Act.

(c) the parties to the agreement are substantially representative of such employees and employers,

(d) the agreement does not conflict with the requirements of the relevant statutory provisions, and

(e) the agreement is in a form suitable for approval".

3–94 Section 24(3) of the 2005 Act provides that the Authority is to direct the parties concerned to publish information on the agreement in such a manner that is likely to bring the application to the notice of all persons concerned. The Authority cannot approve a joint safety and health agreement until one month after its publication and if any objection is received within that period, the Authority must consider the objection and cannot approve the agreement if it does not comply with the requirements of the Authority previously alluded to.[105] Where the Authority approves a joint safety and health agreement, it must publish a notice of approval in Iris Oifigiúil and in at least two daily newspapers.

3–95 Section 24(7) of the 2005 Act requires the parties to a joint safety and health agreement to make copies of the agreement available for inspection by any person affected. An approved joint safety and health agreement can be taken into account by the Authority in assessing compliance with health and safety laws, whether or not an employer, in an employment sector covered by the agreement is a party to it.[106] This does not, however, mean that compliance with a joint safety and health agreement provides a defence to an employer's failure to comply with his or her general duties under the 2005 Act.

SAFETY REPRESENTATIVES AND SAFETY CONSULTATION

3–96 Part 4 of the 2005 Act places a special emphasis on safety representatives and re-enacts the provisions in the 1989 Act on the consultation of workers. This part of the 2005 Act includes an important new provision whereby an employer cannot penalise an employee for acting in good faith in the interests of health and safety.

3–97 Under Part 4 of the 2005 Act, every employer must consult with his or her employees on safety, health and welfare matters at work.[107] In so far as is "reasonably practicable", he or she must take into account representations made by his or her employees. The 2005 Act confers the right on employees to make representations to their employer on matters of safety, health and welfare and to appoint a safety representative from among their number to act on their own behalf. This safety representative has a right to information, and to investigate accidents, potential hazards and complaints.

---

[105] See s.24(2) of the 2005 Act.

[106] Section 24(8) of the 2005 Act.

[107] See also "Guidelines on Safety Consultation and Safety Representatives" (Health and Safety Authority, 1994) and videos on the Safety Representative (Health and Safety Authority, 1991).

3–98 Section 25 of the 2005 Act enhances the rights of worker safety representatives. This section confers the right on employees to elect a safety representative, or more than one, if the employer agrees, from among their number, to represent them in consultations with the employer on matters of safety, health and welfare. This safety representative has wide powers to inspect, investigate accidents or dangerous occurrences, accompany an inspector who is carrying out an inspection and make oral and written submissions. It should be noted that employees do not have to appoint safety representatives. This is an issue entirely for the employees themselves.

3–99 Section 25(2)(a) of the 2005 Act provides that the safety representative has the right to inspect the place of work after giving reasonable notice to the employer. The safety representative, however, may inspect immediately if there is an accident, dangerous occurrence or imminent danger or risk to safety, health and welfare. Section 25(2)(b) enables a safety representative to investigate accidents and dangerous occurrences provided this does not interfere with another person carrying out duties under health and safety laws.

3–100 Section 25(4) of the 2005 Act requires an employer to consider representations made to him or her by the safety representative(s) concerning matters of safety, health and welfare at work "of his or her employees and, so far as is reasonably practicable, take any action that he or she considers necessary or appropriate with regard to those representations." It should be noted that s.25(5) imposes an obligation on an employer to give safety representative(s) such time off from his or her work as is reasonable without loss of remuneration, for the purposes of acquiring the knowledge and training necessary to discharge his or her functions as a safety representative(s).

3–101 Section 26 of the 2005 Act provides for consultation and participation of employees in discussions on all questions relating to health and safety at work. It implements Art.12 of the 1989 Framework Directive, which provides as follows:

> "1. Employers shall consult workers and/or their representatives and allow them to take part in discussions on all questions relating to safety and health at work.
>   This presupposes:
>   – the consultation of workers,
>   – the right of workers and/or their representatives to make proposals,
>   – balanced participation in accordance with national laws and/or practices.
> 2. Workers or workers' representatives with specific responsibility for the safety and health of workers shall take part in a balanced way, in accordance with national laws and/or practices, or shall be consulted in advance and in good time by the employer …
> 3. Workers' representatives with specific responsibility for the safety and health of workers shall have the right to ask the employer to take appropriate measures and to submit proposals to him to that end to mitigate hazards for workers and/or to remove sources of danger.

4. The workers referred to in paragraph 2 and the workers' representatives referred to in paragraphs 2 and 3 may not be placed at a disadvantage because of their respective activities referred to in paragraphs 2 and 3.

5. Employers must allow workers' representatives with specific responsibility for the safety and health of workers adequate time off work, without loss of pay, and provide them with the necessary means to enable such representatives to exercise their rights and functions deriving from this Directive.

6. Workers and/or their representatives are entitled to appeal, in accordance with national law and/or practice to the authority responsible for safety and health protection at work if they consider that the measures taken and the means employed by the employer are inadequate for the purposes of ensuring safety and health at work.

Workers' representatives must be given the opportunity to submit their observations during inspection visits by the competent authority."

3–102   Section 26 places a duty on employers to consult with their employees so as to make and maintain arrangements to enable employers and employees to co-operate to promote and develop safety, health and welfare and to monitor the effectiveness of those arrangements. As part of the aforementioned arrangements, employers must consult employees, their safety representatives or both, "as appropriate", "in advance" and "in good time" on any measure "proposed to be taken in the place of work which may substantially affect the safety, health and welfare" of employees.[108] It is clear from the use of the words "as appropriate" in s.26(1)(b) that there is no obligation on employers to consult with both their employees and a safety representative. In some cases the employer may deem it sufficient and more efficient to consult only with the safety representatives. The extent of the information and consultation requirement was recently clarified by the European Court of Justice (ECJ) in *Irmtraud Junk v Wolfgang Kühnel*,[109] a case that dealt with consultation and information in the context of collective redundancies. The ECJ referred, with approval, to Art.2 of Council Directive 98/59/EC of 20 July 1998, which establishes the "obligation to negotiate" and seemed to impose a standard or requirement of "meaningful consultation". An even more onerous obligation is likely to be imposed by the ECJ on employers in respect of information and consultation in the safety and health context.

3–103   Section 26(3) of the 2005 Act is an innovation in the 2005 Act in that it provides, with the agreement of an employer, for the establishment of a Safety Committee. The Safety Committee, where it is established, exists in place of the aforementioned provisions on consultation and participation. Schedule 4 of the 2005 Act outlines the rules governing the composition and functions of a Safety Committee. For example, it provides that a Safety Committee shall comprise not less than 3 members:

"2. The number of members of a safety committee shall not be less than 3 and shall not exceed one for every 20 persons employed in a place of work at the time when the committee is appointed or 10, whichever is less."

---

[108] See s.26(1)(b) of the 2005 Act.
[109] Case C-188/03, January 27, 2005.

It is clear from the wording of this subsection that, while desirable, an employer is not obliged to agree to the establishment of a Safety Committee. As the consultation requirement is related to the employees at a place of work (and not to a particular undertaking), an employer with multiple places of work must engage in consultation in each place of work on local matters.

Protection against penalisation

3–104   Section 27 of the 2005 Act includes an important new provision that employees should not be penalised for acting in good faith in the interests of health and safety. This section prohibits an employer from penalising an employee for:

* being a safety representative;
* complying with health and safety legislation;
* making a complaint or a representation about health and safety to the safety representative or to the employer or to an inspector;
* giving evidence in enforcement proceedings; and
* leaving, or while the danger persisted, refusing to return to his or her work in the face of serious or imminent danger.[110]

It is to be noted that under s.27 of the 2005 Act penalisation includes any act or omission by an employer, or person acting on behalf of an employer, that affects to his or her detriment, an employee with respect to any term or condition of his or her employment including:

* suspension;
* lay-off;
* dismissal;
* demotion;
* loss of opportunity for promotion;
* transfer of duties;
* change of location of place of work;
* reduction in wages;
* change in working hours;
* imposition of any discipline;
* imposition of any reprimand or other penalty; and
* coercion or intimidation.

This would certainly cover emerging health and safety issues such as stress and bullying. Disagreements as to whether or not an issue concerns a breach of health and safety law are to be determined by the rights commissioner.

3–105   The s.27 penalisation provision broadly mirrors ss. 44, 48 and 49 of the English Employment Rights Act 1996. That said, the Irish penalisation section is broader in scope than the equivalent English provision in that it affords protection to all employees making a complaint. The English equivalent applies only to an employee who can demonstrate that there was no safety representative or safety committee or there was such a representative or safety

---

[110] See s.27(3) of the 2005 Act.

committee but it was not reasonably practicable for the employee to raise the matter by those means.

3–106   If liability is to be imposed on an employer for penalisation, then the employee will have to prove:

1. he or she suffered detriment in respect of any term or condition of his or her employment within the terms of s.27(1) or (2) of the 2005 Act;
2. he or she has acted in compliance with s.27(3) of the 2005 Act; and
3. that the reason the employer penalised the employee by imposing the detriment was one of the protected activities detailed in s.27(3).

In *Shamoon v Chief Constable of the Royal Ulster Constabulary*[111] Lord Hope of Craighead held that the word "detriment" had an objective meaning stating as follows:

> "As May LJ put it in *De Souza v Automobile Association* [1986] IRLR 103, 107, the court or tribunal must find that by reason of the act or acts complained of a reasonable worker would or might take the view that he had thereby been disadvantaged in the circumstances in which he had thereafter to work.
>
> But once this requirement is satisfied, the only other limitation that can be read into the word is that indicated by Lord Brightman. As he put it in *Ministry of Defence v Jeremiah* [1979] IRLR 436, 440 one must take all the circumstances into account. This is a test of materiality. Is the treatment of such a kind that a reasonable worker would or might take the view that in all the circumstances it was to his detriment? An unjustified sense of grievance cannot amount to 'detriment'. *Barclays Bank plc v Kapur & Ors* [1995] IRLR 87. But contrary to the view that was expressed in *Lord Chancellor v Coker and Osamor* [2001] IRLR 116, on which the Court of Appeal relied, it is not necessary to demonstrate some physical or economic consequence. As Lord Hoffmann pointed out in Khan's case, at p.835, paragraph 52, the employment tribunal has jurisdiction to award compensation for injury to feelings whether or not compensation is to be awarded under any other head."

3–107   The dismissal of an employee following penalisation will be deemed to be unfair under the Unfair Dismissal Acts 1977–2001. Therefore, the normal rules obtaining in respect of an employee claiming unfair dismissal[112] do not apply. However, in such a case relief can only be sought under the 2005 Act or the Unfair Dismissal Acts.[113] Section 27(7) should also be noted in that it provides that if an employee is dismissed, the employee shall not be regarded as unfairly dismissed if the employer shows that it was (or would have been) so negligent for the employee to take the steps which he or she took (or proposed to take) that a reasonable employer might have dismissed him or her for taking (or proposing to take) them.

3–108   Sections 28, 29 and 30 of the 2005 Act introduce a profound change in the way in which dispute resolution about health and safety issues are dealt

---

[111] [2003] IRLR 286.
[112] For example, the requirement of 12 months continuous service.
[113] See s.27(5) of the 2005 Act.

with. Under the new complaints procedure an employer who breaches the aforementioned s.27 of the 2005 Act may have to defend his or her actions before a rights commissioner. Section 28 of the 2005 Act provides that a rights commissioner can:

> "(a) give the parties an opportunity to be heard ... and ... present any evidence relevant to the complaint;
> (b) give a decision in writing in relation to [the complaint]; and
> (c) communicate the decision to the parties".

A rights commissioner can declare that the complaint was, or as the case may be, was not well-founded. Alternatively, the Commissioner could direct the employer to take a specific course of action or to pay compensation.

3–109   The Rights Commissioner is given considerable discretion in awarding compensation. The Commissioner is merely required to pay such compensation "as is just and equitable having regard to all the circumstances." A Rights Commissioner must receive a complaint within the period of six months, beginning on the date of the contravention to which the complaint relates, or such further period not exceeding six months as the Rights Commissioner considers reasonable.

A complaint is made by giving notice of it in writing to a Rights Commissioner. The complaint, which must be given to the defendant by the Rights Commissioner, must contain such particulars and be in such form as may be specified from time to time by the Minister for Enterprise, Trade and Employment. A Rights Commissioner will find for a complainant only where all three elements of the aforementioned test for the imposition of liability for penalisation are proven. All proceedings before the Rights Commissioner are conducted *in camera*. Any decision of the Rights Commissioner must be furnished to the Labour Court.

Section 29 of the 2005 Act provides that a decision of a rights commissioner can be appealed to the Labour Court. The appeal, which must be made within six weeks of the date on which the decision of the Rights Commissioner has been communicated to the parties, amounts to a new hearing, with the Labour Court empowered to affirm, vary or set aside the decision of a Rights Commissioner. Section 29(6) of the 2005 Act should be noted in that it provides that an appeal from the Labour Court to the High Court is only possible on a point of law. A determination of the Labour Court can be enforced in the Circuit Court.[114]

THE AUTHORITY

3–110   Part 5 of the 2005 Act deals with the Authority. Section 34(1) of the 2005 Act states that the general functions of the Authority are:

> "(a) to promote, encourage and foster the prevention of accidents, dangerous occurrences and personal injury at work in accordance with the relevant statutory provisions,
> (b) to promote, encourage, foster and provide education and training in the safety, health and welfare of persons at work,

---

[114] See s.30 of the 2005 Act.

(c) to encourage and foster measures promoting the safety, health and welfare of persons at work,

(d) subject to [section 34](2) and section 33 [of the 2005 Act], to make adequate arrangements for the enforcement of the relevant statutory provisions,

(e) to monitor, evaluate and make recommendations to the Minister regarding implementation of and compliance with-

   (i) the relevant statutory provisions, and

   (ii) best practice relating to safety, health and welfare at work, and the review and maintenance of relevant records by employers,

(f) to promote, encourage and foster co-operation with and between persons or bodies of persons that represent employees and employers and any other persons or bodies of persons, as appropriate, as regards the prevention of risks to safety, health and welfare at work in accordance with the relevant statutory provisions,

(g) to make any arrangements that it considers appropriate for providing information and advice on matters relating to safety, health and welfare at work,

(h) to make any arrangements that it considers appropriate to conduct, commission, promote, support and evaluate research, surveys and studies on matters relating to the functions of the Authority and for this purpose-

   (i) to foster and promote contacts and the exchange of information with other persons or bodies of persons involved in safety, health and welfare at work in and outside the State, and

   (ii) as it considers appropriate, to publish in the form and manner that the Authority thinks fit, results arising out of such research, studies and surveys,

(i) in accordance with section 43 [of the 2005 Act], to prepare and adopt a strategy statement and to monitor its implementation,

(j) in accordance with section 44 [of the 2005 Act], to prepare and adopt a work programme,

(k) to comply with any directions in writing, whether general or particular, relating to its functions, that the Minister may from time to time give to the Authority,

(l) to give to the Minister any information relating to the performance of its functions that the Minister may from time to time require, and

(m) to perform any additional functions conferred on the Authority by order under section 35 [of the 2005 Act]."

3–111 The matters detailed in subsections (1)(e), (1)(g), (1)(h), (1)(i), (1)(j), (1)(k) and (1)(m) above are new functions of the Authority. Section 34(1)(k) of the 2005 Act is to be regretted in that it undermines the independence of the Authority in that it requires the Authority to comply with any "directions" that the Minister may give to the Authority.

REGULATIONS AND CODES OF PRACTICE

3–112 Part 6 of the 2005 Act is devoted to the making of regulations and codes of practice, and enforcement. It also requires the Authority to review on a regular basis all relevant health and safety legislation.[115]

---

[115] Section 57 of the 2005 Act.

Codes of practice

3–113   Section 60 of the 2005 Act empowers the Authority, with the consent of the Minister for Enterprise, Trade and Employment, to prepare or approve technical specifications in the guise of Approved Codes of Practice to support the detailed statutory provisions. The requirement that the Authority obtain the consent of the Minister before publishing or approving a code of practice is a new provision in the 2005 Act. The Authority may publish, in such a manner as the Authority considers appropriate, a draft of the code of practice, in full or in part, and must give persons one month from the date of publication to make written representations. Where the Authority publishes or approves a code of practice, or any part of it, it must publish a notice in Iris Oifigiúil, identifying the code, outlining the safety, health and welfare matters in respect of which the code is published and specifying the date on which the code will come into operation. Following the consultation and, where relevant, having considered the representations, if any, made, the Authority must submit the draft code to the Minister for his or her consent, with or without modification. Section 60(7) of the 2005 Act should be noted in that it ensures that existing codes of practice remain in force notwithstanding the repeal of the 1989 Act under which they were introduced.

3–114   Section 31 of the 1989 Act provided that a failure to observe any part of a code of practice would not, of itself, render a person liable to criminal proceedings. No corresponding provision appears in the 2005 Act. That said, failure to observe a code of practice does not, as such, render a person liable under the 2005 Act.

Section 61 of the 2005 Act applies to those codes of practice issued for the purpose of ensuring compliance with a statutory provision. It provides that the provisions of such codes shall be admissible in evidence in criminal proceedings:

> "[w]here it is proved that any act or omission of the defendant alleged to consti-
> tute the contravention–
>
> (i)   is a failure to observe a code of practice ..., or
> (ii) is a compliance with that code of practice."

It can be seen from the foregoing that the special legal standing accorded to the code of practice means that if you are prosecuted for a breach of health and safety law, and it is proven that you did not "observe" the relevant provisions of the code of practice, you will need to demonstrate that you have complied with the law in some other manner or a court will find you liable.

MISCELLANEOUS

3–115   Part 8 of the 2005 Act addresses several miscellaneous matters.

3–116   Section 86 of the 2005 Act states that the Authority shall provide an indemnity for inspectors who carry out their duties under the 2005 Act in a bona fide manner against all actions or claims, howsoever arising, in respect of the carrying out by them of these duties.

3–117 Section 88 of the 2005 Act enables the Minister for Enterprise, Trade and Employment to prescribe any work activity to which the provisions of the 2005 Act apply as being an activity which may not be undertaken except in accordance with the terms or conditions of a licence issued by the Authority or a prescribed person. The type of work activity that will be prescribed under this section is likely to be confined to high-risk work activities.

The terms or conditions that may attach to a licence include those relating to its expiry or revocation. Section 88(5) requires the Authority or a prescribed person to keep an up to date register of all licences granted. The Authority can publish details of any licence application and invite representations concerning it from interested parties. If the Authority or a prescribed person refuses to grant a licence, or grants a licence subject to conditions which the applicant is dissatisfied with, then the applicant may appeal the decision of the Authority to the High Court. A further appeal can be made to the Supreme Court on a point of law.

SCHEDULES

3–118 There are seven schedules to the 2005 Act. Schedule 1 identifies associated statutory provisions upon which the Authority is in a position to comment. Schedule 2 contains a list of "existing enactments"[116].Schedule 3 identifies the general principles of prevention. Broadly, these relate to the evaluation and avoidance of risk, the adaptation of the workplace and system of work, giving priority to collective protective measures over individual protective measures, the development of an adequate prevention policy in relation to safety, health and welfare at work and the provision of appropriate training and instructions to employees. Schedule 4 outlines the conditions attaching to safety committees. Schedule 5 covers appointments to and procedures for the Board of the Authority while Schedule 6 deals with the appointment and functions of the chief executive of the Authority. Schedule 7, as previously stated, sets out matters which can be covered in Regulations.

---

[116] See the definition of existing enactments in s.2 of the 2005 Act. Also s.4 of the 2005 Act.

CHAPTER 4

BULLYING, HARASSMENT AND STRESS AS HEALTH AND SAFETY ISSUES

INTRODUCTION

4–01   The Safety, Health and Welfare at Work Act 2005 imposes an obligation on every employer to provide systems of work that are planned, organised, performed, maintained and revised as appropriate so as to be, as far as is reasonably practicable, safe and without risk to health.[1]

4–02   An employer's duty of care to look after the health and safety of employees includes the reasonable prevention of harassment, bullying and stress-related injuries in the workplace. This duty of care is implied into the contract of employment by the Safety, Health and Welfare at Work Act 2005. Breach of this duty may be treated as a breach of the contract of employment, enabling the employee to claim constructive dismissal.[2] Constructive dismissal should only be availed of where an employee is left with no option other than to resign.[3] Consequently, it is important that the employee exhausts any grievance procedure before adopting this course of action. In dismissing a constructive dismissal claim in the leading case of *Conway v Ulster Bank Ltd*,[4] the Employment Appeals Tribunal (EAT) focused on the employer's grievance procedure and the employee's failure to utilise its provisions:

> "By majority the Tribunal considers that the [employee] did not act reasonably in resigning without first having substantially utilised the grievance procedure to attempt to remedy her complaints. An elaborate grievance procedure existed but the [employee] did not use it. It is not for the Tribunal to say whether using this procedure would have produced a decision more favourable to her, but it is

---

[1]   See, in particular, s.8(2)(e) of the Safety, Health and Welfare at Work Act 2005.

[2]   Section 1 of the Unfair Dismissals Act 1993 defines constructive dismissal as "the termination by the employee of his contract of employment with his employer, whether prior notice of the termination was or was not given to the employer, in circumstances in which, because of the conduct of the employer, the employee was or would have been entitled, or it was or would have been reasonable for the employee to terminate the contract of employment without giving prior notice of the termination to the employer".

[3]   See *Kennedy v Foxfield Inns Ltd t/a The Imperial Hotel*, unreported, Employment Appeals Tribunal, 1995.

[4]   Unreported, UD 474/1981.

possible. She did contact [the] Deputy Regional Personnel Controller, to enquire why she was being transferred. She was told the reason and she felt aggrieved. [The Deputy Regional Personnel Controller] asked her to state a case in writing, but she did not do so. She resigned by letter, which resignation was accepted. The Tribunal by majority determines ... that the appellant was not constructively dismissed from her employment and accordingly we dismiss her appeal and her claim."

Similarly, in *Wyse v St. Margaret's Country Club Ltd*.[5]

4–03 In the determination of the EAT in *Liz Allen v Independent Newspapers (Ireland) Ltd,*[6] the EAT awarded the claimant £70,500 compensation. Significantly, the EAT included compensation for constructive dismissal because of work-related stress injuries and was satisfied that it had to consider "the extent to which the claimant's financial loss [was] attributable to any act or omission or conduct by or on behalf of the respondent prior to dismissal".[7] Until this decision employees could not claim for loss of earnings, even if the employee was too ill to work due to the stress.

The *Allen* case provides useful general guidance on the duties of employers and employees where allegations of bullying and harassment arise in the workplace. Of particular note is the repeated reference by the Tribunal to the requirement that the perceptions of an employee that he or she has been bullied or harassed must be reasonable. The Tribunal also held that it was not unreasonable for the claimant to take into account in deciding to resign "the likely effect on her health and well-being were she to remain in the work environment".[8] The use by the Tribunal of the words "the claimant did not act unreasonably" implies that an objective test will apply when the Tribunal or a Court considers a claimant's concern to remove himself or herself from the employer's workforce in the interests of his or her health and safety. It should also be noted that the Tribunal placed particular emphasis on the employer's response to the claimant's complaint:

"The Tribunal is ... satisfied that at various stages throughout her employment and more particularly in September 2000 Ms Allen brought her complaints to senior management level within the respondent newspaper."

BULLYING

4–04 The Safety, Health and Welfare at Work Act 2005 provides that employers shall carry out a risk assessment at their place of work in the preparation of a safety statement. Such an assessment should include the risks associated with bullying. Procedures or preventative measures should follow this risk assessment in order to eliminate the risk or reduce the level of risk to

5   Unreported, June 3, 1999, UD 577/1999. See, however, *Liz Allen v Independent Newspapers (Ireland) Ltd* [2002] E.L.R. 84.
6   [2002] E.L.R. 84.
7   *ibid.* at 105.
8   *ibid.* at 102.

an acceptable level. Section 19 of the Safety, Health and Welfare at Work Act 2005 requires employers to document the results of the risk assessment.

4–05 There is no statute addressing bullying in the workplace, as there is with most other causes of action in employment law. Indeed, one of the problems with bullying is the absence of an accepted definition. The 2001 Task Force Report defined bullying in the following terms:

> "Workplace bullying is repeated inappropriate behaviour, direct or indirect, whether verbal, physical or otherwise, conducted by one or more persons against another or others, at the place of work and/or in the course of employment, which could reasonably be regarded as undermining the individual's right to dignity at work.
>
> An isolated incident of the behaviour described in this definition may be an affront to dignity at work but as a once off incident is not considered to be bullying".

The Report of the Expert Advisory Group on Workplace Bullying of July 2005 and the recent 2007 Health and Safety Authority Code of Practice[9] have adopted this definition of bullying.

The Task Force definition provides that bullying is aggressive behaviour which is systematic and ongoing and does not relate to isolated, once-off incidents of aggression. Johnson J. in the High Court case of *Nicola Mulvey (A Minor) Suing by her Mother and Next Friend Margaret Mulvey v Martin McDonagh*[10] accepted and adopted the September 1993 definition of bullying in the *Guidelines on Encountering Bullying Behaviour in Primary and Post Primary Schools*. These guidelines define bullying as follows:

> "Bullying is repeated aggression, verbal, psychological or physical conducted by an individual or group against others. Isolated incidents of aggressive behaviour which should not be condoned can scarcely be described as bullying.
>
> However when the behaviour is systematic and ongoing it is bullying".

4–06 The Health and Safety Authority's 2007 *Code of Practice for Employers and Employees on the Prevention and Resolution of Bullying at Work* came into effect on May 1, 2007, replacing its predecessor the 2002 *Code of Practice on the Prevention of Workplace Bullying*. It provides invaluable guidance on preparing a Bullying Prevention Policy in the workplace as well as dealing with a bullying complaint. The focus in the Code is on the resolution of incidents of bullying internally with the assistance, if required, of the Mediation Services of the Labour Relations Commission.

The 2007 Code gives the following non-exhaustive examples of types of bullying:

- Exclusion with negative consequences
- Verbal abuse/insults

---

[9]　See *Code of Practice for Employers and Employees on the Prevention and Resolution of Bullying at Work* (Health and Safety Authority, 2007). This Code is in operation since May 1, 2007.

[10]　[2004] 1 I.R. 497.

- Physical abuse
- Being treated less favourably than colleagues
- Intrusion-pestering, spying or stalking
- Menacing behaviour
- Intimidation
- Aggression
- Undermining behaviour
- Excessive monitoring of work
- Humiliation
- Withholding work-related information
- Repeatedly manipulating a person's job content and targets
- Blame for things beyond the person's control

Significantly, one of the preventative measures recommended by the 2007 Code is having in place a bullying prevention policy, which adequately addresses the risks that have been assessed in the risk assessment carried out pursuant to s.19 of the 2005 Act. The Code sets out further preventative measures which include the nomination of a "contact person", either internal or external, to serve as a first point of contact for a person who claims he or she is being bullied.

4–07   Where bullying occurs in the workplace it will, in general, lead to an increased level of anxiety and stress for the victims. This may result in an inability to concentrate causing errors and accidents.

4–08   Claims of bullying and harassment are usually brought as either constructive unfair dismissal claims, personal injury actions or under the Industrial Relations Act.

4–09   An employer is obliged to take reasonable care and proper steps in investigating and dealing with allegations of bullying in the workplace.[11] In *Joseph Monaghan v Sherry Brothers Limited*, the EAT, having regard to the judgment in the *Allen* case, identified two issues to be considered by the Tribunal in any case of workplace bullying:

> "The question is whether the applicant notified his employer and whether the response to such notification was adequate in all the circumstances".[12]

The Tribunal in the instant case held that management had failed to adequately respond to the instances of bullying and intimidation made known to it. It stated:

> "There is no doubt, in this case, that the employer was notified of the systematic teasing and isolation undergone by the applicant. Indeed, in the evidence proffered by the respondent's floor manager, it is confirmed that the applicant came to him on a number of occasions describing what he had to endure. The response by the employer was completely inadequate in all the circumstances".

---

[11]   See also *Saeham Media Ireland v A Worker* [1999] E.L.R. 41.
[12]   [2003] E.L.R. 293.

It can be seen from the foregoing that where an employee brings allegations of bullying to the attention of his or her employer and his or her employer fails to act, a court is likely to find the employer to have fallen below the standard to be properly expected of a reasonable and prudent employer. Lavan J. in *Matt Quigley v Complex Tooling and Moulding* stated the position in the following terms:

> "It is my opinion, that the action of the defendant in not preventing any further injury to the plaintiffs mental health by taking no action whatsoever against the bullying, falls short of the standard of a reasonable prudent employer".[13]

4–10   In cases of injury sustained by reason of bullying in the workplace, the requirement of foreseeability is likely to create evidential problems for plaintiff employees. Unless the plaintiff employee has some particular susceptibility which was or ought to have been known to the employer, he will have difficulty in securing an award of damages by way of compensation for a work-related mental injury. Colman J. in *Walker v Northumberland County Council*[14] stated that for the risk of injury to be a reasonably foreseeable risk, the plaintiff must be able to demonstrate a "materially substantial risk". In *Walker*,[15] this was held to be "a risk of mental illness materially higher than that which would ordinarily affect a social services middle manager in his position with a really heavy workload". That said, the "egg-shell skull" rule will serve to reduce the obstacle created by the foreseeability rule in bullying cases. In summary, this rule requires a defendant to take his victim (*i.e.* plaintiff) as he finds him. Thus, once an employer can foresee a particular type of injury to his employee, the employer will be liable for all the injury that follows by reason of the employee's vulnerability. Consequently, an employer who is on notice of a particular employee's sensitive/vulnerable disposition will have a higher duty to that employee. Clarke J. in *Maher v Jabil Global Services Limited* held that an injury could be foreseeable "in respect of an individual employee having regard to any particular vulnerability to injury known to the employer in respect of that employee".[16]

4–11   Where the person doing the bullying is a co-employee, the plaintiff may rely on vicarious liability. A relevant and instructive case is that of *Michael Shanley v Sligo County Council*.[17] In this case the plaintiff was "systematically abused, bullied, and belittled" over a protracted period of time (*i.e.* eight years) by a superior officer. The abuse had been so severe that the plaintiff had contemplated suicide. It was noted that the plaintiff had filed complaints with senior management, who had failed to act. Butler J. assessed damages at £65,000, the defendant Council having admitted liability.

---

[13]   [2005] I.E.H.C. 71 at pp.22–23.
[14]   [1995] 1 All E.R. 737.
[15]   *ibid.*
[16]   Unreported, High Court, May 12, 2005 at p.19.
[17]   Unreported, High Court, Butler J., October 10, 2001.

4–12 In many cases, the employer will not be involved in the bullying and will not even be aware that such bullying is taking place in the workplace. The employer is, however, liable for injury sustained by an employee who has been subjected to bullying by fellow employees. The general vicarious liability principle is that the law imposes liability for acts done "within the scope of the employee's employment". In *A Health Board v B.C. and the Labour Court*,[18] Costello J. summarised the legal position in this jurisdiction as follows:

> "In the absence of express statutory provision the law in this country in relation to the liability of an employer for the tortious acts (including statutory torts) of his employee is perfectly clear – an employer is vicariously liable where the act is committed by his employee within the scope of his employment".

4–13 In general, the courts have adopted a wide definition of scope of employment. A relevant and instructive case is the decision of the House of Lords in *Lister v Hesley Hall Ltd*[19] wherein Lord Steyn stated the position in the following terms:

> "For nearly a century, English judges have adopted Salmond's statement of the applicable test as correct. Salmond said that a wrongful act is deemed to be done by a 'servant' in the course of his employment if 'it is either (a) a wrongful act authorised by the master or, (b) a wrongful and unauthorised mode of doing some act authorised by the master'... Situation (a) causes no problems. The difficulty arises in respect of cases under (b). Salmond did, however, offer an explanation which has sometimes been overlooked. He said ...'that a master ... is liable even for acts which he has not authorised, provided that they are so connected with acts which he has authorised, that they may rightly be regarded as modes – although improper modes – of doing them'."

It remains to be seen whether the Irish courts will adopt this broader definition of "within the scope of employment" as quoted above in the Health Service Executive case. Relevant factors include where the bullying occurs, whether the bullied is subordinate to the person doing the bullying and works in the same department, and what the alleged acts of bullying consist of. For example, where a manager bullies a subordinate by excessive and unreasonable criticism of that person in the workplace, then vicarious liability, it is suggested, would clearly be established.

4–14 Not many successful claims have been brought on the basis of workplace bullying. In *O'Byrne v Dunnes Stores*,[20] Smyth J. held in favour of the plaintiff and allowed him to recover for the mental distress ensuing from the breach of his contract, which breach arose from the plaintiff being told to move location without any notice or chance to object. The case also concerned an incident of bullying which was described by the court as "inexcusably offensive". Smyth J. held that he was in no doubt that the plaintiff was being forced to move "by diktat" and that "an effort was being sought to bully him into a situation of getting out." The learned judge stated that "there was no question

---

[18] [1994] E.L.R. 27.
[19] [2001] I.R.L.R. 472.
[20] [2003] E.L.R. 297.

of any form of discussion, reasons tendered and no reasons apparently tendered until the trial of [the] action".

In a case in March 2005, the High Court held that the plaintiff had suffered personal injury as a direct result of a breach of the defendant's duty to prevent workplace bullying.[21] What was particularly interesting about this case was the fact that Lavan J. made reference to the Safety, Health and Welfare at Work Act 1989 and the 1993 General Application Regulations. The learned judge stated:

> "The Safety, Health and Welfare at Work Act 1989 ("the 1989 Act") and the Safety, Health and Welfare at Work Regulations 1993 impose an obligation on every employer to provide systems of work that are, as far as is reasonably practicable, safe and without risk to health … Section 6(1) of the Safety, Health and Welfare at Work Act 1989 states that:
>
> 'It shall be the duty of every employer to ensure, so far as is reasonably practicable, the safety, health and welfare at work of all his employees' ….
>
> It has been a fairly recent movement towards the thinking that an employer must take care not only of the physical health of their employees, for example by providing safe equipment, but also must take reasonable care to protect them against mental injury, such as is complained of by the plaintiff in this case.
>
> It follows on from this that employers now have an obligation to prevent their employees from such that would cause mental injury, i.e. stress, harassment and bullying in the workplace … In this case, the plaintiff has given evidence of treatment by servants of the defendant which the plaintiff claims amounted to bullying in the workplace, and by not preventing such as is claimed by the plaintiff, the defendant, as employers, were negligent and in breach of their duty."

4–15 A number of successful bullying cases have been brought in the United Kingdom. In *Ratcliffe v Dyfed County Council*,[22] for example, the plaintiff was a teacher who claimed he had been bullied for a lengthy period of time by the head teacher and, as a result, had suffered a nervous breakdown. The case was settled for £100,000. In *Waters v Commissioner of Police for the Metropolis*, the position in the United Kingdom was summarised by Lord Steyn as follows:

> "If an employer knows that acts being done by his employees during their employment may cause mental or physical harm to a particular fellow employee and he does nothing to supervise or prevent such acts, when it is in his power to do so, it is clearly arguable he may be in breach of his duty to that employee".[23]

4–16 In *Helen Green v DB Group Services (UK) Limited*,[24] the English High Court awarded £80,000 to a secretary in a commercial bank in London who was subjected to a campaign of harassment at the hands of four women with

---

[21] See *Matt Quigley v Complex Tooling and Moulding* [2005] I.E.H.C. 71.

[22] English High Court, 1998. See also *McLeod v Test Valley Borough Council*, Q.B.D., January 11, 2000, which settled for £200,000, wherein the plaintiff claimed damages for harassment and bullying by his manager resulting in stress causing a nervous breakdown, chronic depression and a persistent delusional disorder. An Irish case which settled was that of *McGlade v County Mayo Radio Ltd t/a Mid West Radio*, Health and Safety Review, January/February 2000, page 14, where a former radio manager held that he was bullied and harassed by the radio station's chief executive.

[23] [2000] I.R.L.R. 720.

[24] [2006] E.W.H.C. 1898.

whom she worked in close proximity. The plaintiff claimed she suffered injury to her mental health because of the "offensive, abusive, intimidating, denigrating, bullying, humiliating, patronising, infantile and insulting words and behaviour" of her co-workers. Mr Justice Owen considered the judgment of the Court of Appeal in *Sutherland v Hatton*,[25] in particular the importance of what Hale L.J. described as the "threshold question" of whether psychiatric injury or illness was reasonably foreseeable:

> "As she said at paragraph 43(3):
> (3) Foreseeability depends upon what the employer knows (or ought reasonably to know) about the individual employee. Because of the nature of mental disorder, it is harder to foresee than physical injury, but may be easier to foresee in a known individual than in the population at large … An employer is usually entitled to assume that the employee can withstand the normal pressures of the job unless he knows of some particular problem or vulnerability".[26]

He placed reliance on the dicta of Gray J. in *Barlow v Borough of Broxbourne* when considering whether bullying and harassment can give rise to a liability in negligence. Mr Justice Owen found para.16 of this judgment to be directly applicable:

> "(i) whether the claimant has established that the conduct complained of in the Particulars of Claim took place and, if so, whether it amounted to bullying or harassment in the ordinary connotation of those terms. In addressing this question it is the cumulative effect of the conduct which has to be considered rather than the individual incidents relied on;
> (ii) did the person or persons involved in the victimisation or bullying know, or ought they reasonably to have known, that their conduct might cause the claimant harm;
> (iii) could they by the exercise of reasonable care, have taken steps which would have avoided that harm; and
> (iv) were their actions so connected with their employment as to render the defendant vicariously responsible for them."[27]

The learned judge concluded that the plaintiff had been subjected to a "relentless campaign of mean and spiteful behaviour designed to cause her distress" which "amounted to a deliberate and concerted campaign of bullying within the ordinary meaning of that term".[28]

On the issue of vicarious liability, Mr Justice Owen relied on the test propounded in *Bernard v Att. Gen. of Jamaica*[29] wherein Lord Steyn held that the correct approach to the issue of vicarious liability was in the following terms:

> "The correct approach is to concentrate on the relative closeness of the connection between the nature of the employment and the particular tort, and to ask whether in looking at the matter in the round, it is just and reasonable to hold the employer vicariously liable."

---

[25] (2001) E.W.C.A. Civ. 76.
[26] At para.5 of the judgment.
[27] [2003] E.W.H.C. 50 Q.B.
[28] At para.99.
[29] [2005] I.R.L.R. 393 para.18.

Applying the foregoing test, Mr Justice Owen concluded that the plaintiff should succeed in that the nature of the employment of the co-workers whose behaviour was in question "was so close that it would be just and reasonable to hold the defendant (company) liable for it".

In the instant case the defendant bank sought to rely on the plaintiff's pre-existing vulnerability to mental illness. The High Court rejected this argument. Mr Justice Owen stated:

> "I am…satisfied that the bullying gave rise to a foreseeable risk of psychiatric injury. Such behaviour when pursued relentlessly on a daily basis has a cumula-tive effect. It is designed to make the working environment intolerable for the victim. The stress that it creates goes far beyond that normally to be expected in the workplace. It is in my judgment plainly foreseeable that some individuals will not be able to withstand such stress and will in consequence suffer some degree of psychiatric injury. Furthermore the claimant was a person who, to the knowledge of the defendant, had suffered depression in the relatively recent past and had been prescribed anti-depressant medication. She was therefore to their knowledge more vulnerable than the population at large."[30]

HARASSMENT

4–17 Irish case law has acknowledged harassment as a form of discrimina-tion since 1985. We have followed American jurisprudence by adopting the discrimination-based approach to harassment.[31] This approach is clearly evi-dent in the Employment Equality Acts 1998–2004, which impose a duty on the employer to ensure that an employee is not exposed to harassment in the work-place.[32] The Employment Equality Act 1998 (as amended by the Equal Status Act 2000 and the Equality Act 2004) outlaws discrimination in employment on nine distinct grounds, namely sex (s.6(2)(a)), marital status (s.6(2)(b)), family status (s.6(2)(c)), sexual orientation (s.6(2)(d)), religion (s.6(2)(e)), age (s.6(2)(f)), disability (s.6(2)(g)), race (s.6(2)(h)) and membership of the travel-ling community (s.6(2)(i)). It outlaws both direct and indirect discrimination. The Act covers all aspects of discrimination in employment and applies to employers in both the public and the private sector, as well as advertising (s.10), employment agencies (s.11), vocational training bodies (s.12) and membership of trade unions and professional bodies (s.13).

4–18 Section 15 of the Employment Equality Act 1998, as amended, placed on a statutory footing what was formerly the practice of imposing vicarious lia-bility on the employer and provides:

---

[30] At para.105.

[31] Harassment is also defined as discrimination in a number of directives: the Equal Treat-ment in Employment and Occupation Directive (Council Directive 2000/78/EC); the Race Directive (Council Directive 2000/43/EC) and the Directive on the Equal Treat-ment for Men and Women in relation to Access to Employment, Vocational Training and Promotion, and Working Conditions (Council Directive 2002/73/EC).

[32] See s.32 of the Employment Equality Act 1998, which came into force on October 18, 1999.

> "(1) Anything done by a person in the course of his/her employment shall be treated for the purpose of this Act as done also by that person's employer, whether or not it was done with the employer's knowledge or approval.
>
> (2) Anything done by a person as agent for another person with the authority (whether express or implied and whether precedent or subsequent) of that other person shall be treated for the purposes of this Act as done also by that other person."

4–19 It is therefore essential that employers take a pro-active approach in implementing the provisions of the Employment Equality Acts. This can be seen from s.15(3) of the Employment Equality Act 1998, as amended, which renders an employer liable for the acts of his employees unless he can prove he took such steps as were reasonably practicable to outlaw the particular harassment complained of:

> "In proceedings brought under this Act against an employer in respect of an act alleged to have been done by an employee of the employer, it shall be a defence for the employer to prove that the employer took such steps as were reasonably practicable to prevent the employee:
> (a) from doing that act;
> (b) from doing in the course of his or her employment acts of that description".

This section affords a defence to the imposition of vicarious liability if the employer can show that he took such steps "as were reasonably practicable" to prevent the harassment complained of. The particular duties of employers are delineated in s.16.

4–20 The Employment Equality Acts 1998–2004 outlaw the harassment of employees, and defines such harassment as:

- any form of unwanted conduct related to any of the discriminatory grounds; and

- sexual harassment in any form of unwanted verbal, non-verbal or physical conduct of a sexual nature.

Section 14A(7) of the Employment Equality Act 1998, as amended, provides that harassment occurs where the foregoing conduct in either case has the purpose or effect of violating a person's dignity and creating an intimidating, hostile, degrading, humiliating or offensive environment for the person.

4–21 The definition of harassment in the Employment Equality Act 1998 combined both an objective and subjective test, since the conduct had to be both unwelcome to the recipient and reasonably capable of being regarded as "offensive, humiliating or intimidating" to him or her. The definition of harassment introduced in the 1998 Act has clearly been expanded by the 2004 Act. In particular, the objective reasonableness test no longer applies as the objective element of the definitions has been removed from the 2004 Act.

4–22 The Employment Equality Acts 1998–2004 make sexual harassment in the workplace an act of discrimination. Section 23(3) of the Employment

Equality Act, 1998 provided an express statutory definition of sexual harassment. It covered acts of physical intimacy, a request for sexual favours, or other acts or conduct including "spoken words, gestures or the production, display or circulation of written words, pictures or other material". A relevant and instructive case is the decision of the Labour Court in *Murray and the Equality Authority v De la Salle College*.[33] Section 23 of the Employment Equality Act, 1998 has been repealed by s.14 of the Equality Act 2004. It should be noted that unlike the Employment Equality Act, 1998, the new definition of sexual harassment introduced in the Equality Act 2004 relates only to conduct of a sexual nature.[34]

4–23   Unlike the situation that obtains in respect of bullying, both the sexual and non-sexual definitions of harassment provide that a single incidence of harassment would appear to be sufficient to constitute discrimination. Consequently, the transmission via e-mail by one employee of sexually suggestive or explicit material to another employee may expose the employer to a claim. Similarly, the transmission of e-mails by an employer to an employee which are critical of his performance or abusive, may constitute harassment and could give rise to a claim that they caused psychiatric injury to the employee. Harassment is not only outlawed in the workplace, and in the course of employment; it is also outlawed where such harassment may include incidents involving persons other than fellow employees such as clients, customers or other business contacts. An employer will be vicariously liable for such acts (s.15) if the employer does not take reasonable steps to prevent such harassment. This alters the common law position to leave the employer in a vulnerable position with regard to breaches of the 1998 Act, as amended. The reference to taking "such steps as are reasonably practicable" in s.15(3) of the 1998 Act, as amended, to prevent the harassment will require an employer to have polices and procedures in place to this end. Adherence to the Code of Practice on Sexual Harassment and Harassment at Work would, of course, significantly assist in defending a claim.[35]

4–24   In *Barbara Atkinson v Hugh Carty & Others*, the Circuit Court found in favour of the plaintiff noting that there were no written procedures in place to provide the plaintiff with an avenue to seek redress for sexual harassment.[36] Judge Delahunt stated as follows:

> "[A]n employer is obliged to provide a safe place of work, a safe system of work and a safe working environment … I do believe that the plaintiff suffered a serious case of sexual harassment … I note that there were no written procedures in place to provide the plaintiff with an avenue to seek redress … The failure of the defendants to have in place adequate procedures renders them liable and by reason of their failure to fulfil their statutory obligation they are responsible and

---

[33] Wicklow, February, 2002.
[34] See s.14A(7) of the Employment Equality Act 1998, as amended.
[35] See Employment Equality Act 1998 (Code of Practice) (Harassment) Order 2002, S.I. No. 78 of 2002.
[36] [2005] E.L.R. 1.

cannot plead immunity from same simply because the plaintiff failed to make a complaint". [37]

The defendants in the instant case were held liable for the actions of the independent contractor who provided services to the defendant. Judge Delahunt awarded damages of €137,000. This award was reduced by 25 per cent as the learned judge held that the plaintiff was guilty of contributory negligence for failing to make a complaint earlier:

> "[T]he plaintiff failed to make [the defendant] aware of her difficulties until September of 2000 even though it is clear from her evidence that she was aware in or around 1997 that she was being sexually harassed in the legal sense as a result of information supplied to her by her husband about the sexual harassment policy that applied in his employment."[38]

4–25 The penalties to be applied in respect of breaches of the provisions of the Act are detailed in ss.98–100 of the Employment Equality Acts 1998–2004. Any breach of the Employment Equality Acts 1998–2004 attracts, on summary conviction, a fine not exceeding €1,905, or imprisonment for a term not exceeding one year, or both. On conviction on indictment, a fine not exceeding €31,743 applies or imprisonment for a term not exceeding two years, or both. Section 41 of the Equality Act 2004 inserts a new s.99A into the Employment Equality Act 1998. It provides the Equality Tribunal and the Labour Court with the power to award expenses of one person against another person in circumstances where such person has obstructed or impeded an investigation or appeal.

4–26 Where an employee claims that he or she has suffered harassment, a case can be brought under the Employment Equality Act, 1998, as amended, to the Office of the Director of Equality Investigations (ODEI), or in limited circumstances, to the Labour Court. The Equality Act 2004 refers to the ODEI as the "Equality Tribunal".[39] A six-month time limit applies in respect of the referral of a complaint to the Equality Tribunal, with s.77(5)(a) of the Employment Equality Act 1998, as amended by s.32 of the Equality Act 2004, providing that a complaint "may not be referred" under the Act "... after the end of the period of 6 months after the date of occurrence, or, as the case may be, [the] most recent occurrence" of the discrimination/harassment. Section 29 of the Equality Act 2004 inserts a new s.74(3) into the Employment Equality Act 1998, which provides that the date of referral of a complaint "is the date on which the reference or appeal is received" by the Equality Tribunal, Labour Court or Circuit Court. Section 78 of the Employment Equality Act 1998, as amended, should be noted in that it requires the Equality Tribunal, prior to

---

[37] [2005] E.L.R. 1 at 3.
[38] *ibid.* at p.4. See also *Allen v Independent Newspapers Ltd* ([2002] E.L.R. 84 at 101) on this point.
[39] See s.30 of the Equality Act 2004 which amends s.75 of the Employment Equality Act 1998.

investigating a complaint, to refer it for mediation if it considers that it could be so resolved.

4–27   Claims for sexual harassment alone can be brought directly to the Circuit Court, but the plaintiff must choose whether to bring the claim to the Equality Tribunal, the Labour Court or the Circuit Court. The Equality Tribunal or Labour Court can award a maximum of two years' remuneration, or €12,700 for a person unemployed, in cases of harassment, while the Circuit Court is at liberty to make various orders including an order for compensation, with no upper limit.[40] Section 36 of the Equality Act 2004 amends s.82 of the Employment Equality Act 1998 and provides that a single ceiling applies where the claim before the Equality Tribunal is of both discrimination and harassment. A significant advantage of electing to pursue an equality claim is that a litigant would not have to resign from his or her employment. That said, the disadvantage of pursuing a claim for equality is that it must be proven clearly that the maltreatment was a result of the pleaded ground of discrimination. The burden of proof in discrimination cases is detailed in the European Communities (Burden of Proof in Gender Discrimination Cases) Regulations 2001,[41] which states:

> "Where in any proceedings facts are established by or on behalf of a person from which it may be presumed that there has been a direct or indirect discrimination in relation to him or her, it shall be for the other party concerned to prove the contrary".

4–28   If a case of alleged harassment is of a serious nature, criminal liability may arise. An offence of "harassment" is committed where a person:

> "seriously interferes with the other's peace and privacy or causes alarm, distress or harm to the other, and his or her acts are such that a reasonable person would realise that the acts would seriously interfere with the other's peace and privacy or cause alarm, distress or harm to the other".[42]

STRESS

4–29   Stress has been acknowledged as the second most serious occupational health problem in the European Union and accounts for over 50 per cent of all workforce absenteeism. The year 2002 was designated "Workplace Stress Prevention Year" throughout the European Union. Ireland was one of many Member States to have become actively involved. In particular, the Health and Safety Authority (Authority) in its *Programme of Work for 2002* conducted a major campaign to tackle the growing problem of workplace stress by increasing awareness of the risks as well as promoting and developing preventative measures.[43] The Authority in 2005 issued a document entitled "Work Positive: Prioritizing Organisational Stress", which includes a valuable step by step

---

[40] See s.82 of the Employment Equality Act 1998.
[41] S.I. No. 337 of 2001.
[42] Section 10 of the Non-Fatal Offences Against the Person Act 1997.
[43] *Programme of Work for 2002*, Health and Safety Authority, January 15, 2002.

guide to assessing risks of stress. It is a laudable attempt to tackle stress as a workplace issue and is a joint initiative between the Authority, Health Scotland and the Health Service Executive.

4–30   The Authority defines workplace stress as arising "when the demands of the job and the working environment on a person exceeds their capacity to meet them". The European Commission defines stress as follows:

> "[Work-related stress is] the emotional, cognitive, behavioural and physiological reaction to aversive and noxious aspects of work, work environments and work organisations."

Work-related stress, the EU Commission document states, "is characterised by high levels of arousal and distress and often by feelings of not coping".[44] The British Health and Safety Executive (HSE) defines stress as "the adverse reaction people have to excessive pressure or other types of demands placed on them".[45]

4–31   The HSA identifies the following as situations that can cause stress in the workplace:

• Poor communication at work

• Poor working relationships

• Poorly organised shiftwork

• Faulty work organisation

• Ill-defined work roles

• Lack of personal control over work

• Machine-paced work

• Highly demanding tasks

• Dull repetitive work

• Dealing directly with the public

The Authority notes that stress can affect the individual at the emotional level (fatigue), the cognitive level (making mistakes), the behavioural level (excess drinking or over eating) and the physiological level (heart disease, reduced resistance to infection and skin problems). At the macro level, a company/organisation may be affected by someone who is suffering from stress through poor industrial relations, increased absenteeism, faulty decision-making and reduced productivity.

4–32   An employer's duty is not to provide a stress-free environment, but to take reasonably practicable steps to shield employees from exposure to stress

---

[44] See the document of the Commission of the European Union (EU), "Guidance on work-related stress".

[45] Workplace Stress (Health and Safety Authority, 1992).

and from the consequences of unreasonably stressful working conditions. Colman J. in *Walker v Northumberland County Council*[46] summarised the position in the following terms:

> "The law does not impose upon [the employer] the duty of an insurer against all injury or damage caused by him, however unlikely or unexpected, and whatever the practical difficulties of guarding against it. It calls for no more than a reasonable response, what is reasonable being measured by the nature of the neighbourhood relationship, the magnitude of the risk of injury which was reasonably foreseeable, the seriousness of the consequence for the person to whom the duty is owed of the risk eventuating and the costs and practicability of preventing the risk."

Limits are therefore placed on the employer's duty of care in that an employer is obliged only to take such steps as are reasonable and prudent. In *Dalton v Frendo*,[47] O'Higgins C.J. stated that "the employer is not an insurer". Similarly in *Christie v Odeon (Ireland) Ltd*,[48] where Kingsmill Moore J. spoke of the employer's duty of care in the following terms:

> "It is of little avail to show, after an accident has happened, that such and such a precaution might in the circumstances have avoided a particular accident. The matter must be considered as it would have appeared to a reasonable and prudent [employer] before the accident."

Scott Baker L.J. in *Hartman v South Essex Mental Health and Community Care NHS Trust* stated the position as follows:

> "It is *foreseeable injury* flowing from the employer's breach of duty that gives rise to the liability. It does not follow that because a claimant suffers *stress* at work and that the employer is in some way in breach of duty in allowing that to occur that the claimant is able to establish a claim in negligence. As Simon Brown LJ put it in *Garrett v Camden London Borough Council* [2001] EWCA Civ 395, paragraph 63: 'Many, alas, suffer breakdowns and depressible illnesses and a significant proportion could doubtless ascribe some at least of their problems to the strains and stresses of their work situation: be it simply overworking, the tension of difficult relationships, career prospect worries, fears or feelings of discrimination or harassment, to take just some examples. Unless, however, there was a real risk of breakdown which the claimant's employers ought reasonably to have foreseen and they ought properly to have averted there can be no liability.'"[49]

4–33   Employers have both a statutory and common law duty of care to protect their staff against stress. Whilst there have been few cases decided on this point, the potential for litigation in this area is growing. This can be seen from the case of *Saehan Media Ireland Ltd v A Worker*,[50] where the Labour Court acknowledged work-related stress as a health and safety issue and held that "employers have an obligation to deal with instances of its occurrence which may be brought to their attention". The issue of foreseeability has, therefore,

---

[46] [1995] 1 All E.R. 737.
[47] Unreported, Supreme Court, December 15, 1977.
[48] (1957) 91 I.L.T.R. 25.
[49] [2005] E.W.C.A. Civ. 06, para.2.
[50] [1999] E.L.R. 41.

been to the forefront in the evolution of the stress at work case law. Once an employer is on notice that a particular employee has a greater susceptibility to stress than others, the employer is under a higher duty as a work-related stress injury is more likely to occur.

4–34 The Safety, Health and Welfare at Work Act 2005 provides that all employers shall ensure safe places and systems of work, including safe plant and equipment. This implies work activities and environments that minimise stress. However, it should be noted that some work is regarded as intrinsically containing certain stressors and the voluntary assumption of such work creates a degree of defence for the employer in civil law.

4–35 Health and safety law requires risks to be eliminated or reduced so far as is reasonably practicable, a concept previously discussed at length. The 2005 Act also requires employers to conduct risk assessments. Any such risk assessments should include assessments of activities that could potentially cause unreasonable stress to workers. Section 19 of the Safety, Health and Welfare at Work Act 2005 provides that the results of these assessments should be documented.

4–36 The distinction between physical and psychiatric injury is no longer either medically or legally defensible. The Safety, Health and Welfare at Work Act 2005 no longer discriminates between physical and psychiatric injury. Section 2 of that Act defines "personal injury" as including "any injury, disability, occupational illness or disease, any impairment of physical or mental condition … that is attributable to work". In *Page v Smith*,[51] Lord Lloyd stated that:

> "It would not be sensible to commit the law to a distinction between physical and psychiatric injury, which may already seem somewhat artificial, and may soon be altogether outmoded. Nothing will be gained by treating them as different 'kinds' of personal injury, so as to require the application of different tests in law".[52]

Scott Baker L.J. in *Hartman v South Essex Mental Health and Community Care NHS Trust* summarised the position as follows:

> "Liability for psychiatric injury caused by stress at work is in general no different in principle from liability for physical injury."[53]

4–37 An employer is now under a duty of care not to cause an employee psychiatric illness by reason of the volume or character of the work required to be performed by the employee. If an employer becomes aware that an employee is suffering from stress, then the employer is under a duty of care to take the necessary steps to remedy his symptoms of stress.

---

[51] [1998] A.C. 155.
[52] See, however, *White v Chief Constable of the South Yorkshire Police* [1999] 1 All E.R. 1 and para.4–42 of this book.
[53] [2005] E.W.C.A. Civ. 06 at para.2.

4–38 If liability is to be imposed on employers for mental strain not amounting to a recognised psychiatric illness, then the litigant will have to show:

1. clear evidence of the damage suffered and the extent of that damage;

2. a clear causal link between the damage suffered and the employment; and

3. that the damage to the litigant was foreseeable by the employer.

ENGLISH AND SCOTTISH CASE LAW

4–39 It is clear from the case law in the neighbouring jurisdiction that stress-related claims can arise where there are excessive hours. In *Johnstone v Bloomsbury Health Authority*,[54] for example, the English Court of Appeal permitted a stress claim by a junior doctor to proceed. Significantly, the court considered the junior doctor's duty to work for up to 88 hours a week and the health authority's duty to take reasonable care not to injure his health. While this case was settled without a full hearing, employers should note that claims arising from excessive work hours can succeed.

4–40 In *Petch v Customs & Excise Commissioners*,[55] the English Court of Appeal held that the employee does not have to establish that his stress was caused solely by the acts or omissions of the employer; rather, the employee must merely prove that they contributed to or exacerbated a number of other factors which may have contributed to the stress-related condition. The court decided, however, that a single mental breakdown due to the volume and stressful character of the work was not reasonably foreseeable. Dillon L.J. summarised the position in the following terms:

> "... I take the view ... that, unless senior management in the defendant's department were aware or ought to have been aware that the plaintiff was showing signs of impending breakdown, or ... that his workload carried a real risk that he would have a breakdown, then the defendants were not negligent in failing to avert the breakdown ...".[56]

4–41 In the leading case of *Walker v Northumberland County Council*,[57] a social work officer employed in an area where there was a high number of child care cases suffered a nervous breakdown owing to pressures of work in November 1986. He returned to work in March 1987 and was promised temporary support. The support was not forthcoming and the plaintiff suffered another nervous breakdown six months later. The English High Court awarded damages against the defendant County Council on the basis that it was in breach of the duty it owed the plaintiff not to subject him to a volume of work that would endanger his health. In his judgment, Colman J. stated:

---

[54] [1991] 2 All E.R. 293.
[55] (1993) I.C.R. 789.
[56] See also *Gillespie v Commonwealth of Australia* (1991) A.C.T.R. 1.
[57] [1995] 1 All E.R. 737.

"It is clear that an employer has a duty to provide his employee with a reasonably safe system of work and to take reasonable steps to protect him from risks which are reasonably foreseeable. Whereas the law on the extent of his duty has developed almost exclusively in cases involving physical injury to the employee as distinct from injury to his mental health, there is no logical reason why risk of psychiatric damage should be excluded from the scope of an employer's duty of care or from the co-extensive implied term in the contract of employment."[58]

4–42   Previously, in *Aston v Imperial Chemical Industries Group*,[59] Rose J. stated:

"It ... seems to me that the employer whose system of work negligently induces psychiatric injury by, for example, excessive noise or flickering lights or psychological pressure, is just as liable as one who causes physical injury because the duty of care exists and the necessary proximity exists by reason of the master and servant relationship."

4–43   A further relevant and instructive case is *Group B Plaintiffs v Medical Research Council*.[60] In that case, the defendant council was conducting special therapeutic trials which carried a risk that the patients might contact Creutzfeldt-Jakob Disease (otherwise known as "CJD"). The plaintiffs were involved in the trials and developed a psychiatric illness as a result of their anxiety that they would develop CJD. The court found in favour of the plaintiffs on the ground that such an outcome was reasonably foreseeable in the circumstances.

4–44   In *White v Chief Constable of South Yorkshire Police*,[61] the plaintiffs were police officers involved in the management and treatment of the injured in the aftermath of the FA Cup semi-final at Hillsborough, in 1989, in which large numbers of people were killed and injured. They suffered symptoms of post-traumatic stress disorder as a result of their exposure to the scenes at the football ground. The House of Lords dismissed their claim for damages on the basis that they were outside the area of physical risk. As they were not rescuers, it was held that it was not reasonably foreseeable that they would suffer non-physical injury. Significantly, the Law Lords stated that there was no general duty of care owed by the employer to his employees in respect of psychiatric illness. The position enunciated by the House of Lords in *White v Chief Constable of South Yorkshire Police* was clearly a departure from *Walker v Northumberland County Council*,[62] which recognised that an employer is under a duty of care not to cause an employee psychiatric illness by reason of the volume or character of the work required to be performed by the employee. *White*, in effect, classified employee claimants, who suffer a negligently inflicted psychiatric illness, as secondary victims. Those victims must satisfy the courts, in addition to the ordinary negligence requirements, that there was

---

[58] *ibid.* at p.749.
[59] Unreported, High Court, May 21, 1992.
[60] (1997) 41 B.M.L.R. 157.
[61] [1999] 1 All E.R. 1.
[62] [1995] 1 All E.R. 737.

a "close" relationship between them and the victim, that they were spatially and temporally near the accident and that they perceived the accident through their own senses.[63]

4–45   Notwithstanding the foregoing, the *White* case may be distinguished from the normal employer/employee case insofar as the policeman there was not a participant or directly involved in the incident, and arguably, was analogous to a bystander and an onlooker. This decision has been widely criticised[64] and may not be followed in this jurisdiction. Indeed, McMahon J. in *Curran v Cadbury (Ireland) Ltd*[65] opined that the Irish courts may not be "overawed by *White* and may choose as it did in *Ward v McMaster*[66] to go its own road, especially since *White* has its critics."

4–46   The case of *Lancaster v Birmingham City Council*[67] concerned a stress claim based on a change of position without training. The defendant Council acknowledged that it had not taken appropriate steps to train the plaintiff in her transfer position as a housing officer, in which she had no experience or qualifications. Consequently, the issue to be decided was not one of liability but was merely in respect of the level of compensation (damages of £67,000 were awarded).

4–47   A relevant and instructive decision on stress at work from the Scottish Outer Court of Session is the case of *Cross v Highlands and Islands Enterprise*[68] wherein Lord MacFayden stated that the duty on an employer to take reasonable care for an employee's safety and health, and to provide and maintain a safe system of work, includes a duty not to subject the employee to work conditions which are reasonably foreseeably likely to cause him or her psychiatric illness or injury. Other cases worthy of note include *Ingram v Worcester County Council*[69] and *Howell v Newport County Borough Council*[70].

4–48   The circumstances in which stress-related psychiatric injury will give rise to liability on the part of an employer were comprehensively considered by the Court of Appeal in *Terence Sutherland v Penelope Hatton*,[71] a case which considered four conjoined appeals against a finding of liability for an employee's psychiatric illness caused by stress at work. The court stated that no job was inherently dangerous to an employee's mental health. In judgments that marked a sea change in compensation awards for stress, the Court of Appeal overturned damages claims by three of the four workers totalling

---

[63] See, however, the House of Lords judgment of Lord Slynn of Hadley in *W and others v Essex County Council and another* [2000] 2 All E.R. 237.
[64] See, *e.g.* Tan Keng Feng, *Liability for Psychiatric Illness* [1999] Tort Law Review 165.
[65] [2000] 18 I.L.T. 140.
[66] [1988] I.R. 337.
[67] Unreported, English County Court, 1999.
[68] [2001] I.R.L.R. 336.
[69] *Health and Safety Review*, March 2000, p.26.
[70] *The Times*, December 5, 2000.
[71] [2002] E.W.C.A. Civ. 76; [2002] 2 All E.R.1.

nearly £200,000.[72] Lady Justice Hale opined that it should not be the responsibility of an employer to make exhaustive investigations into the mental
health of employees. Instead, the onus was on the stressed worker to decide
whether to leave the job or carry on working and accept the risk of a mental
breakdown. Hale L.J. stated:

> "[W]hen considering what the reasonable employer should make of the informa-
> tion which is available to him, from whatever source, what assumptions is he
> entitled to make about his employee and to what extent is he bound to probe fur-
> ther into what he is told? *Unless he knows of some particular problem or vulner-
> ability, an employer is usually entitled to assume that his employee is up to the
> normal pressures of the job.* It is only if there is something specific about the job
> or the employee or the combination of the two that he has to think harder. But
> thinking harder does not necessarily mean that he has to make searching or intru-
> sive enquiries. *Generally he is entitled to take what he is told by or on behalf of
> the employee at face value.*
>
> In some cases the only effective way of safeguarding the employee would be
> to dismiss or demote him. There may be no other work at the same level of pay
> which it is reasonable to expect the employer to offer him. *In principle the law
> should not be saying to an employer that it is his duty to sack an employee who
> wants to go on working for him for the employer's own good* ... If there is no
> alternative solution, it has to be for the employee to decide whether or not to
> carry on in the same employment and take the risk of a breakdown in his health
> or whether to leave that employment and look for work elsewhere before he
> becomes unemployable".[73]

4–49   In summary, the court listed 16 guidelines in order to determine liability for stress-induced injury. The guidelines are as follows:

4–50   (1) There are no specific or individual rules governing claims for psychiatric illness or injury arising from work-related stress. The ordinary principles of employer's liability apply.

4–51   (2) The threshold question is whether this kind of harm (*i.e.* injury arising from work-related stress) suffered by a particular employee was reasonably foreseeable. This has two components:

a)   an injury to health, as distinct from occupational stress, which

b)   is attributable to stress at work, as distinct from other factors.

4–52   (3) Foreseeability depends upon what the employer knows (or ought
reasonably to know) about the individual employee. Unless an employer knows
of a particular problem or vulnerability, he or she is usually entitled to assume
that an employee can withstand the normal pressures of a particular job.

---

[72] See *Sutherland v Hatton, Somerset County Council v Barber, Sandwell Metropolitan
Borough Council v Jones* and *Barker Refectories Ltd v Bishop*, unreported, Court of
Appeal (Brooke, Hale, Kay L.JJ.), February 5, 2002; [2002] E.W.C.A. Civ. 76.
[73] pp.14–16. Emphasis added.

4–53   (4) The test is the same whatever the occupation. No one occupation should be regarded as intrinsically dangerous to mental health.

4–54   (5) Factors likely to be relevant in determining whether the harm suffered was reasonably foreseeable include the following:

a)   The nature and extent of the work done by the employee. Is the workload much more than is normal for the particular job? Is the work particularly intellectually or emotionally demanding for this employee? Are demands being made of this employee unreasonable when compared with the demands made of others in the same or comparable job? Or are there signs that others doing the job are suffering from harmful levels of stress? Is there an abnormal level of sickness or absenteeism in the same job or the same department?

b)   Signs from the employee of impending harm to health. Has he or she a particular problem or vulnerability? Has he or she already suffered from illness attributable to stress at work? Have there recently been frequent or prolonged absences which are uncharacteristic of him or her? Is there reason to think that these are attributable to stress at work, for example, because of complaints or warnings from him or her or others?

4–55   (6) An employer is generally entitled to take what he is told by his employee at face value, unless he has good reason to think to the contrary and need not generally have to make searching enquires of the employee or seek permission to make further enquires of his or her medical advisers.

4–56   (7) The duty to take steps is triggered by indicators of impending harm to health arising from stress at work which must be plain enough for any reasonable employer to realise that he or she has to respond.

4–57   (8) A breach of duty only arises if the employer fails to take the steps that are reasonable in the circumstances, having regard to the magnitude of the risk of harm occurring, the gravity of the harm which may occur, the costs and practicability of preventing it, and the justifications for running the risk.

4–58   (9) The employer's size, scope and resources, and the demands of his or her operation are relevant in deciding what is reasonable, including, for example, the need to treat other employees fairly in any redistribution of duties.

4–59   (10) An employer is only expected to take steps which are likely to do some good and the court can require expert evidence on this.

4–60   (11) An employer who offers confidential help to employees, with referral to appropriate counselling or treatment services, is unlikely to be found in breach of duty.

4–61   (12) If the only reasonable and effective action to prevent injury would be to dismiss or demote the employee, the employer will not be in breach of duty for allowing a willing employee to continue in the job.

4–62 (13) In all cases, it is necessary to identify the steps that the employer both should or could have taken before finding him or her to be in breach of his or her duty of care.

4–63 (14) The employee must show that the breach of duty has caused or materially contributed to the harm suffered. It is not sufficient to merely demonstrate that occupational stress of itself caused the harm.

4–64 (15) Where the harm suffered has more than one cause, the employer should only be liable for that part of the harm suffered which is attributable to his or her wrongdoing, unless the harm is truly indivisible. It is for the defendant to raise the question of apportionment. Hale L.J. in *Hatton* cites with approval Clarke L.J. in *Holtby v Brigham & Cowan (Hull) Ltd,*[74] wherein she quotes the following portion of his judgment where he commented:

> "It seems to me that once the claimant has shown that the dependant's breach of duty has made a material contribution to his disease, justice requires that he should be entitled to recover in full from those defendants unless they show the extent to which some other factor, whether it be 'innocent' dust or tortious dust caused by others also contributed".

4–65 (16) Assessment of damages shall take account of any pre-existing disorders or vulnerability and of the possibility that the employee/claimant would have suffered a stress-related disorder in any event.

4–66 One of the appellants before the Court of Appeal, Leon Alan Barber, appealed the decision of the Court of Appeal to the House of Lords, while the other three cases were not appealed. On April 1, 2004, the House of Lords delivered its decision in *Barber v Somerset County Council.*[75] While the decision of the Court of Appeal was reversed, there was broad acceptance of the sixteen principles set out in *Hatton.*

4–67 The House of Lords decision in *Barber* has tempered the *Hatton* decision and has tilted the balance in favour of the employees' position to a greater degree. Moreover, the House of Lords stated that although the 16 guidelines set down by the Court of Appeal were useful, it stated that the best statement of general principle continued to be that set out in *Stokes v Guest, Keen and Nefflefold (Bolts and Nuts) Ltd,*[76] where it was stated that:

> "... the overall test is still the conduct of the reasonable and prudent employer, taking positive thought for the safety of his workers in the light of what he knows or ought to know; where there is a recognised and general practice which has been followed for a substantial period in similar circumstances without mishap, he is entitled to follow it, unless in the light of common sense or newer knowledge it is clearly bad; but, where there is developing knowledge, he must keep reasonably abreast of it and not be too slow to apply it; and where he has in fact

---

[74] [2000] P.I.Q.R.Q. 305.
[75] [2004] U.K.H.L. 13; [2004] 2 All E.R. 385.
[76] [1968] 1 W.L.R. 1776 at 1783.

greater than average knowledge of the risks, he may be thereby obliged to take more than the average or standard precautious. He must weigh up the risk in terms of the likelihood of injury occurring and the potential consequences if it does; and he must balance against this the probable effectiveness of the precautions that can be taken to meet it and the expense and inconvenience they involve. If he is found to have fallen below the standard to be properly expected of a reasonable and prudent employer in these respects, he is negligent".

4–68   In January 2005, the Court of Appeal in *Hartman v South Essex Mental Health and Community Care NHS Trust*[77] was once again considering the circumstances in which occupational stress resulting in psychiatric injury will give rise to liability on the part of an employer. The *Hartman* judgment related to six conjoined appeals (four defendant's appeals and two claimant's appeals) involving claims for damages for psychiatric injury due to stress at work. One general issue to which Scott Baker L.J. refers is to the fact that only where the risk of injury to the employee was one that was sufficiently foreseeable would the employee succeed:

> "[A]s Buxton LJ put it in *Pratley v Surrey County Council* [2004] 1CR159 at paragraph 32, having referred to *Overseas Tankship (UK) Ltd v Morts Dock & Engineering Co Ltd (The Wagon Mound)* [1961] AC 388:
> "It is not the act but the consequences on which tortious liability is founded. The defendant will be deemed liable for those consequences, not because he has caused them in the course of some careless or otherwise undesirable activity, but only if they were caused by his failure to take precautions against a foreseen or foreseeable and legally relevant danger".[78]

4–69   The reference to *Pratley* is interesting as the Court of Appeal in that case held that although there was a foreseeable risk of injury to the employee in the long-term if her work overload continued, "what was unforeseen and unforeseeable was the immediate collapse that occurred". As there was no foreseeable risk of imminent injury, there was no liability and the plaintiff employee's action did not succeed. Buxon L.J. held that to impose liability for a foreseeable risk of injury to an employee in the long-term "would indeed be to impose liability for negligence in the air".[79]

4–70   In the first of the six joint appeals, the claimant contended that the risk of psychiatric injury to her was reasonably foreseeable in that four other employees had left the employment of the defendant Trust due to work-related stress. The trial judge, without considering whether the fact that other employees had left the Trust due to stress was evidence that the claimant's psychiatric injury was reasonably foreseeable, held:

> "[N]o less than four people ... had left [the Trust] through stress for one reason or another and accepting that such problems are perhaps usually multi-factorial one is bound to say along with Lady Bracknell that to lose one member of staff

---

[77] [2005] E.W.C.A. Civ. 06.
[78] *ibid.* at para.2.
[79] *ibid.* at para.41.

to stress is perhaps misfortunate but to lose three or possibly four is care-lessness."

The Court of Appeal rejected the foregoing and stated that the trial judge had failed to identify in what respect the claimant's injury was attributable to a breach of duty on the part of the defendant employers Trust. Rejecting the plaintiff's claim, the Court of Appeal held that her particular injuries were not reasonably foreseeable.

4–71   In the second of the six joint appeals, the Court of Appeal cited *Hatton* and held that the availability of a counselling service was a relevant matter to consider in work-related stress cases.[80] This was the position even if the claim-ant had availed of counselling and it had made no difference. The claimant did not avail of the counselling service in the instant case, pleading that "he may have been naïve enough to think he did not need counselling at the time". This prompted the Court of Appeal to comment that if the claimant did not think he needed counselling at the time, "how could his employers be in a better posi-tion?" It is interesting to note that the Court of Appeal in allowing the appeal in this case commented that the availability of a counselling service does not of itself imply that the employer acknowledges and has therefore foreseen the risk of impending harm to health arising from stress in his or her employment operation.

4–72   In the third of the six joint appeals, a part-time employee whose work averaged 17½ hours per week successfully brought an action against the defendant bank for injury due to stress in the workplace.[81] The Court of Appeal attached particular weight to the fact that the defendant bank had failed to act upon its own medical evidence and thereby allowed the claimant's stress to continue. Scott Baker L.J. summarised the position as follows:

> "[I]t will only be in exceptional circumstances that someone working for 2 or 3 days a week for limited hours will make good a claim for injury caused by stress at work. But despite the unusual circumstances the ordinary principles of employer's liability pass to be applied."[82]

IRISH CASE LAW

4–73   There are relatively few reported Irish decisions in this area. Anecdotal evidence suggests that this is not attributable to the number of cases taken, but rather reflects the fact that stress-related cases seem to settle prior to the full hearing. That said, the Irish courts have not been reluctant, in the few cases that have been considered, in imposing liability in circumstances where employers failed to recognise manifestations of stress when they should have or where they have failed to properly deal with or treat this condition.

---

[80] *Best v Staffordshire University* [2005] E.W.C.A. Civ. 06.
[81] *Wheeldon v HSBC Bank Ltd* [2005] E.W.C.A. Civ. 06.
[82] *ibid.* at para.87.

4–74   If an employer's system of work exposes an employee to hazardous work conditions which, while it does not result in physical injury, nonetheless induces psychological injury, then the employer will be as liable as if physical injury resulted. A relevant and instructive case is *O'Byrne v B and I Line plc*,[83] where the plaintiff was awarded damages in the amount of £35,000 in respect of the stress-related illness he had developed arising from the anxiety of his exposure to asbestos in the course of his employment. Significantly, the plaintiff had no physical symptoms of mesothelioma, the asbestos-related cancer, which has a long latency period.

4–75   Case law on work-related stress injuries has significantly developed since the decision of the Supreme Court in *Sullivan v Southern Health Board*.[84] The plaintiff in this case was a medical consultant employed by the defendant health service executive; he claimed that he was overworked because at the time there was not another medical consultant working with him whereas there had been when he had commenced his employment. It was held that the plaintiff was entitled to be compensated in the amount of £15,000 "for the stress and anxiety caused to him in both his professional and domestic life by the persistent failure of the Board to remedy his legitimate complaints".[85]

4–76   In the high profile case of *McHugh v Minister for Defence*,[86] Budd J. held that the defendant employer had been negligent in failing, firstly, to recognise and then to treat the post traumatic stress syndrome which the plaintiff employee had suffered in the course of his employment. The defendant's negligence was not that McHugh suffered from stress but that the army failed to ensure that the plaintiff received medical attention despite his abnormal and out-of-character behaviour. Later that year in the case of *Quinn v Servier Laboratories (Ireland) Ltd*,[87] the plaintiff settled a claim, reportedly for a "six figure sum", in respect of two nervous break-downs suffered, which he submitted were brought on by his excessive workload.

4–77   In *Hyland v Bestfood Services*,[88] the plaintiff was a factory supervisor who felt under pressure at work because there were staff shortages and a large number of orders to be processed. She took sick leave from work and attended her doctor who told her that she was suffering from such stress that she was liable to have a heart attack. Her employer dismissed her during her period of sick leave. The EAT held that she had been unfairly dismissed and awarded her £26,650.

---

[83] Unreported, High Court, January 12, 1996.
[84] [1997] 3 I.R. 123.
[85] *ibid.* at 136.
[86] Unreported, High Court, January 28, 1999.
[87] *Irish Times*, April 28, 1999.
[88] Unreported, UD 485/99.

4–78 In *Kerwin v Aughinish Alumina*,[89] the High Court awarded the plaintiff compensation, of which £50,000 was for stress and health problems he had suffered as a result of intimidation by his supervisors.

4–79 In *McGrath v Minister for Justice*,[90] the plaintiff, a member of the Garda Síochána, was awarded compensation in the amount of £40,000 for stress. This stress occurred following his suspension on suspicion of criminal embezzlement, of which he was found not guilty, because the suspension continued for an inordinate period of time and was, moreover, longer than that within which it would have been reasonably practicable to have held a full hearing into the suspension. Morris J. referred, in particular, to the established negligence of the defendant, which seems to suggest that a claim for stress may now be successful if the defendant's negligence is established and the plaintiff claims that anxiety was caused by the negligence. Significantly, the High Court made no reference to whether the stress and anxiety suffered by the plaintiff was reasonably foreseeable by the plaintiff's employer.

4–80 In the Circuit Court decision of *Curran v Cadbury (Ireland) Ltd*,[91] which concerned an action in damages for psychiatric injury taken by a factory operative against her employers, McMahon J. held that the duty of the employer towards his employee extends to protecting the employee from non-physical injury such as psychiatric injury, or the mental illness that might result from negligence or from harassment or bullying in the workplace. The learned Judge held "that the defendant owed the plaintiff a duty of care in the circumstances; that there was a breach of its common law duty to take care; and finally that the plaintiff suffered a compensatable injury, which was reasonably foreseeable in the circumstances". He referred to *Walker v Northumberland County Council*,[92] a case discussed at para 4.41, in which the English courts imposed liability where the plaintiff foreseeably suffered a nervous breakdown because of unreasonably stressful working conditions imposed on him by his employer, and stated that there was no reason to suspect that courts in Ireland would not adopt this approach. McMahon J. held that the plaintiff could recover since her employer owed her a duty of care not to expose her to a reasonably foreseeable psychiatric illness caused by the employer's negligence.

4–81 McMahon J. also found that the defendant company had breached para.13 of the Fifth Schedule to the Safety, Health and Welfare at Work (General Application) Regulations 1993, which stated as follows:

> "13(a) Where possible maintenance operations shall be carried out when equipment is shut down.

---

[89] Unreported, High Court, O'Neill J., 2000 and Health and Safety Review, December 2000, p.1.
[90] [2000] E.L.R. 15.
[91] (2000) 18 I.L.T. 140.
[92] [1995] 1 All E.R. 737.

(b) Where this is not possible, it shall be necessary to take appropriate
protection measures for the carrying out of such operations or for such
operations to be carried out outside the area of danger".

The judge held that since the defendant company should have foreseen that the
plaintiff might have suffered psychiatric illness as a result of its breach of the
foregoing provision, the plaintiff was also entitled to recover on the ground of
breach of statutory duty. Significantly, McMahon J. held that in defining
"personal injury", s.2 of the Safety, Health and Welfare at Work Act 1989
included "any disease and any impairment of a person's physical or mental
condition". He awarded the claimant a total of £18,700, which included
£12,000 general damages.

4–82   In *John Ledwith v Bus Átha Cliath/Dublin Bus*, a bus conductor who
suffered extreme post-traumatic stress disorder (PTSD) following physical and
verbal abuse by two intoxicated passengers was awarded €426,186 by the High
Court.[93] The case was later appealed to the Supreme Court, where it was
upheld.[94]

4–83   *In James McGrath v Trintech Technologies Limited and Trintech
Group PLC*,[95] the High Court cited with approval the 16 "practical propositions" set down by the English Court of Appeal in *Terence Sutherland v
Penelope Hatton*.[96] This case concerned an employee who was posted to a
demanding position in Uruguay in November 2002 following a medical examination to ensure he was fit for the role. The plaintiff claimed that he was not
provided with the necessary support or information to perform the job he had
been assigned. He also submitted that he had advised his line manager, Mr
Downes, that his doctor "thought that there might have been 'something going
on with my head'" and that Mr Downes' response was that he should "keep his
mouth shut".

Shortly after the plaintiff's arrival in Uruguay an all-out strike broke out
which he had to deal with, causing him "grave work-related stress and pressure
which resulted in injury to his psychological health and well-being". The
plaintiff had not at any stage disclosed his psychological history to his
employer. On his return in June 2003 the plaintiff took certified sick leave, and
in August 2003 he was advised that, following restructuring, he was one of the
twelve out of one hundred and thirty employees being made redundant from
26th September 2003.

4–84   Laffoy J., in dismissing the plaintiff's claim, held that an employer
could not be held liable for psychological injury caused by work-related stress
in circumstances where the employer "did not have actual knowledge of the
plaintiff's vulnerability to psychological injury or harm". At no point did the
plaintiff make a complaint to his employer in relation to work-related stress

---

[93]   Unreported, High Court, Finlay-Geoghegan J., February 28, 2003.
[94]   Unreported (*ex tempore*) judgment of Keane C.J., June 24, 2003.
[95]   [2004] I.E.H.C. 342.
[96]   [2002] 2 All E.R. 1.

prior to travelling to Uruguay, while in Uruguay or after his time in Uruguay. Laffoy J. stated:

> "On the evidence, in my view, there was no sign or warning which the defendant's personnel ought to have picked up that the plaintiff was prone to psychological injury attributable to work-related stress … The plaintiff had not [advised] the defendant of his psychological history. He had made no complaints in relation to work-related stress before he went to Uruguay. He made no direct complaints while there or on his return. In my view, the conversation with Mr. Downes in November was a casual conversation, which did not put Mr. Downes on any further inquiry as to the plaintiff's psychological condition".[97]

The plaintiff claimed that his failure to raise work-related stress was attributable to the fact that he was not aware himself that he was suffering from a stress-related injury while in Uruguay. Laffoy J. held that:

> "It would be wholly unreasonable to impute to the defendant knowledge of a vulnerability or condition of which the plaintiff was unaware in circumstances in which the defendant had not been appraised of the plaintiff's psychological history and the existence of the vulnerability and the likelihood of psychological harm was not ascertained through [medical] examination and inquiries".[98]

4–85   On the foreseeability issue, Laffoy J. was critical of the plaintiff's failure to adduce expert evidence. Referring to the *Hatton* judgment, the learned judge stated that while expert evidence may be helpful, it can never be determinative of what a reasonable employer should have foreseen.

4–86   The court concluded that the plaintiff failed in his claim for damages for work-related stress on the basis that the risk of psychological injury or harm to the plaintiff was not reasonably foreseeable. The court held as follows:

> "My general conclusion is that the plaintiff has not crossed the foreseeability threshold. The risk of psychological harm to the plaintiff was not reasonably foreseeable. The fundamental test is whether the defendant fell below the standard to be properly expected of a reasonable and prudent employer. In my view it did not".[99]

4–87   The 16 "practical propositions" set down by the Court of Appeal in *Hatton* and as endorsed by Laffoy J. in the High Court in *Trintech* were further considered by Clarke J. in *Michael Maher v Jabil Global Services Limited*.[100] This case follows the reasonable foreseeability test which the court sought to apply in *Trintech* and, in fact, increased the burden on an employee claiming damages for stress at work on the basis that the risk of psychological harm to him or her was reasonably foreseeable.

4–88   The plaintiff in this case was employed by the defendant as a supervisor on a production line in the early months of 2001. Following rapid

---

[97]   *ibid.* at p.74.
[98]   *ibid.* at p.75.
[99]   *ibid.* at p.76.
[100]   [2005] I.E.H.C. 130.

expansion by the defendant company during 2001, the plaintiff was appointed a shift manager, which amounted to a promotion. Shortly after taking up the position of shift manager the plaintiff began to suffer stress as a consequence of the pressure to achieve what he described as unrealistic targets. This led to the plaintiff being absent from work on stress-related leave from October 19, 2001 until the end of that year. Up to this time, the plaintiff had not complained to his employer about his excessive workload nor had he complained about work-related stress. Following a medical assessment as to the plaintiff's fitness to return to work on behalf of the defendant company, the plaintiff returned to work in January 2002. The defendant company's own doctor recommended that the plaintiff should not return to the position which had led to the stress, but rather to some other position within the defendant company that would not cause stress. The defendant company's doctor did, however, caution that the plaintiff was likely to have "ego problems" with being moved to a position "that might be perceived to be lower than the one he had formerly held." The plaintiff agreed to move to a different production area which was less demanding and was perceived by many, including the plaintiff, as a demotion. It was argued by the plaintiff, though not accepted by the court, that the move to the alternative position was agreed on the basis that it was to be on a provisional basis, with the plaintiff having the opportunity to return to his original role at some point.

The plaintiff made a number of requests to be allowed to return to his original role claiming that the role to which he returned in 2002 was a demotion with very little work to be done. Given the available medical evidence and advice, including absences from work on a regular basis, the defendant company refused his requests. The plaintiff continued on in the alternative position until March 12, 2002 when he went out on relatively permanent sick leave. This lasted until he resigned in mid-October 2002.

4–89   The plaintiff in the instant case claimed that the defendant company were liable for his stress-related illness as the defendant company knew or ought to have known that the pressure he was put under to achieve the targets set by the defendant company was likely to cause psychiatric injury to him. He further claimed that the new role assigned to him constituted not only a demotion but a concentrated effort by the defendant company to force him to resign, which merely added to his stress.

4–90   The High Court stated that the starting point for any consideration of liability in assessing psychological injury or harm was to ask the following questions:

> "a) has the plaintiff suffered an injury to his or her health as opposed to what might be described as ordinary occupational stress;
>
> b) if so is that injury attributable to the workplace, and
>
> c) if so was the harm suffered to the particular employee concerned reasonably foreseeable in all the circumstances."[101]

---

[101] *ibid.* at p.18.

4–91   Applying *Hatton*, Clarke J. stated that injuries could be foreseeable in two circumstances. First, injuries that may arise because:

> "having regard to the burden of work or other conditions in which the employee is required to work the risk of such injury ought to be anticipated generally by a prudent employer. Such a factor would potentially be applicable to all employees on the basis that it was foreseeable that any normal employee might suffer mental injury as a result of being exposed to the work and other practices concerned."[102]

An injury to a vulnerable employee could also be foreseeable in circumstances where the employer is on notice of that vulnerability:

> "Alternatively injury may be foreseeable in respect of an individual employee having regard to any particular vulnerability to injury known to the employer in respect of that employee."[103]

4–92   Clarke J. held that the plaintiff was precluded from recovering damages for stress at work as the plaintiff had made no complaints to his employer of excessive workload prior to taking sick leave in October such as would have led his employer to have had reasonable grounds for believing "that his continuance in that job would be likely to lead to psychological harm".[104] The plaintiff's injuries were not therefore reasonably foreseeable, so that there had been no breach of duty on the part of the defendant employer. Laffoy J. in Trintech adopted a similar approach:

> "The issue is not whether the stress the plaintiff suffered was caused by work, but whether the stress-induced injury was a consequence of a breach by the defendant of its statutory duties. Where an employee is injured because of the malfunction of a faulty piece of equipment given to him by his employer, the causative link is obvious. The injury would not have been inflicted if the faulty piece of equipment had not been given to the employee. The question which arises here is whether it can be said, as a matter of probability, that if the defendant took all of the steps which the plaintiff contends it was statutorily obliged to take (dealing with workplace stress in the safety statement, having in place a system for monitoring stress and an employee assistance programme and providing further training for the plaintiff) the plaintiff would not have suffered psychological injury. In my view it cannot.
>
> By way of general observation, if the submissions made on behalf of the plaintiff were correct, in my view, the law would impose a wholly unrealistic burden on employers."[105]

4–93   Both *Trintech* and *Maher* are significant in that together they signpost a high threshold for employees to meet in seeking to establish a breach of duty on the part of an employer in psychological injury or harm cases.

---

[102] *ibid.* at p.19.
[103] *ibid.* at p.19.
[104] *ibid.* at p.17.
[105] *ibid.* at p.78.

4–94   Clarke J. noted that no expert evidence had been provided "from which it might be concluded"[106] that a particular workload might expose a typical employee to an unreasonable level of stress. Objective expert evidence from which it might be concluded that a workload was unreasonable is therefore now an essential proof for establishing liability for stress-related illness to an employee.

4–95   As in *Trintech* and *Hatton*, Clarke J. held that where, as in this case, an employer offers a confidential service, with appropriate counselling or treatment services, that employer is unlikely to be held in breach of duty:

> "subject to a caveat that if the Court was satisfied that notwithstanding the provision of such a service the truth was that an employer was intent on removing an employee the availability of such a service might be regarded as being more a matter of form than substance."[107]

4–96   In summary, the decisions in both *Trintech* and *Maher* have placed a much higher burden on employees seeking to recover in stress related illness cases and should be carefully considered by legal practitioners in assessing an employee's chance of success in any such case.

EMPLOYMENT APPEALS TRIBUNAL

4–97   While the majority of cases to date for psychological injury caused by work-related stress have been personal injuries actions taken in the High Court, an employee could also issue a claim for constructive dismissal under the Unfair Dismissals Acts 1977–2001. In *Riehn v Dublin Society for the Prevention of Cruelty to Animals*, the EAT, applying the principles set down in *Hatton* and *Trintech*, awarded €30,000 to an employee, because "the severe stress on the employee was job-related and should have been noticed by the employer".[108] It should be noted that Lavan J. in *Matt Quigley v Complex Tooling and Moulding Limited* held that an employee who suffers psychological injury or harm as a consequence of excessive occupational stress could, in certain circumstances, pursue two separate sets of proceedings.[109] He or she could pursue proceedings for personal injuries before the High Court as well as being in a position to issue a claim for constructive dismissal under the Unfair Dismissals Acts 1977–2001. Lavan J. stated the position as follows:

> "[T]he plaintiff does not seek to challenge his dismissal but rather contends that the conduct of the defendant during the course of his employment was such as to amount to a breach of an implied duty to maintain trust and confidence during the employment relationship and this caused him injury. In the plaintiff's case the remedy ordered by the EAT was re-engagement. Accordingly it was submitted that there is no basis for precluding the plaintiff in these proceedings from claiming compensation for personal injuries. In doing so, he cannot be accused

---

[106] *ibid* at p.6.
[107] *ibid* at pp.21–22. See also *Pickering v Microsoft Ireland Operations Ltd* (unreported, High Court, Smyth J., December 21, 2005).
[108] [2004] E.L.R. 2005.
[109] [2005] I.E.H.C. 71.

of having 'a second bite at the cherry', as per Nicholls LD in Eastwood at paragraph 23 … I would accept the plaintiff's argument that the claim for injuries resulting from harassment in the workplace is a separate and distinct cause of action to his claim for unfair dismissal."

4–98 In *Pickering v Microsoft Ireland Operations Ltd*, the plaintiff claimed damages for wrongful dismissal owing to the repudiation of the contract of employment by the defendant.[110] The plaintiff was a software engineer for the defendant company and in 1999 was appointed Director of Localisation throughout Europe. Ms L.B. held a similar position for the defendant company in the United States.

In June 1999, the defendant company decided to merge the European and United States localisation departments into one department to be based in the United States. The plaintiff was offered the position of head of this unified department by Mr S. on behalf of the defendant company. Although interested in the position, she did not want to relocate to the United States and therefore turned down the promotion. In September 2000, L.B. was appointed head of the unified department. Under the new structure the plaintiff and her team were to continue to operate, though they would now report to L.B. The plaintiff contended that following L.B.'s appointment as head of the unified department, she was effectively "frozen out" of the company. She claimed that from October 2000 until January 2001, her role and position in the defendant company were undermined and the mutual trust and confidence between her and the defendant company had been eroded.

At a meeting in the United States on January 11, 2001 the plaintiff stated that L.B. agreed the plaintiff's job was effectively no longer in existence. She communicated the contents of this meeting to Mr S., the corporative vice-president of the defendant company, on January 26, 2001, though L.B. denied stating that the plaintiff's job was no longer in existence. The plaintiff was advised by Mr S. that she could not avail of a Reduction in Force package. She claimed she was very distressed by events. In particular, she claimed that news that she would not be able to avail of a Reduction in Force package triggered a nervous breakdown. The plaintiff left her employment on sick leave at the end of January and eventually resigned on August 16, 2001. There was no offer of a severance package by the defendant company.

Smyth J. formulated the following questions to assist him in determining the issues arising in the case:

> "(a) Did the plaintiff suffer a psychological injury to her health which was of a more serious kind and character than what might be described as ordinary occupational stress?
> (b) If so, was this harm attributable to the breach of contract and breach of duty on the part of the defendant?
> (c) If so, was the harm to the particular employee concerned, reasonably foreseeable?"

Applying the principles in *Hatton v Sutherland*,[111] the learned judge held that the defendant company had unlawfully terminated and/or constructively

---

[110] [2006] E.L.R. 65.
[111] [2002] All E.R. 1.

dismissed the plaintiff. Smyth J. stated that she had suffered a psychological injury to her health that was attributable to a breach of contract and breach of duty caused by the actions of the defendant company. Moreover, he held that the depressive illness suffered by the plaintiff was reasonably foreseeable from the time when the defendant company became aware that the plaintiff was suffering from stress. Significantly, Smyth J. held that the failure to negotiate with the plaintiff while on stress leave was a breach of contract. Damages in the amount of €348,000 were awarded against the defendant company for constructively dismissing the plaintiff. The judge granted €149,000 for not being able to cash in stock options. The award also included €100,000 for past and future pain and suffering. A further €69,000 was allowed in relation to salary; €1,348 for medication; €7,757 for flights, €800 for car hire and a hotel bill for the duration of the 12-day hearing of more than €3,000. Smyth J. directed that €200,000 be paid out immediately and he put a stay on the payment of the remainder in the event of an appeal. The case is currently on appeal to the Supreme Court. This is an important decision demonstrating that an employee can succeed in his/her claim for wrongful dismissal even though she/he has resigned.

4–99   The Supreme Court has yet to consider the circumstances in which occupational stress resulting in psychological injury or harm will give rise to liability on the part of an employer. It has, however, considered psychological injury alleged to have been negligently inflicted in the contexts of "nervous shock"[112] and "fear of disease"[113].

MINIMISING LIABILITY TO WORK-RELATED BULLYING,
HARASSMENT AND STRESS CLAIMS

4–100   There is a detectable movement towards encouraging employers to manage health and safety issues and this is particularly pertinent when addressing the identification of bullying, harassment and stress in the work-place. Such an approach involves *inter alia* the employer carrying out a risk assessment on an ongoing basis. The risk assessment must now form part of the safety statement. This statement should aver, not merely to the physical hazards, but also to the potential hazards of stress, harassment and bullying.

4–101   In the Scottish Outer Court of Session case of *Cross v Highlands and Islands Enterprise*,[114] Lord MacFayden alluded to the many publications and guidelines on stress at work which emphasise that "stress should be treated like any other health hazard". Consequently, he held that it is "strongly arguable that today a reasonable employer would carry out assessments of the risk of injury to their employees of stress at work".

---

[112] See *Kelly v Hennessy* [1996] 1 I.L.R.M. 321.
[113] *Fletcher v Commissioner for Public Works* [2003] 1 I.R. 465. See also Chap.8.
[114] [2001] I.R.L.R. 336.

4–102   The British Health and Safety Executive hold that work-related stress is not an individual weakness but a symptom of an organisational problem. It needs to be addressed as a partnership between workers, managers and employers. Using stress-management programmes is, therefore, good human resources practice for employers as well as being advantageous for a number of economic reasons detailed previously.[115] At a minimum, organisations should have a stress-management policy in place.

4–103   Employers should not ignore sicknotes which give work-related stress as the reason for the employee's absence. Stress-related sicknotes may signpost a risk to an employee's health attributable to his or her inability to cope with the work assigned to him or her.

4–104   The employer should assess the individual employee's ability to do the work for which he is employed. This will enable the employer to claim that not only was he unaware that the employee was suffering stress, but that the approach he adopted in relation to the management of the employee was such that if the employee had been suffering stress it would have been uncovered. To be in a position to argue the foregoing, the employer must monitor the employee on a regular basis. Failure to do so can have far-reaching consequences. A relevant and instructive case is *Reed and Ball Information Systems Ltd v Stedman*[116] where it was stated:

> "[S]ince the applicant had made complaints to other colleagues at work, it was incumbent on the employers to investigate the matter, and … their failure to investigate was enough to justify a finding of breach of trust and confidence."

The employer should also carry out a structured performance appraisal on an annual basis. Any such appraisal should consist of two-way communication.

4–105   Bullying and harassment procedures and policies are essential in the defence of a bullying, harassment and stress claim by an employee arising out of alleged harassment or bullying. Indeed, many employers now have procedures in place not just to deal with harassment on the prohibited grounds in the Employment Equality Acts 1998–2004, but also to deal with bullying more generally. In respect of bullying, for example, the sanctions to be taken against those found to be in breach of the Anti-Bullying Policy should be clearly stated. In fact, the Health and Safety Authority's booklet recommends that a rigorous bullying prevention policy be incorporated into the company's safety statement. In *Joseph Monaghan v Sherry Brothers Limited*, the EAT noted that "the grievance procedure and/or the disciplinary procedure was hopelessly inadequate" for dealing with claims of alleged bullying and harassment.[117] The 2001 Task Force Report on the Prevention of Workplace Bullying recommended that every workplace should have a Dignity at Work Charter (Part IV of this book), in addition to a separate and specific written Anti-Bullying Policy designed to

---

[115] See para.4–29.
[116] (1999) I.R.L.R. 299.
[117] [2003] E.L.R. 295.

suit each organisation's requirements.[118] The Report provided detailed guidelines on both. In the Report of the Expert Advisory Group on Workplace Bullying of July 2005, it was stated:

> "The inclusion of bullying as a risk together with policies and procedures to mitigate that risk should be mandatory in every employer's Safety Statement. The Health and Safety Authority will be charged with ensuring that this is enforced".[119]

4–106   Three separate codes of practice on the prevention of workplace bullying have been introduced pursuant to a recommendation of the aforementioned Taskforce on the Prevention of Workplace Bullying. The codes of practice made under the Industrial Relations Act 1990, the Employment Equality Act 1998 and the Safety, Health and Welfare at Work Act 2005 detail procedures for identifying, preventing and processing allegations of bullying in the workplace. In particular, the codes provide instruction on preparing an Anti-Bullying Policy. They outline procedures for addressing allegations of workplace bullying. Such procedures must include written complaints being examined by a designated member of management, culminating in an investigation either by management or an agreed third party.

The code of practice[120] introduced under s.60 of the Safety, Health and Welfare at Work Act 2005 provides valuable guidance on how to identify and prevent workplace bullying and replaces the 2002 Code of Practice entitled *Code of Practice on the Prevention of Workplace Bullying*[121]. It should be noted that the code of practice introduced under the industrial relations legislation underlines the importance of training for those dealing with workplace bullying. The code of practice introduced under the Employment Equality Act 1998 sets out procedures for addressing and preventing harassment in the workplace.

4–107   To be effective, bullying and harassment policies and procedures should be brought to the attention of every employee before he or she enters into a contract with the employer. Regular evaluation of the effectiveness of such policies and procedures is also essential.

Formal grievance procedures should be put in place to ensure access to management. Such procedures are central to the avoidance of bullying, harassment and stress-related claims in that they impose an obligation on the employee to alert the employer to the existence of a bullying, harassment and stress-related problem. Each complaint must be comprehensively investigated. Failure to adopt this approach can have serious consequences. A relevant and instructive case is *A. v Shropshire County Council*.[122] The case arose as a result

---

[118] The Task Force Report on the Prevention of Workplace Bullying was established by the former Minister for Labour, Trade and Consumer Affairs, Mr Tom Kitt, T.D., in September 1999, under the auspices of the Health and Safety Authority, and the Report of its findings was launched on April 10, 2001.

[119] "Report of the Expert Advisory Group on Workplace Bullying", July 2005 at p.9.

[120] See *Code of Practice for Employers and Employees on the Prevention and Resolution of Bullying at Work* (Health and Safety Authority, 2007).

[121] See para.4–06.

[122] English High Court, June, 2000.

of the introduction by a new head teacher of new disciplinary procedures for students, which were a failure. The lack of discipline that followed the introduction of the new regime led to the plaintiff suffering stress symptoms that endured for some time. The warning signs were ignored by the plaintiff's employers. The plaintiff was eventually diagnosed as having suffered a nervous breakdown. A substantial settlement of £300,000 was made in the case.

4–108 Not only should grievance procedures be spelt out for those employees alleging bullying or harassment, it is also clear from previous case law that a person against whom an allegation of bullying or harassment is made is entitled to the benefit of fair procedures.[123] In this regard, the workplace disciplinary procedure should specify "harassment" and "bullying" as grounds of misconduct on which a person may be subjected to disciplinary procedures, and on which the person may ultimately be dismissed. Even where the complaint of bullying or harassment is supported by the employer's investigation, disciplinary and dismissal procedures should include a number of steps. In particular, the sanction will have to be measured so as to meet the circumstances of the particular case.[124]

4–109 Where an employer becomes aware that an employee is exposed to work-related stress, the employer should relieve the employee of his or her duties on full salary and obtain advice from health professionals. Such an approach will enable the employer to investigate the matter and discharge his or her duty to take reasonable care for his or her employees' health and safety. The foregoing procedure was adopted in *Nolan v Ryan Hotels plc t/a The Gresham Hotel*,[125] where the EAT held that "the employer acted in a proper manner in investigating the matter".

4–110 Employers should make sure that they have sufficient liability insurance to cover work-related stress illnesses. It is also essential that employers comply with the Organisation of Working Time Act 1997 as regards daily, weekly and annual breaks.

---

[123] See *Maher v Irish Permanent plc (No.1)* [1998] E.L.R. 77.
[124] See *Timmons v Oglesby and Butler Ltd* (1999) E.L.R. 119.
[125] [1999] E.L.R. 214.

CHAPTER 5

REGULATIONS IMPLEMENTED UNDER THE SAFETY, HEALTH AND WELFARE AT WORK ACT 2005

5–01 Section 58 of the Safety, Health and Welfare at Work Act 2005 empowers the Minister for Enterprise, Trade and Employment to make regulations relating to any matter referred to in the 2005 Act or prescribed or to be prescribed for the purposes of giving full effect to the Act or in respect of any of the matters in Sch.7 to the 2005 Act. The expanded list of matters identified in Sch.7 in respect of which the Minister for Enterprise, Trade and Employment can introduce Regulations pursuant to s.58 of the 2005 Act, should be noted. Of particular significance is art.4 of Sch.7 which states that the Minister may introduce Regulations on the:

> "requirements to be imposed on an employee in relation to conduct or behaviour likely to endanger his or her own safety, health and welfare at work or that of any other person including as regards intoxication and submission to reasonable and proportionate tests …".

This provision is broadly drawn and could be invoked to address the growing problem of bullying and stress in the workplace.

5–02 It is reasonable to suppose that in time very detailed Regulations will be promulgated governing all parties in the workplace. Crucially, the nature of the duties imposed under certain Regulations currently in force appear to be absolute in nature. That is to say they require the result imposed by virtue of the statutory provision to be achieved by the person or body upon whom the duty is imposed. It is not a defence to state that reasonable care was taken, or alternatively, that it was not "reasonably practicable" or practicable to achieve the required result. At best, this absolute standard of care might be considered unfair and, at worst, *ultra vires* the Act. After all, the duty imposed under the 2005 Act is, depending on the section, one of reasonable practicability.

5–03 Section 58(8) of the 2005 Act should be noted in that it ensures that Regulations introduced under s.28 of the 1989 Act (*i.e.* the 1993 Regulations) remain in force[1] and are deemed to have been made under s.58 of the 2005 Act.

---

[1] See s.4(4) of the 2005 Act.

5–04 To date, a number of Regulations have been implemented under the 2005 Act. The main Regulations are the Safety, Health and Welfare at Work (General Application) Regulations 2007[2] and the Safety, Health and Welfare at Work (Construction) Regulations 2006[3].

---

[2] S.I. No. 299 of 2007.
[3] S.I. No. 504 of 2006.

CHAPTER 6

SAFETY, HEALTH AND WELFARE AT WORK (GENERAL APPLICATION) REGULATIONS 2007

6–01 The Safety, Health and Welfare at Work (General Application) Regulations 2007 ("the 2007 General Application Regulations")[1] impose certain absolute duties and are divided into 8 parts and 10 schedules, each of which now fall to be considered. The 2007 General Application Regulations, which replace and largely repeal[2] the 1993 General Application Regulations[3], complement the Safety, Health and Welfare at Work Act 2005. They were signed on June 14, 2007 by the then Minister for Labour Affairs, Mr. Tony Killeen TD and come into operation on 1 November 2007 subject to a small number of exceptions[4]. The 2007 General Application Regulations revoke and replace twenty statutory instruments in full[5] and retranspose 14 EU Directives on health and

---

[1] S.I. No. 299 of 2007.
[2] Part X and the Twelfth Schedule to the 1993 Regulations continue in force.
[3] S.I. No. 44 of 1993. The 2007 General Application Regulations also revoke and replace the Safety, Health and Welfare at Work (General Application)(Amendment) Regulations 2001 (S.I. No. 188 of 2001).
[4] See regs 9(2), 122, 134 and 160(2).
[5] (a) Factories (Report of Examination of Hoists and Lifts) Regulations 1956 (S.I. No. 182 of 1956),
(b) Factories Act 1955 (Hoists and Lifts) (Exemption) Order 1957 (S.I. No. 80 of 1957),
(c) Factories Act 1955 (Lifts) (Exemption) Order 1960 (S.I. No. 129 of 1960),
(d) Regulations 22 to 35 and 37 and 38 and the Schedule to the Docks (Safety, Health and Welfare) Regulations 1960 (S.I. No. 279 of 1960),
(e) Factories Act, 1955 (Hoistways) (Exemption) Order 1962 (S.I. No. 211 of 1962),
(f) Quarries (Electricity) Regulations 1972 (S.I. No. 50 of 1972),
(g) Mines (Electricity) Regulations 1972 (S.I. No. 51 of 1972),
(h) Quarries (General) Regulations 1974 (S.I. No. 146 of 1974) to the extent of in Regulation 3, the definitions of "lifting appliance" and "safe working load", Regulations 40 and 41, in the First Schedule "FORM No. 3" and "FORM No. 5" and the Second Schedule,
(i) Shipbuilding and Ship-Repairing (Safety, Health and Welfare) Regulations 1975 (S.I. No. 322 of 1975) to the extent of in Regulation 3(1), the definitions of "lifting equipment" and "lifting gear" and Regulations 32 to 48,
(j) Factories Act 1955 (Hoistways) (Exemption) Order 1976 (S.I. No. 236 of 1976),
(k) Factories Act 1955 (Hoists) (Exemption) Order 1977 (S.I. No. 13 of 1977),
(l) Mines (Electricity) (Amendment) Regulations 1979 (S.I. No. 125 of 1979),
(m) Quarries (Electricity) (Amendment) Regulations 1979 (S.I. No. 126 of 1979), and

safety[6]. They maintain the general substance of the provisions in the 1993 General Application Regulations while introducing a number of modifications. The use of the term "general application" in the title of the Regulations indicates that they apply, as does the Safety, Health and Welfare at Work Act 2005, to all employments.

PART 1 – INTERPRETATION AND GENERAL

6–02 The Safety, Health and Welfare at Work (General Application) (Revocation) Regulations 2005 revoke the definitions of "fixed term employee" and "temporary employee" in reg.2(1) of the General Application Regulations 1993.[7] It seems clear that "employee" in the Regulations bears the same

---

(n) Safety in Industry Acts 1955 and 1980 (Hoists and Hoistways) (Exemption) Order 1985 (S.I. No. 100 of 1985).

[6] (a) Council Directive 89/654/EEC of November 30, 1989 concerning the minimum safety and health requirements for the workplace;

(b) Council Directive 89/655/EEC of November 30, 1989 concerning the minimum safety and health requirements for the use of work equipment by workers at work, as amended by Council Directive 95/63/EC of December 5, 1995, amending Directive 89/655/EEC;

(c) Council Directive 89/656/EEC of November 30, 1989 on the minimum health and safety requirements for use by workers of personal protective equipment;

(d) Council Directive 90/269/EEC of May 29, 1990 on the minimum health and safety requirements for the manual handling of loads where there is a risk particularly of back injury to workers;

(e) Council Directive 90/270/EEC of May 29, 1990 on the minimum safety and health requirements for work with display screen equipment;

(f) Directive 2001/45/EC of the European Parliament and of the Council of June 27, 2001 amending Council Directive 89/655/EEC relating to the use of work equipment when carrying out work at a height;

(g) Directive 2003/10/EC of the European Parliament and of the Council of February 6, 2003 on the minimum health and safety requirements regarding the exposure of workers to the risks arising from physical agents (noise);

(h) Directive 2002/44/EC of the European Parliament and of the Council of June 25, 2002 on the minimum health and safety requirements regarding the exposure of workers to the risks arising from physical agents (vibration);

(i) the health and safety aspects of Council Directive 94/33/EC of June 22, 1994 on the protection of young people at work;

(j) the occupational safety and health provisions of Council Directive 92/85/EEC of October 19, 1992 on the introduction of measures to encourage improvements in the safetyand health at work of pregnant workers and workers who have recently given birth or are breastfeeding;

(k) in respect of night workers and shift workers, the safety and health protection provisions of Article 9 of Council Directive 93/104/EC of November 23, 1993 concerning certain aspects of the organisation of working time;

(l) Council Directive 92/58/EEC of June 24, 1992 on the minimum requirements for the provision of safety and/or health signs at work;

(m) Directive 1999/92/EC of the European Parliament and of the Council of December 16, 1999 on minimum requirements for improving the safety and health protection of workers potentially at risk from explosive atmospheres.

[7] See the Schedule to the Safety, Health and Welfare at Work (General Application) (Revocation) Regulations 2005 (S.I. No. 392 of 2005).

meaning as in the 2005 Act under which the Regulations were enacted. Section 2(1) of the 2005 Act defines an employee as a person:

> "who has entered into or works under (or, where the employment has ceased, entered into or worked under) a contract of employment and includes a fixed-term employee and a temporary employee and references, in relation to an employer, to an employee [are to] be construed as references to an employee employed by that employer ...".

Regulation 2(3) is worthy of note in that it requires an employer carrying out a risk assessment under s.19 of the 2005 Act to have regard, in particular, to the risks affecting employees working alone at a place of work or working in isolation at remote locations.

PART 2 – WORKPLACE AND WORK EQUIPMENT

Chapter 1 – Workplace

6–03   Regulation 4 of the 2007 General Application Regulations defines a place of work in the following manner:

> "'[p]lace of work' means a place of work intended to house workstations on the premises of the undertaking and any other place within the area of the undertaking to which an employee has access in the course of his or her employment but does not include:
>
> (a)   means of transport used outside the undertaking or a place of work inside a means of transport,
> (b)   temporary or mobile work sites, including construction sites,
> (c)   extractive industries,
> (d)   fishing boats,
> (e)   fields, woods and land forming part of an agricultural or forestry undertaking but situated away from the undertaking's buildings."

It is clear from the foregoing that temporary or mobile work sites are now excluded.

6–04   Chapter 1 broadly sets out employer duties in respect of places of work on several matters. For example, the employer's duty to ensure the structural stability of buildings which house places of work is set out in reg.5. Regulations 6 to 8 of the 2007 General Application Regulations cover a number of workplace standards on ventilation, room temperature, and natural and artificial room lighting that must be in place. The setting of temperatures for workrooms is new and should be noted. Regulations 9, 10 and 11 set out employer requirements as regards floors, walls, ceilings and roofs, windows and skylights and doors and gates. Chapter 1 also covers emergency routes and exits[8] and fire detection and fire fighting[9].

   Space allocation is covered in reg.17. It requires an employer to ensure sufficient space to allow employees to perform their work safely and without risk

---

[8]   Regulation 12.
[9]   Regulation 13.

to their health. Regulations 18 to 26 provide for a number of employer duties and repeal the Safety, Health and Welfare at Work (Miscellaneous Welfare Provisions) Regulations 1995.[10] They impose an obligation on employers to provide a safe and comfortable place of work. The employer duties include, *inter alia*, keeping a place of work in a clean state, providing facilities for sitting where practicable, ensuring an adequate supply of potable drinking water and the provision of adequate and suitable sanitary and washing facilities for the use of employees. Regulation 22 covers accommodation for employees while reg.26 introduces a new provision enabling a tenant or landlord to apply to the Circuit Court for an order allowing the carrying out of any structural or other alterations to the premises necessary to enable the employer to comply with the 2007 General Application Regulations.

Chapter 2 – Use of Work Equipment

6–05   In this part of the Regulations and Sch. 1 to the 2007 General Application Regulations sets out the requirements governing the use of work equipment. Regulations 28 to 30 detail general provisions for all work equipment. Regulations 32-61 inclusive outline the additional minimum requirements applicable to specific types of work equipment including control devices, guards and protection devices, drive systems of mobile work equipment, combustion engines of mobile work equipment, fork-lift trucks, self-propelled work equipment, work equipment for lifting loads, cranes, work equipment for lifting goods or persons, hoists and lifts, winch-operated hoists and lifts, lifting accessories, work equipment for lifting non-guided loads, lifting equipment, excavators, draglines, telehandlers, loaders, and scotch and guy derrick cranes.

Chapter 2 of Pt 2 sets down the minimum requirements for mobile work equipment, whether or not self-propelled and specifically fulfils Ireland's requirements in respect of lifting equipment and lifting operations under Council Directive 96/63/EC. It also addresses the requirements of work equipment for lifting loads. Provisions concerning work equipment for lifting non-guided loads are covered in this part of the 2007 General Application Regulations as are fishing vessels.

Regulation 27 defines the selection, installation and use of work equipment as "any activity involving work equipment, including starting or stopping the equipment, its use, transport, repair, modification, maintenance and servicing and cleaning". Regulation 28 outlines the duties of employers regarding the use of work equipment by their employees. All work equipment for use by employees at a place of work must comply with the provisions of any legislation implementing a specific EU Directive relating to work equipment with respect to health and safety. Employer responsibilities also include risk assessment[11] and ensuring that the necessary measures are taken so that the work equipment is suitable for the work to be carried out. Regulation 28 sets down requirements, such as ergonomic risk assessments, in respect of all work equipment. In particular, reg.28(f) requires employers to ensure that:

---

[10]   S.I. No. 358 of 1995.
[11]   Regulation 28(b).

"the working posture and position of employees while using work equipment, and ergonomic requirements, are taken into account having regard to the safety and health of the employees."

6–06 The provision of adequate information and instruction relating to the proper use of the work equipment is a requirement of reg.29. In *Crane v Premier Prison Services Ltd,*[12] the courts in the neighbouring jurisdiction, considering the English equivalent of reg.29 of the 2007 General Application Regulations, held that the suitablity of equipment is an issue which takes precedence over the adequacy of training in its use.

6–07 The inspection of work equipment is a requirement of reg.30 which introduces a new requirement to carry out periodic examination and, where applicable, testing of work equipment subject to deterioration.

Where a defect in work equipment is potentially hazardous, records of any inspections and maintenance should be kept for a period of five years.[13] This is a requirement for gas equipment.

6–08 All work equipment supplied must be maintained to the requisite standard throughout its working life.[14] A maintenance log concerning the maintenance of work equipment should be kept and the level of such maintenance should be sufficient to continue to meet the requirements of Ch.2 of Pt 2 of the 2007 General Application Regulations. In the case of *Doherty v Bowaters Irish Wallboard Mills Ltd,*[15] a load suspended from a travelling crane fell, injuring the plaintiff. The cause of the accident was a latent defect in the hook, of which the defendant correctly protested he could not have been aware. The Supreme Court held that the requirement in s.34(1) of the Factories Act 1955, that the hook be of adequate strength, was an absolute duty. The mere fact that the hook broke and caused injury was sufficient of itself to impose liability for the accident upon the employer. It can be seen from the case of *Everitt v Thorsman (Irl) Ltd*[16] that this absolute standard has been maintained in regs 28 and 31 of the 2007 General Application Regulations. In that case Kearns J. stated:

"[W]hile there is no blameworthiness in any meaningful sense of the word on the part of the employers in this case, these Regulations do exist for sound policy reasons at least, namely, to ensure that an employee who suffers an injury at work through no fault of his own by using defective equipment should not be left without a remedy. [A]n employer in such a situation may usually, though not always, be in a position to seek indemnity from the third party who supplied the work equipment."

6–09 The onerous duty imposed upon employers in relation to work equipment was addressed in the case of *Eamon Stakelum v The Governor and Company of the Bank of Ireland.*[17] In summary, the High Court held that employers

---

[12] Q.B.D., January 26, 2001.
[13] Regulation 30(b) and (d).
[14] Regulation 31.
[15] [1968] I.R. 277.
[16] Unreported, High Court, June 23, 1999.
[17] Unreported, High Court, O'Donovan J., April 27, 1999.

have a duty to ensure that any equipment used by an employee in the course of his work is free from defects and suitable for the purposes for which it is used. O'Donovan J. placed particular emphasis on the employer's duty to submit equipment used by an employee in the course of his employment to risk/safety assessment. A further relevant and instructive case is that of *Gilna v Maguire*.[18] In that case, the plaintiff, a 25-year-old radiographer employed in Beaumont Hospital, experienced a shock from a laser image processor, supplied by the second named defendant, 3M Ireland Ltd. The shock catapulted her across the room causing her personal injury. Her injuries endured for some time notwithstanding intensive physical treatment. The High Court held that the first named defendant, who was the representative of Beaumont Hospital in the proceedings, as the employer, had failed to provide safe equipment to the plaintiff. The court also held that the manufacturer had been negligent in selling a machine in a condition that caused the plaintiff to experience an electrostatic shock. Damages of £664,203 were awarded.[19]

6–10   The European Communities (Machinery) Regulations 2001[20] detail particular safety provisions for machinery to be marked within the EU. Employers purchasing machinery should seek to locate the appropriate CE mark and required back up documentation indicating that the machinery complies with the essential safety requirements of the underlying directive (98/37/EC).

Chapter 3 – Personal Protective Equipment

6–11   This Part of the 2007 General Application Regulations and Sch.2 to the Regulations requires employers, where risk to health and safety cannot be avoided by technical measures and procedures, to provide personal protective equipment for use by their employees. Prior to the supply and use of personal protective equipment, the employer must carry out an assessment to ensure that the equipment is effective against the risks identified and compatible with other equipment. Further, every employer must also ensure that the personal protective equipment supplied by him or her is maintained at all times in good working order and in a satisfactory hygienic condition. The employer must also give information, training and instruction to the employee in the use of the personal protective equipment.[21] It is a requirement of reg.67 to inform the employee of the level of protection afforded by the personal protective equipment provided for his or her use. These duties are absolute in nature. It would appear that the Regulations do not impose a duty on an employer to enforce the use of the personal safety equipment that he or she is obliged to provide to his

---

[18]   Unreported, High Court, Johnson J., May 19, 1999.

[19]   See also *Everitt v Thorsman (Irl) Ltd and Jumbo Bins and Sludge Disposals Ltd* (unreported, High Court, Kearns J., June 23, 1999, discussed above) and *Michael Armstrong v William J. Dawn & Sons Ltd* (unreported, High Court, February 8, 1999) where Morris J. held a garage solely liable for injuries sustained by the plaintiff as a result of the negligent manner in which repairs to his vehicle had been carried out.

[20]   S.I. No. 518 of 2001.

[21]   Regulation 67. See *Magee v Ideal Cleaning Services Ltd* [1999] E.L.R. 218.

or her employees. A common law duty is imposed on an employer in this regard, however, through the tort of negligence. Sections 8 and 13 of the 2005 Act, discussed in Ch.3, should be considered alongside this part of the 2007 General Application Regulations. These sections impose duties on employers to supply personal protective equipment and on employees to make correct use of personal protective equipment, having been provided with suitable information, instruction and training to enable them to make proper and effective use of the personal protective equipment provided.

Chapter 4 – Manual Handling of Loads

6–12   Lifting manual loads in the workplace was formerly regulated by the Factories Act 1955 (Manual Labour) (Maximum Weights and Transport) Regulations 1972. By virtue of the Safety, Health and Welfare at Work Act 1989 (Repeals and Revocations) Order 1995, which came into force on December 21, 1995, Part VI and the Eighth and Ninth Schedules of the 1993 Regulations replaced the 1972 Regulations. Chapter 4 of Pt 2 and the related Sch.3 of 2007 General Application Regulations repeal the provisions in the 1993 General Application Regulations and deal with the manual handling of loads.   Regulation 68 defines what constitutes the manual handling of loads:

> "'Manual handling of loads' means any transporting or supporting of a load by one or more employees and includes lifting, putting down, pushing, pulling, carrying or moving a load, which, by reason of its characteristics or of unfavourable ergonomic conditions, involves risk, particularly of back injury, to employees."

6–13   Chapter 4 envisages the manual handling of loads by employees as a last resort. Where such manual handling is required, an employer is obliged to minimise the risk involved and provide, where possible, precise information concerning the weight and centre of gravity of a load to the employee.[22] In *Darrell Grant Hawkes v London Borough of Southwark*,[23] the English Court of Appeal held that an employer who failed to reduce the risk to an employee carrying out manual handling operations to the lowest level practicable was liable in damages for the personal injuries that followed. The English equivalent of reg.69(d) was considered in *Alan Swain v Denso Marston Ltd*.[24] The plaintiff in this case was injured in an industrial accident on August 8, 1996. As part of his work, he had to strip down part of a conveyor belt and remove a roller. The plaintiff expected the roller to be hollow but it was solid, weighing 20 kg. As he removed the last bolt, the roller dropped and trapped his hand causing an injury. Under reg.4(1)(b)(iii) (the equivalent of reg.69(d) of the 2007 Irish Regulations), the employer was required to take appropriate steps to provide employees with general indications and, where reasonably practicable to do so, precise information on the weight of each load. The Court of Appeal noted that there had been no risk assessment. It stated that had there

---

[22]   See reg.69(d).
[23]   Unreported, Court of Appeal, February 20, 1998.
[24]   [2000] I.C.R. 1079; [2000] P.I.Q.R. 129.

been any proper assessment, it would have considered what manual handling tasks were involved in repairs and non-routine maintenance. If no brochure or specification had been available, the court considered that the assessment might have involved making inquiries of the manufacturer. If these inquiries failed to disclose the weight of the roller, their Lordships stated prudence would have dictated the assumption that it might be unexpectedly heavy. The Court of Appeal concluded that the latter assumption might have been communicated to employees who were entitled to that information under reg.4(1)(b)(iii), the equivalent of reg.69(d) of the 2007 General Application Regulations.

6–14　The Third Schedule details the five factors that must be taken into account by an employer for the manual handling of loads. These are:

1.　the characteristics of the load;
2.　the physical effort required;
3.　the characteristics of the working environment;
4.　the requirements of the activity; and
5.　individual risk factors.

Schedule 3 identifies, in particular, individual risk factors in the manual handling of loads. It provides that an employee may be at risk if he or she is physically unsuited to perform the task in question, is wearing unsuitable clothing[25] and does not have the adequate or appropriate knowledge or training.

6–15　In *Fiona Stone v Metropolitan Police Commissioner*,[26] the plaintiff, a 28–year-old woman, was awarded £400,000 for the soft tissue lower back injury she suffered as a result of lifting and transporting heavy loads whilst at work. This was a cumulative injury over time and not a single event. Significantly, reg.69 and Sch.3 anticipate such injuries.

6–16　On a literal interpretation of the Regulations an employer would be under an absolute duty to eliminate all manual handling of goods. The logical consequence of such an interpretation would be to mechanise a system and remove the need for employees altogether. Perhaps the greatest defect in this section is one of omission. Whereas the 1972 Regulations included a list of maximum weights, broken down by age and sex, the 2007 General Application Regulations are silent on this point.[27] This has resulted in considerable uncertainty. That said, the Health and Safety Authority has produced an excellent guidance leaflet on manual handling, which has useful examples as well as figures for lifting weights at various heights and at various distances from the body. Appendix 4 of the Authority guide provides a very useful example of a

---

[25]　Schedule 3 provides that wearing unsuitable footwear or other personal effects may put an employee at risk.

[26]　Unreported, Milton Keynes County Court, Serota J., September 16, 1999; L.T.L.P.I. September 27, 1999.

[27]　The 1972 Regulations were abolished by the Safety, Health and Welfare at Work Act 1989 (Repeals and Revocations) Order 1995.

manual handling risk assessment. Section 10(1)(c) of the 2005 Act should also be noted insofar as it requires the employer to assess whether the individual employee is able to lift a particular weight.

6–17 Regular manual handling training will reduce the exposure of an employer to a claim. A relevant and instructive case is *Gorry v British Midland Airways Ltd*[28].[29] Judge Dunne, citing Pt VI of the repealed General Application Regulations 1993, noted that all reasonable precautions were required. The learned judge held that, even where employees were performing a task on a daily basis, they acquired bad habits and needed to be provided with regular training so as to carry out their tasks safely. A similar approach was adopted in *O'Connor v North Eastern Health Board*,[30] wherein the High Court found the Health Service Executive was in breach of its duty to provide training. The plaintiff was awarded £112,000 in general damages and £145,500 in special damages.[31]

Work-Related Upper Limb Disorders

6–18 It is worth noting that this section, considering the characteristics specified in s.4 of the Third Schedule, which refers, *inter alia*, to "over-frequent or over prolonged physical effort involving in particular the spine", could be pleaded in claims involving Work-Related Upper Limb Disorders ("WRULDs"). WRULD is a term covering all kinds of work-related injuries to the muscles, nerves and tendons of the upper limbs.[32] While its recognition as a medical disorder has been slow, there is ample authority to conclude that its existence has been acknowledged at Circuit Court and High Court level in this jurisdiction. In *Sammon v Flemming GmbH*,[33] the plaintiff alleged that she was suffering tennis elbow as a result of her employment. Her work involved screwing caps by hand onto phials on a production line. Barron J. accepted on the evidence that the repetitive nature of the work required of her was the probable cause of her condition. He dismissed the claim, however, on the basis that:

> "[t]he Defendant acted reasonably and could not reasonably be expected to have anticipated that the particular work which the Plaintiff was doing would lead to such an abuse of the muscles of her forearm that she would sustain an injury".[34]

This case pre-dated the 2007 Regulations so they were not considered. The 2007 Regulations now oblige employers to evaluate the potential risk to their employees and review their safety policies. In the above case, the plaintiff first

---

[28] (1999) 17 I.L.T. 224.
[29] On training, see also s.10 of the 2005 Act.
[30] Unreported, High Court, 1999.
[31] For manual handling training prior to the 2007 General Application Regulations, see *Catherine Firth v South Eastern Health Board* (unreported, High Court, Barr J., July 27, 1994).
[32] In the United States, "Cumulative Trauma Disorder" is used to describe WRULD. The British Health and Safety Executive (HSE) have also adopted the term "Work Related Upper Limb Disorder". The HSE has published some useful guidelines on this topic. See, in particular, the HSE's risk filter.
[33] Unreported, High Court, Barron J., November 23, 1993.
[34] See, however, *Paul Bolger v Quealy Pig Slaughtering Ltd*, unreported, High Court, Barron J., March 8, 1996.

complained in 1987, 20 years prior to the enactment of the 2007 Regulations. Knowledge of WRULD is now widely publicised, and may thus be said to be a known risk factor, which should fall to be considered by an employer.[35] It is contended that it would now be open to an employee in a similar situation to *Sammon* to claim and to utilise the higher standard imposed by statute.

6–19   In *Brennan v Telemecanique Ltd*,[36] a case concerning a WRULD sustained during assembly work, Lynch J. held that the overuse by the plaintiff of her middle finger caused the injury. Further, he held that the overuse of the finger was foreseeable by the defendant. Consequently, the employer was held to be in breach of his duty to provide a safe system of work. It is unclear whether the now repealed 1993 General Application Regulations and/or breach of statutory duty were pleaded or relied upon in this case.

6–20   In May 1999, a typist was awarded record damages (£100,000) by the English High Court in the landmark case of *McPherson v Camden Council*.[37] Thornton J., in the course of his judgment, stated that the Council should have provided a wrist rest and a flat keyboard to prevent the onset of the plaintiff's condition, and criticised it for its failure to ensure regular breaks from typing.

   While only of persuasive authority in this jurisdiction, this case shows that employers can now ill afford to ignore WRULD. Indeed, in the short-term and the medium-term, it is widely believed that the number of WRULD claims will continue to rise.

6–21   In WRULD cases much depends upon evidence of the system of work operated by an employer. It would be difficult for a judge, faced with evidence of repetitive work, few breaks and inadequate rotation[38] to find, on the balance of probabilities, that work practices were not to blame. Employers must be pro-active in risk prevention and control. Indeed, the Safety, Health and Welfare at Work Act 2005 and the 2007 General Application Regulations have firmly placed the onus on the employer for analysis and prevention of WRULD risks. For example, where WRULD risks are found following a general risk assessment, a full risk assessment should be carried out of the jobs most at risk, leading to subsequent action to eliminate or reduce the risks. WRULD can be prevented by ergonomic analysis of workstations, changing the manner in which work is managed, treatment by physiotherapy and rest.

6–22   The issue of WRULD is not one that is likely to disappear and employers must take care in advising their staff. This is borne out by the English Court of Appeal decision in *Pickford v ICI*,[39] where it was held that a typist who

---

[35] This was a key factor in the decision of the judge in the English case of *McSherry and Lodge v British Telecommunications plc* [1992] 3 Med. L.R. 129, in holding for the plaintiffs.

[36] Unreported, Eastern Circuit Court, Lynch J., January 1997; [1997] I.L.L.W. 254.

[37] English High Court, May, 1999.

[38] See Organisation of Working Time Act 1997.

[39] [1998] 3 All E.R. 462.

worked a seven-hour day could claim against her employer for injury caused
by excessive typing for lengthy periods without proper breaks or rest periods;
this was because the employer had not given her the same instructions as he
had other typists to take regular breaks.

6–23   From an insurance perspective it is the employer's liability insurance
that will pay for any successful WRULD claims. A policy will generally cover
the compensation awarded by a court, all costs and expenses of litigation
incurred by both the defendant and plaintiff and all other costs.

6–24   In line with the more onerous duties imposed upon employers by the
Safety, Health and Welfare at Work Act 2005 and the Regulations implemented thereunder, the future will undoubtedly result in a wider duty of care
on the employer coupled with a more burdensome standard of care—an
employer will be required to consider even more contingencies to an even
greater depth. This is likely to have an impact upon the legal position of
WRULD and will necessitate the determination of a general date of knowledge. This is the date that the employer should have known that there was a
danger to his employees and thus should have done something to protect them.
Causation will, however, continue to be a significant obstacle to the employee
asserting WRULD. In short, the employee must not only establish a breach of
duty on the part of his employer, but must also satisfy the court that he is suffering from a clinically recognised condition caused by his employment.

Chapter 5 – Display Screen Equipment

6–25   Chapter 5 of Part 2 and Sch. 4 to the 2007 General Application Regulations impose duties on an employer to protect an employee "who habitually uses
display screen equipment as a significant part of his or her normal work …".[40]
Regulation 71 excludes the following:

> "(a)   drivers' cabs or control cabs for vehicles or machinery,
> (b)   computer systems on board a means of transport,
> (c)   computer systems mainly intended for public use,
> (d)   portable display screen equipment not in prolonged use at a workstation,
> (e)   calculators, cash registers and any equipment having a small data or meas-
>   urement display required for direct use of the equipment, and
> (f)   typewriters of traditional design, of the type known as 'typewriter with
>   window'."

It is obvious from the foregoing that portable or laptop computers, as well as
conventional typewriters, are excluded from the remit of these Regulations.
Regulation 72 imposes specific duties on employers to, *inter alia*, assess the
risk presented by display screen equipment, and, on the basis of that evaluation, take appropriate measures to remedy any risks found, taking account of:

(i)   the minimum requirements set out in Sch. 4 to the 2007 Regulations, and

---

[40]   Regulation 70.

(ii) any additional or combined effects of any risks found.

Employers are also required to plan employees' activities to provide breaks and provide training, information and advice to employees on the proper use of the equipment.

The provision of eye tests before commencing display screen work and at regular intervals thereafter, and the provision of special corrective appliances, where necessary, are dealt with in reg.73.

PART 3 – ELECTRICITY

6–26 Part 3 of the 2007 General Application Regulations, which is framework in nature and contains a number of new provisions, applies, *inter alia*, to the generation, storage, transmission and provision of electrical energy to all places of work except mines. This part of the 2007 General Application Regulations should be considered alongside the Safety, Health and Welfare at Work (Offshore Installations) (Operations) Regulations 1991, which also contain provisions for electrical safety.[41] It requires an assessment of risks, which ensures that all items of electrical equipment are properly designed, constructed, installed, maintained and used so as to prevent danger. Regulation 76 is worthy of particular note in that it imposes absolute duties on an employer:

> "All electrical equipment and electrical installations shall at all times be so:-
>
> (a) designed,
> (b) constructed,
> (c) installed,
> (d) maintained,
> (e) protected, and
> (f) used
>
> so as to prevent danger."

Regulation 81 imposes new obligations regarding the checking and inspection of electrical portable equipment. Mobile tools used in confined spaces are not allowed to exceed 125 volts if they have a rating of less than 2 kilovolt amperes.[42] Portable hand lamps are not allowed to exceed 25 volts AC or 50 volts DC in confined spaces.[43]

Regulation 91 imposes new obligations on employers regarding substations and main switch rooms. It provides that an employer must ensure that they are suitably constructed and arranged so that only an authorised person can enter. Regulation 93(2) imposes more onerous obligations regarding work near overhead electricity lines. Such work can no longer be carried out until–

(a) the supply to the overhead line is isolated,
(b) if such isolation is not practicable, the overhead line is diverted,
(c) if such isolation or diversion is not practicable, adequate

---

[41] See S.I. No. 16 of 1991.
[42] Regulation 81(4)(a).
[43] Regulation 81(4)(b).

(i)   barriers,
(ii) protective measures,
(iii) warnings, or
(iv) other suitable means,

are, in so far as is reasonably practicable, put in place to minimise the risk of contact with the overhead line.

PART 4 – WORK AT HEIGHT

6–27   Part 4 and Sch.5 to the 2007 General Application Regulations repeal the Safety, Health and Welfare at Work (Work at Height) Regulations 2006 ("the 2006 Work at Height Regulations")[44] which transposed into Irish law the provisions of Council Directive 89/955/EEC as amended by Directive 95/63/EC and Directive 2001/45/EC on the use of work equipment when carrying out work at a height. The primary aim of this part of the Regulations is to reduce deaths and fatalities at work caused by falls from heights. It sets out basic principles and introduces new rules for safe working at height, based on risk assessment for all work conducted at height in all sectors of employment.

6–28   Part 4 of the 2007 Regulations requires employers to avoid work at height so far as reasonably practicable. Where work at height is necessary, and where such work can be carried out safely and without risk to health, safe systems of work for organising, planning and performing work at height should take place. Planning of work for the purposes of Pt 4 of the 2007 Regulations includes the selection of work equipment, an appropriate risk assessment and preparing for emergencies and rescues.

6–29   In summary, Pt 4 of the 2007 Regulations imposes specific requirements for the organisation, planning and risk assessment of work at height,[45] the avoidance of risks from work at height,[46] the selection of work equipment for work at height,[47] the choice of equipment for work at height,[48] fragile surfaces,[49] falling objects,[50] danger areas[51] and the inspection of work equipment.[52]

6–30   Regulation 100 is of particular significance as it provides that, in addition to taking account of the risk assessment in the selection of the most suitable equipment for work at height, collective protection measures should

---

[44]   S.I. No. 318 of 2006.
[45]   Regulation 95.
[46]   Regulation 98.
[47]   Regulation 100.
[48]   Regulations 103 to 114.
[49]   Regulation 115.
[50]   Regulation 116.
[51]   Regulation 117.
[52]   Regulation 119.

be given priority over personal protection meas~~ ~~ also
requires an employer in selecting equipment for
regard to the following:

1. the working conditions and the risks to '
   at the place where the work equipme~
2. in the case of work equipment fo'
   height to be negotiated;
3. the distance of a potential fall and the ri~
4. the duration and frequency of use of the equ~
5. the need for easy and timely evacuation and resc~
6. any additional risk posed by the use, installation or i~
   equipment or by evacuation and rescue from it.

The detailed requirements as regards the condition of surfaces fo~
ing structures, guard-rails, all working platforms, collective safeguaru~
arresting falls, additional requirements for scaffolding, all personal fall protection systems, work restraint systems and ladders, are set out in regs 101 to 114.

The 2007 General Application Regulations require regular and routine
inspection of all work equipment for work at height to identify whether the
equipment is fit for its purpose.[53] Regulation 119(4) provides that the
employer must record such inspections of work equipment in a manner that
is accessible.

PART 5 – PHYSICAL AGENTS

Chapter 1 – Control of Noise at Work

6–31 The Personal Protective Equipment Regulations[54] overlap with this
part of the 2007 General Application Regulations. Hearing loss cases will generally fall for consideration under this part of the Regulations. Noise-induced
hearing loss is the most frequently reported occupational disease in the EU.

6–32 Assessing a noise exposure case involves more than simply looking at
the noise level. Duration is the other part of the equation. It was previously
reflected in the 1975 Regulations, though it was addressed in a more comprehensive manner in the 1990 Regulations, which detailed additional, lower,
action levels.[55] In summary, noise dose or daily personal noise exposure determines liability. Directive 2003/10/EC of the European Parliament and the
Council of February 6, 2003 on the minimum health and safety requirements
regarding the exposure of employees to the risk arising from noise, were
brought into force as a stand-alone set of Regulations on July 13, 2006.[56] The
2007 General Application Regulations revoke the 2006 Noise Regulations.

---

[53] Regulation 119.
[54] Chapter 3 of Pt.2 and Sch.2 to the 2007 General Application Regulations.
[55] See regs 4, 5 and 6 and the First Schedule to the 1990 Regulations.
[56] S.I. No. 371 of 2006.

Chapter 1 of Pt 5 of the 2007 General Application Regulations, however, re-enact the 2006 Noise Regulations, without any significant change. The 2007 General Application Regulations revoke and replace the European Communities (Protection of Workers) (Exposure to Noise) Regulations 1990,[57] subject to those Regulations continuing to apply to the music and entertainment sectors until February 15, 2008.[58] Regulation 122(1) also provides that the exposure limit value in reg.128 of the 2007 General Application Regulations shall not apply to personnel on board seagoing vessels until February 15, 2011.

6–33   The appropriate test for measuring hearing loss is to be found in the "Green Book", the main recommendations of which were incorporated into the Civil Liability (Assessment of Hearing Injury) Act 1998.[59] Section 2 of the 1998 Act states that the provisions of the Act apply to all proceedings before a court, whether commenced before or after the coming into force of the Act.[60]

6–34   Chapter 1 of Part 5 of the 2007 Regulations applies to all work activities in which employees are or are likely to be exposed to risks to their safety and health arising from exposure to noise during their work. The Regulations seek to prevent the exposure of employees to harmful noise at work and should be read in addition to the range of general provisions with this aim in the Safety, Health and Welfare at Work Act 2005.[61]

Regulation 123 specifies the exposure limit values and exposure action values in respect of the exposure of any employee to noise at work. The exposure limit value means for any worker the level of daily noise exposure or peak sound pressure that must not be exceeded for any employee. The exposure action values mean for any worker the level of daily noise exposure or peak pressure level, which, if exceeded, requires specified action to be taken to reduce risk to any employee.

Regulation 124 requires an employer to conduct a risk assessment where employees are liable to be exposed to noise at work above a lower action value, which may include the need to carry out noise measurements.[62] The aim of this risk assessment is to inform the employer of what action, if any, is necessary to prevent or adequately control exposure of his or her employees to noise at work. Regulation 124(e) provides that an employer should give particular attention when carrying out a risk assessment on noise exposure to the following:

(a)   the level, type and duration of exposure, including any exposure to impulsive noise,

(b)   the exposure limit values and the exposure action values,

---

[57]   S.I. No. 157 of 1990.
[58]   Regulation 122(2).
[59]   S.I. No. 12 of 1998, in force from May 11, 1998.
[60]   See *Greene v Minister for Defence* (unreported, High Court, Lavan J., 1998) and *Hanley v Minister for Defence* (unreported, Supreme Court, 1999). Also *Medical Guidance Notes on Hearing Checks and Audiometry* (Health and Safety Authority, 1992).
[61]   See ss.8, 9, 10, 13, 14, 19 and 22 of the 2005 Act.
[62]   Regulation 124(b).

(c) the effects of exposure to noise on employees whose safety or health is at particular risk from such exposure,

(d) any information on noise emission provided by the manufacturers of the work equipment,

(e) the availability of alternative equipment designed to reduce noise emission,

(f) appropriate information obtained from health surveillance, and

(g) the availability of hearing protectors with adequate attenuation characteristics.

Regulation 125 provides that an employer must ensure, so far as is reasonably practicable, that the risk arising from exposure of his or her employees to noise is either eliminated at source or reduced to a minimum. If a risk assessment indicates that any employee is likely to be exposed to noise at or above an upper exposure action value, the employer must establish and implement a programme of technical and/or organisational measures, excluding the provision of personal hearing protectors, designed to reduce exposure to noise.[63] Regulation 128(b) provides that if exposure above the exposure limit value is detected by an employer he or she must immediately:

• take action to reduce exposure to noise to below the limit value,

• identify the reasons for that limit being exceeded, and

• amend the organisational and technical measures taken to prevent it being reached or exceeded again.

Regulation 131 of the 2007 General Application Regulations requires an employer to make available appropriate health surveillance to those employees for whom a risk to their health has been identified by a risk assessment carried out under reg.124.

The 2007 General Application Regulations require the provision of hearing protection after all efforts to eliminate or reduce the source of the noise have been exhausted.[64] An employee must use the individual hearing protectors provided where noise exposure equals or exceeds the upper exposure action values.[65] Regulation 131(1) provides for audiometric hearing checks for employees where noise exposure exceeds either an upper exposure action value or a lower exposure action value. Information and training must be provided by the employer where his or her employees are exposed to noise at work at or above the lower exposure action value.[66]

6–35 The European Communities (Noise Emissions for Equipment for Use Outdoors) (Amendment) Regulations 2006[67] amend the European Communities (Noise Emission by Equipment for Use Outdoors) Regulations 2001[68] and came into force on January 3, 2006. The use of particular equipment, which prior to January 3, 2006 could not be used, is now permitted. This can be seen

---

[63] Regulation 126.
[64] Regulation 129(1).
[65] Regulation 129(2).
[66] Regulation 130.
[67] S.I. No. 241 of 2006.
[68] S.I. No. 632 of 2001.

from the new Table in Part A of the Schedule to the 2006 Regulations which refers to a range of equipment, including compaction machines, tracked dozers, wheeled dozers, excavators, tower cranes, compressors, power generators and lawn mowers.

Chapter 2 – Control of Vibration at Work

6–36   Chapter 2 of Pt 5 and Sch.6 to the 2007 General Application Regulations re-enact, without significant change, the Safety, Health and Welfare at Work (Control of Vibration at Work) Regulations 2006.[69] Regulations 133 to 142 transpose into Irish law the provisions of Council Directive 2002/44/EC on the minimum health and safety requirements for employees exposed to vibration at work.

This part of the 2007 General Application Regulations sets down minimum standards for the health and safety of workers exposed to hand-arm vibration ("HAV")[70] and whole body vibration ("WBV")[71] by prescribing measures to be taken to protect them from the risks arising from such vibrations.

Where employees are exposed or are likely to be exposed to vibration, an employer must carry out a risk assessment to assess and, if necessary, measure the levels of mechanical vibration[72] to which employees are exposed.[73] Measurement of the extent of the mechanical vibration to which employees are liable to be exposed must be carried out on the basis set out in Schedule 6 to the 2007 General Application Regulations.

Where employees are exposed to risk from mechanical vibration, their employer must provide them, or their safety representative, with "suitable and sufficient information, instruction and training".[74] Chapter 2 of Pt 5 of the 2007 General Application Regulations requires appropriate health surveillance to be made available to employees for whom a risk assessment reveals a risk to their safety and health. Such a risk may arise where, for example, an employee is exposed to mechanical vibration in excess of an exposure action value. Regulation 135 sets out the exposure limit values and action values for HAV and WBV.

PART 7 – FIRST-AID

6–37   Chapter 2 of Pt 7 of the 2007 General Application Regulations imposes a duty on an employer in respect of first aid at places of work including the

---

[69]   The 2007 General Application Regulations revoke the Safety, Health and Welfare at Work (Control of Vibration at Work) Regulations 2006 (S.I. No. 370 of 2006).

[70]   Regulation 133 defines "hand-arm vibration" as "mechanical vibration that, when transmitted to the human hand-arm system, entails risks to the safety and health of employees, in particular vascular, bone or joint, neurological or muscular disorders".

[71]   Regulation 133 defines "whole-body vibration" as "mechanical vibration that, when transmitted to the whole body, entails risks to the safety and health of employees, in particular lower-back morbidity and trauma of the spine".

[72]   Regulation 133 defines "mechanical vibration" as "vibration occurring in a piece of machinery or equipment, or in a vehicle as a result of its operation".

[73]   Regulation 136.

[74]   Regulation 140.

provision of first-aid equipment,[75] occupational first-aiders[76] and first-aid rooms[77]. Regulation 163 provides a definition for first-aid:

> "'first-aid' means–
>
> (a) in a case where a person requires treatment from a registered medical practitioner or a registered general nurse, treatment for the purpose of preserving life or minimising the consequences of injury or illness until the services of a practitioner or nurse are obtained, or
> (b) in a case of a minor injury which would otherwise receive no treatment or which does not need treatment by a registered medical practitioner or registered general nurse, treatment of such an injury; ..."

First-aid does not cover the administration of drugs or medication.

In defining "occupational first-aider", reg.163 also identifies the need for the training of first-aiders. Regulation 165 explicitly requires that the first aid equipment provided for use by occupational first aiders is adequate. First-aid equipment requirements will depend on the work activity involved. That said, every employee should have easy access to first aid boxes, kits and facilities. First aid needs can only be determined by the carrying out of a risk assessment at the workplace. Regulation 166 requires a first-aid room at every place of work if the risk assessment carried out under s.19 of the 2005 Act shows it to be necessary. First-aid rooms are not required for the following:

> "(a) means of transport used outside the undertaking or a place of work inside a means of transport,
> (b) fishing boats,
> (c) a field, wood or land forming part of an agricultural or forestry undertaking which is situated away from the undertaking's buildings".[78]

The Authority guide recommends that the following minimum facilities and equipment should be provided in first-aid rooms:

• wash hand basin with running hot and cold water;

• drinking water and disposable cups;

• soap;

• paper towels;

• smooth topped working surfaces;

• a store for first-aid equipment and materials;

• first-aid equipment;

• refuse containers;

• a couch (with a waterproof surface) and a clean pillow and blankets;

---

[75] Regulation 165(1)(a).
[76] Regulation 165(1)(b).
[77] Regulation 166.
[78] Regulation 164.

- clean protective garments for use by first-aiders;

- a chair; and

- a first-aid treatment record book.

NOTIFICATION OF ACCIDENTS AND DANGEROUS OCCURRENCES

6–38   Part X and the Twelfth Schedule to the 1993 Regulations remain in force. They impose requirements with respect to the notification of accidents[79] and dangerous occurrences,[80] the maintenance of records relating to accidents and dangerous occurrences, and the examination and tests to be effected in their investigation. Regulation 59 provides that accidents or incidents at a place of work are reportable to the Authority in the following circumstances:

- there is a dangerous occurrence[81];

- death of an employee or a self-employed person;

- an injury to an employee where he or she cannot perform his or her work for more than three days (excluding the date of the accident but including Saturdays and Sundays and other days which would not have been working days); and

- any injury to a visitor or member of the public where medical treatment is required.

It is a defence under reg.62, however, to any proceedings under reg.59, for a person to prove that he or she has taken all reasonable steps to have all incidence of accidents and dangerous occurrences brought to his or her notice and that he or she was not aware of the accident or dangerous occurrence which was the subject matter of the prosecution.[82]

---

[79] Section 2 of the 2005 Act provides that accident means "an accident arising out of or in the course of employment which, in the case of a person carrying out work, results in personal injury". The Authority should be notified immediately of a work-related injury causing death or a life-threatening injury. In the case of any other reportable injury, the Authority must be notified within 14 days of an employer becoming aware of the accident.

[80] See paras 3–09 and 3–27.

[81] See para 3–09.

[82] See Approved Forms for Reporting Accidents and Dangerous Occurrences: IR 1 and IR 3.

CHAPTER 7

SAFETY, HEALTH AND WELFARE AT WORK (CONSTRUCTION) REGULATIONS 2006

7–01 The Safety, Health and Welfare at Work (Construction) Regulations 2006[1] ("the 2006 Construction Regulations") replace and revoke the Safety, Health and Welfare at Work (Construction) Regulations 2001[2] and the Safety, Health and Welfare at Work (Construction)(Amendment) Regulations 2003[3] (except for regs 4 and 6 of the 2001 Regulations[4] and the Regulations applicable to lifting (regs 80 to 123 of the 2001 Regulations)). The substantive changes are to be found in Parts I, II and III of the 2006 Construction Regulations which address the management of safety, health and welfare on construction projects.[5] The 2006 Construction Regulations implement and give further effect to EC Council Directive 92/57/EEC[6] on the implementation of minimum safety and health requirements at temporary or mobile construction sites. In summary, they prescribe the main requirements for the protection of the safety, health and welfare of persons working on construction sites. Moreover, the 2006 Construction Regulations clarify and strengthen the duties of those responsible for ensuring safety, health and welfare in construction work, namely Clients, Project Supervisors Design Process (formerly titled Project Supervisors Design Stage), Project Supervisors Construction Stage, Designers, Contractors and Employees. The Regulations came into force on November 6, 2006, though certain transitional provisions are set out in reg.1.[7] The 2006 Construction Regulations will not therefore apply fully until May 5, 2008 and should be considered alongside Pt 4 of the 2007 General Application Regulations applicable to working at heights.[8]

---

[1] S.I. No. 504 of 2006.
[2] S.I. No. 481 of 2001.
[3] S.I. No. 277 of 2003.
[4] These Regulations apply to protect supervisors appointed prior to the commencement of the 2006 Construction Regulations on November 6, 2006.
[5] See *Guidelines on the Design and Management of Construction Projects*, (Health and Safety Authority, 2006); *Guidelines on the Procurement, Design and Management Requirements of the Safety, Health and Welfare at Work (Construction) Regulations 2006*, (Health and Safety Authority, 2006); and *Regulatory Impact Assessment: Safety, Health and Welfare at Work (Construction) Regulations 2006*, (Department of Enterprise, Trade and Employment, 2006).
[6] O.J. L245/6 of August 26, 1992.
[7] See reg.1 of S.I. No. 504 of 2006.
[8] Safety, Health and Welfare at Work (General Application) Regulations 2007 [S.I. No. 299 of 2007].

CERTIFIED TRAINING

7–02   The 2006 Construction Regulations prescribe the principal requirements for the protection of the safety, health and welfare of persons on
construction sites and building projects. They incorporate the key recommendations of the Construction Safety Partnership in the areas of safety training,
safety representation and welfare facilities on construction sites. In the light
of the large number of deaths on construction sites, the new Regulations
require that training for construction workers be certified as per regs 19 and
25 and the Fourth Schedule to the Safety, Health and Welfare at Work (Construction) Regulations 2006. The 2006 Regulations impose a mandatory
requirement that each construction worker receive a basic health and safety
course under the "Safe Pass" training programme and is in possession of a
current registration card. Safe Pass is mandatory for all craft and general construction workers,[9] drivers of vehicles delivering building materials on construction sites, and on-site security personnel. While site office staff, visiting
architects/engineers and visiting inspectors are not specifically required under
the 2006 Construction Regulations to receive Safe Pass training, the *Guidelines on the Design and Management of Construction Projects 2006* strongly
recommend that they do so. In summary, the Safe Pass training is a qualification required by workers to be admitted to a construction project site. In addition, workers who are obliged to carry out specified critical safety duties are
required to be in possession of a Construction Skills Certification Scheme
registration card indicating that they have successfully completed training
approved by the Further Education and Training Awards Council (FETAC)
under the Construction Skills Certification Scheme (CSCS). The tasks in
which training can lead to the issue of a FETAC award identified in the Fourth
Schedule are as follows:

• Scaffolding – basic;

• Scaffolding – advanced;

• Mobile tower scaffold;

• Tower crane operation;

• Self-erecting tower crane operation;

• Slinging/signalling;

• Telescopic handler operation;

• Tractor/dozer operation;

• Mobile crane operation;

• Crawler crane operation;

• Articulated dumper operation;

• Site dumper operation;

• 180° excavator operation;

---

[9]   Regulation 2(1) does not define either "craft" or "general construction".

- Mini-digger operation;
- 360° excavator operation;
- Roof and wall cladding/sheeting;
- Built-up roof felting;
- Signing, lighting and guarding on roads;
- Locating underground services;
- Shotfiring; and
- Such other construction-related tasks as may be prescribed from time to time by the Minister for Enterprise, Trade and Employment and published in *Iris Oifigiúil*.

7–03 The project supervisor for the construction stage is responsible, jointly with the contractors, for ensuring that a site worker has a valid Safe Pass, or an equal and approved registration card or, where required, a valid skills certificate. Surprisingly, there is no set renewal interval for the specified health and safety courses under the Regulations, although there is a refresher requirement.

CONSTRUCTION WORK

7–04 The 2006 Construction Regulations apply to all construction projects together with the maintenance of buildings. "Construction work" and "structure"[10] are very broadly defined in the 2006 Construction Regulations. Construction work includes site clearance, excavation and the erection of a new structure, the demolition and removal of structures, as well as extensions to, and the maintenance of, existing buildings.[11] Window cleaning, painting and decorating projects as well as routine maintenance works are all, to some degree, affected by these Regulations. The erection of a single private dwelling, a development akin to the Financial Services Centre in Dublin, and all construction sites in between fall within the parameters of the 2006 Construction Regulations. It should be noted that reg.2(1) of the 2006 Construction Regulations provides that construction work does not include drilling and extraction in the extractive industries.[12]

DUTIES AND RESPONSIBILITIES IN THE CONSTRUCTION PROCESS

7–05 Parts 2 and 3 of the 2006 Construction Regulations specify the duties of the Client,[13] the Project Supervisor for the Design Process,[14]

---

[10] Regulation 2.
[11] Regulation 2.
[12] This area is governed by the Safety, Health and Welfare at Work (Extractive Industries) Regulations 1997 (S.I. No. 467 of 1997), and more generally by the Mines and Quarries Act 1965 (S.I. No. 7 of 1965) and the Safety, Health and Welfare (Offshore Installations) Act 1987 (S.I. No. 18 of 1987).
[13] Regulations 9 and 10.
[14] Regulations 11, 12, 13 and 14.

Designers,[15] the Project Supervisor for the Construction Stage[16] and the Contractor.[17]

Clients

7–06   Regulation 2 of the 2006 Construction Regulations defines a "client" as follows:

> "'client' means a person for whom a project is carried out, in the course or furtherance of a trade, business or undertaking, or who undertakes a project directly in the course or furtherance of such trade, business or undertaking".

Therefore "clients" range from the owners of a small building carrying out maintenance work to public developers carrying out major works. Regulation 6 requires the client to appoint in writing a competent person or persons to act as project supervisor for the design process and construction stage of every project.[18] Section 17(1) of the 2005 Act should also be noted.[19]

The one person may hold both positions if suitably qualified.[20] The client may appoint as project supervisor:

- an individual or a body corporate;[21]

- different companies or individuals to act as a project supervisor for each stage;

- himself or herself for either or both of the stages if competent to undertake the duties involved.[22]

Confirmation of their appointment must be obtained in writing and the Health and Safety Authority must be notified of such appointments. The project supervisor for the design process must be appointed at or before the commencement of the design work. Regulation 2(1) defines "design process" as meaning "the process for preparing and designing a project, including alterations to the design and the design of temporary works to facilitate construction of the project". It is clear from the foregoing that the project supervisor for the design process will have a role for the entire project, which will not cease on the appointment of the project supervisor for the construction stage. The project supervisor for the construction stage must be appointed prior to the commencement of the construction work. As previously stated, "construction work" is broadly defined and "means the carrying out of any building, civil

---

[15] Regulation 15.
[16] Regulations 16, 17, 18, 19, 20, 21, 22 and 23.
[17] Regulations 24, 25, 26, 27 and 28.
[18] The word "project" is defined widely in reg. 2 as meaning "an activity which includes or is intended to include construction work". It includes all developments regardless of size.
[19] See para. 3–61.
[20] Regulation 6(2)(b).
[21] Regulation 2.
[22] Regulation 6(2)(a).

engineering or engineering work, other than drilling and extraction in the extractive industries." Significantly, reg.7(3) provides that a client cannot appoint a project supervisor for the design stage or construction stage in respect of a project unless the client is reasonably satisfied that the person whom the client intends to appoint has allocated or will allocate sufficient resources to enable the person to perform the duties of the project supervisor for the design or construction process. A similar duty applies in respect of any designers and contractors. Therefore, not only must the client ensure that the project supervisor for the design and construction stage, designer and contractor are competent, but the client must be satisfied that such person has allocated or will allocate sufficient resources. Specific duties are imposed on both of the project supervisors. Regulation 6(4) of the 2006 Construction Regulations states that the appointment of project supervisors "shall, as necessary, be made, terminated, changed or renewed."

7–07   The project supervisors, designers and contractors appointed by the client must be competent. What does this mean? The 2006 Construction Regulations do not, as such, define competency. Section 2(2) of the 2005 Act, however, defines "competent person" as follows:

> "For the purposes of the relevant statutory provisions, a person is deemed to be a competent person where, having regard to the task he or she is required to perform and taking account of the size or hazards (or both of them) of the undertaking or establishment in which he or she undertakes work, the person possesses sufficient training, experience and knowledge appropriate to the nature of the work undertaken.
>
> Account shall be taken, as appropriate … of the framework of qualifications referred to in the Qualifications (Education and Training) Act 1999."

It is clear from the foregoing that a competent person is a person who has sufficient training, experience and knowledge appropriate to the project and nature of the work to be undertaken. This places a heavy burden on the client in that it assumes that the client has sufficient knowledge of the role of the project supervisor to enable him/her to assess whether the person to be appointed is competent. A FETAC-recognised qualification will be considered in assessing whether a person is a competent person. At present, there are currently no FETAC recognised qualifications for acting as a project supervisor for the design process or project supervisor for the construction stage.

The Authority's guidance on the subject of assessing the competence of the parties responsible for securing safety, health and welfare in construction work should also be noted. It provides as follows:

> "When assessing competence, the following general guidelines should be considered:
>
> - Only those competencies and resources that relate to the duties of the person being assessed need to be considered;
> - The matter to be considered is the capacity of the person being assessed to comply with the duties that they would carry under the Regulations;
> - The assessment should relate to the project under consideration but may also focus on previous projects executed and experience gained elsewhere;

- The assessment should be proportionate and should concentrate on the main issues, rather than being generic;
- It follows that a relatively minimal assessment should suffice for what will clearly be a relatively low-risk project;
- An extensive assessment should not be necessary when dealing with a person who you have recently subjected to the process on a similar project;
- An excellent guide should be a proven track record of competence within the duty holder's field".

As a minimum, a client should make reasonable enquiries about competence not only from potential appointees, but also from other persons who will be in a position to supply relevant information.

7–08   Regulation 8(1) requires the client to keep available any safety file prepared for inspection by any person who may need information in the file for the purpose of compliance with any of the statutory duties imposed.[23] Regulation 8(4) now requires the client to co-operate with the project supervisor for the design process and the project supervisor for the construction stage in relation to the period of time required for the completion of the project. Moreover, the client is required to provide information to the project supervisors to enable the relevant project supervisor to comply with the 2006 Construction Regulations. The information required to be provided is information relating to the state or condition of any structure, including information in a safety file that is:

"(a) prepared in accordance with the relevant statutory provisions,
 (b) relevant to the duties of the project supervisors under the Regulations, and
 (c) either in the client's possession or could be obtained by the client making enquiries which it is reasonable for a person in the client's position to make."[24]

Under the repealed 2001 Construction Regulations it was the duty of the Project Supervisor for the Design Stage to provide the preliminary health and safety plan. Regulation 9 now requires the client to provide at the time of project preparation, a copy of the preliminary safety and health plan to every person being considered or tendering for the role of project supervisor for the construction stage. This, as stated above, was previously the duty of the project supervisor for the design stage who had to provide the preliminary health and safety plan to the project supervisor for the construction stage prior to the commencement of construction work.

7–09   Where more than one client is involved in a construction project, the clients can agree in writing which of them is to be subject to the duties of the 2006 Construction Regulations.[25] The only duty the other client(s) will be subject to is to keep and maintain a safety file.

---

[23]   For further information on the safety file, see para.7.11.
[24]   Regulation 8(5).
[25]   Regulation 6(7).

7–10 A client is required to notify the Authority in writing where construction work has a planned duration of greater than 30 working days or a total work volume greater than 500 person days; this notice is to be in an approved form and should be sent either by registered post or as may be directed by the Authority. It should contain the particulars of the client and details of those appointed as project supervisors.

The project supervisor appointed for the design process

7–11 Under the 2006 Construction Regulations, the Project Supervisor for the Design Stage is replaced by the appointment of a Project Supervisor for the Design Process who is required to co-ordinate health and safety amongst designers. This change is significant in that the appointment is no longer for a stage but for the entire design process. Regulation 2 of the 2006 Construction Regulations defines "design process" as "the process for preparing and designing a project, including alterations to the design and the design of temporary works to facilitate construction of the project." It is clear from this definition that the project supervisor for the design process may now be involved right up to the completion of the project. The project supervisor for the design process should be appointed on or before the commencement of the project. Regulations 11 to 14 of the 2006 Construction Regulations specify the duties of the project supervisor for the design process, the most significant of which are the following:

1. Take into account the general principles of prevention detailed in Sch.3 to the Safety, Health and Welfare at Work Act 2005 during the various stages of the design and preparation of a project, in particular when either, or both, technical or organisational aspects are being decided, in order to plan the various items or stages of work which are to take place simultaneously or in succession.[26] Of particular importance in Sch.3 is the reference to the following principles:

   - the replacement of dangerous articles, substances or systems of work by safe or less dangerous articles, substances or systems of work; and

   - the development of an adequate prevention policy in relation to safety, health and welfare at work, which takes account of technology, organisation of work, working conditions, social factors and the influence of factors related to the working environment.

   It should also be noted that the general principles of prevention should be taken into account when determining the time required for completion of a project "and, where appropriate, for stages of a project".

2. Organise co-operation between designers so far as is reasonably practicable and ensure coordination of design activities. This imposes a much higher duty than existed under the repealed 2001 and 2003 Regulations which merely required the project supervisor for the design stage to co-ordinate the

---

[26] Regulation 11(1)(a).

activities of the design team in relation to safety. The vague nature of the new duty is problematic having regard to the fact that it is to be exercised "so far as is reasonably practicable"[27].

3. Prepare on a preliminary basis a safety and health plan specific to the project and pass this on in sufficient time to every person being considered or tendering for the role of project supervisor for the construction stage.[28] The safety and health plan attempts to identify risks and hazards at an early stage with the objective of having those risks and hazards designed out. A safety and health plan is required for those projects that are either notifiable,[29] or that involve a particular risk,[30] such as work involving the assembly or dismantling of heavy prefabricated components. Regulation 12(1)(a) specifies that a preliminary safety and health plan must include the following:

    (i)   a general description of the project and an estimate of the period of time required for completion of the project;
    (ii) appropriate information on any other work activities taking place on the site;
    (iii) where appropriate, a description of work related to the project which will involve particular risks to the safety and health of persons at work, as detailed in Sch.1 to the 2006 Construction Regulations;
    (iv) the basis upon which the period of time in (i) above was established;
    (v)   the conclusions drawn by designers and the project supervisor for the design process as regards the taking into account the general principles of prevention as specified in Sch.3 to the 2005 Act and any relevant safety and health plan or safety file; and
    (vi) the location of electricity, water and sewage connections to facilitate adequate welfare facilities.

4. Keep the preliminary safety and health plan available for inspection by an inspector for a period of five years after its preparation.

5. Prepare a safety file, which was formerly the responsibility of the project supervisor for the construction stage. A safety file is a file containing pertinent health and safety information about the building to be taken into account during any subsequent construction work following completion of the project. It will contain, for example, electrical circuit diagrams and structural load calculations. On completion of the construction project, the project supervisor for the design process should hand over the safety file to the client. This file is to be made available for inspection by any person requiring such information for safety reasons.[31] The file should

---

[27] See paras 3–12–3–15.
[28] Regulation 12(1)(a).
[29] A project is notifiable where construction work is planned to last longer than 30 working days or the volume of work is scheduled to exceed 500 person days. See reg.10.
[30] Schedule 1 to the 2006 Construction Regulations sets out a non-exhaustive list of particular risks.
[31] Regulation 13.

be passed on to any person that acquires an interest in the property. The foregoing duties do not appear to apply to the average householder, though the courts have not yet adjudicated upon the matter.[32]

6. Issue directions to any designer, contractor or other relevant person in order to assist him or her to discharge his or her duties. Any such directions should be confirmed in writing, including a timeframe for their execution. If the directions are not carried out, the project supervisor for the design process must notify in writing the client, the health and safety authority and the person to whom the direction was given.

7–12   The project supervisor for the design process may delegate duties to a competent health and safety co-ordinator for the design process to assist in undertaking the duties outlined above.[33] A question arises therefore as to who is ultimately responsible. The likely answer to this question is the project supervisor for the design process though the health and safety co-ordinator may be liable under s.80 of the 2005 Act.

Designers

7–13   Designers, namely engineers and architects, translate, by means of drawings and specifications, the requirements of the client in respect of the finished product. The designer must ensure, so far as is reasonably practicable, that the project is designed and can be constructed safely. Regulation 2 provides a very wide definition of "design", to include not only the preparation of drawings or specifications for the end product, but of any other "expressions of purpose, according to which a project, or any part or component of a project, is to be executed". Regulation 15 places duties on designers, the most significant of which is to take account of "the general principles of prevention" and the relevant safety and health plan or safety file. The general principles of prevention, as previously stated, are a generic hierarchy of risk control measures applicable to all places of work. Regulation 7(5) should be noted in that it imposes an onerous duty on a client, prior to the appointment of a designer, to ensure that sufficient resources are allocated to enable compliance by the designer with the 2006 Construction Regulations.

7–14   Consideration of health and safety should form an integral part of the design process. To this end, designers are required to assess the design at the various stages as the project develops. If any significant hazard is identified, the design should be altered to eliminate the risk where reasonably practicable, or otherwise to reduce the risk to an acceptable level.[34]

---

[32]   See the *Law Society Gazette*, November 1999.

[33]   Regulation 11(2).

[34]   For what amounts to "reasonably practicable", see para.3–12 of this book. On the designers' duties under the analogous British Regulations, see the Construction (Design and Management) Regulations 1994, also *R v Paul Wurth SA*, unreported, Court of Appeal, 2000 cited in Byrne, R., *Safety, Health & Welfare at Work in Ireland: A Guide* (Dublin, NIFAST, 2001), p.126.

The Authority guidelines provide designers with the following advice on risk assessment:

> "Eliminating hazards and reducing risk, if feasible, at design stage is the first step in managing health and safety on construction projects. All designers must take into account the existing hazards on the project relevant to his areas of concern and consider these with respect to the potential new hazards generated by the design process for construction workers, end users and members of the public."[35]

Regulation 15(2)(a) requires designers to co-operate with the project supervisor for the design process or the project supervisor for the construction stage. The guidelines provide that:

> "This co-operation could be in the form of provision of information or in attendance at meetings or revisions of designs to improve aspects of health and safety on site".[36]

Significantly, the 2006 Construction Regulations do not expressly define whose safety is to be considered by the designer. It should be noted that the duties of designers under the Regulations are in addition to those arising under s.16 of the Safety, Health and Welfare at Work Act 2005.[37]

Construction stage

7–15   Different duties are imposed at the design and construction stages of a construction project. Regulation 2 of the 2006 Construction Regulations defines the "construction stage" as meaning the period of time starting "when preparation of the construction site begins and ending when construction work on the project is completed".

The project supervisor appointed for the construction stage

7–16   The project supervisor for the construction stage has responsibility for the management of safety on the site. This applies to all aspects of safety, including training, access to and within the construction site, the protection of visitors to the site and the wearing of personal protective equipment (*e.g.* hard hats, safety boots, high visibility jackets and, where required, eye, hand and ear protection, respiratory equipment, and fall, arrest and safety harness equipment).[38] Under the 2006 Construction Regulations, the project supervisor for the construction stage is to be appointed prior to the commencement of construction work.

---

[35] See *Guidelines on the Design and Management of Construction Projects, 2006* (Health and Safety Authority, 2006).

[36] See *Guidelines on the Design and Management of Construction Projects, 2006* (Health and Safety Authority 2006).

[37] See para.3–56 of this book.

[38] See also the 2007 General Application Regulations and paras 6–06 to 6–29 of this book.

(1) Safety and health plan

7–17 Regulation 16(1) requires the project supervisor for the construction stage to prepare a safety and health plan, using the plan prepared on a preliminary basis by the project supervisor for the design process and taking into account the requirements of s.20 of the 2005 Act, which imposes an obligation on every employer to prepare or cause to be prepared a safety statement.[39] A safety and health plan is required in the following situations:

- where the work is planned to last longer than 30 working days or the volume of work is scheduled to exceed 500 person days,[40] or

- where the construction work concerned involves a particular risk, including but not limited to any of those referred to in Sch.1 to the 2006 Construction Regulations[41].

7–18 The safety and health plan should address, *inter alia*, discrete site safety issues and operations with significant hazard potential. Specific risk assessments should be undertaken to control the risks identified in the preparation of the safety and health plan. The plan should include a process by which safety and health concerns can be communicated to site management, and as such, is a safety management document.[42] For the larger sites, the safety and health plan should include a formal traffic safety procedure. The life span of the plan is the duration of the construction project.

(2) Safety adviser

7–19 The project supervisor for the construction stage must appoint a full-time safety adviser where more than 100 people are at work on a construction site at any one time.[43] He is to be appointed in writing by the project supervisor for the construction stage to:

(a) advise the project supervisor and contractors as appropriate as to the observance of the requirements of the relevant statutory provisions, and

(b) exercise a general supervision of the observance of those requirements and the promotion of the safe conduct of work generally.

The appointment of a safety adviser is a new requirement and will provide a further level of supervision for large construction projects.

(3) Other duties

7–20 Other duties of the project supervisor for the construction stage include:

---

[39] See para.3–72 of this book.

[40] Regulation 10.

[41] Regulations 12(2) and 16(d).

[42] See *Guidelines to the Safety, Health and Welfare at Work (Construction) Regulations, 2001* (Health and Safety Authority, 2001).

[43] Regulation 18.

- Co-ordinating the activities of the construction team in relation to safety taking into account the general principles of prevention specified in Sch.3 to the 2005 Act.[44]

- Co-ordinating arrangements for the provision and maintenance of site welfare facilities for all persons at work on the construction site.[45]

- Co-ordinating arrangements ensuring that persons at work on the site have a valid Safe Pass registration, or an equal and approved, card, or where required, a valid skills certificate, and keeping records of same available for inspection[46].[47]

The project supervisor for the construction stage may delegate duties to a competent health and safety co-ordinator.[48]

The project supervisor for the construction stage is required, by virtue of reg.21(2), to prepare a safety file where a Project Supervisor for the Design Process has not been appointed.

Site safety representative and consultation

7–21   Regulation 23 and Sch.5 to the 2006 Construction Regulations provide that the project supervisor for the construction stage must facilitate the election of a site safety representative where 20 or more persons are likely to be working on the site.[49] The project supervisor for the construction stage is also required to facilitate the site safety representative in carrying out his duties, including notifying him when a health and safety inspector is undertaking an inspection.[50] Furthermore, the project supervisor for the construction stage must take account of representations made by the site safety representative on any matter affecting the safety, health and welfare at work of any person at work at the construction site.[51] A construction site safety representative has the same rights as with other places of work (although these rights are defined in reg.23(2)). It is to be noted that the role of the site safety representative is distinct from, and in addition to, that of any safety representatives appointed by employers of individual contractors. The project supervisor for the construction stage assumes the role of an employer (on a construction site there can be numerous employers), with the workplace being the construction site.

---

[44] On the personal criminal liability of the project supervisor for the construction stage, where a court finds that there has been inadequate co-ordination of safety, health and welfare on a construction project, see *National Authority for Occupational Safety and Health v Inchagoill Contractors (Salthill) Ltd*, unreported, Galway District Court, 2001, cited in Byrne, R., *Safety, Health & Welfare at Work in Ireland: A Guide* (Dublin, NIFAST, 2001), p.132.
[45] Regulation 17(3).
[46] The project supervisor for the construction stage must now keep appropriate records, including safety cards, for 5 years after the date of preparation.
[47] Regulation 19(1) and Schs. 3 and 4.
[48] Regulation 17(2) of the 2006 Construction Regulations.
[49] Regulation 23(1)(b).
[50] Regulation 23(3).
[51] Regulation 23(9).

Notification of projects

7–22　A project is notifiable by the project supervisor for the construction stage to the Authority in writing if it has a planned duration of greater than 30 working days, or a total work volume greater than 500 person days; this notice is to be in an approved form and should be sent either by registered post or as may be directed by the Authority.[52] It is to be noted that notification to the Authority must include the dates on which the preliminary and developed safety and health plan were prepared. A copy of the notice should be displayed on the site by the project supervisor for the construction stage.[53]

Contractor

7–23　Regulation 2 of the 2006 Construction Regulations defines a "contractor" as follows:

> "'contractor' means a contractor or an employer whose employees undertake, carry out or manage construction work, or a person who carries out or manages construction work for a fixed or other sum, and supplies materials, labour or both, (whether the contractor's own labour or that of another) to carry out the work".

The contractor decides, *inter alia*, on the method of construction, the number of workers to be employed, the management and supervisory procedures for the construction operations, the plant and equipment to be used, the layout of the building site, and the sequence and programme of the work stages. The contractor, therefore, takes possession of, and has total control of, the construction site. He is responsible for ensuring the day-to-day safety, health and welfare of his employees and/or those whom he supplies as labour to a construction project. As the contractor is in control of the workplace, he must carry out a risk assessment and implement the necessary safety controls and precautions. In summary, control of the site and of the risks on the site are the responsibility of the contractor. Regulation 7(4) should be noted in that it imposes an onerous duty on a client, prior to the appointment of a contractor, to ensure the contractor has the competence to carry out the construction work and has allocated or will allocate sufficient resources to enable compliance by the contractor with the 2006 Construction Regulations.

7–24　Regulation 24 imposes a number of obligations on contractors, the more important of which are the following:

- Provide the project supervisor for the construction stage, without delay, with any information which is likely to affect the health, welfare or safety of any person at work on the construction site or which might justify a review of the safety and health plan[54];

---

[52]　See Form PF.1A. See also reg.22 of the 2006 Construction Regulations.
[53]　Regulation 22(2).
[54]　Regulation 24(c).

- Co-operate with the project supervisor for the construction stage in relation to compliance with the pertinent statutory provisions[55] and notification of deaths, accidents and dangerous occurrences[56];

- Ensure all persons under their direct control are trained and are in possession of a current registration card and, where required, a skills certificate and can provide written evidence of this to the project supervisor for the construction stage.[57]

Regulation 25(1)(c) imposes a new obligation on Contractors and should be noted. It provides as follows:–

> "Every contractor or other person under whose direct control persons work on a construction site shall ensure that each of those persons ... has received site-specific safety induction instruction."

The foregoing obligation applies not merely to the main contractor but to all contractors.

Safety officer

7–25   Any contractor who normally has more than 20 persons under his direct control at any one time on any one site is obliged under reg.26 to appoint a qualified safety officer (this figure includes sub-contractors, the self-employed and direct employees). Where the contractor employs more than 30 persons in construction work, a safety officer should also be appointed by the contractor to facilitate compliance with the 2006 Construction Regulations.[58]

Erection and installation of plant and equipment

7–26   Particular provision is made in reg.27 in respect of the erection, installation and modification of plant and equipment, and in particular scaffolding.[59] The duties imposed under reg.27 apply to every contractor. He must ensure that scaffolding is erected, installed and modified by competent scaffolding contractors. Scaffolding should be inspected on a weekly basis or as required.

Information and consultation

7–27   Additional requirements for scaffolding are set out in the 2007 General Application Regulations.[60] Regulation 107(g) of those Regulations requires scaffolds to be designed, assembled, altered and dismantled by a competent person.

---

[55] Regulation 24(b).
[56] Regulation 24(d).
[57] Regulation 25.
[58] Regulation 26(1).
[59] See *Code of Practice for Access and Working on Scaffolds* (Health and Safety Authority, 1999) for comprehensive guidance on the requisite standards for scaffolding and access work.
[60] Regulation 107 and Ch.6.

7–28   Contractors are required to provide safety information to employees and safety representatives, and are obliged to ensure that such information is comprehensible.[61] Regulation 28 provides that contractors must also ensure proper consultation with their staff and/or their safety representatives.[62]

Duties of employees

7–29   Employees under these regulations must co-operate with the employer on matters affecting health and safety, report defects in plant and equipment "without unreasonable delay", and make proper use of the protective equipment provided.[63] To comply with the 2006 Construction Regulations employees are required to:

- undertake training with regard to Safe Pass and Construction Skills Certification without loss of pay; and

- produce Safe Pass and relevant FETAC accredited CSCS cards when requested to do so by the project supervisor for the construction stage or by their employer.[64]

Miscellaneous matters

7–30   Regulations 30–105 are concerned with health and safety requirements relating to the construction site itself, and to specific risks, such as the use of lifting equipment or demolition work. These requirements will, in general, be the responsibility of the contractor(s).[65] Part 9 of the 2006 Regulations is worthy of particular mention, in that it requires that where a person is to be exposed to a dangerous or unhealthy atmosphere, appropriate preventative measures should be taken against such exposure. It makes specific reference to the disposal of waste and the use of internal combustion engines.

7–31   In common with all Regulations made pursuant to s.58 of the Safety, Health and Welfare at Work Act 2005, civil, as well as criminal, sanctions attach for failure to comply with the 2006 Construction Regulations. Obviously in respect of civil actions, there must be a causal connection between the breach of the duty alleged and the loss or injury sustained.

7–32   The 2006 Construction Regulations should be read alongside s.17 of the Safety, Health and Welfare at Work Act 2005. It should be noted that the provisions of the Safety, Health and Welfare at Work (Construction) Regulations 2006 are in addition to the provisions of the Safety, Health and Welfare at Work Act 2005 and the Safety, Health and Welfare at Work (General Application) Regulations 2007.

---

[61]   Regulation 28 and s.9 of the 2005 Act.
[62]   See s.26 of the 2005 Act.
[63]   Regulation 29.
[64]   Regulation 29(g).
[65]   Regulation 24.

CHEMICAL AGENTS AND DANGEROUS SUBSTANCES

8–01 The Safety, Heath and Welfare at Work (Chemical Agents) Regulations 2001[1] implemented the 1998[2] and 2000 EU Directives[3] on chemical agents and replace the Safety, Health and Welfare at Work (Chemical Agents) Regulations 1994.[4] These Regulations came into force on December 19, 2001 and now form a basic framework for all legislation relating to chemical agents including carcinogens, lead, asbestos, and flammable/explosive materials. They should be read in conjunction with the 2002 Code of Practice for the Safety, Health and Welfare at Work (Chemical Agents) Regulations 2001.[5] This Code provides excellent guidance on compliance with regs 4(1)(e), 4(5)(d), 6(1)(c) and 10(3) of the 2001 Regulations. In summary, the Safety, Health and Welfare at Work (Chemical Agents) Regulations 2001 require that before any worker is exposed to a hazardous substance, it is to be subject to an assessment so that appropriate precautions can be taken.

Regulation 2 defines, *inter alia*, activity, biological limit value, chemical agent, hazard, hazardous chemical agent, health surveillance, occupational exposure limit value and risk. Regulation 4 of the 2001 Regulations imposes a duty on an employer to determine what substances in the workplace constitute a risk to health and regs 5 and 6 require the employer to either eliminate such a risk or reduce it to an acceptable level. Measuring the level of risk associated with a chemical agent will generally involve measuring the level of airborne particles a person is, or may be, exposed to (using a recognised scientific measurement technique). This should then be compared with a maximum level as defined in the Regulations or Code of Practice, which cannot be exceeded. Regulation 10 requires the employer to make available health surveillance for employees whose exposure reveals a risk to their health and refers to this requirement as being without prejudice to the general requirement for health surveillance contained in s.22 of the 2005 Act.

Regulation 7 imposes duties on employees, particularly in respect of the proper use of personal protective equipment. Regulation 9 requires employers to provide information and training to employees in relation to the risks

---

[1] S.I. No. 619 of 2001.
[2] Council Directive 98/24/EC of April 7, 1998, O.J. No. L131, 5.5.1998, p.11.
[3] Commission Directive 2000/39/EC of June 8, 2000, O.J. No. L142, 16.6.2000, p.47.
[4] S.I. No. 445 of 2001.
[5] S.I. No. 619 of 2001.

associated with the use of any chemical agent in the workplace and the means whereby such risks are reduced (including the correct use of personal protective equipment). The results of any risk assessment should be made available to the employee (including any measurements). Employers must consult with employees and/or their safety representatives in relation to implementing the Safety, Health and Welfare at Work (Chemical Agents) Regulations 2001, and in particular, in selecting personal protective equipment. Regulation 8 imposes a duty on employers to make arrangements to deal with accidents, incidents and emergencies.[6] It should be noted that reg.11 provides for prohibitions and exemptions relating to the production, manufacture or use at work of chemical agents identified in Sch.3 to the Safety, Health and Welfare at Work (Chemical Agents) Regulations 2001.

8–02　The Safety, Health and Welfare at Work (Carcinogens) Regulations 2001[7] expand on the requirements of the Safety, Health and Welfare at Work (Chemical Agents) Regulations 2001 in relation to carcinogens. Where a carcinogen is identified in a working environment it must be risk assessed and appropriate precautions taken. Staff that are exposed to carcinogens in the course of their work must be offered health surveillance and a record should be kept of such surveillances for a period of 40 years after their exposure.

8–03　The Safety, Health and Welfare at Work (Exposure to Asbestos) Regulations 2006[8] ("the 2006 Exposure to Asbestos Regulations") revoke and replace the European Communities (Protection of Workers) (Exposure to Asbestos) Regulations 1989[9] and the European Communities (Protection of Workers) (Exposure to Asbestos) (Amendment) Regulations 1993[10] and 2000.[11] They apply to all work activities in which employees are, or are likely to be, exposed to dust arising from either or both asbestos and materials containing asbestos.[12] The 2006 Exposure to Asbestos Regulations transpose Directive 2003/18/EC of the European Parliament and of the Council of March 27, 2003, amending Council Directive 83/477/EEC, as previously amended by Council Directive 91/382/EEC on the protection of workers from the risks related to exposure to asbestos at work, both of which Directives are retransposed. The 2006 Exposure to Asbestos Regulations also retranspose Art.12 of Council Directive 87/217/EEC on the prevention and reduction of environmental pollution by asbestos.

The 2006 Exposure to Asbestos Regulations require employers to prevent the exposure of employees to asbestos fibres. If this is not possible, employers are required to ensure that no employee is exposed to an airborne concentration of asbestos in excess of 0.1 fibres per cm^3 as an eight-hour

---

[6]　See also para 8–10 and the European Communities (Control of Major Accident Hazards Involving Dangerous Substances) Regulations 2006. [S.I. No. 74 of 2006].
[7]　S.I. No. 78 of 2001.
[8]　S.I. No. 386 of 2006.
[9]　S.I. No. 34 of 1989.
[10]　S.I. No. 276 of 1993.
[11]　S.I. No. 74 of 2000.
[12]　Regulation 3.

time-weighted average.[13] The introduction of a single lower control limit for all work activities where exposure to asbestos dust in the air at a place of work may arise is one of the key changes in the Regulations. Work that is likely to expose employees to dust from either or both asbestos or materials containing asbestos must be risk assessed and the necessary steps must be taken to ensure that the exposure of employees is reduced to the lowest level reasonably practicable.[14] Where an employee's exposure is sporadic and of low intensity, and when it is clear from the results of the risk assessment that the exposure limit value for asbestos will not be exceeded in the air in the working area, it may not be necessary to notify the Authority, perform a health assessment or maintain medical records where the work involves:

- short, non-continuous maintenance activities in which only non-friable materials are handled;

- removal without deterioration of non-degraded materials in which the asbestos fibres are firmly linked in a matrix;

- encapsulation or sealing of asbestos-containing materials which are in good condition; or

... and sufficient assessment of the risk created by the exposure to asbestos to the health of the employees and the steps that need to be taken to prevent or minimise the exposure;

(c) record the significant findings of the risk assessment;

(d) determine the degree and nature of exposure to asbestos which may occur during the course of the work; and

(e) consider the results of monitoring of exposure and relevant medical surveillance.

[15] Regulation 14.
[16] S.I. No. 504 of 2006.
[17] See para.7–17 of this book.

practicable before demolition techniques are applied or major refurbishment of a premises commences, except where this would create a greater risk to employees than if the asbestos or asbestos-containing products, or both, had been left in place. When the asbestos demolition or removal work has been completed, the employer who has carried out this work must obtain from a competent person a written verification that the premises, or part of the premises where the work has been carried out, has been cleared and is suitable for reoccupation. Regulation 16 is a welcome new provision that requires employers, contractors, asbestos removal firms and persons working in the asbestos sector to provide evidence to the Authority of their ability to do demolition and asbestos removal activities in a safe way to ensure the protection of employees. A non-exhaustive list of information to be provided as evidence of ability to perform asbestos work can be found in Sch.4 to the 2006 Exposure to Asbestos Regulations.

Regulation 17 requires employers to provide appropriate training and adequate information for all employees who are, or are likely to be, exposed to asbestos-containing dust.

Where employees are engaged by employers in activities at a place of work where they are, or may be, exposed in the course of their work to dust arising from asbestos or materials containing asbestos, such employers are required to make arrangements to enable the employees to avail of health assessments.[18] Regulation 21 provides that the medical records of such assessments are to be maintained by the appropriate responsible medical practitioner.

Regulation 25 of the 2006 Exposure to Asbestos Regulations requires an employer to keep and thereafter maintain an "occupational health register" where the exposure limit value is reached or exceeded. The employer must keep and maintain the occupational health register for at least 40 years following the end of the exposure.

8–05 The issue of employers' obligations in the context of exposure to asbestos has been considered by the Irish Supreme Court in *Stephen Fletcher v Commissioners of Public Works in Ireland*[19] and *Packenham v Irish Ferries Limited (formerly known as B&I Limited)*[20].[21] In both *Fletcher* and *Packenham*, the plaintiff held that they had been exposed to asbestos and claimed damages in negligence for this despite not yet showing signs of having developed any recognised illness such as mesothelioma asbestosis[22].

8–06 In *Fletcher* the Supreme Court allowed an appeal by the Commissioners of Public Works in Ireland in relation to a judgment of the High Court

---

[18] Regulation 20.

[19] [2003] 1 I.R. 465; [2003] 2 I.L.R.M. 94 (SC).

[20] Unreported, Supreme Court, ex tempore, January 31, 2005.

[21] Exposure to asbestos in Ireland arose in a stress-related claim in *O'Byrne v B and I Line plc*, unreported, High Court, January 12, 1996 and para.4–74 of this book. Relevant and instructive English cases include *R v Brintons* (English Court of Appeal, 1999) and *O'Toole v Iarnród Éireann* (English High Court, 1999).

[22] An asbestos-related cancer, which has a long latency period.

awarding the plaintiff €48,000 in respect of the stress-related illness he had developed arising from the anxiety caused as a result of his exposure to asbestos in the course of his employment. Significantly, the plaintiff in this case had no physical symptoms of mesothelioma and was advised by a consultant respiratory physician that the risk of contracting the asbestos-related cancer was very remote. The fact that his medical experts acknowledged that he only had a remote chance of developing mesothelioma as a result of his exposure to asbestos weakened the claim by the plaintiff that he had suffered a recognised psychiatric injury. The court denied the plaintiff recovery on public policy and fairness grounds. Keane C.J., as he then was, summarised the position in the following manner:

> "[T]he law would be in an unjust and anomalous state if a plaintiff who was medically advised that he would probably suffer from mesothelioma as a result of his negligent exposure to asbestos could not recover damages for a recognisable psychiatric illness which was the result of his being so informed. I am also satisfied, however, that in cases where there is no more than a very remote risk that he will contract the disease, recovery should not be allowed for such a psychiatric illness."[23]

8–07   Unlike in *Fletcher*, little effort was made in *Packenham* to establish that the plaintiff had suffered a recognised psychiatric injury (as defined by the courts and discussed in Ch. 4 of this book). *Packenham* like *Fletcher*, also concerned a plaintiff who had been negligently exposed to asbestos at work and who claimed damages in respect of an injury for which he had manifested no physical sign of having developed.

In the wake of *Fletcher*, the defendant company in *Packenham* brought an application before the High Court to have the claim struck out. Finnegan J. ordered that the claim be stayed indefinitely.[24] The learned judge stated that in determining whether or not to dismiss proceedings:

> "the Court should have regard to whether on a successful application for amendment, the Plaintiff's claim might be sustainable: *Keaveny v. Geraghty*[25]. Again the Court should be slow to exercise its jurisdiction to dismiss the action: *Sun Fat Chan v. Osseous Ltd*[26].[27]

The case was appealed to the Supreme Court which delivered an *ex tempore* judgment on January 31, 2005. In reversing the decision of Finnegan P., the court held that the plaintiff had no claim as he had not to date suffered a legally recognised head of damage, though it was stated that if an actual physical injury did manifest itself at a future date that a claim would not be *res judicata*. The result was hardly surprising given the approach of the Supreme Court to the asbestos litigation in *Fletcher*.

---

[23]   [2003] 2 I.L.R.M. 114.
[24]   Unreported, High Court, February 26, 2004.
[25]   [1965] I.R. 551 at 562 *per* Walsh J.
[26]   [1992] 1 I.R. 425.
[27]   Unreported, High Court, February 26, 2004 at pp.2–3.

8–08   In *Fairchild v Glenhaven Funeral Services Ltd*[28] the House of Lords held that a worker who had contracted mesothelioma after being wrongfully exposed to significant quantities of asbestos dust at different periods by more than one employer could sue any of them, even though the claimant could not establish which exposure had caused the disease. On the question of the apportionment of damages between the employers, the House of Lords held that each defendant was liable in full for the damages but could seek contributions from other defendants. Liability was not imposed on any of the defendants because his/her breach of duty had caused the mesothelioma that its former employee had contracted as this causative link had not been proven against any of them. It was imposed due to the fact that each, by its breach of duty, had materially increased the risk that the employee would contract the asbestos-related cancer. That said, the House of Lords emphasised the exceptional nature of the liability in this case and held that the general rule continued to be that it must be proven on the balance of probability that the defendant's conduct did cause the damage in the sense that it would not otherwise have happened. What was left undecided in *Fairchild*, however, was the question of what were the limits of the exception created in that case and what is the extent of the liability?

These questions and others were recently considered by the House of Lords in *Barker v Saint Gobain Pipelines Plc*.[29] In *Barker*, the claimant's husband had died of mesothelioma, a cancer caused by exposure to asbestos. He had been exposed to asbestos dust in the course of three periods of employment: the first, when working for an employer other than the defendant company; the second, when working for the defendant company; and the third when he was self-employed for a period. The plaintiff brought proceedings against the defendant company and relied on the decision of the House of Lords in *Fairchild*. An interesting question arose as to whether the deceased could be held contributory negligent for causing himself to be exposed to asbestos while self-employed. Lord Scott of Foscote, who was in agreement with the leading judgment of Lord Hoffmann in this case, succinctly summarises the questions to be considered about the scope of the *Fairchild* decision in the following terms:

"(i)   Does the *Fairchild* principle apply where the period of the victim's exposure to the injurious agent that has caused the disease has been in part during his employment by one or more employers and in part during a period of self-employment or, perhaps, while carrying out domestic chores such as demolishing outbuildings with asbestos roofs?

(2)   Does the *Fairchild* principle apply where the period of the victim's exposure has been in part during his employment by an employer who has not been negligent?

(3)   If the *Fairchild* principle does apply notwithstanding that some of the periods of exposure have been periods when the victim has not been employed by a negligent employer, what is the effect, if any, of those periods of

---

[28]   [2002] U.K.H.L. 22; [2003] 1 A.C. 32.
[29]   [2006] U.K.H.L. 20; [2006] 2 WLR 1027.

exposure on the quantum of damages for which the negligent employers are liable?

(4) There is a fourth question ... almost inevitably prompted by the previous three questions, namely, does the *Fairchild* principle apply only where exposure to a single injurious agent has caused the risk of the disease that the victim has eventually contracted or can it also apply where the victim has been exposed to more than one injurious agent each of which has subjected the victim to a risk of the outcome and it cannot be ascertained which agent has been responsible?"

The learned judge answers questions (1) and (2) in the affirmative. The effect of question one being answered in the affirmative is that the *Fairchild* principle does not cease to apply even when some of the harmful exposure to asbestos dust has occurred when a claimant is self-employed. On the third question of apportionment of liability for the damages between the various employers, Lord Scott held "that the extent of the liability of each defendant in a *Fairchild* type of case, where it cannot be shown which defendant's breach of duty caused the damage but where each defendant, in breach of duty, has exposed the claimant to a significant risk of the eventual damage, should be liability commensurate with the degree of risk for which the defendant was responsible". The learned judge held that the degree of risk would be linked to the amount of exposure for which each negligent defendant was responsible compared with the total amount of the claimant's exposure to the offending agent. Lord Hoffman adopted a similar approach. In remitting the case back to the High Court for that Court to redetermine the damages, the House of Lords held that damages are payable "by reference to the share of risk attributable to the breaches of duty by the defendants". Lord Scott answered the fourth question in the negative holding that the *Fairchild* principle did not cover multi-agent cases.

In summary, *Barker* is a significant decision of the House of Lords which establishes that employers are only liable to employees who contract mesothelioma in proportion to the risk to which they exposed employees.

8–09 The European Communities (Classification, Packaging, Labelling and Notification of Dangerous Substances) Regulations 2003 and 2006[30] limit the use of asbestos to particular products and require that all goods and waste containing asbestos are labelled in a particular manner. Essentially, these Regulations impose an obligation on every manufacturer, importer or other person intending to place a new chemical on the market to submit to the Hazardous Substances Unit of the Authority a "notification dossier" outlining the tests to which the substance has been subjected. They also require details of the proposed classification and labelling of the substance. Suppliers are obliged under the Regulations to place warning labels on containers for dangerous substances and to ensure that such containers are designed, constructed and secured to prevent "spillage or seepage" during normal use. The Regulations require "safety data sheets" for all dangerous substances covered under them.

---

[30] S.I. No. 25 of 2006.

8–10 The European Communities (Control of Major Accident Hazards Involving Dangerous Substances) Regulations 2006 transpose into Irish law the provisions of Council Directive 96/82/EC as amended by Council Directive 2003/105/EC on the control of major accident hazards involving dangerous substances. These Regulations revoke and replace the European Communities (Control of Major Accident Hazards Involving Dangerous Substances) Regulations 2000[31] and the European Communities (Control of Major Accident Hazards Involving Dangerous Substances) (Amendment) Regulations 2003[32] and apply to "establishments where dangerous substances are present in amounts equal to or exceeding the application thresholds."

The definition of dangerous substance has been changed to reflect more accurately the definition in Council Directive 96/82/EC. Significantly, the word "establishment" now covers a situation where two or more areas are under the control of the same person and are separated only by a road, railway or inland waterway. Such a place shall be treated as the one area.

In summary, these Regulations impose duties on the operators of establishments to take all the necessary steps to prevent the occurrence of major accidents and to curtail the consequences of accidents for people and the environment. The Regulations set out duties in respect of safety management systems, preparation of safety reports and emergency preparedness.

8–11 The European Communities (Dangerous Substances and Preparations) (Marketing and Use) Regulations 2003[33] effectively limit or prohibit the use of particular substances and/or preparations in products. They also provide that all products containing certain substances must display a particular warning on the label. Moreover, in certain cases, the Regulations ban products from being placed on the market if they contain specific dangerous substances or preparations.

The European Communities (Dangerous Substances and Preparations) (Marketing and Use) (Amendment) Regulations 2006 transpose into Irish law:

• Council Directive 2005/59/EC, placing restrictions on the marketing and use of toluene and trichlorobenzene;

• Council Directive 2005/69/EC, placing restrictions on the marketing and use of polycyclic aromatic hydrocarbons in extender oils and tyres;

• Council Directive 2005/84/EC, placing restrictions on the marketing and use of phthalates in toys and child care articles; and

• Council Directive 2005/90/EC, placing restrictions on the marketing and use of certain substances and preparations classified as carcinogenic, mutagenic or toxic to reproduction.

The 2006 Regulations amend Schs 1 and 3 to the European Communities (Dangerous Substances and Preparations) (Marketing and Use) Regulations 2003.

---

[31] S.I. No. 476 of 2000.
[32] S.I. No. 402 of 2003.
[33] S.I. No. 220 of 2003.

8–12   The European Communities (Classification, Packaging and Labelling of Dangerous Preparations) Regulations 2004[34] and the European Communities (Classification, Packaging and Labelling of Dangerous Preparations) (Amendment) Regulations 2007[35] detail how information about hazardous preparations is to be documented by suppliers. The Regulations, known as the European Communities (Classification, Packaging and Labelling of Dangerous Preparations) Regulations 2004 and 2007, came into force in Ireland on March 1, 2007. They set out onerous obligations for companies relating to the classification, packaging and labelling of hazardous preparations that will protect human health from the harmful effects of such preparations. In particular, the Regulations require each manufacturer, importer or distributor of a dangerous preparation to classify and label it according to its inherent hazards and to provide safety data sheets.

REACH

8–13   During 2005, the Authority was designated as the competent authority for REACH, the new omnibus Regulation which entered into force on June 1, 2007 with key milestones taking effect from June 1, 2008 to June 1, 2018. REACH is an acronym for Registration, Evaluation and Authorisation of Chemicals, reflecting the key elements of this far reaching Regulation. It will significantly alter the manner in which industry registers, evaluates, authorises and restricts chemical products throughout the EU and applies to all chemical substances which are manufactured, imported, placed on the market or used within the Member States of the EU, either on their own, or in a preparation, or in an article.

Article 2 of the REACH Regulation sets out a list of exemptions from the obligations imposed under the Regulation. Such exemptions apply generally to radioactive substances, non-isolated intermediates, waste and substances in transit under custom supervision. They also extend to substances of low risk, such as water, oxygen, noble gases and cellulose pulp.

In summary, REACH is likely to have a profound effect on businesses and industry and is likely to lead to better and earlier identification of the properties of chemical substances.

8–14   REACH switches responsibility for the control and safety of chemicals from authorities to industry (i.e. those that manufacture, import and use chemicals). Manufacturers and importers will now be obliged to collect information on the properties of their substances and to register the information in a central database.

The aim of REACH is to "improve the protection of human health and the environment while maintaining competitiveness, and enhancing the innovative capability of the EU chemicals industry." REACH will also give greater responsibility to industry to manage the risks from chemicals and to provide safety information that will be passed down the supply chain. Downstream users are required to communicate information up the supply chain to the

---

[34]   S.I. No. 62 of 2004.
[35]   S.I. No. 76 of 2007.

suppliers/importers on the uses to which chemical substances supplied by them are put. For the first time, the benefits of upstream communication in the supply chain are addressed.

REACH will require the registration of all chemical substances manufactured or imported in amounts of one tonne or more per manufacturer or importer per year. Failure to register each chemical substance with the European Chemicals Agency, to be located in Helsinki, Finland, means that the substance cannot be manufactured or imported into the EU market. "Existing" substances (i.e. those already on the EU Market) are to be registered on a phased basis and within certain quality thresholds.

Two types of evaluation are provided under REACH, namely dossier evaluation and substance evaluation. All dossiers registered may be subject to compliance checks with the requirements of registration by the European Chemicals Agency. Substance evaluation may be performed by the Competent Authority (i.e. Health and Safety Authority) to clarify a suspicion of risk to human health or the environment.

Authorisation applies to manufacturers, importers and downstream users who place substances of very high concern on the market. All authorisations granted by the European Commission will be subject to a time-limited review.

The decision to restrict the manufacture, marketing and use of a substance can be taken by the European Commission in consultation with the Member States. This process is intended to provide a safety net to manage risks which have not been addressed by other elements of REACH. Restrictions may apply to a substance on its own, in a preparation or in an article.

Safety Data Sheets must be provided where a substance or preparation is classified as dangerous in accordance with EU Directives 67/548/EEC or 1999/45/EC, or the substance is a PBT[36] or vPvB[37]. These sheets must be provided by a supplier of that substance or preparation.

Key REACH Milestones

- 1 June 2007—REACH enters into force

- 1 June 2008—European Chemicals Agency opens and the main titles of REACH will be enforced

- 1 June 2008—"New" substance registration

- 1 June 2008 to November 2008—Re-registration for phase-in of existing substances

- November 2010—1st phase-in substance deadline

- June 2013—2nd phase-in substance deadline

- June 2018—3rd phase-in substance deadline

---

[36] A substance which is Persistent, Bioaccumulative and Toxic.
[37] A substance which is very Persistent and very Bioaccumulative.

CHAPTER 9

THE BAN ON SMOKING
IN THE WORKPLACE

INTRODUCTION

9–01 The ban on smoking in the workplace introduced by the Tobacco Smoking (Prohibition) Regulations 2003 and the amendments thereto should be considered alongside the employer's responsibility in respect of smoking under the Safety, Health and Welfare at Work Act 2005 and Chapter 1 of Pt II of the 2007 General Application Regulations. In particular, s.8 of the Safety, Health and Welfare at Work Act 2005 requires all employers to provide safe places of work, which includes a working environment free from tobacco smoke.

While there is a deficit of case law on passive smoking claims in Ireland, the matter has been considered on a number of occasions in the neighbouring jurisdiction. In *Waltons and Morse v Dorrington*,[1] for example, it was stated that "… the employer will provide and monitor for his employees, so far as is reasonably practicable, a working environment which is reasonably suitable for the performance by them of their contractual duties". An employee in that case was, therefore, in a position to resign and claim constructive dismissal because of the failure of her employer to remove her from a working environment polluted by tobacco smoke.[2] A further relevant and instructive case is *Rae v Strathclyde Joint Police Board*,[3] where Lord Bonomy stated that:

> "… smoking is a non-industrial activity indeed, a social activity indulged in by workers and tolerated by employers which has got absolutely nothing to do with the industrial process. If to the knowledge of an employer smoking in the workplace gives rise to the risk that an employee will contract illness through working regularly in close proximity to smokers, then it may well, depending on the circumstances, be very easy to regard the employer as under a duty to stamp out smoking, or at the very least mitigate the effects of smoking since there may well in the circumstances be no difficult issues of practicability or expenses to be weighed against the risk."[4]

---

[1] [1997] I.R.L.R. 488.

[2] For the legal implications of passive smoking in the workplace see Andoh, "Passive Smoking at Work – Legal Implications for the Employer", (1998) 3(10) *Health Law*, November, pp.4–7, and (1998) 4(1) *Health Law*, pp.5–6.

[3] (OH) (1999) S.C.L.R. 793.

[4] See also *Dryden v Greater Glasgow Health Board* [1992] I.R.L.R. 669; and *Bland v Stockport Borough Council*, New Law Journal, February 13, 1993.

9–02   The Tobacco Smoking (Prohibition) Regulations 2003 ("the 2003 Regulations")[5] and the amendments thereto, came into force on March 29, 2004. The 2003 Regulations effectively ban smoking in the workplace with limited exceptions relating to those workplaces that are used as dwellings or for accommodation, more of which later. The 2003 Regulations revoke the Tobacco (Health Promotion and Protection) Regulations 1995,[6] which merely outlawed smoking in cinemas, museums, bingo halls, banks, schools, hospitals and buses.

9–03   The 2003 Regulations add to a number of existing legal requirements applicable to smoking in the workplace. These legislative provisions should be viewed alongside the common law duty imposed on an employer to provide a safe place and system of work to an employee who could, as mentioned in para.9–01, argue that his or her health suffered as a result of passive smoking. A 2003 report commissioned by the Health and Safety Authority and the Office of Tobacco Control would appear to support such an argument by an employee, noting that working with smoking co-workers increases the risk of lung cancer in non-smokers by up to 30 per cent.[7]

The Safety, Health and Welfare at Work Act 2005 and the 2007 Regulations

9–04   The employer's responsibility in respect of smoking arises both under the Safety, Health and Welfare at Work Act 2005 and Chapter 1 of Pt II of the 2007 Regulations. Section 8(2)(d) of the 2005 Act obliges employers, so far as is reasonably practicable, to ensure the safety and health at work of employees in connection with "the use of any article or substance or the exposure to noise, vibration or ionising or other radiations or any other physical agent".

The Chemical Agents Regulations 2001

9–05   Regulation 4 of the Chemical Agents Regulations, 2001 imposes a duty on employers to determine those substances present in the place of work that constitute a hazard to their employees and to take measures to eliminate or reduce the risk associated with exposure to the substances to an acceptable level. Tobacco smoke falls within the scope of the 2001 Regulations, as it is dangerous to a person's health when present in the workplace.

---

[5]   S.I. No. 481 of 2003.
[6]   S.I. No. 359 of 1995, made under the Tobacco (Health Promotion and Protection) Act 1988.
[7]   "Report on the health effects of environmental tobacco smoke (ETS) in the workplace" (January 2003).

The Public Health (Tobacco) Act 2002

9–06   The Public Health (Tobacco) Act 2002 ("the 2002 Act")[8] signed into law on March 27, 2002, had as its overarching objective the "prohibition or restriction of tobacco smoking in certain places". The 2002 Act itself became law by ministerial order. Part 2 of the 2002 Act, which came into force on May 31, 2002, established the Office of Tobacco Control, which is now overseeing the implementation of the Act by undertaking a variety of measures aimed at limiting the use of tobacco products generally.[9] It empowers the Minister for Health and Children to make Regulations that will control the use of tobacco-related products in the workplace.

The Tobacco Smoking (Prohibition) Regulations 2003[10]

9–07   The Tobacco Smoking (Prohibition) Regulations 2003, and subsequent amendments, came into force on March 29, 2004 and have been made pursuant to s.47 of the Public Health (Tobacco) Act 2002, as amended by s.16 of the Public Health (Tobacco) (Amendment) Act 2004 ("the 2004 Amendment Act"). They replace and revoke the Tobacco (Health Promotion and Protection) Regulations 1995, which outlawed smoking only in a limited number of premises or parts of a premises. The legislative vehicle by which the ban on smoking was introduced was therefore the 2004 Amendment Act, which is to be read in conjunction with the Public Health Tobacco Act 2002.[11] The amended s.47(6) of the 2002 Act, as inserted by s.16 of the 2004 Amendment Act, identifies the explicit rationale for the making of the 2003 Regulations:

> "This section has been enacted for the purposes of reducing the risk to and protecting the health of persons."

9–08   Since March 29, 2004, smoking has been banned in virtually every "place of work". Regulation 2 of the 2003 Regulations provides that "the smoking of tobacco products in a place or premises (other than a dwelling) specified in the Schedule to these Regulations is prohibited." The places identified in the Schedule are:

• a place of work;

• an aircraft, train, ship or other vessel, a public service vehicle or other vehicle used for the carriage of members of the public for reward, in so far as it is a place of work;

---

8   No. 6 of 2002.
9   See s.10 of the 2002 Act.
10   S.I. No. 481 of 2003.
11   See the Public Health (Tobacco) Act 2002 (Commencement) Order 2004 (S.I. 110 of 2004) and the Public Health (Tobacco) (Amendment) Act 2004 (Commencement) Order 2004 (S.I. 111 of 2004).

- a place or premises to which paras (c), (d), (e), (f) and (g) of s.47(8) of the Public Health (Tobacco) Act 2002, as amended by the 2004 Amendment Act, applies, in so far as it is a place of work;

- a licensed premises, in so far as it is a place of work; and

- a registered club, in so far as it is a place of work.

9–09   The Public Health (Tobacco) (Amendment) Act 2004 defines "place of work" widely and broadly gives it the same meaning as it has in the Safety, Health and Welfare at Work Act, 2005.[12] It therefore includes any "place, land or other location at, in, upon or near which, work is carried on whether occasionally or otherwise". It is also to be noted from the definition of "place of work" that smoking is now banned in company cars and trucks. The 2004 Amendment Act provides that "smoking" includes sucking, sniffing or chewing any tobacco product. As "tobacco product" includes "any cigarette paper or filter", having an unlit cigarette in your mouth would render you liable under the legislation.[13]

9–10   Smoking is now banned in all enclosed places of work,[14] with the following limited exceptions[15]: dwellings, prisons, including St. Patrick's Institution; Garda station detention areas; the Central Mental Hospital in Dundrum; psychiatric hospitals; nursing homes; hospices; religious order homes; maternity homes, hotel, guesthouse and B&B bedrooms; and residential areas where third-level education is provided.

9–11   The legislation covers only enclosed areas and does not apply to outdoor work areas. An outdoor work area is defined as a place or premises, or part of a place or premises "covered by a fixed or movable roof, provided that not more than 50 per cent of the perimeter is surrounded by one or more walls or similar structures (inclusive of windows, doors, gates or other means of access to or egress from that part)".[16]

9–12   The smoking ban in the workplace has enjoyed a high level of compliance to date with authorised officers under the Public Health (Tobacco) Acts 2002 and 2004 having responsibility for the enforcement of the smoking ban. A fine of up to €3,000 can be imposed for failing to comply with the legislation. It is a defence to any proceedings in respect of an offence under the Public Health (Tobacco) Acts, 2002 and 2004 for an employer to show that "he or she made all reasonable efforts to ensure compliance" with the smoking ban.[17]

---

[12] See s.16 of the 2004 Amendment Act. Also s.2(1) of the Safety, Health and Welfare at Work Act 2005.

[13] See s.2 of the 2004 Amendment Act.

[14] This includes an individual's own office as this comes within the definition of an enclosed workplace.

[15] See Tobacco Smoking (Prohibition) Regulations 2003.

[16] See s.16 of the 2004 Amendment Act.

[17] ibid.

9–13 A number of prosecutions have been initiated under the Public Health (Tobacco) Acts 2002 and 2004. In May 2007, for example, the HSE South sucessfully prosecuted a Cork County licensed premises for having a non-compliant enclosed "smoking area" on the premises.

Smoking policy

9–14 Every employer should formulate a policy on smoking in the workplace to suit the individual needs of his or her workplace. The purpose of such a policy is to determine the manner in which the organisation manages tobacco smoking. It should be noted that an employer is not obliged to provide an outdoor smoking facility. If such a facility is provided, it should not be within "six metres of all entrance(s), exit(s), open windows, ventilation intake systems and covered entryways of any building".[18] Work breaks are governed by the Organisation of Working Time Act 1997 and are not affected by the ban on smoking in the workplace, even if staff must now leave the building to smoke during breaks.

Guidance

9–15 1. *Guidance for Employers, Public Health (Tobacco) Acts, 2002 and 2004*, Office of Tobacco Control, 2004.

2.   Office of Tobacco Control
    Clane Shopping Centre
    Clane
    Co. Kildare
    Tel: 045 892015
    Fax: 045 892649
    Web: www.otc.ie
    Email: info@otc.ie.

---

[18] See HSA Guidance.

CHAPTER 10

FIRE, SIGNS, EXPLOSIVE ATMOSPHERES AT PLACES OF WORK AND EMERGENCIES

Fire

10–01   The Fire Services Acts 1981 and 2003[1] place a responsibility on the occupiers or owners of buildings to safeguard against the outbreak of fires on the premises, and to ensure the safety of persons on the premises in the event of an outbreak of fire. In practice, this will involve the existence and enforcement of a fire prevention policy. It will also involve ensuring that the following are adequate:

1. fire alarm(s);

2. emergency procedures;

3. emergency exits (including emergency lighting where appropriate); and

4. available fire fighting equipment.

   Section 29 of the Licensing of Indoor Events Act 2003 amends s.18 of the Fire Safety Act 1981 to bring "any workplace" within the scope of s.18 insofar as the general obligations regarding fire safety are concerned. It also provides that it is the duty of a person having control over a premises to:

(a)   take all reasonable measures to guard against the outbreak of a fire on the premises;

(b)   provide reasonable fire safety measures for a premises and prepare and provide appropriate fire safety procedures to ensure the safety of persons on the premises;

(c)   ensure fire safety measures and procedures are applied at all times; and

(d)   ensure, as far as is reasonably practicable, the safety of persons on the premises in the event of an outbreak of fire, whether or not an outbreak of fire has actually occurred.

   Section 20A(2) of the Fire Services Acts 1981 and 2003 allows an authorised officer[2] to serve a closure notice on a person who owns, occupies or is in

---

[1]   The Fire Services Act 1981 and Part 3 of the Licensing of Indoor Events Act 2003 are cited as the Fire Services Acts 1981 and 2003.

[2]   See s.28 of the Licensing of Indoor Events Act 2003.

control of a building if he or she is of the opinion that a building or premises poses, or is likely to pose, a very serious and immediate risk to the safety of persons in or on a premises or building. This section also details the procedures for the issue of a closure notice as well as the bringing of an appeal against a closure notice.

10–02   The Fire Safety in Places of Assembly (Ease of Escape) Regulations 1985[3] require the occupiers or owners of publicly used buildings to ensure that emergency exists are not obstructed, chained or locked, and are available for use.

10–03   The Building Regulations 1997[4] and the Building Control Regulations 1997,[5] as amended by the Building Control (Amendment) Regulations 2004,[6] require all new buildings or buildings that are to be materially altered to have a Fire Safety Certificate (issued by the local authority) prior to work commencing. To obtain this certificate such buildings must comply with the fire safety requirements as detailed in the Building Regulations 1997–2006 and guidance documentation. The Building Control (Amendment) Regulations 2000[7] detail the particulars that must be furnished to the local authority when applying for a Fire Safety Certificate. These particulars were previously detailed in the Building Control Regulations 1997.

10–04   The Safety, Heath and Welfare at Work Act 2005 imposes a duty of care on all users of the premises to have regard for their own and others' safety. Section 11 of the 2005 Act imposes an obligation on an employer to make provision and take measures that cover, *inter alia,* fire fighting and the evacuation of employees and any other individual present in the workplace in the case of an emergency or serious and imminent danger.

10–05   The primary responsibility for ensuring the fire safety of all buildings rests on the owners and occupiers of premises, and in the case of new buildings on those who design and construct them. Having a fire safety certificate does not imply an immunity.

Safety Signs

10–06   Chapter 1 of Part 7 and Sch. 9 to the General Application Regulations 2007 specify the type of signs and signals to be used at places of work when hazards cannot be avoided or adequately reduced. Such signs and signals are used for prohibiting activities causing a fire hazard (*e.g.* no smoking signs), warning signs of flammable, explosive materials, electricity, as well as emergency escape and fire fighting signs. The requirements of this part of the 2007

---

[3]   S.I. No. 249 of 1985. See also reg.12 of the 2007 General Application Regulations.
[4]   S.I. No. 497 of 1997.
[5]   S.I. No. 496 of 1997.
[6]   S.I. No. 85 of 2004.
[7]   S.I. No. 10 of 2000.

General Application Regulations are in addition to the provisions of ss.8–11, 13, 14, 18–23 and 25–31 of the Safety, Health and Welfare at Work Act 2005.

10–07   Regulation 160 of the 2007 General Application Regulations places a duty on every employer to put in place any safety or health signs (or both) where hazards in the workplace require them for the protection of employees because such hazards cannot be avoided or adequately reduced "by techniques for collective protection or measures, methods or procedures used in the organisation of work".

Every employer must ensure that a safety or health sign used at a place of work complies with Sch.9 to the 2007 General Application Regulations. Schedule 9 relates to safety signs at places of work and is to be found in Part III of this book. Regulation 158 defines "signboard" as meaning "a sign which provides specific information or instructions by a combination of a geometric shape, colours and a symbol or pictogram, *without written words,*[8] which is rendered visible by lighting of sufficient intensity". Therefore, safety signs used after November 1, 2007 are not to contain any written words. Regulation 160(2) is a transitional provision for a signboard in use before November 1, 2007. It provides as follows:

> "Where a signboard is in place (at 1 November 2007) which, solely because it includes a word or words, is not a signboard as defined in Regulation 158, an employer may leave that signboard in place until 1 January 2011".

Regulation 161 requires employees to be provided with information and instruction on the meaning of the signs and signals. Words may be included on a supplementary signboard[9] so long as they do not negatively impact on the message communicated by the safety signboard.

Explosive Atmospheres at Places of Work

10–08   Part 8 and Sch.10 to the General Application Regulations 2007 bring the Safety, Health and Welfare at Work (Explosive Atmosphere) Regulations 2003[10] into the General Application Regulations. In particular, regs 167 to 175 of the Safety, Health and Welfare at Work (General Application) Regulations 2007 set down specific requirements to manage fire and explosion risks where flammable substances are stored or used, and are in addition to the general requirements detailed in the Safety, Health and Welfare at Work Act 2005. Regulation 169 of the 2007 General Application Regulations requires employers to carry out a risk assessment of any work that involves flammable substances. The findings of such risk assessment are to be recorded in an explosion protection document, which may be incorporated into the safety statement. The explosion protection document must specify the following:

---

[8]   The emphasis added is that of the author.
[9]   Regulation 158 defines "supplementary signboard" as meaning "a signboard used together with one of the signs covered by the definition of "signboard" and which gives supplementary information, including, where appropriate, information in writing".
[10]   S.I. No. 258 of 2003.

(a)   that the explosion risks have been determined and assessed,

(b)   that adequate measures have been or will be taken,

(c)   the areas which have been classified into hazardous zones,

(d)   that the work equipment being used is adequate,

(e)   the coordination arrangements between employers where they share work places.

In summary, Pt 8 of the 2007 General Application Regulations details the requirements relating to the assessment of explosion risk, the preparation of an explosion protection document, classification of places where explosive atmospheres may occur, prevention against explosion, safety of plant, equipment and protective systems, training instructions, permits to work, protection of employees from explosion and co-ordination at workplaces.

CHAPTER 11

PREGNANT, POST NATAL AND BREASTFEEDING EMPLOYEES

MATERNITY PROTECTION ACT 1994

11–01 The Maternity Protection Act 1994,[1] as amended by the Maternity Protection (Amendment) Act 2004,[2] provides that all employers shall carry out risk assessments taking particular account of risks to new and expectant mothers. The Act specifically provides for a reduction of risks where practicable, changes in working arrangements, the offer of suitable alternative employment, or, if that is not possible, paid leave for the employee concerned for as long as is necessary to protect her health and safety, or that of her child. It should be noted that reg.24 of the 2007 General Application Regulations imposes an obligation upon employers to provide suitable facilities for pregnant, postnatal and breastfeeding employees. In summary, this involves the provision of a quiet and private area where rests may be taken during the working day, and where a breastfeeding mother may feed her baby during such a break. Indeed, s.15B of the Maternity Protection Act 1994, introduced by s.9 of the Maternity Protection (Amendment) Act 2004, creates an entitlement to time off from work or a reduction of working hours for an employee who is breastfeeding.

11–02 A relevant and instructive case on the Maternity Protection Act 1994 is *Pauline Mulcahy v The Minister for Justice, Equality and Law Reform and Waterford Leader Partnership Limited.*[3]

2007 General Application Regulations

11–03 Chapter 2 of Pt 6 and Sch.8 to the 2007 General Application Regulations contains measures to promote improvement in the health and safety at work of pregnant workers and workers who have recently given birth. These Regulations revoke and replace the Safety, Health and Welfare at Work

---

[1] See S.I. No. 34 of 1994.
[2] S.I. No. 28 of 2004.
[3] Unreported, High Court, O'Sullivan J., October 26, 2001.

(Pregnant Employees etc.) Regulations 2000.[4] They require employers to take such steps as, having regard to the nature of the work, are necessary for the protection of the health and safety at work of pregnant workers and workers who have recently given birth or are breastfeeding.

11–04 Regulation 149 of the 2007 General Application Regulations requires an employer to carry out a risk assessment to determine any possible effects on the pregnancy of, or breastfeeding by, employees resulting from any activity at the employer's place of work. While s.19 of the 2005 Act requires employers to carry out risk assessments in respect of their employees, reg.149 of the 2007 General Application Regulations requires a specific risk assessment on receiving notification that an employee is pregnant. This will involve the employer assessing the specific risks to that employee and taking whatever action of a preventive or protective nature that is necessary to ensure that the pregnant employee is not exposed to any agent, process or working condition that will have a negative effect on either her health or that of her unborn infant. Having regard to the provisions of the Safety, Health and Welfare at Work (Chemical Agents) Regulations 2001,[5] the employer must assess whether in the course of her duties the pregnant employee or the employee who is breastfeeding may be exposed to the non-exhaustive hazards detailed in Sch.8 of the Safety, Health and Welfare at Work (General Application) Regulations 2007. If the assessment reveals there is a risk, the employer cannot require her to perform duties for which the assessment reveals such risk.

11–05 Regulation 152 of the 2007 General Application Regulations requires every employer to ensure that a pregnant employee or employee who is breastfeeding and/or the Safety Representative are provided with information on the outcome of the risk assessment and any corrective measures to be taken concerning the employees' safety and health.

11–06 Regulation 151 of the 2007 General Application Regulations states that if a pregnant employee is certified by a medical practitioner as not being able to perform night work during pregnancy, or for 14 weeks after childbirth, the employer shall endeavour to find day employment for her. If this is not possible, the employer must grant the employee health and safety leave or extend the period of maternity leave. Regulation 151(1) defines "night work" as follows:

> "In this Regulation "night work" means work in the period between the hours of 11p.m. on any day and 6a.m. on the next following day, where-
>
> (a) the employee works at least three hours in that period as a normal course, or
> (b) at least 25 per cent of the employee's monthly working time is performed in that period".

---

[4] S.I. No. 218 of 2000.
[5] See Chap.8.

CHAPTER 12

PROTECTION OF YOUNG PERSONS AND CHILDREN

PROTECTION OF YOUNG PERSONS (EMPLOYMENT) ACT 1996

12–01 The Safety, Health and Welfare at Work Act 2005 obliges employers to provide safe places and systems of work for all staff, including young persons. The Protection of Young Persons (Employment) Act 1996 ("the 1996 Act") in effect, limits the employment of young persons under the age of 18, but over 16, and restricts the employment of children under 16. In general, no child under the age of 14 is permitted to work. A child over 14 years is allowed to do non-industrial work during school holidays so long as it is not harmful to health, development or schooling, and may be employed as part of an approved work experience or education programme. A child over 15 years can also engage in light work for up to 8 hours a week during the school term. Any child under 16 years can be employed in film, theatre, advertising activities or sports under licence from the Minister who must take cognisance of matters such as the safety, health, welfare and education of the child in granting such a licence.

12–02 The Protection of Young Persons (Employment) Act 1996 requires the employer to receive a copy of the birth certificate of anyone he wishes to employ who is under 18. In the case of a child under 16, the employer must obtain written permission from the parent or guardian of the child, prior to the commencement of employment. The employer must maintain a register of employed young persons (including children) which outlines the times of attendance at work for each day, the rate of pay and the total amount paid in wages. Section 35 of the Organisation of Working Time Act 1997 amends the Protection of Young Persons (Employment) Act 1996 to extend to situations where a young person has more than one job.

2007 General Application Regulations

12–03 Chapter 1 of Part 6 and Sch.7 to the 2007 General Application Regulations requires the employer to carry out a risk assessment that takes cognisance of the particular risks to young persons or children if they are employed by the employer. The risk assessment is to include an assessment of the exposure to certain physical, chemical and biological agents, as well as particular work activities, which are detailed in Sch.7 to the 2007 General Application

Regulations. Regulation 144 of the 2007 General Application Regulations provides that an employer must ensure that any risk to the safety or health of a child or young person, or to his or her development, is assessed having regard to the increased risk arising from the child's or young person's "lack of experience, absence of awareness of existing or potential risks or lack of maturity". The risk assessment must therefore not only take cognisance of the safety and health of the child or young person, but should also take account of his or her physical and mental development.

12–04   The employer must carry out a risk assessment before a child or young person commences employment, and when there is a major change in the place of work which could affect the health or safety of a child or young person. Regulation 144(c) of the 2007 Regulations provides that the risk assessment should take account of the following:

(i)   the fitting-out and the layout of the workplace and the individual workstation,

(ii)   any likelihood of exposure to any physical, chemical or biological agent,

(iii) any machines, apparatus and devices which may put the health and safety of the child or young person at risk,

(iv)   the work processes and the manner in which they are organised, and

(v)   the training, instruction and level of supervision provided to a child or young person at the place of work.

12–05   Where the results of a risk assessment confirm that particular work activities may cause harm to a child or young person, he or she shall not be employed in any such activity.[1] In particular, where a risk assessment reveals that the work involved is work which would put the safety and health of the child at risk because the work is beyond the physical or psychological capacity of the child, or exposes him or her to agents which are toxic, carcinogenic or involve harmful exposure to radiation, or otherwise places him or her at undue risk, the employer cannot employ a child or young person.

12–06   The employer must provide protective and preventive measures and inform any child or young person employed of these measures and of the risks that he or she is being protected from.[2]

12–07   Where an assessment shows that a child or young person may be exposed to a risk to his or her physical or mental development, health surveillance must be made available to him or her without charge. If the work involves night work, the employer must provide health assessment without charge prior to the commencement of night work and at regular intervals there-

---

[1]   Regulation 145.
[2]   Regulation 144(e).

after.[3] The parents or guardians of children must be informed of the results of health surveillances or assessments.

EMPLOYMENT OF YOUNG PERSONS IN LICENSED PREMISES

12–08 The Protection of Young Persons (Employment) Act 1996 (Employment of Licensed Premises) Regulations 2001[4] not only reinforce the working hours as detailed in the 1996 Act, but also contain a detailed code of practice concerning the employment of young persons in licensed premises, the terms of which are set out in the Schedule of the Regulations.

12–09 The Protection of Young Persons (Employment) Act 1996 (Bar Apprentices) Regulations 2001[5] relax the restricted hours of work for full-time bar apprentices, permitting 16- and 17-year-old bar apprentices to work in a bar until midnight, provided they are supervised by an adult and they are not starting work prior to 8am the following morning.

12–10 In *National Authority for Occupational Safety and Health v Carabine Joinery Ltd*[6] the defendant company was convicted of a breach of the Safety, Health and Welfare at Work (Children and Young Persons) Regulations 1998. The case resulted from an accident where a 17-year-old seriously injured his left hand when he was removing a spanner from an automatic spindle moulder machine. Judge Devins fined the defendant company €2,000 and awarded costs and expenses totalling €1,065. This case highlights not only the dangers associated with machinery but, more specifically, how important it is for all employers to address the specific risk to the safety and health of a young person. The level of any such risk should be assessed for each workplace as part of the process of preparing a safety statement.[7]

---

[3] However, under the Protection of Young Persons (Employment) Act 1996, young persons are expressly precluded from being employed after 11pm or before 7am. Similarly, children cannot be employed after 8pm or before 8am the next morning.
[4] S.I. No. 350 of 2001.
[5] S.I. No. 351 of 2001.
[6] Unreported, Ballina District Court, February 12, 2002.
[7] See paras 3–73 to 3–88 of this book.

CHAPTER 13

NIGHT WORK
AND SHIFT WORK

13–01   The principal elements of the 1993 EC Working Time Directive[1] were implemented by the Organisation of Working Time Act 1997. Articles 9 and 13 of the 1993 Directive, which concern those aspects of the organisation of working time dealing with night workers and shift workers were implemented by Ch. 3 of Pt 6 of the 2007 General Application Regulations.

13–02   Regulation 153 of the 2007 General Application Regulations oblige employers to take such steps as, having regard to the nature of the work, are appropriate for the protection of the health and safety of night workers and shift workers.

13–03   Regulation 155 of the 2007 General Application Regulations defines "night work" and "night worker". Night work is the time between midnight and 7am the following day. Night worker has the same meaning as in the Organisation of Working Time Act 1997[2] and refers to an employee who normally works a minimum of three hours of their daily working time during night time and his or her annual number of hours worked at night equals or exceeds 50 per cent of his or her annual working time.

13–04   Regulation 155 of the 2007 General Application Regulations requires an employer to carry out a risk assessment to determine if any night workers are exposed to special hazards or a heavy physical or mental strain.[3] The risk assessment must take account of the specific effects and hazards of night work and have regard to the risk assessment requirements detailed in s.19 of the Safety, Health and Welfare at Work Act 2005.[4]

13–05   Regulation 157(1) of the 2007 General Application Regulations obliges employers before an employee is employed to do night work, and at regular intervals thereafter, to make available to the employee, free of charge, an assessment of the effects of night work, if any, on the employee's health. It states that the health assessment must be conducted by a registered medical

---

[1]   93/104/EC.
[2]   No. 20 of 1997.
[3]   See also s.16(2)(a) and (b) of the Organisation of Working Time Act 1997.
[4]   See para.3–69 of this book.

practitioner or a person acting under his or her supervision. The employer must facilitate the employee in his or her availing of himself or herself of an entitlement to an assessment.[5] The employer and employee are to be advised by the person carrying out the assessment of his or her opinion as to whether the employee is fit or unfit to perform the night work concerned, or whether the employee is fit to perform night work in limited circumstances.[6] If the person carrying out the assessment is of the opinion that the employee is unfit for night work by virtue only of the particular conditions under which it is performed, the employer and employee are to be informed of the person's opinion of what changes could be made which would result in his or her being able to consider the employee fit to perform that work.[7] Regulation 157(4) provides that the health assessment must comply with the requirements of medical confidentiality.

13–06 Regulation 157(5) of the 2007 General Application Regulations requires employers, whose night workers become ill or otherwise exhibit symptoms of ill-health which are recognised as being connected with the fact that they perform night work, to re-assign such workers to day work suited to them whenever possible.

Trainee doctors

13–07 The Regulations regarding the working hours of trainee doctors are to be found in the European Communities (Organisation of Working Time) (Activities of Doctors in Training) Regulations 2004.[8] These Regulations are operative since August 1, 2004 and apply to the activities of trainee doctors. In summary, these Regulations prescribe maximum hours of work and minimum hours of rest for trainee doctors. Article 9 of the Regulations provide that between August 1, 2004 and July 31, 2007, an employer cannot require a trainee doctor to work for more than 58 hours a week, averaged over a maximum reference period of 12 months. From August 1, 2007 to July 31, 2009, an employer cannot require a trainee doctor to work for more than 56 hours a week, averaged over a maximum reference period of six months. From August 1, 2009, a 48-hour average working week is to be introduced for all trainee doctors.

---

[5] Regulation 157(2)(b).
[6] Regulation 157(3)(b).
[7] Regulation 157(3)(b).
[8] S.I. No. 494 of 2004. Also Directive 2000/34/EC, June 22, 2000; O.J. L195, 01.08.2000, p.41.

CHAPTER 14

EUROPEAN COMMUNITIES (HYGIENE OF FOODSTUFFS) REGULATIONS 2006

14–01 The European Communities (Hygiene of Foodstuffs) Regulations 2006[1] revoke and replace the European Communities (Hygiene of Foodstuffs) Regulations 2000[2] and the European Communities (Hygiene of Foodstuffs) (Amendment) Regulations 2005[3]. These Regulations apply to all undertakings "whether for profit or not and whether public or private, carrying out any or all of the following: preparation, processing, manufacturing, packaging, storing, transportation, distribution, handling, or offering for sale or supply of foodstuffs". The Regulations require the proprietor of the food business to ensure the business is carried out in a hygienic manner. This includes all aspects of the business from the storage and transport of food, to its final preparation for sale or supply. The Regulations impose requirements in respect of premises, equipment, personal hygiene and training. Insofar as safety is concerned, the proprietor is required to carry out a risk assessment. In particular, he or she is required to identify all significant hazards and implement procedures and controls to eliminate or control these hazards based on the principles of hazard analysis and critical control point. The Regulations also impose obligations on food business proprietors in respect of registration.

14–02 The local health service executive enforces these Regulations. The penalties, enforcement and authorised officer provisions are set out in the Regulations. An Environmental Health Officer, on behalf of the health service executive, may inspect food premises at any time, in order to ensure compliance with the Regulations. A relevant and instructive case on the labelling of foodstuffs is *East Coast Area Health Board v O'Kane Foods (Ireland)*.[4]

---

[1] S.I. No. 369 of 2006.
[2] S.I. No. 165 of 2000.
[3] S.I. No. 67 of 2005.
[4] Unreported, High Court, Ó Caoimh J., April 12, 2002.

CHAPTER 15

SAFETY, HEALTH AND WELFARE AT WORK (CONFINED SPACES) REGULATIONS 2001

15–01   The Safety, Health and Welfare at Work (Confined Spaces) Regulations 2001[1] came into force on August 31, 2001.[2] The definition of a confined space expanded significantly under the 2001 Confined Spaces Regulations. The 2001 Regulations apply to all workplaces where confined spaces are present, though mining and diving activities are excluded.[3] Regulation 2 defines confined space as:

> "any place which, by virtue of its enclosed nature creates conditions which give rise to a likelihood of accident, harm or injury of such a nature as to require emergency action due to–
>
> (a) the presence or the reasonably foreseeable presence of
>   (i)   flammable or explosive atmospheres,
>   (ii) harmful gas, fume, or vapour,
>   (iii) free flowing solid or an increasing level of liquid,
>   (iv) excess of oxygen,
>   (v)   excessively high temperature,
> (b) lack or reasonably foreseeable lack of oxygen; …".

The objective of the 2001 Regulations is to bring the health and safety management of work in confined spaces into line with the modern risk assessment based, goal setting approach. The 2001 Regulations require that employers avoid the need to enter confined spaces where reasonably practicable. If entry is required, all risks must be assessed so that a safe system of work is established; furthermore, persons entering the confined space must be provided with sufficient information, instruction and training for the work activity prior to entry. The Regulations require that no person shall enter a confined space

---

[1] S.I. No. 218 of 2001.
[2] It should be noted that the Safety, Health and Welfare at Work Act 1989 (Repeal of Section 38 of Factories Act 1955) (Commencement) Order 2001 [S.I. No. 219 of 2001] came into operation on the same day. This Order repealed s.38 of the Factories Act 1955 (as provided for in ss.1(2) and 4(3) of the Safety, Health and Welfare at Work Act 1989), as amended by s.21 of the Safety in Industry Act 1980, on the coming into force of the Safety, Health and Welfare at Work (Confined Spaces) Regulations 2001.
[3] Regulation 3(2).

unless sufficient arrangements have been made for the rescue of such person in the event of an emergency.

15–02   The Health and Safety Authority has produced an approved code of practice relating to working in confined spaces.[4]

15–03   The risks associated with excavations are significant. To ensure the safety of those involved in this type of work, it has "to be properly planned, managed, supervised and executed in order to prevent accidents". In January 2007 the Health and Safety Authority updated its 2004 Guide to Safety in Excavations to reflect the requirements of the Safety, Health and Welfare at Work Act 2005 and the 2006 Construction Regulations. The 2007 Guide aims "to assist persons in controlling the risks associated with excavations", having regard to the new duties imposed under the 2005 Act and 2006 Regulations.

---

[4]   *Code of Practice for Working in Confined Spaces* (Health and Safety Authority, 2001).

CHAPTER 16

TRANSPORT OF DANGEROUS GOODS BY ROAD AND RAIL

16–01 Section 2 of the Safety, Health and Welfare at Work Act 2005 defines a vehicle as a place of work. Accordingly, the Carriage of Dangerous Goods by Road Regulations 2007[1] fall to be considered as part of a review of health and safety legislation. The Carriage of Dangerous Goods by Road Regulations 2007 were signed by the Minister for Enterprise, Trade and Employment on June 13, 2007.[2] They revoke and replace the European Communities (Carriage of Dangerous Goods by Road) (ADR Miscellaneous Provisions) Regulations 2006.[3] The 2006 Carriage of Dangerous Goods by Road Regulations revoked the European Communities (Safety Advisers for the Transport of Dangerous Goods by Road and Rail) Regulations 2001[4] in so far as they related to the transport of dangerous goods by road.[5]

Rail

16–02 In summary, the European Communities (Safety Advisers for the Transport of Dangerous Goods by Road and Rail) Regulations 2001 require any person or undertaking involved in the transport of dangerous goods by rail, subject to certain limited exceptions, to appoint a Dangerous Goods Safety Adviser. The adviser must be in possession of a Community-type Vocational Training Certificate for rail transport. The Minister for Enter-

---

[1] S.I. No. 288 of 2007.

[2] S.I. Nos. 288 to 291 of 2007.

[3] S.I. No. 406 of 2006.

[4] S.I. No. 6 of 2001.

[5] See also the Dangerous Substances Act 1972 (No. 10 of 1972), the Road Traffic Acts, 1961 to 1995 (No. 7 of 1995), the Carriage of Dangerous Goods by Road Act 1998 (No. 43 of 1998), the European Communities (Road Transport) (Recording Equipment) Regulations 2006 (S.I. No. 89 of 2006), the Carriage of Dangerous Goods by Road Regulations 2007 (S.I. No. 288 of 2007), the European Communities (Carriage of Dangerous Goods by Road) (ADR Miscellaneous Provisions) Regulations 2007 (S.I. No. 289 of 2007), the Carriage of Dangerous Goods by Road Act 1998 (Appointment of Competent Authorities) Order 2007 (S.I. No. 290 of 2007), the Carriage of Dangerous Goods by Road (Fees) Regulations 2007 (S.I. No. 291 of 2007), the Carriage of Dangerous Goods by Road Act 1998 (Commencement) Order 2001 (S.I. No. 495 of 2001) and the Dangerous Substances (Retail and Private Petroleum Stores) (Amendment) Regulations 2001 (S.I. No. 584 of 2001).

prise is the national competent authority for the transport of dangerous goods by rail.[6]

Road

16–03   In relation to the transport of dangerous goods by road, the Carriage of Dangerous Goods by Road Regulations 2007 apply since June 13, 2007. Regulation 4 provides that these Regulations apply to the carriage of dangerous goods by road "whether on international carriage or national transport only, in or on a vehicle". This includes the packing, loading, filling and unloading of the dangerous goods in relation to their carriage.

The 2007 Carriage of Dangerous Goods by Road Regulations impose specific duties on those participants involved in the transport of dangerous goods (including their loading and unloading). Such participants are identified in reg.13 of the 2007 Carriage of Dangerous Goods by Road Regulations and the European Agreement concerning the international carriage of dangerous goods by road. They include the following:

- loaders;

- packers;

- fillers;

- consignors;

- carriers;

- drivers;

- vehicle crew;

- unloaders; and

- consignees.

The 2007 Carriage Regulations require drivers and those involved in the transport of dangerous goods by road to be adequately trained. Drivers are required to hold certificates of such training.

---

[6]   See *Guidance on European Communities (Safety Advisers for the Transport of Dangerous Goods by Road and Rail) Regulations, 2001* (Health and Safety Authority, 2001).

CHAPTER 17

OCCUPIERS' LIABILITY

17–01   The occupier of a premises is obliged to take reasonable precautions in terms of the general condition of the premises. This is termed occupiers' liability and is largely governed by the Occupiers' Liability Act 1995.

17–02   The rights and obligations of the occupiers of both land and property have undergone a total transformation through the centuries. Not too long ago, a trespasser risked forfeiting his life for venturing onto the land of another. However, the law has moved on from that time. Indeed, throughout the centuries the rights of occupiers of land have been gradually eroded, while at the same time, the obligations imposed upon them have increased exponentially. In essence, the law has held an occupier of land primarily liable by virtue of the fact that he is in actual *control* of the land and premises and is usually the person in the best position to control who enters the land and to remedy defects.

17–03   Prior to July 17, 1995, the old common law position pertained. Essentially, apart from contractual entrants, three distinct categories existed: invitees, licensees and trespassers. These entrants were categorised with reference to the benefit they conferred on the occupier; the greater the benefit conferred on the occupier the greater the duty imposed upon him.

17–04   In the absence of express contractual provisions, the occupier owed the contractual entrant an implied duty of reasonable care that the premises were in a reasonably safe state. To the invitee, an occupier was obliged to take reasonable care to ensure that the invitee was protected from unusual dangers of which the occupier was actually aware, or ought reasonably, in the circumstances, to have been aware. With respect to licensees, an occupier was not liable for obvious defects on the premises, however dangerous. The occupier was liable only for traps or concealed dangers. Finally, trespassers were positioned at the bottom of the hierarchy and the only obligation imposed upon the occupier was not to undertake any act which might intentionally or recklessly injure the trespasser, whose presence was either known, or ought reasonably to have been known. These categories survived, by and large, until the late 1960s.

17–05   In two seminal cases, *Purtill v Athlone Urban District Council*[1] and *McNamara v Electricity Supply Board*,[2] the pendulum continued to swing

---

[1]   [1968] I.R. 205.
[2]   [1975] I.R. 1.

towards the entrants. In the latter, and more celebrated case, an 11-year-old was seriously injured when, in an effort to reach a drain pipe and slide down from a flat roof extension into an electrical transformer station, his hand came into contact with a high tension cable adjacent to the pipe. On any application of the above categories, the plaintiff could only be defined as a trespasser. As such, the only duty the Electricity Supply Board owed to him was not to injure him intentionally, or to act with reckless disregard for his safety whilst on the premises. The matter was complicated, somewhat, by virtue of the fact that the wire fence surrounding the sub-station was undergoing repair at the time. This facilitated the plaintiff's entry. The Supreme Court held that the Electricity Supply Board did owe a duty of care towards the plaintiff. The court held that an occupier of land owed a duty of care to a trespasser whose presence was reasonably foreseeable and who was in a sufficiently proximate relationship with the occupier. It held that the duty of care deemed to be owed was to take such reasonable care as the circumstances demanded. The Supreme Court did not expressly abolish the old common law categories but rather redefined them.[3]

17–06   The effect of this judgment was immediate. Land owners, farmers, hotel owners, schools, hospitals and restaurants, rightly or wrongly, envisaged themselves as automatically liable for all personal injuries, loss and damage sustained by any trespasser who entered onto their land or premises. Many organisations, most notably the Irish Farmers Association, lobbied for a withdrawal from this new "onerous" duty of care imposed upon them. Significant pressure was brought to bear on the political establishment, and in 1992, the Attorney General requested that the Law Reform Commission conduct research pertaining to the issue of occupiers' liability.

OCCUPIERS' LIABILITY ACT 1995

17–07   The Occupiers' Liability Act 1995, which came into force on July 17, 1995, constituted a sweeping transformation of the existing law at that time. It created three new categories of entrants: visitors, recreational users and trespassers.

17–08   The Law Reform Commission in its Consultation Paper,[4] and subsequent Report,[5] stated that an "occupier" ought to be:

"(i) a person who is in physical possession of premises; or
(ii) a person who has responsibility for, and control over, the condition of the premises, the activities conducted on those premises and the persons allowed to enter the premises, and that, for the purpose of the legislation, there may be more than one occupier of the same premises."

---

[3] See also *Keane v Electricity Supply Board*, unreported, Supreme Court, 1980.
[4] The Law Reform Commission, *Consultation Paper On Occupiers' Liability* (Dublin, The Law Reform Commission, June, 1993) para.4.139.
[5] The Law Reform Commission, *Report On Occupiers' Liability* (Number 46) (Dublin, The Law Reform Commission, 1994) p.37.

Section (1)(1) of the 1995 Act defines an "occupier" in relation to any premises as:

"a person exercising such control over the state of the premises that it is reasonable to impose upon that person a duty towards an entrant in respect of a particular danger thereon and, where there is more than one occupier of the same premises, the extent of the duty of each occupier towards an entrant depends on the degree of control each of them has over the state of the premises and the particular danger thereon and whether, as respects each of them, the entrant concerned is a visitor, recreational user or trespasser; ..."

The Act therefore places emphasis on "control" as opposed to occupation. This approach, however, pre-dated the 1995 Act. In an earlier case, *Keegan v Owens and McMahon*,[6] control and occupation were clearly distinguished. In that case, an order of nuns obtained permission to use a field to hold a carnival for the purpose of fund raising. The actual management and running of the carnival was assigned to a committee. Keegan, the plaintiff in the case, was a carpenter. As such, he was ordinarily employed by the nuns. On the occasion in question, he was requested to assist with the carnival set-up on completion of his normal working hours. While assisting, however, a nail in one of the swings operated by him injured him. He subsequently brought an action against the order of nuns alleging that they were liable for the accident, *inter alia*, as occupiers. The Supreme Court held that the nuns were not the occupiers of the field and a new trial was ordered against the co-defendant. In reaching this conclusion the Supreme Court incorporated the control test enunciated and developed by the common law.

17–09 In summary, an occupier, for the purposes of the 1995 Act, is an individual who is in actual occupation of the premises for the time being and, as such, has immediate supervision and *control* over those premises, as well as the power to either admit or refuse entry to other persons. In certain circumstances, it is possible for more than one occupier to exist. This may occur where the owner of a premises grants a licence which allows part of the premises to be used by another individual while, at the same time, the owner retains certain rights in relation to those premises. In such a situation, it is possible that each of the occupiers will owe different duties to the entrant who may be a trespasser *vis-à-vis* one and a visitor *vis-à-vis* the other.

PREMISES AND SCOPE OF LIABILITY

(1) What is covered?

17–10 Section 1(1) of the 1995 Act defines premises as including:

"[l]and, water and any fixed or moveable structures thereon and also includes vessels, vehicles, trains, aircraft and other means of transport; ..."

Thus, the Act may be seen to be very broad in its application, covering, as it does, not only land but also structures on both land and water, as well as means

---

6   [1953] I.R. 267.

of transport. For example, "premises" in s.(1)(1) of the 1995 Act covers not only dwelling houses, farmland, forest parks and supermarkets but also includes objects on land such as scaffolding and electricity pylons.

17–11   Traditionally, the duties of an occupier have focused upon the static condition of the premises as opposed to the activities conducted on them. Crucially, however, the legislation limits liability to dangers due to the state of the premises only.[7] To explain this, it is necessary to distinguish between such terms as "state" and "activity". If a poorly constructed wall on a premises collapses, causing injury, it can clearly be seen that the injury resulted from the actual state of the premises. Were that same plaintiff to have been injured, however, by a forklift moving pallets within the premises, the damage results not from the state of the premises but rather from the activity carried on within the premises.[8]

17–12   In many cases, however, a situation will arise whereby the plaintiff may well have sustained injury due both to the state of the premises and the activity carried on therein. Take the hypothetical scenario of a warehouse where containers are transported by means of a forklift and which has a floor surface coated with a substance that becomes extremely slippery when wet. If a forklift skids on liquid negligently spilt from a container, and consequently collides with and causes injury to an employee, liability could be said to arise out of both the activity carried on in the premises and the state of the premises. Liability in such a situation could well be imposed under both the general common law principle of negligence and the statutory requirements of the 1995 Act. As Professor William Binchy so succinctly observed:

> "The problem here is that, for the past two decades and more, Irish courts have not been required to make the conceptual distinction between 'activity' and 'occupancy' duties because frankly the outcome of the case would not be affected by it. A trespasser who was owed the duty of care could invoke the negligence standard however the facts were characterised."[9]

The new categories

17–13   Section 2 of the Occupiers' Liability Act 1995 abolished the common law classifications and introduced three new categories of entrants: visitors, recreational users and trespassers. The abolition of the common law categories is subject to s.8 of the 1995 Act. This section makes it clear that nothing in the 1995 legislation is to be construed as affecting any enactment or rule of law relating to:

---

[7]   A relevant and instructive case is that of *Angela Sheehy v The Devil's Glen Tours Equestrian Centre Ltd*, unreported, High Court, Lavan J., December 10, 2001. See, in particular, p.5 of the judgment.

[8]   See *McGovern v Dunnes Stores*, unreported, Circuit Court, McMahon J., March 6, 2003.

[9]   Binchy W., *Practical Implications of the Occupiers' Liability Act, 1995*, Continuing Legal Education Seminar of the Law Society of Ireland, March 13, 1996, p.9.

"(a) self-defence, the defence of others or the defence of property,

(b) any liability imposed on an occupier as a member of a particular class of persons including the following classes of persons:

    (i) persons by virtue of a contract for the hire of, or for the carriage for reward of persons or property in, any vessel, vehicle, train, aircraft or other means of transport;

    (ii) persons by virtue of a contract of bailment; and

    (iii) employers in respect of their duties towards their employees, or

(c) any liability imposed on an occupier for a tort committed by another person in circumstances where the duty imposed on the occupier is of such a nature that its performance may not be delegated to another person".

These new categories supplanted the old system of classification whereby an entrant was assigned to a particular category depending, in part, on the nature of the benefit which the entrant conferred upon the occupier.

(1) Visitor

17–14   A visitor is defined in s.1(1) of the 1995 Act as:

"(a) an entrant, other than a recreational user, who is present on premises at the invitation, or with the permission, of the occupier or any other entrant specified in *paragraph (a), (b)* or *(c)* of the definition of "recreational user",[10]

(b) an entrant, other than a recreational user, who is present on premises by virtue of an express or implied term in a contract,[11] and

(c) an entrant as of right,[12]

while he or she is so present, as the case may be, for the purpose for which he or she is invited or permitted to be there, for the purpose of the performance of the contract or for the purpose of the exercise of the right, and includes any such entrant whose presence on premises has become unlawful after entry thereon and who is taking reasonable steps to leave."

Therefore, a visitor is a person whose presence on the premises is lawful. The term covers those invited onto a premises by an occupier as well as those permitted by the occupier to be there. It also embraces, as of right, those authorised under statute to enter a premises for some official purpose.

17–15   The status of visitor is conferred by virtue of the purpose of the visit. Therefore, a shop customer who engages in an act of theft would be engaged in an activity inconsistent with the purpose for which he or she is on the premises, namely to view or purchase goods. By engaging in the act of theft, the status of a visitor is lost. It is interesting to note s.4(3) of the 1995 Act in this context. This section provides that an occupier shall not be liable for a breach of the duty imposed by s.4(1)(b) where a person enters a premises, or while present thereon commits an offence, save where the court determines otherwise in the interests of justice. Barry Doherty, in his

---

[10] For example, a customer in a shop.
[11] For example, a theatre goer.
[12] For example, a firefighter.

annotation to the Act, outlines a pertinent example where s.4(3) might usefully be relied upon.[13] Where a person attains the status of a visitor by lawfully entering a public house during normal licensing hours and remains in the public house after closing time, he is committing a criminal offence. In that particular case, it might be in the interests of justice that he be entitled to recover. It is also to be noted that a visitor whose status has altered, to the extent that his presence on the land or premises becomes unlawful, maintains the status of visitor whilst taking reasonable steps to leave. A "visitor" to a restaurant, who becomes unruly and boisterous, may well be requested to leave by the management. If that visitor insists on remaining on the premises he becomes an effective trespasser. However, if the unruly visitor, having been requested to vacate the premises, turns to leave and trips over a tray lying negligently on the ground, he will be deemed to have retained the status of a visitor.

17–16   Section 3 of the 1995 Act establishes the duty of care which is owed by occupiers of premises to visitors:

> "3. (1) An occupier of premises owes a duty of care ('the common duty of care') towards a visitor thereto except in so far as the occupier extends, restricts, modifies or excludes that duty in accordance with section 5.
>
> (2) In this section 'the common duty of care' means a duty to take such care as is reasonable in all the circumstances (having regard to the care which a visitor may reasonably be expected to take for his or her own safety and, if the visitor is on the premises in the company of another person, the extent of the supervision and control the latter person may reasonably be expected to exercise over the visitor's activities) to ensure that a visitor to the premises does not suffer injury or damage by reason of any danger existing thereon."

17–17   In summary, the duty is the "common duty of care". Consequently, there is an obligation on the occupier to take reasonable care to ensure that the visitor does not suffer personal injury, or damage to his property, as a result of any danger existing on the premises. The "common duty of care" is, in fact, similar to the negligence standard at common law. Therefore, the effect of this provision is to apply general negligence principles to this area of the law. Consequently, before any liability may be imposed, there must be a breach of the duty which an occupier owes to a visitor and the damage suffered by the visitor must be caused by that breach. The duty owed will depend on the facts of each particular case and what is reasonable in all the circumstances.

17–18   The section appears to make particular provision for the care of children accompanied by an adult. It is reasonable for an occupier of a premises to assume that a child visitor, in the company of an adult visitor, will be supervised and controlled to some degree. However, it is most unlikely that this section will operate to relieve an occupier of any duty of care towards a child. It should be noted that historically the judicial approach in all courts towards the infant plaintiff has been sympathetic, to say the least, and

---

[13] *Irish Current Law Statutes Annotated* (Dublin, Round Hall Sweet and Maxwell, 1995), para.10–04.

particularly so where the infant plaintiff has suffered serious injury. An instructive case on the issue of child supervision and the standard of the care owed by an occupier is *Coffey v Moffit*.[14]

(2) Recreational user

17–19   An entirely new concept of recreational user was introduced in the 1995 Act. This creation resulted directly from representations and submissions from the farming lobby who feared being sued by such persons as hill walkers or persons visiting sites or buildings of historical significance. As McMahon J. in *Heaves v Westmeath County Council*[15] stated: "The [1995] Act was primarily introduced to reverse *McNamara v E.S.B.* [1975] IR 1 in respect of trespassers, and to create a new category for recreational users who were causing some concern to the agricultural community who feared that the common law might treat them too leniently by according to them the duty of reasonable care." The 1995 Act defines a "recreational user" as:

> "an entrant who, with or without the occupier's permission or at the occupier's implied invitation, is present on premises without a charge (other than a reasonable charge in respect of the cost of providing vehicle parking facilities) being imposed for the purpose of engaging in a recreational activity, including an entrant admitted without charge to a national monument pursuant to section 16(1) of the National Monuments Act, 1930, but not including an entrant who is so present and is-
>
> (a) a member of the occupier's family who is ordinarily resident on the premises,
> (b) an entrant who is present at the express invitation of the occupier or such a member, or
> (c) an entrant who is present with the permission of the occupier or such a member for social reasons connected with the occupier or such a member; ..."

17–20   The Act further defines recreational activity as:

> "any recreational activity conducted, whether alone or with others, in the open air (including any sporting activity), scientific research and nature study so conducted, exploring caves and visiting sites and buildings of historical, architectural, traditional, artistic, archaeological or scientific importance; ..."

Therefore, recreational users are those persons who, without payment of any charge, enter onto premises to engage in a recreational activity which is carried on in the open air. Such recreational users include individuals who engage in hill walking, hunting or swimming as well as a team sport such as football. The recreational user classification applies to those who visit sites or buildings of historical, national or scientific significance. It is worth noting that the fact that an occupier permits a recreational activity to be engaged in will not automatically result in the elevation of an entrant to the visitor status. This altered the common law position which pertained prior to July 17, 1995.

---

[14] Unreported, Circuit Court, McMahon J., June 17, 2005.
[15] Circuit Court, Mullingar, McMahon J., October 17, 2001.

17–21   Under the 1995 Act, to be classified as a recreational user the party in question must not pay in any way for the privilege of entry, save for a vehicle parking fee. It is noteworthy that the Act refers to a reasonable charge only. Consequently, a stately home which permits free entry to the house and grounds, but levies an exorbitant parking fee, would be most unlikely to fall within the ambit of the protection of this provision. A relevant and instructive case discussed at paragraph 17–54 is *Heaves v Westmeath County Council*.[16]

17–22   There will be cases where the distinction between visitor and recreational user will be unclear. For example, the status of a visitor to a scenic area who receives detailed guidelines and directions from the occupier or a member of his family, and on following the advice, sustains injury, could be open to question. This could well be construed as an "express invitation", thus elevating the recreational user to the status of visitor. It would be reasonable to conclude, however, that mere advice or the erection of a sign should not constitute an "express invitation", *urbi et orbi*, thus elevating the status of an entrant from recreational user to visitor.[17]

(3) Trespassers

17–23   A trespasser is defined in s.1(1) of the 1995 Act as an entrant other than a recreational user or visitor.[18]

(4) Duty owed to recreational users and trespassers

17–24   Section 4(1) of the 1995 Act provides that an occupier owes recreational users or trespassers on a premises a restricted duty not to impose injury or cause injury to be imposed on them. Further, he owes them a duty not to damage their property intentionally and not to act with reckless disregard for them or their property unless, and in so far as, the occupier has extended his duty in accordance with s.5 of the 1995 Act. In this category, negligence principles do not apply and the duty of the occupier is pitched at a lower level. In summary, this section adopts the approach that trespassers and recreational users should largely be able to take care of themselves. Therefore, occupiers will not be levied with liability under the 1995 Act, save where they intentionally cause injury to an entrant or behave with reckless disregard for the presence of an entrant. Landowners with national monuments on their property, which, of their nature, attract visitors are slow to accept responsibility for any injuries which such visitors might sustain, especially where no entrance fee is imposed for the visit. The fact that the monuments may not be

---

[16]   Circuit Court, Mullingar, McMahon J., October 17, 2001.

[17]   This should logically follow from the decision of Fitzgibbon J. in *Kenny v Electricity Supply Board* [1932] I.R. 73 at 84, wherein he commented that "an open gate or an unfenced field does not amount to an invitation or licence *urbi et orbi* to enter upon private property".

[18]   For a relevant and instructive case, see *Keith Williams v T.P. Wallace Construction Ltd*, unreported, High Court, Morris J., November 23, 2001, and, in particular, p.4 of the judgment.

in the best structural condition augments the concern of such landowners. It is submitted that the 1995 Act has remedied this situation.

17–25   In many cases, where intention is not necessarily clear cut, the greatest source of potential litigation will arise in determining whether an occupier has acted with reckless disregard for a recreational user or trespasser.

17–26   The Law Reform Commission in its Consultation Paper provisionally recommended that:

> "the duty of an occupier towards a trespasser (over 15 years of age) should be a duty not to injure the trespasser intentionally or to act with gross negligence towards the trespasser."[19]

The Law Reform Commission, in its final report, adhered to its provisional recommendation and advocated that this approach be adopted.[20] The legislature, however, more realistically adopted the reckless disregard standard. This duty of care, it is submitted, is less burdensome for the occupier. Interestingly, the duty imposed on similar classes of persons in the analogous UK legislation, the UK Occupiers' Liability Act 1984, is higher.

17–27   What is reckless disregard? Henchy J. in *People (DPP) v Murray*[21] stated that recklessness exists in circumstances where a person "consciously disregards a substantial and unjustifiable risk. Such a risk must involve culpability to a high degree". Having discussed the concept of recklessness, the act of recklessness is to be determined according to a range of factors specified in s.4(2) of the 1995 Act.

(a) Recklessness and the factors specified in section 4(2)
17–28   "**(a) Whether the occupier knew of or had reasonable grounds for believing that a danger existed on the premises**"

It falls to be considered what level of foresight is required by the phrase "knew" or "had reasonable grounds for believing". The test to be adopted would appear to be objective as opposed to subjective. That said, is "knew" or "ought to have known" not a higher standard than "knew" or "reasonable grounds"? Clearly, this applies to several other factors.

17–29   "**(b) Whether the occupier knew or had reasonable grounds for believing that the person and, in the case of damage, property of the person, was or was likely to be on the premises**"

and

---

[19] The Law Reform Commission, *Consultation Paper On Occupiers' Liability* (Dublin, The Law Reform Commission, June, 1993) p.9.

[20] The Law Reform Commission, *Report On Occupiers' Liability* (Number 46) (Dublin, The Law Reform Commission, 1994), p.38.

[21] [1977] I.R. 360 at 403.

> **"(c) Whether the occupier knew or had reasonable grounds for believing that the person or property of the person was in, or was likely to be in, the vicinity of the place where the danger existed"**

With regard to (b) and (c) there is no obligation imposed upon a court under s.4(2) to dismiss a case by either a trespasser or a recreational user whose presence on the premises, or in the vicinity of the premises, was not highly foreseeable. Under the common law rules that pertained prior to July 17, 1995, the judiciary demanded a high degree of forseeability.

17–30   **"(d) Whether the danger was one against which, in all the circumstances, the occupier might reasonably be expected to provide protection for the person and property of the person"**

and

> **"(e) The burden on the occupier of eliminating the danger or of protecting the person and property of the person from the danger, taking into account the difficulty, expense or impracticability, having regard to the character of the premises and the degree of the danger, of so doing"**

Both (d) and (e) can be considered together and merely demand the usual balancing test that is a requirement in any assessment of what constitutes negligence. In fact, (d) virtually replicates a provision in s.1(3) of the UK Occupiers' Liability Act 1984. Interestingly, (d) could be viewed as incorporating in spirit the test enunciated by Hand J., where he suggested that the formula $B < P \times L$ be utilised in negligence assessment.[22] In this equation, B denotes the liability if the event occurs, P the cost of remedying the defect before the harm is caused and L the risk of that harm occurring.

The application of factors (d) and (e) will vary, depending on the situation. For example, in so far as trespassers may be a danger on the premises, that danger must be one against which an occupier might reasonably be expected to provide full protection. Mounting an ordinary fence would not be such a danger. Further, the burden on the occupier of eliminating the danger, bearing in mind its degree, must be balanced against the difficulty, expense or impracticability of doing so. For example, an occupier with a large lake on his premises would not be expected to erect a wall around it to ensure that a recreational user or trespasser did not fall in.

17–31   **"(f) The character of the premises including, in relation to premises of such a character as to be likely to be used for recreational activity, the desirability of maintaining the tradition of open access to premises of such a character for such an activity"**

The central factor to be taken into account in ground (f) is the character of the premises and the desirability of maintaining open access for those premises where they are likely to be used for recreational activities. Therefore, the same burden of protection will not be expected of the occupier of a working farm or wilderness as will be expected in the case of the occupier of a building which

---

[22] See *United States v Carol Towing* Co. 159 F.201 169 (Second Circuit, January 9, 1947).

was specifically designed to attract visitors. Further, where structures are provided permanently for recreational use, there is an obligation on the occupier to take reasonable care to ensure that they are maintained in a safe condition. It should be mentioned that such structures do not include gates and stiles which would be used in the ordinary course of farming. Rather, they include such structures as benches in parks on which people may sit, secured viewing points in scenic areas and equipment provided for use in playgrounds.

17–32   This clause embodies the spirit and purpose of the legislation. It should act as a reminder to the court that if too onerous a duty is imposed on occupiers under this heading, the inevitable result will be the withdrawal by occupiers of admittance to their lands, thus defeating one of the primary purposes of the 1995 Act.

17–33   **"(g)   The conduct of the person, and the care which he or she may reasonably be expected to take for his or her own safety, while on the premises, having regard to the extent of his or her knowledge thereof"**

and

      "(h)   The nature of any warning given by the occupier or another person of the danger"

and

      "(i)   Whether or not the person was on the premises in the company of another person and, if so, the extent of the supervision and control the latter person might reasonably be expected to exercise over the other's activities"

Barry Doherty, in his annotations to the Act, observes that a specific clause in this section governing minors and the disabled was omitted at a late stage in the passage of the then Bill through the Oireachtas.[23] Clauses (g) to (i) were then inserted to remedy this perceived defect in the legislation. Together, unlike the paragraphs considered previously, these sections collectively call for a subjective test as opposed to the objective test mentioned in paragraphs (a), (b) and (c) above.

17–34   In particular, paragraph (g) would appear to have some relevance to the case of so-called "guilty" trespassers. Paragraph (h), while not requiring a warning, makes provision for credit to be given to occupiers who provide warnings; always assuming that such warnings are adequate and reasonable in the circumstances. Further, unlike the other paragraphs in s.4(2), this paragraph has greater relevance to visitors. Paragraph (i) transfers some responsibility to parents and guardians in the care and control of minors, which would have the practical implication of reducing, however slight, the onus or duty of care on occupiers. Previously, the position in this area is that regard had to be

---

[23]   *Irish Current Law Statutes Annotated* (Dublin, Round Hall Sweet and Maxwell, 1995), para.10–06.

had both to the age and to the ability to appreciate the danger, in circumstances where minors were, in what would be regarded under the 1995 Act as, recreational users or trespassers. The 1995 Act does not state that an occupier owes a minor a common duty of care. Nor does it mention that the occupier is strictly liable for whatever accident may befall such an entrant. Indeed, the Act introduced additional criteria which make it clear that in circumstances where a minor is on the premises and is in the company of another person, the extent of the supervision and control which that person might reasonably be expected to exercise over the minor's activities will be relevant in determining whether an occupier has acted with reckless disregard.

Modification of occupiers' duties to entrants

17–35   Under s.5(1) of the 1995 Act an occupier of a premises may, by express agreement or notice, extend his duty towards entrants under ss.3 and 4. Trespassers are the category most likely to rely on this particular section as the duty of care owing to them is quite low. "Agreement" in s.1(1) of the 1995 Act is not defined. That said, it could be contended that in the absence of an express or written agreement extending the duty, the courts should be reluctant to find that the duty has, in fact, been extended by the occupier. In reality, occupiers are most unlikely to voluntarily assume a higher duty of care towards entrants than that provided for in the legislation.

17–36   Section 5(2) of the 1995 Act provides that an occupier may restrict, modify or exclude his duty towards visitors under s.3. This restriction is clearly stated to be applicable to visitors only and does not apply to recreational users or trespassers. In effect, by complying with the section, occupiers may reduce the duties they owe to visitors to the level owed to recreational users and trespassers. However, s.5(3) states, irrespective of a danger existing on the premises, the restrictions, modifications or exclusions referred to in s.5(2) shall not allow an occupier to injure a visitor, or damage his or her property intentionally, or to act with reckless disregard for a visitor or his or her property. This section enshrines the absolute minimum duty of care owed by an occupier to an entrant. The duty owing to a visitor may never fall below that owing to recreational users or trespassers. In summary, an occupier is precluded from excluding liability.

17–37   Under s.5(2)(b), a modification or exclusion *shall not* be binding on a visitor unless: (1) it is reasonable in all the circumstances, and (2) the occupier has taken reasonable steps to bring the notice to the attention of the visitor. Adequacy and sufficiency of notice in particular cases has long troubled the judicial mind. In relation to exclusion clauses, Lord Denning M.R. stated for certain notices to be effective the equivalent of a "red hand" would be required before the court would uphold such a clause.[24] Perhaps, with this in mind, the legislature provided in s.5(2)(c) that, for the purposes of s.5(2)(b)(ii), an occupier

---

[24] See *Spurling Ltd v Bradshaw* [1956] 1 W.L.R. 461 at 466.

shall be presumed, unless the contrary is shown, to have taken reasonable steps to bring a notice to the attention of a visitor if it is prominently displayed at the normal means of access to the premises. Nonetheless, this is a rebuttable presumption. It should not be taken to mean, even if a prominent notice was not displayed at the normal means of access, that a visitor can never be alerted by other means. For example, if a large geographical area is involved, with numerous unauthorised means of access, the mere erection of notices might not only be impractical but also insufficient.

17–38   Section 5(5) provides:

> "Where injury or damage is caused to a visitor or property of a visitor by a danger of which the visitor had been warned by the occupier or another person, the warning is not, without more, to be treated as absolving the occupier from liability unless, in all the circumstances, it was enough to enable the visitor, by having regard to the warning, to avoid the injury or damage so caused."

Considering the matter of notices, Professor William Binchy reflected on how a court should view a situation where an occupier puts up a notice which states:

> "No liability shall attach to the occupiers of these lands in respect of any injury sustained on these lands by any visitor, recreational user or trespasser, howsoever caused."[25]

It is clear from s.5(3) of the 1995 Act that the effect of a proper notice, assuming it is effective and binding, can only operate to reduce the duty of care owed to visitors to that lower and more restricted duty which is owed to recreational users and trespassers. Yet, this sample notice purports to exclude liability. It is conceivable that a visitor on seeing such a notice could reasonably form the view that the notice was so badly drafted that it could not possibly be correct; thus, conceivably, the visitor could assume that it had no legal value and could proceed to ignore it altogether. Professor Binchy considers and rejects this interpretation and proffers the view that the notice should be effective but interpreted as restricting the occupiers' liability in so far as s.5(3) permits, but no further. In *Marcelle Baldwin v Grainne Foy and Forest Way Riding Holidays Ltd*,[26] Laffoy J. considered two notices present on a premises. The first notice from the Association of Irish Riding Establishments excluded liability for any accident whatsoever arising out of the activity carried out on the premises:

> "The Association of Irish Riding Establishments Scheme for the registration of riding establishments is a voluntary non-statutory scheme under which the Association has set up and maintains a register of riding establishments which have been inspected by the Association and the owners of which have been advised of A.I.R.E.'s minimum requirements in relation to the provision of facilities, equipment, supervision, safety requirements, insurance, etc. Non-compliance by a riding establishment with these standards would automatically result in cancellation of the registration of that riding establishment. The A.I.R.E. wishes

---

[25] Binchy W., *Practical Implications of the Occupiers' Liability Act, 1995*, Continuing Legal Education Seminar of the Law Society of Ireland, March 13, 1996, p.25.

[26] Unreported, High Court, Laffoy J., July 1, 1997.

to make it clear that it cannot accept legal liability in respect of any accident, howsoever caused, arising out of the operation of any riding establishment."

The second notice stated:

"Riding is a risk sport. Your choice to ride is voluntary. We take care to provide suitable and safe horses and ponies for our customers, but all animals can be unpredictable. We strongly advise you to take out full personal accident cover."

Laffoy J. held that the foregoing notices did not exclude liability for negligence. It would appear therefore that to benefit from the notice procedure available under s.5(2) of the 1995 Act, a notice must be clear, unambiguous and specific.[27]

Duty of occupiers to strangers to contracts

17–39   There are many situations, particularly large developments or schemes of work involving local authorities, schools, hospitals, housing developments and such like, where an occupier of land will enter into a contract with a main contractor or master builder to effect certain works. These contracts should, and no doubt often do, avail of the 1995 Act to modify the liability that would otherwise arise pursuant to s.3 of that Act. The main contractor may then enter into subsequent agreements with independent contractors, builders, plumbers, electricians, block layers and such like, who will enter onto the premises, and, in many cases, undertake a significant proportion of the work. Often, the original contract between the occupier and main contractor will envisage or even require that these independent contractors enter onto the property of the occupier. That said, there is no direct contractual nexus or connection between the occupier and these third parties. In short, there is no privity of contract.

17–40   Section 6(1) of the 1995 Act provides that the duty which an occupier of premises owes to an entrant shall not be capable of being modified or excluded by a contract to which the entrant is a stranger. Enshrined in s.6 is the basic principle, which is now common to most other European jurisdictions, namely, that strangers to a contract should not have their status adversely affected by contracts to which they themselves are not a party. This is the position irrespective of whether or not the occupier is bound by the contract to permit the entrant to enter onto or use the premises. (It is interesting to note that s.6 is retrospective.) The Act is silent, however, as to a situation where the principal contract between the occupier and the main contractor provides that the main contractor's subsequent contracts with these strangers shall modify the liability that would otherwise arise not only for the main contractor but also the occupier. However, it is worth noting that an occupier may still achieve the same result by utilising s.5 of the 1995 Act. In particular, the occupier could avail of the notice procedure described previously or enter into express agreements limiting liability.

---

[27] For sample notice, see Part II of this book.

17–41   Section 5(2)(b)(i), which provides that a restriction, modification or exclusion *shall not* bind a visitor, unless it is reasonable in all the circumstances, might be used to challenge either the notice procedure or direct agreements between occupiers and independent contractors. It is arguable that it would be open to an independent contractor under s.6(1) of the 1995 Act to contend that the duty under the Act is not capable of being modified or excluded and, that to allow an occupier to achieve indirectly what he would be unable to achieve directly, should not be permissible. A defence to this submission would appear to be that the Act expressly provides for both the notice procedure and for modification by agreement. Safeguards have also been inserted in the notice and agreement opt-out provisions. For example, such notices and agreements must be "reasonable in all the circumstances", reasonable steps must be taken to bring the notice to the attention of the visitor and the standard of care owing to a visitor can never be reduced below that owing to recreational users and trespassers.

Liability of occupiers for the negligence of independent contractors

17–42   Under s.7 of the 1995 Act an occupier of premises shall not be liable for injury or damage caused to an entrant or his property by reason of a danger existing on the premises due to the negligence of an independent contractor employed by the occupier, provided that the occupier has taken all reasonable care in the circumstances. The section specifies that reasonable care includes the occupier taking such steps as he ought reasonably to take. In drafting this section the legislature followed the same principle as was manifest in an analogous provision in s.6(1) of Ontario's Occupiers' Liability Act 1980. Section 7 of the 1995 Act, while extending some comfort and protection to occupiers, in so far as independent contractors are concerned, does not provide a complete defence to occupiers where their independent contractors are negligent. Essentially, the occupier must take reasonable steps to ensure that the independent contractor is competent. In many respects, s.7 is somewhat academic as, in practice, many independent contractors will be exercising control over the state of the premises while working therein. Therefore, pursuant to s.1(1) of the 1995 Act, independent contractors could themselves fall within the definition of an occupier. An independent contractor would always incur liability under the ordinary rules of negligence.

Retention of other enactments and rules of law

17–43   Section 8 of the 1995 Act has been referred to previously and is worthy of more detailed analysis. The whole purpose of the Occupiers' Liability Act 1995 was to redress what was perceived as the unreasonable imposition of burdensome obligations on occupiers. It is clear that the legislature in their efforts to achieve this objective were concerned that other protections for entrants onto land would remain unaffected. It was for this reason that s.8 was inserted. The section identifies three specific areas, which now fall to be considered.

(1) Self defence, the defence of others or the defence of property

17–44 Section 8(a) retains the pre-existing law that an occupier is permitted to use reasonable and proportionate force to defend his or her property.

(2) Any liability imposed on an occupier as a member of a particular class of persons

17–45 Three examples are listed in s.8(b). It should be noted that this list is not exhaustive. The Law Reform Commission in its Report identifies hotel proprietors as an example of a class of persons to be considered under this subsection.[28] Hotel proprietors are not, however, mentioned specifically in the 1995 Act. Section 4 of the Hotel Proprietors Act 1963 provides that where a person is received as a guest at a hotel, the proprietor is under a duty to take reasonable care of the person of the guest and to ensure that for the purpose of personal use by the guest, the premises are "as safe as reasonable care and skill can make them". Section 6 of the 1963 Act relates to liability for property of the guest. Section 8 of the 1995 Act specifically provides that the foregoing duties are independent of any liability of the proprietor as occupier of the premises. In summary, the saver contained in s.8(b) of the 1995 Act clearly leaves the protections included in the 1963 Act intact.

17–46 Section 8(b) also provides for the retention of the common law duty of care an employer owes to an employee. For example, employers owe a specific duty to their employees to provide them with safe premises, independently of any duty they may owe to them as occupiers.[29] Section 8 makes it clear that the statutory prescription of occupiers' liability does not affect this type of duty.

(3) Ultra-hazardous activities

17–47 Section 8(c) copper-fastens the protection which employees have at common law where ultra-hazardous activities are concerned. Where such ultra-hazardous activities are involved, the occupier may not delegate his obligations at common law to, for example, an independent contractor.

Occupiers' Liability Act 1995 – its operation since inception

17–48 The Occupiers' Liability Act 1995, as previously stated, came into effect on July 17, 1995. McCracken J., delivering judgment in the High Court in the case of *Ann Thomas v The County Council of the County of Leitrim,*[30]

---

[28] The Law Reform Commission, *Report On Occupiers' Liability* (No. 46) (Dublin, The Law Reform Commission, 1994) p.40.

[29] This duty has already been alluded to in detail at para.3–22 of this book.

[30] Unreported, High Court, 1995.

held that while the Occupiers' Liability Act 1995 abolished the old distinctions between licensees and invitees, the 1995 Act could not be applied retrospectively in that case.[31]

17–49   Since the Occupiers' Liability Act 1995 came into operation it has given rise to a distinctive body of jurisprudence. It must be noted as a preliminary point that the plaintiff must prove that the facts allow for the application of the Act. As has already been noted, the ideology of the Act has been to hand power back to the occupier and this has certainly been carried out in practice.

One may have to ask the question "who is an occupier?" Section 1(1) of the Act seeks to define the word in the following terms:

> "a person exercising such control over the state of the premises that it is reasonable to impose upon that person a duty towards an entrant in respect of a particular danger thereon and, where there is more than one occupier of the same premises, the extent of the duty of each occupier towards an entrant depends on the degree of control each of them has over the state of the premises and the particular danger thereon and whether, as respects each of them, the entrant concerned is a visitor, recreational user or trespasser".

17–50   This issue was adverted to by McMahon J. in *Ashmore v Dublin Land Securities Ltd and Dublin Corporation*.[32] Although the incident occurred prior to the commencement of the Act, the approach of McMahon J. is instructive. Here, the plaintiff sustained personal injuries while walking across an uneven forecourt. He relied on the concept of control to define who "occupied" the premises. On the facts, it was held that Dublin Corporation had no case to answer as the Corporation had no dealings with the premises. McMahon J. also indicated that if it had carried out repair or other maintenance works in such a way as to have caused the plaintiff to trip, then it could not be said to have assumed control of the premises for the purposes of the common law rules. The first named defendant, Dublin Land Securities Ltd, was the owner of the forecourt but had no other material dealings with it. It was submitted that the Act's definition of occupier essentially equated with the common law concept of control. The submission was rejected in the following terms:

> "I am not convinced that the new statutory definition reflects exactly the common law position in this regard. It may be true that in determining what control is required to bring one within the definition, the pre-1995 emphasis on the ability to exclude and the ability to fix the defect will be helpful, but the amalgam of the responsibility and control issues in the new definition complicates the threshold characterisation that was the primary concern of the common law. In particular, when addressing the position where there is more than one occupier of the same premises, the definition states that the extent of the duty may vary from occupier to occupier depending on the variety of factors listed under section 3. I am not, therefore, prepared to assume, without further argument, that the effect of the legislation was only to confirm the common law definition and for this

---

[31] See Gayer S., "Visitor to Tourist Amenity is Invitee Under Former Occupiers' Liability Law" *The Irish Times*, April 6, 1998.
[32] Unreported, Circuit Court, McMahon J., January 14, 2003.

reason, I am not prepared to rely on the statutory definition to retrospectively inform the court as to what the pre-1995 definition was in that regard. No doubt the definition of occupier given in the new Act will engage courts in the future, but, given the task I am faced with in this case, I do not find the statutory definition to be of any assistance. If I were pushed and if the same factual situation had arisen after the Act came into force, I would, at first blush, conclude that the first defendant was also an occupier under the Act."[33]

Although the above statement is speculative in nature and thus *obiter*, the passage is useful in that it clarifies the distinction between the common law and legislative rules. Whereas the issue of control was determinative under the previous regime, the new rules emphasise responsibility as well as mere control. This has particular implications for plaintiffs seeking to join more than one party to an action.

17–51   In terms of the types of premises covered by the Act, *Weldon v Fingal Coaches*[34] is instructive. Ó Caoimh J. noted how the Act applies to vehicles as well as premises in the more traditional sense. This case concerned injuries sustained by the plaintiff when he fell out of the luggage compartment of a mini bus while coming home from a night club as was the practice among some night club patrons. The incident was held to come within the remit of the Act given the wide meaning of premises.

17–52   Of crucial importance in the new legislative scheme is the concept of structural defects. Instructive in this regard is *Sheehy v Devils Glen*.[35] In this case the plaintiff was visiting the defendant's premises when she tripped and fell over a door saddle resulting in severe personal injuries. Lavan J. held that the door saddle did constitute a danger due to the state of the premises. Consequently the defendant was held liable.

17–53   One of the most interesting cases to have been decided in this area is *McGovern v Dunnes Stores*.[36] In this case the plaintiff sought damages having tripped over a plastic clothes hanger which was lying on the floor of the defendant's premises. McMahon J. held that the Act did not apply given that the cause of the accident was not due to a structural defect. The passage is worth quoting in full, as the issue addressed has major implications for litigation in this area:

> "At the outset, it is important to note that this is not a case which falls to be determined under the provisions of the Occupiers' Liability Act, 1995. That Act sets out the principles that apply when a person is injured because of a structural defect on the occupier's premises. The plaintiff's allegation here is that she tripped or slipped on a clothes hanger which was lying on the floor of the store. There was no complaint about a structural defect in this case and so ordinary negligence principles govern the situation."[37]

---

[33] *ibid.* p.5.
[34] Unreported, High Court, Ó Caoimh J., January 25, 2001.
[35] Unreported, High Court, Lavan J., December 10, 2001.
[36] Unreported, Circuit Court, McMahon J., March 6, 2003.
[37] *ibid.* p.2.

What this demonstrates is that any act or omission on the part of an occupier, short of one relating to the structural state of the premises, will not fall to be considered within the Occupiers' Liability Act 1995. Consequently, the general principles of negligence set out by the Supreme Court in *Glencar Exploration plc v Mayo County Council (No. 2)*[38] apply to such cases.

17–54   The next issue which may pose a difficulty for a plaintiff is the category that he or she may fall into. This has implications for the nature of the duty owed to him or her—the highest duty is owed visitors; the lowest to trespassers. While the Occupiers' Liability Act 1995 provides definitions on how one may qualify as a particular kind of entrant, case law is also instructive. For example, *Heaves v Westmeath County Council*[39] considered this issue. In this case the plaintiff lawfully entered onto property owned by the defendant. While there, he slipped and suffered injury. The main issue at the trial was over his status—was he a visitor or recreational user? It was submitted by counsel for the plaintiff that he was squarely within the definition of visitor, whereas the defence argued in the alternative based on the payment of a fee, which they claimed was a parking fee, and not an entrance fee. However, as the fee would have been payable in the event that the plaintiff had not availed of car parking facilities, it could not under any logical construction of the statute be considered to be a parking fee. Thus, the plaintiff was held to be a visitor. McMahon J. made an important observation on the law as follows:

> "[E]ngaging in a recreational activity does not necessarily and invariably make him a recreational user. The Act is clear in declaring that if an entrant comes to the premises under a contract and pays a charge he is a visitor, and only a visitor. In this legislative classification it is important to remember that there are three, and only three categories; these categories are exhaustive; there are no more categories. Furthermore, it is equally important to realise that an entrant cannot be in two categories at the same time."[40]

17–55   With regard to the distinction between visitor and trespasser, notice should be taken of *Williams v T.P. Wallace Construction Ltd.*[41] The plaintiff claimed that he had been present on a roof at the defendant's construction site with the permission of one of their workmen. Morris J. held on the basis of the evidence that he did not have the requisite permission to ground a claim as a visitor and therefore was held to be a trespasser. Despite the learned judge not indulging in any dissection of the legal principles involved, his approach to the issue is illuminating in that it shows current judicial attitudes and approaches to the issue. The plaintiff will have to adduce evidence, on the balance of probabilities, that he or she falls within a particular category. The finding as to which category he or she belongs to at law will be based on the oral testimony received at trial and counsel's submissions will have limited impact upon this determination. However, once the appropriate categorisation is determined,

---

[38] [2002] 1 I.R. 84.
[39] Circuit Court, Mullingar, McMahon J., October 17, 2001.
[40] *ibid.* p.4.
[41] Unreported, High Court, Morris J., 23 November 2001.

judges must then follow the scheme of the Act in determining the duty owed. The question of whether or not this duty was breached will also be an issue of evidence. Thus, it is clear that unlike the common law of negligence or other torts, there is little room for judicial creativity or activism in standard setting.

17–56   The case of *Geraldine Weir-Rogers v The S.F. Trust Ltd*[42] deals with the concept of recklessness under the Occupiers' Liability Act 1995. Here, the plaintiff was walking on a cliff owned by the defendant. She entered onto a part of the cliff at which there was broken fencing, and trodden grass leading her to believe that there was a path leading to the edge. She took this route before she rested in the area for some time. She then decided to go back to the restaurant where she had been dining. However, on standing up she slipped and slid down the stony gradient of the cliff face. In the High Court, Herbert J. found her to have been a recreational user, and that the defendant was liable and awarded the plaintiff €113,000, to be reduced by the plaintiff's contributory negligence of 25 per cent. In particular, he noted that the defendant should have erected a notice warning the public of the danger posed by the cliff, but rejected the contention that there should have been a fence erected so as to prevent the public gaining access to it. In the Supreme Court, Geoghegan J. held for the appellant trust. He held the test of recklessness in the context of the Act to mean objective, and not subjective, recklessness. As a result, it was held by the court that the respondent was not acting recklessly in not having erected full protective fencing or indeed erecting a warning notice. Geoghegan J. took cognisance of the argument that someone who uses land adjoining the sea should be aware of the potential dangers which would ordinarily arise from such use:

> "It is perfectly obvious to all users of land higher than sea level but adjoining the sea that there may well be a dangerous cliff edge and, in those circumstances, the occupier of the lands cannot be held to be unreasonable in not putting up a warning notice."[43]

Exceptional circumstances may in some cases raise the duty on occupiers to bring the danger to the attention of the user, but this should not ordinarily be the case:

> "The person sitting down near a cliff must be prepared for oddities in the cliff's structure or in the structure of the ground adjacent to the cliff and he or she assumes the inherent risks associated therewith. There could, of course, be something quite exceptionally unusual and dangerous in the state of a particular piece of ground which would impose a duty on the occupier the effect of which would be that if he did not put up a warning notice he would be treated as having reckless disregard."[44]

The successful appeal is of major importance to individual users and occupiers concerned with the "right to roam". It essentially states that unless some inherent danger on the land is known to the occupier and is not readily detectable by the user using common sense, then no liability will fall on the occupier because the

---

[42] [2005] 1 I.R. 47.
[43] *ibid.* at p.57.
[44] *ibid.* at p.58.

Oireachtas has chosen reckless disregard as the appropriate standard of care applicable to recreational users and trespassers.

The *ex tempore* judgment of the Supreme Court in *Raleigh v Iarnród Éireann*[45] provides further evidence that plaintiffs face significant obstacles in establishing that an occupier has acted with reckless disregard pursuant to s.4 of the 2005 Act. In that case, the plaintiff failed in his action to obtain compensation for injuries he sustained when he was hit by a train after he fell asleep close to a railway track, having consumed "a feed of alcoholic drink".

17–57 The Occupiers' Liability Act 1995 is broadly similar to the Occupiers' Liability Act 1984 (U.K.), which substantially amended the provisions of the Occupiers' Liability Act 1957 (UK). Thus, it might prove instructive to consider decisions handed down by the courts in that jurisdiction. It should be mentioned, however, that such decisions are not binding upon our courts. That said, such decisions, particularly of the House of Lords, would be of persuasive authority in this jurisdiction.

17–58 The duty owed to persons engaged in outdoor activities was addressed by the House of Lords in *Tomlinson v Congleton Borough Council*.[46] Lord Hutton cited with approval the Scottish case of *Stevenson v Corporation of Glasgow* where Lord M'Laren stated:

> "in a town, as well as in the country, there are physical features which may be productive of injury to careless persons or to young children against which it is impossible to guard by protective measures. The situation of a town on the banks of a river is a familiar feature; and whether the stream be sluggish like the Clyde at Glasgow, or swift and variable like the Ness at Inverness, or the Tay at Perth, there is always danger to the individual who may be so unfortunate as to fall into the stream. But in none of these places has it been found necessary to fence the river to prevent children or careless persons from falling into the water. Now, as the common law is just the formal statement of the results and conclusions of the common sense of mankind, I come without difficulty to the conclusion that precautions which have been rejected by common sense as unnecessary and inconvenient are not required by the law."[47]

17–59 In this regard, the Northern Irish case of *McGeown v Northern Ireland Housing Executive*[48] is worthy of consideration. The facts of the case are easily stated. Josephine McGeown, the plaintiff, resided on the Twinbrook estate in Belfast and was the wife of the tenant of number 3, Juniper Court. The defendants were the owners and occupiers of a public area and pathway which they had provided as a means of access for the plaintiff to her residence. In December of 1985, whilst walking along that public area, Mrs McGeown tripped in a hole and fell, sustaining serious personal injury. The land on which the accident occurred was partly flagged, and partly grass covered, and was in the ownership of the defendants. This land was crossed by three footpaths.

---

[45] *Ex tempore* judgment of the Supreme Court of 30 November 2006.
[46] [2004] A.C. 46.
[47] 1908, S.C. 1034 at p.1039.
[48] [1994] 3 W.L.R. 187.

It was found as a fact by the trial judge that the public had acquired a right of way over these footpaths. The accident occurred on the most central of these footpaths.

17–60   Mrs McGeown sued the Northern Ireland Housing Executive claiming, *inter alia*, that she was a "visitor", and as such, was owed the duty of care provided for by ss.1 and 2 of the Occupiers' Liability (Northern Ireland) Act 1957. The defendants denied liability. Both the lower court and the Court of Appeal dismissed her contention that she was a visitor and the case came before the House of Lords. Lord Keith of Kinkel, in dismissing the appeal, relied heavily on *Greenhalgh v British Railways Board*[49] and *Gautret v Egerton*[50]. The case of *Gautret v Egerton* is a long-standing authority for the proposition that the owner of land over which a public right of way passes is under no liability for negligent non-feasance towards members of the public using it. The House of Lords provided that if Mrs McGeown was a visitor she was owed a duty of care under the 1957 Act. Lord Keith of Kinkel referred to Lord Denning M.R. in *Greenhalgh v British Railways Board*:

> "A person is a 'visitor' if at common law he would be regarded as an invitee or licensee; or be treated as such, as for instance, a person lawfully using premises provided for the use of the public, e.g., a public park, or a person entering by lawful authority, e.g., a policeman with a search warrant. But a 'visitor' does not include a person who crosses land in pursuance of a public or private right of way. Such a person was never regarded as an invitee or licensee, or treated as such."[51]

Lord Denning M.R. further stated that s.2 of the 1957 Act only defines the extent of the occupiers' duty to acknowledged visitors:

> "It does not extend the range of persons who are to be treated as visitors. Section 2(6) applies, for instance, to persons who enter a public park, or a policeman who enters on a search warrant, for they enter in the exercise of a right conferred by law and are treated as if they were invitees or licensees. They are acknowledged 'visitors'. ... Applying these considerations, it is apparent that Mrs. Greenhalgh was not a 'visitor' of the railways board. She was a person who was exercising a public right of way and to her the board owed no duty under the Occupiers' Liability Act."[52]

Lord Keith held:

> "If the pathway on which the plaintiff fell in the present case had not become subject to a public right of way it seems clear that the defendants would have owed her the common duty of care under the Act of 1957 and would have been liable accordingly."[53]

---

[49] [1969] 2 Q.B. 286.
[50] (1867) L.R. 2 C.P. 371.
[51] [1969] 2 Q.B. 286 at 292–293.
[52] [1994] 3 W.L.R. 187.
[53] *ibid.* at 192.

Therefore, the plaintiff was held not to be a "visitor" within the meaning of the Act and her claim was dismissed. Reverting to the Irish Occupiers' Liability Act 1995, it is clear that the Irish definition of "visitor" (leaving aside a consideration of "recreational user" for the moment) also incorporates the concept of invitation and permission of the occupier. Would it not then be the situation that a similar case on similar facts would have a similar outcome in this jurisdiction? When one considers the vast areas in Ireland over which the public enjoy a right of way or the right to pass, this would appear to exclude significant areas from the remit of the 1995 Act.

17–61   Unlike the United Kingdom, the Irish 1995 Act incorporates the concept of recreational user. Would Mrs McGeown have come within the definition of recreational user in this jurisdiction? The plaintiff in that case was walking to her house. It is, therefore, not certain that this purpose would necessarily fall within the definition of "recreational activity" in s.1(1) of the Occupiers' Liability Act 1995. Further, even if a plaintiff, such as Mrs McGeown, was to fall within the definition of recreational user in this jurisdiction, the duty owed to her by the occupier would only be not to injure her, or damage her property intentionally, or act with reckless disregard for her personal safety or that of her property.

17–62   Lord Browne-Wilkinson, in *McGeown*, while concurring in the dismissal of the appeal, was concerned by this issue. He noted, for example, that the public can acquire a public right of way over a shopping centre.[54] Lord Browne-Wilkinson stated:

> "To my mind it would be unfortunate if, as a result of the decision in this case, the owner of a railway bridge or shopping centre could, by expressly dedicating the land as a public highway or submitting to long public user, free himself from all liability to users whose presence he had encouraged. Who, other than the occupier, is to maintain these artificial structures and protect from injury those encouraged to use them by the occupier for the occupier's own business reasons?

> For these reasons, I am reluctant to reach a conclusion which will leave unprotected those who, for purposes linked to the business of the owners of the soil, are encouraged, expressly or impliedly, to use facilities which the owner has provided."[55]

However, the view of the author is that the Irish courts are likely to interpret the 1995 Act in a broader manner than the House of Lords did in the foregoing case.

Occupiers' Liability Act 1995 – the underwriting experience

17–63   The Occupiers' Liability Act 1995 makes generous provisions for occupiers of land who wish to modify or limit the duty of care owing by them

---

[54] See *Cumbernauld and Kilsyth District Council v Dollor Land (Cumbernauld) Ltd* (1993) S.L.T. 1318.
[55] [1994] 3 W.L.R. 197.

to "visitors". This modification may be achieved by express agreement or by notice. The use of notices is not new. Section 7 of the Hotel Proprietors Act 1963 provides for the limitation of liability of hotel owners by the erection of a notice in the form prescribed in the First Schedule to that Act. The hotel industry has been assiduous in encouraging its members to avail of the benefits of the Hotel Proprietors Act 1963.

17–64   As a matter of general observation, occupiers do not appear to have utilised the possible benefits to them of the 1995 Act. It may be the case that as occupiers become more aware of the benefits available under the Act, perhaps through the passage of time, or the public attention consequent on a future High Court case, this will change.

17–65   Insurance companies do not appear to have encouraged compliance with the 1995 Act. The writer knows of no scheme where insurance companies offer discounts or other benefits to occupiers who seek to limit their (and their insurers) duty of care to visitors under the Act. It is worth noting that, irrespective of the attitude of insurance companies, it would benefit occupiers directly to avail of the benefits provided for under the Act. The fewer the claims against an occupier, the lower his or her annual premium will be. Further, many policies provide for the payment of an excess premium by an occupier, and if an insurance company can defeat a claim by using the Act, this will directly benefit the occupier in that he will not be liable for the excess premium. There is anecdotal evidence to suggest that insurance companies do not give credit to occupiers for compliance with the Act. Rather, they are primarily concerned with the use to which the land is put, the turnover of the business, the number of employees and, above all, the claims history.

17–66   The insurance industry view would appear to be that the Occupiers' Liability Act 1995 has not had an impact upon the level and frequency of claims. It is debatable whether this is attributable to any deficiencies in the Act or is, rather, a complete failure by all interested parties to utilise the benefits of the Act.

CHAPTER 18

ENFORCEMENT

INTRODUCTION

18–01   The sanctions provided under the Safety Health and Welfare at Work Act 2005 are significantly greater than those provided under the 1989 Act. Given the fact that breaches would be technical in nature, it was logical for the 1989 Act to vest responsibility for enforcement in a new administrative body, namely the National Authority for Occupational Safety and Health. Part V of the 2005 Act provides for the continuance in being of the National Authority for Occupational Safety and Health, although it is now to be known as the Health and Safety Authority (the Authority). Section 33 of the 2005 Act enables the Minister to prescribe persons, natural or legal, to perform functions in lieu of the Authority.[1] To date, however, only the Authority itself has been so authorised to enforce the provisions of the Act. Under s.34 of the 2005 Act, the principal functions of the Authority include the enforcement of the relevant statutory provisions and the prevention of accidents. Parts VI and VII of the 2005 Act provide the Authority with its metaphorical teeth.

Inspectors

18–02   As under the 1989 Act, the responsibility for enforcement is entrusted to the Authority and certain other persons prescribed by the Minister for Enterprise, Trade and Employment. Under the 1989 Act, such other persons were described as "enforcing agencies" and were appointed by the Minister under s.32 of the 1989 Act. Such terminology is not retained in the 2005 Act, with s.33(1) of the 2005 Act providing that the Minister "may prescribe persons to perform such functions in lieu of the Authority in respect of the implementation of any of the relevant statutory provisions, and to the extent as may be prescribed".

18–03   Inspectors are appointed under s.62 of the 2005 Act to enforce the provisions of the Act. As under the 1989 Act, the Authority or person prescribed may appoint persons as inspectors by issuing such persons with a certificate of authorisation.[2] When requested, an inspector must produce this certificate or a copy of it and a form of personal identification. Inspectors appointed under the 1989 Act continue to act as such, despite the repeal of the Act.[3]

---

[1]   Section 33(1) of the Safety, Health and Welfare at Work Act 2005.
[2]   Section 62(1) and (2) the 2005 Act.
[3]   Section 62(4) of the 2005 Act.

18–04   The powers of the inspector are set out in s.64 of the 2005 Act, which enlarges and refines many of the powers under the 1989 Act.[4] Very wide powers of entry, inspection, examination, search, seizure and analysis are entrusted to the appointed inspectors. Among the particular powers of the inspector is the authority to issue improvement directions and plans, improvement notices and prohibition notices, which powers will be examined in detail later. Under s.71 of the 2005 Act, the Authority may apply *ex parte* to the High Court for an order when it considers that the risk to the health and safety of persons is so serious "that the use of the place of work" or part thereof should be restricted or should be immediately prohibited "until specified measures have been taken to reduce the risk to a reasonable level".

18–05   Some comparison can be made with the powers of inspectors under statutory regimes who can enter places of work. These may include the inspectors under the Companies Act 1990 and inspectors under the Competition Act 2002. Although the role of such inspectors is somewhat different, there are certain similarities in the scope of their powers.

18–06   The powers of the inspectors are augmented by criminal sanctions, with section 77 creating certain offences in relation to the exercise of powers by inspectors. These include an offence where a person "prevents, obstructs, impedes or delays an inspector from exercising any functions conferred on him or her by [the 2005 Act]"[5] or where a person "fails to comply with a bona fide request, instruction or directions from an inspector in the exercise of his or her statutory functions"[6].

18–07   The powers of the inspectors must be read subject to rights of persons affected by such powers. Such rights may include rights arising under the Constitution and rights under the European Convention on Human Rights [ECHR]. Relevant privileges may include legal professional privilege and the privilege against self-incrimination. Since the enactment of the 1989 Act, the ECHR has gained some force in domestic law by means of the European Convention on Human Rights Act 2003. The case law of the European Court of Human Rights ("ECt.HR") has developed the notion of privilege under Art.6 of the ECHR. Other areas of uncertainty include whether there is a constitutional right to have a lawyer present when an inspection is being carried out.

Powers of entry

18–08   As regards the power of entry, s.64(1)(a) of the 2005 Act enlarges the circumstances in which an inspector may enter by adding two other circumstances. In addition to the power to enter where the inspector has reasonable grounds for believing a place is used as a place of work, the inspector may also enter any place:

---

[4]   Section 34 of the 1989 Act.
[5]   Section 77(2)(d) of the 2005 Act.
[6]   Section 77(2)(e) of the 2005 Act.

"(ii) in which he or she has reasonable grounds for believing that articles or substances or records are kept, or

(iii) to which the relevant statutory provisions apply, ..."

It is therefore no longer an essential condition of entry that the place is used as
a place of work. The rather wide-ranging scope of the power of entry is, however, restricted by considering the relevant definition of "article" which relates
to use at work. Section 2 of the 2005 Act provides that:

"'article' means–

(a) any plant, machine, machinery, appliance, apparatus, tool or any other
work equipment for use or operation (whether exclusively or not) by
persons at work,

(b) any article designed for use as a component in, part of or to control any
such plant, machine, machinery, appliance, apparatus, work equipment, tool or any other work equipment, and

(c) any other product used by persons at work; ..."

However, the definition of "substance" or "record" is not specifically defined
in terms of use at work. Section 2 of the 2005 Act, for example, defines
"record" as follows:

""record" includes any memorandum, book, report, statement, register, plan,
chart, map, drawing, specification, diagram, pictorial or graphic work or other
document, any photograph, film or recording (whether of sound or images or
both), any form in which data (within the meaning of the Data Protection Acts
1988-2003) are held, any form (including machine-readable form) or thing in
which information is held or stored manually, mechanically or electronically,
and anything that is a part or copy, in any form, of any of, or any combination of,
the foregoing."

It would seem appropriate to adopt a purposive interpretation to these powers
of entry in terms of the object of the Act. It is submitted that to adopt any other
approach would render the powers of entry constitutionally vulnerable.

18–09   Section 64(5) of the 2005 Act limits the ability of the inspector to enter
any dwelling and provides that an inspector shall not enter a dwelling without
the consent of an owner or a District Court warrant. This reference to dwelling,
however, underlines that the power of entry is not restricted to places of work.
Of some relevance in this respect is Art.8, ECHR which guarantees respect for
private and family life, home and correspondence. Article 8, ECHR protects not
only dwellings but also, it would appear, business premises. In *Niemietz v Ger-
many*,[7] the ECt.HR held that to interpret "private life" and "home" as "including
certain professional or business activities or premises would be consonant with
the essential object and purpose of Art.8, namely to protect the individual
against arbitrary interference by the public authorities". Although the
premises searched in that case was a lawyer's home, in *Tamosius v United Kingdom*,[8] the ECt.HR accepted that Art.8 applied to a search of a lawyer's office.

---

7   [1992] 16 E.H.R.R. 97.
8   Application 062002/00, judgment September 19, 2002; See also *Veeber v Estonia (no. 1)*
(Application 37571/97), judgment of November 7, 2002.

18–10   Under s.34(1)(d) of the 1989 Act, a warrant could issue where an inspector had reasonable cause to believe an offence under the Act "has or is being committed". However, s.64(7) of the 2005 Act allows for the issue of such a warrant where there are reasonable grounds for believing that:

> "(a) there are any articles or substances being used in a place of work or any records (including documents stored in a non-legible form) or information, relating to a place of work, that the inspector requires to inspect for the purposes of the relevant statutory provisions, held in, at or on any place or any part of any place, or
>
> (b) there is, or such an inspection is likely to disclose, evidence of a contravention of the relevant statutory provisions, …".

It is therefore no longer necessary to show that an offence has or is being committed and it appears that a warrant can be issued in any circumstances where the inspector seeks to exercise his powers of entry, so long as there are "reasonable grounds" for either of the aforementioned two circumstances obtaining. The warrant may authorise the use of reasonable force where necessary.

18–11   It appears that the conditions for issue of a search warrant must be strictly met. In *Simple Imports v The Revenue Commissioners*,[9] Keane J. stated in relation to the general power to issue search warrants:

> "These are powers which the police and other authorities must enjoy in defined circumstances for the protection of society, but since they authorise the forcible invasion of a person's property, the courts must always be concerned to ensure that the conditions imposed by the legislature before such powers can be validly exercised are strictly met".

18–12   As under the 1989 Act,[10] an inspector may be accompanied by a member of the Garda Síochána where "he or she has reasonable cause to apprehend any serious obstruction in the execution" of his or her duty.[11]

18–13   The power in s.64(1)(a) of the 2005 Act also includes an expanded list of activities which can be carried out once the inspector has entered the place of work. While the corresponding provision in the 1989 Act referred simply to "enter, inspect, examine and search …", s.64(1)(a) of the 2005 Act allows the inspector to enter the place:

> "and inquire into, search, examine and inspect that place and any work activity, installation, process or procedure at that place which is subject to the relevant statutory provisions and any such articles, substances or records to ascertain whether the relevant statutory provisions have been or are being complied with and for those purposes take with him or her and use any equipment or materials required for those purposes".

Despite such a significantly expanded list, the object of the change is largely to clarify and make explicit the scope of the activity which can be

---

9   [2000] 2 I.R. 243.
10   Section 34(1)(b) of the 1989 Act.
11   Section 64(8) of the 2005 Act.

carried out by the inspector as opposed to any fundamental expansion in his or her powers.

Request for information/examination

18–14   The power of the inspector to request information under s.64(1)(i) of the 2005 Act differs from the corresponding provision in s.34(1)(g) of the 1989 Act. While the 1989 Act required "any person" to provide the information, the 2005 Act merely requires "the employer, owner, person in charge of the place or any employee" to give the information. A number of provisions in the 1989 Act are not retained under the 2005 Act, including the references to such persons answering "either alone or in the presence of any person", the signing of a declaration of truth of the answers and also the qualification that "no one shall be required to answer any question or to give any evidence tending to incriminate himself". However, s.64(9) of the 2005 Act provides that no person is required on examination or inquiry to give any answer or information tending to incriminate that person.

18–15   Similar to subsections 34(f) and (g) of the 1989 Act, the inspector may "examine" any person who the inspector believes to be able to give information. The inspector may require such person to answer any questions and sign a declaration of truth of the answers.

18–16   Under s.64(10) of the 2005 Act, where an inspector has reasonable grounds to believe that a person has committed an offence under Act, he or she may require that person to provide him or her with his or her name and the address at which he or she ordinarily resides.

18–17   As regards criminal offences, s.77(1)(b) of the 2005 Act provides that it is an offence where a person prevents or attempts to prevent any person from answering any question to which an inspector may require an answer pursuant to his or her powers under s.64 of the 2005 Act. Section 77(2)(e) makes it an offence where a person "fails to comply with a bona fide request, instruction or directions from an inspector in the exercise of his or her statutory functions". Similarly, s.77(2)(f) makes it an offence:

> "where any person makes a statement to an inspector which he or she knows to be false or recklessly makes a statement which is false where the statement is made—
>
> (i)   in purported compliance with a requirement to furnish any information imposed by or under any of the relevant statutory provisions, or
> (ii) for the purpose of obtaining the issue of a document under any of the relevant statutory provisions to himself or herself or another person, …".

18–18   As regards the rights of persons subject to requests or examination, of particular relevance is the privilege against self-incrimination. In *Re National Irish Banks Ltd*,[12] in the context of company inspectors, a similar restriction on

---

the privilege against self-incrimination was upheld as being proportionate. However, the admission of information contained in compelled answers provided under such powers may not be permitted in any subsequent criminal trial and might be classified as involuntary statements. A further relevant and instructive case is *Saunders v United Kingdom*.[13] It appears therefore that the powers of inspectors under s.64 of the 2005 Act may be upheld as proportionate interference in the public interest. However, the admissibility of information obtained at any criminal trial is more doubtful.

18–19   Other relevant privileges include legal professional privilege. The doctrine of legal professional privilege includes both legal advice privilege and litigation privilege. This is another matter which requires to be weighed against the exercise of the powers by the inspector.

18–20   Under s.72 of the 2005 Act, the Authority or prescribed person (as opposed to the inspector) may serve a notice requiring a person to provide information specified in the notice.

Records

18–21   The 2005 Act affords the inspector a significantly expanded list of powers in relation to records. Under s.34(f) of the 1989 Act, an inspector had the power to "require the production of any books, registers, records, whether kept in manual form or otherwise, certificates, notices, documents, maps and plans." Under the 2005 Act, the inspector's powers in relation to records include the power:

–   to require the production of records and to require information in a non-legible form to be reproduced in a legible form[14];
–   to inspect and take copies of or extracts from records, including those records in non-legible form where reproduced in a legible form[15];
–   where a computer is used to produce or store records, to require a person having charge of, or otherwise concerned with the operation of the computer, to provide reasonable assistance to the inspector[16]; and
–   to require records to be maintained for a reasonable period of time[17].

The power in relation to records is augmented by certain criminal sanctions. For example, s.77(2)(e) of the 2005 Act makes it an offence to fail to comply with a bona fide request, instruction or directions from an inspector in the exercise of his or her statutory functions while s.77(2)(h) provides that it is an offence where a person, "produces or causes to be produced or allows to be produced to an inspector any record which is false or misleading in any respect knowing it to be so false or misleading".

---

[13]   [1997] 23 E.H.R.R. 313.
[14]   Section 64(1)(d) of the 2005 Act.
[15]   Section 64(1)(e) of the 2005 Act.
[16]   Section 64(1)(f) of the 2005 Act.
[17]   Section 64(1)(h) of the 2005 Act.

Other powers

18–22 Many of the powers of inspectors which existed under the 1989 Act are re-enacted under the 2005 Act. Such powers include the following:

- the power to direct that a place be left undisturbed for so long as is reasonably necessary for the purpose of an inspection or investigation in s.64(1)(b) of the 2005 Act which power largely corresponds to the former s.34(1)(h) of the 1989 Act;
- the power to take measurements, photographs or recordings formerly in s.34(1)(m) of the 1989 Act is re-enacted in s.64(1)(n) of the 2005 Act;
- the power under s.34(1)(n) of the 1989 Act to require a person to give such "assistance and facilities" within the person's control or responsibilities as is reasonably necessary is now contained in s.64(1)(j) of the 2005 Act;
- the power to take samples in s.64(1)(r) of the 2005 Act which power largely corresponds to the former s.34(1)(l) of the 1989 Act;
- the power under s.34(1)(k) of the 1989 Act to remove and retain any article or substance for examination mirrors the new s.64(1)(s) of the 2005 Act; and
- the power to cause any article or substance which appears to have caused danger to safety and health to be dismantled or subject to any process detailed in s.34(1)(j) of the 1989 Act, is now to be found at s.64(1)(q) of the 2005 Act.

18–23 Although similar to the former s.34(1)(i) of the 1989 Act, s.64(1)(p) of the 2005 Act has been somewhat expanded. It concerns the power to test and examine any article or substance found "at the place". The new provision makes explicit that the testing can be carried out at the place or elsewhere, with the addition of the words "there or at any other place". The former provision simply required a person to supply "samples" for testing or examination. The new provision allows the inspector to request that any article or substance itself (as opposed to simply samples) be supplied or removed for testing. Surprisingly, there are no specified limitations regarding the length of time an article or substance can be retained by the inspectors.

18–24 New powers granted by the 2005 Act include:

- s.64(1)(c) which establishes the power to direct that a safety statement be amended in accordance with s.20(5)(c) of the 2005 Act;
- s.64(1)(m) which establishes the power to require any article to be operated or set in motion or that a procedure be carried out "that may be relevant to any search, examination, investigation, inspection, or inquiry"; and
- s.64(1)(o) which establishes the power to install, use and maintain monitoring equipment and seals.

Under s.64(2) of the 2005 Act the inspector may request that the name and address of the supplier of an article or substance be provided. This section mirrors s.10(13) of the 1989 Act. A significant new power of the inspector under s.64(1)(k) of the 2005 Act is to summon any employer, employee, the owner or person in charge of the place, by written notice, at a specified time and place, to give any information which the inspector may reasonably require in relation to the "place, article or substance, work activity, installation or procedure". In addition, the summons may require such person to produce any records in that person's power or control.

Powers

18–25   Sections 65–69 of the 2005 Act replace ss.35–39 of the 1989 Act with a number of important additions. These sections provide inspectors with a wide range of powers to enforce the provisions of the 2005 Act. Such powers include a direction to an employer requiring submission of an improvement plan, an improvement notice and a prohibition notice.

Improvement directions

18–26   The inspector, as previously stated, has the power to issue improvement directions requiring the submission of an improvement plan, improvement notices and prohibition notices. On foot of 13,549 inspections carried out by the Authority in 2005, 10 directions for an improvement plan were issued.

Improvement plans

18–27   Section 65 of the 2005 Act allows an inspector to issue written directions requiring the submission of an improvement plan where he or she discovers work activities which involve a risk to safety, health or welfare of persons. The s.65 direction for the improvement plan must detail how the work activity referred to is connected to any particular duty arising under the 2005 Act. This is significant in that the provisions of the 2005 Act may only be invoked to enforce a duty set out in the 2005 Act. The use of "persons" is significant in that an inspector may give a direction for an improvement plan in the case of an activity presenting a risk to persons other than employees. This section introduces changes to the corresponding s.35 of the 1989 Act. In addition to changes in the language and layout of the section, such as a clearer statement of the contents of a direction for an improvement plan[18] and the procedure on receipt of submissions for an improvement plan,[19] more substantive changes include:

–   a requirement to make the submission of an improvement plan within one month specifying the remedial action to be taken, while the former section simply required submission "within a time specified in the direction"[20];

–   a detailed procedure on receipt of submissions. The section now prescribes an acknowledgement type procedure, whereby within one month

---

[18]   Section 65(2) of the 2005 Act.
[19]   Section 65(4) of the 2005 Act.
[20]   Section 35(3) of the 1989 Act.

of receipt of the submission, the inspector must confirm whether or not he or she is satisfied with the plan or if dissatisfied may direct that a revised plan be resubmitted within a specified period. In the former corresponding s.35 of the 1989, there was no such confirmation procedure. It simply provided that where the inspector was not satisfied with the plan he or she could direct a revised plan be resubmitted[21];

— a requirement for the inspector to give a copy of the direction to any safety representative in the place of work.

18–28 It is an offence under s.77(1)(c) of the 2005 Act where a person fails to submit an improvement plan to an inspector within the time specified in a direction under s.65, and under s.77(1)(d) where a person fails to implement an improvement plan, the adequacy of which has been confirmed to be in accordance with s.65. The precise procedure for the issuing of a direction must therefore be strictly followed.

Improvement notices

18–29 Section 66 of the 2005 Act provides for the service of a written notice known as an improvement notice. An improvement notice is the first and least intrusive of the arsenal that the inspector has at his or her disposal and is issued in circumstances where there is a breach of health and safety law that requires addressing, but is not sufficiently serious as to require a work stoppage. The Authority issued 458 improvement notices in 2005.

Content of improvement notice

18–30 An improvement notice can be issued in two situations. The first is where an inspector is of the opinion that a person is contravening or has contravened a provision of the 2005 Act. Secondly, an improvement notice can be served in circumstances where a person has failed to comply with a previous direction to submit an improvement plan or has failed to implement an improvement plan. It may be served "on the person who has or may reasonably be presumed to have control over the work activity concerned." It should be stated that s.66 does not appear to sanction the service of an improvement notice on the ground that a revised improvement plan was inadequate.

The procedure following the issuing of an improvement notice and the contents of such a notice is now contained in s.66 of the 2005 Act (formerly s.36 of the 1989 Act). In addition to changes in the language and the layout of the section, s.66(2) contains a more detailed description of the content of the improvement notice. The main changes include:

1. There is now a requirement to give reasons for the inspector's opinion that there has been a contravention or failure to implement an improvement plan,[22] as well as a separate requirement to give reasons for the opinion in respect of the relevant statutory provision.[23] While there

---

21 Section 35(3) of the 1989 Act.
22 Section 66(2)(b) of the 2005 Act.
23 Section 66(2)(d) of the 2005 Act. Formerly s.36(1)(b) of the 1989 Act.

would appear to be some duplication in such separate requirements to give reasons, the changes appear to require a more expansive statement of reasons.

2. The improvement notice must now include information regarding the making of an appeal.[24] The time limit for the bringing of an appeal is 14 days from the date of service of the notice.

3. The notice may include other requirements the inspector considers appropriate[25] and must be signed and dated[26].

The contents of the improvement notice specified in s.66(2) are mandatory (suggested by use of the word "shall") and must be strictly complied with. This follows from the fact that failure to comply with an improvement notice may result in a criminal offence under s.77(3)(k), which makes it an offence to contravene an improvement notice. In this respect guidance can be obtained from the approach adopted by the High Court to the service of an enforcement notice in planning law, where in *Dundalk Town Council v Lawlor*,[27] O'Neill J. quashed an enforcement notice issued under s.154 of the Planning and Development Act 2000 due to the enforcement notice lacking sufficient precision and clarity as to what steps the recipient should take. The learned judge held as follows:

> "The first thing that has to be borne in mind here is that a failure to comply with an Enforcement Notice is a criminal offence. It is well settled that criminal offences must be defined with clarity and precision so that a person can know whether his conduct is or is not a commission of an offence.[28]

Section 66(2)(e), which mirrors s.36(1)(d) of the 1989 Act, should be noted in that it requires the contravention of the matters identified in the improvement notice to be remedied by a specified date.

18–31 Other new provisions require that a copy of the improvement notice must be given to a safety representative in the place of work, who must also be informed where an improvement notice is withdrawn.[29] The section also prescribes a new procedure regarding compliance with such a notice. A person on whom an improvement notice has been served who believes the notice has been complied with, must confirm to the inspector in writing that the matters have been remedied and a copy of such confirmation must be given to the safety representative.[30] Where the inspector is satisfied that the matters have been remedied, the inspector must issue a written notice of such compliance within one month of receipt of the confirmation notice.[31]

---

24 Section 66(2)(f) of the 2005 Act.
25 Section 66(2)(g) of the 2005 Act.
26 Section 66(2)(h) of the 2005 Act.
27 [2005] 2 I.L.R.M. 106.
28 See *King v Attorney General* [1981] I.R. 233.
29 Section 66(4) of the 2005 Act.
30 Section 66(5) of the 2005 Act.
31 Section 66(6) of the 2005 Act.

Significantly, the 2005 Act does not require the Authority to re-inspect the workplace prior to confirming that the employer has complied with the improvement notice.

18–32   The procedure regarding an appeal against an improvement notice[32] is the same as under the 1989 Act.[33] In summary, an appeal against an improvement notice lies to the District Court within 14 days beginning on the day on which the notice is served. An appeal effectively acts as a stay on the improvement notice. A person appealing an improvement notice must notify the Authority of the appeal and the grounds for the appeal. The Authority is entitled to appear, be heard and adduce evidence on the hearing of the appeal. In determining the appeal, the judge may confirm, vary or cancel the improvement notice.

18–33   The form of notice that must be used by a person appealing to the District Court against an improvement notice is prescribed in the Safety, Health and Welfare at Work Act 2005 (Appeals Forms) Rules 2005.[34]

18–34   Where there is no appeal against the improvement notice, the notice takes effect on the later of:

> "(a)   the end of the period for making an appeal, or
> (b)   the day specified in the notice."

Prohibition notice

18–35   The provisions regarding prohibition notices are contained in s.67 of the 2005 Act. A prohibition notice can be served where an inspector is of the opinion that at any place of work there is occurring, or is likely to occur, any activity which involves or is likely to involve "a risk of serious personal injury to any person". A prohibition notice prohibits the carrying on of an activity until the matters which have given rise to or are likely to give rise to the risk are eliminated. In 2005, the Authority issued 494 prohibition notices.

18–36   Section 67 makes limited changes compared to the corresponding s.37 of the 1989, with certain changes in language and layout largely for the sake of clarity. A prohibition notice may be served "on the person who has or who may reasonably be presumed to have control over the activity concerned". This is a more succinct description compared to the former s.37(1), which has been deleted, with the addition of "or who may reasonably be presumed to have". The contents of the prohibition notice are mandatory and are set out in s.67(2) which declares that it shall:

> "(*a*)   state the [inspector's opinion],
> (*b*)   state the reasons for that opinion,

---

[32]   Subsections 66(7) to (11) of the 2005 Act.
[33]   Subsections 36(4) to (7) of the 1989 Act.
[34]   S.I. No. 548 of 2005. Also the District Court (Safety, Health and Welfare at Work Act 2005) Rules 2006 (S.I. No. 209 of 2006) and Part III of this book.

(c) specify the activity in respect of which that opinion is held,

(d) where in his or her opinion the activity involves a contravention, or likely contravention, of any of the relevant statutory provisions, specify the relevant statutory provision,

(e) prohibit the carrying on of the activity concerned until the matters which give rise or are likely to give rise to the risk are remedied, and

(f) be signed and dated by the inspector".

The changes in the above compared to s.37(3) of the 1989 Act are largely minor. In summary, they include the following:

– the requirement to give reasons is given a separate paragraph in s.67(2)(b) of the 2005 Act, while it was formerly combined in the 1989 Act[35] in the paragraph corresponding to s.67(2)(d) of the 2005 Act;

– paragraph 67(2)(e) of the 2005 Act uses the word "prohibit" with regard to the carrying on of the activity concerned as opposed to the word "direct", which was used in s.37(3)(d) of the 1989 Act; and

– paragraph 67(2)(f) of the 2005 Act requiring the notice to be signed and dated is new.

18–37 It is a criminal offence to fail to comply with a prohibition notice under s.77(2)(l) of the 2005 Act. As was stated in connection with an improvement notice, the requirements of a prohibition notice must be strictly satisfied.[36]

18–38 A new s.67(3) of the 2005 Act provides that a prohibition notice may include directions as to the measures to remedy the contravention or matter to which the notice relates. This is, however, a discretionary matter as opposed to the matters set out in s.67(2) which are mandatory. Section 67(4) is new and requires (as with an improvement notice) that a copy of the prohibition notice must be given to a safety representative in the place of work, who must also be informed when a prohibition notice is withdrawn. The procedure concerning an appeal against a prohibition notice is largely the same as under the 1989 Act. Unlike an appeal against an improvement notice, an appeal does not have the effect of suspending the operation of the notice. That said, the appellant may apply to Court to have the operation of the prohibition notice suspended until the appeal is disposed of. The appeal against a prohibition notice lies to the District Court within seven days beginning on the day on which the notice is served. In determining the appeal, the judge may confirm, vary or cancel the notice.

18–39 The form of notice that must be used by a person appealing to the District Court against a prohibition notice is prescribed in the Safety, Health and Welfare at Work Act 2005 (Appeals Forms) Rules 2005.[37]

---

[35] See s.37(3)(c) of the 1989 Act which refers to giving "particulars of the reasons".

[36] See *Dundalk Town Council v Lawlor*, unreported, High Court, O'Neill J., March 18, 2005.

[37] S.I. No. 548 of 2005. Also the District Court (Safety, Health and Welfare at Work Act 2005) Rules 2006 (S.I. No. 209 of 2006) and Part III of this book.

18–40 An application concerning the suspension of a notice is given a separate subsection,[38] although it was combined with an appeal against a prohibition notice in s.37 of the 1989 Act. The form of notice that must be used by a person appealing to the District Court to have the operation of a prohibition notice suspended is prescribed in the Safety, Health and Welfare at Work Act 2005 (Appeals Forms) Rules 2005.[39] Rule 5 provides as follows:

> "Upon issuing a Notice of Appeal against a prohibition notice which said prohibition notice is declared to take effect immediately it is received by the person on whom it is served, or at any time thereafter, the appellant may apply, at any sitting of the District Court for the district court district in which the appeal is listed for hearing, under section 67(6) of the Act of 2005 to have the operation of the said prohibition notice suspended until the appeal is disposed of, provided the appellant first gives 48 hours notice of the application (in the form set out in Part 2 of the Schedule [see S.I. 548 of 2005], or a form to like effect) to each party directly affected by the appeal and lodges the original of Form 2, together with a statutory declaration as to service thereof, with the district court clerk and such form may, where appropriate, be served at the same time as, and together with, the Notice of Appeal."

Also new are subsections 67(10) and (11), which create a new procedure regarding compliance with a prohibition notice and confirmation of such by the inspector.[40]

18–41 Subsections 67(12) to (14) of the 2005 Act outline more detailed provisions regarding the withdrawal of a prohibition notice, while the former s.37(8) of the 1989 Act simply stated that an inspector could revoke the notice. Section 67(12) provides that an inspector may withdraw a notice where the activity no longer involves a risk of serious injury or where the notice was issued in error or was incorrect. A notice is withdrawn when the withdrawal notice is given to the person on whom the prohibition was served.[41] The withdrawal of a notice does not, however, prevent the service of other prohibition notices.[42] It may be observed that as a notice can only be withdrawn under s.67(12) where there is no longer a risk or where the notice was issued in error or was incorrect, a notice is unlikely to be issued concerning the same matter, unless there is another change in circumstances. However, if the notice was, for example, issued addressed to the wrong person, a new notice could immediately be issued.

A person appealing a prohibition notice or applying for suspension of the notice must notify the Authority of the appeal and the grounds for the appeal. The Authority is entitled to appear, be heard and adduce evidence on the hearing of the appeal or the application for suspension of the notice.

18–42 The procedure concerning an application for contravention of a prohibition notice to the High Court, formerly contained in s.37(9) of the 1989 Act, is contained in a separate section,[43] although there is no change in the substance.

---

[38] Section 67(8) of the 2005 Act.
[39] S.I. No. 548 of 2005. Also Part III of this book.
[40] The procedure is similar to that which applies in respect of an improvement notice.
[41] Section 67(13) of the 2005 Act.
[42] Section 67(14) of the 2005 Act.
[43] Section 68 of the 2005 Act.

General provisions and the requirement to display notices

18–43   Section 3 of the 2005 Act sets out the procedure for the service of a notice or document under the provisions of the 2005 Act.

18–44   A new provision provides that where an improvement or prohibition notice is served, the person to whom it is addressed must:

> "(*a*) bring the notice to the attention of any person whose work is affected by the notice, and
>
> (*b*) display the notice or a copy of the notice in a prominent place at or near any place of work, article or substance affected by the notice."[44]

Investigations and special reports

18–45   Section 70 of the 2005 Act invests the Authority with the power to direct any of its staff or any other competent person to investigate the circumstances surrounding any accident, disease, occurrence, situation or any other matters. It sets out the procedure for investigations and reports concerning "the causes and circumstances surrounding any accident, incident, personal injury, occurrence or situation or any other matter related to the general purposes" of the 2005 Act. The difference with the former corresponding s.46 of the 1989 Act are largely stylistic and for the sake of clarity, with the former s.46(1)(a) referring to investigations concerning "the circumstances surrounding any accident, disease, occurrence, situation or any other matter related to the general purposes" of the 1989 Act. The only other changes concern making explicit the requirement to present the report to the Minister for Enterprise, Trade and Employment "as soon as practicable"[45] and the reference to certain other statutory provisions regarding the matters which require the consent of the Minister, before an investigation can be carried out.[46]

At the end of the process the inspector must produce a special report. The precise nature of such a report in terms of findings is not entirely clear. No specific procedures are described as to how such an investigation is to be conducted. However, as such an investigation may result in findings of fact which may be damaging to certain persons, arguably some form of fair procedures ought to apply. An analogy can be made with an inspector under the Companies Acts, where fair procedures have been held not to apply to the first stage of information gathering but only apply to the second stage, when the evidence is being assessed for the purposes of making findings. This was so held in *Re National Irish Bank Ltd. (No. 1)*[47] and in *Re National Irish Bank Ltd (No. 2)*.[48] Arguably the investigations under s.70 of the 2005 Act simply concern information gathering rather than fact-finding, in which case a requirement for fair procedures will not apply. It should be noted that

---

[44]   Section 69 of the 2005 Act.
[45]   Section 70(5) of the 2005 Act.
[46]   Section 70(6) of the 2005 Act.
[47]   [1999] 3 I.R. 145.
[48]   [1999] 3 I.R. 190.

the Authority may publish a special report "in such manner as it considers appropriate".[49]

Order of High Court as to use of place of work

18–46 Section 71 prescribes the procedure, formerly contained in s.39 of the 1989 Act, whereby the Authority or prescribed persons, can seek a court order restricting or prohibiting the use of a place or part of place of work, where the Authority or prescribed persons consider that;

> "…the risk to the safety, health or welfare of persons is so serious that the use of a place of work or part of a place of work should be restricted or immediately prohibited until specified measures have been taken to reduce the risk to a reasonable level, …".

There are no differences in substance with the former s.39 save for the fact that s.77(5) of the 2005 Act makes it an offence to contravene any order or orders made under s.71. The High Court can make an interim or interlocutory order as it sees it. There is no requirement for a prohibition notice to have been issued, so it is distinct from the procedure under s.68 of the 2005 Act, although the practice and procedure for application to the High Court is the same.

It appears that the procedure under s.71 should only be invoked in exceptional circumstances in cases of urgency. A court order obtained without notices interferes with the constitutional right to earn a livelihood and the constitutional right to the enjoyment of property. The service of a prohibition notice at least provides some form of notice and opportunity for compliance, which is absent from the s.71 procedure. It will therefore be a necessary proof in any such application to demonstrate that the service of a prohibition notice was not appropriate.

Obtaining and disclosure of information

18–47 Section 72 of the 2005 Act sets out a procedure for the Authority or prescribed persons, to require a person to provide specified information, which was formerly contained in s.42 of the 1989 Act. Section 72(2) is a new provision and provides that the period specified in the information notice can be extended at the discretion of the Authority on the written application of the person on whom the notice is served. A person on whom an information notice is served can appeal against the notice within seven days to the District Court.[50] In determining the appeal, the judge can confirm, vary or cancel the notice.

18–48 Section 73 of the 2005 Act constitutes a more streamlined provision concerning the prohibition on unauthorised disclosure of confidential information, compared to the corresponding s.45 of the 1989 Act. In particular, s.73 concerns the prohibition on disclosure of "confidential information", while the

---

[49] Section 70(5) of the 2005 Act.
[50] See the District Court (Safety, Health and Welfare at Work Act 2005) Rules 2006 (S.I. No. 209 of 2006).

former s.45 prohibited disclosure of "relevant information". Under s.73(1), such prohibition does not apply where a person is "duly authorised by the Authority", although there is no definition of such. Section 73 does not re-enact s.45(3), which sets out specified circumstances in which disclosure could be made. Section 73(2), however, provides that there is no prohibition on disclosure of information, though only by means of a report:

(*a*) to the Authority,

(*b*) to the Minister, by or on behalf of the Authority, or

(*c*) to a coroner holding an inquest under the Coroners Act 1962 on the body of a person whose death may have been caused through personal injury.

While s.45(3)(a) of the 1989 Act allowed disclosure to the Authority and a Minister, there was no mention of a coroner.

18–49 Section 74 of the 2005 Act amends section 46(1) of the Freedom of Information Act 1997, by inserting the following:

> "a record held or created under the relevant statutory provisions by the Health and Safety Authority or an employee of the Authority, relating to or arising from its enforcement functions (other than a record concerning any other functions of the Authority or the general administration of the Authority), …".

The foregoing has particular significance for the solicitor seeking sight of the Authority file in that it excludes from the jurisdiction of the Freedom of Information Act 1997 (as amended) any record held or created by the Authority, relating to or arising from its enforcement functions. The only means of accessing an Authority file will now be through a third party discovery order.

18–50 Section 75 of the 2005 Act contains a more expanded list of bodies, which may disclose information to the Authority relevant to the performance of certain of its duties. While disclosure by the Revenue Commissioners was also authorised by s.43 of the 1989 Act, there was no similar provision concerning disclosure by the Minister for Health and Children and the Minister for Social and Family Affairs, a member of an Garda Síochána and persons prescribed by the Minister for Enterprise, Trade and Employment.

18–51 Subsections 76(1) and (2) of the 2005 Act allow for disclosure by an inspector of information to employees in certain circumstances and correspond to s.45(7) of the 1989 Act, with certain minor changes in language. Section 76(3)(a) of the 2005 Act provides enhanced protection to certain types of information. While s.45(7) of the 1989 Act simply protected trade secrets, s.76(3)(a) refers to "any manufacturing, trade or commercial secrets or other processes". Such types of information are not, however, afforded absolute protection, as s.76(3)(b) provides that disclosure is permitted (i) for the purpose of the inspectors functions under the 2005 Act, (ii) where it is made with the relevant consent, or (iii) for the purposes of any legal proceedings or of any investigation or special report under s.70 of the 2005 Act.

CHAPTER 19

OFFENCES AND PENALTIES

INTRODUCTION

19–01   Part 7 of the 2005 Act deals with offences and penalties. It is important that the sanctions available under the 2005 Act have a correlation to the seriousness of the offences created under the Act.

19–02   There is little possibility of escaping responsibility for breaches of the Safety, Health and Welfare at Work Act 2005 as employers, the self-employed, employees, and manufacturers, designers and builders, may all be prosecuted for breaches of the Act. Both individuals and corporate bodies may be prosecuted. In most cases the company itself will be prosecuted. However, s.80 of the 2005 Act specifically provides for the prosecution of the officers and management of a company or other body. Where an offence has been committed by "an undertaking", and that offence is shown to have been committed with the consent or authorisation of, or to have been attributable to connivance or any neglect on the part of any director, manager, other similar officer, or a person who purports to act in such capacity, that person may be prosecuted in addition to the undertaking. This approach has been taken in England and Wales since the introduction in that jurisdiction of a similar provision in 1974.[1] In the case of *R v Boal*,[2] for example, an inspection of a bookshop identified serious breaches of the Fire Precautions Act 1971. That Act contained a provision similar to s.80 of the 2005 Act. Mr Boal held the position of assistant manager in the bookshop and was only in charge when the manager was absent. The manager was absent on the particular day of the inspection. The case against Mr Boal was dismissed, as it was held that, although he was in charge of the store on the particular day of the inspection, he had no control over the fire safety policy of the shop. That said, the owners were successfully prosecuted.[3] Consequently, it would appear that, for the imposition of personal liability on an officer or manager of a company, some element of control over corporate policy is required. Control is, therefore, a critical concept under existing health and safety legislation, and equals responsibility. The application of s.80(1) of the 2005 Act, formerly s.28(19) of the 1989 Act, in Ireland can be seen in the November 1998 case of *National Authority for Occupational Safety and Health v Noel Frisby Construction Ltd and Noel Frisby* and *National Authority*

---

[1]   Section 37 of the Health and Safety at Work Act 1974 (UK).
[2]   [1992] Q.B. 591.
[3]   See *Armour v Skeen* [1977] I.R.L.R. 310.

for Occupational Safety and Health v F & S Property Development Ltd and Mr James Clancy.

Offences

19–03 Section 77 of the 2005 Act contains an enlarged list of offences, which were formerly contained in s.48 of the 1989 Act. Many of the offences are the same although a different layout is provided in the section.

Section 77(1) sets out a number of less serious offences for which a person is liable on summary conviction to a maximum fine of €3,000.[4] In particular, s.77(1)(a) creates certain additional offences in respect of the duties of the safety representative[5] and also regarding consultation and participation of employees in safety committees.[6]

The other offences in s.77(1) of the 2005 Act were also offences under the 1989 Act and arise where a person:

(*b*)   prevents or attempts to prevent any person from answering any question to which an inspector may require an answer under s.64;[7]

(*c*)   fails to submit an improvement plan to an inspector within the time specified in a direction under s.65;[8]

(*d*)   fails to implement an improvement plan, the adequacy of which has been confirmed in accordance with s.65;[9]

(*e*)   contravenes any requirement imposed by a notice requiring information under s.72;[10] and

(*f*)   prevents, obstructs, impedes, or delays an officer of customs and excise in the exercise of any of the powers conferred on him or her by s.87.[11]

In relation to s.77(1)(c) and (d) above, the former defence to such offences contained in s.48(4), "if it can be shown that other measures providing at least equal protection were taken", is omitted.

19–04 Section 77 of the 2005 Act should be read with s.78 of the Act.

19–05 Section 77(2) to (8) and (9)(a) are offences arising for breaches of the general duties in the 2005 Act and the numerous Regulations made under the

---

4   Section 78(1) of the 2005 Act.
5   Section 25 of the 2005 Act.
6   Section 26 of the 2005 Act.
7   Formerly s.48(3) of the 1989 Act.
8   Formerly s.48(4) of the 1989 Act.
9   Formerly s.48(4) of the 1989 Act.
10   Formerly s.48(6) of the 1989 Act.
11   Formerly s.48(7) of the 1989 Act.

2005 Act. They are dealt with either summarily in the District Court[12] or on conviction on indictment in the Circuit Criminal Court[13].

19–06 Section 77(2)(a) criminalises:

- a failure to discharge a duty by employers,[14] employees and persons in control of work[15];
- a failure to discharge a duty by designers, manufacturers, importers and suppliers[16];
- a failure to discharge duties relating to construction work[17]; and
- a failure to discharge certain protective and preventive measures.[18]

As Part 2 of the 2005 Act sets out an expanded list of responsibilities and duties of employers, there is a corresponding expanded set of offences.[19]

19–07 The other offences in s.77(2) of the 2005 Act arise where a person:

(*b*) contravenes s.14 of the 2005 Act[20];

(*c*) except for the provisions of this section as they apply to the 2005 Act, contravenes the relevant statutory provisions;

(*d*) prevents, obstructs, impedes or delays an inspector from exercising any functions conferred on him or her by the 2005 Act[21];

(*e*) fails to comply with a bona fide request, instruction or directions from an inspector in the exercise of his or her statutory functions[22];

(*f*) makes a statement to an inspector, which he or she knows to be false, or recklessly makes a statement, which is false where the statement is made—

    (i) in purported compliance with a requirement to furnish any information imposed by or under any of the relevant statutory provisions, or

    (ii) for the purpose of obtaining the issue of a document under any of the relevant statutory provisions to himself or herself or another person[23];

(*g*) makes a false entry intentionally in any register, book, notice or other document required by or under any of the relevant statutory provisions to be kept, served or given or, with intent to deceive, makes use of any such entry which he or she knows to be false[24];

---

[12] On summary conviction in the District Court a person guilty of such an offence is liable to a fine not exceeding €3,000 or imprisonment for a term not exceeding six months or both.

[13] On conviction on indictment in the Circuit Criminal Court a person guilty of such an offence is liable to a fine not exceeding €3,000,000 or imprisonment not exceeding two years or both.

[14] Part 2, Chap.1 of the 2005 Act.

[15] Part 2, Chap.2 of the 2005 Act.

[16] Section 16 of the 2005 Act.

[17] Section 17 of the 2005 Act.

[18] Section 18 of the 2005 Act.

[19] The corresponding offences were set out in s.48(1)(a) of the 1989 Act.

[20] Formerly included in s.48(1)(b) of the 1989 Act.

[21] Formerly included in s.48(2) of the 1989 Act.

[22] Formerly included in s.48(2) of the 1989 Act.

[23] Formerly included in s.48(12) of the 1989 Act.

[24] Formerly included in s.48(13) of the 1989 Act.

(*h*) produces or causes to be produced or allows to be produced to an inspector any record which is false or misleading in any respect knowing it to be so false or misleading;

(*i*) forges or uses a document issued or authorised to be issued under any of the relevant statutory provisions or required for any purpose under the relevant statutory provisions with the intent to deceive, or makes or has in his or her possession a document so closely resembling any such document as to be calculated to deceive[25];

(*j*) falsely represents himself or herself to be an inspector[26];

(*k*) contravenes any requirement of an improvement notice served under s.66 of the 2005 Act[27];

(*l*) carries on any activity in contravention of a prohibition notice served under s.67 of the 2005 Act.[28]

19–08 Section 77(3) of the 2005 Act creates a new offence where a person removes, alters, damages or defaces a notice or document without lawful authority at any time during the period of three months after a notice or document is affixed under s.3(1)(d) of the 2005 Act. Section 77(4) creates certain new procedural offences where a person:

> "(*a*) obstructs or impedes a member of the Garda Síochána in the exercise of a power conferred on him or her or by a warrant under section 64(7) [of the 2005 Act],
>
> (*b*) refuses to produce any record that an inspector lawfully requires him or her to produce, or
>
> (*c*) gives to an inspector information that the person knows is false or misleading."

19–09 Section 77(5) of the 2005 Act inserts on a statutory basis the offence of contempt of court in respect of orders made, and in particular, orders made under s.71 of the 2005 Act.[29]

19–10 A person who fails to comply with a requirement in an information notice or who, in purported compliance with this requirement, furnishes information to the Authority that the person knows to be false or misleading shall be guilty of an offence.[30]

19–11 Section 77(8) is to be noted in that it provides in addition to any fine, for a power whereby a convicted person may be ordered to remedy within a specified time health and safety matters.

19–12 Other Offences in s.48 of the 1989 Act, re-enacted in s.77 of the 2005 Act, include subsections 77(9) and (10) of the latter Act.

---

[25] Formerly included in s.48(14) of the 1989 Act.
[26] Formerly included in s.48(15) of the 1989 Act.
[27] Formerly included in s.48(5) of the 1989 Act.
[28] Formerly included in s.48(6) of the 1989 Act.
[29] An order of the High Court as to the use of a place of work.
[30] Section 77(6) of the 2005 Act.

Section 77(9) of the 2005 Act somewhat mirrors s.48(17) of the 1989 Act. A separate offence is committed under s.77(9) by a person on whom a duty is imposed by ss.8 to 12 inclusive and ss.14 to 17 inclusive of the 2005 Act where a person suffers any personal injury as a consequence of the contravention of any of these provisions. It is not a separate offence if the act or default by which the personal injury was caused has been heard and dismissed by a court before the personal injury occurred or if the injury was not a direct result of a breach of the 2005 Act. Section 77(9)(b)(ii) of the 2005 Act excludes such a defence where the personal injury results in death.

Section 77(10)(a) of the 2005 Act mirrors s.48(18)(a) of the 1989 Act in that it allows a person charged summarily with an offence to have brought to court the person whom he or she believes to be the true offender.

19–13 It should be noted that an employer cannot defend himself or herself by claiming that responsibility should lie with either an employee or a competent person appointed by the employer under s.18 of the 2005 Act.[31]

Offences under the 2005 Act

19–14 The 2005 Act creates three categories of offences. They are:

1. a small number of summary offences for which a fine (not exceeding €3,000) only can be imposed[32];

2. summary offences for which a fine (not exceeding €3,000) and/or imprisonment (not exceeding 6 months) can be imposed[33];

3. indictable offences punishable by the imposition of a fine (not exceeding €3,000,000) and/or imprisonment (not exceeding two years).[34]

In summary, the first category applies to less serious matters and the second and third categories cover the more serious offences. In addition, the person convicted can be ordered to pay the Authority's costs and expenses. Section 78(4) of the 2005 Act provides:

> "where a person is convicted of an offence under the relevant statutory provisions in proceedings brought by the Authority …, the court shall, unless it is satisfied that there are special and substantial reasons for not so doing, order the person to pay to the Authority … the costs and expenses measured by the court, incurred by the Authority … in relation to the investigation, detection and prosecution of the offence including costs and expenses incurred in the taking of samples, the carrying out of tests, examinations and analyses and in respect of the remuneration and other expenses of employees of or consultants and advisers engaged by the Authority…".

19–15 The categories of offences differ somewhat to the position which pertained under the 1989 Act, where they included: summary offences attracting

---

[31] Section 77(12) of the 2005 Act.
[32] Section 78(1) of the 2005 Act.
[33] Section 78(2)(c)(i) of the 2005 Act.
[34] Section 78(2)(c)(ii) of the 2005 Act.

merely a fine (not exceeding €1905);[35] indictable offences which attracted merely a fine[36]; and indictable offences which attracted a fine and imprisonment for up to two years. The main changes under the 2005 Act therefore include a significant increase in the level of fines and also the fact that certain summary offences can attract a prison sentence of up to six months. Under the 1989 Act only three of the indictable offences were punishable by a term of imprisonment.[37] As noted below, the number of offences punishable by a term of imprisonment has been increased by the 2005 Act. While breaches of s.48(1) of the 1989 Act[38] could be prosecuted on indictment, the maximum penalty was merely a fine.

19–16 Significantly, s.60(1)(a) of the 1989 Act has been omitted from the 2005 Act in what is a fundamental departure from the approach adopted under the 1989 Act. This section provided that a failure to comply with the general duties of employers and self-employed persons did not give rise to a cause of action in civil proceedings. Contravention of these general duties merely attracted criminal sanctions.[39] The removal of the civil liability exemption in respect of a failure by an employer to comply with his or her general duties will necessitate increased vigilance on the part of employers to ensure compliance with the expanded list of general duties imposed on employers under the 2005 Act.

---

[35] Section 49(1) and (2)(a) of the 1989 Act. Also s.49(3)(c) of the 1989 Act.

[36] Section 49(2)(b) of the 1989 Act.

[37] Activities in contravention of a prohibition notice (an offence prescribed in s.48(6) of the 1989 Act). A relevant and instructive case is *The People (DPP) v Dwyer* (discussed in the Annual Report of the Authority in 2004) where the Circuit Criminal Court imposed a 12 month suspended sentence on the defendant for two breaches of prohibition notices. See also s.49(3)(a) of the 1989 Act: disclosure of information in contravention of section 45 of the 1989 Act (an offence prescribed in s.48(9) of the 1989 Act). See s.49(3)(b) of the 1989 Act: offences regarding activities that breach safety legislation if carried on without a licence. Also s.49(c) of the 1989 Act.

[38] Offences under s.48(1) of the 1989 Act included failure to discharge duties pursuant to s.6 of the 1989 Act (general duties of employers to their employees), s.7 (general duties of employers and self-employed to persons other than their employees), s.8 (general duties of persons concerned with places of work to persons other than their employees), s.9(1) (duty of every employee while at work to take reasonable care for his or her own safety, health and welfare and that of any other person who may be affected by his or her acts or omissions while at work), s.9(2) (intentional or reckless misuse of protective clothing, appliances etc.), s.10 (general duties of designers, manufacturers, etc., as regards articles and substances for use at work), s.11 (general duties of persons who design or construct places of work), s.12(1) (duty of employer to prepare a safety statement), s.12(4) (duty to include certain particulars in the safety statement), s.12(5) (failure to comply with a direction from an inspector to amend a safety statement), s.12(6) (failure to set out in the director's report the extent to which a safety statement has been fulfilled), s.12(7) (duty of self employed person to prepare a safety statement), s.12(8) (duty of self employed and employers to bring a safety statement to the attention of employees and other persons at the place of work), s.13(1) (duty to arrange to consult his or her employees for the purpose of arrangements which will enable him or her and his or her employees to co-operate effectively in promoting and developing safety measures) and s.13(5) (duty of employers to inform a safety representative of an inspector's visit).

[39] See s.48 of the 1989 Act.

1. Summary offences: fine only

19–17 The offences comprised in this category are set out in s.78(1) of 2005 Act. They are:

(a) an offence under s.39(17)(e) of the Redundancy Payments Act 1967 (incorporated by s.29(7) of the 2005 Act). This section provides that a person shall be guilty of an offence where he or she fails to comply with a summons by the Labour Court to give evidence or produce a document; and

(b) any of the aforementioned six offences described in s.77(1) of the 2005 Act.

2. Summary offences: fine and/or imprisonment

19–18 These include:

(a) any of the offences set out in subsections 77(2) to (8) and 9(a) of the 2005 Act;

(b) where a licence is required under the Act, an offence consisting of doing something for which a licence is necessary, without obtaining such a licence; and

(c) an offence consisting of breaching the terms or conditions of such a licence.

It is to be noted that a breach of the general duties owed by employers to employees is covered under s.77(2) of the 2005 Act and can therefore now attract on conviction in the District Court a maximum fine of €3,000 and/or imprisonment not exceeding six months.

3. Indictable offences: fine and/or imprisonment

19–19 Any of the summary offences set out above which can attract a fine and/or imprisonment can also be prosecuted on indictment. It is a matter for the DPP to decide whether such contraventions are serious enough to justify a prosecution on indictment. The largest fine imposed to date in Ireland was in a prosecution against Smurfit News Press Limited on October 29, 2004. It was fined €1 million following two serious accidents at its premises. The level of the fine reflected the fact that the circumstances of both accidents were virtually identical and occurred over a two-week period. Significantly, the court concluded that the second accident would never have occurred had the first accident been properly dealt with.

19–20 In *Daly v P.J. Hegarty and Sons*, the High Court awarded the plaintiff, a construction worker, €900,000 in respect of a head injury sustained when a steel cage was being lowered into a trench by a tower crane.[40]

Damages of €745,000 were awarded to the family of a former ESB employee who was killed when an electric circuit breaker exploded at the ESB's Tarbert generating station in 1993.

---

[40] Unreported, High Court, 2005.

19–21 In July 2003 in the *Oran Pre-Cast* case, where a man was killed when he fell 11 metres in the middle of repairing guttering in a factory in County Galway, the Circuit Court fined Oran Pre-Cast Limited €500,000 for breaches of the 1989 Act and the 1995 Construction Regulations.[41] Hardiman J. in the Court of Criminal Appeal reduced the fine of half a million euros imposed at first instance to €100,000. The learned judge stated:

> "I would repeat what [the Supreme Court] said before in a case where there is no limit on the power of the Court, the Court has to weigh all the aggravating factors but it has to also balance them with questions as to the actual degree of fault and not yield to a purely emotional reaction to the fact that there has been a fatality. The principal factor in assessing a penalty in this case is the degree of fault. The second factor is the context of the Company itself, that is to say its record and how it behaved since these events. And the third factor, which may not be a factor at all in some certain cases, is the ability of the company to pay any particular fine."[42]

19–22 In *DPP v O'Flynn Construction Company Limited*,[43] the Court of Criminal Appeal recently dismissed an appeal by a large construction company against a fine of €200,000 imposed on it for failing to conduct its business in such a way as to ensure, so far as is reasonably practicable, that persons not in its employment who might be affected were not exposed to risks to their safety or health and failing to signpost and lay out the surroundings and perimeter of a construction site. The incident giving rise to the two charges was the death of a nine-year old boy, who while playing on the construction site of the defendant company, caught fire after a barrel of wood preservative exploded.

Murray C.J., delivering the judgment of the Court of Criminal Appeal, held that while there was no recklessness on the part of the defendant company, "there was a serious degree of culpability on its part"[44]. The learned judge stated:

> "It is notorious that building sites, particularly those adjacent to where young people live, are frequently if not invariably an attraction for children and teenagers to enter upon, play and explore. It is entirely foreseeable that when children or teenagers enter upon a building site that they will get up to mischief or engage in dangerous activity which a reasonable or prudent adult would not do. This may include climbing on scaffolding, into and around partially constructed buildings, interference with plant or machinery, tools or materials on a building site".

In the concluding portion of the judgment, the Chief Justice considers the severity of the fine. In dismissing the appeal he makes the following observations:

[41] *The People (DPP) v Oran Pre-Cast Ltd*, Circuit Criminal Court, Castlebar, July 3, 2003.

[42] *Ex tempore* judgment of the Court of Criminal Appeal delivered by Hardiman J. on December 16, 2003. See p.10 of the judgment. Also *The People (DPP) v Redmond* [2001] 3 I.R. 390 where Hardiman J. stated that a fine of £7,500 was neither lenient nor harsh "but only in terms of the circumstances of the person who must pay it" (at p.29).

[43] [2006] I.E.C.C.A. 56.

[44] *ibid.* at p.6.

"[T]he trial judge was nonetheless entitled and indeed bound to impose a penalty that reflected the seriousness of the offence so that it applied appropriate punitive and deterrent elements. Among the elements to be taken into account in assessing the severity of a fine, whether imposed on an individual or a corporate entity, is the wealth or resources of the person or company concerned. As was found by the learned trial judge the defendants in this case are a substantial company who were involved in a very substantial construction project. It could not be said to be disproportionate to their means and resources.

More importantly, the Court is of the view that the fine imposed is proportionate to and reflects the seriousness of the default of the defendant in committing the offences to which they pleaded guilty".

Summary offences under the 2005 Act

19–23 Either of the two categories of summary offences above (*i.e.* those attracting a fine only and those which can attract a fine and/or imprisonment) can be brought by the Authority or a person prescribed under s.33 of the 2005 Act.[45] As with all summary offences, these are prosecuted in the District Court.

19–24 Prosecutions must be brought, pursuant to s.82(3) of the Safety Health and Welfare at Work Act 2005, within one year from the date of the offence. Section 82(4) provides that where a statutory report on foot of an investigation is required, pursuant to s.70 of the 2005 Act, summary proceedings on the findings of the report must be brought within six months of the making of the report or 12 months after the date of the contravention, whichever is the later.

19–25 As stated above, s.82(3) of the 2005 Act extends the normal time prescribed in the Petty Sessions Act 1851 for instituting summary proceedings, from 6 months to 12 months. It provides that summary proceedings must be brought "within 12 months from the date on which the offence was committed".[46] Proceedings are instituted by the issue of a summons. As with any summons, it appears while the summons must be issued within the time limit, it is not necessary that it be served within such a 12-month period.

19–26 Section 83 of the 2005 Act mirrors s.52 of the 1989 Act and provides that an appeal lies to the Circuit Court against any order made by the District Court under the 2005 Act. The decision of the judge of the Circuit Court on any such appeal is final and conclusive.

Fixed charge penalties

19–27 Section 79 of the 2005 Act, which is not yet in force, introduces a new procedure for the imposition of fixed charge penalties on both employees and

---

[45] See s.82 of the 2005 Act.
[46] See s.82(3) of the 2005 Act.

employers by an inspector in lieu of a prosecution.[47] Section 79(1) provides that where an inspector has reasonable grounds for believing that a person is committing or has committed a prescribed offence under the relevant statutory provision, he or she may serve the person with a notice in the prescribed form. The maximum on-the-spot fine which can be imposed is €1,000, which is to be paid "during the period of 21 days beginning on the day of the notice".[48]

19–28 The level of the fine will be detailed in Regulations along with the minor offences and employment sectors to which this fine will apply. A necessary precondition for the exercise of the fine is that the inspector must:

(a) have reasonable grounds to believe a prescribed offence is being committed; and

(b) serves a valid prescribed notice.

As previously stated, a person has 21 days from the service of the notice to pay the fine. If the fine is not paid during the 21-day period, the Authority can proceed to a prosecution.

The advantages of such a scheme include administrative convenience by removing the cost, risk and delay of bringing a prosecution in the District Court. The advantage for the perpetrator in paying the fine include a reduced level of fine compared to a fine which may be imposed in the District Court if the charge is contested. In any prosecution for non-payment under the 2005 Act, the onus is on the accused to prove that the payment has been made.

Liability of directors

19–29 Section 80 of the 2005 Act introduces new offences for directors, employers, officers and senior managers who, for the first time, could be personally liable for breaches of health and safety legislation, and could face either two years imprisonment or a maximum fine of up to €3,000,000 per offence, or both, on conviction on indictment. In summary, s.80 of the 2005 Act adopts an evidence-based approach.

Section 48(19) of the 1989 Act provided for the prosecution of the senior officers and management of a company or other body as follows:

> "(a) Where an offence under any of the relevant statutory provisions committed by a body corporate is proved to have been committed with the consent or connivance of, or to have been attributable to any neglect on the part of any director, manager, secretary or other similar officer of the body corporate or a person who was purporting to act in any such capacity, he as well as the body corporate shall be guilty of that offence and shall be liable to be [prosecuted] against and punished accordingly;
>
> (b) Where the affairs of a body corporate are managed by its members, *paragraph (a)* shall apply in relation to the acts and defaults of a member in

---

[47]   Regulations on this issue are expected in 2007.
[48]   Section 79(2) of the 2005 Act.

connection with his functions of management as if he were a director of the body corporate."

Section 80 of the 2005 Act replaces s.48(19) with some important additions.

19–30   Section 80(1) of the 2005 Act is broadly similar to s.48(19) of the 1989 Act. It attributes liability to a director, manager or other similar officer in the undertaking or a person purporting to act in such capacity, as well as the undertaking, when an offence is committed by an undertaking and the acts involved were authorised or consented to, or were attributable to connivance or neglect by those persons. The reference to a person "who purports to act in any such capacity" renders a person who does not have management functions but purports to act in such capacity liable to prosecution.

19–31   Section 80(2) of the 2005 Act is a significant provision in that it introduces a new presumption. It is presumed by virtue of this provision, until the contrary is proven, that at the material time, the acts resulting in the offence were authorised, consented to or were attributable to connivance or neglect on the part of a director or a person significantly influencing the management of a company.[49] This provision refers to the management of a company and therefore may not apply to safety officers. It was imported from corporate enforcement law and introduces a presumption that a director consented or was neglectful in his or her duties under the 2005 Act unless he or she can disprove this. The existence of such a rebuttable presumption makes the task of prosecution somewhat easier and is likely to be very useful to the Authority and the DPP in initiating prosecutions under the Act. It underlines the importance of senior management taking ownership of health and safety.

The presumption may, however, be rebutted and where this is the case, the prosecutor must then prove the matters beyond all reasonable doubt. For the presumption to be rebutted it is not entirely clear what standard of evidence the defendant must adduce. The phrase it shall be presumed "until the contrary is proved", in a criminal context, normally places a burden on the accused to prove on the balance of probabilities.[50] Therefore to simply raise a reasonable doubt or to discharge an evidential burden of "sufficient evidence" would appear not to be sufficient to amount to a rebuttal. Where a defendant has rebutted the presumption, the Authority must prove the matter beyond all reasonable doubt by producing additional evidence.

A question may be raised about the constitutionality of s.80(2) of the 2005 Act, which is in essence a "guilty until proven innocent" provision. It may be argued that it reverses the normal burden on the prosecution to prove all the elements of the offence beyond reasonable doubt. However, it is submitted that this argument would not be successful especially in the light of the Supreme Court judgments in *Hardy v Ireland*[51] and, in particular, *O'Leary v Attorney General*.[52] In *O'Leary v Attorney General*,[53] where the statute provided that

---

[49]   Section 80(2) of the 2005 Act.
[50]   See Adrian Keane, *The Modern Law of Evidence* (2000), 5th ed. at p.77.
[51]   [1994] 2 I.R. 550.
[52]   [1993] 1 I.R. 102.

possession of an incriminating document was "evidence until the contrary is proved", the Supreme Court upheld the constitutionality of the section and stated that the provision merely shifted the evidential burden and not the legal burden.[54]

19–32 Where the affairs of a body corporate are managed by its members, the foregoing provisions apply to the acts or defaults of a member as if he or she were a director of the body corporate.[55]

Onus of proof

19–33 Section 81 of the 2005 Act mirrors s.50 of the 1989 Act. It provides that in any criminal prosecution for an offence consisting of a failure to comply with a duty or requirement to do something under a relevant statutory provision, it is for the accused to prove that it was not practicable or was not reasonably practicable to do more than was in fact done to satisfy this duty or requirement.[56]

Evidence

19–34 Section 84(1) of the 2005 Act introduces a statutory presumption of fact that any person found to be carrying on a work activity in any place of work at any time shall be deemed to be an employee of the person who has or who may reasonably be presumed to have overall control of the work activities concerned. The section appears to introduce a presumption as to the status of a person carrying on work activities at a place of work.

19–35 Section 84(2) of the 2005 Act provides that where an entry in a record is required under the Act, that the entry made by an employer or on behalf of the employer, shall be admissible against the employer as *prima facie* evidence of the facts contained therein. The absence of such a record shall be admissible that such an entry was not made. This section constitutes a statutory qualification to the rule against hearsay, which generally precludes the introduction of documentary evidence as proof of the facts contained in them. Section 84(2) of the 2005 Act may raise presumptions regarding external acts described in the documents and therefore constitutes a significant modification of the rules against hearsay. The most significant previous modification of this rule was contained in s.5 of the Criminal Evidence Act 1992, which made admissible certain business records where strict conditions were satisfied. Section 5 of the 1992 Act provides that information contained in a document shall be admissi-

[53] [1993] 1 I.R. 102.

[54] The presumption introduced by s.80(2) of the 2005 Act also applies to members responsible for the management of an undertaking. See s.80(3) of the 2005 Act.

[55] Section 80(3) of the 2005 Act.

[56] See para.3–15 of this book. Also *O'Leary v Attorney General* [1993] 1 I.R. 102 and *Boyle v Marathon Petroleum (Ireland) Ltd* [1999] 2 I.R. 640.

ble in any criminal proceedings as evidence of any fact contained therein of which direct oral evidence would be admissible if the information:

(a) was compiled in the ordinary course of a business,

(b) was supplied by a person (whether or not he or she so compiled it and is identifiable) who had, or may reasonably be supposed to have had, personal knowledge of the matters dealt with, and

(c) in the case of information in non-legible form that has been reproduced in permanent legible form, was reproduced in the course of the normal operation of the reproduction system concerned.

Insofar as s.84(2) of the 2005 Act is concerned, there are two similar preconditions to the use of the records as evidence of the facts contained therein: (1) the entry of the record must be required by the relevant statute; and (2) the entry must be by or on the behalf of the employer.

The phrase *prima facie* evidence connotes that such evidence may be rebutted by merely discharging an evidential burden which is a lesser standard than the balance of probabilities. This therefore may be contrasted with the presumptions under ss.80(2) and 84(1) of the 2005 Act.

19–36 Section 84(3) of the 2005 Act should also be noted. It provides that in any proceedings, a copy record may be given in evidence and stands as *prima facie* evidence if the court is satisfied that the system used to make the copy record and the original entry on which it was based is reliable.

Naming and shaming

19–37 Section 85 of the 2005 Act provides that the Authority can compile a list of persons upon whom a fine or penalty has been imposed, upon whom a prohibition notice has been served or in respect of whom an interim or interlocutory order has been made by a court. This list must include:

> "(a) the matter occasioning any fine, penalty, notice or order, as the case may be, imposed on the person, and
> (b) any fine, penalty, notice or order occasioned by the matter referred to in *paragraph (a)*".

The concept of naming and shaming is not new to the Irish legal system. It already exists in company and revenue law. For example, the Companies Registration Office publicises the names of defaulters in the submission of annual returns under the Companies Acts and the Revenue Commissioners publish the names of certain tax defaulters with whom they have made settlements.

CHAPTER 20

THE FUTURE OF HEALTH AND SAFETY LEGISLATION AND MANAGEMENT STANDARDS

20–01 There has been a powerful movement towards greater protection of the safety, health and welfare of employees at work. Certainly, there would be few who would disagree that we have come a long way from the 1802 Act for the Preservation of the Health and Morals of Apprentices and Others.[1] It is probable that many more Regulations, affecting all aspects of the workplace and all those persons connected with it, will be introduced pursuant to s.58 of the Safety, Health and Welfare at Work Act 2005. These Regulations will, no doubt, impose more extensive obligations upon employers as a whole. The cost of complying with these Regulations will also increase.

20–02 The leading question that remains to be addressed is what duty of care will be imposed on employers in the future. Currently, the protection afforded by statute is in excess of that at present afforded by the common law. The provisions of the 2005 Act require the high standard of reasonable practicability from employers. Surprisingly, very few references are made to this standard of reasonable practicability in the General Application Regulations. In fact, the General Application Regulations impose certain absolute duties (see regs 28 and 76). Is it likely, therefore, that future Regulations will impose a higher standard of care on employers than the 2005 Act?

20–03 It has been suggested that the duty of care imposed under future Regulations should be one of absolute liability.[2] A number of reasons for this approach are proffered. Most Regulations commence life as directives from Europe, which this State is obliged, pursuant to its treaty obligations, to implement. Directives set down minimum standards not maximum ones and do not preclude the imposition of a higher duty of care. Accordingly, it is always open to a court to hold that the Regulations impose a higher standard than that provided for under the 2005 Act. In addition, in some cases, absolute duties

---

[1] See para.1–03.
[2] Strict liability is not to be equated with absolute liability. Defences may be pleaded in respect of a strict liability standard, whereas no defence is available to a standard of absolute liability. This standard is higher than that of reasonable practicability under the 2005 Act.

have already been in existence in Irish law since the Factories Act 1955, and to withdraw or recoil from that now would be to reduce the level of protection available to employees under the 2005 Act. This would be totally contrary to the intention of the legislature and the spirit of the legislation. Further, many of the Regulations are general in nature and, indeed, are vague in parts. This would, and should, militate against too strict an interpretation of the Regulations by the courts.

20–04 A relevant and instructive case is *Stark v The Post Office*.[3] In that case a postman was injured when part of the brake mechanism on his bike failed. The front wheel jammed, catapulting him over the handlebars. The defendant unsuccessfully relied on the Directive, which imposed a duty that was not absolute in nature. The claimant pleaded reg.6(1) of the English Provision and Use of Work Equipment Regulations 1992, which imposed an absolute duty on employers to ensure that work equipment was maintained in an efficient state, in efficient working order and in good repair. The Court of Appeal stated that European directives impose minimum, not maximum standards.

20–05 With the passage of time, the Safety, Health and Welfare at Work Act 2005, the Regulations implemented under that Act and the Occupiers' Liability Act 1995 will improve the health and safety standards which employees enjoy in the workplace. This should result in fewer accidents. Consequently, the number and cost of claims should fall. This increased protection may raise the expectations of society as a whole in so far as safety, health and welfare at work are concerned. It may serve, in time, to impact upon the common law duty of care. In other words, what is reasonable now may not be deemed reasonable in the future. In summary, the greater protection afforded by statute may become no more than merely declaratory of the common law position.

20–06 Society and the courts are already reflecting this increased awareness of health and safety. In a case heard in May 1998, namely *DPP v Cullagh*, the operator of a funfair was prosecuted for, and convicted of, criminal negligence arising out of the death of a member of the public.[4] The defendant was given a three-year suspended sentence (on appeal, the Court of Criminal Appeal upheld the conviction). This case was not taken under the health and safety legislation, but rather, under the common law. It was the first case of its type in Irish legal history. The initiation of manslaughter charges by the Director of Public Prosecutions against the managing director of a company (arising from the death of two employees at work), in a case in 1999, was hailed as a milestone; this is because it signposted the fact that workplace fatalities were no longer to be discounted as a minor matter for the District Court. The case resulted in fines of almost a quarter of a million pounds; moreover, a sub-contractor with the company received an 18-month suspended prison sentence

---

[3] Unreported, Court of Appeal, March 2, 2000.
[4] Unreported, Circuit Court, 1998; Court of Criminal Appeal, March 15, 1999 (*ex tempore* judgment of Murphy J.). See also "Man Found Guilty of Funfair Death" *Irish Times*, May 15, 1998.

after he pleaded guilty to a charge of reckless endangerment under the Non-Fatal Offences Against the Person Act 1997.[5] Mr Tom Beegan, then Director General of the Health and Safety Authority, commenting on the case, stated:

> "The message which must go out to employers in all sectors, and not just the construction industry, is that they have a statutory obligation to proactively manage safety in the workplace including the preparation of an adequate Safety Statement".

The Court of Criminal Appeal refused leave to appeal in this case.[6] Significantly, it held that where death was the consequence of a criminal act, the penalty should reflect public disquiet at the unnecessary loss of life. Reliance was placed on the English case of *R. v F. Howe & Sons (Engineers) Ltd*,[7] and in particular the following paragraph from p.254 of that judgment:

> "[I]t is often a matter of chance whether death or serious injury results from even a serious breach. Generally where death is the consequence of a criminal act it is regarded as an aggravating feature of the offence. The penalty should reflect public disquiet at the unnecessary loss of life".

CONCLUSION

20–07   This duty to proactively manage safety in the workplace emerges as a central theme in the Safety, Health and Welfare at Work Act 2005. The general provisions of the 2005 Act, which include on-the-spot fines, increased sentences and fines, the naming and shaming by the Authority, testing for intoxicants, employers' duties, safety statements, safety representatives, codes of practice and joint safety and health agreements will improve the safety and health standards which employees enjoy in the workplace. However, the success of the 2005 Act is dependent not only on ensuring compliance with the new statutory provisions but will also depend on changing existing attitudes.

20–08   The 2005 Act encourages employers to manage health and safety issues, a theme which also emerges from a report published by the European Agency for Safety and Health at Work.[8] This report, which is based on a study of a range of European Businesses, outlines ten occupational safety and health criteria that should form part of a well-structured corporate social responsibility strategy. It highlights the need to integrate occupational health and safety into areas such as marketing and human resources. One of the key criteria identified in the report underlines the importance of linking occupational safety and health goals with a business's long-term strategic and environmental objectives.

20–09   In the future, it is likely that individual members of management will face criminal charges arising out of deaths and injuries at work where it is

---

[5] *DPP v Roseberry Construction Co. Ltd*, unreported, Naas Circuit Criminal Court, November 21, 2001.

[6] *DPP v Roseberry Construction Limited* [2003] 4 I.R. 338.

[7] [1999] 2 All E.R. 249.

[8] See www.osha.eu.int.

possible to connect the individual failures of senior executives with the corporate body. A safety management system must be in place for directors to avoid conviction. Such a system will involve directors identifying hazards, putting appropriate control measures in place and monitoring these control measures to ensure effectiveness. There is now a strong case for express statutory provision for the offence of corporate manslaughter. Where someone loses his or her life through employer negligence, the offence of corporate manslaughter is likely to apply if such an offence is introduced in Ireland.

20–10 In October 2005 the Law Reform Commission published its final report on corporate killing.[9] It recommended in that report that corporations should be subject to criminal liability for corporate killing. The Law Reform Commission's report identified the Stardust nightclub fire, the Whiddy Island disaster and the train crashes at Buttevant and Cherryville as instances where organisational failures in Ireland resulted in death. It also made reference to the Blood Transfusion Service Board, which breached its own rules when it neglected to investigate complaints adequately and to recall contaminated batches of blood produce, leading to the infection of large numbers of people.

20–11 The Law Reform Commission has recommended the introduction of a new statutory offence of "corporate manslaughter", "which would make an organisation responsible for a death arising from its gross recklessness". This offence would facilitate the prosecution of company directors and individual managers if they:

- knew or ought reasonably to have known of a substantial risk of serious personal harm or death;

- failed to make reasonable efforts to eliminate that risk; and

- were aware that such failure fell far below what could reasonably be expected in the circumstances.

Significantly, it would render them liable for unlimited fines and imprisonment for up to 12 years ("as well as possible disqualification from acting as a manager in an undertaking") in circumstances where they are found to have neglected the health and safety of those affected by their activities.[10] The offence of corporate manslaughter, as outlined in the draft Bill appended to the Law Reform Commission's report, requires gross negligence, which means recklessness as to the danger involved in an act or omission when the danger would have been obvious to any reasonable person.

---

[9] See *Report on Corporate Killing* (LRC CP 26-2005) October 2005.

[10] Such an offence was proposed in the United Kingdom by the Law Commission in 1996. Law Com. No. 237, Legislating the Criminal Code: Involuntary Manslaughter, H.M.S.O., 1996. In May 2000, the Home Office issued its consultation paper *Reforming the Law on Involuntary Manslaughter: The Government's Proposals*. This led to the passage by the British Government in 2007 of the Corporate Manslaughter and Corporate Homicide Act 2007. The Act will come into force on 6 April 2008 and will render both small and large companies liable for manslaughter in circumstances where gross failures in management cause death.

PART II

Legal requirements : format? SS

Reporting
methods

Ibed → central
National

International

Global

Colour
coded syste

Braille

which section

for whom

How do g find?

S9.

Corporate style chart

colours - S.mgmt
M.mgnt.
Admin
Service
Domestic

ref.
material?

Samples?

Contacts

info sources

8

GUIDELINES FOR DRAFTING
A SAFETY STATEMENT

SUMMARY

1. The Safety Statement says:

    (a) What the employer wants to achieve in the area of safety, health and welfare at work—it includes a statement of general policy on safety and health, which is signed by a member of senior management and is dated.
    (b) Who is to do it—the means by which everyone in the company/organisation is made aware of the things they are expected to do to help achieve a safe and healthy workplace.
    (c) How it is to be done—the employer's arrangements for safety and health.
    (d) When and what is to be checked—planned review and revision as required.

2. The completed Safety Statement must be relevant to the business activities, the location and workforce.

3. It must be brought to the notice of every employee annually, before he/she enters into a contract with the employer, as must any revisions. (See s.20(3) of the 2005 Act and para.3–78 of this book).

4. Representatives of the workforce must be consulted in good time on matters affecting safety and health. Employees must be consulted where the workforce has not selected a safety representative.

5. Although the general contents are specified by the Safety, Health and Welfare at Work Act 2005 ("the Act"), there is no legally required format for a safety statement. (See para.3–74 of this book.) Extensive guidance on the subject has been published by the Authority. (See www.hsa.ie and Pt IV of this book).

It is also good practice for the Safety Statement to:

6. Stress the need for co-operation between management and workforce before the policy can be effective and ensure the employer can comply with s.8 duties set out in the Act.

7. Draw the attention of employees to their own responsibilities under s.13 of the Act. (See para.3–49 of this book).

8. Cover the safety and health of visitors and contractors, where they could be affected by the business activities and also to cover the safety

and health of employees where they could be affected by the work of visitors and contractors.

9. Cover occupational health matters such as stress, bullying, harassment, fatigue, eyestrain and musculoskeletal disorders.

10. Refer to environmental responsibilities, if relevant to the business activities.

Introduction

A–01 Under s.20 of the 2005 Act, every employer must as soon as possible, prepare or cause to be prepared, a statement in writing which is known as a Safety Statement. This statement specifies the manner in which safety, health and welfare shall be secured in the workplace. The purpose of the document is to require employers to assess the workplace over which they have control and to identify the hazards to safety, health and welfare in that place of work. The risks posed by these hazards are assessed, eliminated where possible, or reduced to acceptable levels. Arrangements are then made to manage the remaining risks at the workplace.

Why do I need a Safety Statement?

A–02 The safety statement is a management tool for managing workplace health and safety. Failure to comply with the s.20 Safety Statement requirement is a criminal offence. Civil liability may also attach.

Key components of a Safety Statement

A–03 There are four main components to a Safety Statement, and these are required under the guidance documentation published by the Authority.

1. **General Policy Statement** – this spells out the commitment of the organisation to safety and health. The reduction/elimination of accidents and the protection of health should be expressly stated as a key feature of the organisation's activities and measure of success.
2. **Organisation** – defining who does what, details the duties/responsibilities of persons in relation to workplace safety, health and welfare.
3. **Arrangements in force** – should characterise the particular arrangements established to achieve the targets set out in the general statement, such as first aid arrangements, training and fire precautions. This will also include a listing of all significant hazards and associated policies and procedures for eliminating or reducing the associated risks.
4. **Review** – all Safety Statements should be subject to periodic review to minimise the risk of the policy falling out of date and failing to address either legal standards or practical issues which arise within the organisation.

COMPONENT 1: THE STATEMENT OF GENERAL POLICY
ON SAFETY AND HEALTH

General Policy Statement

A–04 The first part of the Safety Statement is a statement of commitment that you will manage your business/company/organisation/firm in such a way that, as far as you are able, the safety of staff, visitors, clients, contractors and members of the public will be assured. This is where you identify all possible stakeholders in a well run operation, and declare your intention to look after their interests and request their co-operation to ensure compliance with the duties detailed in s.8 of the Act.

Organisation

A–05   The second section should outline the management organisation, describing who is responsible for delivering the commitments that you have made in the opening statement. This is an opportunity to inform individual members of staff what they are expected to do. Staff need to know what is expected of them in the area of workplace health and safety – and this may be defined in the Safety Statement. This should be repeated in job descriptions and should be raised at staff reviews.

Arrangements

A–06   The final section is the most specific—detailing what you do in practice for first aid, accident reporting, fire safety, hazardous substances, manual handling, machinery/equipment safety, electrical safety, and all other specific issues that should have been picked up as critical in the hazard identification and subsequent risk assessments. Under s.18 of the Act, the employer is required to retain the services of a competent advisor in safety and health. This part of the safety statement is an ideal place to document whatever has been arranged for managers and staff in terms of safe systems of work, information, instructions, advice and training for competence.

Reviews

A–07   The Safety Statement needs to be audited, to ensure that it remains up to date taking into consideration any changes at the workplace, the introduction of new equipment or systems of work, or developments in technology and standards.

A–08   When drafting the policy statement, in order to make a realistic commitment to safety and health, statements should be included that say:

(a)   the business/company/organisation/firm has a commitment to achieving high standards of safety and health;
(b)   it will manage the workplace and work to ensure the safety of employees and that of others who may be affected by its activities;
(c)   safe conditions, equipment and systems of work will be provided and maintained;
(d)   sufficient instruction, information and training will be provided to enable employees to work safely;
(e)   people in the organisation have specific safety responsibilities (and where these are listed);
(f)   it will be reviewed periodically, and revised if necessary.

COMPONENT 2: THE EMPLOYER'S ORGANISATION
FOR SAFETY AND HEALTH

A–09   This part of the Safety Statement is the means by which everyone in the business/company/organisation/firm is made aware of the things they are expected to do to help achieve a safe and healthy workplace—*i.e.* it sets out their responsibilities. There is no legally prescribed method for stating the management responsibilities which make up an employer's organisation for safety and health, but it must be relevant to the business/company/organisation/ firm. It is critical to the success of the Safety Statement that people are only given responsibilities for matters over which they have control and adequate expertise.

A–10   Management accountability starts at the top, from the person identified in the Safety Statement as having control of the firm. Smaller organisations may simply nominate named individuals. This helps those people and other employees identify with their responsibilities directly, rather than in a general job description.

Allocating core responsibilities

A–11   Ensure that someone has responsibility for:

- making employees aware of the Safety Statement and how it applies to them;

- ensuring that subordinates are discharging their safety responsibilities properly;

- receiving information from staff about dangers and giving information about hazards of the business;

- investigating, recording and reporting injuries, ill health and certain dangerous occurrences to the Authority when necessary;

- confirming mechanical and electrical safety, even if these are done by contractors;

- fire safety, including drills, alarm checks, extinguishers, emergency lighting and other fire fighting equipment;

- First Aid provisions, such as training First Aiders and ensuring there are adequate contents in the First Aid boxes;

- ensuring that staff are given adequate instruction, information and training to perform their job safely;

- carrying out an adequate general risk assessment of the workplace, with more specific detailed risk assessments if required;

- ensuring that any building or maintenance work on the premises complies with the requirements of the Safety, Health and Welfare at Work (Construction) Regulations 2006.

Employer responsibilities

A–12   The legal responsibilities of the employer (under s.8 of the Act) are as listed below:

- manage and conduct work activities in such a way as to ensure the safety, health and welfare at work of his or her employees;
- manage and conduct work activities in such a way as to prevent any improper conduct or behaviour likely to put the safety, health or welfare at work of his or her employees at risk;
- provide a properly designed and maintained place of work such that it is safe and without risk to health;
- provide a properly designed and maintained means of egress from and access to the place of work;
- provide a properly planned, organised, performed and maintained system of work such that it is safe and without risk to health;
- provide such information, instruction, training and supervision as is necessary for ensuring the safety and health of his/her employees;
- prepare and revise adequate plans to be followed in emergencies;
- provide and maintain facilities to ensure the welfare of his/her employees; and
- obtain the services of a competent person for the purposes of ensuring the safety and health of employees. (See also paras 3–19 to 3–31 of this book).

Employee responsibilities

A–13   An employee's legal responsibilities (under s.13 of the Act) are:

- not to be under the influence of an intoxicant at the place of work to the extent that the state he or she is in, is likely to endanger his or her own safety, health or welfare at work or that of any other person;
- if reasonably required by his or her employer, to submit to any appropriate, reasonable and proportionate tests for intoxicants by, or under the supervision of, a registered medical practitioner who is a competent person;
- not to engage in improper conduct or behaviour that is likely to endanger his or her own safety or that of any other person;
- to attend such training and, as appropriate, undergo such assessment as may reasonably be required by his or her employer relating to safety, health and welfare at work or relating to the work carried out by the employee;
- not, on entering into a contract of employment, to misrepresent himself or herself to an employer with regard to the level of training he or she may have;
- to take reasonable care of his or her own safety and health and that of others who may be affected by his or her actions;

- to co-operate with management to meet the employer's legal duties;

- to use any device or protective equipment intended to help secure his or her health or safety;

- to report to management any defects in equipment or other dangers immediately, or as soon as it is safe to do so; and

- not to interfere intentionally or recklessly with or to misuse anything provided in the interest of health, safety or welfare. (See also paras 3–49 to 3–52 of this book.)

COMPONENT 3: THE EMPLOYERS' ARRANGEMENTS FOR SAFETY AND HEALTH

A–14 The arrangements component of the Safety Statement is prepared after carrying out a detailed risk analysis of the workplace. Each hazard is identified and eliminated where possible. Where a remaining hazard can potentially cause a significant danger to a person's health or safety, the degree of risk is quantified and arrangements, precautions and procedures are developed to reduce the level of risk to an acceptable level. These arrangements and precautions to minimise the risks must be written down in the Safety Statement.

Arrangements and procedures can involve any combination of:

- design;

- specification;

- inspection;

- maintenance;

- operating procedures and systems of work; and

- training, supervision or monitoring procedures,

which are needed to control an identified risk (see below).

This part of the Safety Statement will detail actual procedures to manage risks and hazards, as outlined below. Before arrangements can be established to control any remaining hazards, they need to be considered in risk assessments.

General Hazard Identification

A–15 An initial hazard identification of any place of work covering access to (and egress from) and within the place of work, all machinery and equipment, all articles and substances, and all activities in the place of work may find many hazards. Where reasonably practicable, hazards identified should be eliminated. Legally, the significant hazards that remain must be written down and incorporated in the Safety Statement.

Specific risk assessments

A–16 Specific risk assessments examining in more detail those dangers discovered in the general risk assessment, will be necessary, for example, these would include:

- fire safety;
- electrical safety;
- mechanical safety, including maintenance and testing;
- display screen equipment;
- manual handling operations;
- noise;
- hazardous substances;
- workplace activities; and
- the workplace environment (heating, lighting, ventilation and toilet facilities).

Checklist for the arrangements for safety

A–17 The following checklist can be completed when checking existing Safety Statement arrangements or setting up new ones.

1. Has a General Hazard Identification been carried out to identify which hazards need arrangements for their elimination or control?
2. Has someone carried out Specific Risk Assessments for each hazard found by the General Hazard Identification?
3. Do the arrangements detail all the hazards for which risk assessments have been done? (For example, have there been checks for noise problems, lifting heavy loads by hand and employees working at computers or employees working away from their base?)
4. Are there procedures laid down for dealing with the identified hazards, including instruction, information and training?
5. Are there procedures for ensuring that non-employees are aware of risks they may face from the business/company/organisation/firm?

COMPONENT 4: REVIEW AND REVISION

A–18 Section 20(5) of the Act requires a Safety Statement's contents to be altered under the direction of an inspector of the Authority if he/she is dissatisfied with the quality of its material. As such, the contents of the Safety Statement need to be revised periodically and as, and when, required. The Authority has recommended this approach in their guidance publications. It is also a statutory requirement. (See s.20(5) of the 2005 Act.)

The Safety Statement must be revised, if significant changes have occurred, such as:

- the creation of a new department;
- the introduction of a new process, such as a solvent-based component cleaning operation;

- transfer of responsibilities from one manager or director to another;

- closing down or selling part of the business/company/organisation/firm, since, given that the Safety Statement must be relevant, so references to a non-existent part of the business/company/organisation/firm must be removed;

- change of premises (which will alter such arrangements as fire safety procedures, evacuation and assembly, or alarm testing);

- changes in Legislation, Approved Codes of Practice, Codes of Practice, Guidance Notes, Irish Standards and International Standards;

- changes in technology that may affect the interpretation of "reasonably practicable".

Note: It is not possible to provide a generic Safety Statement as the risks in each workplace will vary depending on the activity being carried out.

GUIDELINES FOR DRAFTING A NOTICE RESTRICTING LIABILITY
UNDER THE OCCUPIERS' LIABILITY ACT 1995

A–19 Notices should clearly specify the relevant information. This includes identifying the category of entrant and what duty the occupier intends to exclude. It is clear from s.5(3) of the Occupiers' Liability Act 1995 that the effect of a proper notice can only operate to reduce the duty of care owed to visitors to that lower and more restricted duty which is owed to recreational users and trespassers.

SAMPLE NOTICE

Occupiers' Liability Act 1995

The Owners of this Premises do not accept any liability for any personal injury, loss or damage caused to any individual on coming into, while present on, or on leaving these premises save where such injury, loss or damage was caused intentionally or recklessly.

All individuals entering onto these premises are responsible for their own safety and must supervise and control children accompanying them.

This notice is merely a sample notice. It is recommended that you seek legal advice in advance of inserting any such notice on your premises.

PART III

OCCUPIERS' LIABILITY ACT, 1995

(No. 10 of 1995)

ARRANGEMENT OF SECTIONS

Act referred to

National Monuments Act, 1930   1930, No. 2

An Act to amend the law relating to the liability of occupiers of premises (including land) in respect of dangers existing on such premises for injury or damage to persons or property while on such premises and to provide for connected matters.   [17th June, 1995]

Be it enacted by the oireachtas as follows:

Interpretation

1.—(1) In this Act, unless the context otherwise requires—

"damage" includes loss of property and injury to an animal;

"danger", in relation to any premises, means a danger due to the state of the premises;

"entrant", in relation to a danger existing on premises, means a person who enters on the premises and is not the sole occupier;

"injury" includes loss of life, any disease and any impairment of physical or mental condition;

"occupier", in relation to any premises, means a person exercising such control over the state of the premises that it is reasonable to impose upon that person a duty towards an entrant in respect of a particular danger thereon and, where there is more than one occupier of the same premises, the extent of the duty of each occupier towards an entrant depends on the degree of control each of them has over the state of the premises and the particular danger thereon and whether, as respects each of them, the entrant concerned is a visitor, recreational user or trespasser;

"premises" includes land, water and any fixed or moveable structures thereon and also includes vessels, vehicles, trains, aircraft and other means of transport;

"property", in relation to an entrant, includes the property of another in the possession or under the control of the entrant while the entrant is on the premises of the occupier;

"recreational activity" means any recreational activity conducted, whether alone or with others, in the open air (including any sporting activity), scientific research and nature study so conducted, exploring caves and visiting sites and buildings of historical, architectural, traditional, artistic, archaeological or scientific importance;

"recreational user" means an entrant who, with or without the occupier's permission or at the occupier's implied invitation, is present on premises without a charge (other than a reasonable charge in respect of the cost of providing vehicle parking facilities) being imposed for the purpose of engaging in a recreational activity, including an entrant admitted without charge to a national monument pursuant to section 16 (1) of the National Monuments Act, 1930, but not including an entrant who is so present and is—

(*a*) a member of the occupier's family who is ordinarily resident on the premises,

(*b*) an entrant who is present at the express invitation of the occupier or such a member, or

(*c*) an entrant who is present with the permission of the occupier or such a member for social reasons connected with the occupier or such a member;

"trespasser" means an entrant other than a recreational user or visitor;
"visitor" means—

(*a*) an entrant, other than a recreational user, who is present on premises at the invitation, or with the permission, of the occupier or any other entrant specified in *paragraph (a), (b)* or *(c)* of the definition of "recreational user",

(*b*) an entrant, other than a recreational user, who is present on premises by virtue of an express or implied term in a contract, and

(*c*) an entrant as of right,

while he or she is so present, as the case may be, for the purpose for which he or she is invited or permitted to be there, for the purpose of the performance of the contract or for the purpose of the exercise of the right, and includes any such entrant whose presence on premises has become unlawful after entry thereon and who is taking reasonable steps to leave.

(2) In this Act—

(*a*) a reference to a section is to a section of this Act, unless it is indicated that reference to some other enactment is intended,

(*b*) a reference to a subsection is to the subsection of the provision in which the reference occurs, unless it is indicated that reference to some other provision is intended, and (*c*) a reference to any enactment shall be construed as a reference to that enactment as amended, adapted or extended by or under any subsequent enactment including this Act.

Replacement of common law rules

2.—(1) Subject to *section 8*, the duties, liabilities and rights provided for by this Act shall have effect in place of the duties, liabilities and rights which heretofore attached by the common law to occupiers of premises as such in respect of dangers existing on their premises to entrants thereon.

(2) This Act does not apply to a cause of action which accrued before the commencement of this Act.

Duty owed to visitors

3.—(1) An occupier of premises owes a duty of care ("the common duty of care") towards a visitor thereto except in so far as the occupier extends, restricts, modifies or excludes that duty in accordance with *section 5*.

(2) In this section "the common duty of care" means a duty to take such care as is reasonable in all the circumstances (having regard to the care which a visitor may reasonably be expected to take for his or her own safety and, if the visitor is on the premises in the company of another person, the extent of the supervision and control the latter person may reasonably be expected to exercise over the visitor's activities) to ensure that a visitor to the premises does not suffer injury or damage by reason of any danger existing thereon.

Duty owed to recreational users or trespassers.

4.—(1) In respect of a danger existing on premises, an occupier owes towards a recreational user of the premises or a trespasser thereon ("the person") a duty—

(*a*) not to injure the person or damage the property of the person intentionally, and

(*b*) not to act with reckless disregard for the person or the property of the person,

except in so far as the occupier extends the duty in accordance with *section 5*.

(2) In determining whether or not an occupier has so acted with reckless disregard, regard shall be had to all the circumstances of the case, including—

(*a*) whether the occupier knew or had reasonable grounds for believing that a danger existed on the premises;

(*b*) whether the occupier knew or had reasonable grounds for believing that the person and, in the case of damage, property of the person, was or was likely to be on the premises;

(*c*) whether the occupier knew or had reasonable grounds for believing that the person or property of the person was in, or was likely to be in, the vicinity of the place where the danger existed;

(*d*) whether the danger was one against which, in all the circumstances, the occupier might reasonably be expected to provide protection for the person and property of the person;

(*e*) the burden on the occupier of eliminating the danger or of protecting the person and property of the person from the danger, taking into account the difficulty, expense or impracticability, having regard to the character of the premises and the degree of the danger, of so doing;

(*f*) the character of the premises including, in relation to premises of such a character as to be likely to be used for recreational activity, the desirability of maintaining the tradition of open access to premises of such a character for such an activity;

(*g*) the conduct of the person, and the care which he or she may reasonably be expected to take for his or her own safety, while on the premises, having regard to the extent of his or her knowledge thereof;

(*h*) the nature of any warning given by the occupier or another person of the danger; and

(*i*) whether or not the person was on the premises in the company of another person and, if so, the extent of the supervision and control the latter person might reasonably be expected to exercise over the other's activities.

(3)(*a*) Where a person enters onto premises for the purpose of committing an offence or, while present thereon, commits an offence, the occupier shall not be liable for a breach of the duty imposed by *subsection (1) (b)* unless a court determines otherwise in the interests of justice.

(*b*) In *paragraph (a)* "offence" includes an attempted offence.

(4) Notwithstanding *subsection (1)*, where a structure on premises is or has been provided for use primarily by recreational users, the occupier shall owe a duty towards such users in respect of such a structure to take reasonable care to maintain the structure in a safe condition:

Provided that, where a stile, gate, footbridge or other similar structure on premises is or has been provided not for use primarily by recreational users, the occupier's duty towards a recreational user thereof in respect of such structure shall not be extended by virtue of this subsection.

Modification of occupiers' duty to entrants

5.—(1) An occupier may by express agreement or notice extend his or her duty towards entrants under *sections 3* and *4*.

(2)(*a*) Subject to this section and to *section 8*, an occupier may by express agreement or notice restrict, modify or exclude his or her duty towards visitors under *section 3*.

(*b*) Such a restriction, modification or exclusion shall not bind a visitor unless—

(i) it is reasonable in all the circumstances, and

(ii) in case the occupier purports by notice to so restrict, modify or exclude that duty, the occupier has taken reasonable steps to bring the notice to the attention of the visitor.

(c) For the purposes of *paragraph (b) (ii)* an occupier shall be presumed, unless the contrary is shown, to have taken reasonable steps to bring a notice to the attention of a visitor if it is prominently displayed at the normal means of access to the premises.

(3) In respect of a danger existing on premises, a restriction, modification or exclusion referred to in *subsection (2)* shall not be taken as allowing an occupier to injure a visitor or damage the property of a visitor intentionally or to act with reckless disregard for a visitor or the property of a visitor.

(4) In determining for the purposes of *subsection (3)* whether or not an occupier has acted with reckless disregard, regard shall be had to all the circumstances of the case including, where appropriate, the matters specified in *subsection (2)* of *section 4.*

(5) Where injury or damage is caused to a visitor or property of a visitor by a danger of which the visitor had been warned by the occupier or another person, the warning is not, without more, to be treated as absolving the occupier from liability unless, in all the circumstances, it was enough to enable the visitor, by having regard to the warning, to avoid the injury or damage so caused.

Duty of occupiers towards strangers to contracts

6.—(1) The duty which an occupier of premises owes to an entrant under this Act shall not be capable of being modified or excluded by a contract to which the entrant is a stranger, whether the occupier is bound by the contract to permit the entrant to enter or use the premises or not.

(2) For the purposes of this section, an entrant shall be deemed to be a stranger to a contract if the entrant is not for the time being entitled to the benefit of the contract as a party to it or as the successor by assignment or otherwise of a party to it, and, accordingly, a party to the contract who has ceased to be so entitled shall be deemed to be a stranger to the contract.

(3) This section applies to contracts entered into before the commencement of this Act, as well as to those entered into after such commencement.

Liability of occupiers for negligence of independent contractors

7.—An occupier of premises shall not be liable to an entrant for injury or damage caused to the entrant or property of the entrant by reason of a danger existing on the premises due to the negligence of an independent contractor employed by the occupier if the occupier has taken all reasonable care in the circumstances (including such steps as the occupier ought reasonably to have taken to satisfy himself or herself that the independent contractor was competent to do the work concerned) unless the occupier has or ought to have had knowledge of the fact that the work was not properly done.

Saver

8.—Nothing in this Act shall be construed as affecting any enactment or any rule of law relating to—

(*a*) self-defence, the defence of others or the defence of property,

(*b*) any liability imposed on an occupier as a member of a particular class of persons including the following classes of persons:

    (i) persons by virtue of a contract for the hire of, or for the carriage for reward of persons or property in, any vessel, vehicle, train, aircraft or other means of transport;

    (ii) persons by virtue of a contract of bailment; and

    (iii) employers in respect of their duties towards their employees, or

(*c*) any liability imposed on an occupier for a tort committed by another person in circumstances where the duty imposed on the occupier is of such a nature that its performance may not be delegated to another person.

Short title and commencement

9.—(1) This Act may be cited as the Occupiers' Liability Act, 1995.

(2) This Act shall come into operation one month after the date of its passing.

SAFETY, HEALTH AND WELFARE AT WORK ACT 2005

Number 10 *of* 2005

ARRANGEMENT OF SECTIONS

PART 1

PRELIMINARY AND GENERAL

PART 2

GENERAL DUTIES

CHAPTER 1

General Duties of Employer

CHAPTER 2

General Duties of Employee and Persons in Control of Places of Work

CHAPTER 3

General Duties of Other Persons

PART 3

PROTECTIVE AND PREVENTIVE MEASURES

PART 4

SAFETY REPRESENTATIVES AND SAFETY CONSULTATION

PART 5

THE AUTHORITY

CHAPTER 1

The Authority

CHAPTER 2

Staff of Authority

PART 6

REGULATIONS, CODES OF PRACTICE AND ENFORCEMENT

CHAPTER 1

Regulations and Codes of Practice

CHAPTER 2

Enforcement

SCHEDULE 4

SAFETY COMMITTEES

SCHEDULE 5

THE AUTHORITY

SCHEDULE 6

THE CHIEF EXECUTIVE

SCHEDULE 7

REGULATIONS

Acts Referred to

Air Navigation and Transport Act 1936	1936, No. 40
Air Pollution Act 1987	1987, No. 6
Boiler Explosions Act 1882	45 & 46 Vict., c. 22
Boiler Explosions Act 1890	53 & 54 Vict., c. 35
Civil Service Regulation Act 1956	1956, No. 46
Companies Acts 1963 to 2003	
Comptroller and Auditor General (Amendment) Act 1993	1993, No. 8
Consumer Information Act 1978	1978, No. 1
Coroners Act 1962	1962, No. 9
Courts Act 1981	1981, No. 11
Dangerous Substances Acts 1972 and 1979	
Data Protection Acts 1988 and 2003	
Defence Act 1954	1954, No. 18
Defence (Amendment) (No. 2) Act 1960	1960, No. 44
Electricity (Supply) Acts 1927 to 2004	
Electronic Commerce Act 2000	2000, No. 27
Employment Agency Act 1971	1971, No. 27
Ethics in Public Office Act 1995	1995, No. 22
European Communities Act 1972	1972, No. 27
European Parliament Elections Act 1997	1997, No. 2
Explosives Act 1875	38 & 39 Vict., c. 17
Fire Services Act 1981	1981, No. 30
Freedom of Information Act 1997	1997, No. 13
Freedom of Information (Amendment) Act 2003	2003, No. 9
Gas Act 1976	1976, No. 30
Gas (Amendment) Act 1987	1987, No. 9
Gas (Interim) (Regulation) Act 2002	2002, No. 10

Licensing of Indoor Events Act 2003	2003, No. 15
Merchant Shipping (Investigation of Marine Casualties) Act 2000	2000, No. 14
Merchant Shipping Acts 1894 to 2000	
Mines and Quarries Act 1965	1965, No. 7
Minimum Notice and Terms of Employment Acts 1973 to 2001	
National Standards Authority of Ireland Act 1996	1996, No. 28
Notice of Accidents Act 1894	57 & 58 Vict., c. 28
Organisation of Working Time Act 1997	1997, No. 20
Petty Sessions (Ireland) Act 1851	14 & 15 Vict., c. 93
Poisons Act 1961	1961, No. 12
Public Offices Fees Act 1879	42 & 43 Vict., c. 58
Qualifications (Education and Training) Act 1999	1999, No. 26
Railway Employment (Prevention of Accidents) Act 1900	63 & 64 Vict., c. 27
Redundancy Payments Act 1967	1967, No. 21
Redundancy Payments Acts 1967 to 2003	
Regulation of Railways Act 1842	5 & 6 Vict., c. 55
Regulation of Railways Act 1871	34 & 35 Vict., c. 78
Road Traffic Acts 1961 to 2004	
Safety in Industry Acts 1955 and 1980	
Safety, Health and Welfare (Offshore Installations) Acts 1987 and 1995	
Safety, Health and Welfare at Work Act 1989	1989, No. 7
Social Welfare (Consolidation) Act 1993	1993, No. 27
Terms of Employment (Information) Acts 1994 and 2001	
Trade Union Act 1941	1941, No. 22
Unfair Dismissals Acts 1977 to 2001	

An act to make further provision for securing the safety, health and welfare of persons at work and for the enforcement of the relevant statutory provisions, to give further effect to council directive 89/391/eec of 12 june 1989[1] on the introduction of measures to encourage improvements in the safety and health of workers at work and council directive 91/383/eec of 25 june 1991[2] on measures to improve the safety and health at work of workers with a fixed-duration or temporary employment relationship, to provide for the further regulation of work activities, to continue in being and confer additional functions on the national authority for occupational safety and health and rename that body as the health and safety authority, to repeal the safety, health and welfare at work act 1989, to provide for the repeal of certain other enactments and the amendment of the national standards authority of ireland act 1996 and to provide for related matters.

[*22nd June*, 2005]

---

[1]   OJ No. L183, 29.6.1989, p.1
[2]   OJ No. L206, 29.7.1991, p.19

NOTE

Although Section 4 of the Safety, Health and Welfare at Work Act 2005 repeals the Safety, Health and Welfare at Work Act 1989, attention is drawn to the following provisions in the 2005 Act

32.—(1) Notwithstanding the repeal of the Act of 1989 by s.4—

(*a*) the National Authority for Occupational Safety and Health shall continue in being and shall from the commencement of this Act be known as the Health and Safety Authority (and in this Act referred to as the "Authority"), and

(*b*) anything commenced but not completed before the commencement of that section by the Authority may be carried on and completed by it after such commencement as if that Act had not been repealed.

37.—(4) Notwithstanding the repeal of the Act of 1989 by s.4, a person who is a member of the Authority immediately before the commencement of that section shall continue in office as such a member for the remainder of the term of office for which he or she was appointed, unless he or she dies or resigns from office or otherwise ceases to hold office in accordance with *Schedule 5*.

38.—(4) Notwithstanding the repeal of the Act of 1989 by s.4, a person who is a member of an advisory committee immediately before the commencement of that section shall continue in office as such a member for the remainder of the term of office for which he or she was appointed, unless he or she dies or resigns from office or otherwise ceases to hold office.

39.—(6) Notwithstanding the repeal of the Act of 1989 by s.4, the Chief Executive of the Authority holding office immediately before the commencement of this Act shall continue in office as Chief Executive for the remainder of the term of office for which he or she was appointed, unless he or she dies or resigns from office or otherwise ceases to hold office.

52.—(4) Notwithstanding the repeal of the Act of 1989 by s.4, every person who, immediately before the commencement of that section, was a member of the staff of the Authority shall continue to be a member of the staff of the Authority and each such person shall not, after such commencement, be subject to less beneficial conditions of service (including conditions in relation to tenure of office) or of remuneration than the conditions of service (including conditions in relation to tenure of office) or remuneration to which he or she was subject immediately before the said commencement.

56.—(5) Notwithstanding the repeal of the Act of 1989 by s.4, any scheme for the granting of superannuation benefits to or in respect of any members of staff of the Authority in operation immediately before the commencement of the said s.4 shall continue in operation after such commencement.

60.—(7) Notwithstanding the repeal of the Act of 1989 by s.4, a code of practice in operation immediately before the commencement of that section continues to be a code of practice as if prepared and published under this section.

62.—(4) Notwithstanding the repeal of the Act of 1989 by s.4, an inspector authorised immediately before the commencement of that section under s.33 of the Act of 1989 continues to be an inspector as if authorised under this section.

SAFETY, HEALTH AND WELFARE AT WORK ACT 2005

PART 1

PRELIMINARY AND GENERAL

Short title and commencement

1.— (1) This Act may be cited as the Safety, Health and Welfare at Work Act 2005.

(2) This Act shall come into operation on such day or days as may be appointed therefor by order or orders of the Minister either generally or with reference to any particular purpose or provision, and different days may be so appointed for different purposes and different provisions of this Act and an order under this subsection may provide for the commencement of *section 4(2)* upon different days as respects different existing enactments and different provisions of existing enactments.

Interpretation

2.—(1) In this Act, unless the context otherwise requires—

"accident" means an accident arising out of or in the course of employment which, in the case of a person carrying out work, results in personal injury;
"Act of 1989" means the Safety, Health and Welfare at Work Act 1989;
"advisory committee" means an advisory committee established under *section 38*;
"approved" means approved in writing for the time being by the Authority or conforming with a specification in writing by the Authority;
"article" means—

> (*a*) any plant, machine, machinery, appliance, apparatus, tool or any other work equipment for use or operation (whether exclusively or not) by persons at work,
> (*b*) any article designed for use as a component in, part of or to control any such plant, machine, machinery, appliance, apparatus, work equipment, tool or any other work equipment, and
> (*c*) any other product used by persons at work;

"associated statutory provisions" means the provisions of the Acts specified in *Schedule 1* and any statutory instruments made under those Acts for the time being in force;
"Authority" means the Health and Safety Authority;
"cash flow statement" means, in relation to a year, an account showing the derivation of all moneys received by the Authority during that year and the purposes to which they were applied;

"code of practice" means a code of practice prepared and published or, as the case may be, approved of, by the Authority in accordance with *section 60*;

"competent person" shall be read in accordance with *subsection (2)*;

"confidential information" includes—

    (*a*) information that is expressed by the Authority or an advisory committee, as the case may be, to be confidential either as regards particular information or as regards information of a particular class or description, and

    (*b*) proposals of a commercial nature or tenders submitted to the Authority by contractors, consultants or any other person;

"construction work" means the carrying out of any building, civil engineering or engineering construction work, as may be prescribed;

"contract of employment" means a contract of employment or service or apprenticeship, whether the contract is express or implied and, if express, whether it is oral or in writing;

"dangerous occurrence" means an occurrence arising from work activities in a place of work that causes or results in—

    (*a*) the collapse, overturning, failure, explosion, bursting, electrical short circuit discharge or overload, or malfunction of any work equipment,

    (*b*) the collapse or partial collapse of any building or structure under construction or in use as a place of work,

    (*c*) the uncontrolled or accidental release, the escape or the ignition of any substance,

    (*d*) a fire involving any substance, or

    (*e*) any unintentional ignition or explosion of explosives,

as may be prescribed;

"director" includes a person in accordance with whose directions or instructions the directors of the undertaking concerned are accustomed to act but does not include such a person if the directors are accustomed to so act by reason only that they do so on advice given by the person in a professional capacity;

"employee" means a person who has entered into or works under (or, where the employment has ceased, entered into or worked under) a contract of employment and includes a fixed-term employee and a temporary employee and references, in relation to an employer, to an employee shall be construed as references to an employee employed by that employer;

"employer", in relation to an employee—

    (*a*) means the person with whom the employee has entered into or for whom the employee works under (or, where the employment has ceased, entered into or worked under) a contract of employment,

    (*b*) includes a person (other than an employee of that person) under whose control and direction an employee works, and

    (*c*) includes where appropriate, the successor of the employer or an associated employer of the employer;

"enactment" includes any instrument made under an enactment.

"existing enactments" means—

> (*a*) the enactments specified in *Part 1 of Schedule 2* and any instruments made under those enactments for the time being in force, and
>
> (*b*) the regulations made under the European Communities Act 1972 for the time being in force specified in *Part 2 of Schedule 2*;

"fixed-term employee" means an employee whose employment is governed by a contract of employment for a fixed-term or for a specified purpose, being a purpose of a kind that the duration of the contract was limited but was, at the time of its making, incapable of precise ascertainment;

"health surveillance" means the periodic review, for the purpose of protecting health and preventing occupationally related disease, of the health of employees, so that any adverse variations in their health that may be related to working conditions are identified as early as possible;

"improvement notice" means a notice served under *section 66*;

"improvement plan" means a plan required to be submitted under *section 65*;

"inspector" means a person authorised under *section 62* by the Authority or by a person prescribed under *section 33*;

"intoxicant" includes alcohol and drugs and any combination of drugs or of drugs and alcohol;

"joint safety and health agreement" shall be read in accordance with *section 24*;

"material interest" has the meaning assigned by section 2(3) of the Ethics in Public Office Act 1995;

"micro-organism" includes any microscopic biological entity which is capable of replication;

"Minister" means the Minister for Enterprise, Trade and Employment;

"penalisation" has the meaning assigned to it by *section 27* and cognate words shall be read accordingly;

"personal injury" includes—

> (*a*) any injury, disease, disability, occupational illness or any impairment of physical or mental condition, or
>
> (*b*) any death,

that is attributable to work;

"place of work" includes any, or any part of any, place (whether or not within or forming part of a building or structure), land or other location at, in, upon or near which, work is carried on whether occasionally or otherwise and in particular includes—

> (*a*) in relation to an extractive industry including exploration activity, the whole area intended to house workstations to which employees have access for the purpose of their work relating to the immediate and ancillary activities and installations of, as appropriate—
>
> > (i) the surface or, as the case may be, underground extractive industry, including overburden dumps and other tips and any accommodation that is provided and, in the case of the underground extractive industry, any working area,

(ii) the extractive industry through drilling onshore including any accommodation that is provided, and

(iii) the extractive industry through drilling offshore, including any accommodation that is provided,

(*b*) a tent, trailer, temporary structure or movable structure, and

(*c*) a vehicle, vessel or aircraft;

"prescribed" means prescribed—

(*a*) by regulations made by the Minister under this Act (other than in the case of *sections 66(7), 67(7)* and *72(3)*, and

(*b*) in the case of sections *66(7), 67(7)* and *72(3)* by rules made by the Minister for Justice, Equality and Law Reform in consultation with the Minister,

and cognate words shall be read accordingly;

"prohibition notice" means a notice served under *section 67*;

"reasonably practicable" has the meaning assigned by *subsection (6)*;

"recognised trade unions and staff associations" means trade unions and staff associations recognised by the Authority for the purposes of negotiations concerned with the remuneration, conditions of employment or working conditions of its employees;

"record" includes any memorandum, book, report, statement, register, plan, chart, map, drawing, specification, diagram, pictorial or graphic work or other document, any photograph, film or recording (whether of sound or images or both), any form in which data (within the meaning of the Data Protection Acts 1988 and 2003) are held, any form (including machine-readable form) or thing in which information is held or stored manually, mechanically or electronically, and anything that is a part or copy, in any form, of any of, or any combination of, the foregoing;

"registered medical practitioner" means a person whose name is entered in the General Register of Medical Practitioners;

"relevant statutory provisions" means existing enactments and this Act and any instrument made under this Act for the time being in force;

"risk assessment" shall be read in accordance with *section 19*;

"safety representative" means a person selected and appointed under *section 25* as a safety representative;

"safety statement" shall be read in accordance with *section 20*;

"self-employed person" means a person who works for profit or gain otherwise than under a contract of employment, whether or not the person employs other persons;

"share fisherman" has the meaning assigned by *subsection (3)(c)*;

"special report" means a report made under *section 70*;

"strategy statement" means the strategy statement of the Authority prepared and adopted under *section 43*;

"substance" includes any natural or artificial substance, preparation or agent in solid or liquid form or in the form of a gas or vapour or as a micro-organism;

"superannuation benefits" means a pension, gratuity or other allowance payable on resignation, retirement or death;

"temporary employee" means an employee who is assigned by a temporary employment business to work for and under the control of another undertaking availing of the employee's services;

"temporary employment business" means a business, including an employment agency within the meaning of the Employment Agency Act 1971, which provides temporary employees to other undertakings availing of the services of those employees;

"trade union" means a trade union which is the holder of a negotiation licence under Part II of the Trade Union Act 1941;

"undertaking" means a person being an individual, a body corporate or an unincorporated body of persons engaged in the production, supply or distribution of goods or the provision of a service (whether carried on by him or her for profit or not);

"use" includes—

> (*a*) in the case of an article, the manufacture, supply, operation, setting, repair, cleaning and maintenance of the article, and
>
> (*b*) in the case of a substance, the manufacture, process, operation, storage, treatment, mixing, packing, conveyance, supply, handling, filling or emptying, loading and unloading of the substance;

"vessel" means a waterborne craft of any type, whether self-propelled or not, and includes an air cushion craft and any structure in or on water or on water and attached to land;

"work programme" means the work programme of the Authority prepared and adopted under *section 44*.

(2) (*a*) For the purposes of the relevant statutory provisions, a person is deemed to be a competent person where, having regard to the task he or she is required to perform and taking account of the size or hazards (or both of them) of the undertaking or establishment in which he or she undertakes work, the person possesses sufficient training, experience and knowledge appropriate to the nature of the work to be undertaken.

> (*b*) Account shall be taken, as appropriate, for the purposes of *paragraph (a)* of the framework of qualifications referred to in the Qualifications (Education and Training) Act 1999.

(3) In this Act references, in relation to an employer, to an employee shall be read as references to an employee employed by that employer, and for the purposes of this Act—

> (*a*) a person holding office under, or in the service of, the State (including a civil servant within the meaning of the Civil Service Regulation Act 1956) is deemed to be an employee employed by the State or Government, as the case may be,
>
> (*b*) an officer or servant of a harbour authority, the Health Service Executive or a vocational educational committee is deemed to be an employee employed by the harbour authority, the Health Service Executive or vocational education committee, as the case may be, and

(*c*) a share fisherman is deemed to be an employee of the owner or skipper, as the case may be, of a fishing vessel whom he or she accompanies on board the fishing vessel, as a member of the crew, to engage in fishing where he or she is remunerated by a share in the catch or the profits or the gross earnings of the working of the vessel.

(4) For the purposes of the relevant statutory provisions, where an individual agrees with a person who is carrying on the business of an employment agency within the meaning of the Employment Agency Act 1971, and is acting in the course of that business to do or perform personally any work or service for another person (whether or not the latter person is a party to the contract and whether or not the latter person pays the wages or salary of the individual in respect of the work or service), then the latter person shall be deemed to be the individual's employer for the purposes of the relevant statutory provisions.

(5) For the purposes of the relevant statutory provisions, a person who is training for employment or receiving work experience, other than when present at a course of study in a university, school or college, shall be deemed to be an employee of the person whose undertaking (whether carried on by him or her for profit or not) is for the time being the immediate provider to that person of training or work experience, and "employee", "employer" and cognate words and expressions shall be read accordingly.

(6) For the purposes of the relevant statutory provisions, "reasonably practicable", in relation to the duties of an employer, means that an employer has exercised all due care by putting in place the necessary protective and preventive measures, having identified the hazards and assessed the risks to safety and health likely to result in accidents or injury to health at the place of work concerned and where the putting in place of any further measures is grossly disproportionate having regard to the unusual, unforeseeable and exceptional nature of any circumstance or occurrence that may result in an accident at work or injury to health at that place of work.

(7) References in the relevant statutory provisions to a risk assessment or safety statement shall be read as including references to an amended risk assessment or amended safety statement, as the case may be.

(8) A financial year of the Authority shall be a period of 12 months ending on 31 December in any year and for the purposes of *sections 45* and *48* the period commencing on the coming into operation of *section 45* and ending on the following 31 December is deemed to be a financial year of the Authority.

(9) In this Act—

(*a*) a reference to a Part, section or Schedule is a reference to a Part or section of, or Schedule to, this Act, unless it is indicated that a reference to some other enactment is intended,

(*b*) a reference to a subsection, paragraph or subparagraph is a reference to the subsection, paragraph or subparagraph of the provision in which the reference occurs, unless it is indicated that a reference to some other provision is intended,

(*c*) a reference to any enactment shall be read as a reference to that enactment as amended by or under any other enactment, including this Act,

(*d*) a reference to a statutory instrument or to Regulations shall be read as a reference to that instrument as amended, adapted or to Regulations extended by any other statutory instrument, and

(*e*) a reference to the performance of functions includes, with respect to powers and duties, a reference to the exercise of powers and the carrying out of duties.

(10) A word or expression that is used in this Act and is also used in Council Directive 89/391/EEC of 12 June 1989 or Council Directive 91/383/EEC of 25 June 1991 has, unless the contrary intention appears, the same meaning in this Act that it has in those Directives.

Service of notices, etc

3.— (1) A notice or other document required or authorised to be served on, sent or given to any person under the relevant statutory provisions shall, subject to *subsection (2)*, be addressed to the person concerned by name, and may be served on, sent or given to the person in one of the following ways:

(*a*) by delivering it to the person;

(*b*) by leaving it at the address at which the person ordinarily resides or, in a case where an address for service has been furnished, at that address;

(*c*) by sending it by post in a prepaid registered letter to the address at which the person ordinarily resides or, in a case in which an address for service has been furnished, to that address;

(*d*) where the address at which the person ordinarily resides cannot be ascertained by reasonable inquiry and the notice or other document is required to be served on, sent or given to him or her in respect of any place of work, by delivering it to a person over the age of 16 years of age resident or employed at the place of work or by affixing it in a conspicuous position on or near the place of work;

(*e*) if the person concerned has agreed to service of notices by means of an electronic communication (within the meaning assigned by section 2 of the Electronic Commerce Act 2000) to that person (being an addressee within the meaning assigned by that section) and provided that there is a facility to confirm receipt of electronic mail and that such receipt has been confirmed, then by that means;

(*f*) where there is a facility for receiving a facsimile of the notice by electronic means at the address at which the person ordinarily resides or carries on business, by transmitting a facsimile of the notice by such means to that address, provided that the notice is also served or given in any of the other ways referred to in this subsection, or

(*g*) by any other means that may be prescribed.

(2) Where a notice or other document required or authorised under the relevant statutory provisions is to be served on, sent or given to a person who is the owner or occupier of a place of work and the name of the person cannot be ascertained by reasonable inquiry, it may be addressed to the person by using the words "the owner" or, as the case may require, "the occupier".

(3) For the purposes of this section, a company within the meaning of the Companies Acts 1963 to 2003 shall be deemed to be ordinarily resident at its registered office, and every other body corporate and every unincorporated body shall be deemed to be ordinarily resident at its principal office or place of business.

Repeals and savings

4.— (1) Sections 38 and 41 of the Organisation of Working Time Act 1997 are repealed.

(2) The existing enactments set out in *Part 1* of *Schedule 2* are repealed.

(3) Where any document refers to an existing enactment repealed by this Act and provision is made by this Act corresponding to that enactment, then, unless the context otherwise requires, that reference shall be construed as or, as the case may be, as including a reference to the corresponding provision of this Act.

(4) Subject to *subsection (3)*, in so far as any instrument (including any order or regulation) made or issued and any other thing done under an existing enactment set out in *Part 1 of Schedule 2* is in force immediately before the repeal of such enactment by *subsection (2)* could have been made, issued or done under a corresponding provision of this Act, it shall not be invalidated by the repeals effected by *subsection (2)* but, except in so far as this Act otherwise provides, shall continue in force as if made, issued or done under this Act.

Expenses

5.—The expenses incurred by the Minister in administering this Act, shall, to such extent as may be sanctioned by the Minister for Finance, be paid out of moneys provided by the Oireachtas.

Application of relevant statutory provisions to certain public service activities

6.—(1) The relevant statutory provisions apply to prisons and places of detention unless their application is incompatible with safe custody, good order and security.

(2) Subject to *section 11*, the relevant statutory provisions apply to members of the Defence Forces except when they are—

(*a*) on active service within the meaning of section 5 of the Defence Act 1954 or deemed to be on active service within the meaning of section 4(1) of the Defence (Amendment) (No. 2) Act 1960, (*b*) engaged in action in the course of operational duties at sea,

(*c*) engaged in operations in aid to the civil power, or

(*d*) engaged in training directly associated with any of the activities specified in *paragraph (a)* to *(c)*.

Application of relevant statutory provisions to self-employed persons

7.—The relevant statutory provisions apply, where appropriate, to a self-employed person as they apply to an employer and as if that self-employed person was an employer and his or her own employee and references in the relevant statutory provisions to an employer shall be read as references to a self-employed person.

PART 2

GENERAL DUTIES

CHAPTER 1

General Duties of Employer

General duties of employer

8.— (1) Every employer shall ensure, so far as is reasonably practicable, the safety, health and welfare at work of his or her employees.

(2) Without prejudice to the generality of *subsection (1)*, the employer's duty extends, in particular, to the following:

(*a*) managing and conducting work activities in such a way as to ensure, so far as is reasonably practicable, the safety, health and welfare at work of his or her employees;

(*b*) managing and conducting work activities in such a way as to prevent, so far as is reasonably practicable, any improper conduct or behaviour likely to put the safety, health or welfare at work of his or her employees at risk;

(*c*) as regards the place of work concerned, ensuring, so far as is reasonably practicable—

(i) the design, provision and maintenance of it in a condition that is safe and without risk to health,

(ii) the design, provision and maintenance of safe means of access to and egress from it, and

(iii) the design, provision and maintenance of plant and machinery or any other articles that are safe and without risk to health;

(*d*) ensuring, so far as it is reasonably practicable, the safety and the prevention of risk to health at work of his or her employees relating to the use of any article or substance or the exposure to noise, vibration or ionising or other radiations or any other physical agent;

(*e*) providing systems of work that are planned, organised, performed, maintained and revised as appropriate so as to be, so far as is reasonably practicable, safe and without risk to health;

(*f*) providing and maintaining facilities and arrangements for the welfare of his or her employees at work;

(*g*) providing the information, instruction, training and supervision necessary to ensure, so far as is reasonably practicable, the safety, health, and welfare at work of his or her employees;

(*h*) determining and implementing the safety, health and welfare measures necessary for the protection of the safety, health and welfare of his or her employees when identifying hazards and carrying out a risk assessment under *section 19* or when preparing a safety statement under *section 20* and ensuring that the measures take account of changing circumstances and the general principles of prevention specified in *Schedule 3*;

(*i*) having regard to the general principles of prevention in *Schedule 3*, where risks cannot be eliminated or adequately controlled or in such circumstances as may be prescribed, providing and maintaining such suitable protective clothing and equipment as is necessary to ensure, so far as is reasonably practicable, the safety, health and welfare at work of his or her employees;

(*j*) preparing and revising, as appropriate, adequate plans and procedures to be followed and measures to be taken in the case of an emergency or serious and imminent danger;

(*k*) reporting accidents and dangerous occurrences, as may be prescribed, to the Authority or to a person prescribed under *section 33*, as appropriate, and

(*l*) obtaining, where necessary, the services of a competent person (whether under a contract of employment or otherwise) for the purpose of ensuring, so far as is reasonably practicable, the safety, health and welfare at work of his or her employees.

(3) Any duty imposed on an employer under the relevant statutory provisions in respect of any of his or her employees shall also apply in respect of the use by him or her of the services of a fixed-term employee or a temporary employee.

(4) For the duration of the assignment of any fixed-term employee or temporary employee working in his or her undertaking, it shall be the duty of every employer to ensure that working conditions are such as will protect the safety, health and welfare at work of such an employee.

(5) Every employer shall ensure that any measures taken by him or her relating to safety, health and welfare at work do not involve financial cost to his or her employees.

Information for employees

9.— (1) Without prejudice to the generality of *section 8*, every employer shall, when providing information to his or her employees under that section on matters relating to their safety, health and welfare at work ensure that the information—

(*a*) is given in a form, manner and, as appropriate, language that is reasonably likely to be understood by the employees concerned, and

(*b*) includes the following information—

(i) the hazards to safety, health and welfare at work and the risks identified by the risk assessment,

(ii) the protective and preventive measures to be taken concerning safety, health and welfare at work under the relevant statutory provisions in respect of the place of work and each specific task to be performed at the place of work, and

(iii) the names of persons designated under *section 11* and of safety representatives selected under *section 25*, if any.

(2) Where an employee of another undertaking is engaged in work activities in an employer's undertaking, that employer shall take measures to ensure that the employee's employer receives adequate information concerning the matters referred to in *subsection (1)*.

(3) Every employer shall ensure that employees appointed under *section 18* and safety representatives, if any, have access, for the purposes of performing their functions relating to the safety, health and welfare of employees, to—

(*a*) the risk assessment carried out under *section 19*,

(*b*) information relating to accidents and dangerous occurrences required to be reported to the Authority or a person prescribed under *section 33* under the relevant statutory provisions, and

(*c*) any information arising from protective and preventive measures taken under the relevant statutory provisions or provided by the Authority, a person prescribed under *section 33*, or a person referred to in *section 34(2)*.

(4) (*a*) Where an employer proposes to use the services of a fixed-term employee or a temporary employee, the employer shall, prior to commencement of employment, give information to the employee relating to—

(i) any potential risks to the safety, health and welfare of the employee at work,

(ii) health surveillance,

(iii) any special occupational qualifications or skills required in the place of work, and

(iv) any increased specific risks which the work may involve.

(*b*) Where an employer proposes to use the services of a temporary employee, the employer shall—

(i) specify to the temporary employment business concerned the occupational qualifications necessary for and the specific features of the work for which such an employee is required, and

(ii) ensure that the temporary employment business gives the information referred to in *paragraph (a)* to the employee.

(5) The temporary employment business referred to in *subsection (4)(b)* shall give to the employee the information referred to in *subsection (4)(b)(i)*.

Instruction, training and supervision of employees

10.— (1) Without prejudice to the generality of *section 8* and having regard to *sections 25* and *26*, every employer shall, when providing instruction, training and supervision to his or her employees in relation to their safety, health and welfare at work, ensure that—

(*a*) instruction, training and supervision is provided in a form, manner and, as appropriate, language that is reasonably likely to be understood by the employee concerned,

(*b*) employees receive, during time off from their work, where appropriate, and without loss of remuneration, adequate safety, health and welfare training, including, in particular, information and instructions relating to the specific task to be performed by the employee and the measures to be taken in an emergency,

(*c*) in relation to any specific task assigned to an employee, that his or her capabilities in relation to safety, health and welfare are taken into account,

(*d*) in the case of—

(i) a class or classes of particularly sensitive employees to whom any of the relevant statutory provisions apply, or

(ii) any employee or group of employees exposed to risks expressly provided for under the relevant statutory provisions,

the employees concerned are protected against the dangers that specifically affect them.

(2) Training under this section shall be adapted to take account of new or changed risks to safety, health and welfare at work and shall, as appropriate, be repeated periodically.

(3) Training under this section shall be provided to employees—

(*a*) on recruitment,

(*b*) in the event of the transfer of an employee or change of task assigned to an employee,

(*c*) on the introduction of new work equipment, systems of work or changes in existing work equipment or systems of work, and

(*d*) on the introduction of new technology.

(4) Where, in respect of any particular work, competency requirements are prescribed, the employer shall provide for the release of employees, during working hours, where appropriate, and without loss of remuneration, for the purpose of attending training in matters relating to safety, health and welfare at work as regards the particular work.

(5) Every employer shall ensure that persons at work in the place of work concerned who are employees of another employer receive instructions relating to any risks to their safety, health and welfare in that place of work as necessary or appropriate.

(6) Every employer who uses the services of a fixed-term employee or a temporary employee shall ensure that the employee receives the training appropriate to the work which he or she is required to carry out having regard to his or her qualifications and experience.

Emergencies and serious and imminent dangers

11.—(1) Without prejudice to the generality of *section 8*, every employer shall, in preparing and revising as necessary adequate plans and procedures to be followed and measures to be taken in the case of an emergency or serious and imminent danger—

(*a*) provide the necessary measures to be taken appropriate to the place of work for first aid, fire-fighting and the evacuation of employees and any other individual present in the place of work, taking account of the nature of the work being carried on and the size of the place of work,

(*b*) arrange any necessary contacts with the appropriate emergency services, in particular with regard to first aid, emergency medical care, rescue work and fire-fighting,

(*c*) for the purposes of implementing the plans, procedures and measures referred to in this section and *section 8*

(i) designate employees who are required to implement those plans, procedures and measures, and

(ii) ensure that the number of those employees, their training and the equipment available to them are adequate, taking into account either or both the size of and specific hazards relating to the place of work.

(2) In the event of an emergency or serious and imminent danger, an employer shall—

(*a*) as soon as possible inform all employees concerned of the risk involved and of the steps taken or to be taken to protect them from it,

(*b*) save in exceptional cases for the reasons specified in the plans and procedures referred to in *subsection (1)*, refrain from requiring employees to carry out or resume work where there is still a serious and imminent danger to their safety and health, and (*c*) ensure that, in the absence of appropriate guidance or instruction and having regard to the knowledge of the employee and the technical means at his or her disposal, and where the employee's immediate superior responsible cannot be contacted, the employee concerned may take appropriate steps to avoid the consequences of the danger.

(3) In the event of serious, imminent and unavoidable danger, an employer shall—

(*a*) take action and give instructions to enable employees to either or both stop work and immediately leave the place of work and to proceed to a safe place, and

(*b*) ensure that an employee who leaves a place of work is not penalised because of such action.

(4) An employer shall ensure that only employees who have received appropriate instructions have access to the area of the place of work where a serious, specific danger exists.

(5) This section does not apply to the following persons when they are engaged in activities relating to civil emergencies, public order, security or an act of war where any such activity prevents compliance with this section:

(*a*) members of the Defence Forces;

(*b*) members of the Garda Síochána;

(*c*) employees of a fire authority (within the meaning of the Fire Services Act 1981); or

(*d*) persons engaged in the activities of civil protection or civil defence.

General duties of employers to persons other than their employees

12.— Every employer shall manage and conduct his or her undertaking in such a way as to ensure, so far as is reasonably practicable, that in the course of the work being carried on, individuals at the place of work (not being his or her employees) are not exposed to risks to their safety, health or welfare.

CHAPTER 2

General Duties of Employee and Persons in Control of Places of Work

Duties of employee

13.—(1) An employee shall, while at work—

(*a*) comply with the relevant statutory provisions, as appropriate, and take reasonable care to protect his or her safety, health and welfare and the safety, health and welfare of any other person who may be affected by the employee's acts or omissions at work, (*b*) ensure that he or she is not under the influence of an intoxicant to the extent that he or she is in such a state as to endanger his or her own safety, health or welfare at work or that of any other person,

(*c*) if reasonably required by his or her employer, submit to any appropriate, reasonable and proportionate tests for intoxicants by, or under the supervision of, a registered medical practitioner who is a competent person, as may be prescribed,

(*d*) co-operate with his or her employer or any other person so far as is necessary to enable his or her employer or the other person to comply with the relevant statutory provisions, as appropriate,

(*e*) not engage in improper conduct or other behaviour that is likely to endanger his or her own safety, health and welfare at work or that of any other person,

(*f*) attend such training and, as appropriate, undergo such assessment as may reasonably be required by his or her employer or as may be prescribed relating to safety, health and welfare at work or relating to the work carried out by the employee,

(*g*) having regard to his or her training and the instructions given by his or her employer, make correct use of any article or substance provided for use by the employee at work or for the protection of his or her safety, health and welfare at work, including protective clothing or equipment,

(*h*) report to his or her employer or to any other appropriate person, as soon as practicable—

  (i) any work being carried on, or likely to be carried on, in a manner which may endanger the safety, health or welfare at work of the employee or that of any other person,

  (ii) any defect in the place of work, the systems of work, any article or substance which might endanger the safety, health or welfare at work of the employee or that of any other person, or

  (iii) any contravention of the relevant statutory provisions which may endanger the safety, health and welfare at work of the employee or that of any other person,

of which he or she is aware.

(2) An employee shall not, on entering into a contract of employment, misrepresent himself or herself to an employer with regard to the level of training as may be prescribed under *subsection (1)(f)*.

Interference, misuse, etc.

14.—A person shall not intentionally, recklessly or without reasonable cause—

(*a*) interfere with, misuse or damage anything provided under the relevant statutory provisions or otherwise for securing the safety, health and welfare of persons at work, or (*b*) place at risk the safety, health or welfare of persons in connection with work activities.

General duties of persons in control of places of work, etc.

15.—(1)This section applies to a person who has control to any extent of—

(*a*) a non-domestic place of work that has been made available as a place of work to persons other than employees of the person to whom this section applies,

(*b*) the means of access to or egress from that place of work, or

(*c*) any article or substance provided for the use of persons at that place of work, other than employees of the person who has control of the article or substance,

including a person who has control of a place of work or part of a place of work in connection with the carrying on by him or her of a trade, undertaking or business (whether for profit or not).

(2) Where a person has, by virtue of any contract, tenancy, licence or other interest, an obligation to any extent—

(*a*) to maintain or repair a place of work or the means of access thereto or egress therefrom, or

(*b*) as regards the safety of, or the absence of risk to health arising from, any article or substance provided for use in, that place of work,

the person is deemed, for the purposes of this section, to be a person to whom this section applies to the extent of his or her obligation.

(3) A person to whom this section applies shall ensure, so far as is reasonably practicable, that the place of work, the means of access thereto, or egress therefrom, and any article or substance provided for use in the place of work, are safe and without risk to health.

CHAPTER 3

General Duties of Other Persons

General duties of designers, manufacturers, importers and suppliers of articles and substances.

16.— (1)A person who designs, manufactures, imports or supplies any article for use at work shall—

(*a*) ensure, so far as is reasonably practicable, that the article is designed and constructed so as—

(i) to be safe and without risk to health when properly used by a person at a place of work, and

(ii) to comply with the relevant statutory provisions and with the provisions of any relevant enactment implementing any relevant directive of the European Communities, (*b*) ensure that the article undergoes appropriate levels of testing and examination to ensure compliance with *paragraph (a)*,

    (*c*) provide or arrange for the provision of adequate information about the article to the persons to whom it is supplied to ensure its safe use,

    (*d*) ensure that persons to whom the article is supplied are provided with any revisions of the information provided under *paragraph (c)* as are necessary by reason of it becoming known that anything relating to the article gives rise to a serious risk to safety or health,

    (*e*) if the person has responsibility under a rental, leasing or other arrangement to do so, maintain the article in a safe condition and in compliance with the relevant statutory provisions,

    (*f*) comply with the relevant statutory provisions.

(2) For the purposes of *subsection (1)(c)*, adequate information includes information relating to—

    (*a*) the use for which the article has been designed, manufactured or tested, as the case may be, and

    (*b*) any conditions necessary to ensure its safe installation, use, maintenance, cleaning, dismantling or disposal without risk to safety or health.

(3) A person who undertakes the design or manufacture of any article for use at work shall carry out or arrange for the carrying out of any necessary research with a view to the discovery and, so far as is reasonably practicable, the elimination or minimisation of any risks to safety or health to which the design or article may give rise.

(4) A person who erects, assembles or installs any article for use at a place of work where that article is to be used by persons at work shall ensure, so far as is reasonably practicable, that nothing in the manner in which it is erected, assembled or installed makes the article unsafe or a risk to health when used at the place of work.

(5) A person who manufactures, imports or supplies a substance for use at work shall—

    (*a*) ensure, so far as is reasonably practicable, that the substance is safe and without risk to health when properly used by a person at a place of work,

    (*b*) ensure that the substance undergoes appropriate levels of testing and examination to ensure compliance with *paragraph (a)*,

    (*c*) provide or arrange for the provision of adequate information about the substance to the persons to whom it is supplied to ensure its safe use, and

    (*d*) comply with the relevant statutory provisions and with the provisions of any relevant enactment implementing any relevant directive of the European Communities.

(6) For the purposes of *subsection (5)(c)*, adequate information includes information relating to—

    (*a*) the identification of the substance,

(*b*) any risk to safety or health associated with its inherent properties,

(*c*) the results of any relevant tests or examination which have been carried out on or in connection with the substance that are relevant to its safe use, and

(*d*) any conditions necessary to ensure its safe use, handling, processing, storing, transportation or disposal without risk to safety or health.

(7) A person who undertakes the manufacture of a substance, or in the case where the manufacture was undertaken outside the State, the importer, shall carry out or arrange for the carrying out of any necessary research with a view to the discovery and, so far as is reasonably practicable, the elimination or minimisation of any risks to safety or health to which the substance may give rise when in use.

(8) Nothing in *subsections (1)* to *(7)* shall be read as requiring a person to repeat any testing, examination or research which has been carried out otherwise than by or on behalf of the person, in so far as it is reasonable for the person to rely on the results of that testing, examination or research, for the purposes of those subsections.

(9) Any duty imposed on a person by *subsections (1)* to *(7)* extends only to things done in the course of a trade, undertaking or business (whether for profit or not) carried on by the person and to matters within his or her control.

(10) Where a person designs, manufactures, imports or supplies an article or substance for use at work and does so for or to another person on the basis of a written undertaking by that other person to take specified steps that are sufficient to ensure, so far as is reasonably practicable, that the article or substance shall be safe and without risk to health or safety when it is used at a place of work, the undertaking has the effect of relieving the person who designs, manufactures, imports or supplies the article or substance from the duty imposed by *paragraphs (a)* and *(b)* of *subsection (1)* and *paragraphs (a)* and *(b)* of *subsection (5)* to such extent as is reasonable having regard to the terms of the undertaking.

(11) Nothing in *subsection (9)* or *(10)* relieves any person who imports any article or substance from any duty in respect of anything which—

(*a*) in the case of an article designed outside the State, was done by and in the course of any trade, profession or other undertaking carried on by, or was within the control of, the person who designed the article, or

(*b*) in the case of an article or substance manufactured outside the State, was done by and in the course of any trade, profession or other undertaking carried on by, or was within the control of, the person who manufactured the article or substance.

(12) Where a person (in this subsection referred to as "the supplier") supplies to another person (in this subsection referred to as "the customer") any

article or substance for use at work under a hire-purchase agreement, a leasing agreement or credit-sale agreement, and the supplier—

(*a*) carried on the business of financing the acquisition of goods by others by means of those agreements, and

(*b*) in the course of that business acquired his or her interest in the article or substance supplied to the customer as a means of financing its acquisition by the customer from a third party,

then that third party and not the supplier shall be treated for the purposes of this section as supplying the article or substance to the customer and any duty imposed by this section on suppliers shall, accordingly, fall on that third party and not on the supplier.

(13) For the purposes of this section, an absence of safety or a risk to health shall be disregarded in so far as the case is or, in relation to which it would arise is shown to be, one the occurrence of which could not reasonably be foreseen and, in determining whether a duty imposed by *paragraphs (a)* and *(b)* of *subsection (1)* or *paragraphs (a)* and *(b)* of *subsection (5)* has been performed, regard shall be had to any relevant information or advice which has been provided to any person by the person who designed, manufactured, imported or supplied the article or by the person who manufactured, imported or supplied the substance.

Duties related to construction work

17.—(1) A person who commissions or procures a project for construction work shall appoint in writing a competent person or persons for the purpose of ensuring, so far as is reasonably practicable, that the project—

(*a*) is designed and is capable of being constructed to be safe and without risk to health,

(*b*) is constructed to be safe and without risk to health,

(*c*) can be maintained safely and without risk to health during subsequent use, and

(*d*) complies in all respects, as appropriate, with the relevant statutory provisions.

(2) A person who designs a project for construction work shall ensure, so far as is reasonably practicable, that the project—

(*a*) is designed and is capable of being constructed to be safe and without risk to health,

(*b*) can be maintained safely and without risk to health during use, and

(*c*) complies in all respects, as appropriate, with the relevant statutory provisions.

(3) A person who carries out construction work shall ensure, so far as is reasonably practicable, that it is constructed to be safe and without risk to health and that it complies in all respects, as appropriate, with the relevant statutory provisions.

(4) For the purposes of this section, 'project' means any development which includes or is intended to include construction work.

PART 3

PROTECTIVE AND PREVENTIVE MEASURES

Protective and Preventive Measures

18.—(1) Without prejudice to the generality of *section 8*, an employer shall, for the purpose of complying with the relevant statutory provisions, appoint one or more competent persons to perform such functions as are specified by the employer, relating to the protection from and the prevention of risks to safety, health and welfare at work.

(2) An employee appointed under *subsection (1)* as a competent person shall be allowed adequate time, with no loss of remuneration, to enable him or her to perform such functions as are specified by the employer.

(3) Every employer shall—

    (*a*) ensure that—

        (i) the number of persons appointed, and

        (ii) the time available to them and the means at their disposal to perform their functions under this section,

    are adequate having regard to the size of the place of work, the risks to which employees are exposed and the distribution of those risks in the place of work, and

    (*b*) make arrangements for ensuring adequate co-operation between those persons and safety representatives (if any) appointed under *section 25* whenever necessary.

(4) Where there is a competent person in the employer's employment, that person shall be appointed for the purposes of this section in preference to a competent person who is not in his or her employment except where the knowledge and experience of the person first referred to is not adequate or appropriate to the functions conferred by this section.

(5) An employer shall provide the competent person appointed under this section who is not in his or her employment with the following information:

    (*a*) the factors known by the employer to affect, or suspected by the employer of affecting, the safety, health and welfare of his or her employees;

    (*b*) the risks to safety, health and welfare and the protective and preventive measures and activities in respect of the place of work and the work carried out there;

    (*c*) the measures for the evacuation of employees and other persons to be taken under *section 11*, including the employees designated to implement the plans and measures referred to in *paragraphs (a)* and *(b)* of *subsection (1)* of that section; and

(*d*) such reasonable information about any person in the place of work concerned who is a fixed-term employee or a temporary employee as is necessary to enable the competent person to perform his or her functions under this section.

Hazard identification and risk assessment

19.—(1) Every employer shall identify the hazards in the place of work under his or her control, assess the risks presented by those hazards and be in possession of a written assessment (to be known and referred to in this Act as a "risk assessment") of the risks to the safety, health and welfare at work of his or her employees, including the safety, health and welfare of any single employee or group or groups of employees who may be exposed to any unusual or other risks under the relevant statutory provisions.

(2) For the purposes of carrying out a risk assessment under *subsection (1)*, the employer shall, taking account of the work being carried on at the place of work, have regard to the duties imposed by the relevant statutory provisions.

(3) The risk assessment shall be reviewed by the employer where—

(*a*) there has been a significant change in the matters to which it relates, or

(*b*) there is another reason to believe that it is no longer valid, and, following the review, the employer shall amend the risk assessment as appropriate.

(4) In relation to the most recent risk assessment carried out by an employer, he or she shall take steps to implement any improvement considered necessary relating to the safety, health and welfare at work of employees and to ensure that any such improvement is implemented in respect of all activities and levels of the place of work.

(5) Every person to whom *sections 12* or *15* applies shall carry out a risk assessment in accordance with this section to the extent that his or her duties under those sections may apply to persons other than his or her employees.

Safety statement

20.—(1) Every employer shall prepare, or cause to be prepared, a written statement (to be known and referred to in this Act as a "safety statement"), based on the identification of the hazards and the risk assessment carried out under *section 19*, specifying the manner in which the safety, health and welfare at work of his or her employees shall be secured and managed.

(2) Without prejudice to the generality of *subsection (1)*, every employer shall ensure that the safety statement specifies—

(a) the hazards identified and the risks assessed,

(b) the protective and preventive measures taken and the resources provided for protecting safety, health and welfare at the place of work to which the safety statement relates,

(c) the plans and procedures to be followed and the measures to be taken in the event of an emergency or serious and imminent danger, in compliance with *sections 8* and *11*,

(d) the duties of his or her employees regarding safety, health and welfare at work, including co-operation with the employer and any persons who have responsibility under the relevant statutory provisions in matters relating to safety, health and welfare at work,

(e) the names and, where applicable, the job title or position held of each person responsible for performing tasks assigned to him or her pursuant to the safety statement, and

(f) the arrangements made regarding the appointment of safety representatives and consultation with, and participation by, employees and safety representatives, in compliance with *sections 25* and *26*, including the names of the safety representative and the members of the safety committee, if appointed.

(3) Every employer shall bring the safety statement, in a form, manner and, as appropriate, language that is reasonably likely to be understood, to the attention of—

(a) his or her employees, at least annually and, at any other time, following its amendment in accordance with this section,

(b) newly-recruited employees upon commencement of employment, and

(c) other persons at the place of work who may be exposed to any specific risk to which the safety statement applies.

(4) Where there are specific tasks being performed at the place of work that pose a serious risk to safety, health or welfare, an employer shall bring to the attention of those affected by that risk relevant extracts of the safety statement setting out—

(a) the risk identified,

(b) the risk assessment, and

(c) the protective and preventive measures taken in accordance with the relevant statutory provisions in relation to that risk.

(5) Every employer shall, taking into account the risk assessment carried out under *section 19*, review the safety statement where—

(a) there has been a significant change in the matters to which it refers,

(b) there is another reason to believe that the safety statement is no longer valid, or

(c) an inspector in the course of an inspection, investigation, examination, inquiry under *section 64* or otherwise directs that the safety statement be amended within 30 days of the giving of that direction, and, following the review, the employer shall amend the safety statement as appropriate.

(6) Every employer who is conducting activities, as may be prescribed in accordance with this subsection, who contracts with another employer for that employer to provide services to him or her shall require that that employer is in possession of an up-to-date safety statement as required under this section.

(7) A copy of a safety statement, or relevant extract of it, shall be kept available for inspection at or near every place of work to which it relates while work is being carried out there.

(8) It shall be sufficient compliance with this section by an employer employing 3 or less employees to observe the terms of a code of practice, if any, relating to safety statements which applies to the class of employment covering the type of work activity carried on by the employer.

(9) Every person to whom *section 12* or *15* applies shall prepare a safety statement in accordance with this section to the extent that his or her duties under those sections may apply to persons other than his or her employees.

Duty of employers to co-operate

21.—Where employers share a place of work, they shall—

(*a*) in relation to safety, health and welfare at work, co-operate in complying with and implementing the relevant statutory provisions,

(*b*) taking into account the nature of the work carried on at the place of work concerned—

(i) co-ordinate their actions in matters relating to the protection from and prevention of risks to safety, health and welfare at work, and

(ii) inform each other and their respective employees and safety representatives (if any) of any risks to their safety, health and welfare arising from the work activity, including by the exchange of safety statements or relevant extracts therefrom relating to hazards and risks to employees.

Health surveillance

22.—(1) Every employer shall ensure that health surveillance appropriate to the risks to safety, health and welfare that may be incurred at the place of work identified by the risk assessment under *section 19*, is made available to his or her employees.

(2) *Subsection (1)* is without prejudice to any more specific requirement for health surveillance which may be in force under the relevant statutory provisions.

Medical fitness to work

23.—(1) An employer may require an employee of a class or classes, as may be prescribed, to undergo an assessment by a registered medical practitioner, nominated by the employèr, of his or her fitness to perform work activities referred to in *subsection (2)* and the employee shall co-operate with such a medical assessment.

(2) An employer shall ensure that employees undergo assessment by a regis-tered medical practitioner of their fitness to perform work activities, as may be prescribed, which, when performed, give rise to serious risks to the safety, health and welfare of persons at work.

(3) Where, following an assessment under *subsection (1)*, a registered medi-cal practitioner is of the opinion that an employee is unfit to perform work activities referred to in *subsection (2)*, he or she shall notify the employer, by the quickest practicable means, of that opinion and the likelihood of early resumption of work for rehabilitative purposes and shall inform the employee accordingly, giving the reasons for that opinion.

(4) If an employee referred to in *subsection (1)* becomes aware that he or she is suffering from any disease or physical or mental impairment which, should he or she perform a work activity referred to in *subsection (2)*, would be likely to cause him or her to expose himself or herself or another person to danger or risk of danger, he or she shall immediately notify the employer concerned or a registered medical practitioner nominated by that employer who shall in turn notify the employer.

(5) Where an employer receives a notification under *subsection (3)* or *(4)*, he or she shall immediately take appropriate action to comply with his or her general duties under *section 8*.

Joint safety and health agreements

24.—(1) A trade union of employees, representing a class or classes of employees, and a trade union of employers may—

　(*a*) enter into or vary an agreement (in this Act referred to as a "joint safety and health agreement") providing practical guidance to the employees and employers with respect to safety, health and welfare at work includ-ing the requirements of the relevant statutory provisions, and

　(*b*) apply to the Authority seeking approval for the agreement or its variation.

(2) The Authority may approve of a joint safety and health agreement where it is satisfied that—

　(*a*) the parties concerned consent to the approval sought,

　(*b*) the agreement is expressed to apply to all employees of a particular class and their employers and the Authority is satisfied that it is nor-mal and desirable that it should so apply,

　(*c*) the parties to the agreement are substantially representative of such employees and employers,

　(*d*) the agreement does not conflict with the requirements of the relevant statutory provisions, and

　(*e*) the agreement is in a form suitable for approval.

(3) Where an application is made to the Authority for approval of a joint safety and health agreement, the Authority shall direct the parties concerned to publish information on the agreement in such a manner that is best calculated to bring the application to the notice of all persons concerned.

(4) The Authority shall not approve of a joint safety and health agreement until one month after its publication under *subsection (3)* and if any objection is received within that period, the Authority shall consider the objection and shall not approve the agreement if it does not comply with *subsection (2)*.

(5) Approval of a joint safety and health agreement may be withdrawn by the Authority if it is satisfied that all parties thereto consent to its withdrawal or if the agreement is terminated by any of the parties concerned.

(6) Where the Authority approves of a joint safety and health agreement, it shall publish a notice of approval in *Iris Oifigiúil* and in at least 2 daily newspapers circulating in the State, and that notice shall—

  (*a*) identify the agreement,

  (*b*) specify the matters relating to safety, health and welfare at work or the relevant statutory provisions in respect of which the agreement is approved and published, and

  (*c*) specify the date on which the agreement shall come into operation.

(7) The parties to a joint safety and health agreement shall make copies of the agreement, or variations thereof, available for inspection by all persons concerned.

(8) A joint safety and health agreement shall, so long as it continues to be approved by the Authority, be taken into account by the Authority or a person prescribed under *section 33* for the purposes of assessing compliance by an employer with the relevant statutory provisions notwithstanding the fact that that employer and the employees concerned are not party to the joint safety and health agreement.

PART 4

SAFETY REPRESENTATIVES AND SAFETY CONSULTATION

Safety representatives

25.—(1) Without prejudice to *section 26*, employees may, from time to time, select and appoint from amongst their number at their place of work a representative (in this Act referred to as a "safety representative") or, by agreement with their employer, more than one safety representative, to represent them at the place of work in consultation with their employer on matters related to safety, health and welfare at the place of work.

(2) A safety representative may—

    (*a*) inspect the whole or any part of the place of work—

        (i) subject to *subsection (3)*, after giving reasonable notice to the employer, or

        (ii) immediately, in the event of an accident, dangerous occurrence or imminent danger or risk to the safety, health and welfare of any person,

    (*b*) investigate accidents and dangerous occurrences provided that he or she does not interfere with or obstruct the performance of any statutory obligation required to be performed by any person under any of the relevant statutory provisions,

    (*c*) after the giving of reasonable notice to the employer, investigate complaints relating to safety, health and welfare at work made by any employee whom he or she represents,

    (*d*) accompany an inspector who is carrying out an inspection of the place of work under *section 64* other than an inspection for the purpose of investigating an accident or dangerous occurrence,

    (*e*) at the discretion of the inspector concerned, accompany an inspector who is carrying out an inspection under *section 64* for the purpose of investigating an accident or dangerous occurrence,

    (*f*) at the discretion of the inspector concerned, where an employee is interviewed by an inspector with respect to an accident or dangerous occurrence at a place of work, attend the interview where the employee so requests,

    (*g*) make representations to the employer on any matter relating to safety, health and welfare at the place of work,

    (*h*) make oral or written representations to inspectors on matters relating to safety, health and welfare at the place of work, including the investigation of accidents or dangerous occurrences,

    (*i*) receive advice and information from inspectors on matters relating to safety, health and welfare at the place of work, or

    (*j*) consult and liaise on matters relating to safety, health and welfare at work with any other safety representatives who may be appointed in the undertaking concerned, whether or not those safety representatives work in the same place of work, in different places of work under the control of the employer or at different times at the place of work.

(3) The employer and the safety representative shall, having regard to the nature and extent of the hazards in the place of work, agree the frequency or schedule of inspections which may be carried out under *subsection (2)(a)(i)*, which agreement shall not be unreasonably withheld by the employer.

(4) Every employer shall consider any representations made to him or her by the safety representative in relation to the matters specified in this section or any other matter relating to the safety, health and welfare at work of his or her employees and, so far as is reasonably practicable, take any action

that he or she considers necessary or appropriate with regard to those representations.

(5) An employer shall give to a safety representative such time off from his or her work as is reasonable having regard to all the circumstances, without loss of remuneration, to enable the safety representative—

(*a*) to acquire, on an ongoing basis, the knowledge and training necessary to discharge his or her functions as a safety representative, and

(*b*) to discharge those functions.

(6) Where an inspector attends at a place of work for the purpose of carrying out an inspection under *section 64*, the employer shall inform the safety representative that the inspection is taking place.

Consultation and participation of employees, safety committees

26.—(1) Every employer shall, for the purpose of promoting and developing measures to ensure the safety, health and welfare at work of his or her employees and ascertaining the effectiveness of those measures—

(*a*) consult his or her employees for the purpose of making and maintaining arrangements which will enable the employer and his or her employees to co-operate effectively for those purposes,

(*b*) in accordance with the arrangements referred to in *paragraph (a)*, consult with his or her employees, their safety representatives or both, as appropriate, in advance and in good time regarding—

(i) any measure proposed to be taken in the place of work which may substantially affect the safety, health and welfare of those employees, including measures to be taken under the relevant statutory provisions,

(ii) the designation of employees under *section 11*,

(iii) activities arising from or related to the protection from and the prevention of risks to safety, health and welfare at work,

(iv) the hazard identification and the risk assessment to be carried out under *section 19*,

(v) the preparation of a safety statement under *section 20*,

(vi) the information to be provided to employees under *section 9*,

(vii) the information required to be kept or notified to the Authority in respect of accidents and dangerous occurrences referred to in *section 8(2)(k)*,

(viii) the appointment of persons referred to in *section 18*,

(ix) the planning and organisation of the training referred to in *section 10*, or

(x) the planning and introduction of new technologies particularly in relation to the consequences of the choice of equipment and working conditions and the working environment for the safety, health and welfare of employees.

(2) Employees shall have the right to make representations to and consult their employer on matters relating to their safety, health and welfare at work, including the matters specified in *subsection (1)*.

(3) Where, in a place of work by agreement of the employer, there is a group of persons (by whatever name known) representative of the employer and the employees that constitutes a safety committee in compliance with *Schedule 4* and that exists for the purpose of consultation regarding the safety, health and welfare at work of the employees, consultation within that group of persons may, to such extent as may be agreed between the employer and his or her employees, fulfil the requirements *of subsections (1)* and *(2)*.

(4) Every employer shall consider any representations made to him or her by his or her employees in relation to the matters specified in this section or any other matter relating to their safety, health or welfare at work and, so far as is reasonably practicable, take any action that he or she considers necessary or appropriate with regard to those representations.

(5) An employer shall give to employees involved in arrangements for consultation referred to in *subsections (1)* and *(3)* such time off from their duties as is reasonable having regard to all the circumstances, without loss of remuneration, to enable those employees—

    (*a*) to acquire the knowledge and training necessary to discharge their functions under this section, and

    (*b*) to discharge those functions.

(6) In an undertaking in which arrangements for joint decision-making exist involving the employer and employees, these arrangements shall include consultation in accordance with this section.

Protection against dismissal and Penalisation

27.—(1) In this section "penalisation" includes any act or omission by an employer or a person acting on behalf of an employer that affects, to his or her detriment, an employee with respect to any term or condition of his or her employment.

(2) Without prejudice to the generality of *subsection (1)*, penalisation includes—

    (*a*) suspension, lay-off or dismissal (including a dismissal within the meaning of the Unfair Dismissals Acts 1977 to 2001), or the threat of suspension, lay-off or dismissal,

    (*b*) demotion or loss of opportunity for promotion,

    (*c*) transfer of duties, change of location of place of work, reduction in wages or change in working hours,

    (*d*) imposition of any discipline, reprimand or other penalty (including a financial penalty), and

    (*e*) coercion or intimidation.

(3) An employer shall not penalise or threaten penalisation against an employee for—

    (*a*) acting in compliance with the relevant statutory provisions,

    (*b*) performing any duty or exercising any right under the relevant statutory provisions,

    (*c*) making a complaint or representation to his or her safety representative or employer or the Authority, as regards any matter relating to safety, health or welfare at work,

    (*d*) giving evidence in proceedings in respect of the enforcement of the relevant statutory provisions,

    (*e*) being a safety representative or an employee designated under *section 11* or appointed under *section 18* to perform functions under this Act, or

    (*f*) subject to *subsection (6)*, in circumstances of danger which the employee reasonably believed to be serious and imminent and which he or she could not reasonably have been expected to avert, leaving (or proposing to leave) or, while the danger persisted, refusing to return to his or her place of work or any dangerous part of his or her place of work, or taking (or proposing to take) appropriate steps to protect himself or herself or other persons from the danger.

(4) The dismissal of an employee shall be deemed, for the purposes of the Unfair Dismissals Acts 1977 to 2001, to be an unfair dismissal if it results wholly or mainly from penalisation as referred to in *subsection (2)(a)*.

(5) If penalisation of an employee, in contravention of *subsection (3)*, constitutes a dismissal of the employee within the meaning of the Unfair Dismissals Acts 1977 to 2001, relief may not be granted to the employee in respect of that penalisation both under this Part and under those Acts.

(6) For the purposes of *subsection (3)(f)*, in determining whether the steps which an employee took (or proposed to take) were appropriate, account shall be taken of all the circumstances and the means and advice available to him or her at the relevant time.

(7) Where the reason (or, if more than one, the principal reason) for the dismissal of an employee is that specified in *subsection (3)(f)*, the employee shall not be regarded as unfairly dismissed if the employer shows that it was (or would have been) so negligent for the employee to take the steps which he or she took (or proposed to take) that a reasonable employer might have dismissed him or her for taking (or proposing to take) them.

Complaints to rights commissioners

28.—(1) Without prejudice to *section 27(4)*, an employee may present a complaint to a rights commissioner that his or her employer has contravened *section 27*.

(2) Where a complaint under *subsection (1)* is made, the rights commissioner shall—

(*a*) give the parties an opportunity to be heard by the commissioner and to present to the commissioner any evidence relevant to the complaint,

(*b*) give a decision in writing in relation to it, and

(*c*) communicate the decision to the parties.

(3) A decision of a rights commissioner under *subsection (2)* shall do one or more of the following:

(*a*) declare that the complaint was or, as the case may be, was not well founded;

(*b*) require the employer to take a specific course of action;

(*c*) require the employer to pay to the employee compensation of such amount (if any) as is just and equitable having regard to all the circumstances.

(4) A rights commissioner shall not entertain a complaint under this section unless it is presented to him or her within the period of 6 months beginning on the date of the contravention to which the complaint relates or such further period not exceeding 6 months as the rights commissioner considers reasonable.

(5) (*a*) A complaint shall be presented by giving notice of it in writing to a rights commissioner and the notice shall contain such particulars and be in such form as may be specified from time to time by the Minister.

(*b*) A copy of a notice under *paragraph (a)* shall be given to the other party concerned by the rights commissioner concerned.

(6) Proceedings under this section before a rights commissioner shall be conducted otherwise than in public.

(7) A rights commissioner shall furnish the Labour Court with a copy of any decision given by the commissioner under *subsection (2)*.

Appeals from and enforcement of decisions of rights commissioner

29.—(1) A party concerned may appeal to the Labour Court from a decision of a rights commissioner under *section 28* and, if the party does so, the Labour Court shall give the parties an opportunity to be heard by it and to present to it any evidence relevant to the appeal, shall make a determination in writing in relation to the appeal affirming, varying or setting aside the decision and shall communicate the determination to the parties.

(2) An appeal under this section shall be initiated by the party concerned, within 6 weeks of the date on which the decision to which it relates was communicated to the party, by giving written notice to the Labour Court under *subsection (4)* stating the intention of the party concerned to appeal against the decision.

(3) A copy of a notice under *subsection (2)* shall be given by the Labour Court to any other party concerned as soon as practicable after the receipt of the notice by the Labour Court.

(4) The following matters, or the procedures to be followed in relation to those matters, shall be determined by the Labour Court, namely—

> (*a*) the initiation and the hearing by the Labour Court of appeals under this section,
> (*b*) the times and places of hearings of such appeals,
> (*c*) the representation of the parties to such appeals,
> (*d*) the publication and notification of determinations of the Labour Court,
> (*e*) the particulars to be contained in a notice under *subsection (2)*, and
> (*f*) any matters consequential on, or incidental to, the matters referred to in *paragraphs (a)* to *(e)*.

(5) The Minister may, at the request of the Labour Court, refer a question of law arising in proceedings before it under this section to the High Court for its determination and the determination of the High Court shall be final and conclusive.

(6) A party to proceedings before the Labour Court under this section may appeal to the High Court from a determination of the Labour Court on a point of law and the determination of the High Court shall be final and conclusive.

(7) Section 39(17) of the Redundancy Payments Act 1967 shall apply in relation to proceedings before the Labour Court under this Part as it applies to matters referred to the Employment Appeals Tribunal under that section with—

> (*a*) the substitution in that provision of references to the Labour Court for references to the Tribunal, and
> (*b*) the substitution in paragraph (*e*) of that provision of "€3,000" for "£150".

(8) Where a decision of a rights commissioner in relation to a complaint under this Act has not been carried out by the employer concerned in accordance with its terms, the time for bringing an appeal against the decision has expired and no appeal has been brought, the employee concerned may bring the complaint before the Labour Court and the Labour Court shall, without hearing the employer concerned or any evidence (other than in relation to the matters aforesaid) make a determination to the like effect as the decision.

(9) The bringing of a complaint before the Labour Court under *subsection (8)* shall be effected by giving to the Labour Court a written notice containing such particulars (if any) as may be determined by the Labour Court.

(10)The Labour Court shall publish, in a manner it considers appropriate, particulars of any determination made by it under *paragraphs (a), (b), (c), (e)* and *(f)* of *subsection (4)* (not being a determination as respects a particular appeal under this section) and *subsection (9)*.

Enforcement of determinations of Labour Court

30.—(1) If an employer fails to carry out in accordance with its terms a determination of the Labour Court in relation to a complaint under *section 28*
within 6 weeks from the date on which the determination is communicated
to the parties, the Circuit Court shall, on application to it in that behalf
by—

    (*a*) the employee concerned,
    (*b*) with the consent of the employee, any trade union of which the
        employee is a member, or
    (*c*) the Minister, if the Minister considers it appropriate to make the
        application having regard to all the circumstances, without hearing
        the employer or any evidence (other than in relation to the matters
        aforesaid), make an order directing the employer to carry out the
        determination in accordance with its terms.

(2) The reference in *subsection (1)* to a determination of the Labour Court is
a reference to a determination in relation to which, at the end of the time
for bringing an appeal against it, no appeal has been brought or, if an
appeal has been brought it has been abandoned and the references to the
date on which the determination is communicated to the parties shall, in a
case where an appeal is abandoned, be read as references to the date of
abandonment.

(3) In an order under this section providing for the payment of compensation, the Circuit Court may, if in all the circumstances it considers it
appropriate to do so, direct the employer concerned to pay to the
employee concerned interest on the compensation at the rate referred to
in section 22 of the Courts Act 1981, in respect of the whole or any part
of the period beginning 6 weeks after the date on which the determination of the Labour Court is communicated to the parties and ending on
the date of the order.

(4) An application under this section to the Circuit Court shall be made to
the judge of the Circuit Court for the circuit in which the employer concerned ordinarily resides or carries on any profession, business or
occupation.

**Evidence of failure to attend before or give evidence or produce documents to
Labour Court**

31.—A document purporting to be signed by the chairperson or a vice-
chairperson of the Labour Court stating that—

    (*a*) a person named in the document was, by a notice under section
        39(17) of the Redundancy Payments Act 1967 as applied to this Act
        by *section 29(7)*, required to attend before the Labour Court on a day
        and at a time and place specified in the document, to give evidence or
        produce a document,

(*b*) a sitting of the Labour Court was held on that day and at that time and place, and

(*c*) the person did not attend before the Labour Court in pursuance of the notice or, as the case may be, having so attended, refused to give evidence or refused or failed to produce the document,

shall, in a prosecution of the person under section 39(17) of the Redundancy Payments Act 1967 as applied to this Act by *section 29(7)*, be evidence of the matters so stated without further proof.

PART 5

THE AUTHORITY

CHAPTER 1

The Authority

Continuance in being of Authority

32.—(1) Notwithstanding the repeal of the Act of 1989 by *section 4*—

(*a*) the National Authority for Occupational Safety and Health shall continue in being and shall from the commencement of this Act be known as the Health and Safety Authority (and in this Act referred to as the "Authority"), and

(*b*) anything commenced but not completed before the commencement of that section by the Authority may be carried on and completed by it after such commencement as if that Act had not been repealed.

(2) Where, immediately before the commencement of *section 4*, any legal proceedings are pending to which the National Authority for Occupational Safety and Health is a party, the name of the Authority shall be substituted in the proceedings for that of the National Authority for Occupational Safety and Health and the proceedings shall not abate by reason of such substitution.

(3) The Authority shall be a body corporate with perpetual succession and an official seal and with power—

(*a*) to sue and be sued in its corporate name, and

(*b*) with the consent of the Minister and the Minister for Finance, to acquire, hold and dispose of land or an interest in land, and to acquire, hold and dispose of any other property.

(4) *Schedule 5* applies to the Authority.

Minister may prescribe persons to perform certain functions

33.—(1) Subject to *section 34*, the Minister, with the consent of the Minister for Finance, and after consultation with any other Minister of the Government that the Minister considers appropriate, may prescribe persons to perform such functions in lieu of the Authority in respect of the implementation of any of the relevant statutory provisions, and to the extent as may be prescribed.

(2) A person prescribed under this section shall, in accordance with any guidelines given to the person by the Authority—

> (*a*) make adequate arrangements for the performance of functions to the extent prescribed under *subsection (1)*,
>
> (*b*) perform any other functions conferred on the person by any of the relevant statutory provisions, and
>
> (*c*) furnish to the Authority an annual report in accordance with *subsection (3)* and such other reports and information relating to his or her functions and activities under this Act, or as prescribed, as the Authority may from time to time require.

(3) As soon as practicable but in any case not later than 2 months after the end of each year, a person prescribed under this section shall prepare and submit a report (in this section referred to as the "annual report") to the appropriate Minister referred to in *subsection (1)* and to the Authority.

(4) The annual report shall be in the form that the Authority may direct and shall include—

> (*a*) information on the performance of the person concerned of his or her functions and activities under this Act or as prescribed, and
>
> (*b*) any other information that the person considers appropriate or as the Minister may require.

Functions of Authority

34.—(1) The general functions of the Authority are—

> (*a*) to promote, encourage and foster the prevention of accidents, dangerous occurrences and personal injury at work in accordance with the relevant statutory provisions,
>
> (*b*) to promote, encourage, foster and provide education and training in the safety, health and welfare of persons at work,
>
> (*c*) to encourage and foster measures promoting the safety, health and welfare of persons at work,
>
> (*d*) subject to *subsection (2)* and *section 33*, to make adequate arrangements for the enforcement of the relevant statutory provisions,
>
> (*e*) to monitor, evaluate and make recommendations to the Minister regarding implementation of and compliance with—
>
>> (i) the relevant statutory provisions, and
>>
>> (ii) best practice relating to safety, health and welfare at work, and the review and maintenance of relevant records by employers,
>
> (*f*) to promote, encourage and foster co-operation with and between persons or bodies of persons that represent employees and employers and any other persons or bodies of persons, as appropriate, as regards

the prevention of risks to safety, health and welfare at work in accordance with the relevant statutory provisions,

(g) to make any arrangements that it considers appropriate for providing information and advice on matters relating to safety, health and welfare at work,

(h) to make any arrangements that it considers appropriate to conduct, commission, promote, support and evaluate research, surveys and studies on matters relating to the functions of the Authority and for this purpose—

(i) to foster and promote contacts and the exchange of information with other persons or bodies of persons involved in safety, health and welfare at work in and outside the State, and

(ii) as it considers appropriate, to publish in the form and manner that the Authority thinks fit, results arising out of such research, studies and surveys,

(*i*) in accordance with *section 43*, to prepare and adopt a strategy statement and to monitor its implementation,

(*j*) in accordance with *section 44*, to prepare and adopt a work programme,

(*k*) to comply with any directions in writing, whether general or particular, relating to its functions, that the Minister may from time to time give to the Authority,

(*l*) to give to the Minister any information relating to the performance of its functions that the Minister may from time to time require, and

(*m*) to perform any additional functions conferred on the Authority by order under *section 35*.

(2) The Authority, subject to the approval of the Minister given with the consent of the Minister for Finance, may make agreements with—

(*a*) any Minister of the Government, or other person, for that Minister or person to perform on behalf of the Authority (with or without payment) any of its functions, or

(*b*) make agreements with any Minister of the Government for the Authority to perform on behalf of that Minister (with or without payment) any functions that may appropriately be performed by the Authority in connection with its functions under this Act.

(3) The Authority shall have all such powers as are necessary or expedient for the performance of its functions.

(4) The Authority may perform any of its functions through or by the Chief Executive or any other member of staff of the Authority duly authorised by the Authority to act in that behalf.

Conferral of additional functions on Authority

35.—(1) The Minister may, with the consent of the Minister for Finance and after consultation with the Authority and any other Minister of the Government that he or she considers appropriate, by order—

(*a*) confer on the Authority any additional functions connected with the functions for the time being of the Authority that the Minister considers appropriate, subject to the conditions (if any) that may be specified in the order, and

(*b*) make such provision as he or she considers necessary or expedient in relation to matters ancillary to or arising out of the conferral of those additional functions.

(2) (*a*) The Minister may by order amend or revoke an order under this section (including an order under this subsection).

(*b*) An order under this subsection shall be made in the like manner, and subject to the same consent and consultations (if any) as the order that it is amending or revoking.

Establishment of subsidiaries

36.—(1) The Authority may, without prejudice to its general responsibilities under this Act, perform any of its functions (other than those set out in *section 34(1)(d)*), provide any of its services or carry on any of its activities through a subsidiary (within the meaning of the Companies Acts 1963 to 2003) which is wholly owned by the Authority and, accordingly, the Authority may, with the consent of the Minister and the Minister for Finance, for the purpose of such performance, provision or carrying on, form and register such a subsidiary.

(2) The memorandum and articles of association of a subsidiary referred to in this section shall be in the form that may be determined by the Authority with the consent of the Minister and the Minister for Finance.

(3) (*a*) The Minister may give to the Authority such directions in writing as he or she considers appropriate in relation to any policy, programme or activity of a subsidiary and the body concerned shall comply or, as may be appropriate, secure compliance with that direction.

(*b*) A direction under *paragraph (a)* shall not apply to any particular undertaking or person (other than a subsidiary).

(4) A direction under *subsection (3)* in relation to the disposal of any assets or profits of a subsidiary shall not be given without the consent of the Minister for Finance.

Membership of Authority

37.—(1) The Authority shall consist of a chairperson and 11 ordinary members who shall be appointed by the Minister, who shall comprise the Board of the Authority.

(2) The ordinary members of the Authority shall be—

(*a*) 3 persons nominated by such organisations representative of employees as the Minister considers appropriate, (*b*) 3 persons nominated by such organisations representative of employers as the Minister considers appropriate,

(*c*) 5 persons as the Minister considers appropriate which shall include one person from the Department under whose auspices the Authority operates.

(3) The Minister shall, for the purposes of *paragraph 13(b)* of *Schedule 5*, designate one of the ordinary members of the Authority to be deputy chairperson of the Authority.

(4) Notwithstanding the repeal of the Act of 1989 by *section 4*, a person who is a member of the Authority immediately before the commencement of that section shall continue in office as such a member for the remainder of the term of office for which he or she was appointed, unless he or she dies or resigns from office or otherwise ceases to hold office in accordance with *Schedule 5*.

Advisory committees

38.—(1) The Authority may from time to time establish advisory committees to advise it in relation to any of its functions and may determine the membership, term of office and terms of reference and regulate the procedure of any such committee.

(2) Where the Authority has appointed an advisory committee, it shall appoint one of the members of the committee as chairperson of that committee and another as deputy chairperson who shall act in the absence of the chairperson.

(3) The members of an advisory committee established under this section shall be paid by the Authority such allowances for expenses incurred by them as the Minister, with the consent of the Minister for Finance, may determine.

(4) Notwithstanding the repeal of the Act of 1989 by *section 4*, a person who is a member of an advisory committee immediately before the commencement of that section shall continue in office as such a member for the remainder of the term of office for which he or she was appointed, unless he or she dies or resigns from office or otherwise ceases to hold office.

Chief Executive

39.—(1) There shall be a chief executive officer of the Authority who shall be known and is referred to in this Act as the "Chief Executive".

(2) The Chief Executive shall be appointed and may be removed from office in accordance with the terms and conditions of his or her appointment by the Authority with the consent of the Minister.

(3) The Authority, with the consent of the Minister and the Minister for Finance, may appoint one or more assistants to the Chief Executive who shall be known and is referred to in this Act as the "Assistant Chief Executive".

(4) The Chief Executive shall carry on, manage and control generally the administration and business of the Authority and perform any other functions that may be conferred on him or her by this Act or as may be determined by the Authority.

(5) The Chief Executive shall—

(a) prepare and submit to the Authority a draft strategy statement in accordance with *section 43* and a draft work programme in accordance with *section 44*,

(b) provide annual and other progress reports to the Authority on the implementation of the strategy statement at such intervals as the Authority may from time to time direct,

(c) provide advice to the Authority with respect to any matter within, affecting or connected with the functions of the Authority,

(d) provide to the Authority any information, including financial information, relating to the performance of his or her functions as the Authority may from time to time require, and

(e) manage all matters relating to appointments, performance, discipline and dismissals of staff below the position of Assistant Chief Executive.

(6) Notwithstanding the repeal of the Act of 1989 by *section 4*, the Chief Executive of the Authority holding office immediately before the commencement of this Act shall continue in office as Chief Executive for the remainder of the term of office for which he or she was appointed, unless he or she dies or resigns from office or otherwise ceases to hold office.

(7) *Schedule 6* applies to the Chief Executive.

Consultants and advisers

40.—(1) The Authority may, from time to time, engage consultants or advisers that it considers necessary or expedient for the performance by it of its functions.

(2) Any fees payable by the Authority to a consultant or adviser engaged under this section shall be paid by it out of moneys at its disposal and it shall have regard to guidelines issued from time to time by the Minister or the Minister for Finance.

(3) The Authority shall comply with any directions with regard to consultants or advisers engaged under this section that the Minister may give to it with the consent of the Minister for Finance.

Disclosure of certain interests by members of Authority

41.—(1) Where at a meeting of the Authority any of the following matters arise, namely—

(a) an arrangement to which the Authority is a party or a proposed such arrangement, or (*b*) a contract or other agreement with the Authority or a proposed such contract or other agreement,

then, any member of the Authority present at the meeting who has a material interest in the matter, otherwise than in his or her capacity as such a member, shall—

    (i) at the meeting, in advance of any consideration of the matter, disclose to the Authority the fact of the interest and the nature of the interest,

   (ii) neither influence nor seek to influence a decision relating to the matter,

  (iii) absent himself or herself from any meeting or that part of the meeting during which the matter is discussed,

  (iv) take no part in any deliberation of the Authority relating to the matter, and

   (v) not vote on a decision relating to the matter.

(2) Where a member discloses a material interest in a matter under this section—

    (*a*) the disclosure shall be recorded in the minutes of the meeting, and

    (*b*) for so long as the matter is being dealt with by the meeting, the member shall not be counted in the quorum for the meeting unless the Authority otherwise determines.

(3) Where, at a meeting of the Authority, a question arises as to whether or not a course of conduct, if pursued by a member of the Authority, would be a failure by the member to comply with the requirements of *subsection (1)*—

    (*a*) the question may, subject to *subsection (4)*, be determined by the chairperson of the meeting, whose decision shall be final, and

    (*b*) where the question is so determined, particulars of the determination shall be recorded in the minutes of the meeting.

(4) Where at a meeting of the Authority, the chairperson of the meeting is the member in respect of which a question to which *subsection (3)* applies is to be determined, then the other members of the Authority attending the meeting shall choose one of their number to be chairperson of the meeting for the purpose of determining the question concerned.

(5) If satisfied that a member of the Authority has contravened *subsection (1)*, the Minister may, if he or she thinks fit, remove that member from office or take any other action that the Minister considers appropriate.

(6) A person who is removed from office under *subsection (5)* is disqualified from membership of the Authority.

Disclosure of certain interests by members of staff of Authority

42.—(1) Where a member of the staff (including the Chief Executive) of the Authority or a consultant, adviser or other person engaged by the

Authority has a material interest, otherwise than in his or her capacity as such a member or as such a consultant, adviser or other person engaged by the Authority, in any contract, agreement or arrangement, or proposed contract, agreement or arrangement, to which the Authority is a party, that person shall—

(a) disclose to the Authority his or her interest and the nature of the interest in advance of any consideration of the matter,

(b) neither influence nor seek to influence a decision relating to the matter nor make any recommendation in relation to the contract, agreement or arrangement, and

(c) take no part in the negotiation of the contract, agreement or arrangement or in any deliberation by the Authority or staff of the Authority relating to the matter.

(2) *Subsection (1)* does not apply to a person as regards a contract or proposed contract of employment of that person as a member of the staff of the Authority.

(3) Where a person contravenes this section the Authority may decide on the appropriate action to be taken including alterations to the person's terms and conditions of employment or contract for services or termination of the person's contract of employment or for services.

Strategy statement

43.—(1) At the times set out in *subsection (2)(f)*, the Authority shall prepare and submit to the Minister for his or her approval, with or without amendment, a strategy statement for the following 3 year period.

(2) A strategy statement shall—

(a) specify the key objectives, outputs and related strategies (including the use of resources) of the Authority,

(b) have regard to the need to ensure the most beneficial, effective and efficient use of the Authority's resources,

(c) except for the first strategy statement, include a review of the outcomes and effectiveness of the preceding strategy statement,

(d) specify the manner in which the Authority proposes to assess its performance in respect of the objectives referred to in *paragraph (a)*, taking account of relevant performance indicators (financial and non-financial),

(e) be prepared in the form and manner that the Minister may from time to time direct,

(f) be prepared and submitted to the Minister not later than—

(i) in the case of the first strategy statement, 4 months after the coming into operation of *section 32*, and

(ii) in the case of each subsequent strategy statement, the third anniversary of the date of submission of the preceding strategy statement, and

(*g*) include any other matters that the Minster may from time to time direct.

(3) When preparing the strategy statement, the Authority may consult such persons or bodies of persons that it considers appropriate.

(4) A strategy statement is deemed to be adopted when it is approved by the Minister.

(5) As soon as practicable after a strategy statement has been approved, the Minister shall cause a copy of the strategy statement to be laid before each House of the Oireachtas and the strategy statement shall be published in the form and manner that the Authority considers appropriate.

Work programme of Authority

44.—(1) The Authority shall prepare and submit to the Minister for his or her approval with or without amendment, at least 2 months before the commencement of each year, a work programme relating to the discharge of its functions, including—

(*a*) having regard to the strategy statement, the objectives of the Authority for that year and its strategy for achieving those objectives,

(*b*) the priorities of the Authority for that year, having regard to those objectives and its available resources, and

(*c*) any other matters that the Minister may from time to time specify when issuing directions or guidelines under *subsection (2)*.

(2) The Minister may, from time to time, issue directions or guidelines to the Authority concerning the preparation of the work programme and the Authority shall comply with those directions and prepare the work programme in accordance with those guidelines.

(3) A work programme is deemed to be adopted when it is approved by the Minister.

Grants to Authority

45.—(1) In each year there may be paid to the Authority out of moneys provided by the Oireachtas a grant or grants of such amount or amounts as the Minister, with the consent of the Minister for Finance, determines for the purposes of expenditure by the Authority in performing its functions.

(2) The Authority may with the consent of the Minister and the Minister for Finance invest money in such manner as it thinks fit.

(3) The Authority may, subject to *sections 46* and *47*, with the prior consent of the Minister and the Minister for Finance, seek and accept moneys from any source and subject to any conditions that the Minister may approve of, from time to time.

Power to borrow

46.—The Authority may, for the purpose of providing for current or capital expenditure, from time to time, borrow money (whether on the security of the assets of the Authority or otherwise), including money in a currency other than the currency of the State, subject to the consent of the Minister and the Minister for Finance and to the conditions they may determine.

Fees for services, etc.

47.—(1) Subject to the approval of the Minister and the Minister for Finance, the Authority may—

    (*a*) determine the amount of such fees as it considers appropriate in consideration of—

        (i) the performance by the Authority of its functions,

        (ii) the provision by it of services (other than a service consisting of the provision of advice to the Minister or another Minister of the Government), and

        (iii) the carrying on by it of activities,

    (*b*) provide for the payment of different fees or for the exemption from the payment of fees or for the waiver, remission or refund (in whole or in part) of fees in different circumstances or classes of circumstances or for different cases or classes of cases,

    (*c*) sell, for such prices as it considers appropriate, anything produced, published, approved or developed by, or in cooperation with, the Authority, and

    (*d*) enter into contracts upon such terms and conditions as it considers appropriate (including terms and conditions relating to payments to the Authority) for the further development and commercial exploitation of anything produced, published or developed by the Authority,

and shall record receipts from such fees, sales or payments as income.

(2) The Authority shall make available on request, free of charge, details of fees determined under this section.

(3) Fees, prices and payments referred to in *subsection (1)* in respect of functions performed, services provided, activities carried on or things sold, shall not, save with the prior approval of the Minister, be less than the cost of the performance of the function, the provision of the service, the carrying on of the activity or the production, publication or development of the thing, as the case may be.

(4) The Authority may recover any amount due and owing to it under *subsection (1)* from the person by whom it is payable as a simple contract debt in any court of competent jurisdiction.

(5) The Public Offices Fees Act 1879 does not apply to fees charged in accordance with this section.

Accounts and audits

48.—(1) The Authority shall keep in such form as may be approved of by the Minister, with the consent of the Minister for Finance, and in respect of each year all proper and usual accounts or other records, including an income and expenditure account, a cash flow statement and a balance sheet, of—

(a) all income received and expenditure by the Authority in performing its functions under this Act,

(b) the sources of the income and the subject matter of the expenditure, and

(c) the property, assets and liabilities of the Authority.

(2) Accounts kept in pursuance of this section shall be submitted not later than 3 months after the end of the year to which they relate by the Authority to the Comptroller and Auditor General for audit and, after the audit—

(a) a copy of the accounts, statement and balance sheet and of any other accounts kept under this section as the Minister, after consultation with the Minister for Finance, may direct, and

(b) a copy of the report of the Comptroller and Auditor General on the accounts,

shall, within one month of receipt by the Authority of the report referred to in *paragraph (b)*, be presented to the Minister.

(3) The Minister shall cause a copy of the accounts and the auditor's report referred to in *subsection (2)* to be laid before each House of the Oireachtas.

Attendance before Committee of Public Accounts

49.—(1) The Chief Executive shall, whenever required in writing to do so by the Committee of Dáil Éireann established under the Standing Orders of Dáil Éireann to examine and report to Dáil Éireann on the appropriation accounts and reports of the Comptroller and Auditor General, give evidence to that Committee on—

(a) the regularity and propriety of the transactions recorded or required to be recorded in any book or other record of account subject to audit by the Comptroller and Auditor General that the Authority is required to prepare under this Act,

(b) the economy and efficiency of the Authority in the use of its resources,

(c) the systems, procedures and practices employed by the Authority for the purpose of evaluating the effectiveness of its operations, and

(d) any matter affecting the Authority referred to in a special report of the Comptroller and Auditor General under section 11(2) of the Comptroller and Auditor General (Amendment) Act 1993 or in any other report of the Comptroller and Auditor General (in so far as it relates to a matter specified in *paragraph (a)*, *(b)* or *(c)*) that is laid before Dáil Éireann.

(2) In the performance of his or her duties under this section and *section 50*, the Chief Executive shall not question or express an opinion on the merits of any policy of the Government or a Minister of the Government or on the merits of the objectives of such a policy.

(3) For the purposes of *sections 46, 47, 48* and this section, "Authority" shall include any subsidiary or subsidiaries of the Authority.

Attendance before other committees of Houses of the Oireachtas

50.—(1) In this section "Committee" means a Committee appointed by either House of the Oireachtas or jointly by both Houses of the Oireachtas, other than—

    (*a*) the Committee referred to in *section 49*,

    (*b*) the Committee on Members' Interests of Dáil Éireann, or

    (*c*) the Committee on Members' Interests of Seanad Éireann,

or a subcommittee of such a Committee.

(2) Subject to *subsection (3)*, the Chief Executive shall, at the request in writing of a Committee, attend before it to account for the general administration of the Authority as may be required by the Committee.

(3) The Chief Executive shall not be required to account to a Committee for any matter which is or has been or may at a future time be the subject of proceedings before a court or tribunal in the State.

(4) Where the Chief Executive is of the opinion that a matter in respect of which the Chief Executive is requested to account to a Committee is a matter to which *subsection (3)* applies, he or she shall inform the Committee of that opinion and the reasons for the opinion and, unless the information is conveyed to the Committee at a time when the Chief Executive is before it, the information shall be so conveyed in writing.

(5) Where the Chief Executive has informed a Committee of his or her opinion in accordance with *subsection (4)* and the Committee does not withdraw the request referred to in *subsection (2)* in so far as it relates to a matter the subject of that opinion—

    (*a*) the Chief Executive may, not later than 21 days after being informed by the Committee of its decision not to do so, apply to the High Court in a summary manner for determination of the question whether the matter is one to which *subsection (3)* applies, or

    (*b*) the chairperson of the Committee may, on behalf of the Committee, make such an application,

and the High Court shall determine the matter.

(6) Pending the determination of an application under *subsection (5)*, the Chief Executive shall not attend before the Committee to account for the matter the subject of the application.

(7) If the High Court determines that the matter concerned is one to which *subsection (3)* applies, the Committee shall withdraw the request referred to in *subsection (2)*, but if the High Court determines that *subsection (3)* does not apply, the Chief Executive shall attend before the Committee to account for the matter.

Reports and information to the Minister

51.—(1) As soon as practicable, but in any case not later than 3 months after the end of each year, the Authority shall prepare and submit a report (in this section referred to as the "annual report") to the Minister and the Minister shall cause copies of the annual report to be laid before each House of the Oireachtas.

(2) The annual report shall be in the form that the Minister may direct and shall include—

    (*a*) information on the performance of the Authority's functions during the year to which the report relates having regard to the strategy statement and work programme of the Authority,

    (*b*) information on the performance of any agreement under *section 34(2)*,

    (*c*) information in relation to any annual report furnished to the Authority under *section 33(3)*, and

    (*d*) any other information that the Authority considers appropriate or that the Minister may require.

(3) The Authority—

    (*a*) may, as it considers appropriate, make any other reports to the Minister relating to its functions, and

    (*b*) shall publish its annual report.

CHAPTER 2

Staff of Authority

Staff of Authority

52.—(1) The Authority may, with the consent of the Minister and the Minister for Finance, appoint such number of persons to be members of the staff of the Authority as it from time to time determines.

(2) A member of the staff of the Authority (other than the Chief Executive) shall—

    (*a*) be employed on the terms and conditions (including terms and conditions relating to remuneration) that the Authority, with the consent of the Minister and the Minister for Finance, may determine, and

    (*b*) be paid out of moneys at the disposal of the Authority the remuneration and allowances for expenses (if any) incurred by him or her as the Authority, with the consent of the Minister and the Minister for Finance, may determine.

(3) The grades of the staff of the Authority, and the numbers of staff in each grade shall be determined by the Authority with the consent of the Minister and the Minister for Finance.

(4) Notwithstanding the repeal of the Act of 1989 by *section 4*, every person who, immediately before the commencement of that section, was a member of the staff of the Authority shall continue to be a member of the staff of the Authority and each such person shall not, after such commencement, be subject to less beneficial conditions of service (including conditions in relation to tenure of office) or of remuneration than the conditions of service (including conditions in relation to tenure of office) or remuneration to which he or she was subject immediately before the said commencement.

Remuneration of staff of Authority

53.—The Authority, in determining the remuneration or allowances for expenses to be paid to members of its staff (including the Chief Executive) or the other terms or conditions subject to which such members hold or are to hold their employment, shall have regard to Government or nationally agreed guidelines which are for the time being extant and to Government policy concerning remuneration and conditions of employment that is so extant and, in addition to the foregoing, the Authority shall comply with any directives with regard to such remuneration, allowances, terms or conditions that the Minister may give to the Authority with the consent of the Minister for Finance.

Transfer of officers etc., to Authority

54.—(1) Every officer of the Minister who has been designated by the Minister at any time before such day as may be appointed by the Minister by order shall, on the day of such designation, be transferred to, and become a member of the staff of, the Authority.

(2) The Minister shall not make an order under *subsection (1)* without having notified in writing the officer concerned and any recognised trade unions or staff associations concerned and the Authority of his or her intention to do so and having considered any representations made by him or her, or by them or by any of them, in relation to the matter within the time specified in the notification.

(3) Save in accordance with a collective agreement negotiated with any recognised trade union or staff association concerned, an officer designated under *subsection (1)*, who is transferred by that subsection to the staff of the Authority shall not, while in the service of the Authority, receive a lesser scale of pay or be subject to less beneficial terms and conditions of service (other than those relating to tenure of office) than the scale of pay to which he or she was entitled and the terms and conditions of service (other than those relating to tenure of office) to which he or she was subject immediately before the day on which he or she was transferred.

(4) Until such time as the scales of pay and the terms and conditions of service (other than those relating to tenure of office) of officers transferred under *subsection (1)* are varied by the Authority, following consultation with any recognised trade unions and staff associations concerned, the scales of pay

to which they were entitled and the terms and conditions of service (other than those relating to tenure of office), restrictions, requirements and obligations to which they were subject immediately before their transfer shall continue to apply to them and may be applied or imposed by the Authority or the Chief Executive, as the case may be, while they are in the service of the Authority, and no such variation shall operate to worsen the scales of pay or the terms or conditions of service applicable to an officer immediately before the day on which he or she was transferred under *subsection (1)*, save in accordance with a collective agreement negotiated with any recognised trade union or staff association concerned.

(5) (*a*) The terms and conditions relating to tenure of office which are granted by the Authority to an officer designated under *subsection (1)* and transferred to its staff shall not, while he or she is in the service of the Authority, be less favourable to him or her than those applicable for the time being in the civil service.

    (*b*) Any alteration in the conditions in regard to tenure of office of any such officer shall not be such as to render those conditions less favourable to him or her than those applicable in the civil service at the time of the alteration, save in accordance with a collective agreement negotiated with any recognised trade unions or staff associations concerned.

    (*c*) If a dispute arises between the Authority and any such officer as to conditions applicable in the civil service, the matter shall be determined by the Minister for Finance after consultation with the Minister.

(6) In relation to officers transferred to the staff of the Authority under *subsection (1)*, previous service in, or service reckonable for the purposes of any superannuation benefits payable by or on behalf of, the civil service shall be reckonable for the purposes of, but subject to any other exceptions or exclusions in, the Redundancy Payments Acts 1967 to 2003, the Organisation of Working Time Act 1997, the Minimum Notice and Terms of Employment Acts 1973 to 2001, the Unfair Dismissals Acts 1977 to 2001 and the Terms of Employment (Information) Acts 1994 and 2001.

Code of conduct

55.—(1) The Authority shall, following consultation with the Minister and the Minister for Finance, draw up a code of conduct in respect of controls on staff interests and ethical behaviour to apply to each member of its staff.

(2) The Authority shall publish any code of conduct drawn up under *subsection (1)*.

Superannuation of staff of Authority

56.—(1) The Authority shall prepare and submit to the Minister a scheme or schemes for the granting of superannuation benefits to or in respect of its staff (including the Chief Executive).

(2) A scheme under this section shall fix the time and conditions of retirement for all persons to or in respect of whom superannuation benefits are payable under the scheme and different times and conditions may be fixed in respect of different classes of person.

(3) The Authority may at any time prepare and submit to the Minister a scheme amending or revoking a scheme previously submitted and approved under this section including a scheme under this subsection or a scheme to which *subsection (5)* applies.

(4) A scheme or amending scheme submitted to the Minister under this section shall, if approved by the Minister with the consent of the Minister for Finance, be carried out by the Authority in accordance with its terms.

(5) Notwithstanding the repeal of the Act of 1989 by *section 4*, any scheme for the granting of superannuation benefits to or in respect of any members of staff of the Authority in operation immediately before the commencement of the said *section 4* shall continue in operation after such commencement.

(6) A scheme or schemes under this section shall, as respects a person transferred under *section 54* to be a member of the staff of the Authority, provide for the granting to or in respect of him or her of superannuation benefits upon and subject to terms and conditions that are not less favourable to him or her than the terms and conditions applied to him or her immediately before the day on which he or she was so transferred in relation to the grant of such benefits.

(7) Where, during the period between commencement of this section and the coming into operation of a scheme under this section, superannuation benefits would have been granted to or in respect of a person transferred by *section 54* to the staff of the Authority in respect of his or her employment as an officer of the Minister, the superannuation benefits shall be granted and paid to or in respect of the person by the Authority and for that purpose his or her pensionable service with the Authority shall be aggregated with his or her previous pensionable service.

(8) Subject to *subsection (7)*, no superannuation benefit shall be granted by the Authority to or in respect of any members of its staff (including the Chief Executive) who are members of a scheme under this section, nor shall any other arrangement be entered into for the provision of any superannuation benefit to such persons, otherwise than in accordance with a scheme submitted and approved under this section or with the consent of the Minister and the Minister for Finance.

(9) If a dispute arises as to the claim of a person to, or the amount of, a superannuation benefit payable in respect of a scheme under this section, the dispute shall be submitted to the Minister who shall refer it to the Minister for Finance.

(10) The Minister shall cause every scheme submitted and approved under this section, including an amendment of a scheme, to be laid before each House of the Oireachtas as soon as practicable after it is approved and, if a resolution annulling the scheme is passed by either House within the next 21 days on which that House has sat after the scheme is laid before it,

the scheme shall be annulled accordingly, but without prejudice to the validity of anything done under the scheme.

PART 6

REGULATIONS, CODES OF PRACTICE AND ENFORCEMENT

CHAPTER 1

Regulations and Codes of Practice

Review of legislation

57.—(1) The Authority shall—

    (*a*) keep under review—

        (i) the relevant statutory provisions, and

        (ii) the associated statutory provisions,

    (*b*) submit, from time to time, to the Minister any proposals that it considers appropriate relating to the relevant statutory provisions or for making or revoking any instruments under those provisions,

    (*c*) submit, from time to time, to the Minister and to the Minister having responsibility for any of the associated statutory provisions any proposals that it considers appropriate relating to those provisions or for making or revoking any instruments under those provisions,

    (*d*) undertake such reviews of relevant statutory provisions as the Minister may direct, and

    (*e*) assist in the preparation of draft legislation as the Minister may direct.

(2) Before submitting proposals to the Minister, the Authority shall consult any other person or body that appears to the Authority to be appropriate having regard to the proposals to be submitted or as directed by the Minister.

Regulations

58.—(1) Subject to *subsections (2)* and *(3)*, the Minister may—

    (*a*) by regulations provide, subject to this Act, for any matter referred to in this Act as prescribed or to be prescribed,

    (*b*) make regulations generally for the purposes of giving full effect to this Act, and

    (*c*) without prejudice to the generality of *paragraph (b)*, make regulations for or in respect of any of the matters set out in *Schedule 7*.

(2) Before making regulations under this Act (other than as a consequence of a proposal made by the Authority under *section 57*), the Minister—

    (*a*) shall consult with the Authority, and

    (*b*) may publish in such manner as the Minister thinks fit notice of the Minister's intention to do so and shall give persons desiring to make representations in relation to the proposed regulations a period of 21 days to do so.

(3) The Minister shall consult with the Authority before making regulations giving effect with modifications to any proposal made by the Authority under *section 57*.

(4) Regulations under this Act may—

    (*a*) contain any incidental, supplementary and consequential provisions that appear to the Minister to be necessary or expedient for the purposes of the regulations,

    (*b*) apply either generally or to a specified class or classes of persons, places of work or work activities, article or substance or to any other matter that the Minister may consider to be appropriate,

    (*c*) include different provisions in relation to different classes of persons, place of work or work activity, article or substance, and

    (*d*) subject to *subsection (5)* and to any conditions that may be prescribed, exempt from all or any of the provisions of the relevant statutory provisions any specified class of work activity, employment, article or substance or any specified class of person or place of work, where, having regard to the class of work activity, employment, article, substance, person or place of work, the Minister is satisfied that the application of those provisions is unnecessary or impracticable and that adequate protective measures are in place.

(5) Regulations made under this Act may apply to all work activities or to particular work activities, and they may also relate to—

    (*a*) one or more chemical, physical or biological agents,

    (*b*) the classification, packaging, labelling, marketing or use of any article or substance,

    (*c*) the control of major accident hazards,

    (*d*) the storage or transport of dangerous substances, or

    (*e*) factories, the extractive industries, office premises or to boilers.

(6) Without prejudice to the generality of *subsections (1)* and *(4)*, regulations under this Act may apply to—

    (*a*) employers or other persons who control places of work or specified places of work,

    (*b*) employees or a particular class of employees,

    (*c*) all work activities or particular work activities,

    (*d*) designers, manufacturers, sellers or suppliers (or any classes thereof) of articles, substances or personal protective clothing or equipment (or any classes thereof),

    (*e*) a specified article or substance or an article or substance of a particular class.

(7) Regulations made under this Act may incorporate, adopt, apply or make prescriptions by reference to, with or without modification, any code of practice issued by the Authority in accordance with *section 60*.

(8) The provisions of this section shall be deemed to have been in operation on the commencement of section 28 of the Act of 1989 and to have been

incorporated in that section from that date and every regulation made in exercise of the powers under that section and not revoked before the commencement of this section shall be deemed to have been made in the exercise of the powers under the provisions of that section, including the provisions of this section deemed to have been incorporated in that section by this subsection.

(9) Every regulation or order (other than an order made under *section 1(2)*) under this Act shall be laid by the Minister before each House of the Oireachtas as soon as may be after it is made and, if a resolution annulling the regulation or order is passed by either House within the next 21 days on which that House has sat after the regulation or order is laid before it, the regulation or order shall be annulled accordingly but without prejudice to the validity of anything previously done under the regulation or order.

(10) The power to make regulations under this section includes power to make provision by regulations to give effect to either—

(*a*) any provision of the treaties of the European Communities, or

(*b*) any act adopted by an institution of the European Communities, which regulates any of the matters set out in *Schedule 7*.

Miscellaneous adaptations

59.—References to the Minister (other than in respect of making rules, regulations, bye-laws, orders, exemptions or exceptions) contained immediately before the commencement of this Act in any existing enactment shall, insofar as they relate to functions exercisable by the Authority under this Act, be construed as references to the Authority.

Codes of practice

60.—(1) For the purpose of providing practical guidance to employers, employees and any other persons to whom this Act applies with respect to safety, health and welfare at work, or the requirements or prohibitions of any of the relevant statutory provisions, the Authority—

(*a*) may, and shall if so requested by the Minister, prepare and publish codes of practice, and

(*b*) may approve of a code of practice or any part of a code of practice made or published by any other body.

(2) Before publishing or approving of a code of practice or any part of a code of practice under this section, the Authority—

(*a*) shall obtain the consent of the Minister,

(*b*) may publish in such manner as the Authority considers appropriate a draft of the code of practice or sections of a draft code of practice and shall give persons one month from the date of publication of the draft code or sections within which to make written representations to the Authority in relation to the draft code or sections of the draft code, or such further period, not exceeding 28 days, as the Authority in its absolute discretion thinks fit, and (*c*) following consultation and, where relevant, having considered the representations, if any, made, shall submit the draft code to the Minister for his or her consent to its publication or approval under this section, with or without modification.

(3) Where the Authority publishes or approves of a code of practice or approves of any part of a code of practice, it shall publish a notice of such publication or approval in *Iris Oifigiúil* and that notice shall—

    (*a*) identify the code,

    (*b*) specify the matters relating to safety, health and welfare at work or the relevant statutory provisions in respect of which the code is published or approved of, and

    (*c*) specify the date on which the code shall come into operation.

(4) The Authority may with the consent of the Minister and following consultation with any other person or body that the Authority considers appropriate or as the Minister directs—

    (*a*) amend or revoke any code of practice or part of any code of practice prepared and published by it under this section, or

    (*b*) withdraw its approval of any code of practice or part of any code of practice approved by it under this section.

(5) Where the Authority amends or revokes, or withdraws its approval of a code of practice or any part of a code of practice published or approved under this section, it shall publish notice of the amendment, revocation or withdrawal, as the case may be, in *Iris Oifigiúil*.

(6) The Authority shall make available for public inspection without charge at its principal office during normal working hours—

    (*a*) a copy of each code of practice published or approved by it, and

    (*b*) where a code of practice has been amended, a copy of the code as so amended.

(7) Notwithstanding the repeal of the Act of 1989 by *section 4*, a code of practice in operation immediately before the commencement of that section continues to be a code of practice as if prepared and published under this section.

Use of codes of practice in criminal proceedings

61.—(1) Where in proceedings for an offence under this Act relating to an alleged contravention of any requirement or prohibition imposed by or under a relevant statutory provision being a provision for which a code of practice had been published or approved by the Authority under *section 60* at the time of the alleged contravention, *subsection (2)* shall have effect with respect to that code of practice in relation to those proceedings.

(2) (*a*) Where a code of practice referred to in *subsection (1)* appears to the court to give practical guidance as to the observance of the requirement or prohibition alleged to have been contravened, the code of practice shall be admissible in evidence.

(*b*) Where it is proved that any act or omission of the defendant alleged to constitute the contravention—

(i) is a failure to observe a code of practice referred to in *subsection (1)*, or

(ii) is a compliance with that code of practice,

then such failure or compliance is admissible in evidence.

(3) A document bearing the seal of the Authority and purporting to be a code of practice or part of a code of practice published or approved of by the Authority under this section shall be admissible as evidence in any proceedings under this Act.

CHAPTER 2

Enforcement

Authorisation of inspectors

62.—(1) The Authority or a person prescribed under *section 33* may authorise such and so many persons as the Authority or person considers appropriate to be inspectors for the purposes of the enforcement of all or any of the relevant statutory provisions within the relevant area of responsibility in accordance with *section 33* or *34*, as the case may be.

(2) (*a*) An inspector shall be furnished with a certificate of authorisation as an inspector.

(*b*) When exercising a power conferred on him or her by this section, an inspector shall, if requested by a person affected, produce the certificate of authorisation or a copy of it to that person and a form of personal identification.

(3) An authorisation under this section shall cease when the Authority or a person prescribed under *section 33*, as the case may be, revokes the authorisation.

(4) Notwithstanding the repeal of the Act of 1989 by *section 4*, an inspector authorised immediately before the commencement of that section under section 33 of the Act of 1989 continues to be an inspector as if authorised under this section.

Medical examinations

63.—(1) The Authority or a person prescribed under *section 33* may designate in writing any person, including an inspector, who is a registered medical practitioner to receive any notice, report or certificate required by any of the relevant statutory provisions to be sent to the Authority or a person prescribed under *section 33* by a registered medical practitioner, and any person so designated may—

(*a*) invite any person who, in his or her opinion, either has been or may be exposed in the course of his or her work to any risk of personal injury or other danger to his or her health, and

(*b*) for the purpose of comparing with that of other persons the state of health of persons employed in different places of work or specified places of work or in different places in the same place of work, invite any person,

to provide biological samples or to be examined medically, or both, at such place as the person so designated shall designate, either by him or her or on his or her behalf or by or on behalf of such other registered medical practitioner as he or she shall specify.

(2) References in the relevant statutory provisions to "occupational medical adviser" shall be read as references to persons designated under this section.

Powers of inspectors

64.—(1) An inspector shall, for the purposes of the relevant statutory provisions have power to do any one or more of the following:

(*a*) subject to *subsection (5)*, at any time enter any place—

  (i) which he or she has reasonable grounds for believing is used as a place of work,
  (ii) in which he or she has reasonable grounds for believing that articles or substances or records are kept, or
  (iii) to which the relevant statutory provisions apply,

and inquire into, search, examine and inspect that place and any work activity, installation, process or procedure at that place which is subject to the relevant statutory provisions and any such articles, substances or records to ascertain whether the relevant statutory provisions have been or are being complied with and for those purposes take with him or her and use any equipment or materials required for those purposes;

(*b*) direct that that place or any part of that place and anything in that place be left undisturbed for so long as is reasonably necessary for the purpose of any search, examination, investigation, inspection or inquiry under the relevant statutory provisions;

(*c*) direct that a safety statement be amended in accordance with *section 20(5)(c)*;

(*d*) require the employer, any employee, the owner or person in charge of the place to produce to the inspector any records and in the case of such information in a nonlegible form to reproduce it in a legible form and to give to the inspector such information as the inspector may reasonably require in relation to any entries in those records;

(*e*) inspect and take copies of or extracts from any such records or any electronic information system at the place, including in the case of information in a non-legible form, copies of or extracts from such information in a permanent legible form or require that such copies be provided;

(*f*) require a person by whom or on whose behalf a computer is or has been used to produce or store records or any person having charge of, or otherwise concerned with the operation of the computer, to afford the inspector all reasonable assistance in relation thereto;

(*g*) remove and retain the records (including documents stored in a non-legible form) and copies taken and detain the records for such period as the inspector reasonably considers to be necessary for further examination or until the conclusion of any legal proceedings;

(*h*) require that records be maintained for such period of time as may be reasonable;

(*i*) require the employer, any employee, the owner or person in charge of the place to give to the inspector any information that the inspector may reasonably require for the purposes of any search, examination, investigation, inspection or inquiry under the relevant statutory provisions;

(*j*) require the employer, owner, any person in charge of the place or any employee to give to the inspector such assistance and facilities within the person's control or responsibilities as are reasonably necessary to enable the inspector to exercise any of his or her powers under the relevant statutory provisions;

(*k*) summon, at a time and place specified by written notice to the person concerned, the employer, any employee, the owner or person in charge of the place to give to the inspector any information which the inspector may reasonably require in relation to the place, any article or substance, work activity, installation or procedure at the place, and to produce to the inspector any records that are in that person's power or control;

(*l*) subject to *subsection (9)*, examine any person whom the inspector reasonably believes to be able to give information relevant to any search, examination, investigation, inspection or inquiry under the relevant statutory provisions and require the person to answer such questions as the inspector may put relative to the search, examination, investigation, inspection or inquiry and to sign a declaration of the truth of the answers;

(*m*) require that any article be operated or set in motion or that a procedure be carried out that may be relevant to any search, examination, investigation, inspection, or inquiry under the relevant statutory provisions;

(*n*) take any measurements or photographs or make any tape, electrical or other recordings which the inspector considers necessary for the purposes of any search, examination, investigation, inspection or inquiry under the relevant statutory provisions;

(*o*) where appropriate, install, use and maintain in, at or on the place monitoring instruments, systems and seals for the purposes of the relevant statutory provisions;

(*p*) there, or at any other place, carry out, or have carried out, such testing, examination or analysis of any article or substance found at the place, as he or she reasonably considers to be necessary, and for that purpose require the employer or owner or person in charge of the place to supply to the inspector without charge any article or substance or samples thereof, or remove any article, substance or samples thereof, for such testing, examination or analysis;

(*q*) cause any article or substance found at the place which appears to the inspector to be or to have been a risk to safety or health, to be dismantled or subjected to any process or test in accordance with *paragraph (p)* (but not so as to damage or destroy it unless this is in the circumstances necessary for the purposes of the relevant statutory provisions) and where an inspector proposes to exercise the power conferred by this paragraph in the case of an article or substance found at any place, he or she shall, if so requested by the employer, owner or person in charge of the place, cause anything which is to be done by virtue of that power to be done in the presence of that person;

(*r*) take samples of the atmosphere in any place of work;

(*s*) in relation to any article or substance found at the place in accordance with *paragraph (q)*, to remove and retain it for such period as is necessary for all or any of the following purposes, namely:

    (i) to examine or arrange for the examination of it and do to it anything which he or she has power to do under *paragraph (q)*;

    (ii) to ensure that it is not tampered with before the examination of it is completed;

    (iii) to ensure that it is available for use as evidence in any proceedings;

(*t*) exercise such other powers as may be necessary for carrying out his or her functions.

(2) Where an article or substance is used at work, and a request is made in that behalf by an inspector in the course of a search, examination, investigation, inspection or inquiry, the employer shall give to the inspector the name and address of the supplier from whom the article or substance was purchased or otherwise obtained.

(3) Before exercising the power conferred by *subsections (1)(p)* and *(q)* in the case of any article or substance, an inspector shall, in so far as it is practicable to do so, consult such persons as appear to him or her to be appropriate for the purpose of ascertaining what dangers, if any, there may be in doing anything which he or she proposes to do under that power.

(4) Where under the power conferred by *subsection (1)(s)* an inspector takes possession of any article or substance found at or in any place of work, he or she shall if it is practicable for him or her to do so, take a sample thereof and give to a responsible person at the place of work a portion of the sample marked in a manner sufficient to identify it.

(5) An inspector shall not enter a dwelling other than—

    (*a*) with the consent of the occupier, or

    (*b*) in accordance with a warrant from a District Court issued under *subsection (7)* authorising such entry.

(6) Where an inspector in the exercise of his or her powers under this section is prevented from entering any place, an application may be made to the District Court for a warrant under *subsection (7)* authorising such entry.

(7) Without prejudice to the powers conferred on an inspector by or under any other provision of this section, if a judge of the District Court is satisfied on the sworn information of an inspector that there are reasonable grounds for believing that—

    (*a*) there are any articles or substances being used in a place of work or any records (including documents stored in a non-legible form) or information, relating to a place of work, that the inspector requires to inspect for the purposes of the relevant statutory provisions, held in, at or on any place or any part of any place, or

    (*b*) there is, or such an inspection is likely to disclose, evidence of a contravention of the relevant statutory provisions,

the judge may issue a warrant authorising an inspector, accompanied by such other inspectors or such other competent persons as may be appropriate or members of the Garda Síochána as may be necessary, at any time or times, within one month from the date of issue of the warrant, on production of the warrant if requested, to enter the place, if need be by reasonable force, and perform the functions conferred on an inspector by or under the relevant statutory provisions.

(8) An inspector, where he or she has reasonable cause to apprehend any serious obstruction in the execution of his or her duty or otherwise considers it necessary, may be accompanied by a member of the Garda Síochána or any other person authorised by the Authority, when performing any functions conferred on an inspector by or under the relevant statutory provisions.

(9) No person is required on examination or inquiry under this section to give any answer or information tending to incriminate that person.

(10) Where an inspector upon reasonable grounds believes that a person has committed an offence under the relevant statutory provisions he or she may require that person to provide him or her with his or her name and the address at which he or she ordinarily resides.

Directions for improvement plan

65.—(1) Where an inspector is of the opinion that there is occurring or likely to occur any activity which involves or is likely to involve a risk to the safety, health or welfare of persons, he or she may give a written direction to the employer concerned requiring submission to him or her of an improvement plan.

(2) A direction given under *subsection (1)* shall—

    (*a*) identify the activity which is or is likely to be a risk,

    (*b*) require the submission to the inspector, within a period of one month, of an improvement plan specifying the remedial action proposed to be taken,

    (*c*) require the employer to implement the plan, and

    (*d*) include any other requirements that the inspector considers necessary.

(3) Where there is a safety representative in a place of work in respect of which a direction is given under *subsection (1)*, the inspector shall give a copy of the direction to the safety representative.

(4) Within one month of receipt of an improvement plan submitted under *subsection (2)*, an inspector, by written notice to the person who submitted the plan—

    (*a*) shall confirm whether or not he or she is satisfied that the plan is adequate, or

    (*b*) may direct that the plan be revised as specified in the notice and resubmitted to the inspector within a period specified in the notice.

Improvement notice

66.—(1) An inspector who is of the opinion that a person—

    (*a*) is contravening or has contravened any of the relevant statutory provisions, or

    (*b*) has failed to comply with a direction under *section 65(1)* to submit an improvement plan or, in the case of a notice under *section 65(4)(b)*, a revised improvement plan, or has failed to implement the improvement plan or revised improvement plan,

may serve a written notice (in this Act referred to as an "improvement notice") on the person who has or may reasonably be presumed to have control over the work activity concerned.

(2) An improvement notice shall—

    (*a*) state that the inspector is of the opinion referred to in *subsection (1)*,

    (*b*) state the reasons for that opinion,

    (*c*) identify the relevant statutory provision in respect of which that opinion is held,

    (*d*) specify the reasons why he or she is of that opinion,

    (*e*) direct the person to remedy the contravention or the matters occasioning that notice by a date specified in the notice, that shall not be earlier than the end of the period within which an appeal may be made under *subsection (7)*,

    (*f*) include information regarding the making of an appeal under *subsection (7)*,

    (*g*) include any other requirement that the inspector considers appropriate, and

    (*h*) be signed and dated by the inspector.

(3) An improvement notice may include directions as to the measures to be taken to remedy any contravention or matter to which the notice relates or to otherwise comply with the notice.

(4) Where there is a safety representative in a place of work in respect of which an improvement notice is served under *subsection (1)*, the inspector shall give a copy of the improvement notice to the safety representative and inform the safety representative in writing where an improvement notice is withdrawn under *subsection (11)*.

(5) A person on whom an improvement notice has been served who is of the opinion that the improvement notice has been complied with shall confirm in writing to the inspector that the matters referred to in the notice have been so remedied and shall give a copy of the confirmation to the safety representative, if any.

(6) Where a person on whom an improvement notice has been served confirms in writing to the inspector in accordance with *subsection (5)* that the matters referred to in the improvement notice have been remedied, the inspector shall, on being satisfied that the matters have been so remedied, within one month of receipt of such confirmation, give written notice to the person concerned of compliance with the improvement notice.

(7) A person aggrieved by an improvement notice may, within 14 days beginning on the day on which the notice is served on him or her, appeal in the prescribed manner against the notice to a judge of the District Court in the district court district in which the notice was served in the prescribed manner and, in determining the appeal the judge may, if he or she is satisfied that it is reasonable to do so, confirm, vary or cancel the notice.

(8) A person who appeals under *subsection (7)* shall at the same time notify the Authority or the person prescribed under *section 33*, as the case may be, of the appeal and the grounds for the appeal and the Authority or the person prescribed under *section 33* shall be entitled to appear, be heard and adduce evidence on the hearing of the appeal.

(9) Where an appeal under *subsection (7)* is taken, and the notice is not cancelled, the notice shall take effect on the later of—

    (*a*) the day next following the day on which the notice is confirmed on appeal or the appeal is withdrawn, or

    (*b*) the day specified in the notice.

(10) Where there is no appeal under *subsection (7)*, the notice shall take effect on the later of—

    (*a*) the end of the period for making an appeal, or

    (*b*) the day specified in the notice.

(11) An inspector may—

    (*a*) withdraw an improvement notice at any time, or

    (*b*) where no appeal is made or pending under *subsection (7)*, extend the period specified under *subsection (2)(e)*.

Prohibition notice

67.—(1) Where an inspector is of the opinion that at any place of work there is occurring or is likely to occur any activity (whether by reference to any article or substance or otherwise) which involves or is likely to involve a risk of serious personal injury to any person, the inspector may serve a written notice (in this Act referred to as a "prohibition notice") on the person who has or who may reasonably be presumed to have control over the activity concerned.

(2)   A prohibition notice shall—

    (*a*) state that the inspector is of the opinion referred to in *subsection (1)*,
    (*b*) state the reasons for that opinion,
    (*c*) specify the activity in respect of which that opinion is held,
    (*d*) where in his or her opinion the activity involves a contravention, or likely contravention, of any of the relevant statutory provisions, specify the relevant statutory provision,
    (*e*) prohibit the carrying on of the activity concerned until the matters which give rise or are likely to give rise to the risk are remedied, and
    (*f*) be signed and dated by the inspector.

(3)   A prohibition notice may include directions as to the measures to be taken to remedy any contravention or matter to which the notice relates or to otherwise comply with the notice.

(4)   Where there is a safety representative in a place of work in respect of which a prohibition notice is served under *subsection (1)*, the inspector shall give a copy of the prohibition notice to the safety representative and inform the safety representative in writing where a prohibition notice is withdrawn under *subsection (12)*.

(5)   A prohibition notice shall take effect—

    (*a*) immediately the notice is received by the person on whom it is served, or
    (*b*) where an appeal is taken, on the later of the day next following the day on which the notice is confirmed on appeal or the appeal is withdrawn or the day specified in the notice.

(6)   The bringing of an appeal against a prohibition notice which is to take effect in accordance with *subsection (5)* shall not have the effect of suspending the operation of the notice but the appellant may apply to the court to have the operation of the notice suspended until the appeal is disposed of and, on such application, the court may, if it thinks proper to do so, direct that the operation of the notice be suspended until the appeal is disposed of.

(7)   A person aggrieved by a prohibition notice may, within 7 days beginning on the day on which the notice is served on him or her, appeal in the prescribed manner against the notice to a judge of the District Court in the district court district in which the notice was served and in

determining the appeal the judge may, if he or she is satisfied that it is reasonable to do so, confirm, vary or cancel the notice.

(8)   Where, on the hearing of an appeal under this section, a prohibition notice is confirmed, notwithstanding *subsection (5)*, the judge by whom the appeal is heard may, on the application of the appellant, suspend the operation of the notice for such period as in the circumstances of the case the judge considers appropriate.

(9)   A person who—

(*a*) appeals under *subsection (7)*, or

(*b*) applies for a direction suspending the application of a prohibition notice under *subsection (8)*,

shall at the same time notify the Authority or a person prescribed under *section 33*, as the case may be, of the appeal or the application and the grounds for the appeal or the application and the Authority or the person prescribed under *section 33* shall be entitled to appear, be heard and adduce evidence on the hearing of the appeal or the application.

(10)   A person on whom a prohibition notice has been served who is of the opinion that the matters referred to in the notice have been remedied by the date specified in the notice shall confirm in writing to the inspector that those matters have been so remedied and shall give a copy of the confirmation to the safety representative, if any.

(11)   Where a person on whom a prohibition notice has been served confirms in writing to the inspector in accordance with *subsection (10)* that the matters referred to in the prohibition notice have been remedied, the inspector shall, on being satisfied that the matters have been so remedied, within one month of receipt of such confirmation, give written notice to the person concerned of compliance with the prohibition notice.

(12)   An inspector may at any time withdraw a prohibition notice by written notice to the person on whom it was served where—

(*a*) the inspector is satisfied that the activity to which the notice relates no longer involves a risk of serious personal injury to any person, or

(*b*) the inspector is satisfied that the notice was issued in error or is incorrect in some material respect.

(13)   The withdrawal of a notice under *subsection (12)* has effect when the notice of withdrawal is given to the person on whom the prohibition notice was served.

(14)   The withdrawal of a notice under this section does not prevent the service of any other prohibition notice.

Contravention of prohibition notice — application to High Court

68.—(1) Where a prohibition notice has been served under *section 67* and activities are carried on in contravention of the notice, the High Court may, on the application of an inspector, by order prohibit the continuance of the activities.

(2) An application to the High Court for an order under *subsection (1)* may be ex parte and the Court, when considering the matter, may make such interim or interlocutory order (if any) as it considers appropriate, and the order by which an application under this subsection is determined may contain such terms and conditions (if any) regarding the payment of costs that the Court considers appropriate.

Notices to be displayed

69.—Where an improvement notice or a prohibition notice is served, the person to whom it is addressed shall on receipt of the notice—

(*a*) bring the notice to the attention of any person whose work is affected by the notice, and

(*b*) display the notice or a copy of the notice in a prominent place at or near any place of work, article or substance affected by the notice.

Investigations and special reports

70.—(1) Without prejudice to this Chapter and subject to *subsection (6)*, the Authority may at any time direct any of its staff or any other competent person as it considers appropriate to—

(*a*) investigate the causes and circumstances surrounding any accident, incident, personal injury, occurrence or situation or any other matter related to the general purposes of this Act, and

(*b*) make a report (in this Act referred to as a "special report") of the investigation to the Authority.

(2) A person, who is not an inspector, carrying out an investigation under this section shall, for the purposes of the investigation, have all the powers of an inspector under this Act.

(3) In the case of a person directed to carry out an investigation and make a special report under *subsection (1)* (other than a member of the staff of the Authority), the Authority may pay to the person such fees and expenses as the Minister may determine with the approval of the Minister for Finance.

(4) The Authority may, to the extent that the Minister may determine, discharge the costs, other than those incurred under *subsection (3)*, if any, incurred in the preparation of a special report.

(5) A copy of a special report made under *subsection (1)* shall be presented to the Minister as soon as practicable and the Authority may cause the report to be made public in such manner as it considers appropriate.

(6) The Authority in discharging its functions under *subsection (1)* shall not, save with the consent of the Minister given with the concurrence of any other Minister of the Government that he or she considers appropriate, investigate, examine or inquire into any of the following—

(*a*) an accident within the meaning of the Air Navigation (Notification and Investigation of Accidents and Incidents) Regulations 1997 (S.I. No. 205 of 1997),

(*b*) a rail accident, or

(*c*) a marine casualty (within the meaning of the Merchant Shipping (Investigation of Marine Casualties) Act 2000).

Order of High Court as to use of place of work

71.—(1) Where the Authority or a person prescribed under *section 33*, as the case may be, considers that the risk to the safety, health or welfare of persons is so serious that the use of a place of work or part of a place of work should be restricted or immediately prohibited until specified measures have been taken to reduce the risk to a reasonable level, the Authority or the person prescribed under *section 33* may apply, exparte, to the High Court for an order restricting or prohibiting the use of the place of work or part of a place of work accordingly.

(2) The Court may make any interim or interlocutory order that it considers appropriate.

(3) Any order made by the Court under this section shall have effect notwithstanding the terms of any permission given under any other enactment for the use of the place of work or part of the place of work to which the application under this section relates.

(4) On an application by any person for the revocation or variation of an order under *subsection (1)*, the Authority or a person prescribed under *section 33*, as appropriate, shall be entitled to be heard.

CHAPTER 3

Obtaining and Disclosure of Information

Power to require information

72.—(1) The Authority or a person prescribed under *section 33* may, by written notice (referred to in this Act as an "information notice") served on a person, require the person to give to the Authority, within such period and in such form as may be specified in the notice, any information specified in the notice that the Authority or the person prescribed under *section 33* may reasonably require in performing its functions.

(2) The period specified in the information notice under *subsection (1)* may be extended at the discretion of the Authority on the written application of the person on whom the notice is served.

(3) A person on whom an information notice is served under this section may, within 7 days beginning on the day on which the notice is served on him or her, appeal in the prescribed manner against the notice to a judge of the District Court in the district court district in which the notice was served

and in determining the appeal the judge may, if he or she is satisfied that it is reasonable to do so, confirm, vary or cancel the notice.

(4) Where, on the hearing of an appeal under *subsection (3)*, a notice is confirmed or varied, the judge of the District Court by whom the appeal is heard may, on the application of the appellant, suspend the operation of the notice for such period as in the circumstances of the case the judge considers appropriate.

(5) A person on whom an information notice is served shall comply with the notice before the later of—

   (*a*) where no appeal is made against the notice under *subsection (3)*—

      (i) the end of the period for bringing an appeal under that subsection,
      (ii) the end of the period specified in the notice for the purpose of giving the specified information, or
      (iii) where the period referred to in *subparagraph (ii)* is extended under *subsection (2)*, the end of that extended period,

   (*b*) where an appeal is made and the information notice is confirmed or varied or the appeal is withdrawn—

      (i) the day following the day on which the notice is confirmed or varied or the appeal is withdrawn,
      (ii) the end of the period specified in the notice, or
      (iii) where the operation of the notice has been suspended in accordance with *subsection (3)*, on the expiration of the period that the judge of the District Court considered appropriate for the purpose of that subsection.

Prohibition on unauthorised disclosure of confidential information

73.—(1) Save as otherwise provided by law and subject to *subsection (2)*, a person shall not, unless duly authorised by the Authority, disclose confidential information obtained by the person while performing or as a result of performing any functions as—

   (*a*) a member of the Authority,
   (*b*) a member of the staff (including the Chief Executive) of the Authority,
   (*c*) a member of an advisory committee, or
   (*d*) a consultant or adviser to the Authority or an employee of such person.

(2) *Subsection (1)* does not prohibit the disclosure of information by means of a report made—

   (*a*) to the Authority,
   (*b*) to the Minister, by or on behalf of the Authority, or
   (*c*) to a coroner holding an inquest under the Coroners Act 1962 on the body of a person whose death may have been caused through personal injury.

(3) The Freedom of Information Act 1997 is amended in the Third Schedule thereto—

  (*a*) by the deletion—

      (i) in column (1), of "No. 7 of 1989",
      (ii) in column (2), of "Safety, Health and Welfare at Work Act 1989.", and
      (iii) in column (3), of "Section 45.", and

  (*b*) by the addition to Part 1 at the end thereof—

      (i) in column (2), of "*Safety, Health and Welfare at Work Act 2005.*", and
      (ii) in column (3), of "*Section 73.*".

Amendment of Freedom of Information Act 1997

74.—The Freedom of Information Act 1997 is amended in section 46(1) (as amended by section 29 of the Freedom of Information (Amendment) Act 2003), by inserting the following after paragraph (*db*):

"(*dc*) a record held or created under the relevant statutory provisions by the Health and Safety Authority or an employee of the Authority, relating to or arising from its enforcement functions (other than a record concerning any other functions of the Authority or the general administration of the Authority),".

Disclosure of information

75.—(1) The Revenue Commissioners may, where they consider it appropriate for the purpose of facilitating the exercise or performance by the Authority or a person prescribed under *section 33* of any of their powers or duties under the relevant statutory provisions, authorise the disclosure to the Authority or to a person prescribed under *section 33* or to an inspector of the Authority or of a person prescribed under *section 33* of any information obtained by the Revenue Commissioners in relation to articles or substances imported into the State.

(2) The Minister for Health and Children and the Minister for Social and Family Affairs may give to the Authority or a person prescribed under *section 33* such information in relation to personal injury to persons at work as may be necessary for promoting the safety, health and welfare of persons at work.

(3) A member of the Garda Síochána may give to the Authority or a person prescribed under *section 33* such information in relation to personal injury to a person at work as may be necessary for enforcement of the relevant statutory provisions.

(4) The Minister, following consultation with any other Minister of the Government that he or she considers appropriate, may prescribe persons requiring them to give to the Authority or a person prescribed under *section 33* such information in relation to personal injury to persons at work

as may be necessary for promoting the safety, health and welfare of persons at work.

Disclosure of information by inspector in certain circumstances

76.—(1) An inspector shall, where he or she considers it necessary to do so for the purpose of providing adequate information to employees and their safety representatives (if any) at any place of work in relation to their safety, health and welfare at work, give to those employees and their safety representatives (if any) the following information—

    (*a*) subject to *subsection (3)*, factual information obtained by the inspector under the relevant statutory provisions relating to the place of work concerned or any article or substance or any activity being carried on in the place of work, and

    (*b*) information with respect to any action which the inspector has taken or proposes to take in or in connection with that place of work in performing his or her functions.

(2) Where an inspector gives any information to employees or their safety representatives under *subsection (1)* he or she shall give the same information to the employer concerned.

(3) (*a*) An inspector shall not disclose any information relating to any manufacturing, trade or commercial secrets or work processes that was obtained by the inspector in the performance of his or her functions under this Act.

    (*b*) *Paragraph (a)* does not prevent the disclosure of information where that disclosure is—

        (i) for the purpose of his or her functions under this Act,

        (ii) made with the relevant consent, or

        (iii) for the purposes of any legal proceedings or of any investigation or special report under *section 70*.

PART 7

OFFENCES AND PENALTIES

Offences

77.—(1) A person commits an offence where he or she—

    (*a*) fails to discharge a duty to which he or she is subject under *sections 25(4),(5)* and *(6)*, *26(1)*, *(4)*, *(5)* and *(6)* and *section 69*,

    (*b*) prevents or attempts to prevent any person from answering any question to which an inspector may require an answer under *section 64*,

    (*c*) fails to submit an improvement plan to an inspector within the time specified in a direction under *section 65*,

    (*d*) fails to implement an improvement plan the adequacy of which has been confirmed in accordance with *section 65*, (*e*) contravenes any requirement imposed by a notice requiring information under *section 72*, or

(*f*) prevents, obstructs, impedes or delays an officer of customs and excise in the exercise of any of the powers conferred on him or her by *section 87*.

(2) A person commits an offence where he or she—

(*a*) fails to discharge a duty to which he or she is subject by virtue of *sections 8, 9, 10, 11(1)* to *(4), 12, 13* and *15* to *23*,

(*b*) contravenes *section 14*,

(*c*) except for the provisions of this section as they apply to this Act, contravenes the relevant statutory provisions,

(*d*) prevents, obstructs, impedes or delays an inspector from exercising any functions conferred on him or her by this Act,

(*e*) fails to comply with a bona fide request, instruction or directions from an inspector in the exercise of his or her statutory functions,

(*f*) where any person makes a statement to an inspector which he or she knows to be false or recklessly makes a statement which is false where the statement is made—

(i) in purported compliance with a requirement to furnish any information imposed by or under any of the relevant statutory provisions, or

(ii) for the purpose of obtaining the issue of a document under any of the relevant statutory provisions to himself or herself or another person,

(*g*) makes a false entry intentionally in any register, book, notice or other document required by or under any of the relevant statutory provisions to be kept, served or given or, with intent to deceive, makes use of any such entry which he or she knows to be false,

(*h*) produces or causes to be produced or allows to be produced to an inspector any record which is false or misleading in any respect knowing it to be so false or misleading,

(*i*) forges or uses a document issued or authorised to be issued under any of the relevant statutory provisions or required for any purpose under the relevant statutory provisions with the intent to deceive, or makes or has in his or her possession a document so closely resembling any such document as to be calculated to deceive,

(*j*) falsely represents himself or herself to be an inspector,

(*k*) contravenes any requirement of an improvement notice served under *section 66*, or

(*l*) carries on any activity in contravention of a prohibition notice served under *section 67*.

(3) A person who, at any time during the period of 3 months after a notice or document is affixed under *section 3(1)(d)* removes, alters, damages or defaces the notice or document without lawful authority, commits an offence.

(4) A person commits an offence if he or she—

    (*a*) obstructs or impedes a member of the Garda Síochána in the exercise of a power conferred on him or her or by a warrant under *section 64(7)*,

    (*b*) refuses to produce any record that an inspector lawfully requires him or her to produce, or

    (*c*) gives to an inspector information that the person knows is false or misleading.

(5) It is an offence to contravene any order or orders made under *section 71*.

(6) A person who, without reasonable cause, fails or refuses to comply with a requirement specified in an information notice or who in purported compliance with such a requirement furnishes information to the Authority that the person knows to be false or misleading in a material respect commits an offence.

(7) A person who contravenes *section 73* commits an offence.

(8) (*a*) A person convicted of an offence under any of the relevant statutory provisions may, in addition to any fine that may be imposed, be ordered to take steps within a specified time to remedy the matters in respect of which the contravention occurred (and may on application extend the time so specified) and any person who fails to comply with any such order within the specified time (as extended) commits an offence.

    (*b*) The time specified under *paragraph (a)* may be extended at the discretion of the court on application made by the person to whom the order is addressed.

(9) (*a*) Subject to *paragraph (b)*, if a person suffers any personal injury as a consequence of the contravention of any of the relevant statutory provisions by a person on whom a duty is imposed by *sections 8 to 12* inclusive and *14* to *17* inclusive, the person on whom the duty is imposed commits an offence.

    (*b*) A person does not commit an offence under *paragraph (a)*—

        (i) if a prosecution against the person in respect of the act or default by which the personal injury was caused has been heard and dismissed before the personal injury occurred, or

        (ii) in the case of personal injury excluding death, where that injury was not caused directly by the alleged contravention.

(10)(*a*) Without prejudice to *subsection (12)*, where a person is charged with a summary offence under any of the relevant statutory provisions, the person is entitled, upon information duly laid by him or her and on giving to the prosecution not less than 3 days notice in writing of his or her intention, to have any other person whom he or she charges as the actual offender brought before the court at the time appointed for hearing the matter (whether or not the other person is his or her employee or agent).

(*b*) If the commission of the offence is proved and the first person charged proves to the satisfaction of the court that he or she used all diligence to enforce the relevant statutory provisions and that the other person whom he or she charges as the actual offender committed the offence without his or her consent, connivance or wilful default, that other person shall be summarily convicted of the offence and the first person is not guilty of the offence, and the person convicted shall, in the discretion of the court, be also liable to pay any costs incidental to the proceedings.

(*c*) The prosecution shall in any case to which this subsection applies have the right to cross-examine the first person charged if he or she gives evidence and any witnesses called by him or her in support of his or her charge, and to adduce rebutting evidence.

(11) Where an offence under any of the relevant statutory provisions is committed by reason of a failure to do something at or within a time fixed by or under any of those provisions, the offence shall be deemed to continue until that thing is done.

(12) Nothing in the relevant statutory provisions shall operate so as to afford an employer a defence in any criminal proceedings for a contravention of those provisions by reason of any act or default of—

(*a*) his or her employee, or
(*b*) a competent person appointed by the employer under section 18.

Penalties

78.—(1) A person guilty of an offence under section 39(17)(*e*) of the Redundancy Payments Act 1967 as applied to this Act by *section 29(7)*, or *77(1)* is liable on summary conviction to a fine not exceeding €3,000.

(2) A person guilty of an offence—

(*a*) under *section 77(2)* to *(8)* and *(9)(a)*,
(*b*) which consists of contravening any of the relevant statutory provisions by doing otherwise than under the authority of a licence issued by the Authority or, a person prescribed under *section 33*, something for the doing of which such a licence is necessary under the relevant statutory provisions, or
(*c*) which consists of contravening a term of or a condition or restriction attached to any such licence as is mentioned in *paragraph (b)*,

is liable—

(i) on summary conviction to a fine not exceeding €3,000 or imprisonment for a term not exceeding 6 months or both, or
(ii) on conviction on indictment to a fine not exceeding €3,000,000 or imprisonment for a term not exceeding 2 years or both.

(3) Nothing in this section shall be construed as creating an indictable offence in respect of regulations made under the European Communities Act 1972.

(4) Where a person is convicted of an offence under the relevant statutory provisions in proceedings brought by the Authority or a prescribed person under *section 33*, the court shall, unless it is satisfied that there are special and substantial reasons for not so doing, order the person to pay to the Authority or the prescribed person under *section 33* the costs and expenses measured by the court, incurred by the Authority or the prescribed person under *section 33* in relation to the investigation, detection and prosecution of the offence including costs and expenses incurred in the taking of samples, the carrying out of tests, examinations and analyses and in respect of the remuneration and other expenses of employees of or consultants and advisers engaged by the Authority or the prescribed person under *section 33*, as the case may be.

Provisions regarding certain offences

79.—(1) If an inspector has reasonable grounds for believing that a person is committing or has committed a prescribed offence under the relevant statutory provisions, he or she may serve the person with a notice in the prescribed form stating that—

(a) the person is alleged to have committed the offence, and

(b) a prosecution in respect of the alleged offence will not be instituted during the period specified in the notice and, if the payment specified in the notice is made during that period, no prosecution in respect of the alleged offence will be instituted.

(2) A person on whom a notice is served under *subsection (1)* may, during the period of 21 days beginning on the day of the notice, make to the Authority or to a person prescribed under *section 33*, as appropriate, at the address specified in the notice a payment not exceeding €1,000 as may be prescribed.

(3) Where a notice is served under *subsection (1)*—

(a) the Authority or a person prescribed under *section 33*, as specified in the notice, may receive the payment, issue a receipt for it and retain the money so paid, and any payment so received shall not be recoverable in any circumstance by the person who made it, and

(b) a prosecution in respect of the alleged offence shall not be instituted in the period specified in the notice, and if the payment so specified is made during that period, no prosecution in respect of the alleged offence shall be instituted.

(4) In a prosecution for an offence under this Act the onus of proving that a payment pursuant to a notice under this section has been made shall lie on the accused.

Liability of directors and officers of undertakings

80.—(1) Where an offence under any of the relevant statutory provisions has been committed by an undertaking and the doing of the acts that constituted the offence has been authorised, or consented to by, or is attributable to connivance or neglect on the part of, a person, being a director, manager or other similar officer of the undertaking, or a person who purports to act in any such capacity, that person as well as the undertaking shall be guilty of an offence and shall be liable to be proceeded against and punished as if he or she were guilty of the first-mentioned offence.

(2) Where a person is proceeded against as aforesaid for such an offence and it is proved that, at the material time, he or she was a director of the undertaking concerned or a person employed by it whose duties included making decisions that, to a significant extent, could have affected the management of the undertaking, or a person who purported to act in any such capacity, it shall be presumed, until the contrary is proved, that the doing of the acts by the undertaking which constituted the commission by it of the offence concerned under any of the relevant statutory provisions was authorised, consented to or attributable to connivance or neglect on the part of that person.

(3) Where the affairs of a body corporate are managed by its members, *subsections (1)* and *(2)* shall apply in relation to the acts or defaults of a member in connection with his or her functions of management as if he or she were a director of the body corporate.

Onus of proof

81.—In any proceedings for an offence under any of the relevant statutory provisions consisting of a failure to comply with a duty or requirement to do something so far as is practicable or so far as is reasonably practicable, or to use the best practicable means to do something, it shall be for the accused to prove (as the case may be) that it was not practicable or not reasonably practicable to do more than was in fact done to satisfy the duty or requirement, or that there was no better practicable means than was in fact used to satisfy the duty or requirement.

Prosecution of offences

82.—(1) Subject to *subsection (2)*, summary proceedings in relation to an offence under any of the relevant statutory provisions may be brought and prosecuted by the Authority.

(2) Summary proceedings in relation to an offence under any of the relevant statutory provisions may be brought and prosecuted by a person prescribed under *section 33* whose function it is, in accordance with any of the relevant statutory provisions, to enforce the provision concerned.

(3) Notwithstanding section 10(4) of the Petty Sessions (Ireland) Act 1851, but without prejudice to *subsection (4)*, summary proceedings for an offence under any of the relevant statutory provisions may be instituted at any time within 12 months from the date on which the offence was committed.

(4) Where a special report on any matter to which *section 70* applies is made and it appears from the report that any of the relevant statutory provisions

was contravened at a time which is material in relation to the subject matter of the report, summary proceedings against any person liable to be proceeded against in respect of the contravention may be instituted at any time within 6 months of the making of the report or 12 months after the date of the contravention, whichever is the later.

Appeals from orders

83.—Any person (including the Authority or a person prescribed under *section 33*) aggrieved by an order made by the District Court on determining a complaint under this Act may appeal therefrom to a judge of the Circuit Court within whose circuit is situated the District Court in which the decision was given, and the decision of the judge of the Circuit Court on any such appeal shall be final and conclusive.

Evidence

84.—(1) If a person is found to be carrying on a work activity in any place of work at any time at which work is being carried on, he or she shall, until the contrary is proved, be deemed for the purposes of this Act to have been employed in that place of work either by the person who has or who may reasonably be presumed to have overall control over the work activity concerned or by another employer carrying on work activities in that place of work.

(2) Where any entry is required by any of the relevant statutory provisions to be made in any record, the entry made by an employer or on behalf of an employer shall, as against the employer, be admissible as evidence of the facts therein stated, and the fact that any entry so required with respect to the observance of any of the relevant statutory provisions has not been made, shall be admissible as evidence that the provision has not been observed.

(3) In any proceedings under this Act a copy record may be given in evidence and shall be prima facie evidence of the facts stated in it, if the court is satisfied as to the reliability of the system used to make the copy record and the original entry on which it was based.

Publication of names of certain persons

85.—(1) The Authority may from time to time compile a list of names and addresses and the description of business or other activity of every person—

    (*a*) on whom a fine or other penalty was imposed by a court under any of the relevant statutory provisions,

    (*b*) on whom a prohibition notice was served under *section 67*, or

    (*c*) in respect of whom an interim or interlocutory order was made under *section 71*.

(2) The Authority may at any time cause any list referred to in *subsection (1)* to be published in such manner as it considers appropriate.

(3) Any list referred to in *subsection (1)* shall specify in respect of each person named in the list such particulars, as the Authority thinks fit, of—

    (*a*) the matter occasioning any fine, penalty, notice or order, as the case may be, imposed on the person, and

    (*b*) any fine, penalty, notice or order occasioned by the matter referred to in *paragraph (a)*.

PART 8

MISCELLANEOUS

Indemnification of inspectors, etc.

86.—(1) Where the Authority or a person prescribed under *section 33* is satisfied that any inspector appointed by the Authority or a person prescribed under *section 33*, or any employee of the Authority or person prescribed under *section 33* has carried out his or her duties in relation to the enforcement of the relevant statutory provisions in a bona fide manner, the Authority or the person prescribed under *section 33*, as the case may be, shall indemnify the inspector or other employee against all actions or claims howsoever arising in respect of the carrying out by him or her of those duties.

(2) No action or other proceedings shall lie or be maintainable against the Authority, any person prescribed under *section 33* or any person referred to in *section 34(2)(a)* for the recovery of damages in respect of any injury to persons, damage to property or other loss alleged to have been caused or contributed to by a failure to perform or to comply with any of the functions imposed on the Authority, any person prescribed under *section 33* or any person referred to in *section 34(2)(a)*.

Powers of officer of customs and excise to detain articles, etc.

87.—For the purpose of facilitating the exercise or performance by the Authority of any powers or duties conferred on it under any of the relevant statutory provisions, an officer of customs and excise, when authorised to do so by the Revenue Commissioners following a written request in that behalf by the Authority or a person prescribed under *section 33*, may detain any article or substance being imported for so long as is reasonably necessary for an inspector to examine it for the purposes of this Act, which period shall not in any case exceed 48 hours from the time when the article or substance concerned is detained.

Licences

88.—(1) The Minister may, for the purpose of protecting the safety, health and welfare of persons at work, prescribe any work activity to which the provisions of the Act apply as being an activity which may not be carried on except in accordance with the terms or conditions of a licence issued by the Authority or a person prescribed under *section 33*, which licence the Authority or the person so prescribed is hereby authorised to issue.

(2) The Authority or a person prescribed under *section 33* may attach such conditions to a licence issued in accordance with *subsection (1)* as it thinks proper including conditions as to its expiry or revocation.

(3) The Authority or a person prescribed under *section 33* may at its discretion grant or refuse an application for a licence under this section.

(4) The Authority or a person prescribed under *section 33* may, if it so thinks proper, publish particulars of an application for a licence under this section and invite representations concerning it from interested persons.

(5) (*a*) The Authority or a person prescribed under *section 33* shall cause a register of all licences granted by it under this section to be kept in such form and containing such particulars as it thinks proper.

   (*b*) Any person, upon payment of a prescribed fee and an inspector, without payment, shall be entitled at all reasonable times to inspect and take copies of or extracts from a register kept under this subsection.

(6) If the Authority or a person prescribed under *section 33* refuses to grant a licence or grants a licence on conditions with which the applicant is dissatisfied, the Authority or person so prescribed shall, at his or her request, deliver to him or her a certificate stating the grounds on which it has refused a licence or attached the conditions.

(7) The applicant may appeal to the High Court from the decision of the Authority or a person prescribed under *section 33* within 10 days after receipt of the certificate or such further time as the High Court may allow.

(8) On the hearing of an appeal from a decision of the Authority or a person prescribed under *section 33* refusing the grant of a licence or granting a licence on conditions with which the applicant is dissatisfied, the High Court may confirm the decision or may direct the Authority or person prescribed under *section 33* to grant the licence, to attach specified conditions to the licence or to amend or delete a condition attached to the licence, as may be appropriate.

(9) A decision of the High Court on an appeal under this section shall be final save that, by leave of that Court, an appeal shall lie to the Supreme Court on a specified question of law.

Amendment of National Standards Authority of Ireland Act 1996

89.—Section 32 of the National Standards Authority of Ireland Act 1996 is amended by inserting the following after subsection (4):

"(5) The powers of prosecution conferred on the Director of Consumer Affairs under this section shall be deemed to be functions of the Director for the purposes of sections 9 and 16 of the Consumer Information Act 1978.".

SCHEDULE 1   *Section 2.*

ASSOCIATED STATUTORY PROVISIONS

Chapter, Number and Year (1)	Short Title (2)	Associated Statutory Provisions (3)
5 & 6 Vict., c. 55	Regulation of Railways Act 1842	The whole Act
34 & 35 Vict., c. 78	Regulation of Railways Act 1871	The whole Act
38 & 39 Vict., c. 17	Explosives Act 1875	The whole Act
	Merchant Shipping Acts 1894 to 2000	The whole Acts
1894 c. 28	Notice of Accidents Act 1894	The whole Act
1900 c. 27	Railway Employment (Prevention of Accidents) Act 1900	The whole Act
	Electricity (Supply) Acts 1927 to 2004	The whole Acts
No. 40 of 1936	Air Navigation and Transport Act 1936	Section 60
No. 12 of 1961	Poisons Act 1961	Sections 14 and 15
	Road Traffic Acts 1961 to 2004	The whole Acts
No. 30 of 1976	Gas Act 1976	Sections 7, 8(2) (as substituted by section 11 of the Gas (Interim) (Regulation) Act 2002 (No. 10 of 2002)) and 38
No. 9 of 1987	Gas (Amendment) Act 1987	Sections 2(1) and (2)
No. 10 of 2002	Gas (Interim) (Regulation) Act 2002	Section 11

No. 27 of 1993	Social Welfare (Consolidation) Act 1993	Chapter 10 of Part II
No. 30 of 1981	Fire Services Act 1981	Section 3 and Parts I, II and III
No. 15 of 2003	Licensing of Indoor Events Act 2003	Part III
No. 6 of 1987	Air Pollution Act 1987	The whole Act

Sections 2 and 4.   SCHEDULE 2

EXISTING ENACTMENTS

PART 1

ENACTMENTS

Chapter, Number and Year (1)	Title (2)
45 & 46 Vict., c. 22	Boiler Explosions Act 1882
53 & 54 Vict., c. 35	Boiler Explosions Act 1890
No. 7 of 1965	Mines and Quarries Act 1965
	Dangerous Substances Acts 1972 and 1979
	Safety in Industry Acts 1955 and 1980
	Safety, Health and Welfare (Offshore Installations) Acts 1987 and 1995
No. 7 of 1989	Safety, Health and Welfare at Work Act 1989

Section 2. PART 2

REGULATIONS MADE UNDER THE EUROPEAN COMMUNITIES ACT 1972 WHICH ARE EXISTING ENACTMENTS

1986 European Communities (Major Accident Hazards of Certain Industrial Activities) Regulations 1986 (S.I. No. 292 of 1986)

1989 European Communities (Protection of Workers) (Exposure to Asbestos) Regulations 1989 (S.I. No. 34)

European Communities (Major Accident Hazards of Certain Industrial Activities) (Amendment) Regulations 1989 (S.I. No. 194 of 1989)

1990 European Communities (Protection of Workers) (Exposure to Noise) Regulations 1990 (S.I. No. 157 of 1990)

1992 European Communities (Major Accident Hazards of Certain Industrial Activities) (Amendment) Regulations 1992 (S.I. No. 21 of 1992)

1993 European Communities (Protection of Workers) (Exposure to Asbestos) (Amendment) Regulations 1993 (S.I. No. 276 of 1993)

1999 European Communities (Equipment and Protective Systems Intended for Use in Potentially Explosive Atmospheres) Regulations 1999 (S.I. No. 83 of 1999)

2000 European Communities (Protection of Workers) (Exposure to Asbestos) (Amendment) Regulations 2000 (S.I. No. 74 of 2000)

European Communities (Control of Major Accident Hazards Involving Dangerous Substances) Regulations 2000 (S.I. No. 476 of 2000)

2001 European Communities (Safety Advisers for Transport of Dangerous Goods by Road and Rail) Regulations 2001 (S.I. No. 6 of 2001)

European Communities (Machinery) Regulations 2001 (S.I. No. 518 of 2001)

2002 European Communities (Export and Import of Certain Dangerous Chemicals) (Industrial Chemicals) (Enforcement) Regulations 2002 (S.I. No. 395 of 2002)

2003   European Communities (Classification, Packaging and
           Labelling and Notification of Dangerous Substances)
           Regulations 2003 (S.I. No. 116 of 2003)

           European Communities (Dangerous Substances and
           Preparations) (Marketing and Use) Regulations 2003
           (S.I. No. 220 of 2003)

           European Communities (Control of Major Accident Hazards
           Involving Dangerous Substances) (Amendment) Regulations
           2003 (S.I. No. 402 of 2003)

           European Communities (Dangerous Substances and
           Preparations) (Marketing and Use) (Amendment) Regulations
           2003 (S.I. No. 503 of 2003)

2004   European Communities (Classification, Packaging and
           Labelling of Dangerous Preparations) Regulations 2004
           (S.I. No. 62 of 2004)

           European Communities (Transportable Pressure Equipment)
           Regulations 2004 (S.I No. 374 of 2004)

           European Communities (Dangerous Substances and
           Preparations) (Marketing and Use) (Amendment) Regulations
           2004 (S.I. No. 852 of 2004)

SCHEDULE 3

GENERAL PRINCIPLES OF PREVENTION

1. The avoidance of risks.

2. The evaluation of unavoidable risks.

3. The combating of risks at source.

4. The adaptation of work to the individual, especially as regards the design of places of work, the choice of work equipment and the choice of systems of work, with a view, in particular, to alleviating monotonous work and work at a predetermined work rate and to reducing the effect of this work on health.

5. The adaptation of the place of work to technical progress.

6. The replacement of dangerous articles, substances or systems of work by safe or less dangerous articles, substances or systems of work.

7. The giving of priority to collective protective measures over individual protective measures.

8. The development of an adequate prevention policy in relation to safety, health and welfare at work, which takes account of technology, organisation of work, working conditions, social factors and the influence of factors related to the working environment.

9. The giving of appropriate training and instructions to employees.

SCHEDULE 4

SAFETY COMMITTEES

1. Should they so wish the employees employed in a place of work to which *section 26* applies may select and appoint from amongst their number members of a safety committee to perform the functions assigned to safety committees under this Act.

2. The number of members of a safety committee shall not be less than 3 and shall not exceed one for every 20 persons employed in a place of work at the time when the committee is appointed or 10, whichever is the less.

3. Where pursuant to *paragraph 2* the number of members of which a safety committee is to be comprised is—

    (*a*) 4 or less, one member of the committee may be appointed by the employer, and the remaining members of the committee may be selected and appointed by the employees,

    (*b*) not more than 8 and not less than 5,2 members of the committee may be appointed by the employer, and the remaining members may be selected and appointed by the employees, and

    (*c*) more than 8, 3 members of the committee may be appointed by the employer and the remaining members may be selected and appointed by the employees.

4. Where, in a place of work, a safety representative or representatives have been appointed under *section 25*, at least one such safety representative shall be selected and appointed by the employees to be a member of the committee.

5. Where a safety committee is appointed under *section 26* the following provisions shall have effect—

    (*a*) the safety committee shall assist the employer and employees concerned in relation to the relevant statutory provisions,

    (*b*) the quorum for a meeting of a safety committee shall be such number, being not less than 3, as shall for the time being be fixed by the committee,

    (*c*) where a member of a safety committee ceases to be employed in the place of work concerned, he or she shall at the same time cease to be a member of the committee,

    (*d*) the employer shall be entitled to attend personally, or to nominate a person or persons to attend on his or her behalf at each meeting of the safety committee,

    (*e*) the employer or his or her nominee or nominees shall attend the first meeting of the safety committee and shall, as soon as may be after it is available, present to the members of the safety committee the statement required under *section 20*, and (*f*) the safety committee shall consider any representations made to it by the employer on matters affecting the safety, health and welfare of persons employed in the place of work.

6. On a request being made in that behalf by a safety committee, the employer shall consult with the safety committee with the object of reaching agreement concerning—

(i) facilities for holding meetings of the safety committee, and
(ii) the frequency, duration and times of meetings of the safety committee.

7. Subject to the terms of any agreement between the employer and a safety committee, meetings of the safety committee shall be held from time to time on such days as the committee shall decide and such meetings may be held during normal working hours, without loss of remuneration to the members of the committee if the following conditions are satisfied, namely:

(i) except in the case of an emergency such meeting shall not be held more frequently than once every three months;
(ii) the duration of each such meeting shall not exceed one hour;
(iii) the number of members of the safety committee attending such a meeting shall be at least such as is required to form a quorum, and
(iv) the times at which the meetings of the safety committee are held shall be compatible with the efficient operation of the place of work.

SCHEDULE 5

THE AUTHORITY

1. In this Schedule, except where the context otherwise requires, "member" means a member of the Authority, including the chairperson.

2. (1) The seal of the Authority shall be authenticated by the signature of—

   (*a*) the chairperson of the Authority or other member authorised by the Authority to act in that behalf, and

   (*b*) the Chief Executive or a member of staff of the Authority authorised by the Authority to act in that behalf.

   (2) Judicial notice shall be taken of the seal of the Authority and every document purporting to be an instrument made by, and to be sealed with the seal of, the Authority (purporting to be authenticated in accordance with *subparagraph (1)*) shall be received in evidence and be deemed to be such instrument without further proof unless the contrary is shown.

3. Subject to this Act, a member shall hold office on the terms and conditions (including terms and conditions relating to remuneration and allowances for expenses) that may be determined by the Minister, with the consent of the Minister for Finance.

4. A member shall be appointed by the Minister in a part-time capacity and shall hold office for 3 years and a member whose term of office expires shall be eligible for reappointment.

5. A member shall not be eligible for reappointment where he or she has served 2 terms of office.

6. A member may resign from office by written notice given to the Minister and the resignation shall take effect on the date specified in the notice or on the date on which the Minister receives the notice, whichever is the later.

7. The Minister may remove a member from office—

   (*a*) if the member becomes incapable through ill-health of effectively performing his or her functions,

   (*b*) for stated misbehaviour, or

   (*c*) if the member's removal appears to the Minister to be necessary for the effective performance by the Authority of its functions,

   and the Minister shall cause to be laid before each House of the Oireachtas a written statement of the reasons for any such removal.

8. A member shall cease to be and shall be disqualified from being a member where the member—

   (*a*) is adjudicated bankrupt,

   (*b*) makes a composition or arrangement with creditors,

   (*c*) is convicted of an indictable offence,

(*d*) is sentenced to a term of imprisonment by a court of competent jurisdiction, or

(*e*) is disqualified or restricted from being a director of any company
(within the meaning of the Companies Acts 1963 to 2003).

9. (1) The Minister may appoint a person to fill a casual vacancy which arises
in the membership of the Authority due to the death, resignation, disqualification or removal from office of a member and the person so appointed
shall be appointed in the same manner as the member who occasioned the
casual vacancy.

(2) A person appointed to be a member under this paragraph shall hold office
for the remainder of the term of office of the member who occasioned the
casual vacancy.

10. (1) A member of the Authority who is—

(*a*) nominated as a member of Seanad Éireann,

(*b*) elected as a member of either House of the Oireachtas or to be a representative in the European Parliament, or

(*c*) regarded pursuant to Part XIII of the Second Schedule to the European Parliament Elections Act 1997 as having been elected to the
European Parliament to fill a vacancy,

thereupon ceases to be a member of the Authority.

(2) A member of the staff of the Authority who is—

(*a*) nominated as a member of Seanad Éireann,

(*b*) elected as a member of either House of the Oireachtas or to be a representative in the European Parliament, or

(*c*) regarded pursuant to Part XIII of the Second Schedule to the European
Parliament Elections Act 1997 as having been elected to the European
Parliament to fill a vacancy,

thereupon stands seconded from employment by the Authority and shall
not be paid by, or be entitled to receive from, the Authority remuneration
or allowances in respect of the period commencing on such nomination or
election, or when he or she is so regarded as having been elected, as the
case may be, and ending when he or she ceases to be a member of either
House or that Parliament.

(3) A period referred to in *subparagraph (2)* shall not be reckoned as service
with the Authority for the purposes of any superannuation benefits, gratu-
ities or other allowances payable on death, retirement or resignation.

(4) A person who is for the time being entitled under the Standing Orders of
either House of the Oireachtas to sit in the House or who is a representative in the European Parliament shall, while he or she is so entitled or is
such a representative, be disqualified from becoming a member of, or from
employment in any capacity by, the Authority.

(5) The Authority shall not employ or otherwise retain in any capacity a person who would otherwise be disqualified under this paragraph from becoming a member of the Authority.

11 (1) The Authority shall hold such and so many meetings as may be necessary for performing its functions but in any case shall meet not less than once in every 3 months.

(2) The arrangements referred to in *paragraph 15* may, with the approval of the Minister, provide for the discharge, under the general direction of the Authority, of any of its functions by a committee of the Authority.

12. The quorum for a meeting of the Authority shall be 6 or such greater number of members as the Authority may from time to time determine.

13. At a meeting of the Authority—

(*a*) the chairperson shall, if present, be the chairperson of the meeting, or

(*b*) if and so long as the chairperson is not present or if the office of chairperson is vacant, the deputy chairperson of the Authority shall be chairperson of the meeting, or

(*c*) if and so long as the chairperson is not present or if the office of chairperson is vacant or the deputy chairperson is not present or the office of deputy chairperson is vacant, the members who are present shall choose one of their number to be chairperson of the meeting.

14. Every question that is to be decided at a meeting of the Authority shall be determined by a majority of the votes of the members present and voting on the question and, in the case of an equal division of votes, the chairperson of the meeting shall have a second or casting vote.

15. Subject to *paragraph 12* the Authority may act notwithstanding one or more than one vacancy among its membership or any deficiency in the appointment of a member that may subsequently be discovered.

16. Subject to this Act, the Authority shall make arrangements for the regulation of its proceedings and business.

SCHEDULE 6

THE CHIEF EXECUTIVE

1. The Chief Executive shall be appointed on the terms and conditions (including terms and conditions relating to duration of contract, performance, remuneration, allowances for expenses and removal from office) that the Authority may from time to time determine with the consent of the Minister and the Minister for Finance.

2. The Chief Executive shall be paid by the Authority out of such moneys at its disposal such remuneration and such allowances for expenses (if any) incurred by him or her as the Authority, with the consent of the Minister and the Minister for Finance, may determine.

3. The Chief Executive shall perform his or her functions subject to such policies as may be determined from time to time by the Authority and shall be accountable to the Authority for the efficient and effective management of the Authority and for the due performance of his or her functions.

4. The Chief Executive may delegate any of his or her functions to an employee of the Authority, subject to such conditions as the Chief Executive considers appropriate, unless they are delegated to the Chief Executive subject to the condition that they shall not be sub-delegated, and the employee concerned shall be accountable to the Chief Executive for the performance of the functions so delegated to him or her.

5. Notwithstanding any delegation under *paragraph 3*, the Chief Executive shall at all times remain accountable to the Authority for the performance of the functions so delegated.

6. The Chief Executive shall not hold any other office or employment or carry on any business without the consent of the Authority.

Section 58.   SCHEDULE 7

REGULATIONS

The Minister may make regulations under *section 58* for or in respect of any matters including the following:

(1)   requirements to be imposed on employers as regards the safety, health and welfare of their employees at work with respect to—

   (*a*) the management and conduct of work activities including the prevention of improper conduct or behaviour,

   (*b*) the design, provision and maintenance of—

       (i)   places of work,
       (ii) safe means of access to and egress from places of work, and
       (iii) plant and machinery and other articles,

   (*c*) the use of any article or substance,

   (*d*) the provision, planning, organisation, performance and maintenance of systems of work,

   (*e*) the provision of information, instruction, training and supervision, including, as appropriate, such provision in an appropriate language or languages,

   (*f*) the determination and implementation of safety, health and welfare measures,

   (*g*) the provision, testing, use and maintenance of protective clothing or equipment,

   (*h*) the preparation and revision of plans and procedures and measures to be taken in emergencies and in the case of serious and imminent danger,

   (*i*) the obtaining of the services of competent persons so as to ensure the safety, health and welfare of persons at work including the training, experience and knowledge required of competent persons,

   (*j*) co-operation in matters relating to safety, health and welfare at work, and

   (*k*) the safety, health and welfare at work of fixed-term or temporary employees;

(2)   requirements to be imposed on employers as regards the conduct of their undertakings to provide that in the course of work being carried on persons at the place of work not in the employment of the said employers are not exposed to risks to their safety, health and welfare at the undertaking;

(3)   requirements to be imposed on persons to whom *section 15* applies in relation to non-domestic places of work as regards such places of work, any article or substance provided for use in such places and as regards access to or egress from such places;

(4)   requirements to be imposed on an employee in relation to conduct or behaviour likely to endanger his or her own safety, health and welfare

at work or that of any other person including as regards intoxication and submission to reasonable and proportionate tests;

(5) requirements to be imposed on persons as regards interference, misuse or damage of anything provided under the relevant statutory provisions or otherwise for securing the safety, health and welfare of persons at work;

(6) requirements to be imposed on an employee as regards his or her own safety, health or welfare at work including requirements as regards the use of any appliance, protective clothing, convenience, equipment or means or thing provided for securing their safety, health or welfare at work and attendance at safety and health training;

(7) requirements to be imposed on persons who design, manufacture, import or supply articles for use at work as regards—

(a) the design, construction, testing, examination or use of any article or prescribed class of article, or

(b) the provision of information relating to the use at work for which any article or prescribed class of article was designed or tested or relating to its being sited, tested, installed, repaired, altered, maintained, dismantled or disposed of in a manner which will be safe and without risk to the health or welfare of persons at work;

(8) requirements to be imposed on persons who design or manufacture articles for use at work as regards the carrying out of research with respect to those articles with a view to the discovery of potential risks or the elimination or minimisation of any risks to the safety, health or welfare of persons at work;

(9) requirements to be imposed on persons who erect or install articles for use at work as regards the erection or installation of those articles so as to be safe and without risks to health or welfare when those articles are used in a place of work;

(10) requirements to be imposed on persons who manufacture, import or supply any substance or prescribed class of substance as regards—

(a) the use, testing or examination of the substance, or

(b) the provision of information about any risk to safety, health or welfare to which the substance may give rise, or

(c) the results of tests on the substance or its use or disposal in a manner which will be safe and without risk to the health or welfare of persons at work;

(11) requirements to be imposed on persons who manufacture, or in a case where the manufacture is undertaken outside the State, import any substances as regards the carrying out of research with a view to the discovery, elimination or minimisation of risks to safety, health or welfare to which the substance may give rise when in use;

(12) requirements to be imposed on persons who commission or procure the construction of places of work as regards the appointment of competent persons to ensure those places are designed, can be constructed, are maintained and comply with the relevant statutory provisions so as to be safe and without risk to the health or welfare of persons at work;

(13) requirements to be imposed on persons who design places of work as regards the design of those places so as to be safe and without risk to the health or welfare of persons at work;

(14) requirements to be imposed on persons who construct places of work as regards the construction of those places so as to be safe and without risk to the health or welfare of persons at work;

(15) requirements to be imposed on employers as regards the identification of hazards and the assessment of risks;

(16) requirements to be imposed on employers as regards safety statements;

(17) requirements to be imposed as regards the regulation, prohibition or control of the use of specified articles for use at work including the guarding, siting, installing, commissioning, protecting, testing, examining, inspecting, altering, adjusting, maintaining or dismantling of any such article;

(18) requirements to be imposed as regards the marking of any article for use at work or designed for use as a component of such article;

(19) requirements to be imposed as regards the regulation, prohibition or control of the use of any specified substance;

(20) requirements to be imposed as regards the testing, examination, classification or labelling of any specified substance including notification of specified particulars in relation to such substance;

(21) requirements to be imposed as regards the prohibition or control of importation or supply of any article or substance for use at work;

(22) requirements to be imposed as regards the prohibition or the regulation of the transport of any article or substance for use at work including requirements as regards the construction, testing and marking of containers and means of transport and the packaging and labelling for transport of those articles or substances;

(23) requirements to be imposed as regards the use or design of specified safety signs at places of work;

(24) requirements to be imposed as regards the making of arrangements for health surveillance of persons at work including medical examinations, biological monitoring or special health surveys;

(25) requirements to be imposed as to the registration in a prescribed register of any specified activity or thing in order to monitor compliance with

safety, health and welfare requirements under the relevant statutory provisions;

(26) requirements to be imposed as to the appointment of prescribed persons or classes of persons to do prescribed things in relation to safety, health or welfare at work or to carry out specific activities or undertake specific responsibilities with safety, health and welfare implications;

(27) requirements to be imposed as to the regulation of or prohibition from prescribed classes of employment of prescribed classes of persons in relation to their safety, health and welfare at work;

(28) requirements to be imposed with respect to any matter affecting the conditions in which persons work, including such matters as the structural condition and stability of premises, the means of access to and egress from the premises, cleanliness, temperature, humidity, lighting, ventilation, overcrowding, noise, vibrations, ionising and other radiations or other physical agent, dust and fumes and exposure to water or other liquids;

(29) regulating or prohibiting atmospheric or other conditions to which an employee may be exposed in a place of work;

(30) prescribing methods, standards or procedures for determining the amount or level of any atmospheric condition or any biological, chemical or physical agent or combination thereof in a place of work;

(31) requirements to be imposed as to facilities or arrangements for welfare at work (including supply of water, sanitary conveniences, washing or bathing facilities, ambulance and first-aid arrangements, cloakroom facilities, seating, refreshment facilities, facilities for the making or taking of meals or, prohibiting the taking of meals or refreshments in specified circumstances);

(32) reuirements to be imposed so as to control or limit—

(*a*) the emission into a place of work of any specified gas, vapour, smoke, dust, or any other specified substance arising from work activities,

(*b*) the emission into the working environment of noise, vibration, any ionising or other radiations,

(*c*) other environmental pollution in the place of work including environmental tobacco smoke, or

(*d*) the monitoring of any such emissions in a place of work;

(33) conferring powers on inspectors in specified circumstances to require persons to submit written particulars of measures proposed to be taken to achieve compliance with any of the relevant statutory provisions;

(34) requirements to be imposed with respect to the keeping and preservation of records relating to compliance with the relevant statutory provisions in relation to safety, health and welfare at work;

(35) requirements to be imposed as regards the safety, health or welfare of persons with respect to the management of animals in or at places of work;

(36) requirements to be imposed as regards any place of work in relation to—

(*a*) precautions to be taken against dangers to which the place of work or persons in the place of work are or may be exposed by reason of conditions (including natural conditions) existing in the vicinity of that place, or

(*b*) securing that persons in a place of work leave that place of work in specified circumstances where there is a risk to their safety or health;

(37) requirements to be imposed as to the doing or prohibition of any specified thing where any accident or other occurrence of a specified kind has occurred;

(38) requirements to be imposed in prescribed circumstances with respect to the taking of precautions in connection with the risk of fire, fire-safety rules and procedures and the provision and maintenance of fire-protection equipment in places of work;

(39) requirements to be imposed with respect to the reporting in the prescribed manner of such matters relating to the safety, health or welfare of persons at work as may be prescribed, or that of other persons arising out of work activities, (including the giving of such information as may be prescribed relating to accidents, personal injuries or dangerous occurrences) to the Authority or a person prescribed under *section 33* or to an inspector of the Authority or of a person prescribed under *section 33* or to any other person as may be prescribed;

(40) requirements to be imposed with respect to the safe lifting or handling by persons at work of any load likely to cause injury to a person so lifting or handling it;

(41) the prohibition of the carrying on of such work activities as may be prescribed except by or under the supervision of persons with prescribed qualifications, training or experience;

(42) requirements to be imposed as regards joint safety and health agreements;

(43) such further requirements, arrangements, modifications or exemptions as the Minister considers necessary, from time to time, in relation to the operation of *sections 25* and *26*;

(44) such fees as may be charged under *section 47*.

SAFETY, HEALTH AND WELFARE AT WORK (CONSTRUCTION) REGULATIONS 2006

S.I. No. 504 of 2006

ARRANGEMENT OF REGULATIONS

PART 1

INTERPRETATION AND GENERAL

PART 2

DESIGN AND MANAGEMENT

PART 3

GENERAL DUTIES OF CONTRACTORS AND OTHERS

PART 4

GENERAL SAFETY PROVISIONS

PART 14

CONSTRUCTION SITE WELFARE FACILITIES

SCHEDULE 1

Non-exhaustive List of Work Involving Particular Risks to the Safety, Health and Welfare of Persons at Work

SCHEDULE 2

Non-Exhaustive List of Matters to be Considered in Particular as regards the Application of the General Principles of Prevention of Construction Work under these Regulations

SCHEDULE 3

Safety Awareness Scheme

SCHEDULE 4

Construction Skills Certification Scheme

SCHEDULE 5

Procedure for Selection of Site Safety Representatives

SCHEDULE 6

List of Vehicles Requiring Auxiliary Devices and Visual Aids

S.I NO.504 OF 2006

SAFETY, HEALTH AND WELFARE AT WORK (CONSTRUCTION) REGULATIONS 2006

I, Tony Killeen, Minister of State at the Department of Enterprise, Trade and Employment, in exercise of the powers conferred on me by section 58 of the

Safety, Health and Welfare at Work Act 2005 (No. 10 of 2005) and the Enterprise, Trade and Employment (Delegation of Ministerial Functions) Order 2005 (S.I. No. 316 of 2005), after consultation with the Health and Safety Authority, hereby make the following regulations:

PART 1

INTERPRETATION AND GENERAL

Citation and Commencement.

1. (1) These Regulations may be cited as the Safety, Health and Welfare at Work (Construction) Regulations 2006.

    (2) These Regulations come into operation on 6 November 2006, in this Regulation called the "effective date".

    (3) If, prior to the effective date,

    (a) a design stage has commenced, and
    (b) a project supervisor for the design stage has been appointed in accordance with the Regulations of 2001 and 2003 and holds that position on that date

    all duties of the client in relation to the appointment of a project supervisor for the design process and all duties assigned in these Regulations to the project supervisor for the design process apply only from 18 months after that date.

    (4) If the client, under Regulation 3(2) of the Regulations of 2001 and 2003, has been self-appointed as project supervisor for the design stage and holds that position on the effective date the duties specified in *Regulation* 6 apply only from 18 months after that date.

    (5) If, from 18 months after the effective date, a client wishes to seek exemption from the duty to appoint a project supervisor for the design process the client may do so—

    (a) only on the basis that a project supervisor for the design stage has been appointed for the project prior to that date and holds that position on that date, and
    (b) by an application made in accordance with *paragraph* (6).

    (6) The application referred to in *paragraph* (5) must be made to the Authority in an approved form outlining the reasons for the exemption and the length of time for which the exemption is sought.

    (7) The Authority may grant an exemption on the basis of an application made under *paragraph* (6), but no exemption may be granted to last longer than 30 months after the effective date.

(8) Nothing in this Regulation prevents the client on and after the effective date from appointing—

    (a) the project supervisor for the design stage as appointed under the Regulations of 2001 and 2003, or

    (b) any other competent person as project supervisor for the design process.

(9) In the case of projects under construction prior to the effective date and where—

    (a) a project supervisor for the construction stage has been appointed before that date,

    (b) notification has been given to the Authority, in accordance with the Regulations of 2001 and 2003, and

    (c) the person appointed under *subparagraph* (a) holds that position on that date all duties of the client in relation to the appointment of a project supervisor for the construction stage and all duties given in these Regulations to the project supervisor for the construct ion stage apply only from 18 months after that date.

(10) Nothing in this Regulation prevents the client on and after the effective date from appointing—

    (a) the project supervisor for the construction stage as appointed under the Regulations of 2001 and 2003, or

    (b) any other competent person as project supervisor for the construction stage under these Regulations.

(11) If the client, under Regulation 3(2) of the Regulations of 2001 and 2003, has been self-appointed as project supervisor for the construction stage, and holds that position on the effective date, the duties specified in *Regulation* 6 apply only from 18 months after that date.

(12) For projects where the design stage commenced before the effective date, if, having regard to this Regulation, a project supervisor for the design process has not been appointed, the project supervisor for the construction stage shall co-ordinate the design of temporary works of facilitate the construction of the project.

(13) For the tasks listed in *Schedule 4, paragraph 1 (1) (c), (e) (n) and (r) to (t), Regulations 19(l) (b), 25(l) (b), 29(l)(g), 74(e) and 97(b) and (c)* apply only from 18 months after the effective date.

Interpretation.

2   (1) In these Regulations, unless the context otherwise requires—

    "Act" means the Safety, Health and Welfare at Work Act 2005 (No. 10 of 2005);

    "Act" of 1875 means the Explosives Act 1875;

"client means a person for whom a project is carried out, in the course of furtherance of a trade, business or undertaking, or who undertakes a project directly in the course or furtherance of such trade, business or undertaking;

"construction site" means any site at which construction work in relation to a project is carried out;

"construction work" means the carrying out of any building, civil engineering or engineering work, other than drilling and extraction in the extractive industries, and includes but is not limited to each of the following:

(a) the doing of one or more of the following with respect to a structure:

    (i) construction;
    (ii) alteration;
    (iii) conversion;
    (iv) fitting out;
    (v) commissioning;
    (vi) renovation:
    (vii) repair;
    (viii) upkeep;
    (ix) redecoration or other maintenance (including cleaning which involves the use of water or an abrasive at high pressure or the use of substances or preparations classified as corrosive or toxic for the purpose of Regulation 8 of the European Communities (Classification, Packaging, Labelling and Notification of Dangerous Substances) Regulation 2003 and 2006 (S.I.116 of 2003 and S.I. 25 of 2006) and Regulation 5 of the European Communities (Classification, Packaging, Labeling and Notification of Dangerous Preparations) Regulations 2004 (S.I. No. 62 of 2004));
    (x) de-commissioning, demolition or dismantling;

(b) the preparation for an intended structure, including but not limited to site clearance, exploration, investigation (but not site survey) and excavation, and he laying or installing of the foundations of an intended structure;

(c) the assembly of prefabricated elements to form a structure, or the disassembly of prefabricated element which, immediately before such disassembly, formed a structure;

(d) the removal of a structure or part of a structure of any product or waste resulting from demolition or dismantling of a structure or disassembly of prefabricated elements which, immediately before such disassembly, formed a structure;

(e) the installation, commissioning, maintenance, repair or removal of mechanical, electrical, gas, compressed air, hydraulic, telecommunication and computer systems, or similar services which are normally fixed within or to a structure;

"contractor" means

> (a) a contractor or an employer whose employees undertake, carry out or manage construction work, or
>
> (b) a person who—
>
>> (i) carries out or manages construction work for a fixed or other sum, and
>>
>> (ii) supplies materials, labour or both, whether the contractor's own labour or that of another, to carry out the work;

"contractor responsible for a construction site" includes a contractor responsible for a part of the site over which the contractor has control;

"design" means the preparation of drawings, particulars, specifications, calculations and bills of quantities in so far as they contain specifications or other expressions of purpose, according to which project, or any par or component of a project, is to be executed;

"designer" means a person engaged in work related to the design of a project;

"design process" means the process for preparing and designing a project, including alterations to the design and the design of temporary works to facilitate construction of the project;

"detonator" means an initiator for explosives that contains a charge of high explosive fired by means of a flame, spark, electric current or shock tube;

"exploder" means a device designed for firing detonators;

"explosives" means explosive articles or explosive substances;

"explosive article" means an article containing one or more explosive substances;

"explosive store" means a

> (a) magazine licensed under sections 6 to 8 of the Act of 1875,
>
> (b) store licensed under section 15 of the Act of 1875, or
>
> (c) premises registered in accordance with section 21 of the Act of 1875;

"explosive substances" means a solid or liquid substance (or a mixture of substances) which is in itself capable of chemical reaction of producing gas at such a temperature and pressure and at such a speed as to cause damage to the surroundings;

"FAS" means An Foras Aiseanna Saothair;

"FETAC" means the Further Education and Training Awards Council;

"footpath" means a over which there is a public right of way for pedestrians only, not being a footway;

"general principles of prevention" means the general principles of prevention specified in Schedule 3 to the Act;

"locomotive" means any self-propelled wheeled vehicle used on a line of rails for the movement of trucks or wagons;

"man-lock" means any air lock or decompression chamber used for the compression or decompression of persons, but does not include an air lock which is only so used in emergency or a medical lock used solely for treatment purposes;

"misfire" means an occurrence in relation to the firing of shots where—

    (a) testing before firing reveals broken continuity which cannot be rectified, or

    (b) a shot or any part of a shot fails to explode when an attempt is made to fire it;

"mobile crane" means a crane capable of traveling under its own power, but does not include such a crane which travels on a line of rails;

"plant or equipment" means any gear, machine, rig, apparatus or appliance, or any part of any plant or equipment.

"project" means an activity which includes or is intended to include construction work;

"project supervisor" means an individual or a body corporate appointed under *Regulation 6(1)* and responsible for carrying out—

    (a) the appropriate duties specified in these Regulations, and

    (b) other duties that are

        (i) assigned to the person by the client at the time of appointment, and

        (ii) necessary to allow the client to comply with section 17(1) of the Act'

"Regulations of 2001 and 2003" means the Safety, Health and Welfare at Work (Construction) Regulations, 2001 (S.I.No. 481 of 2001) as amended by the Safety, Health and Welfare at Work (Construction) (Amendment) Regulations 2003 (S.I.No. 277 of 2003);

"road" means a road over which a public right of way exists;

"rolling stock" means a train or any other vehicle with flanged wheels which is designed to operate on rails or a railway;

"safety and health plan" means a plan in writing prepare and developed in accordance with *Regulation 12* and *16*;

"safety file" means a safety file prepared and completed in accordance with *Regulations 13* and *21*;

"safety fuse" means a flexible cord that contains an internal burning medium by which fire is conveyed at a continuous and uniform rate for the purpose of firing plain detonators or black powder, without initiating burning in a similar fuse that may be in lateral contact alongside;

"shot" means a single shot or a series of shots fired as part of one blast;

"shotfirer" means a person appointed pursuant to *Regulation* 74 to be responsible for shotfiring operations;

"shotfiring operations" includes—

    (a) checking to ensure that the blasting specification is still appropriate for the site conditions at the time the blasting is to take place,

    (b) mixing explosives,

    (c) priming a cartridge,

    (d) charging and stemming a shothole,

    (e) linking or connecting a round of shots,

    (f) withdrawal and sheltering of persons,

(g) inspecting and testing a shotfiring circuit,

(h) firing a shot.

(i) checking for misfires, and

(j) destroying surplus explosives;

"structure" means—

(a) any building, railway line or siding, tramway line, dock, harbor, inland navigation systems, tunnel, bridge, viaduct, waterworks, reservoir, pipe-line (whatever it contains or is intended to contain), underground or over ground cables, aqueduct, sewer, sewage works, gasholder, road, airfield, sea defence works, river works, drainage works, earthworks, lagoon, dam, wall, caisson, mast, tower, pylon, underground tank, earth retaining element or assembly of elements, or element or assembly of elements designed to preserve or alter any natural feature, and any other structure similar to the foregoing,

(b) any formwork, false work, scaffold or other element or assembly of elements designed or used to provide support or means of access during construction work, or

(c) any fixed plant in respect of work which is installation, commissioning, de-commissioning or dismantling.

(2) Without limiting the application of the definition of "reasonably practicable" in section 2 of the Act in relation to the duties of employers, that definition also applies, for the purposes of these Regulations, in relation to the duties under these Regulations of other persons.

(3) Where, under these Regulations, a person is required to give directions or make rules, such directions and such rules shall be reasonable in the context of the duty with which the person is required to comply.

(4) Taking account of the European Communities (Recognition of Qualifications and Experience) Regulations 2003 (S.I.No. 372 of 2003) and in compliance with Directive 2005/36/EC[1], FÁS is responsible for the issue of valid construction skills registration cards, with photographic identification, under *Schedule* 4 and for the maintenance of a register of the cards issued.

Keeping records.

3 (1) Subject to *paragraph* (2), the relevant contractor shall ensure that the records, reports, certificates and other documents required by these Regulations—

(a) are kept on the site to which they are relevant, or

(b) when no relevant works are being carried out on the site, are kept at an appropriate office of—

---

[1] OJ L 255/22 of 30th September 2005.

      (i) the contractor for whom the report was made or the certificate or document was obtained, or

     (ii) the owner of the plant or equipment to which the certificate relates.

(2) In the case of a construction site where a contractor has reasonable grounds for believing that the work will be completed in a period of less than 30 working days, the records, reports, certificates and other documents referred to in *paragraph (1)* may be kept, in lieu of being kept at that site, at an appropriate office of the contractor.

(3) The person having custody of the records required by these Regulations—

    (a) shall ensure that the records are open to inspection by an inspector at all reasonable times, and

    (b) forthwith shall send to any such inspector such extracts from them or copies of them as the inspector may from time to time require for the purpose of the execution of the inspector duties under the Act.

(4) Subject to *paragraph (5)*, where under these Regulations records, reports, certificates or other documents are required to be made and kept, it is sufficient compliance with the requirement if the person concerned—

    (a) enters the record, report, certificate or other document in an approved form in a computer, and

    (b) duly authenticates it as soon as is practicable afterwards.

(5) Where under these Regulations records are required to be made and kept by designers, it is sufficient compliance with the requirement if the records are kept in a computer.

Application.

4. (1) Subject to *paragraph* (2), these Regulations apply to and in relation to construction work.

    (2) Subject to *paragraph (3), Schedule* 3 applies to—

        (a) craft and general construction workers,
        (b) persons undertaking on-site security work, and
        (c) persons or classes of persons as may be prescribed by the Minister.

    (3) *Schedule* 3 does not apply to person involved in the installation, commissioning, maintenance, repair or removal of mechanical, electrical, gas, compressed air, hydraulic, telecommunication and computer systems, or similar services, where—

        (a) the person is normally domiciled outside the State,
        (b) the person's normal place of employment is outside the State and

    (c) the person has not been working on the project for a period in excess of 20 working days in any 12 month period.

(4) A person mentioned in *paragraph (3)* shall be in possession of a letter in the English or Irish language from the relevant employer, which letter—

    (a) describes the work to be undertaken,

    (b) states the competence of the person to undertake that work, and

    (c) specifies the commencement date and the anticipated completion date of that work.

(5) *Regulation 87 (1)(e)* applies to—

    (a) all vehicles that are in use immediately before the coming into operation of these Regulations and are listed in *Schedule 6,* from 18 months after the coming into operation of these Regulations, and

    (b) for all vehicles that are first used after the coming into operation of these Regulations and are listed in *Schedule 6* from 6 months after the coming into operation of these Regulations.

Revocations and savings.

5. The Regulations of 2001 and 2003, other than—

    (a) Regulations 80 to 123, and

    (b) subject to *Regulation 1(3)* to *(5), (7), (9)* and *(11)* of these Regulations, Regulations 4 and 6 of the Regulations of 2001 and 2003 insofar as Regulation 4 and 6 apply to a project supervisor for the design stage and a project supervisor for the construction stage respectively, appointed in accordance with the Regulations of 2001 and 2003,

are revoked.

PART 2

DESIGN AND MANAGEMENT

Duties of clients, appointments of project supervisors.

6. (1) Except as provide for in *paragraph (5)* and *(6)*, a client shall appoint, in writing, for every project—

    (a) a competent project supervisor for the design process, and

    (b) a competent project supervisor for the construction stage, and the client shall obtain written confirmation of acceptance of each of the appointments.

(2) Nothing in *paragraph (1)* prevents—

(a) a client being self-appointed as project supervisor if competent to undertake the duties involved, or

(b) a client appointing one individual or body corporate as project supervisor for both the design process and construction stage if that individual or body corporate is competent to undertake duties involved.

(3) A client shall appoint the project supervisor—

(a) for the design process at or before the start of the design process, and

(b) for the construction stage before commencement of the construction work.

(4) An appointment under *paragraph (1)* shall, as necessary, be made, terminated, changed or renewed.

(5) *Paragraph (1)* does not apply to routine maintenance, cleaning, decoration and repair within or to a structure unless—

(a) the work involves a particular risk including but not limited to a risk referred to in *Schedule 1,*

(b) more than one contractor is involved, or

(c) *Regulation 10* applies

(6) In accordance with section 58(4)(d) of the Act and without prejudice to the duties of a contractor undertaking construction work under these Regulations, section 17(1) of the Act does not apply to or in respect of project if—

(a) a person commissions or procures the project in relation to the person's domestic dwelling, and

(b) the project is not for the purpose or furtherance of a trade, business or undertaking after the completion of construction work.

(7) If all of the clients involved in a project agree in writing that one or more but not all of them shall be treated as the client for the purposes of these Regulations—

(a) the client or clients agreed on shall be subject to all the duties of a client under these Regulations, and

(b) after that agreement is made, the others shall not be subject to the duties of a client under these Regulations, except the duties under *Regulations 8 (1)* and (3).

Duties to ascertain suitability of project supervisor, designer and contractor appointees.

7. (1) A client shall not appoint a person as project supervisor for the design process for a project unless reasonably satisfied that the person has allocated or will allocate adequate resources to enable the person to

perform the duties imposed under these Regulation for that project supervisor position.

(2) A client shall not arrange for a designer to prepare a design unless reasonably satisfied that the designer has allocated or will allocate adequate resources to enable the designer to comply with *Regulation 15*.

(3) A client shall not appoint a person as project supervisor for the construction stage for a project unless reasonably satisfied that the person has allocated or will allocate adequate resources to enable the person to perform the duties imposed under these Regulations for that project supervisor position.

(4) A client shall not arrange for a contractor to carry out or manage construction work unless reasonably satisfied that the contractor has the competence to carry out or, as the case may be, manage that construction work and has allocated or will allocate adequate resources to enable the contractor to comply with the requirements and prohibitions imposed on the contractor by or under the relevant statutory provisions.

(5) A person to whom these Regulations apply shall not arrange for a designer to prepare a design unless reasonably satisfied that the designer has the competence to prepare the design and has allocated or will allocate adequate resources to enable the designer to comply with *Regulation 15*.

(6) A person to whom these Regulations apply shall not arrange for a contractor to carry out or manage construction work unless reasonably satisfied that the contractor has the competence to carry out or, as the case may be, manage that construction work and has allocated or will allocate adequate resources to enable the contractor to comply with the requirements and prohibitions imposed on the contractor by or under the relevant stautory provisions.

Duties of clients, safety file.

8. (1) A client shall keep available—

    (a) any safety file referred to in *Regulation 13 or 21*, and
    (b) any information delivered to a client in relation to the file.

for inspection by any person who may need information in the file for—

    (i) the purpose of compliance by that person with any duties imposed under the relevant statutory provisions, or

    (ii) for that person's own information when carrying out any construction work on the structure to which the safety file relates.

(2) It is sufficient compliance with *paragraph (1)* by a client and every subsequent owner of a structure who disposes of the client's or owner's interest in the structure involved if the client or subsequent

owner deliver the safety file for that structure to the person who acquires the interest.

(3) A person to whom a safety file is delivered in accordance with *paragraph (2)* shall keep the safety file available for inspection in accordance with *paragraph (1)*

(4) A client shall co-operate with the project supervisor for the design process and the project supervisor for the construction stage, as appropriate, including in relation to the time required for the completion of the project and by providing information to enable the relevant project supervisor to comply with these Regulations.

(5) The information required to be provided under *paragraph (4)* is information relating to the state or condition of any structure, including information is safety file that is—

(a) prepared in accordance with the relevant statutory provisions,
(b) relevant to the duties of the project supervisors under these Regulations, and
(c) either in the client's possession or could be obtained by the client making enquiries which it is reasonable for a person in the client's position to make.

Duties of clients, safety and health plan.

9.   A client shall provide or arrange to have provided a copy of the safety and health plan prepared under *Regulation 12* or every person—

(a) being considered for the role of project supervisor for the construction stage, or
(b) tendering for that role.

Duties of clients, notification to the Authority.

10.   If construction work is planned to last longer than 30 working days or the volume of work is scheduled to exceed 500 person days, a client shall promptly give notice in writing to the Authority in an approved form, sent either—

(a) by registered post, or
(b) as may be directed from time to time by the Authority, of those particulars as are known or can be reasonably known about the appointments made in accordance with *Regulation 6.*

Duties of project supervisor for the design process, co-ordination and cooperation.

11.   (1) The project supervisor for the design process shall—

(a) take account of the general principles of prevention during the various stages of the design and preparation of a project, in particular—

    (i) when either, or both, technical or organisational aspects are being decided, in order to plan the various items or stages of work which are to take place simultaneously or in succession, and

    (ii) when estimating the time required for completion of a project and, wher appropriate, for stages of a project

(b) take account of any safety and health plan or safety file, and

(c) organise co-operation between designers on the same project and, so far as it reasonably practicable, ensure, co-ordination of their activities in relation to the design of the project with a view to protecting the safety, health and welfare of persons involved in construction work.

(2) The project supervisor for the design process may appoint a competent person as health and safety co-ordinator for the design process to assist in the undertaking of the duties specified in paragraph(*1*).

Duties of project supervisor for the design process, safety and health plan.

12.   (1) The project supervisor for the design process shall—

(a) subject to *paragraph (2)*, on a preliminary basis and for the purpose of providing information for the project supervisor for the construction stage, prepare a written safety and health plan that specifies—

    (i) a general description of the project and of the time within which it is intended that the project will be completed,

    (ii) appropriate information on any other work activities taking place on the site,

    (iii) where appropriate, work related to the project which will involve particular risks to the safety, health and welfare of persons at work including but not limited to those referred to in *Schedule 1,*

    (iv) the basis upon which the time in *subparagraph (i)* was established, taking into account *Regulation 11(1)(a),*

    (v) the conclusions drawn by designers and the project supervisor for the design process as regards the taking account of the general principles of prevention and any relevant safety and health plan or safety file, and

    (vi) the location of electricity, water and sewage connections, where appropriate, to facilitate adequate welfare facilities,

(b) prepare the safety and health plan referred to in *subparagraph (a)* in time to enable it to be provided in compliance with *Regulation 9* to every person being considered or tendering for the role of project supervisor for the construction stage, and

(c) keep a copy of the safety and health plan referred to in *subparagraph (a)* available for inspection by an inspector for a period of 5 years after its preparation.

(2) Where notification is not required under *Regulation 10,* a safety and health plan is required only for sites where the work concerned involved a particular risk, including but not limited to any of those referred to in *Schedule 1.*

Duties of project supervisor for the design process, safety file.

13. The project supervisor for the design process shall—

(a) prepare safety file appropriate to the characteristics of the project, containing relevant safety and health information, including any information provided under *Regulation 21,* to be taken into account during any subsequent construction work following completion of the project, and

(b) promptly deliver the safety file to the client on completion of the project.

Powers of project supervisor for the design process to issue directions.

14. (1) The project supervisor for the design process, so far as in necessary,

(a) may give directions to each person who is a designer, contractor or other relevant person, which direction, if carried out, will assist or enable compliance by the project supervisor with the duties imposed by these Regulations on the project supervisor, and

(b) shall confirm the directions in writing, including a time frame for their execution, it the project supervisor considers that the person to whom the directions were given has not carried out the directions.

(2) If, in the opinion of the project supervisor for the design process, a designer, contractor or other relevant person has not carried out directions confirmed in writing under *paragraph(1) (b),* the project supervisor for the design process shall—

(a) notify in writing the Authority, the client and the person to whom the direction was given of the opinion of the project supervisor, and

(b) include with the notification—

(i) a copy of the written confirmation under *paragraph (1)(b),* and

(ii) particulars of the response, if any, made by the designer, contractor or other relevant person to the directions.

(3) The project supervisor for the design process shall ensure that—

(a) each confirmation in writing of a direction given under *paragraph (1) (b),* and

  (b) a copy of each associated notification to the Authority referred
   to in *paragraph(2)* is retained with the safety and health plan.

Duties of designers.

15. (1) In carrying out work related to the design of a particular project, a
   designer shall—

   (a) take account of—

    (i) the general principles of prevention, and

    (ii) the relevant—

    (I) safety and health plan, and
    (II) safety file

  prepared in accordance with these Regulation, and

   (b) provide in writing to the project supervisor for the design process
    all relevant information necessary for the project supervisor to
    carry out the project supervisor's duties under these Regulations.

  (2) In carrying out work related to the design of a particular project, a
   designer shall—

   (a) co-operate with the project supervisor for the design process or
    the project supervisor for the construction stage, as appro-
    priate, to enable that project supervisor to comply with these
    Regulations,
   (b) co-operate with other designers, as appropriate, to enable them to
    comply with these Regulation in relation to the project, and
   (c) comply with al directions from the project supervisor for the
    design process or the project supervisor for the construction
    stage, that are issued pursuant to *Regulation 14 or 20*, as appro-
    priate.

  (3) In carrying out work related to the design of a particular project, a
   designer shall promptly provide in writing to the project supervisor
   for the design process or for the construction stage, whichever is
   appropriate, all information—

   (a) about the project that is known to the designer regarding particu-
    lar risks to the safety, health and welfare of persons at work,
    including but not limited to the risks referred to in *Schedule 1,*
   (b) regarding the nature and scope of the project to the extent neces-
    sary to enable the project supervisor to comply with these
    Regulations,
   (c) about the project that is necessary for that project supervisor to
    prepare the safety file, and
   (d) that is known to that person and is necessary to ensure, so far as
    is reasonably practicable, the safe construction of the design for
    the project.

(4) For the purposes of *paragraph (3),* if no project supervisor is known to the designer to have been appointed for the project, the designer shall provide the information referred to in that provision to the appropriate contractor instead of to a project supervisor.

(5) If a designer is not aware of the appointment of a project supervisor for the design process, the designer shall promptly inform the client of the client's duties under *Regulation 6.*

Duties of the project supervisor for the construction stage, safety and health plan.

16.   The project supervisor for the construction stage shall—

(a) further develop, as necessary, before the commencement of the construction work, the safety and health plan for the construction site prepared under *Regulation 12,* in the Regulation called "the plan",

(b) make adjustments to the plan where required to take account of the progress of the work and any changes which occur,

(c) take account as regards the plan, at all times during the construction stage, of section 20 of the Act and of other work activities taking place on the site,

(d) include in the plan specific measures concerning work which involves a particular risk, including but not limited to any risk referred to in *Schedule 1,*

(e) include in the plan, rules for the execution of the construction work which rules are required for the purposes of the safety, health and welfare of persons at work, and

(f) ensure that the plan and any rules contained in it are in writing and that they are brought to the attention of all contractors and other relevant persons who may be affected by them.

Duties of the project supervisor for the construction stage, co-ordination and cooperation.

17.   (1) If more than one contractor is engaged in a project, the project supervisor for the construction stage shall—

(a) co-ordinate the implementation during construction of the general principles of prevention when—

(i) deciding technical or organizational aspects, and

(ii) estimating the time required for completing the work or work stages

(b) co-ordinate the implementation of any requirements of these Regulations in order that contractors and others—

(i) apply the general principles of prevention in a consistent manner, in particular as regards the matters specified in *schedule 2* to these Regulations,

    (ii) monitor the consistent application of *subparagraph (i),* and

   (iii) where required, follow the provisions of the safety and health plan,

  (c) organise cooperation between contractors (including successive contractors on the same site) and others and the co-ordination of their activities in relation to a project with a view to protecting persons at work and preventing accidents and injury to health and monitor such cooperation and co-ordination

  (d) organize the implementation of section 21 of the Act, in particular in relation to the provision of information, monitor such implementation and, if information provided is inadequate, take appropriate corrective action as set out in *Regulation 20.*

  (e) coordinate the implementation by contractors of *Regulation 24 (d)* in relation to any accident or dangerous occurrence and keep available for inspection a record of any information provided to the project supervisor under that Regulation, and

    (i) monitor such coordination, and

    (ii) if the Authority requests information in relation to that record, comply with the request as soon as possible,

  (f) provide access to appropriate information regarding safety, health and welfare required under this Regulation to the site safety representative,

  (g) coordinate arrangements for checking the implementation of safe working procedures and monitor the implementation of those arrangements, and

  (h) coordinate measures to permit authorized persons only on to the construction site and monitor such coordination.

(2) The project supervisor for the construction stage may appoint a competent person as health and safety co-ordinator for the construction stage to assist in undertaking the duties specified in *Regulation 16* and this Regulation.

(3) The project supervisor for the construction stage shall—

  (a) coordinate arrangements which facilitate the provision and maintenance, in an appropriate condition, of site welfare facilities for all persons at work on the construction site, in accordance with *Part 14,* and

  (b) monitor the implementation of the arrangements.

(4) The project supervisor for the construction stage shall take appropriate corrective action as set out in *Regulation 20* where contractors or others donot comply with one or more *paragraphs (1)(b)* to *(g)* and *(h)* and*(3) (b)* of this Regulation.

(5) The project supervisor for the construction stage shall maintain and keep available for inspection a record of the names of person at work

at the construction site to whom *Regulation 19* applies as provided by each contractor under *Regulation 25(2)*

(6) The project supervisor for the construction stage shall keep appropriate records and copies of relevant documents in relation to *paragraphs (1)(e)* and *(4)* and *Regulations 16* and *22* for 5 years after the date of preparation of the records or documents

(7) The project supervisor for the construction stage shall also comply with *Regulation 87 (2)*, if applicable.

Duties of the project supervisor for the construction stage, safety adviser.

18.   If there are normally more than 100 persons on a construction site at any one time engaged in construction work, the project supervisor for the construction stage shall appoint in writing a full-time competent safety adviser for that site to—

(a) advise the project supervisor and contractors as appropriate as to the observance of the requirements of the relevant statutory provisions, and

(b) exercise a general supervision of the observance of those requirements and the promotion of the safe conduct of work generally.

Duties of the project supervisor for the construction stage, safety awareness and skills certification.

19.   (1) The project supervisor for the construction stage shall—

(a) coordinate arrangements to ensure that persons at work on the construction site to whom *Regulation 4 (2)* applies are each in possession of a valid safety awareness registration card referred to in *Schedule 3,*

(b) coordinate arrangements to ensure that those persons who engage in tasks specified in *Schedule 4* are each in possession of an appropriate valid construction skills registration card referred to in that Schedule, and

(c) monitor the implementation of the arrangements and take any necessary corrective action as set out in *Regulation 20.*

Powers of the project supervisor for the construction stage to issue directions.

20.   (1) The project supervisor for the construction stage, so far as is necessary,

(a) may give directions to each person who is a contractor, designer, or other relevant person, which directions, if carried out, will assist or enable compliance by the project supervisor with the duties imposed by these Regulations on the project supervisor, and

(b) shall confirm the directions in writing including a time frame for their execution, if the project supervisor considers that the person to whom the directions were given has not carried out the directions.

(2) If, in the opinion of the project supervisor for the construction stage, a contractor, designer, or other relevant person has not carried out directions confirmed in writing under *paragraph (1)(b)*, the project supervisor shall—

(a) notify in writing the Authority, the client and the person to whom the direction was given of the alleged failure, and

(b) include with the notification—

(i) a copy of the written confirmation under *paragraph (i)(b)*, and

(ii) particulars of the response, if any, made by the contractor, designer or other relevant person to the directions.

(3) The project supervisor for the construction stage shall ensure that a copy of each—

(a) confirmation in writing of a direction given under *paragraph (1)*, and

(b) associated notification to the Authority referred to in *paragraph (2)* is retained with the safety and health plan.

Duties of the project supervisor for the construction stage, safety file.

21. (1) The project supervisor for the construction stage of a project shall—

(a) coordinate arrangements among contractors to ensure the provision of relevant information, in writing, necessary for the project supervisor for the design process to complete the safety file referred to in *Regulation 13*, monitor the implementation of the arrangements and take any necessary corrective action, as set out in *Regulation 20*, and

(b) provide in writing to the project supervisor for the design process all relevant information necessary for that project supervisor to complete the safety file referred to in *Regulation 13*.

(2) For projects where the design stage commenced before the coming into operation of these Regulations if, having regard to *Regulation 1(3)*, a project supervisor for the design process has not been appointed, the project supervisor for the construction stage shall prepare the safety file as required by *Regulation 13*.

Duties of the project supervisor for the construction stage, notification to the Authority.

22. (1) If construction work on a construction site is planned to last longer than 30 working days or the volume or work is scheduled to exceed 500 person-days, the project supervisor for the construction stage, before the work begins, shall give notice promptly to the Authority in an approved form, sent either—

(a) by registered post, or

(b) as may be directed from time to time by the Authority.

(2) The project supervisor for the construction stage shall cause to be clearly displayed on the construction site and, if necessary, periodically cause to be updated the particulars required to be in any notice under *paragraph (1)*.

Site safety representative.

23. (1) The project supervisor for the construction stage shall—

(a) co-ordinate the development and application by contractors of arrangements, made in consultation with their employees, which will enable them and their employees to co-operate effectively in promoting and developing measures in relation to their safety, health and welfare on the construction site and in ascertaining the effectiveness of such measures, taking account of section 26 of the Act, and

(b) facilitate, where more than 20 persons are normally employed at any one time on a construction site at any stage of a project, in co-operation with contractors and persons employed on the project, the appointment of a site safety representative from among the employees of the contractor or contractors undertaking the project in accordance with the procedure outlined in *Schedule 5*.

(2) The project supervisor for the construction stage shall ensure that a site safety representative, for the purposes of performing functions relation to safety, health and welfare at a construction site, has access to—

(a) the risk assessment carried out under section 19 of the Act,

(b) information relating to accidents and dangerous occurrences required to be reported under the relevant statutory provisions, and

(c) any information arising from protective and preventive measures taken under the relevant statutory provisions or provided by—

(i) the Authority,

(ii) a person prescribed under section 33 of the Act, or

(iii) a person referred to in section 34(2) of the Act.

(3) The project supervisor for the construction stage shall inform the site safety representative when an inspector enters the construction site for the purpose of carrying out an inspection.

(4) The project supervisor for the construction stage shall—

(a) inform the site safety representative of the time and venue of all site safety meetings, and

    (b) facilitate the attendance of the site safety representative at the meetings.

(5) A site safety representative for a construction site may inspect the whole or any part of the construction site—

    (a) after giving reasonable notice to the project supervisor for the construction stage and to the contractor employing the site safety representative, or

    (b) immediately, in the event of an accident, dangerous occurrence or imminent danger or risk to the safety, health welfare of any person.

(6) The project supervisor for the construction stage the contractor employing the site safety representative and the site safety representative, having regard to the nature and extent of the hazards at the construction site, shall agree as to the frequency of inspections ot be carried out under *paragraph (5),* which agreement shall not be unreasonably withheld by the project supervisor or the contractor.

(7) A site safety representative may—

    (a) investigate accidents and dangerous occurrences provided that the or she does not interfere with or obstruct the performance of any statutory obligation required to be performed by any person under any of the relevant statutory provisions,

    (b) after giving of reasonable notice to the project supervisor for the construction stage and to the contractor employing the site safety representative, investigate complaints relating to safety, health and welfare at work made by any employee whom he or she represents.

    (c) accompany an inspector who is carrying out an inspection of the construction site under section 64 of the Act other than an inspection for the purpose of investigating an accident or dangerous occurrence,

    (d) at the discretion of the inspector concerned, accompany on inspector who is carrying out an inspection of the construction site under section 64 of the Act for the purpose of investigating an accident or dangerous occurrence,

    (e) at the discretion of the inspector concerned, where an employee is interviewed by an inspector with respect to an accident or dangerous occurrence at the construction site, attend the interview at the request of the employee,

    (f) on any mater relating to safety, health and welfare at the construction site, make representative to the project supervisor for the construction stage and to any contractor on the construction site,

    (g) make oral or written representations to inspectors on matters relating to safety, health and welfare at the construction site including, but not limited to, the investigation of accidents or dangerous occurrences,

(h) receive advice and information from inspectors on matters relating to safety, health and welfare at the construction site, or

(i) consult and liaise on matters relating to safety, health and welfare at work with any other safety representatives who may be appointed at the construction site concerned.

(9) The project supervisor for the construction stage and, as appropriate, any contractor involved in the project shall take account of any representations made to the project supervisor by a site safety representative on any matter affecting the safety, health and welfare at work of any person at work at the construction site.

(10) The contractor employing a site safety representative shall afford the site safety representative such time off from his or her duties as may be reasonable having regard to all the circumstances, without loss of remuneration, to enable the representative to—

(a) acquire the knowledge necessary to discharge his or her functions as a site safety representative, and

(b) discharge his or her functions as a site safety representative under this Regulation.

PART 3

GENERAL DUTIES OF CONTRACTORS AND OTHERS

Duties of contractors.

24. A contractor shall—

(a) comply with *Parts 2* to *14,*

(b) co-operate with the project supervisor for the construction stage to enable the project supervisor to comply with the relevant statutory provisions,

(c) provide promptly to the project supervisor for the construction stage any information (including a copy of any relevant safety statement prepared under section 20 of the Act) which—

(i) is likely to affect the safety, health or welfare of any person at work on the construction site, or

(ii) might justify a review of the safety and health plan,

(d) provide the project supervisor for the construction stage with—

(i) information in relation to any accident or dangerous occurrence of which the contractor is required, under the relevant statutory provisions, to give notification or to report, and

(ii) a copy of the required notification or report,

(e) promptly provide the project supervisor for the construction stage, in writing, with all relevant information necessary to prepare the safety file,

(f) comply with directions given under these Regulations by the project supervisor for the design process or by the project supervisor for the construction stage,

(g) bring to the attention of the contractor's employees any rules applicable to them contained in the safety and health plan,

(h) comply with the safety and health plan and any rules in the plan that are applicable to the contractor or to the contractor's employees,

(i) ensure, so far as is reasonably practicable, compliance by the contractor's employees with the rules referred to in *paragraph (h),*

(j) apply, where appropriate, the general principles of prevention in a consistent manner, in particular in relation to the matters specified in *Schedule 2*, in order to protect the safety, health and welfare of persons at work, and

(k) facilitate the performance by the site safety representative of the functions of the site safety representative under *Regulation 23.*

Safety awareness and skills certification.

25. (1) Every contractor or other person under whose direct control persons work on a construction site shall ensure that each of those persons, in this Regulation called a "worker"—

(a) is in possession of a valid safety awareness registration card referred to in *Schedule 3* if *Regulation 4(2)* applies to the worker,

(b) is in possession of an appropriate valid construction skills registration card referred to in *Schedule 4* if the worker engages in any of the tasks specified in that Schedule, and

(c) has received site-specific safety induction instruction if *Regulation 4(3)* applies to the worker.

(2) On the date upon which a worker first starts work on a construction site, the contractor or other person under whose direct control the worker is working shall—

(a) ask to see the appropriate valid registration card referred to in *paragraph (1),* and

(b) furnish to the project supervisor for the construction stage written confirmation that the worker is in possession of—

(i) the valid registration card, and

(ii) other relevant certificates and documentation required under the relevant statutory provisions.

Appointment of safety officers.

26. (1) Every contractor who normally has under direct control at any one time more than 20 persons on a construction site, or 30 persons engaged in construction work, shall appoint in writing, taking into account section 18 of the Act, one or more competent persons, as may be appropriate, as safety officers to undertake the following duties:

(a) to advise the contractor as to the observance of the requirements of the relevant statutory provisions;

(b) to exercise a general supervision of the observance of the requirements of the relevant statutory provisions and the promotion of the safe conduct of work generally;

(c) to co-operate with any safety adviser appointed under *Regulation 18* in relation to safety, health and welfare at work on the project.

(2) The duties assigned to any person appointed *under paragraph (1)*, including duties other than those mentioned in *paragraph (1)*, shall not be such as to prevent that person from discharging with reasonable efficiency duties assigned under that paragraph.

(3) Nothing in these Regulations shall be construed as preventing the same person or persons being appointed as safety officer under this Regulation for a group of sites or 2 or more contractors from jointly so appointing the same person or persons.

(4) Nothing in these Regulations shall be construed as preventing a person appointed as a safety adviser under *Regulation 18* on a particular site being appointed as a safety officer for that site in accordance with this Regulation.

Erection and installation of plant or equipment.

27.   The relevant contractor shall —

(a) erect, install, modify, work or use any plant or equipment to which any of the relevant statutory provisions apply in a manner which complies with those provisions, and

(b) erect or alter any scaffold in a manner which complies with any relevant requirements of any of the relevant statutory provisions, having regard to the purpose or purposes for which the scaffold is designed at the time of erection or alteration.

Consultation.

28.   The relevant contractor shall ensure consultation on the construction site with the contractor's employees, their safety representative and the site safety representative in relation to the requirements of these Regulations in accordance with the provisions of section 26 of the Act, taking account of the need, whenever necessary, for co-operation and coordination among —

(a) employees,

(b) the safety representatives of the different contractors, and

(c) the site safety representative

with a view to promoting and developing measures for protecting safety, health and welfare of persons at work on the site.

Duties of employees and other persons at work.

29. (1) Every person engaged in work to which these Regulations apply shall—

(a) comply with these Regulations,

(b) co-operate in carrying out the requirements of these Regulations,

(c) report without unreasonable delay any defect, discovered by the person, in the plant or equipment to which these Regulations apply, which might endanger safety, health and welfare, to the person's employer or immediate supervisor, or to the contractor responsible for the plant or equipment,

(d) comply with all rules applicable to the person in the safety and health plan,

(e) make proper use of any safety helmet, harness or any other personal protective equipment provided for the person's safety and health,

(f) make proper use of any work equipment supplied, and

(g) show relevant registration cards referred to in *Regulations 19* and *25* when requested by the person's employer or the project supervisor for the construction stage.

(2) A person shall not—

(a) in applying for a registration card or certificate as referred to in *Schedules 3* and *4,* make a statement which the person applying knows to be false,

(b) with intent to deceive, forge or alter a registration card or certificate referred to in *paragraph (a),* or

(c) with intent to deceive, make, supply or possess any document closely resembling a registration card or certificate required in accordance with these Regulations.

PART 4

GENERAL SAFETY PROVISIONS

Site safety and access to construction sites.

30. (1) A contractor responsible for a construction site shall take all appropriate precautions, so far as is reasonably practicable, to ensure that the site is safe and without risk of injury to the safety, health and welfare of persons at work, taking into account these Regulations.

(2) A contractor responsible for a construction site shall ensure for that site that—

(a) the surroundings and the perimeter are signposted and laid out so as to be clearly visible and identifiable,

(b) safe means of access to and egress from are —

(i) provided and maintained, and

(ii) indicated where appropriate, and

(c) appropriate precautions are taken to protect persons present, at or in the vicinity of the site, from risks which may arise from such site, for example, by the provision of appropriate barriers, where necessary, to prevent unauthorised entry.

Emergency routes and exits.

31. (1) The application of this Regulation is without prejudice to the Fire Services Acts 1981 and 2003 (No. 30 of 1981 and No. 15 of 2003) and other relevant legislation.

(2) A contractor responsible for a construction site shall ensure for that site that —

(a) emergency routes and exits remain clear of obstruction and lead as directly as possible to a safe area,

(b) in the event of danger, it is possible for persons to evacuate their workstations quickly and as safely as possible,

(c) the number, distribution and dimensions of emergency routes and exits are adequate, taking into account the use, equipment and dimensions of the site and of the rooms and the maximum number of persons that may be present,

(d) specific emergency routes and exits are indicated by signs in accordance with the relevant statutory provisions applying to safety and health signs at work,

(e) emergency routes and exits, and the traffic routes and doors giving access to them, are free from obstruction so that they can be used at any time without hindrance, and

(f) emergency routes and exits requiring illumination are provided with emergency lighting of adequate intensity in case the lighting fails.

Doors and gates.

32. A contractor responsible for a construction site shall ensure for that site that—

(a) sliding doors are fitted with safety devices to prevent them from being derailed and falling over,

(b) doors and gates opening upwards are fitted with a mechanism to secure them against falling back,

(c) doors and gates along escape routes are appropriately marked,

(d) in the immediate vicinity of gates intended primarily for vehicle traffic, there are doors for pedestrian traffic, unless it is safe for pedestrians to cross, and such doors are clearly marked and kept free at all times,

(e) mechanical doors and gates operate without any risk of accident to persons at work,

(f) doors and gates are fitted with stop devices which are easily identifiable and accessible and, unless they open automatically in the event of a power-cut, it is possible for them to be opened manually, and

(g) in the case of indoor workstations on construction sites—

    (i) the position, number and dimensions of doors and gates, and the materials used in their construction, are determined by the nature and use of the rooms or areas,

    (ii) transparent doors are appropriately marked at a conspicuous level, and swing doors and gates are transparent or have see-through panels,

    (iii) if transparent or translucent surfaces in doors and gates are not made of safety material and if there is a danger that persons at work may be injured if a door or gate should shatter, the surfaces are protected against breakage,

    (iv) emergency doors open outwards,

    (v) emergency doors are not so locked or fastened that they cannot be easily and immediately opened by any person at work who may require to use them in an emergency, and

    (vi) sliding or revolving doors are not used as emergency exits.

Traffic routes and danger areas.

33. (1) A contractor responsible for a construction site shall ensure for that site that

    (a) traffic routes, including stairs, fixed ladders and loading bays and ramps, are designed, located, laid out and made negotiable to ensure easy, safe and appropriate access in such a way as not to endanger persons working in the vicinity of these traffic routes,

    (b) routes used for pedestrian traffic or goods traffic, or for both, including those used for loading and unloading are dimensioned in accordance with the number of potential users and the type of activity concerned,

    (c) if means of transport are used on traffic routes, a sufficient safety clearance or adequate protective devices are provided for other site users, and routes are clearly marked, regularly checked and properly maintained,

    (d) sufficient clearance is allowed between vehicle traffic routes and doors, gates, passages for pedestrians, corridors and staircases,

    (e) if the site includes limited access areas, these are—

        (i) equipped with devices to prevent persons at work who are not authorised to enter such areas from entering,

        (ii) appropriate measures are taken to protect persons who are authorised to enter the danger areas, and

        (iii) danger areas are clearly signposted, and

    (f) traffic routes are clearly identified where the use and equipment of rooms in indoor workstations on construction sites so requires for the protection of persons at work.

Stability and solidity.

34. (1) A contractor responsible for a construction site shall ensure for that
site that—

(a) materials, equipment and any component which, when moving
in any way, may affect the safety, health and welfare of persons
at work are stabilised in an appropriate and safe manner,

(b) access to any surface involving insufficiently resistant materials is
not authorised unless appropriate equipment or means are provided to enable the work to be carried out safely, and

(c) ahigh-level or low-level movable or fixed outdoor workstations are
solid and stable, taking account of the—

(i) number of persons occupying them,

(ii) maximum loads they may have to bear and the weight distribution, and

(iii) outside influences to which they may be subject.

(2) If the support and the other components of the workstations referred
to in *paragraph (1)(c)* are not intrinsically stable, the relevant contractor shall ensure that—

(a) atheir stability is ensured by appropriate and safe methods of fixing to avoid any untimely or spontaneous movement of the whole
or of parts of the workstations, and

(b) atheir stability and solidity are checked appropriately, especially
after any change in the height or depth of the workstation.

(3) The relevant contractor shall ensure that premises containing indoor
workstations on construction sites have a structure and stability
appropriate to the nature of their use.

Protection from falling material and protective safety helmets.

35. (1) A contractor responsible for a construction site shall ensure for that
site that

(a) adequate measures are taken to prevent persons at work from
being struck by any falling material or article,

(b) where technically feasible, persons are protected by collective
methods against falling objects,

(c) materials and equipment are laid out or stacked in such a way as
to prevent their collapsing or overturning, and

(d) where necessary, there are covered passageways on the site or
access to danger areas is prevented.

(2) Every contractor shall ensure that every person under the contractor's direct control who is carrying out construction work is provided
with a suitable—

(a) protective safety helmet, or

    (b) other head protection unless there is no foreseeable risk of injury to the head other than by falling.

(3) Every contractor shall ensure that—

    (a) every protective safety helmet or other head protection that is provided pursuant to this Regulation for use on a construction site is marked with a distinguishing mark used to identify it in relation to the person to whom it has been issued, and

    (b) the helmet or other head protection is not issued to any other person unless and until it has been cleaned and disinfected.

(4) On a construction site, a person shall not throw, drop or allow to be shot or ejected downwards any scaffold materials or tools or any other materials or objects, including waste materials, from a height where they are liable to cause injury.

(5) Where practicable a person who moves any scaffold materials, tools or other objects, including waste materials, from a height on a construction site where they are liable to cause injury, shall cause them to be properly lowered.

(6) A contractor responsible for a construction site shall ensure for that site that adequate steps are taken to protect persons at work from falling or flying debris where—

    (a) proper lowering under *paragrah (5)* is not practicable, or

    (b) any part of a building or other structure is being demolished or removed.

Loading bays and ramps.

36. A contractor responsible for a construction site shall ensure for that site that—

    (a) loading bays and ramps are suitable for the dimensions of the loads to be transported,

    (b) loading bays have at least one exist point, and

    (c) loading ramps are sufficiently safe to prevent persons at work from falling off.

Installations, machinery and equipment

37. A contractor responsible for a construction site shall ensure for that site that all installations, machinery and equipment hand tools, whether power-operated or not, used on a construction site, are—

    (a) properly designed and constructed, taking account, as far as possible, of the principles of ergonomics,

    (b) maintained in proper working order,

    (c) used only for the work for which they were designed, and

    (d) operated only by persons who have received appropriate training.

Wet paint on ironwork or steelwork.

38. (1) Except as regards moving or manipulating in connection with the painting of ironwork or steelwork on a construction site, a person shall not, on a construction site, move or manipulate any ironwork or steelwork which has been painted unless all the paint on it. other than paint for the purpose of joining, is dry.

    (2) A person shall not walk or work or require or permit another person to walk or work on erected—

      (a) ironwork, or
      (b) steelwork

on which the paint, other than paint for the purpose of jointing, is wet.

Helmets or crowns for pile driving.

39. A contractor responsible for a construction site shall ensure for that site that every helmet or crown used in connection with pile driving is good construction, of sound and suitable material, of adequate strength and free from patent defect.

Lighting of work places.

40. A contractor responsible for a construction site shall ensure for that site that –

    (a) every place and the approach to that place on that site is adequately and suitably lighted if, at that place –

      (i) persons are at work and, in particular, every such place and approach where raising or lowering operations with the use of a lifting appliance are in progress, or
      (ii) there are openings dangerous to persons at work,

    (b) workstations, rooms and traffic routes are provided with—

      (i) sufficient natural lighting, as far as possible, and
      (ii) appropriate and sufficient artificial lighting at night and when natural daylight is inadequate,

    (c) where necessary portable light sources that are protected against impact are used,
    (d) indoor workstations on construction sites—

      (i) as far as possible, have natural light, and
      (ii) are equipped with the means of providing artificial lighting

        which is sufficient for the purpose of protecting the safety, health and welfare of persons at work,

    (e) the colour of artificial light used on the construction site does not alter or affect the perception of signals or signposts in any way that endangers the safety and health of persons at work,

(f) lighting installations for rooms, workstations and traffic routes are placed in such a way that there is no risk of accidents to persons at work as a result of the type of lighting fitted, and

(g) rooms, workstations and traffic routes, where persons at work are especially exposed to risks in the event of failure of artificial lighting, are provided with emergency lighting of adequate intensity.

Prevention of electrocution.

41. A contractor responsible for a construction site shall ensure for that site that—

(a) whenever possible, where overhead power lines exist, they are redirected away from the area of the site or else that the current is cut off,

(b) if compliance with *paragraph (a)* is not possible, barriers and notices are provided, as appropriate, to ensure that vehicles and installations are kept away,

(c) suitable warnings and suspended protections are provided where vehicles have to pass beneath overhead power lines,

(d) energy distribution installations are designed, constructed and used so as not to present a fire or explosion hazard,

(e) persons at work are adequately protected against the risk of electrocution caused by direct or indirect contact,

(f) the design, construction and choice of equipment and protection devices take account of the type and power of the energy distributed, external conditions and the competence of persons with access to parts of the installation,

(g) on-site outdoor energy distribution installations are regularly checked and maintained, and

(h) outdoor installations existing on the site before the construction work began are identified, checked and clearly signposted.

Projecting nails and loose material.

42. A constructor responsible for a construction site shall ensure for that site that timber or material with projecting nails—

(a) is not used in any work to which these Regulations apply if the timber or material is a source of danger to persons at work, and

(b) is not allowed to remain in any place where it is a source of danger to persons at work.

Construction of temporary structures.

43. A contractor responsible for a construction site shall ensure for that site that any temporary structure erected for the purpose of construction work, having regard to the purpose for which the temporary structure is used,

(a) is of good design and construction and of adequate strength and stability, and

(b) is of sound material, free from patent defect and properly maintained.

Avoidance of danger from collapse of structure.

44. A contractor responsible for a construction site shall ensure for that site that—

(a) metal or concrete frameworks and their components, shutterings, prefabricated components, temporary supports, false work and buttresses are erected and dismantled only under the supervision of a competent person,

(b) all practicable precautions are taken by the use of temporary guys, stays, supports and fixings, or otherwise, where necessary to prevent danger to any person at work through the collapse of any part of a building or other structure during any temporary state of weakness or instability of the building or structure, or part thereof, before the whole building or structure is completed,

(c) any guys, stays, supports, fixings or other devices provided under *paragraph (b)* are designed, installed and maintained so as to safely withstand any strains and stresses which may be placed on them, and

(d) all practicable precautions are taken by shoring, or otherwise, to prevent danger to any person at work from—

    (i) the collapse of a building or structure, or

    (ii) the fall of any part of a building or structure

       where any work is likely to reduce the security or stability of any part of an existing building or structure or of a building or structure in the course of construction.

Fire detection and fire fighting.

45. (1) The application of this Regulation is without prejudice to the Fire Services Acts 1981 and 2003 (No. 30 of 1981 and No. 15 of 2003) and other relevant legislation.

(2) A contractor responsible for a construction site, depending on the characteristics of the site, the dimensions and use of rooms, the on-site equipment, the physical and chemical properties of the substances present and the maximum potential number of persons at work present, shall provide or cause to be provided on the site an adequate number of—

    (a) appropriate fire-fighting devices, and

    (b) where required, fire detectors and alarm systems.

(3) A contractor responsible for a construction site shall ensure for that site that—

    (a) fire-fighting devices, fire detectors and alarm systems are regularly checked and properly maintained,

(b) appropriate tests and drills take place at regular intervals,

(c) non-automatic fire-fighting equipment is easily accessible and easy to use, and

(d) fire fighting equipment is indicated by signs in accordance with the relevant statutory provisions applying to safety and health signs at work.

Floors, walls, ceilings and roofs of rooms.

46. A contractor responsible for a construction site shall ensure for that site that—

(a) in the case of indoor workstations, the floors have no dangerous bumps, holes or slopes and are fixed, stable and not slippery,

(b) the surfaces of floors, walls and ceilings in rooms can be cleaned or refurbished to an appropriate standard of hygiene, and

(c) transparent or translucent walls, in particular all-glass partitions, in rooms or in the vicinity of workstations and traffic routes are—

(i) clearly indicated,

(ii) made of safety material, or

(iii) shielded from workstations and traffic routes to prevent persons at work from coming into contact with walls or being injured if the walls shatter.

Windows and skylights.

47. (1) In the case of indoor workstations, a contractor responsible for a construction site shall ensure for that site that—

(a) it is possible for persons at work to open, close, adjust or secure windows, skylights and ventilators in a safe manner, and

(b) the windows, skylights and ventilators when open are not positioned so as to constitute a hazard to persons at work.

(2) A contractor responsible for a construction site shall ensure for that site that windows and skylights are—

(a) of a design, or

(b) are otherwise fitted with devices

so that when used in conjunction with equipment that may be cleaned without risk to the safety, health or welfare of persons carrying out this work or of other persons present.

Freedom of movement at the workstation.

48. A contractor responsible for a construction site shall ensure that the floor area at a workstation on the site allows persons sufficient freedom of movement to perform their work, taking account of any necessary equipment or appliances present.

Room dimensions and air space in rooms.

49.   A contractor responsible for a construction site shall ensure that workrooms on the site have sufficient surface area and height to allow persons to perform their work without risk to their safety, health or welfare.

Specific measures for escalators and travelators.

50.   A contractor responsible for a construction site shall ensure for that site that—

>   (a) escalators and travelators function safely, and
>   (b) are equipped with any necessary safety devices and with easily identifiable and accessible emergency shut-down devices.

PART 5

EXCAVATIONS, SHAFTS, EARTHWORKS,
UNDERGROUND WORKS AND TUNNELS

Safety precautions.

51.   (1) A contractor responsible for a construction site shall ensure for that site that adequate precautions are taken in any excavation, shaft, earthwork, underground works or tunnel to—

>   (a) guard against danger to persons at work from fall or dislodgement of earth, rock or other material by suitable shoring or otherwise,
>   (b) guard against dangers arising from the fall of material or objects or the inrush of water into the excavation, shaft, earthworks underground works or tunnel,
>   (c) secure adequate ventilation at all workstations so as to maintain an atmosphere fit for respiration and to limit any fumes, gases, vapours, dust or other impurities to levels which are not dangerous or injurious to health,
>   (d) guard against the occurrence of fire or flooding.
>   (e) enable persons at work to reach safety in the event of fire or an inrush of water or materials,
>   (f) avoid risk to persons at work arising from possible underground dangers such as underground cables or other distribution systems, the circulation of fluids or the presence of pockets of gas, by undertaking appropriate investigations to locate them before excavation begins, and
>   (g) provide safe means of access to and egress from each place of work.

(2) *Paragraph (1)(a)* does not apply to any excavation, shaft or earthwork where, having regard to the nature and slope of the sides of the excavation, shaft or earthwork and other circumstances, a fall or dislodgement of earth or other material which would bury or trap a person from a height of more than 1.25 meters is not liable to occur.

(3) Where a person is engaged in shoring or other work carried out for the purpose of compliance with *paragraph (1) (a)*, the relevant contractor shall take measures to ensure, so far as reasonably practicable, that appropriate precautions are taken to ensure the safety and health of the person so engaged.

Inspection and examination.

52. (1) Subject to *paragraph (4)*, a contractor responsible for a construction site shall ensure for that site that—

    (a) every part of any excavation, shaft, earthwork, underground works or tunnel where persons are at work is inspected by a competent person at least once is every day during which persons are at work therein, and

    (b) the face of every tunnel, the working end of every trench more than 2 meters deep and the base and crown of every shaft are each inspected by a competent person at the commencement of every shift.

(2) Subject to *paragraph (4)*, a contractor responsible for a construction site shall ensure for that site that no person is permitted to work in any excavation, shaft, earthwork, underground work or tunnel unless a thorough examination has been carried out by a competent person—

    (a) of those part of it and in particular any shoring or other support, in the region of a blast after explosives have been used in or near the excavation, shaft, earthwork, underground work or tunnel in a manner likely to have affected the strength or stability of that shoring or other support of any part of it,

    (b) of those parts of it in the region of any shoring or other support of any part of it that has been substantially damaged and in the region of any unexpected fall of rock or earth or other material, and

    (c) of every part of it within the immediately preceding 7 days.

(3) On the day of an examination required under *paragraph (2)*, the person carrying out the examination shall make and sign a report of the results of the examination in an approved form.

(4) This Regulation does not apply on a construction site—

    (a) to any excavation, shaft or earthwork where, having regard to the nature and slope of the sides of the excavation, shaft or earthwork and other circumstances, a fall or dislodgement of earth or other material which—

(i) would bury or trap a person, or
(ii) would strike a person from a height of more than 1.25 meters
is not likely to occur, or

(b) in relation to persons carrying out inspections or examinations required by this Regulation or engaged in shoring or other work for the purpose of making a place safe, if appropriate precautions are taken, so far as is reasonably practicable, to ensure their safety and health.

Supervision and execution of shoring and other work.

53. A contractor responsible for a construction site shall ensure for that site that—

(a) shoring or other support for any part of an excavation, shaft, earthwork, underground work or tunnel is not erected, substantially added to, altered or dismantled, except—

(i) under the direction of a competent person, and
(ii) so far as is practicable, by persons possessing adequate experience of such work,

(b) all material for shoring or other support as described in *paragraph (a)* is inspected by a competent person on each occasion before being taken into use,
(c) material found defective in any respect is not used,
(d) shoring or other support for any part of an excavation, shaft, earthwork, underground work or tunnel is of good construction, sound material, free from patent defect and of adequate strength for the purpose for which it is used and is properly maintained, and
(e) all struts and braces in any excavation, shaft, earthwork, underground work or tunnel are properly and adequately secured so as to prevent their accidental displacement or fall.

Excavations etc. likely to reduce security of a structure.

54. A contractor responsible for a construction site shall not—

(a) commence or continue, or
(b) allow to be commenced or continued

on that site, any excavation, shaft, earthwork, underground works or tunnel likely to endanger any employee or other person at work by reducing the security or stability of any part of any temporary or permanent structure, on or adjacent to the site, unless adequate steps are taken, both before and during the progress of the work, to prevent danger to the employee or other person from collapse of the structure or the fall of any part of it.

Fencing of excavations, etc.

55. (1) A contractor responsible for a construction site shall ensure for that site that every accessible part of an excavation, shaft, pit or opening in the ground near to which persons are working and into or down which a person is liable to fall a distance liable to cause personal injury—

    (a) has a suitable barrier placed as close as is practicable to the edge, or

    (b) is securely covered.

(2) *Paragraph (1)* does not apply to any part of an excavation, shaft, pit or opening while, and to the extent to which—

    (a) the absence of the barrier and covering is necessary for the access of persons or for the movement of plant or equipment or materials, or

    (b) it has not up to then been practicable to erect the barrier or covering since the formation of that part of the excavation, shaft, pit or opening.

(3) Where such barriers or coverings are not yet in place, the relevant contractor shall ensure that all appropriate measures are taken, so far as is reasonably practicable to prevent persons from falling into the shaft, pit or opening.

Safeguarding edges of excavations, etc.

56. A contractor responsible for a construction site—

    (a) shall ensure that material is not placed or stacked on the site near the edge of any excitation, shaft, pit or opening in the ground where it is likely to endanger persons at work below,

    (b) shall not on the site—

        (i) place or move, or

        (ii) allow to be placed or moved

    any load, vehicle, plant or equipment near the edge of any excavation, shaft, pit or opening in the ground where it is likely to cause a collapse of the side of the excavation, shaft, pit or opening and thereby endanger any person at work, and

    (c) if necessary, shall ensure that appropriate barriers are provided.

PART 6

COFFERDAMS AND CAISSIONS

Construction and maintenance.

57. A contractor responsible for a construction site shall ensure for that site that every cofferdam or caisson and every part of one is—

(a) of good construction,
(b) of suitable and sound material,
(c) free from patent defect,
(d) of adequate strength, and
(e) properly maintained.

Means of egress in case of flooding.

58. A contractor responsible for a construction site shall ensure for that site that every cofferdam or caisson is provided with adequate means for each person at work to reach a place of safety in the event of an inrush of water or material.

Supervision of work and inspection of material.

59. A contractor responsible for a construction site shall ensure for that site that—

(a) no cofferdam caisson or part of one is constructed, placed in position, substantially added to, altered or dismantled, except—

(i) under the immediate supervision of a competent person, and
(ii) so far as is practicable by persons possessing adequate experience of the work,

(b) all material used for the construction or fixing of a cofferdam or caisson is inspected by a competent person on each occasion before being taken into such use, and

(c) material which is unsuitable or defective in any respect is not used.

Inspections and examinations.

60. (1) Subject to *paragraph (3)*, a contractor responsible for a construction site shall ensure for that site that any cofferdam or caisson in which persons are at work is—

(a) inspected by a competent person at least once every day during which persons are working in the cofferdam or caisson, and

(b) thoroughly examined by a competent person—

   (i) in case explosives have been used in or near the cofferdam or caisson in a manner likely to have affected the strength or stability of the cofferdam or caisson or any part thereof, since the use of the explosives,

   (ii) where the cofferdam or caisson has been substantially damaged, and

   (iii) in any other case, at least once within the immediately preceding 7 days.

 (2) A person who carries out an examination made pursuant to this Regulation shall, on the day of the examination, make and sign a report, in an approved form, of the results of the examination.

 (3) Where persons are engaged on a construction site in the construction, placing, repairing or alteration of a cofferdam or caisson or carrying out inspections or examinations required by *paragraph (1)*, this Regulation does not apply if appropriate precautions are taken, so far as is reasonably practicable, to ensure their safety and health.

PART 7

COMPRESSED AIR

Interpretation for this Part.

61. In this Part and in *Schedule 1*, "compressed air" means air compressed above atmospheric pressure, measured in kg/cm^2.

Safety precautions and supervision.

62. A contractor responsible for a construction site shall ensure for that site that where persons are required to work in compressed air—

 (a) appropriate precautions, arrangements and procedures are adopted, and

 (b) the work is planned and undertaken only under the supervision of a competent person.

Plant and equipment.

63. A contractor responsible for a construction site shall ensure for that site that all plant and equipment, including man-lock and air supply plant, and all parts and fittings thereof provided for use in relation to work in compressed air are—

 (a) of good design and construction,

 (b) of sound material and adequate strength,

    (c) free from patent defect,
    (d) properly maintained and used, and
    (e) suitable for the purpose for which they are used.

Fitness to work and supervision.

64. A contractor responsible for a construction site shall ensure for that site that—
    (a) work in compressed air is carried out only by persons who have been medically examined and found fit for the work,
    (b) work in compressed air is carried out only when a competent person is present to supervise and take charge of the operations, and
    (c) no person is permitted to work in compressed air unless properly instructed and informed as to the precautions to be taken in connection with the work.

Maximum pressure and records.

65. A contractor responsible for a construction site shall ensure for that site that—
    (a) no person working in compressed air is subjected to pressure exceeding 3.5 kg/cm^2 except in emergencies, and
    (b) for every shift a record is kept showing the time each person working in compressed air spends in the working chamber and the time taken for decompression.

Medical examinations and first aid.

66. (1) Without prejudice to *paragraph (2)*, a contractor responsible for a construction site shall not require or permit any person to work in compressed air, on that site, where the air pressure exceeds 1.25 kg/cm^2 unless the person has been—

    (a) medically examined, within the previous 4 weeks, by a registered medical practitioner familiar with compressed air work, and
    (b) certified by the registered medical practitioner as being fit for such work.

  (2) A contractor responsible for a construction site shall ensure that persons who work continuously for more than 10 hours per week in compressed air on the site—

    (a) at a pressure of not more than 1.5 kg/cm^2 are medically re-examined every 2 months, or
    (b) at a pressure of more than 1.5 kg/cm^2 are medically re-examined at intervals to be assessed by a registered medical practitioner to the extent that a shorter interval than under *subparagraph (a)* is considered appropriate.

(3) A contractor responsible for a construction site shall ensure that—

    (a) Persons are medically re-examined if they have been absent from work in compressed air for any period due to illness or for 10 days or more for reasons other than illness,

    (b) for every project where persons work in compressed air, a registered medical practitioner, a nurse, or a trained first-aid attendant, familiar with compressed air work, shall be available at all times, and

    (c) When persons work in compressed air at a pressure exceeding 1.25 kg/cm^2, a neighbouring hospital is informed of the location of the site and of the name and address of the registered medical practitioner exercising medical supervision.

Identification badge.

67. A contractor responsible for a construction site shall ensure for that site that every person who works in compressed air at a pressure exceeding 1.25 kg/cm^2 is provided with an identification badge to be worn on the body—

    (a) indicating that the person has worked in compressed air and giving the address of the medical lock at the place of work, and

    (b) stating that the wearer, if ill, should be taken to the medical lock and not to a hospital.

Compressions and decompressions.

68. A contractor responsible for a construction site shall ensure for that site that—

    (a) adequate and suitable facilities for remaining on the site after decompression, including shelters with seats, are provided for persons working in compressed air,

    (b) any person who has not previously worked in compressed air is not subjected to compressed air unless accompanied in the man-lock by a person competent to advise as to the appropriate conduct of persons during compressions,

    (c) the pressure is not raised during compression to more than 0.35 kg/cm^2 until the man-lock attendant has ascertained that no person is complaining of discomfort, and thereafter the pressure is raised at a rate not exceeding 0.7 kg/cm^2 per minute, and

    (d) if during compression any person is suffering from discomfort, compression is stopped and the pressure gradually reduced.

Working chambers.

69. A contractor responsible for a construction site shall ensure for that site that, where persons are required to work in compressed air,

    (a) every working chamber is provided with a wet-bulb thermometer,

(b) work under pressure when the wet-bulb temperature exceeds 28°C is restricted unless it is absolutely necessary, and

(c) while any person is in a working chamber, the door between the chamber and a man-lock leading to a lower pressure, so far as is practicable, is kept open if the lock is not in use.

Medical locks.

70.   A contractor responsible for a construction site shall ensure for the site that, where persons are required to work in compressed air,

(a) if the pressure in a working chamber ordinary exceeds 1.25 kg/cm², a suitable medical lock conveniently situated is provided solely for the treatment of persons at work in compressed air,

(b) the medical lock has 2 components so that it can be entered under pressure, and

(c) while any person is at work in compressed air a medical lock is in the charge of a suitably qualified person.

Man-locks.

71.   (1) A contractor responsible for a construction site shall ensure for that site that every man-lock on a construction site is of adequate internal dimensions and is equipped with—

(a) pressure gauges that indicate to the man-lock attendant the pressure in the man-lock and in each working chamber to which it affords direct or indirect access and indicate to the persons in the man-lock the pressure in it,

(b) a clock or clocks so placed that the man-lock attendant and the persons in the man-lock can readily ascertain the time,

(c) efficient means of verbal communication between the man-lock attendant, the man-lock and the working chamber or chambers,

(d) means of enabling the persons in the man-lock to convey visible or other non-verbal signals to the man-lock attendant, and

(e) efficient means enabling the man-lock attendant, from outside the man-lock, to reduce or cut off the supply of compressed air to the man-lock.

(2) The relevant contractor shall ensure that persons in every man-lock on a construction site are not able to reduce the air pressure except—

(a) under the control of the man-lock attendant, or

(b) in an emergency, by special means that should normally be kept sealed or locked.

(3) The relevant contractor shall ensure that in every man-lock on a construction site there is a suitable notice indicating the precautions to be taken by persons during compression and decompression, and after decompression.

(4) The relevant contractor shall ensure that every man-lock on a construction site, while any person is in the man-lock or in any working chamber to which it affords direct or indirect access, is in the charge of an attendant who—

    (a) controls compression and decompression in the man-lock, and

    (b) if the pressure exceeds 1.25 kg/cm^2, keeps a register showing—

        (i) the times at which each person enters and leaves the man-lock,

        (ii) the pressures at the times of entering and leaving, and

        (iii) the times taken to decompress each person.

Air-supply.

72. A contractor responsible for a construction site on which persons are required to work in compressed air shall provide, or cause to be provided, compressed air installations with an air supply plant capable of supplying any working chamber with sufficient fresh uncontaminated air—

    (a) at the pressure in the chamber, and

    (b) at not less than 0.3 m^3 per minute per person in the chamber.

PART 8

EXPLOSIVES

Application of Part 8.

73. This part applied to the storage, transport, use and disposal of explosives at a construction site.

Duties of contractor.

74. A contractor responsible for a construction site shall—

    (a) so far as is reasonably practicable, ensure that all explosives used or to be used on the site are stored, transported, used and disposed of safely and securely,

    (b) appoint in writing one or more competent persons, each known in these Regulations as an "Explosives Supervisor" to organise and supervise all work at the site involving the use of explosives and obtain confirmation in writing of acceptance of the appointments,

    (c) ensure that at no time is there more than one person acting as the Explosives Supervisor at the site,

    (d) ensure that shotfiring operations on the site are carried out by a competent shotfirer or, subject to *Regulation 75*, by a trainee shotfirer acting under the close personal supervision of a competent shotfirer,

(e) ensure that the competent shotfirer is in possession of a valid constructions skills registration card for that task as referred to in Schedule 4,

(f) ensure that suitable and sufficient rules, known in these Regulations as "shotfiring rules", are made which lay down in writing procedure for—

(i)   shotfiring operations at the site,
(ii) appointing shotfirers, trainee shotfirers and storekeepers,
(iii) authorising other persons who will be involved with the storage, transport, use or disposal of explosives,
(iv) dealing with misfires, and
(v) ensuring, so far as is reasonably practicable, that such rules are complied with,

(g) ensure that an adequate written blast specification based on an assessment of the risks (whether or not produced by the contractor) is prepared for each shotfiring at the site to ensure, so far as is reasonably practicable, that when such firing occurs it will not give rise to danger,

(h) ensure that a copy of any relevant information contained in the blast specification referred to in *subparagraph (g)* is given to any person upon whom it imposes duties,

(i) ensure that operation involving the storage, transport, use or disposal of explosives are carried out by—

(i) a duly authorised and competent person, or
(ii) a trainee under the close supervision of a duly authorised and competent person as referred to in *Regulation 75,*

(j) ensure that such facilities and equipment as are necessary to enable shotfiring operations to be carried out safely are provided,

(k) ensure that any vehicle which is provided for use in relation to shot-firing operation is safe for use and so marked as to be readily identifiable from a distance,

(l) ensure that detonators are stored in separate containers from other explosives,

(m) ensure that explosives are kept at all time either in a locked explosives store or under the supervision of a suitable person, and

(n) ensure, so far as is reasonably practicable, that each shotfiring operation is carried out safely and in accordance with the shotfiring rules required to be made under *subparagraph (f)* and any blast specification required to be prepared under *subparagraph (g).*

Supervision of shotfiring operation and trainee shotfirers and records of appointment.

75. (1) A contractor responsible for a construction site shall ensure that—

(a) a trainee shotfirer at the site does not fire shots and is not required to fire shots, except when he or she is under the close person supervision of a shotfirer, until the contractor is satisfied that he or she has completed a suitable period of training and has appropriate practical experience and is competent, and

(b) all shotfiring operations at the site are carried out under the close personal supervision of the shotfirer.

(2) The relevant contractor for a construction site shall ensure that a record of the appointment at the site of any shotfirer or trainee shotfirer is kept at a suitable place until 3 years after that shotfirer's or, as the case may be, trainee shotfirer's, employment at the site ends.

Duties of Explosives Supervisor and shotfirer.

76. (1) The Explosives Supervisor and shotfirer shall ensure that any shotfiring operation on a construction site is carried out in accordance with any shotfiring rules required by *Regulation 74* and any blast specification prepared pursuant to *Regulation 74*.

(2) Before a short is fired on a construction site, a shorter shall—

(a) ensure that no person is within, or may enter within, the danger zone specified in the blast specification prepared pursuant to *Regulation 74* when the shot is being fired,

(b) check the shotfiring system or circuit to ensure that it has been connected correctly,

(c) where electrical detonators are used, ensure that they have been correctly connected to the shotfiring system or circuit and that the shotfiring system or circuit is tested with an instrument suitable for the purpose,

(d) where appropriate, ensure that the electrical integrity of the shotfiring system or circuit is such as to make a misfire unlikely, and

(e) ensure that the short is fired from a safe place.

Misfires.

77. In the event of a misfire the relevant contractor for a construction site shall ensure, so far as is reasonably practicable that—

(a) no person other than the Explosives Supervisor, shotfirer, trainee shotfirer or any other person authorised any of them enters the danger area—

(i) where the shot was fired by means of safety fuse, until a period of 30 minutes had elapsed since the misfire, or

(ii) where the shot was fired by other means, until a period of 5 minutes has elapsed since the misfire and any shotfiring apparatus has been disconnected from the shot,

(b) appropriate steps are taken to determine the cause of and to deal with the misfire, and

(c) a suitable record is kept of the misfire.

Prohibited activities.

78. (1) No person other than a person engaged in the transport of explosives to or from a construction site, a shotfirer, trainee shotfirer, a person authorised to handle explosives at the site or a person appointed to be in charge of the explosives store shall handle explosives at the site.

(2) No person other than a shotfirer or a trainee shotfirer shall handle detonators at a construction site.

(3) No person shall—

(a) bring any substance or article (other than explosives) likely to cause an unintended explosion or file, or
(b) except for the purpose of lighting an igniter cord or a safety fuse, take any naked flame

within 100 meters of any explosives.

(4) No person shall forcibly remove any detonator lead, safety fuse or other system for initiating shots from a shothole after the shothole has been charged and primed.

(5) No person shall charge or fire a shot or a construction site—

(a) unless there is sufficient visibility to ensure that work preparatory to shotfiring, the shotfiring operation and any site inspection after the shot is fired can be carried out safely, or
(b) in a shothole which has previously been fired, unless the person is dealing with a misfire in accordance with action taken under *Regulation 77(b)*.

(6) No person shall fire a shot on a construction site—

(a) unless the person is a shotfirer or trainee shotfirer, and
(b) does so only by means of a suitable exploder or suitable safety fuse.

(7) No person on a construction site shall cap a safety fuse with a detonator unless the person—

(a) is using equipment designed for the purpose, and
(b) is in a suitably sheltered place designated by the relevant contractor for the purpose.

(8) No person other than a shotfirer or a trainee shotfirer shall by detonation or burning dispose of surplus explosives, detonators, accessories or packaging remaining following shorfiring operations at a construction site.

PART 9

GENERAL HEALTH HAZARDS

Health hazards.

79. (1) A contractor responsible for a construction site, where persons are liable to be exposed to any chemical, physical or biological hazard to such an extent as is liable to be dangerous to health, shall ensure that appropriate preventive measures are taken on the site against that exposure.

(2) The preventive measures referred to in *Paragraph (1)* shall comprise—

(a) wherever possible, the replacement of hazardous substance by a harmless or less hazardous substance,

(b) technical measures applied to the plant, machinery, equipment or process, or

(c) Where it is not possible to comply with *subparagraph (a)* or *(b)*, other effective measures, including the use of personal protective equipment and protective clothing.

Atmospheric influences.

80. A contractor responsible for a construction site shall ensure for that site that persons working outdoors are protected against atmospheric influences which could affect their safety and health.

Ventilation.

81. (1) A contractor responsible for a construction site shall ensure for that site that—

(a) steps are taken to ensure that there is sufficient fresh air provided, having regard to the working methods used and the physical demands placed on the persons at work,

(b) if a forced ventilation system is used, it is maintained in working order and shall not expose persons at work to draughts which are harmful to health, and

(c) any breakdown in a forced ventilation system is indicated by a control system, if necessary for the health of persons at work.

(2) In indoor workstations on construction sites the relevant contractor shall ensure that—

(a) if air conditioning or mechanical ventilation installations are used, they operate in such a way that persons at work are not exposed to draughts which cause discomfort, and

(b) any deposit or dirt likely to create an immediate danger to the health of persons at work by polluting the atmosphere is removed without delay.

Temperature.

82. A contractor responsible for a construction site shall ensure for that site that—

(a) during working hours, the temperature is appropriate for human beings, having regard to the working methods used and the physical demands placed on the persons at work, and

(b) in indoor workstations on the site—

    (i) the temperature is rest areas, rooms for duty staff, sanitary facilities, canteens and first-aid rooms is appropriate to the particular purpose of such areas, and

    (ii) windows, skylights and glass partitions allow excessive effects of sunlight to be avoided, having regard to the nature of the work and use of them.

Disposal of waste.

83. A contractor responsible for a construction site shall ensure that waste in respect of the site is not—

(a) destroyed, or

(b) otherwise disposed of

in a manner liable to be injurious to safety and health.

Internal combustion engines or dangerous gas.

84. A contractor responsible for a construction site shall ensure that—

(a) no stationary internal combustion engine is used on the site in any enclosed or confined place unless specific provision is made for conducting the exhaust gases from the engine into the open air, or

(b) the site is adequately ventilated so as to prevent danger to health from the exhaust gases.

PART 10

CONSTRUCTION WORK ON OR ADJACENT TO WATER

Transport by water.

85. A contractor responsible for a construction site shall ensure for that site that—

(a) when any person at work is conveyed to or from any place of work on water, proper measures are taken to provide for the person's safe transport, and

(b) vessels used to convey persons as described in *paragraph (a)* are—

    (i) of suitable construction,

    (ii) properly maintained,

    (iii) in the change of a competent person, and

    (iv) not overcrowded or overloaded.

Prevention of drowning.

86. (1) A contractor responsible fo'r a constructions site shall ensure that—

    (a) where, on or adjacent to the site, there is water into which a person, in the course of his or her work, is liable to fall with risk of drowning—

        (i) suitable rescue equipment is provided and kept in an efficient state, ready for use, and

        (ii) arrangements are made for the prompt rescue of any such person who is in danger of drowning, and

    (b) personal flotation devices conforming to European Norm (EN) or equivalent standards, as appropriate, are provided and worn at all times on the site.

(2) A contractor responsible for a construction site shall ensure for that site that personal flotation devices provided in pursuance of this Regulation are—

    (a) properly maintained,

    (b) checked before each use,

    (c) inspected in accordance with the manufacturer's instructions, and

    (d) subjected to a thorough examination every 12 months.

(3) On the day of a required inspection or examination under *paragraph (2)*, the person who carries out the inspection or examination, as the case may be, shall—

    (a) make a report of the results in an approved form, and

    (b) sign the report.

(4) Where, on a construction site, there is special risk of a fall from the edge of adjacent land from—

    (a) a structure adjacent to or above the water, or

    (b) a floating state,

the relevant contractor shall ensure that secure fencing is provided near the edge to prevent such a fall.

(5) To the extent necessary for the access of persons or the movement of materials, *paragraph (4)* does not apply if appropriate precautions are taken, so far as is reasonably practicable, to ensure the safety and health of persons.

PART 11

TRANSPORT, EARTHMOVING AND MATERIALS-HANDLING
MACHINERY AND LOCOMOTIVES

Safe operation of vehicles.

87. (1) A contractor responsible for a construction site shall ensure for that site that, if used for the purposes of construction work, all transport vehicles, earth-moving machinery, materials-handling machinery and locomotives, as set out in *Schedule 6,*

 (a) are of good design and construction taking into account as far as possible ergonomic principles,
 (b) are maintained in good working order,
 (c) are properly used,
 (d) are not operated otherwise than by a competent person who has attained the age of 18 years, unless operation is by a person for the purpose of his or her training under the close personal supervision of a competent person, and
 (e) in circumstances where the operator's visibility is restricted, have auxiliary devices as listed in *Schedule 6* installed to improve visibility, unless a risk assessment shows that the auxiliary devices are not required.

 (2) On all construction sites on which transport vehicles, earth-moving or materials-handling machinery or locomotives are used, the project supervisor for the construction stage shall ensure that—

 (a) safe and suitable access ways are provided for them, and
 (b) traffic and pedestrian routes are so organised and controlled, including, where appropriate, by the provision of a traffic and pedestrain management plan, as to secure their safe operation.

Rails and rail tracks.

88. (1) A contractor responsible for a construction site shall ensure for that site that all rails on a construction site on which any locomotive, truck, wagon or rolling stock moves—

 (a) have an even running surface, are sufficiently and adequately supported and are of adequate length and guage,
 (b) are securely jointed,
 (c) are securely fastened to sleepers or bearers,

(d) are supported on a surface sufficiently firm to prevent undue movement of the rails,

(e) are laid in straight lines or in curves of such radii that the locomotive, truck, wagon or rolling stock can be moved freely and without danger of derailment, and

(f) are provided with an adequate stop or buffer on each rail at each end of the track.

(2) The relevant contractor for a construction site shall ensure that all rails and equipment referred to in this Regulation are properly maintained, but *paragraph (1) (b)* and *(c)* do not apply if other adequate steps are taken—

(a) to ensure the proper junction of the rails,

(b) to prevent any material variation in the gauge of the rails, and

(c) to arrest any locomotive, truck, wagon or rolling stock running out of control.

Clearance.

89. (1) A contractor responsible for a construction site shall ensure for that site in connection with the erection, installation, working or use of any line of rails on which any locomotive, truck, wagon or rolling stock moves, that there is adequate clearance so that persons are not likely to be crushed or trapped—

(a) by any locomotive, truck, wagon or rolling stock, or

(b) by any part of a load on any locomotive, truck, wagon or rolling stock.

(2) Where it is not practicable to provided clearance in accordance with *paragraph (1),* the relevant contractor shall provide or cause to be provided such suitable arrangements as are necessary to ensure that persons at work are not exposed to unnecessary risks.

Riding in insecure positions on vehicles, etc.

90. (1) No person at work on a construction site shall ride, and no person supervising a person at work on a construction site shall require or permit another person to ride, on the buffer, step, running board or any other insecure position on any—

(a) transport vehicle, earthmoving or materials-handling machinery, or

(b) locomotive, truck, wagon or rolling stock.

(2) A person at work on a construction site shall ride only on the part of any—

(a) transport vehicle, earthmoving or materials-handling machinery, or

(b) locomotive, truck, wagon or rolling stock

designed and intended for that purpose.

Vehicles near edge of excavations, etc.

91. A contractor responsible for a construction site shall ensure that adequate measures are taken, where necessary, so as to prevent any vehicle or machinery on the site from overturning or overunning the edge of an excavation, shaft, embankment or earthwork when the vehicle or equipment is used for tipping material—

(a) into the excavation or shaft,
(b) over the edge of any embankment or earthwork, or
(c) into water.

Protection of driver.

92. A contractor responsible for a construction site shall ensure for that site that, where appropriate, excavating machinery and materials-handling machinery comply with any relevant Directive of the European Communities which is applicable as regards the protection of the driver—

(a) against being crushed if the machine overturns, and
(b) against falling objects.

PART 12

DEMOLITION

Application of Part 12.

93. This Part applies to the demolition of the whole or any substantial part a structure.

Safety precautions and supervision.

94. A contractor responsible for a construction site shall ensure for that site that when the demolition of any structure is likely to present danger to persons at work or others, that—

(a) appropriate precautions, methods and written procedures are adopted, including those for the disposal of waste or residues, and
(b) the work is planned and undertaken only under the supervision of a competent person.

Fire and flooding.

95. A contractor responsible for a construction site shall ensure for that site, before demolition work is commenced and during the progress of the work, that appropriate steps are taken to prevent danger to persons at work and others on the site from risk of—

(a) fire or explosion through leakage or accumulation of gas or vapur, and

(b) flooding.

Precautions in connection with demolition.

96. (1) A contractor responsible for a construction site shall ensure for that site that no part of a structure where demolition is carried out is so overloaded with debris or materials as to render in unsafe to any person.

(2) A contractor responsible for a construction site shall ensure for that site that the following operations are carried out under the direction of a competent person and only by persons trained and experienced in the kind of work involved:

(a) the actual demolition of a structure or part thereof, except where there is no risk of a collapse of any part of the structure in the course of, or as a result of, the demolition which would endanger any person;

(b) the actual demolition of any part of structure where there is a risk of collapse, whether of that or of any part of the structure in the course of, or as a result of, the demolition;

(c) the cutting of reinforced or prestressed concrete, steelwork or ironwork forming part of the structure which is being demolished.

(3) Before any steelwork or ironwork is cut or released on a construction site, the relevant contractor shall ensure that precautions are taken to avoid danger from any sudden twist, spring or collapse.

(4) Where demolition is being carried out on a construction site, the relevant contractor shall ensure that all appropriate precautions are taken to avoid danger from collapse of a structure when any party of the framing is removed from a framed or partly framed structure.

(5) The relevant contractor on a construction site shall ensure that, before demolition is commenced and during the progress of the work on the site, precautions, where necessary, are taken by adequate shoring or otherwise to prevent the accidental collapse of—

(a) any part of the relevant structure, or

(b) any adjoining structure,

which may endanger any person.

(6) *paragraph (5)* does not apply in relation to any person actually engaged in erecting or placing shoring or other safeguards for the

purpose of compliance with *paragraph (5)*, if appropriate precautions, so far as is reasonably practicable, are taken to ensure the person's safety and health.

(7) The relevant contractor on a construction site—

(a) before demolition is commenced, and
(b) during the progress of the work

shall take or cause to be taken appropriate steps on the site to ensure that there is no danger to any person from electric cables, gas pipes, water mains, sewers or other underground watercourses.

(8) The relevant contractor shall ensure that appropriate steps are taken to suppress, either by water sprays or other means, any dust generated during the process of demolition.

PART 13

ROADS, ETC.

Works on roads, footpaths and cycle tracks.

97. A contractor responsible for a construction site, on which, any part of a road, footpath or cycle track is opened, excavated, broken up or obstructed by plant or equipment or by materials for the purpose of performing construction work, shall ensure for that site that the following measures are taken to protect the safety of persons at work and others in the course of the work being carried on:

(a) adequate guarding and lighting is provided, and traffic signs are placed and maintained, and where necessary operated, as reasonably required for the safe guidance or direction of persons, having regard, in particular, to the needs of people with disabilities;
(b) the works are supervised by a competent person who has been issued with a valid construction skills registration card as referred to in *Schedule 4*;
(c) there is on site, at all times when the works are in progress, at least one person who has been issued with a valid construction skills registration card as referred to in *Schedule 4*.

PART 14

CONSTRUCTION SITE WELFARE FACILITIES

Shelters and accommodation for clothing and for taking meals.

98. (1) Subject to *paragraphs (2)* and *(3)*, a contractor responsible for a construction site, shall provide or cause to be provided at or in the immediate vicinity of the site for the use of persons at work and conveniently accessible to them—

(a) adequate and suitable enclosed accommodation for taking shelter during interruptions of work owing to bad weather and for depositing clothing not worn during working hours, being accommodation containing—

    (i) where there are more than 5 persons at work, adequate and suitable means of enabling them to warm themselves and to dry wet clothing, or

    (ii) where there are 5 persons or less at work, such arrangements as are practicable for enabling them to warm themselves and for drying wet clothing,

(b) adequate and suitable accommodation for the deposit of protective clothing used for work and kept, when not in use, at or in the immediate vicinity, with such arrangements as are practicable for drying the clothing if it becomes wet,

(c) adequate and suitable accommodation affording protection from the weather and including sufficient tables with impermeable surfaces and seats with backs, for taking meals,

(d) facilities for boiling water and, where there are more than 5 persons at work and heated food is not otherwise available, adequate facilities for heating food and, where appropriate, for preparing food, and

(e) an adequate supply of potable drinking water and, where appropriate another suitable non-alcoholic beverage, at a convenient point or convenient points.

(2) In determining whether accommodation of any kind provided in pursuance of *paragraph (1)(c)* at any time and place is adequate, regard shall be had to the number of the persons at work who appear to be likely to use such accommodation at that time and place.

(3) For the purpose of *paragraph (1),* in determining whether accommodation is conveniently accessible account shall be taken of any transport provided by the relevant contractor for the persons at work.

(4) The relevant contractor shall ensure that all accommodation provided in pursuance of *paragraph (1)* is—

(a) properly ventilated, adequately lighted, kept in a clean, hygienic and orderly condition, and

(b) not used for the deposit or storage of building materials or plant.

Changing rooms and lockers.

99. (1) A contractor responsible for a construction site shall ensure for that site that—

(a) appropriate changing rooms are provided for persons at work if they have to wear special work clothes and if, for reasons of health or propriety, they cannot be expected to change in another area, and

(b) the changing rooms are easily accessible, are of sufficient capacity and are provided with seating.

(2) If circumstances so require where work clothes are likely to be contaminated by dangerous substances, atmospheric conditions or the place of work, the relevant contractor shall provide or cause to be provided—

(a) facilities to enable working clothes to be kept in a place separate from personal clothing and effects, and

(b) separate changing rooms or separate use of changing rooms for men and women.

(3) If changing rooms are not required as referred to in *paragraph (1)*, the relevant contractor shall ensure that every person at work is provided with a place to lock away his or her own clothes and personal effects.

Washing facilities.

100. (1) A contractor responsible for a construction site shall ensure for that site that adequate and suitable facilities for washing appropriate to the numbers of persons at work and the nature and duration of the work are provided.

(2) Subject to paragraph (4), a contractor responsible for a construction site where there are reasonable grounds for believing that the work to be undertaken on the site will not be completed within 30 working days after its commencement, shall ensure that the facilities for washing referred to in *paragraph (1)* include—

(a) adequate troughs or basins having in every case a smooth impervious internal surface,

(b) adequate and suitable means of cleaning and drying, being either soap and towels or other means, as the case may require, and

(c) a sufficient supply of hot and cold or warm running water.

(3) Subject to *paragraph (4)*, where there are

(a) more than 100 persons at work on a construction site, and

(b) reasonable grounds for believing that the work to be undertaken on the site will not be completed within 12 months after its commencement,

in lieu of providing troughs or basins mentioned in *paragraph (2) (a)*, the contractor responsible for the site shall ensure that washbasins are provided on the following scale, that is to say, 6 with the additional of one for every unit 20 persons at work by which the number of persons exceeds 100, any fraction of a unit 20 persons being treated as one.

(4) A contractor responsible for a construction site on which persons are at work in a process in which a dangerous substance is used shall for that site—

    (a) provide an adequate number of nail brushes, and

    (b) for the purpose of *paragraph (2) (a)* or *(3)*, as may be appropriate provide one trough, basin, or washbasin as may be appropriate, every 5 persons at work.

(5) A contractor responsible for a construction site shall ensure for that site that—

    (a) the washing facilities provided are conveniently accessible from the accommodation for taking meals and shall be adequately lighted, properly ventilated and kept in a clean and orderly condition,

    (b) seperate washbasins, or separate use of washbasins for men and women are provided, when so required for reasons of propriety,

    (c) suitable showers in sufficient numbers are provided for persons at work if required by the nature of the work or for health reasons,

    (d) provision is made for separate shower rooms or separate use of shower rooms for men and women,

    (e) the shower rooms are sufficiently large to permit each person to wash without hindrance in conditions of an appropriate standard of hygiene,

    (f) the showers are equipped with hot and cold running water, and

    (g) where the rooms housing the showers or washbasins are separate from the changing rooms, there is easy communication between them.

Sanitary conveniences.

101. (1) A contractor responsible for a construction site shall ensure for that site—

    (a) that subject to *subparagraph (d)*, at least one suitable sanitary convenience is provided, not being a convenience suitable only as an urinal, for every 20 persons at work at work on the site,

    (b) that every sanitary convenience required under these Regulations—

        (i) if practicable, discharges into main sewer,

        (ii) is sufficiently ventilated and does not communicate with any workroom or messroom except through the open air or through an intervening ventilated space,

        (iii) is under cover and so partitioned off as to secure privacy,

> (iv) other than a convenience suitable only as an urinal, has a proper door and fastening,
>
> (v) is conveniently accessible to persons at work at all times while they are at the site and, where practicable, is convenient to the washing facilities, and
>
> (vi) is maintained in a clean and hygienic condition,
>
> (c) that provision is made for separate sanitary conveniences or separate use of sanitary conveniences for men and women, and
>
> (d) where there are more then 100 persons at work on the site and sufficient urinal accommodation is provided, that there is at least one suitable sanitary convenience as described in *subparagraph (a)*—
>
> > (i) for every 25 persons at work on the site up to and including the first 100, and
> >
> > (ii) for every 35 persons at work on the site after the first 100.
>
> (2) In calculating the number of conveniences required—
>
> > (a) by *paragraph (1)(a)*, any number of persons—
> >
> > > (i) less than 20 shall be reckoned as 20, and
> > >
> > > (ii) any number a multiple of 20 shall be reckoned as being the nearest lower number which is a multiple of 20, and
> >
> > (b) by *paragraph (1)(d)* any number of persons—
> >
> > > (i) less than 25 or 35, as may be appropriate, shall be reckoned as 25 or 35, and
> > >
> > > (ii) any number not a multiple of 25 or 35, may be appropriate, shall be reckoned as being the nearest lower number which is a multiple of 25 or 35.

Accommodation areas.

102. A contractor responsible for a construction site shall ensure that fixed living accommodation areas on the site, unless used only in exceptional cases,

> (a) have sufficient sanitary equipment, a rest room and a leisure room,
>
> (b) are equipped with beds, cupboards, tables and seats with backs, taking account of the number of persons at work, and
>
> (c) are allocated taking account, where appropriate, of the presence of persons of both sexes.

Safe access to places where facilities are provided.

103. A contractor responsible for a construction site shall ensure for the site that—

(a) safe means of access and egress are provided and maintained to and from every place at which any of the facilities referred to in this Part are situated, and

(b) every such place is made safe and kept safe for persons using the facilities.

Pregnant women and nursing mothers.

104. A contractor responsible for a construction site shall ensure that pregnant women and nursing mothers at work on the site are provided with appropriate facilities as set out in other relevant legislation.

Persons with disabilities.

105. A contractor responsible for a construction site shall ensure for that construction site that places of work, where necessary, are organized to take account of persons at work with disabilities, in particular as regards doors, passageways, staircases, washbasins, lavatories and work-stations used or occupied directly by those persons.

Regulations 12, 15 and 16   SCHEDULE 1

NON-EXHAUSTIVE LIST OF WORK INVOLVING PARTICULAR RISKS TO THE SAFETY,
HEALTH AND WELFARE OF PERSONS AT WORK

1.   Work which puts persons at work at risk of—

(a) falling from a height,
(b) burial under earthfalls, or
(c) engulfment in swampland,

where the risk is particularly aggravated by the nature of the work or processes used or by the environment at the place of work or construction site.

2.   Work which puts persons at work at risk from chemical or biological substances constituting a particular danger to the safety and health of such persons or involving a Statutory requirement for health monitoring.

3.   Work with ionizing radiation requiring the designation of controlled or supervised areas as defined in Directive 96/29/Euratom[2].

4.   Work near high voltage power lines.

5.   Work exposing persons at work to the risk of drowning.

6.   Work on wells, underground earthworks and tunnels.

7.   Work carried out by divers at work having a system of air supply.

8.   Work carried out in a caisson with a compressed-air atmosphere.

9.   Work involving the use of explosives.

10. Work involving the assembly or dismantling of heavy prefabricated components.

---

[2]   OJ L159 29th June 1996

SCHEDULE 2

NON-EXHAUSTIVE LIST OF MATTERS TO BE CONSIDERED IN PARTICULAR AS REGARDS THE APPLICATION OF THE GENERAL PRINCIPLES OF PREVENTION TO CONSTRUCTION WORK UNDER THESE REGULATIONS

1. Keeping the construction site in good order and in a satisfactory state of cleanliness.

2. Choosing the location of workstations bearing in mind how access to them is obtained, and determining routes or areas for the passage and movement of equipment.

3. The conditions under which various materials are handled.

4. Technical maintenance, pro-commissioning checks and regular checks on installations and equipment with a view to correcting any faults which might affect the safety, health and welfare of persons at work.

5. The demarcation and laying-out of areas for the storage of various materials, in particular where dangerous materials or substances are concerned.

6. The conditions under which the dangerous materials used are removed.

7. The storage and disposal or removal of waste and debris.

8. The adaptation, based on progress made on the construction site, of the actual time to be allocated for the various types of work or work stages.

9. Co-operation between employers and self-employed persons.

10. Interaction with industrial activities at the place within which or in the vicinity of which the construction site is located.

Safety Awareness Scheme

The requirements under these Regulations for the issue of a valid safety awareness registration card are successful completion of any one of the following:

(a) the FÁS Safe Pass training programme;

(b) an equivalent safety awareness scheme approved by FÁS;

(c) an equivalent safety awareness scheme in another Member State of the European Communities approved by FÁS.

(2) A valid safety awareness registration card is one of the following:

(a) the FÁS Safe Pass registration card;

(b) a registration card, with photographic identification, issued by such body as may be prescribed by the Minister, for the purpose of the issuing of safety awareness cards;

(c) a registration card issued in association with a scheme referred to in *paragraph 1(c)*.

CONSTRUCTION SKILLS CERTIFICATION SCHEME

1. (1) The requirement for the issue of a FETAC award under the Construction Skills Certification Scheme is successful completion of training under the scheme in any of the following tasks:

    (a) Scaffolding – basic;
    (b) Scaffolding – advanced;
    (c) Mobile tower scaffold – where the employee has not been trained in the task referred to at *subparagraphs (a)* or *(b);*
    (d) Tower crane operation;
    (e) Self erecting tower crane operation – where the employee has not been trained in the task referred to at *subparagraph (d)*;
    (f) Slinging/signalling;
    (g) Telescopic handler operation;
    (h) Tractor/dozer operation;
    (i) Mobile crane operation;
    (j) Crawler crane operation;
    (k) Articulated dumper operation;
    (l) Site dumper operation;
    (m) 180° excavator operation;
    (n) Mini-digger operation – where the employee has not been trained in the task referred to at *subparagraph (m);*
    (o) 360° excavator operation;
    (p) Roof and wall cladding/sheeting;
    (q) Built-up roof felting;
    (r) Signing, lighting and guarding on roads
    (s) Locating under-ground services;
    (t) Shotfiring;
    (u) Such other construction related tasks as may be prescribed by the Minister.

    (2) Where it is necessary to gain experience prior to undertaking a programme related to the tasks listed at *paragraph (1)* it is permissible for a person to undertake those tasks during the training period required by the programme if—

        (a) the person concerned is at all times under the close personal supervision of a person who is in possession of a valid construction skills registration card relevant to the task concerned, and
        (b) the person concerned is in possession of an appropriate identification identifying the person as a trainee in the relevant skills and an associated documented log-book recording experience gained in the skill in which the person is undergoing training.

2. The requirements for the issue of a valid construction skills registration card under the Construction Skills Certification Scheme are possession of—

(a) the relevant FETAC award under the Construction Skills Certification Scheme,

(b) an equivalent FETAC award, or

(c) an equivalent award approved by a body in another Member State of the European Communities recognised by FÁS as equivalent to the FETAC award under the Construction Skills Certification Scheme.

3. (1) "Scaffolding – basic" listed in *paragraph 1(1)(a)* means general scaffolding operations (other than those covered by "Scaffolding – advanced" listed in *paragraph 1(1)(b))*.

(2) "Scaffolding – advanced" listed in *paragraph 1(I)(b)* includes any or all of the following:

(a) construction of special scaffolds as may be specified in a relevant code of practice;

(b) construction of scaffolds that may require design or calculation, including any such scaffold as may be specified in a relevant code of practice;

(c) such other tasks as may be prescribed by the Minister.

Regulation 23 SCHEDULE 5

PROCEDURE FOR SELECTION OF SITE REPRESENTATIVES

The selection of a site safety representative shall proceed as follows:

(1) If a site safety representative is selected by the persons at work on a construction site at any time after commencement of activities on the site, that person shall be recognised as such by the project supervisor for the construction stage. The particulars listed at *paragraph 6* shall be noted in writing by the project supervisor for the construction stage.

(2) If a safety representative has previously been selected under section 25 of the Act by the employees of any of the contractors on the construction site, the views of all persons at work on the site at the time must be taken into account when confirming that person as site safety representative.

(3) If, at the time the number of persons at work on the construction site normally exceeds 20 and there is no site safety representative the project supervisor for the construction stage shall invite all persons working on the site at that time to elect a site safety representative from amongst their number. If those working on the site are unwilling to organise a selection process themselves and request the project supervisor for the construction stage to do so the project supervisor shall organise the election.

(4) If a site safety representative is not selected under *paragraph 3* the project supervisor for the construction stage shall invite persons working on the construction site or their representatives to nominate persons willing to undertake the role. If more than one name is put forward the project supervisor for the construction stage shall determine which candidate has the most support from all persons employed on the site. The person who has the most support shall be deemed selected.

(5) If no site safety representative has been selected under *paragraphs 1* to *4*, the project supervisor for the construction stage shall nominate a provisional site safety representative. If subsequently a site safety representative is selected by a process involving more than 50 per cent of the person working on the construction site a particular time then that person shall be deemed to be the site safety representative.

(6) The project supervisor for the construction stage shall take steps to inform all persons who are at work on the construction site at the time of the selection and subsequently of the name of the site safety representative. The project supervisor for the construction stage must keep available for inspection by an inspector a record of the name of the site safety representative and details of the selection process.

LIST OF VEHICLES REQUIRING AUXILIARY DEVICES AND VISUAL AIDS.

Machine type	Reversing and visual aids required
Off-road dump trucks (trailer to rear of driver), payload greater than 7 Tonnes	Reversing alarm and flashing beacon with CCTV or convex mirrors or a combination of both to allow vision from the driver's seat of all points more than 1 metre high and 1 metre from the machine at each side and at rear of driver
Dumpers (front tip) no cab	Reversing alarm and flashing beacon
Dumpers (front tip) with cab	Convex mirrors; reversing alarm and flashing beacon
Wheel loaders (loading shovels), including skid steer loaders.	Reversing alarm and flashing beacon with CCTV or convex mirrors or a combination of both to allow vision from the driver's seat of all points more than 1 metre high and 1 metre from the machine at each side and at rear of driver
Backhoe loaders	Convex mirrors; reversing alarm and flashing beacon
All 360° excavators	Movement alarm and flashing beacon with CCTV or convex mirrors or a combination of both to allow vision from the driver's seat (without slewing) at all points more than 1 metre high and 1 metre from the machine
Scrapers	Reversing alarm and flashing beacon with CCTV or convex mirrors or a combination of both to allow vision from the driver's seat of all points more than 1 metre high and 1 metre from the machine at each side and at rear of driver
All tracked type tractors (bulldozers)	Reversing alarm and flashing beacon with CCTV or convex mirrors a combination of both to allow vision at all points more than 1 metre high and 1 metre from the machine at each side and at rear of driver
Graders	CCTV, convex mirrors, reversing alarm and flashing beacon

(Continued)

Telescopic handlers	Reversing alarm and flashing beacon with CCTV or convex mirrors or a combination of both to allow vision from the driver's seat of all points more than 1 metre high and 1 metre from the machine at each side and at rear of driver
Compactors/rollers without cab and seat to rear	Reversing alarm and flashing beacon
Compactors/rollers with cab and seat to rear	Convex mirrors, reversing alarm and flashing beacon
All compactors/ rollers	Reversing alarm and flashing beacon with CCTV or convex mirrors, or a combination of both, to allow vision at all points more than 1 metre high and 1 metre from the machine at each side and at rear of driver
Road planer	Convex mirrors, reversing alarm and flashing beacon
Road pavers	Convex mirrors, reversing alarm and flashing beacon

GIVEN under my hand,
28th September 2006.

Tony Killeen
Minister for State at the
Department of Enterprise,
Trade and Employment.

HEALTH AND SAFETY AUTHORITY

Safety, Health and Welfare at Work (Construction) Regulations, 2006

Approved Form (AF 2)   Regulation 22

Particulars to be notified by Project Supervisor for the Construction Stage to the Health and Safety Authority before the construction work begins

NOTE:

This form is to be used to notify the Health & Safety Authority of any project covered by the Safety, Health and Welfare at Work (Construction) Regulations 2006, which will last longer than 30 days or 500 person days. It can also be used to provide changes to initial notification of projects.

Any day on which construction work is carried out (including holidays and weekends) should be counted, even if the work on that day is of short duration. A person day is one individual, including supervisors and specialists, carrying out construction work for one normal working shift.

This Notification is to be made by Registered Post to HSA, Metropolitan Building, James Joyce Street, Dublin 1; or as may be directed by the Authority.

The project supervisor for the construction stage shall clearly display on the construction site a copy of this form.

1 **Client:** Provide name, full address, telephone number and e-mail address for the Client. If more than one Client, please attach details of all Clients on a separate sheet.

Name:	
Address:	
Telephone:	E-Mail:

2 **Project Supervisor Design Process and Health & Safety Coordinator:** Provide name, full address, telephone number and e-mail address for the PSDP and Health & Safety Coordinator for the Design Process.

PSDP Name:		H&S C. Name:	
Address:		Address:	
Telephone:		Telephone:	
E-Mail:		E-Mail:	

3 **Project Supervisor Construction Stage and Health & Safety Coordinator:** Provide name, full address, telephone number and e-mail address for the PSCS and Health & Safety Coordinator for the Construction Stage.

PSCS Name:		H&S C. Name:	
Address:		Address:	
Telephone:		Telephone:	
E-Mail:		E-Mail:	

4 **Information on Construction Work:** Please provide your details / estimates for the following.

Description of Project:	
Address of Site:	

The planned date for the commencement of the construction work:	
How long the construction work is expected to take (in weeks):	
The maximum number of people carrying out construction work on site at any one time.	
The number of Contractors expected to work on site.	

5 **Information on Construction Work:** Provide name, full address & telephone number of those selected to work on this project (if required continue on a separate sheet).

Name	Address	Telephone and Email

Signed:	by or on behalf of the Project Supervisor for the Construction Stage
Position:	Date:

SAFETY, HEALTH AND WELFARE AT WORK (GENERAL APPLICATION) REGULATIONS 2007[*]

S.I. No. 299 of 2007

ARRANGEMENT OF REGULATIONS

PART 1

INTERPRETATION AND GENERAL

PART 2

WORKPLACE AND WORK EQUIPMENT

CHAPTER 1 — WORKPLACE

---

[*] All images reproduced in Schs 9 and 10 of these Regulations appear in black and white. To view the colour images, please consult the official version of the Regulations, as published by the Stationary Office and which can be downloaded at www.hsa.ie.

CHAPTER 2 — CONTROL OF VIBRATION AT WORK

PART 6

SENSITIVE RISK GROUPS

CHAPTER 1 — PROTECTION OF CHILDREN AND YOUNG PERSONS

CHAPTER 2 — PROTECTION OF PREGNANT, POST NATAL AND BREASTFEEDING EMPLOYEES

CHAPTER 3 — NIGHT WORK AND SHIFT WORK

Part D — Equipment that has a lifting function, is subject to Regulation 30 and is not subject to Regulation 52

Part E — Information to be contained in report of thorough examination

SCHEDULE 2

PERSONAL PROTECTIVE EQUIPMENT

Part A — Guide list of activities and sectors of activity which may require provision of personal protective equipment

Part B — Guide list of items of personal protective equipment

SCHEDULE 3

RISK FACTORS FOR MANUAL HANDLING OF LOADS

SCHEDULE 4

MINIMUM REQUIREMENTS FOR ALL DISPLAY SCREEN EQUIPMENT

SCHEDULE 5

PARTICULARS TO BE INCLUDED IN A REPORT OF INSPECTION

SCHEDULE 6

HAND-ARM VIBRATION AND WHOLE-BODY VIBRATION

Part A — Hand-arm vibration

Part B — Whole-body vibration

SCHEDULE 7

PROTECTION OF CHILDREN AND YOUNG PERSONS

Part A — Guide list of agents, processes and work

Part B — Processes and work

SCHEDULE 8

LISTS OF AGENTS, PROCESSES AND WORKING CONDITIONS RELATING TO PREGNANT, POST NATAL AND BREASTFEEDING EMPLOYEES

Part A — Pregnant, post natal and breastfeeding employees

Part B — Pregnant employees

Part C — Employees who are breastfeeding

SCHEDULE 9

SAFETY AND HEALTH SIGNS AT WORK

Part A — General requirements
Part B — Signboards
Part C — Signs on containers and pipes
Part D — Identification and location of fire-fighting equipment used exclusively for fire-fighting purposes
Part E — Signs used for obstacles and dangerous locations and for marking traffic routes
Part F — Illuminated signs
Part G — Acoustic signs
Part H — Verbal communication
Part I — Hand signals

SCHEDULE 10

EXPLOSIVE ATMOSPHERES

Part A — Classification of places where explosive atmospheres may occur
Part B — Warning sign for places where explosive atmospheres may occur

SAFETY, HEALTH AND WELFARE AT WORK
(GENERAL APPLICATION) REGULATIONS 2007

I, Tony Killeen, Minister of State at the Department of Enterprise, Trade and Employment, in exercise of powers conferred on me by section 58 of the Safety, Health and Welfare at Work Act 2005 (No. 10 of 2005) and the Enterprise, Trade and Employment (Delegation of Ministerial Functions) Order 2005 (S.I. No. 316 of 2005), after consultation with the Health and Safety Authority, hereby make the following regulations-

PART 1

INTERPRETATION AND GENERAL

Citation and commencement

1. (1) These Regulations may be cited as the Safety, Health and Welfare at Work (General Application) Regulations 2007.
    (2) These Regulations come into operation on 1 November 2007.

Interpretation

2. (1) In these Regulations:

    "Act" means the Safety, Health and Welfare at Work Act 2005 (No. 10 of 2005);

"lifting equipment" means work equipment for lifting, lowering loads or pile driving, and includes anything used for anchoring, fixing or supporting such equipment;

"personal protective equipment" means all equipment designed to be worn or held by an employee for protection against one or more hazards likely to endanger the employee's safety and health at work, and includes any additions and accessories to the equipment, if so designed, but does not include—

    (a) ordinary working clothes and uniforms not specifically designed to protect the safety and health of an employee,

    (b) personal protective equipment for the purposes of road transport,

    (c) sports equipment,

    (d) self-defence equipment or deterrent equipment, or

    (e) portable devices for detecting and signalling risks and nuisances;

"public road" means a road the responsibility for the maintenance of which lies on a road authority;

"road authority" means a county council, a city council or a town council (within the meaning of the Local Government Act 2001 (No. 37 of 2001)) other than the council of a town mentioned in Part 2 of Schedule 6 to that Act;

"work equipment" means any machinery, appliance, apparatus, tool or installation for use at work.

(2) An employer shall ensure that, where activities mentioned in sections 6 and 11(5) of the Act are being carried out, the safety, health and welfare of the employer's employees are protected as far as possible, taking account of the relevant statutory provisions.

(3) Without prejudice to the generality of section 19 of the Act, an employer shall, in identifying hazards and assessing risks under that section, take account of particular risks, if any, affecting employees working alone at the place of work or working in isolation at remote locations.

(4) Any reference in these Regulations to provisions encompassed in the generality of the Act shall be without prejudice to the requirements of those provisions in the Act.

Revocations and savings

3. (1) The following are revoked:

    (a) Factories (Report of Examination of Hoists and Lifts) Regulations 1956 (S.I. No. 182 of 1956),

    (b) Factories Act 1955 (Hoists and Lifts) (Exemption) Order 1957 (S.I. No. 80 of 1957),

    (c) Factories Act 1955 (Lifts) (Exemption) Order 1960 (S.I. No. 129 of 1960),

(d) Regulations 22 to 35 and 37 and 38 and the Schedule to the Docks (Safety, Health and Welfare) Regulations 1960 (S.I. No. 279 of 1960),

(e) Factories Act, 1955 (Hoistways) (Exemption) Order 1962 (S.I. No. 211 of 1962),

(f) Quarries (Electricity) Regulations 1972 (S.I. No. 50 of 1972),

(g) Mines (Electricity) Regulations 1972 (S.I. No. 51 of 1972),

(h) Quarries (General) Regulations 1974 (S.I. No. 146 of 1974) to the extent of in Regulation 3, the definitions of "lifting appliance" and "safe working load", Regulations 40 and 41, in the First Schedule "FORM No. 3" and "FORM No. 5" and the Second Schedule,

(i) Shipbuilding and Ship-Repairing (Safety, Health and Welfare) Regulations 1975 (S.I. No. 322 of 1975) to the extent of in Regulation 3(1), the definitions of "lifting equipment" and "lifting gear" and Regulations 32 to 48,

(j) Factories Act 1955 (Hoistways) (Exemption) Order 1976 (S.I. No. 236 of 1976),

(k) Factories Act 1955 (Hoists) (Exemption) Order 1977 (S.I. No. 13 of 1977),

(l) Mines (Electricity) (Amendment) Regulations 1979 (S.I. No. 125 of 1979),

(m) Quarries (Electricity) (Amendment) Regulations 1979 (S.I. No. 126 of 1979),

(n) Safety in Industry Acts 1955 and 1980 (Hoists and Hoistways) (Exemption) Order 1985 (S.I. No. 100 of 1985),

(o) Safety, Health and Welfare at Work (General Application) Regulations 1993 (S.I. No. 44 of 1993), other than Part X and the Twelfth Schedule,

(p) Safety, Health and Welfare at Work (Signs) Regulations 1995 (S.I. No. 132 of 1995),

(q) Safety, Health and Welfare at Work (Miscellaneous Welfare Provisions) Regulations 1995 (S.I. No. 358 of 1995),

(r) Safety, Health and Welfare at Work (Children and Young Persons) Regulations 1998 (S.I. No. 504 of 1998),

(s) Safety, Health and Welfare at Work (Night Work and Shift Work) Regulations 2000 (S.I. No. 11 of 2000),

(t) Safety, Health and Welfare at Work (Pregnant Employees etc.) Regulations 2000 (S.I. No. 218 of 2000),

(u) Safety, Health and Welfare at Work (General Application) (Amendment) Regulations 2001 (S.I. No. 188 of 2001),

(v) Regulations 80 to 123 of the Safety, Health and Welfare at Work (Construction) Regulations 2001 (S.I. No. 481 of 2001),

(w) Safety, Health and Welfare at Work (Explosive Atmospheres) Regulations 2003 (S.I. No. 258 of 2003),

(x) Safety, Health and Welfare at Work (Work at Height) Regulations 2006 (S.I. No. 318 of 2006),

(y) Safety, Health and Welfare at Work (Control of Vibration at Work) Regulations 2006 (S.I. No. 370 of 2006), and

(z) Safety, Health and Welfare at Work (Control of Noise at Work) Regulations 2006 (S.I. No. 371 of 2006), except Regulation 11(3) of those Regulations.

(2) Regulation 11(3) of the Safety, Health and Welfare at Work (Control of Noise at Work) Regulations 2006 (S.I. No. 371 of 2006) is revoked on 14 February, 2008.

PART 2

WORKPLACE AND WORK EQUIPMENT

CHAPTER 1 — WORKPLACE

Interpretation for Chapter 1

4. In this Chapter—

"place of work" means a place of work intended to house workstations on the premises of an undertaking and any other place within the area of the undertaking to which an employee has access in the course of his or her employment but does not include—

(a) means of transport used outside the undertaking or a place of work inside a means of transport,

(b) temporary or mobile work sites, including construction sites,

(c) extractive industries,

(d) fishing boats,

(e) fields, woods and land forming part of an agricultural or forestry undertaking but situated away from the undertaking's buildings.

Stability and solidity

5. An employer shall ensure that buildings which house places of work shall have a structure and solidity appropriate to the nature of their use.

Ventilation of enclosed places of work

6. An employer shall ensure that—

(a) sufficient fresh air is provided in enclosed places of work, having regard to the working methods used and the physical demands placed on the employer's employees,

(b) if a forced ventilation system is used, it is maintained in working order and any breakdown is indicated by a control system if necessary for the safety and health of employees,

(c) if air-conditioning or mechanical ventilation installations are used, they operate in such a way that employees are not exposed to draughts which cause discomfort, and

(d) any deposit or dirt likely to create an immediate danger to the safety and health of employees by polluting the atmosphere is removed without delay.

Room temperature

7. (1) An employer shall ensure that—

(a) during working hours, the temperature in rooms containing workstations is appropriate for human beings, having regard to the working methods being used and the physical demands placed on the employees,

(b) for sedentary office work, a minimum temperature of 17.5°C, so far as is reasonably practicable, is achieved and maintained at every workstation after the first hour's work,

(c) for other sedentary work, at every workstation where a substantial proportion of the work is done sitting and does not involve serious physical effort, a minimum temperature of 16°C is, so far as is reasonably practicable, achieved and maintained after the first hour's work,

(d) means are available to enable persons at work to measure the temperature in any workplace inside a building,

(e) the temperature in rest areas, rooms for duty staff, sanitary facilities, canteens and first-aid rooms is appropriate to the particular purpose of such areas, and

(f) in relation to windows, skylights and glass partitions, excessive effects of sunlight are avoided in places of work, having regard to the nature of the work and the characteristics of the place of work.

(2) The temperature referred to in paragraphs (1)(b) and (c) shall be a dry bulb temperature taken at the working position of the employee at 1.1 m above the floor surface.

(3) Where, due to process requirements, a workplace temperature below 16°C is necessary, the employer shall assess the risks and take any necessary measures to ensure the safety, health and welfare of the employer's employees.

Natural and artificial lighting

8. An employer shall ensure that—

(a) places of work receive, as far as possible, sufficient natural light and are equipped with artificial lighting adequate for the protection of the safety and health of the employer's employees,

(b) lighting installations in rooms containing workstations and in passageways are placed in such a way that there is no risk of accident to the employer's employees as a result of the type of lighting fitted, and

(c) places of work in which the employer's employees are especially exposed to risks in the event of failure of artificial lighting are provided with emergency lighting of adequate intensity.

Floors, walls, ceilings and roofs of rooms

9. (1) An employer shall ensure that—

(a) the floors of rooms have no dangerous bumps, holes or slopes and are fixed, stable and, so far as is reasonably practicable, not slippery,

(b) the surfaces of floors, walls and ceilings in rooms are such that they can be cleaned or refurbished to an appropriate standard of hygiene,

(c) access to roofs and suspended ceilings made of materials of insufficient strength is not permitted unless—

    (i) equipment is provided to ensure that the work can be carried out in a safe manner, and

    (ii) appropriate warning signs in accordance with Part 7, Chapter 1 are placed at such access points,

(d) transparent and translucent walls, in particular all-glass partitions, in rooms or in the vicinity of workstations and traffic routes are—

    (i) clearly indicated,

    (ii) made of safety material, or

    (iii) shielded from such places or traffic routes,

    to prevent employees from coming into contact with the walls or being injured should the walls shatter, and

(e) places of work containing workstations are adequately thermally insulated, bearing in mind the type of undertaking involved and the physical activity of the employees.

(2) Paragraph (1)(e) does not apply to places of work in use prior to 31 December 1992 except as regards modifications, extensions or conversions made after that date.

Windows and skylights

10. An employer shall ensure that—

(a) where it is possible for employees to open, close, adjust or secure windows, skylights and ventilators—

> (i)   it may be done safely, and
> (ii)   when open, such windows, skylights and ventilators are not positioned so as to constitute a hazard to employees, and
>
> (b) windows and skylights can be cleaned without risk to the safety, health or welfare of persons carrying out this work or of other persons present—
>
> (i)   by design,
> (ii)   by being fitted with devices, or
> (iii) in conjunction with the use of equipment.

Doors and gates

11.   An employer shall ensure that—

> (a) the position, number and dimensions of doors and gates, and the materials used in their construction, are determined by the nature and use of the rooms or areas and are appropriate for the safety, health and welfare of employees,
> (b) swing doors and swing gates are transparent or have see-through panels,
> (c) transparent doors are appropriately marked at a conspicuous level,
> (d) if transparent or translucent surfaces in doors and gates are not made of safety material and, if there is a danger that employees may be injured if a door or gate should shatter, the surfaces are protected against breakage,
> (e) sliding doors and sliding gates are fitted with a safety device to prevent them from being derailed or falling over,
> (f) doors and gates opening upwards are fitted with a mechanism to secure them against falling back,
> (g) there are doors or gates for pedestrian traffic in the immediate vicinity of gates intended primarily for vehicle traffic, unless it is safe for pedestrians to pass through, and such doors or gates are clearly marked and kept unobstructed at all times, and
> (h) mechanical doors and gates—
>
> (i)   function in such a way that there is no risk of accident to employees,
> (ii)   are fitted with easily identifiable and accessible emergency shut-down devices, and
> (iii) can be opened manually where they operate as an emergency exit, unless they open automatically in the event of a power failure.

Emergency routes and exits

12.   Without predjudice to section 11 of the Act, the Fire Services Acts 1981 and 2003 (No. 30 of 1981 and No.15 of 2003) and other relevant legislation, an employer shall ensure that—

(a) emergency routes to emergency exits and the exits themselves are kept clear at all times and lead as directly as possible to the open air or to a safe area,

(b) in the event of danger, it is possible for employees to evacuate all workstations quickly and as safely as possible,

(c) the number, distribution and dimensions of the emergency routes and exits are adequate for the use, equipment and dimensions of the place of work and the maximum number of persons that may be present,

(d) emergency exit doors open outwards,

(e) any sliding or revolving doors that are fitted are not used, or intended to be used, as emergency exits,

(f) emergency doors and gates are not so locked or fastened that they cannot be easily and immediately opened by any person who may need to use them in an emergency,

(g) specific emergency routes and exits are indicated by signs in accordance with Part 7, Chapter 1 and such signs are placed at appropriate points and are adequately durable,

(h) emergency routes and exits, and the traffic routes and doors giving access to them, are free from obstruction so that they can be used at any time without hindrance, and

(i) emergency routes and exits requiring illumination are provided with emergency lighting of adequate intensity in case the lighting fails.

Fire detection and fire fighting

13. Without predjudice to section 11 of the Act, the Fire Services Acts 1981 and 2003 (No. 30 of 1981 and No.15 of 2003) and other relevant legislation, an employer shall ensure that—

(a) a place of work is equipped with appropriate fire-fighting equipment and, as necessary, fire detectors and an alarm system, taking account of—

   (i) the dimensions and use of the buildings,
   (ii) the equipment they contain,
   (iii) the physical and chemical characteristics of the substances present, and
   (iv) the maximum potential number of people present,

(b) non-automatic fire-fighting equipment is—

   (i) easily accessible and simple to use, and
   (ii) indicated by signs in accordance with Part 7, Chapter 1 and the signs are placed at appropriate points and are adequately durable, and

(c) fire detection equipment and fire-fighting equipment is—

(i)   inspected and maintained as frequently as necessary to ensure that it is in good working order, and

(ii) serviced by a competent person as frequently as necessary.

Movement of pedestrians and vehicles in danger areas

14.   An employer shall ensure that—

(a)   outdoor and indoor places of work are organised in such a way that pedestrians and vehicles can circulate in a safe manner,

(b)   traffic routes, including stairs, fixed ladders and loading bays and ramps, are designed, located and dimensioned to ensure easy, safe and appropriate access for pedestrians or vehicles in such a way as not to endanger employees employed in the vicinity of such routes,

(c)   routes used for pedestrian traffic or goods traffic, or for both, are dimensioned in accordance with the number of potential users and the type of undertaking,

(d)   sufficient safety clearance is provided for pedestrians if means of transport are used on traffic routes,

(e)   sufficient clearance is allowed between vehicle traffic routes and doors, gates, passages for pedestrians, corridors and staircases,

(f)   pedestrian routes and traffic routes are clearly identified for the protection of employees, where the use and equipment of places of work so require, and

(g)   if the places of work contain danger areas in which, owing to the nature of the work, there is a risk of an employee or objects falling, these are—

(i)   equipped, as far as possible, with devices preventing unauthorised employees from entering those areas, and

(ii) clearly indicated, and

appropriate measures are taken to protect employees authorised to enter danger areas.

Specific measures for escalators and travelators

15.   An employer shall ensure that escalators and travelators—

(a)   function safely,

(b)   are equipped with any necessary safety devices, and

(c)   are fitted with easily identifiable and accessible emergency shutdown devices.

Loading bays and ramps

16.   An employer shall ensure that—

(a)   loading bays and ramps are suitable for the dimensions of the loads to be transported,

(b) loading ramps are, as far as possible, safe enough to prevent employees from falling off,

(c) loading bays have at least one exit point, and

(d) loading bays longer than the width of 5 vehicles have an exit point at each end where technically feasible, or alternatively an appropriate refuge is provided which may be used to avoid persons at work being struck or crushed by a vehicle.

Room dimensions and air space in rooms and freedom of movement at the workstation

17.   An employer shall ensure that—

(a) workrooms have sufficient surface area, height and air space to allow employees to perform their work without risk to their safety, health or welfare, and

(b) the dimensions of the free unoccupied area at a workstation are calculated to allow employees sufficient freedom of movement to perform their work and, where this is not possible for reasons specific to the workstation, the employee is provided with sufficient freedom of movement near his or her workstation.

General welfare requirements

18.   An employer shall ensure that—

(a) every place of work is kept in a clean state and accumulations of dirt, refuse, trade refuse and waste are removed by a suitable method as frequently as necessary to maintain an appropriate level of safety and health,

(b) the floor of every workroom is cleaned by a suitable method as frequently as necessary to maintain an appropriate level of safety and health,

(c) where any employees have in the course of their employment reasonable opportunities for sitting without detriment to their work or, where a substantial proportion of any work done by employees can properly be done sitting,

   (i)   suitable facilities for sitting are provided and maintained for their use, or

   (ii)   if this is not practical, they are otherwise ergonomically supported,

(d) an adequate supply of potable drinking water is provided and maintained at suitable points conveniently accessible to all employees,

(e) suitable and adequate facilities for boiling water and taking meals are provided and maintained for the use of employees, or that employees have reasonable access to other suitable and adequate facilities for the taking of meals, and

(f) the taking of meals by employees is prohibited at any location in the place of work where there is likely to be a risk to safety, health or welfare.

Rest rooms and rest areas

19. An employer shall ensure that—

    (a) where, because of—

        (i) the type of activity carried out, or
        (ii) the presence of more than a certain number of employees, and
        (iii) the safety, health and welfare of employees so requires, employees are provided with an easily accessible rest room or appropriate rest area, except where the employees are employed in offices or similar workrooms providing relaxation during breaks,

    (b) rest rooms are large enough and equipped with tables with easily cleaned surfaces and seats with backs, adequate for the number of employees, and

    (c) if working hours are regularly and frequently interrupted and there is no rest room, other rooms are provided in which employees can stay during such interruptions, wherever this is required for the safety, health or welfare of employees.

Sanitary and washing facilities

20. An employer shall provide and maintain and keep in a clean state—

    (a) adequate and suitable sanitary and washing facilities for the use of employees,

    (b) an adequate number of lavatories and washbasins, with hot and cold running water, in the vicinity of workstations, rest rooms, changing rooms and rooms housing showers,

    (c) separate use of lavatories or washbasins for men and women, when so required for reasons of propriety,

    (d) adequate and suitable showers for employees if required by the nature of the work or for health reasons related thereto, and in such case—

        (i) separate shower rooms or separate use of shower rooms for men and women,
        (ii) shower rooms which are sufficiently large to permit each employee to wash without hindrance in satisfactory conditions of hygiene, and
        (iii) showers which are equipped with hot and cold running water, and

    (e) easy access between the rooms housing showers or washbasins where they are separate from the changing rooms.

Changing rooms and lockers

21. (1) An employer shall provide or cause to be provided—

  (a) appropriate changing rooms for persons at work if they have to wear special work clothes and if, for reasons of health or propriety, they cannot be expected to change in another area, which are—

   (i) easily accessible,
   (ii) of sufficient capacity, and
   (iii) provided with seating,

  (b) separate changing rooms or separate use of changing rooms for men and women, and

  (c) adequate provision for drying wet or damp work clothes.

  (2) If circumstances so require where work clothes are likely to be contaminated by dangerous substances, atmospheric conditions or the conditions of the place of work, an employer shall provide, or cause to be provided, facilities in changing rooms to enable working clothes to be kept in a place separate from personal clothing and effects.

  (3) If changing rooms are not required as referred to in paragraph (1), the employer shall ensure that every person at work is provided with a place to store his or her own clothes and personal effects.

Accommodation areas at a place of work

22. An employer shall ensure that fixed living accommodation areas provided for employees at a place of work—

  (a) are safe and without risk to health, and

  (b) unless used in exceptional cases—

   (i) have sufficient sanitary equipment,
   (ii) are equipped with beds, cupboards, tables and seats with backs, taking account of the number of persons at work, and
   (iii) are allocated taking account, where appropriate, of the presence of persons of both sexes.

Outdoor places of work, special provisions

23. An employer shall ensure that when employees are employed at outdoor workstations, the workstations are, as far as possible, arranged so that employees—

  (a) are protected against inclement weather conditions,

  (b) are not exposed to harmful influences such as gases, vapours or dust, in compliance with the relevant statutory provisions, and

  (c) cannot slip or fall.

Pregnant, postnatal and breastfeeding employees

24. An employer shall ensure that pregnant, postnatal and breastfeeding employees are able to lie down to rest in appropriate conditions.

Employees with disabilities

25. An employer shall ensure that places of work, where necessary, are organised to take account of persons at work with disabilities, in particular as regards doors, passageways, staircases, showers, washbasins, lavatories and workstations used or occupied directly by those persons.

Agreements as to a premises used as a place of work

26. (1) If, by reason of an agreement between the owner of a premises used as a place of work and an employer, the owner or employer is prevented from carrying out any structural or other alterations in the premises which are necessary to enable the employer to comply with these Regulations,

    (a) the owner or employer may apply to the Circuit Court for an order under this Regulation, and

    (b) the Court, after hearing the parties and any witnesses whom they desire to call, may make an order setting aside or modifying the terms of the agreement, as the Court considers appropriate in the circumstances of the case.

(2) Where, in any premises, the whole or any part of which has been let as a place of work,

    (a) any structural or other alterations are required in order to comply with any provision of these Regulations, and

    (b) the owner or employer, as the case may be, alleges that the whole or any part of the expenses of the alterations ought to be borne by the employer or owner,

the owner or employer may apply to the Circuit Court for an order under this Regulation and, after hearing the parties and any witnesses whom they desire to call, the Court—

    (i) may make such an order concerning the expenses, or their apportionment, as the Court considers appropriate in the circumstances of the case, regard being had to the terms of any contract between the parties, or,

    (ii) in the alternative, at the request of the owner or employer, may determine the lease on such terms, having regard to the provisions of the lease, as the Court considers appropriate.

CHAPTER 2 — USE OF WORK EQUIPMENT

Interpretation for Chapter 2

27. In this Chapter:

"carrier" means the device by which persons or goods, or both, are supported in order to be lifted, lowered or moved;

"danger zone" means any zone within or around work equipment in which an employee is subject to a risk to his or her safety or health;

"EC declaration of conformity" refers to a declaration of conformity issued pursuant to Directive 98/37/EC[1] or Directive 2006/42/EC[2] of the European Parliament and of the Council on the approximation of the laws of the Member States relating to machinery;

"exposed employee" means any employee wholly or partially in a danger zone;

"fishing vessel" means a vessel to which the Safety, Health and Welfare at Work (Fishing Vessels) Regulations 1999 (S.I. No. 325 of 1999) apply;

"hoist or lift" means a lifting machine which has its direction of movement restricted by a guide or guides but, for the purpose of this Chapter, does not include a fork lift truck, order picker, self- propelled variable reach truck or similar type equipment;

"lifting accessories" include clamps and similar attachments, chain slings, rope slings, rings, hooks, shackles, swivels, spreader beams, spreader frames and any other item placed between lifting equipment and the load or on the load in order to attach it, but excluding features of the load used for its lifting;

"load" includes a person;

"non-integrated cage or basket" means one which is not equipped with controls that control its movement;

"selection, installation and use of work equipment" means any activity involving work equipment, including starting or stopping the equipment, its use, transport, repair, modification, maintenance and servicing and cleaning;

"thorough examination" includes testing if—

(a) a competent person considers it to be necessary for the purpose of the examination, or

(b) testing is required pursuant to Regulation 52 and Schedule 1.

Duties of employer, use of work equipment

28. An employer shall ensure that—

(a) any work equipment provided for use by employees at a place of work complies, as appropriate, with the provisions of any relevant

---

[1] Official Journal L 207, 23.7.98, p. 1–46;

[2] Official Journal L 157, 9.6.2006, p. 24–86

enactment implementing any relevant Directive of the European Communities relating to work equipment with respect to safety and health,

(b) in selecting the work equipment, account is taken of the specific working conditions, characteristics and hazards in the place of work having regard to the safety and health of the employees and any additional hazards posed by the use of such work equipment,

(c) the necessary measures are taken so that the work equipment is installed and located and is suitable for the work to be carried out, or is properly adapted for that purpose, and may be used by employees without risk to their safety and health,

(d) where it is not possible fully to ensure that work equipment can be used by employees without risk to their safety or health, appropriate measures are taken to minimise any such risk,

(e) sufficient space to reduce such risks is provided between moving parts of work equipment and fixed or moving parts in its environment,

(f) where the use of work equipment is likely to involve a specific risk to the safety or health of employees—

    (i) the use of such work equipment is restricted to those employees required to use it, and

    (ii) in cases of work involving repairs, modifications, maintenance or servicing of such work equipment, the employees concerned are competent to carry out such work,

(g) the working posture and position of employees while using work equipment, and any ergonomic requirements, are taken into account having regard to the safety and health of the employees,

(h) areas and points for working on, or maintenance of, work equipment are suitably lit having regard to the operation to be carried out,

(i) work equipment parts at high or very low temperature are, where appropriate, protected to avoid the risk of employees coming into contact or coming too close,

(j) work equipment bears warnings and markings essential to ensure the safety and health of employees,

(k) employees have safe means of access to, and egress from, and are able to remain safely in, all the areas necessary for production, adjustment and maintenance operations,

(l) work equipment is used only for operations and under conditions for which it is appropriate,

(m) all work equipment is appropriate for protecting employees against the risk of the work equipment catching fire or overheating, or of discharges of gas, dust, liquid, vapour or other substances produced, used or stored in the work equipment,

(n) all work equipment is appropriate for preventing the risk of explosion of the work equipment or of substances produced, used or stored in the work equipment,

(o) work equipment is erected or dismantled under safe conditions in particular observing any instructions which may have been provided by the manufacturer,

(p) work equipment which may be struck by lightning while being used is protected by devices or appropriate means against the effects of lightning, and

(q) all forms of energy, substances and articles used or produced with work equipment are supplied or removed in a safe manner.

Information and instruction

29.   An employer shall ensure that—

(a) the necessary measures are taken so that employees have at their disposal adequate information and, where appropriate, written instructions on the work equipment containing at least adequate safety and health information concerning—

(i) the conditions of use of work equipment,

(ii) foreseeable abnormal situations, and

(iii) the conclusions to be drawn from experience, where appropriate, in using such work equipment, and

(b) employees are made aware of safety and health risks relevant to them associated with work equipment located at or near their workstation or to any changes relating to that work equipment, even if they do not use the equipment.

Inspection of work equipment

30.   An employer shall ensure that—

(a) where the safety of work equipment depends on the installation conditions—

(i) an initial inspection is carried out after installation is completed and before it is first put into service, and

(ii) an inspection is carried out after assembly at any new site or in any new location, and that the work equipment is installed correctly and is operating properly,

(b) in the case of work equipment which is exposed to conditions causing deterioration liable to result in a danger to safety or health—

(i) periodic inspections and, where appropriate, testing is carried out,

(ii) special inspections are carried out when exceptional circumstances arise which are liable to make the work equipment unsafe, including modification work, accidents, natural phenomena or prolonged inactivity, and

(iii) deterioration is detected and remedied in good time,

(c) inspections carried out under paragraphs (a) and (b) are carried out by a competent person and are appropriate to the nature, location and use of the work equipment,

(d) the results of inspections carried out under paragraphs (a) and (b) are recorded and kept available for 5 years from the date of inspection, for inspection by an inspector, and access to these records is made available to users of the work equipment upon request, and

(e) when work equipment is used in another place of work, it is accompanied by evidence of the last inspection carried out under paragraphs (a) and (b).

Maintenance

31. An employer shall ensure that—

(a) throughout its working life work equipment is kept, by means of adequate maintenance, at a level such that it complies with the provisions of this Chapter,

(b) where possible, maintenance operations are carried out when work equipment is shut down, and where this is not possible, appropriate protection measures are taken for the carrying out of such operations or such operations are carried out outside the area of danger,

(c) work equipment is maintained in such a way as to reduce the risks to users of the work equipment and to other persons at work, and

(d) a maintenance log for any machine is kept up to date.

Control devices

32. (1) An employer shall ensure that—

(a) work equipment control devices which affect safety and health are clearly visible and identifiable and appropriately marked where necessary,

(b) control devices are located outside danger zones except where necessary,

(c) the operation of control devices cannot cause additional hazard,

(d) the operation of control devices cannot give rise to any hazard as a result of any unintentional operation,

(e) the absence of persons in the danger zones is verifiable from the main control position if necessary,

(f) where it is impracticable to comply with paragraph (e), a safe system such as an audible or visible warning signal, or such a signal that is both audible and visible, is given automatically whenever the machinery is about to start,

(g) an exposed employee has the time, the means, or both, quickly to avoid hazards caused by the starting or stopping, or both, of the work equipment,

(h) control systems are safe, and are chosen making appropriate allowances for the failures, faults and constraints to be expected in the planned circumstances of use,

(i) it is possible to start work equipment only by deliberate action on a control provided for the purpose,

(j) a control is included in work equipment to—

    (i)   restart it after a stoppage for whatever reason, and

    (ii)   to control a significant change in the operating conditions

unless such a restart or change does not subject exposed employees to any hazard,

(k) all work equipment is fitted with a control to stop it completely and safely,

(l) each workstation is fitted with a control to stop some or all of the work equipment, depending on the type of hazard, so that the equipment is in a safe state,

(m) the equipment's stop control has priority over the start controls and, when the work equipment or the dangerous parts of it have stopped, the energy supply of the actuators concerned is switched off, and

(n) where appropriate, and depending on the hazards the equipment presents and its normal stopping time, work equipment is fitted with an emergency stop device.

(2) Paragraph (1)(j) does not apply to restarting or a change in operating conditions as a result of a normal operating cycle of an automatic device.

Guards and protection devices

33. An employer shall ensure that—

(a) work equipment presenting risk due to falling objects or projections is fitted with appropriate safety devices corresponding to the risk,

(b) work equipment presenting hazards due to emissions of gas, vapour, liquid or dust is fitted with appropriate containment devices, extraction devices, or both, near the sources of the hazard,

(c) work equipment and parts of such equipment are, where necessary for the safety and health of employees, stabilised by clamping or some other means,

(d) where there is a risk of rupture or disintegration of parts of work equipment, likely to pose significant danger to the safety and health of employees, appropriate protection measures are taken,

(e) where there is a risk of physical contact with moving parts of work equipment which could lead to accidents, those parts are provided with guards or protection devices to prevent access to danger zones or to halt movement of dangerous parts before the danger zones are reached,

(f) guards and protection devices where required under subparagraph (e)—

    (i) are of robust construction,

    (ii) do not give rise to any additional hazard,

    (iii) are not easily removed or rendered inoperative,

    (iv) are situated at sufficient distance from the danger zone,

    (v) do not restrict more than necessary the view of the operating cycle of the equipment,

    (vi) allow operations necessary to fit or replace parts, and

    (vii) restrict access for maintenance work only to the area where the work is to be carried out, if possible, without removal of the guard or protection device,

(g) warning devices on work equipment are unambiguous and easily perceived and understood, and

(h) any part of a stock-bar which projects beyond the headstock of a lathe is securely fenced unless it is in such a position as to be safe to employees as it would be if securely fenced.

Connection to energy sources

34. An employer shall ensure that—

(a) all work equipment is fitted with clearly identifiable means to isolate it from all its energy sources, and

(b) the reconnecting of the work equipment to its energy sources poses no risk to the employees concerned.

Contact with wheels or tracks of mobile work equipment

35. An employer shall ensure that work equipment with ride-on employees is fitted out in such a way as to reduce the risks for employees during the journey, including risk of contact with or trapping by wheels or tracks.

Drive systems of mobile work equipment

36. An employer shall ensure that—

(a) where an inadvertent seizure of the drive unit between an item of mobile work equipment and its accessories or anything towed, or both, creates a specific risk, the work equipment is equipped or adapted to prevent blockages of the drive units and where such seizure cannot be avoided, every possible measure is taken to avoid any adverse effects on employees, and

(b) where drive shafts for the transmission of energy between mobile items of work equipment can become soiled or damaged by trailing on the ground, facilities are available for fixing them.

Combustion engines of mobile work equipment

37. An employer shall ensure that mobile work equipment with a combustion engine is not used in working areas unless –

(a) specific provision is made for conducting the exhaust gases from the engine into the open air, or

(b) the working area is adequately ventilated so as to prevent danger to health from the exhaust gases.

Roll-over of mobile work equipment

38. (1) An employer shall ensure that mobile work equipment with ride-on employees is designed to restrict, under actual conditions of use, the risks arising from roll over of work equipment either by—

(a) a protection structure to ensure that the equipment does not tilt by more than a quarter turn,

(b) a structure giving sufficient clearance around the ride-on employees if the tilting movement can continue beyond a quarter turn, or

(c) by some other device of equivalent effect.

(2) The protection structures referred to in paragraph (1) may be an integral part of the work equipment but are not required when the work equipment is stabilised during operation or where the design makes roll over impossible.

(3) An employer shall ensure that where there is a risk of a ride-on employee being crushed between parts of the work equipment and the ground should the equipment roll over a restraining system for the ride-on employees is installed.

Fork-lift trucks

39. An employer shall ensure that a fork-lift truck carrying one or more employees is equipped or adapted to limit the risk of it overturning—

(a) by the installation of an enclosure for the driver,

(b) by a structure preventing the fork-lift truck from overturning,

(c) by a structure ensuring that, if the fork-lift truck overturns, sufficient clearance remains between the ground and appropriate parts of the fork-lift truck for the employees carried, or

(d) by a structure restraining the employees on the driving seat so as to prevent them from being crushed by parts of the fork-lift truck which overturns.

Safety of self-propelled work equipment

40. An employer shall ensure that—

(a) self-propelled work equipment is operated only by competent persons who have been appropriately trained, and

(b) self-propelled work equipment, which when in motion may create risks for persons—

(i) has facilities for preventing unauthorised start-up;

(ii) has appropriate facilities for minimising the consequences of a collision where there is more than one item of track-mounted work equipment in motion at the same time;

(iii) has a device for braking and stopping equipment;

(iv) in the event of failure of the main facility for braking and stopping equipment, where safety constraints so require, has available emergency facilities operated by readily accessible controls or automatic systems for braking and stopping the equipment;

(v) has adequate auxiliary devices installed to improve visibility where the driver's direct field of vision is inadequate;

(vi) is equipped with lighting appropriate to the work to be carried out and ensures sufficient safety for employees where designed for use at night or in dark places;

(vii) is equipped with appropriate fire-fighting appliances where such appliances are not available sufficiently nearby at the place of use, where such work equipment constitutes a fire hazard, either on its own or in respect of whatever it is towing or carrying, or both, and is liable to endanger employees;

(viii) if remote-controlled, stops automatically once it leaves the control range;

(ix) if it

(I) is remote-controlled, and

(II) creates, in normal conditions a crushing or impact hazard, has facilities to guard against that hazard, unless other appropriate devices are present to control the hazard.

Traffic rules for mobile work equipment

41. An employer shall ensure that—

(a) if work equipment is moving around in a work area, appropriate traffic rules are drawn up and followed,

(b) organisational measures are taken to prevent employees on foot coming within the area of operation of self-propelled work equipment and, if work can be done properly only if employees on foot are present, appropriate measures are taken to prevent them from being injured by the equipment, and

(c) the transport of employees on mechanically driven mobile work equipment is only permitted where safe facilities are provided to this effect and if work is carried out during the journey, speeds are adjusted as necessary.

Work equipment for lifting loads

42.   An employer shall ensure that—

(a) all lifting operations are properly planned, appropriately supervised and carried out to protect the safety of employees,

(b) when work equipment for lifting loads is installed permanently, its strength and stability during use is assured, having regard to the loads to be lifted and the stress induced at the mounting or fixing points of the structure,

(c) lifting equipment designed for low frequency use is not installed where its anticipated use will render the equipment unsuitable,

(d) machinery for lifting loads is clearly marked to indicate its safe working load, and where appropriate the safe working load for each configuration of the machinery,

(e) work equipment which is not designed for lifting persons is appropriately and clearly marked to this effect,

(f) every drum or pulley round which the chain or wire rope of any lifting equipment is carried is of suitable diameter and construction for the chain or rope used,

(g) every chain or rope which terminates at the winding drum of any lifting equipment is properly secured thereto and at least two turns of such chains or rope remain on such drum in every operating position of the equipment,

(h) permanently installed work equipment is installed in such a way as to reduce the risk of the load—

   (i)   striking employees,

   (ii) drifting dangerously or falling freely, and

   (iii) being released unintentionally,

(i) work equipment which is mobile or can be dismantled and which is designed for lifting loads is used in such a way as to ensure the stability of the work equipment during use under all foreseeable conditions, taking into account the nature of the ground,

(j) lifting equipment is not used beyond its safe working load except when being tested under the direction of a competent person,

(k) unless required for the effective operation of the work, measures are taken to ensure that employees are not present under suspended loads,

(l) loads are not moved above unprotected workplaces usually occupied by employees, and

(m) if the hazards referred to in paragraphs (k) and (l) cannot be avoided, appropriate procedures are laid down and applied where work cannot be carried out properly any other way.

Cranes.

43. (1) An employer shall ensure that, without prejudice to Regulations 42 and 45,

(a) every crane of variable operating radius, before it is taken into use—

(i)   has plainly marked upon it or within the cab the safe working load at various radii of the jib, trolley or crab, and in the case of a crane with a derricking jib, the maximum radius at which the jib may be worked,

(ii) is fitted with a suitable accurate automatic safe load indicator or rated capacity indicator, clearly visible to the driver showing at any time the radius of the jib, trolley or crab and the safe working load corresponding to that radius unless–

(I)   it is a guy derrick crane (being a crane of which the mast is held upright solely by means of ropes with the necessary fittings and tightening screws),

(II) it is a hand crane which is being solely used for erecting or dismantling another crane, or

(III) it has been assigned by a competent person a safe working load of 1,000 kg or less, and

(iii) has an automatic safe load indicator or rated capacity indicator, if required under subparagraph (ii), which is—

(I)   properly maintained,

(II) correctly used, and

(III) tested by a competent person after erection, installation or alteration of the crane for the purpose of any work before the crane is taken into use or returned to use as the case may be,

(b) in the case of a crane which is on occasion dismantled or partially dismantled any jib or boom which is separated from the crane in dismantling is clearly marked so as to indicate the crane of which it is a part,

(c) cranes with derricking jibs are provided with—

(i)   such means as will minimise the risk of the accidental raising or lowering of the jib, and

(ii) a jib that does not exceed the maximum radius specified by the manufacturer, or by a competent person in a report pursuant to Regulation 53,

(d) a crane travelling on rails is provided with deflector plates to remove from the rails any loose material likely to cause danger,

(e) where the safety of work equipment depends on the installation conditions on a construction site—

(i) after each assembly of a tower crane or after any adjustment to any member which may affect the strength or stability of the crane, and before it is put into use, it is subject to a static test with a test coefficient of 1.25 and a dynamic test with a test coefficient of 1.1, taking account of any direction from the machine manufacturer, and

(ii) where the stability of a crane is secured by means of removable weights, a diagram or notice indicating the amount and position of such weights is affixed on the crane so that it can be readily seen and each such removable weight is clearly marked with its correct weight, and

(f) notwithstanding any other provisions of this Chapter, lifting equipment used on a construction site is examined weekly by the user as regards features related to its safe working and a record of the results is kept in a suitable form which is kept available for inspection by an inspector for 3 months from the date of examination.

(2) The use of an excavator, telehandler, loader or combined excavator/loader as a crane is subject to Part C of Schedule 1.

Support of lifting equipment

44. An employer shall ensure that every platform or support, whether fixed or mobile, upon or from which lifting equipment is mounted or supported is suitable for the purpose.

Work equipment for lifting goods or persons

45. An employer shall ensure that—

(a) persons may be lifted only by means of work equipment and accessories suitable for this purpose, and

(b) work equipment for lifting or moving persons or for lifting goods is, where applicable, provided such as to—

(i) prevent the risk of the carrier falling, where one exists, by the use of suitable devices,

(ii) prevent the risk of the user falling from the carrier, where one exists,

(iii) prevent the risk of persons being crushed, trapped or struck, in particular through inadvertent contact with objects,

(iv) where the carrier has a roof, be equipped with a suitable inspection control station and stopping device,

(v)   where, in respect of a carrier with a roof, a hazard exists by virtue of the free distance in the horizontal plane beyond and perpendicular to the carrier's outer edge exceeding 0.30 m, measures to address the hazard, and

(vi)   ensure that persons trapped in the carrier in the event of an incident are not exposed to danger, can raise the alarm and can be freed, and

(c) where, for reasons inherent in the site and height differences, the risks referred to in subparagraph (b)(i) cannot be avoided by other safety measures, an enhanced safety coefficient suspension rope is installed and checked every working day.

Hoists and lifts

46. (1) Without prejudice to Regulations 42 and 45, this Regulation applies to a hoist, lift, hoistway or liftway subject to the conditional exemptions under Part A of Schedule 1.

(2) An employer shall ensure that—

(a) every hoistway or liftway is efficiently protected by a substantial enclosure fitted with gates so as to prevent, when the gates are shut,

(i)   any person falling down the way, or
(ii)   coming into contact with any moving part of the hoist or lift,

(b) any gate referred to in subparagraph (a) is fitted with efficient interlocking or other devices to ensure that the gate cannot be opened except when the carrier is at the landing and that the carrier cannot be moved away from the landing until the gate is closed,

(c) every hoist or lift and every such enclosure as is referred to in subparagraph (a) is constructed so as to prevent any part of any person or any goods carried in the hoist or lift being trapped between—

(i)   any part of the hoist or lift and any fixed structure, or
(ii)   between the counterbalance weight and any other moving part of the hoist or lift,

(d) efficient devices which will support the carrier together with its safe working load in the event of failure of the hoisting system are provided and maintained, where practicable, in connection with every hoist or lift,

(e) efficient automatic devices are provided and maintained in connection with every hoist or lift which will ensure that the carrier does not overrun the highest point set for its intended travel,

(f) every hoist or lift is installed so that it can be operated at any one time only from one position and is not operated from the carrier unless the requirements of subparagraph (h) are complied with,

(g) the carrier bears an easily visible plate clearly showing the rated load in kilograms and, if applicable, the maximum number of passengers which may be carried, and

(h) in the case of hoists and lifts used for carrying persons, whether together with goods or otherwise,

   (i) efficient automatic devices are provided and maintained to prevent the carrier overrunning,

   (ii) every carrier on each side from which access is afforded to a landing is fitted with a gate and, in connection with every such gate, efficient devices are provided to secure that, when persons or goods are in the carrier, the carrier cannot be raised or lowered unless the gate is closed and comes to rest when the gate is opened,

   (iii) in the case of a hoist or lift where the carrier is suspended by rope or chain, there are at least two ropes or chains separately connected to the carrier, each rope or chain and its attachments being capable of carrying the whole weight of the carrier and its maximum working load,

   (iv) efficient devices are provided and maintained which will support the carrier with its maximum working load in the event of a breakage of the ropes or chains or any of their attachments, and

   (v) suitable efficient automatic devices are provided which will ensure that the carrier comes to rest at a point above the lowest point to which the carrier can travel.

(3) This Regulation applies to a hoist, lift, hoistway or liftway, subject to the conditional exemptions under Part A of Schedule 1, and any reference to a gate includes reference to a door where the context so requires.

(4) An employer shall ensure that hoists or lifts or hoistways or liftways of a class or description specified in Part A of Schedule 1 are subject to the conditions set out therein

Winch-operated hoists and lifts

47. An employer shall ensure that—

(a) where a hoist or lift is operated by means of a winch, the winch is so constructed that the brake is applied when the control device is not held in the operating position, and

(b) a hoist is not operated by a winch where it is fitted with a pawl and ratchet gear on which the pawl has to be disengaged before the carrier can be lowered.

Conditions regarding lifting of persons

48. (1) An employer shall ensure that work equipment not specifically designed for the purpose of lifting persons is not used to this effect other than in exceptional circumstances and subject to the following conditions:

(a) appropriate action including adequate supervision is taken to ensure safety;

(b) while employees are on work equipment designed for lifting loads, the control position is manned at all times;

(c) persons being lifted have reliable means of communication;

(d) in the event of danger, there is reliable means of evacuating persons from lifting equipment;

(e) the ground underneath the equipment is even and reasonably flat;

(f) the equipment is stable under all circumstances;

(g) persons in a nonintegrated cage or basket cannot reach the controls or other dangerous parts of the lifting machine;

(h) the cage/basket is properly secured to the lifting machine;

(i) the total load is less than half the rated capacity of the lifting equipment;

(j) the lifting equipment has a capacity not less than 1,000 kg unless its manufacturer indicates that the machine is suitable for such use;

(k) hydraulically-operated machines are fitted with check valves on the hydraulic lifting cylinders, or some other suitable device, to prevent a gravity fall of the load in the event of a hydraulic failure.

(2) An employer shall ensure that lifting equipment with provision for free fall is not used to lift persons.

Lifting accessories

49. An employer shall ensure that—

(a) lifting accessories are selected as a function of the loads to be handled, gripping points, attachment tackle and the atmospheric conditions, having regard to the mode and configuration of slinging,

(b) lifting accessories are stored in a way that ensures that they will not be damaged or degraded, and

(c) lifting accessories are marked in such a way that it is possible to identify the characteristics essential for safe use, having regard to Regulation 57.

Work equipment for lifting non-guided loads

50. An employer shall ensure that—

(a) when two or more items of work equipment used for lifting non-guided loads are installed or erected on a site in such a way that their working radii overlap, appropriate measures are taken to avoid collision between loads or the work equipment parts themselves, or both,

(b) when using mobile work equipment for lifting non-guided loads,

    (i) measures are taken to prevent the equipment from tilting, overturning or, if necessary, moving or slipping, and

    (ii) checks are made to ensure that the measures are executed properly,

(c) if the operator of work equipment designed for lifting non-guided loads cannot observe the full path of the load either directly or by means of auxiliary equipment providing the necessary information,

    (i) a competent person is in communication with the operator to guide him or her, and

    (ii) organisational measures are taken to prevent collisions of the load which could endanger employees,

(d) work is organised in such a way that, when an employee is attaching or detaching a load by hand, it can be done safely, in particular through the employee retaining direct or indirect control of the work equipment,

(e) if a load has to be lifted by two or more pieces of work equipment for lifting non-guided loads simultaneously, a procedure is established and applied to ensure good co-ordination on the part of the operators,

(f) if work equipment designed for lifting non-guided loads cannot maintain its hold on the load in the event of a complete or partial power failure, appropriate measures are taken to avoid exposing employees to any resultant risks,

(g) suspended loads are not left without surveillance unless access to the danger zone is prevented and the load has been safely suspended and is safely held,

(h) open air use of work equipment designed for lifting non-guided loads is halted when meteorological conditions deteriorate to the point of jeopardising the safe use of the equipment and exposing employees to risks, and

(i) adequate protection measures, in particular to avoid work equipment turning over, are taken to avoid any risks to employees.

Lifting equipment—signalling and operation

51. An employer shall ensure that—

(a) lifting equipment is operated by a competent person or by a person who is under the direct supervision of a competent person for the purpose of training,

(b) no person under 18 years of age is employed to—

(i) give signals to the operator of lifting equipment driven by mechanical power, or

(ii) to operate any such equipment,

(c) every signal given for directing the movement of lifting equipment—

(i) is distinctive in character, and

(ii) such that the person to whom it is given is able to hear or see it easily, and

(d) signalling devices are—

(i) properly maintained, and

(ii) the means of communication are adequately protected from accidental interference.

Examination and testing of lifting equipment

52. (1) An employer shall ensure that, without prejudice to Regulation 30,

(a) fixed work equipment for lifting loads, including rail mounted work equipment for lifting loads, is not taken into use for the first time unless—

(i) it has been tested and thoroughly examined by a competent person, and

(ii) a certificate of test and examination specifying the safe working load and, if appropriate, the maximum numbers of persons permitted has been obtained,

(b) mobile work equipment for lifting loads is not taken into use in any place of work for the first time unless—

(i) it has been examined and certified in accordance with this Regulation, or

(ii) it is a new machine and which—

(I) is CE marked in accordance with the relevant directives of the European Communities,

(II) is accompanied by an EC declaration of conformity in accordance with the relevant directives of the European Communities,

(III) is accompanied by a certificate of test and examination for that machine signed by the person making the test, specifying the safe working load, and

(IV) has not been reassembled since dispatch from the manufacturer,

(c) where

(i) any alteration or repair is carried out to lifting equipment or a lifting accessory, and

      (ii)   the alterations or repairs are relevant to the safe operation of the equipment, the equipment is examined by a competent person in compliance with this Regulation before the equipment's return to service, and

  (d) where a report of an examination pursuant to paragraph (3) specifies conditions for the safe working of the equipment, the equipment is used only in accordance with those conditions.

(2) In the case of work equipment to which paragraph (1)(b)(ii) applies, the period to the first examination pursuant to paragraph (3) shall be determined by reference to the date of the certificate referred to in paragraph (1)(b)(ii)(III).

(3) Without prejudice to Regulation 30, an employer shall ensure that work equipment of a type or class listed in column 1 of Parts B or C of Schedule 1 is not used unless it has been examined by a competent person at least once in the period specified in column 2 of Parts B or C of that Schedule or as required under the other circumstances described in Part C.

(4) Where equipment referred to in paragraph (3) has already been thoroughly examined in accordance with the relevant statutory provisions in force prior to the introduction of these Regulations, the beginning of the period referred to in paragraph (3) shall be deemed to be the date of the last such examination.

(5) The requirements of this Regulation do not apply to the work equipment listed under Part D of Schedule 1.

(6) Where a thorough examination has been carried out in compliance with the relevant statutory provisions in force immediately before the commencement of these Regulations, the examination shall be regarded as being in compliance with this Chapter and this Regulation does not apply until after the expiry of the period specified under those statutory provisions.

(7) An employer shall ensure that a thorough examination is carried out as soon as practicable if one is outstanding under the relevant statutory provisions from the period before the commencement of these Regulations.

Reports by competent persons

53.   (1) A competent person carrying out an examination under Regulation 52 shall—

  (a) prepare a report of the result of every examination and test as referred to in Regulation 52 containing the particulars that are set out in Part E of Schedule 1,

   (b) where work equipment is examined pursuant to Regulation 52 and the examination reveals that the equipment can only be used safely if certain repairs are carried out or if the person making the examination foresees a need for such repairs—

     (i) inform in writing the owner and user of the need for such repairs or the potential need,

     (ii) not later than 20 days after the completion of the examination, send a copy of the report of the examination to the Authority where immediate cessation of the work has been advised, and

     (iii) in the case of potential need for repairs, specify the period within which, in his or her opinion, the repairs shall be carried out.

(2) A competent person carrying out an examination under Regulation 52(3) may specify a period less than that in column 2 of Parts B or C of Schedule 1 if in that person's opinion a more frequent examination is required but, if this is done, he or she shall provide the reason for the opinion in writing to the owner and user of the work equipment.

Keeping of records and registers of lifting equipment

54. (1) An employer shall ensure that a report produced under Regulation 53, or a copy of it—

   (a) is kept at the place of work when the lifting equipment is permanently located there,

   (b) in the case of lifting equipment on a construction site, is kept at the site office or at the business address of the contractor for whom the report was made, and

   (c) in the case of mobile equipment, is kept on the equipment in addition to being available for inspection at the address of the equipment owner.

(2) An employer shall ensure that—

   (a) a register of lifting equipment and lifting accessories containing details of the equipment, distinguishing number, date of first use and date of last thorough examination and testing is maintained and kept available for inspection by an inspector, and

   (b) if the equipment does not have a distinguishing number or mark, one of long lasting duration is provided.

Safe working loads for excavators, draglines, telehandlers, loaders or combined excavators and loaders when used as cranes

55. (1) In this Regulation, reference to "machine" is a reference to an "excavator, dragline, telehandler, loader or combined excavator and loader when used as a crane".

(2) An employer shall ensure that—

(a) before a machine to which this Regulation applies is first used, a competent person—

   (i) specifies the safe working load or loads which may be raised and lowered by the machine, or where its safe working load depends on the configuration of the machine, its safe working load for the different configurations are determined, and

   (ii) provides a signed certificate specifying the safe working load and any necessary safety provisions,

(b) the certificate referred to in subparagraph (a)(ii) is kept available for inspection with the machine,

(c) a machine is not loaded beyond the relevant safe working load specified in the certificate required by subparagraph (a)(ii),

(d) the specified safe working load or loads and the outrigger position and the length of jib or boom to which the safe working loads relate is either plainly marked on the machine or a copy of the table relating safe working loads to the distance worked is affixed in a clearly visible position in the driver's cab,

(e) if, after the issue of the certificate required by subparagraph (a)(ii), a machine undergoes any substantial alteration or repair likely to affect the specified safe working loads, that certificate is cancelled and a new certificate is obtained,

(f) hydraulically-operated machines, except for machines with a maximum rated lift capacity of a 1,000 kg or less, are fitted with check valves on the cylinders used for lifting or by another means to prevent a gravity fall of the load in the event of a hydraulic failure,

(g) in the case of a telehandler, the safe working load is not greater than 1,000 kg unless fitted with an automatic safe load indicator or rated capacity indicator,

(h) unless a machine is fitted with an automatic safe load indicator or a rated capacity indicator, the safe working load is the same for all radii at which a jib or boom is operated and is not greater than the load which the machine in its least stable configuration is designed to lift with that jib or boom,

(i) means of identification are plainly marked on machines to which this Regulation applies, and

(j) machines to which this Regulation applies are examined and tested periodically in accordance with Parts B and C of Schedule 1.

Specific requirements for scotch and guy derrick cranes.

56. An employer shall ensure that, where a scotch and guy derrick crane is to be used,

(a) the jib of a scotch derrick crane is not erected between the back stays of the crane,

(b) a load which lies in the angle between the back stays of a scotch derrick crane is not moved by that crane,

(c) appropriate measures are taken to prevent the foot of the king post of any scotch derrick crane from being lifted out of its socket or support whilst in use, and

(d) where the guys of a guy derrick crane cannot be fixed at approximately equal inclinations to the mast so that the angles between adjacent pairs of guys are approximately equal, such other measures are taken as will ensure the stability of the crane.

Construction, testing, examination and safe working load of lifting accessories

57. (1) An employer shall ensure that—

(a) subject to paragraph (2), a chain, rope or other lifting accessory is not used in raising or lowering or as a means of suspension unless—

(i) it is of good construction, sound material, adequate strength, suitable quality and free from patent defect,

(ii) it is properly installed and used,

(iii) it is properly maintained,

(iv) it is used only for the purpose for which it was intended,

(v) except in the case of a fibre rope or fibre rope sling, it has been tested and examined by a competent person and there has been obtained a certificate of such test and examination specifying the safe working load and signed by the person making, or responsible for, the carrying out of the test and examination,

(vi) in the case of a fibre rope or fibre rope sling, information from the manufacturer on its safe working load is available, and

(vii) it is marked in plain legible figures and letters with the safe working load and a means of identification, unless paragraph (2) applies to the safe working load,

(b) a chain, rope or lifting gear is not loaded beyond its safe working load except for testing purposes as specified by, and under the direction of, a competent person appointed to carry out the tests,

(c) a hook used for raising or lowering or as a means of suspension is either—

(i) provided with an efficient device to prevent the displacement of the sling or load from the hook, or

(ii) of such shape as to reduce as far as possible the risk of such displacement,

(d) a sling used for raising or lowering on a lifting appliance is securely attached to the appliance and the method of attachment is not a method likely to result in damage to any part of the sling or to any lifting gear supporting it,

(e) a double or multiple sling is not used for raising or lowering if—

    (i) the upper ends of the sling legs are not connected by means of a shackle, ring or link of adequate strength, or

    (ii) the safe working load of any sling leg is exceeded because of the angle between the sling legs,

(f) where a load is being lifted or otherwise moved, adequate steps are taken by the use of suitable packing, or otherwise, to prevent the edges of the load from coming into contact with a sling, rope or chain, where this would involve risk of personal injury,

(g) a load is not raised, lowered or suspended on a chain or wire rope which has a knot tied in any part of the chain or rope under direct tension,

(h) a chain which is shortened or joined to another chain by means of bolts and nuts inserted through the links is not used for raising, lowering or suspending any load, and

(i) where a chain or lifting gear is made of such material that would require annealing or a form of heat treatment to ensure its safety, the chain or lifting gear—

    (i) is effectively annealed or subjected to an appropriate form of heat treatment under the supervision of a competent person and at intervals as specified by a competent person, and

    (ii) is not used in raising or lowering or as a means of suspension unless a report has been made in writing of every annealing or appropriate heat treatment signed by the competent person under whose supervision the annealing or heat treatment was carried out.

(2) Where the safe working load of a rope or rope sling is—

(a) contained in the report made pursuant to Regulation 53 and the rope or sling is so marked as to enable its safe working load as specified in that report to be ascertained from the report, or

(b) in the case of a fibre rope or a fibre rope sling, contained in a table of safe working loads clearly visible in a prominent position at the workplace

the ropes or rope slings do not need to be marked with their safe working load.

Delivery of loads with lifting accessories attached

58. Where—

(a) any article, material or other load intended for use in construction work is delivered at, or adjacent to, a construction site with a chain, rope or other lifting accessory attached thereto and designed for use as a means of raising and lowering that class of load when removing the same from the point of delivery to a position on the site, and

(b) the chain, rope or gear is free from patent defect whether of construction or quality and is not owned or hired by any contractor who is undertaking construction work on the site,

this Chapter does not apply in respect of the use of such chain, rope or lifting gear for raising or lowering the load so long as the chain, rope or gear remains attached to the article, material or load.

Duty of persons who hire lifting equipment to others

59. Without prejudice to section 16 of the Act, a person who hires out lifting equipment for use by others, shall comply with the duties set out in Regulations 52 and 54.

Duty of the master of a ship in respect of examination of lifting equipment

60. The master of a ship shall comply with the duties set out in Regulations 52 and 54.

Duty of the owner of a fishing vessel in respect of examination of lifting equipment

61. The owner of a fishing vessel shall comply with the duties set out in Regulations 52 and 54.

CHAPTER 3 — PERSONAL PROTECTIVE EQUIPMENT

Provision of personal protective equipment

62. (1) An employer shall ensure that, without prejudice to section 8 of the Act, personal protective equipment is provided for use by the employer's employees where risks at a place of work to the safety or health of employees cannot be avoided or sufficiently limited by technical means of collective protection or by measures, methods or procedures of work organisation.

(2) Without prejudice to the generality of paragraph (1), an employer when providing personal protective equipment shall take into account the appropriate matters specified in Schedule 2.

(3) Without prejudice to section 16 of the Act, an employer shall ensure that personal protective equipment provided under these Regulations complies with relevant European Community directives regarding design and manufacture of personal protective equipment with respect to safety and health.

Assessment of personal protective equipment

63. (1) Before choosing any personal protective equipment required to be provided under Regulation 62, an employer shall make an assessment to determine whether such equipment satisfies the requirements of this Regulation and Regulations 62 and 64.

(2) The assessment required by paragraph (1) shall consist of—

    (a) an analysis and assessment of risks present which cannot be avoided by other means,

    (b) the definition of the characteristics which personal protective equipment must have in order to be effective against the risks referred to in subparagraph (a), taking into account any risks which this equipment itself may create, and

    (c) comparison of the characteristics of the personal protective equipment available with the characteristics referred to in sub-paragraph (b).

(3) An employer shall review forthwith the assessment required by paragraph (1) if any alteration takes place in any of the matters referred to in paragraph (2) and, where as a result of this review changes in the assessment are required, such changes shall be made.

Conditions of use and compatibility

64. (1) Where it is necessary for an employee to use personal protective equipment, the employer shall determine the conditions of use of such equipment, in particular the period for which it is worn, on the basis of—

    (a) the seriousness of the risk,

    (b) the frequency of the exposure to the risk,

    (c) the characteristics of the workstation of the employee, and

    (d) the adequacy of the personal protective equipment.

(2) An employer shall ensure that personal protective equipment is used only for the purposes specified, except in specific and exceptional circumstances.

(3) Where it is necessary for an employee to wear simultaneously more than one item of personal protective equipment, the employer shall ensure that such items of personal protective equipment are compatible with each other and continue to be effective against the risks involved.

Personal use

65. (1) An employer shall ensure that—

    (a) the use of an item of personal protective equipment provided by the employer under Regulation 62 is normally confined to one employee, and

    (b) where it is necessary for an item of personal protective equipment to be worn by more than one employee, such use does not create health or hygiene problems for any user.

(2) An employee to whom personal protective equipment is made available under these Regulations shall take all reasonable steps to ensure that such equipment is returned to storage after use by him or her.

Maintenance and replacement

66. An employer shall ensure that any personal protective equipment provided by the employer under Regulation 62 is maintained at all times in good working order and in a satisfactory hygienic condition by means of any necessary storage, maintenance, repair or replacement.

Information, training and instruction

67. Where an employer provides personal protective equipment for use by an employee under Regulation 62, the employer, without prejudice to sections 9 and 10 of the Act, shall—

    (a) inform the employee of the risks against which the wearing of the equipment protects him or her,

    (b) provide the employee with adequate information on the personal protective equipment provided,

    (c) inform the employee of the level of protection afforded by the personal protective equipment provided for his or her use,

    (d) provide the employee with instruction on the use of such personal protective equipment, and

    (e) arrange for training and, if appropriate, organise demonstrations in the wearing of such equipment.

CHAPTER 4 — MANUAL HANDLING OF LOADS

Interpretation for Chapter 4

68. In this Chapter, "manual handling of loads" means any transporting or supporting of a load by one or more employees and includes lifting, putting down, pushing, pulling, carrying or moving a load, which, by reason of its characteristics or of unfavourable ergonomic conditions, involves risk, particularly of back injury, to employees.

Duties of employer

69. An employer shall—

    (a) take appropriate organisational measures, or use the appropriate means, in particular mechanical equipment, to avoid the need for the manual handling of loads by the employer's employees,

    (b) where the need for the manual handling of loads by the employer's employees cannot be avoided, take appropriate organisational measures, use appropriate means or provide the employer's employees with such means in order to reduce the risk involved in the manual handling of such loads, having regard to the risk factors specified in Schedule 3,

(c) wherever the need for manual handling of loads by the employer's employees cannot be avoided, organise workstations in such a way as to make such handling as safe and healthy as possible, and—

   (i)   taking account of the risk factors for the manual handling of loads specified in Schedule 3, assess the health and safety conditions of the type of work involved and take appropriate measures to avoid or reduce the risk, particularly of back injury, to the employer's employees,

   (ii)   ensure that particularly sensitive risk groups of employees are protected against any dangers which specifically affect them in relation to the manual handling of loads and the individual risk factors, having regard to the risk factors set out in Schedule 3,

   (iii) ensure that where tasks are entrusted to an employee, his or her capabilities in relation to safety and health are taken into account, including, in relation to the manual handling of loads by employees, the individual risk factors set out in Schedule 3, and

   (iv)   when carrying out health surveillance in relation to the manual handling of loads by employees, take account of the appropriate risk factors set out in Schedule 3, and

(d) without prejudice to section 9 of the Act, ensure that those of the employer's employees who are involved in manual handling of loads receive general indications and, where possible, precise information on—

   (i)   the weight of each load, and

   (ii)   the centre of gravity of the heaviest side when a package is eccentrically loaded.

CHAPTER 5 — DISPLAY SCREEN EQUIPMENT

Interpretation for Chapter 5

70. In this Chapter:

"display screen equipment" means any alphanumeric or graphic display screen, regardless of the display process involved;

"employee" means an employee who habitually uses display screen equipment as a significant part of his or her normal work;

"workstation" means an assembly comprising display screen equipment, which may be provided with a keyboard or input device or software, or a combination of the foregoing, determining the operator and machine interface, and includes—

    (a) a work chair and work desk or work surface,

    (b) any optional accessories and peripherals, and

    (c) the immediate work environment of the display screen equipment.

Non-application of Chapter 5

71.   This Chapter does not apply to—

    (a) drivers' cabs or control cabs for vehicles or machinery,

    (b) computer systems on board a means of transport,

    (c) computer systems mainly intended for public use,

    (d) portable display screen equipment not in prolonged use at a work-station,

    (e) calculators, cash registers and any equipment having a small data or measurement display required for direct use of the equipment, and

    (f) typewriters of traditional design, of the type known as "typewriter with window".

Duties of employer

72.   (1) An employer, when providing display screen equipment for use by an employee at a workstation, shall—

    (a) ensure that the general use of the equipment is not a source of risk for the employee,

    (b) perform an analysis of the workstation in order to evaluate the safety and health conditions to which it gives rise for the employees, particularly as regards possible risks to eyesight, physical problems and problems of mental stress, and, on the basis of that evaluation, take appropriate measures to remedy any risks found, taking account of—

        (i)   the minimum requirements specified in Schedule 4, and

        (ii) any additional or combined effects of any such risks so found,

    (c) plan the activities of the employer's employees in such a way that daily work on display screen equipment is periodically interrupted by breaks or changes of activity which reduce workload at the display screen,

    (d) without prejudice to section 9 of the Act, provide information to the employer's employees in relation to the measures applicable to workstations which have been implemented under this Regulation and Regulation 73,

    (e) without prejudice to section 10 of the Act, provide training to employees in the use of workstations before commencing work with display screen equipment and whenever the organisation of the workstation is substantially modified, and

(f) perform a further analysis of the workstation as referred to in sub-paragraph (b) where—

    (i) an employee transfers to a new workstation, or

    (ii) significant new work equipment, change of equipment or new technology is introduced at an individual's workstation.

(2) Schedule 4 applies only to the extent that the components concerned are present at a workstation and that the inherent requirements or characteristics of the work do not preclude such application.

Provision of eye tests and corrective appliances

73. An employer shall, taking into account any entitlement which an employee may have to any tests and appliances provided by the State relating to eyesight and appliances, ensure that—

(a) the provision of an appropriate eye and eyesight test, carried out by a competent person, is made known to and is made available to every employee—

    (i) before commencing display screen work,

    (ii) at regular intervals thereafter, and

    (iii) if an employee experiences visual difficulties which may be due to display screen work,

(b) if the results of a test under this Regulation show that it is necessary, an ophthalmologic examination is carried out on the employee concerned, and

(c) where the results of a test or an examination under this Regulation show that it is necessary, and if normal corrective appliances cannot be used, the employee concerned is provided with special corrective appliances appropriate to his or her work.

PART 3

ELECTRICITY

Interpretation for Part 3

74. In this Part:

"authorised person" means a person who is—

(a) competent for the purpose of this Part, in relation to which the expression is used,

(b) either an employer, a self-employed person, or an employee appointed or selected by the employer or self-employed person, and

(c) engaged in work or duties incidental to the generation, transformation, conversion, switching, controlling, regulating, rectification, storage, transmission, distribution, provision, measurement or use of electrical energy;

"circuit" means part of an electrical installation supplied from the same origin, which may be protected against overcurrents by the same protective device;

"circuit breaker" means an electro-mechanical device capable of making, carrying and breaking currents under normal circuit conditions and also capable of making, carrying for a specified time, and breaking currents under specified abnormal circuit conditions such as those of short circuit;

"conductive part" means a part capable of conducting current although not necessarily used for carrying current in normal conditions;

"conductor" means a conductor of electrical energy;

"danger" means risk of personal injury from—

(a) electric shock, electric burn, electrical explosion or arcing,

(b) fire or explosion caused by the use of electricity, or

(c) mechanical movement of electrically driven equipment,

and preventing danger in this Part shall be construed as preventing danger so far as is reasonably practicable;

"earthing" means the connection of the exposed conductive parts of an installation to the conductive mass of the earth;

"electrical equipment" includes any conductor or electric cable and any part of any machine, apparatus or appliance intended to be used or installed for use for the generation, transformation, conversion, switching, controlling, regulating, rectification, storage, transmission, distribution, provision, measurement or use of electrical energy;

"electrical installation" means an assembly of associated electrical equipment fulfilling a specific purpose or purposes and having co-ordinated characteristics;

"higher voltage" means any voltage exceeding—

(a) 1,000 volts alternating current, or

(b) 1,500 volts direct current;

"isolation" means the disconnection and separation of electrical equipment from every source of electrical energy in such a way that the disconnection and separation is secure;

"live" means electrically energised;

"medical electrical equipment" means medical electrical equipment as defined in the Electro-Technical Council of Ireland (ETCI) document entitled "National Rules for Electrical Installations in Medically Used Rooms" or other equipment as may be prescribed by the Minister;

"overcurrent" means any current exceeding the rated value of the electrical equipment concerned;

"overhead line" means any electric line suspended above ground carrying or intended to carry electrical energy at a voltage exceeding 80 volts to earth;

"portable equipment" means equipment, including hand-held portable equipment, which—

(a) because of the manner in which it is to be used, requires to be moved while it is working,

(b) is designed so that it can be moved while it is working, or

(c) is moved from time to time between the periods during which it is working;

"residual current device" means an electro mechanical switching device intended to disconnect a circuit when the residual current attains a stated value under specific conditions;

"substation" means any building, enclosure or other structure, or any part thereof, which—

(a) is large enough to enable a person to enter after the electrical equipment therein is in position, and

(b) contains equipment for transforming or converting electrical energy either to or from higher voltage (not being equipment for transforming or converting electrical energy solely for the operation of switchgear or instruments),

and includes that equipment, together with any other equipment for switching, controlling or otherwise regulating electrical energy;

"switch room" means a room intended primarily to house electrical switching and distribution equipment for a building;

"underground cable" means any electric cable below ground carrying or intended to carry electrical energy at a voltage exceeding 80 volts to earth.

Application of Part 3

75. (1) This Part, without prejudice to section 16 of the Act, applies as appropriate to persons who design, install, maintain, use, or are in control to any extent of—

(a) an electrical installation or part of an electrical installation in a place of work, or

(b) an electrical network, including the generation, transformation, conversion, switching, controlling, regulating, rectification, storage, transmission, distribution, provision, measurement or use of electrical energy at a place of work.

(2) This Part does not apply to—

(a) any electrical equipment or electrical installation used exclusively for electrical testing or research purposes, or

(b) medical electrical equipment,

but persons using equipment referred to in subparagraph (b) shall ensure that the equipment or installation is constructed, installed, maintained, protected and used, with adequate precautions being taken, so as to prevent danger.

Suitability of electrical equipment and installations

76. An employer shall ensure that—

    (a) all electrical equipment and electrical installations are—

        (i)   designed,
        (ii)   constructed,
        (iii) installed,
        (iv) maintained,
        (v)   protected, and
        (vi) used

so as to prevent danger, and

    (b) all electrical equipment and electrical installations, including distribution boards, sockets, transformers and connections, are suitably protected from ingress of moisture or of particles and foreseeable impacts, as appropriate to the location, without prejudice to Regulation 77.

Adverse or hazardous environments

77. An employer shall ensure that electrical equipment which may foreseeably be exposed to adverse or hazardous environments, including in particular—

    (a) mechanical damage,
    (b) the effects of weather, natural hazards, temperature or pressure,
    (c) the effects of wet, dirty, dusty or corrosive conditions, and
    (d) any flammable or potentially explosive atmosphere, including any mixture of air and a flammable substance in the form of gas, vapour, mist or dust,

is constructed, installed, maintained and modified or so protected as to prevent danger arising from the exposure.

Identification and marking

78. An employer shall ensure that—

    (a) all electrical equipment is suitably identified where necessary to prevent danger,
    (b) all electrical equipment, other than cables and overhead lines, displays the maker's name together with all ratings necessary to show that it is suitable for the purpose for which it is used, and
    (c) all electrical circuits are suitably identified at their source to allow those circuits to be safely and securely de-energised and isolated.

Protection against electric shock in normal conditions

79. An employer shall ensure that all live parts which may cause danger—

    (a) are suitably covered with insulating material and so protected as to prevent danger, or

(b) are the subject of precautions taken to prevent danger, including, where appropriate, the live parts being suitably placed to prevent danger.

Protection against electric shock in fault conditions

80. An employer shall ensure that—

    (a) precautions are taken, either by—

        (i) earthing and automatic disconnection of the supply of electricity, or

        (ii) other suitable means,

to prevent danger arising where any exposed conductive part may become live,

    (b) in adverse or potentially hazardous conditions and where all of an electrical installation is dependant on one or more residual current devices in a single location for earth fault protection, precautions are taken to prevent the transmission of dangerous voltage levels in the installation caused by a fault upstream of the protective device or devices by—

        (i) installing it or them in a non-conducting enclosure, or

        (ii) using equally effective means, and

    (c) all electrical circuits supplying—

        (i) electric water heating devices,

        (ii) electrically heated showers, and

        (iii) pumps for electrically operated showers,

which are located in zone (1), as defined by the Electro-Technical Council of Ireland "National Rules for Electrical Installations", of rooms in a place of work containing a bath or shower basin, are protected by a residual current device having a tripping current not exceeding 30 milliamperes operating within such period of time so as to provide the necessary protection to prevent danger to any person coming into direct or indirect contact with any live part of the circuit.

Portable equipment

81. (1) An employer shall ensure that—

    (a) a circuit supplying portable equipment or a socket outlet intended to supply portable equipment, including any circuit supplied by an electrical generator, and in which is used alternating current at a voltage—

(i)   exceeding 125 volts, and
(ii)   not exceeding 1,000 volts,

is protected by one or more residual current devices having a tripping current not exceeding 30 milliamperes operating within such period of time so as to provide the necessary protection to prevent danger to any person coming into direct or indirect contact with any live part of the circuit,

(b) portable equipment is maintained in a manner fit for safe use, and
(c) portable equipment which is—

   (i)   exposed to conditions causing deterioration liable to result in danger, and
   (ii)   supplied at a voltage exceeding 125 volts alternating current, is—

      (I)   visually checked by the user before use, and
      (II) periodically inspected by a competent person, appropriate to the nature, location and use of the equipment.

(2) An employer shall ensure, where appropriate, that a competent person—

   (a) tests any portable equipment described in paragraph (1)(c)(i) and (ii), and
   (b) certifies whether or not the portable equipment (including any cables and plugs) was, on the day of test, as far as could reasonably be ascertained, safe and without risk to persons coming into direct or indirect contact with any live part of the equipment.

(3) If the certificate of the competent person referred to in paragraph (2) indicates that the portable equipment tested was not, on the day of the test, safe and without risk, as described in that paragraph, the employer shall ensure that the equipment is not used until it is made safe and certified as such in compliance with paragraph (2).

(4) An employer shall ensure that—

   (a) portable equipment, other than portable transformers and portable generators, supplied at a voltage exceeding 125 volts alternating current is not used in—

      (i)   construction work,
      (ii)   external quarrying activities, or
      (iii) damp or confined locations,

   unless its rating exceeds 2 kilovolt amperes,

   (b) portable hand lamps supplied at a voltage exceeding 25 volts alternating current or 50 volts direct current is not used in—

      (i)   construction work,
      (ii)   external quarrying activities, or
      (iii) damp or confined locations, and

    (c) where a transformer or generator is used to supply electricity to portable equipment at a voltage greater than 25 volts, but not exceeding 125 volts, alternating current,

        (i)   the centre point, electrically, or

        (ii) neutral (star) point in the case of three phase of the output voltage or secondary winding,

is connected to earth and the transformer or generator is of the double wound type.

Connections and cables

82.   An employer shall ensure that—

    (a) an electrical joint and connection is of adequate construction as regards conductance, insulation, mechanical strength and protection so as to prevent danger,

    (b) where a cable is used in construction work or in external quarrying operations, it is appropriately protected and insulated for the voltage of the cable to prevent danger, and

    (c) a cable for portable equipment—

        (i)   is connected to the equipment and to the system either by efficient permanent joints or by a properly constructed connector, and

        (ii) is arranged so that tension in the cable cannot be transmitted through the conductors to the terminals at either end of the cable.

Overcurrent protection

83.   An employer shall ensure that effective means suitably located are provided to protect all electrical equipment and electrical installations from overcurrent so as to prevent danger.

Auxiliary generator and battery supply

84.   An employer shall ensure that—

    (a) appropriate precautions are taken to prevent danger—

        (i)   when operating, installing, maintaining, transporting or storing auxiliary power supply batteries or auxiliary generators, and

        (ii) to persons who install, maintain or use an electrical installation where auxiliary batteries or generators have been fitted or are intended to be fitted, and

    (b) where auxiliary batteries or generators have been fitted or are intended to be fitted, appropriate precautions are taken to prevent danger to persons working on the external electrical network supplying an electrical installation.

Switching and isolation for work on equipment made dead

85.   (1) An employer shall ensure that—

   (a) subject to paragraph (2), where necessary to prevent danger, suitable means (including, where appropriate, methods of identifying circuits) are available to switch off the supply of electricity to any electrical equipment and to isolate any electrical equipment,

   (b) every switch, circuit breaker or other control device provided under subparagraph (a) is, where necessary to prevent danger,

   (i)   clearly marked to indicate the "ON" and "OFF" positions, unless these are otherwise self-evident, and

   (ii)   readily accessible for authorised persons and in a suitable and adequately lit location, and

   (c) adequate precautions are taken to prevent the operation of any switch while carrying current where that switch is not capable of safely interrupting normal load current.

   (2) Paragraph (1) does not apply to electrical equipment which is itself a source of electrical energy, provided that adequate precautions are taken to prevent danger.

Precautions for work on electrical equipment

86.   (1) An employer shall ensure that—

   (a) work activity, including the operation, use and maintenance of electrical equipment or electrical installations, is carried out in a manner that prevents danger,

   (b) before work is carried out on live electrical equipment the equipment is, where appropriate, made dead so as to prevent danger,

   (c) adequate precautions are taken to prevent danger arising from—

   (i)   electrical equipment which has been made dead becoming live while work is carried out on or near that equipment, and

   (ii)   any electrical equipment inadvertently becoming live,

   (d) where it is necessary for work to be carried out on or near any live part, other than one suitably covered with insulating material so as to prevent danger, of electrical equipment, a person is not engaged in work activity unless—

   (i)   it is unreasonable in the circumstances for it to be dead,

   (ii)   it is reasonable in the circumstances for such person to be at work on or near it while it is live, and

   (iii)   suitable precautions are taken to prevent danger, including, where necessary, the provision of protective equipment.

   (2) An employer shall ensure that any equipment provided under this Part for the purpose of protecting employees, or others to whom

the relevant statutory provisions apply, near electrical equipment is—

(a) suitable for the use for which it is provided,
(b) maintained in a condition suitable for that use, and
(c) properly used.

Working space, access and lighting

87. An employer shall ensure that—

(a) adequate working space, adequate means of access and egress and adequate lighting are provided at all electrical equipment on which, or near which, work is being done in circumstances which may cause danger, and
(b) emergency lighting is fitted in all switchrooms in order to give an adequate degree of lighting in the event of a loss of electrical supply.

Persons to be competent to prevent danger

88. An employer shall ensure that no person is engaged in any work activity to which this Part relates where technical knowledge and experience is necessary to prevent danger unless that person is competent or is under such degree of supervision as is appropriate, having regard to the nature of the work.

Testing and inspection

89. An employer shall ensure that—

(a) a new electrical installation and a major alteration of, or extension to, an existing electrical installation is, after completion, inspected and tested by a competent person and a report of the test is completed verifying that the relevant requirements of this Part have been complied with,
(b) an existing electrical installation is inspected and tested annually, or if an inspector so requires, by a competent person and a report of the test is completed verifying that the relevant requirements of this Part have been complied with,
(c) the advice of an inspector, or competent person, on the necessity for further testing of an electrical installation is acted upon having regard to the condition of the installation and the outcome of any tests referred to in paragraphs (a) and (b), and
(d) all defects found during the testing and inspection of an electrical installation are rectified promptly so as to prevent danger.

Earth leakage protection for higher voltage

90. An employer shall ensure that effective means are provided in relation to every circuit in which higher voltage is used to prevent danger arising from leakage currents to earth.

Substation and main switch room

91. (1) An employer shall ensure that a substation or a main switch room is—

    (a) suitably constructed,

    (b) arranged, so far as is reasonably practicable, so that no person can obtain access thereto otherwise than by the intended entrance,

    (c) arranged, so far as is reasonably practicable, so that a person cannot interfere with the equipment or conductors therein from outside,

    (d) provided with efficient means of ventilation and kept dry if under cover, and

    (e) as appropriate to the tasks being undertaken, under the control of an authorised person or authorised persons.

  (2) An employer shall ensure that only an authorised person or a person acting with his or her consent, or under his or her supervision, can enter any part of a substation or switch room in which there may be danger.

Fencing of outdoor equipment

92. An employer shall ensure that, wherever any transformer or switchgear in which higher voltage is used is installed otherwise than in a building, the transformer or switchgear is adequately protected either by—

    (a) suitable fencing not less than 2.4 m high, or

    (b) some other effective means for preventing any unauthorised person gaining access to the equipment or to anything connected thereto which is used as a conductor

unless it is completely enclosed by—

    (i) a metal casing which is connected to earth, or

    (ii) some other equally suitable non-metal casing.

Overhead lines and underground cables

93. (1) An employer shall ensure that—

    (a) all overhead lines and their supporting structures and underground cables are constructed, installed, connected and maintained in a manner suitable for the work and conditions under which they are to be operated to prevent danger,

    (b) where cables to be installed underground are to be enclosed in ducting of any material, other than in concrete ducts or in floor voids or floor slabs, such ducting—

        (i) is coloured red,

        (ii) has a high resistance to impact, and

        (iii) is covered with suitable warning tape embedded in the ground above the duct,

    (c) all overhead lines and other current-carrying parts connected to or containing part of overhead lines are arranged so that adequate clearance is provided from the ground or other accessible place to prevent dangerous contact with a person, article, substance or any conducting material,

    (d) means are provided to prevent danger—

        (i)   in the event of any live conductor accidentally falling due to breakage or otherwise, and

        (ii) from excessive voltage on overhead lines arising from accidental contact with or leakage from any other overhead line or otherwise, and

    (e) where excavation work is to be carried out in the proximity of a known or suspected underground cable—

        (i)   where reasonably practicable, the electrical supply to the underground cable is isolated,

        (ii) the position of the underground cable is accurately determined, so far as is reasonably practicable, and

        (iii) material immediately surrounding the underground cable is excavated only using an appropriate and safe system of work to prevent danger.

(2) A person in control to any extent of a place of work or any item at that place shall take such action, so far as is reasonably practicable, to ensure that any work activity carried out in the proximity of live overhead lines that would expose persons to any risk to their safety and health is not carried out until—

    (a) the supply to the overhead line is isolated,

    (b) if such isolation is not practicable, the overhead line is diverted,

    (c) if such isolation or diversion is not practicable, adequate

        (i)   barriers,

        (ii) protective measures,

        (iii) warnings, or

        (iv) other suitable means,

are, in so far as is reasonably practicable, put in place to minimise the risk of contact with the overhead line.

(3) The owner of a new or known underground cable, where practicable, shall determine the position of the cable and record the position on a plan to prevent dangerous contact with any person, article, substance or any conducting material.

PART 4

WORK AT HEIGHT

Interpretation for Part 4.

94.   (1) In this Part:

"access" and "egress" include ascent and descent;

"fragile surface" means a surface, including fittings, that would be liable to fail if a person's weight were to be applied to it in reasonably foreseeable circumstances;

"ladder" includes a fixed ladder and a stepladder;

"line" includes rope, chain or webbing;

"personal fall protection system" means—

(a) a fall prevention, work restraint, work positioning, fall arrest or rescue system, other than a system in which the only safeguards are collective safeguards, or

(b) rope access and positioning techniques;

"scaffold" means any temporary structure, including its supporting components, whether fixed, suspended or mobile, that is used—

(a) for supporting employees and materials, or

(b) to gain access to any structure,

and includes a working platform, a working stage, a gangway, a run and a ladder or step-ladder (other than an independent ladder or step-ladder that does not form part of such a structure), together with any guard-rail, toe-board or other such safeguard and all fixings thereon, but does not include—

(i)   lifting equipment, or

(ii)   a structure used only to support another structure or equipment (including lifting equipment),

and "scaffolding" shall be construed accordingly;

"supporting structure" means any structure used for the purpose of supporting a working platform and includes any plant used for that purpose;

"work at height" means work in any place, including a place—

(a) in the course of obtaining access to or egress from any place, except by a staircase in a permanent place of work, or

(b) at or below ground level,

from which, if measures required by this Part were not taken, an employee could fall a distance liable to cause personal injury and any reference to carrying out work at height includes obtaining access to or egress from such place while at work;

"work equipment" means any machine, appliance, apparatus, tool or installation for use at work (whether exclusively or not) and includes anything to which Regulations 101 to 114 apply;

"working platform" means any platform used as a place of work or as a means of access to or egress from a place of work, including any scaffold, suspended scaffold, cradle, mobile platform, trestle, gangway, gantry and stairway that is so used.

(2) Any reference in this Part to the keeping of a copy of a report or plan includes reference to it being kept in a form in which it is —

(a) capable of being reproduced as a printed copy when required, and

(b) secure from loss or unauthorised interference.

Organisation, planning and risk assessment

95. (1) An employer shall ensure that—

(a) work at height is properly planned, appropriately supervised and carried out in a manner that is, so far as is reasonably practicable, safe and without risk to health, and

(b) in planning work at height—

(i) the selection of work equipment is in accordance with Regulation 100,

(ii) an appropriate risk assessment and safety statement pursuant to sections 19 and 20 of the Act are prepared, and

(iii) a plan is prepared for emergencies and rescues, without prejudice to section 11 of the Act.

(2) In identifying measures to comply with this Part, an employer shall take account of the risk assessment.

Checking of places of work at height

96. An employer shall ensure that the surface and every parapet, permanent rail or other such fall protection measure at every place of work at height are checked visually prior to use and at appropriate intervals during use.

Weather conditions

97. An employer shall ensure that work at height is carried out only when weather conditions do not place the safety and health of employees at risk.

Avoidance of risks from work at height

98. Taking account of the general principles of prevention in Schedule 3 to the Act, an employer shall—

(a) ensure that work is not carried out at height where it is reasonably practicable to carry out the work safely and without risk to health otherwise than at height,

(b) without prejudice to the generality of paragraph (a), ensure that work is not carried out at height unless it is reasonably practicable to do so safely and without risk to health,

(c) where, having regard to paragraphs (a) and (b), it is necessary to carry out work at height, take suitable and sufficient measures to prevent an employee falling a distance liable to cause personal injury, including—

    (i)   ensuring that the work is carried out—

        (I)   from an existing place of work, or

        (II) in the case of obtaining access or egress, by using an existing means of access or egress,

    in compliance with this Part, where it is practicable to do so safely and under appropriate ergonomic conditions, and

    (ii) where it is not practicable for the work to be carried out in accordance with subparagraph (i), ensuring that suitable and sufficient work equipment, in compliance with Regulation 100, is provided to prevent a fall occurring,

(d) where the measures taken under paragraph (c) do not eliminate the risk of a fall occurring—

    (i)   provide sufficient work equipment, in compliance with Regulation 100, to minimise the distance of a potential fall and the risk of personal injury, and

    (ii) without prejudice to the generality of paragraph (c), provide such additional training and instruction or take other additional suitable and sufficient measures to prevent, so far as is practicable, any employee falling a distance liable to cause personal injury.

Protection of places of work at height

99. An employer shall ensure that a place of work, or means of access or egress thereto, at which work at height is, or is to be, carried on—

    (a) is stable and of sufficient strength and rigidity for the purpose for which it is intended to be or is being used,

    (b) where applicable, rests on a stable, sufficiently strong surface,

    (c) is of sufficient dimensions to permit the safe passage of employees and the safe use of any plant or materials required to be used and provide a safe working area having regard to the work to be carried out there,

    (d) is provided with suitable and sufficient edge protection,

    (e) possesses a surface that has no gap—

        (i)   through which an employee could fall,

        (ii) through which any material or object could fall and injure an employee, or

        (iii) giving rise to other risk of injury to any employee, unless measures have been taken to ensure that no employee could be so injured,

(f) is so constructed, used and maintained in such condition as to prevent, so far as is reasonably practicable—

(i) the risk of slipping or tripping, or
(ii) any employee being caught between it and any adjacent
structure, and

(g) where it has moving parts, is prevented by appropriate devices
from moving inadvertently during work at height.

Selection of work equipment for work at height

100. An employer shall—

(a) in selecting work equipment for use in work at height—

(i) give collective protection measures priority over personal
protection measures, and
(ii) take account of the following:

(I) the working conditions and the risks to the safety and
health of employees at the place where the work equipment is to be used;
(II) in the case of work equipment for access and egress, the
distance and height to be negotiated;
(III) the distance of a potential fall and the risk of personal
injury;
(IV) the duration and frequency of use of the equipment;
(V) the need for easy and timely evacuation and rescue in an
emergency;
(VI) any additional risk posed by the use, installation or
removal of that work equipment or by evacuation and
rescue from it;
(VII) the other requirements of this Part, and

(b) select work equipment for work at height that—

(i) has characteristics, including dimensions, that are appropriate to the nature of the work to be performed and the foreseeable loadings,
(ii) allows safe passage, and
(iii) in other respects, is the most suitable work equipment, having regard in particular to Regulation 98.

Condition of surfaces for supporting structures

101. An employer shall ensure that a surface upon which any supporting
structure rests is stable, of sufficient strength and of suitable composition to support safely the supporting structure, the working platform and
any loading intended to be placed on the working platform.

Stability of supporting structure

102. An employer shall ensure that a supporting structure is—

    (a) suitable and of sufficient strength and rigidity for the purpose for which it is being used,

    (b) in the case of a mobile structure, prevented by appropriate devices from moving inadvertently during work at height,

    (c) in a case other than a mobile structure, prevented from slipping by secure attachment to the bearing surface or to another structure, by provision of an effective anti-slip device, or by other means of equivalent effectiveness,

    (d) stable while being erected, used and dismantled, and

    (e) when altered or modified, so altered or modified as to ensure that it remains stable.

Guard-rails, toe-boards, barriers, etc

103. (1) A reference in this Regulation to a means of protection is to a guard-rail, toe-board, barrier or other similar means of protection.

    (2) An employer shall ensure that a means of protection is—

    (a) of sufficient dimensions, strength and rigidity for the purposes for which it is being used and is otherwise suitable,

    (b) so placed, secured and used as to ensure, so far as is practicable, that it does not become accidentally displaced,

    (c) so placed as to prevent, so far as is practicable, the fall of any employee, or any material or object from any place of work,

    (d) in relation to work at height involved in construction work such that—

        (i) the top guard-rail or other similar means of protection is at least 950 mm above the edge from which any employee is liable to fall,

        (ii) toe-boards provided are suitable and sufficient to prevent the fall of any employee, or any material or object, from any place of work, and

        (iii) any intermediate guard-rail or similar means of protection is positioned so that any gap between it and other means of protection does not exceed 470 mm.

    (3) An employer shall ensure that—

    (a) any structure or part of a structure that supports a means of protection, or to which a means of protection is attached, is of sufficient strength and suitable for the purpose of that support or attachment,

    (b) subject to paragraph (2)(d), there is not a lateral opening in a means of protection other than at a point of access to a ladder or stairway where an opening is necessary,

(c) a means of protection may be removed only for the time, and to the extent necessary, to gain access or egress, or for the performance of a particular task, and is replaced as soon as practicable, and

(d) the particular task is not performed while the means of protection is removed, unless effective compensatory safety measures are in place.

Stability of working platforms

104. An employver shall ensure that a working platform is—

(a) suitable and of sufficient strength and rigidity for the purpose for which it is intended to be used or is being used,

(b) so erected and used as to ensure that its components do not become accidentally displaced so as to endanger any employee,

(c) when altered or modified, so altered or modified as to ensure that it remains stable,

(d) where it has moving parts, prevented by appropriate devices from moving inadvertently during work at height, and

(e) dismantled in such a way as to prevent accidental displacement.

Safety on workving platforms

105. An employer shall ensure that a working platform—

(a) is of sufficient dimensions to permit the safe passage of employees and the safe use of any plant or materials required to be used, and provides a safe working area, having regard to the work being carried out there,

(b) possesses a suitable surface and, in particular, is so constructed that the surface of the working platform has no gap—

    (i) through which an employee could fall,

    (ii) through which any material or object could fall and injure an employee, or

    (iii) giving rise to other risk of injury to any employee, unless measures have been taken to ensure that no employee could be so injured, and

(c) is so erected and used, and maintained in such condition, as to prevent, so far as is reasonably practicable—

    (i) the risk of slipping or tripping, or

    (ii) any employee being caught between the working platform and any adjacent structure.

Loading of working platform and supporting structures

106. An employer shall ensure that a working platform or a supporting structure is not so loaded as to give rise to a risk of collapse or to any deformation that could affect its safe use.

Scaffolding, additional requirements

107.   An employer shall ensure that—

  (a) every scaffold and every part of it is of good design and construc-
      tion, composed of suitable and sound material and is of adequate
      strength for the purpose for which it is used or intended to be used,
  (b) strength and stability calculations for scaffolding are carried out
      unless—

      (i)   a record of the calculations covering the structural arrange-
            ments contemplated is available, or
      (ii) it is assembled in conformity with a generally recognised
            standard configuration,

  (c) depending on the complexity of the scaffolding selected, an
      assembly, use and dismantling plan is drawn up by a competent
      person, which plan may be in the form of a standard plan supple-
      mented by information on the scaffolding in question,
  (d) a copy of the plan referred to in paragraph (c), including any
      instructions it may contain, is kept available for the use of persons
      concerned in the assembly, use, dismantling or alteration of scaf-
      folding until it has been dismantled,
  (e) the dimensions, form and layout of scaffolding decks are appro-
      priate to the nature of the work to be performed, suitable for the
      loads to be carried and permit work and passage in safety,
  (f) while a scaffold is not available for use, including during its
      assembly, dismantling or alteration, it is marked with warning
      signs in accordance with the requirements of Part 7, Chapter 1
      and, where appropriate, is protected by barriers or other suitable
      means from unauthorised access or use, and
  (g) any scaffolding assembled, dismantled or significantly altered is
      only carried out under the supervision of a competent person and
      by persons who have received appropriate and specific training in
      the operations envisaged that addresses specific risks that the oper-
      ations may entail and precautions to be taken, and, in particular—

      (i)   in understanding the plan referred to in paragraph (c) for the
            assembly, dismantling or alteration of the scaffolding con-
            cerned,
      (ii) the need for safety during the assembly, dismantling or
            alteration of the scaffolding concerned,
      (iii) measures to prevent the risk of persons, materials or objects
            falling,
      (iv) safety measures in the event of changing weather conditions
            that could adversely affect the safety of the scaffolding con-
            cerned,
      (v)   permissible loadings, and
      (vi) any other risks that the assembly, dismantling or alteration
            of the scaffolding concerned may entail.

Collective safeguards for arresting falls

108. (1) Any reference in this Regulation to a safeguard is to a collective safeguard for arresting falls.

(2) An employer shall ensure that—

(a) a safeguard may be used only if—

    (i) the risk assessment has demonstrated that the work activity can, so far as is reasonably practicable, be performed safely while using it and without affecting its effectiveness,

    (ii) the use of other, safer work equipment is not practicable, and

    (iii) a sufficient number of persons are available, if required, to assist with any aspect of the safeguard's operation and have received adequate training specific to the safeguard, including rescue procedures,

(b) a safeguard is suitable and of sufficient strength to arrest safely the fall of any employee who is liable to fall,

(c) a safeguard—

    (i) in the case of a safeguard that is designed to be attached—

        (I) is securely attached to all the required anchors, and

        (II) has anchors, and the means of attachment thereto, that are suitable and of sufficient strength and stability for the purpose of safely supporting the foreseeable loading in arresting any fall or during any subsequent rescue,

    (ii) in the case of an airbag, landing mat or other similar safeguard, is stable, and

    (iii) in the case of a safeguard that expands when arresting a fall, affords sufficient clearance, and

(d) suitable and sufficient steps are taken to ensure, so far as is practicable, that in the event of a fall by any employee, the safeguard itself does not cause injury to that employee.

Personal fall protection systems.

109. An employer shall ensure that—

(a) a personal fall protection system is only used by an employee if—

    (i) the risk assessment has demonstrated that—

        (I) the work can, so far as is reasonably practicable, be performed safely while using that system, and

        (II) the use of other, safer work equipment is not practicable, and

    (ii) the user and a sufficient number of persons are available, if required, to assist with any aspect of the operations envisaged and have received adequate training specific to the operations envisaged, including immediate rescue procedures,

(b) a personal fall protection system is suitable and of sufficient strength for the purposes for which it is being used, having regard to the work being carried out and any foreseeable loading,

(c) where appropriate, a personal fall protection system—

(i) fits the employee,

(ii) is correctly fitted,

(iii) is adjustable to minimise injury to the user if a fall occurs, and

(iv) is so designed, installed and used as to prevent unplanned or uncontrolled movement of the user,

(d) where designed for use with an anchor, a personal fall protection system is securely attached to at least one anchor, and each anchor and the means of attachment thereto is suitable and of sufficient strength and stability for the purpose of supporting any foreseeable loading,

(e) suitable and sufficient steps are taken to prevent any employee falling or slipping from a personal fall protection system, and

(f) suitable and sufficient steps are taken to ensure, so far as is practicable, that in the event of a fall by any employee, an injury from the personal fall protection system is minimised.

Work positioning systems

110. An employer shall ensure that—

(a) a work positioning system is used only if—

(i) the system includes a suitable backup system for preventing or arresting a fall, and

(ii) where the system includes a line as a backup system, the user is connected to it, and

(b) if not practicable to comply with paragraph (a), all reasonably practicable measures are taken to ensure that the work positioning system does not fail.

Rope access or positioning technique

111. An employer shall ensure that—

(a) a rope access or positioning technique is used only if—

(i) it involves a system comprised of at least two separately anchored lines, of which one (known in this Regulation as "the working line") is used as a means of access, egress and support, and the other is the safety line,

      (ii)   the user is provided with a suitable harness and is connected by it to the working line and the safety line,

      (iii) the working line is equipped with safe means of ascent and descent and has a self-locking system to prevent the user falling should he or she lose control of his or her movements, and

      (iv) the safety line is equipped with a mobile fall protection system that is connected to, and travels with, the user of the system,

  (b) provision is made for a seat with appropriate accessories depending, in particular, on the duration of the job and the ergonomic constraints, and

  (c) the system referred to in paragraph (a)(i) does not comprise a single line, except where—

      (i)   the risk assessment has demonstrated that the use of a second line would entail higher risk to employees, and

      (ii) appropriate measures have been taken to ensure safety.

Fall arrest systems

112.   An employer shall ensure that—

  (a) a fall arrest system incorporates means of absorbing energy and limiting the force applied to the user's body, and

  (b) a fall arrest system is not used in a manner that—

      (i)   involves the risk of a line being cut,

      (ii) where its safe use requires a clear zone (allowing for any pendulum effect), does not afford such zone, or

      (iii) otherwise inhibits its performance or renders its use unsafe.

Work restraint systems

113.   An employer shall ensure that a work restraint system is only used if it is—

  (a) designed so that, if used correctly, it prevents the user from getting into a position in which a fall can occur, and

  (b) used correctly.

Ladders

114.   An employer shall ensure that—

  (a) a ladder is used for work at height only if the risk assessment has demonstrated that the use of more suitable work equipment is not justified because—

      (i)   the level of risk is low, and

      (ii) the duration of use is short, or

      (iii) existing features at the place of work cannot be altered,

(b) any surface upon which a ladder rests is stable, firm, of sufficient strength and of suitable composition to support safely the ladder, so that the ladder's rungs or steps and any loading intended to be placed on it remain horizontal,

(c) a ladder is so positioned as to ensure its stability during use,

(d) a suspended ladder is attached in a secure manner so that, with the exception of a flexible ladder, it cannot be displaced and swinging is prevented,

(e) a portable ladder is prevented from slipping during use by—

   (i)   securing the stiles at or near their upper or lower ends,

   (ii) effective anti-slip or other effective stability devices, or

   (iii) any other arrangement of equivalent effectiveness,

(f) a ladder used for access is long enough to protrude sufficiently above the place of landing to which it provides access, unless other measures have been taken to ensure a firm handhold,

(g) no interlocking or extension ladder is used unless its sections are prevented from moving relative to each other while in use,

(h) a mobile ladder is prevented from moving before it is used,

(i) where a ladder, or run of ladders, rises a vertical distance of 9 m or more above its base, sufficient safe landing areas or rest platforms are provided at suitable intervals, where reasonably practicable, and

(j) a ladder is used in such a way that—

   (i)   a secure handhold and secure support are always available to the employee, and

   (ii) the employee can maintain a safe handhold when carrying a load unless, in the case of a step ladder, the maintenance of a handhold is not practicable when a load is carried, and the risk assessment has demonstrated that the use of a stepladder is justified because—

       (I)   the level of risk is low, and

       (II) the duration of use is short.

Fragile surfaces

115. An employer shall—

(a) ensure that no employee passes across or near, or works on, from or near, a fragile surface, where work can be carried out safely and under appropriate ergonomic conditions without his or her doing so,

(b) where it is necessary to pass across or near, or work on, from or near a fragile surface—

   (i)   ensure, so far as is reasonably practicable, that suitable and sufficient platforms, coverings, guard rails or other similar means of support or protection are provided and used so that any foreseeable loading is supported by such supports or borne by such protection, and

(ii) where a risk of an employee falling remains despite the measures taken under this Regulation, take suitable and sufficient measures to minimise the distance of a potential fall and the risk of personal injury, and

(c) where an employee may pass across or near, or work on, from or near a fragile surface, ensure that—

(i) prominent warning notices are affixed at the approach to the place where the fragile surface is situated, or

(ii) where that is not practicable, such employee is made aware of it by other means.

Falling objects

116. An employer shall—

(a) take suitable and sufficient steps to prevent, so far as is reasonably practicable, the fall of any material or object where necessary to prevent injury to any employee,

(b) where it is not practicable to prevent the fall of any material or object as referred to in paragraph (a), take suitable and sufficient steps to prevent any person being struck by any falling material or object that is liable to cause injury,

(c) ensure that no material or object is thrown or tipped from height in circumstances where it is liable to cause injury to any person, and

(d) ensure that materials and objects are stored in such a way as to prevent risk to any employee arising from the collapse, overturning or unintended movement of the materials or objects.

Danger areas

117. An employer shall ensure, without prejudice to the preceding requirements of this Part, that, where a place of work contains an area in which, owing to the nature of the work, there is a risk of any employee suffering personal injury by—

(a) falling a distance, or

(b) being struck by a falling object,

the place of work, so far as is practicable, is equipped with devices preventing unauthorised employees from entering the area and that the area is clearly indicated by warning signs or other appropriate means.

Interpretation for Regulation 119

118. (1) Subject to paragraph (2), in this Regulation and Regulation 119, "inspection" means such visual or more rigorous inspection by a competent person as is appropriate for safety purposes and includes any testing appropriate for those purposes.

(2) Where a thorough examination has been made of lifting equipment under a specific requirement of any of the relevant statutory provisions—

(a) the examination, for the purposes of Regulation 119, other than paragraph (1)(c) of that Regulation, shall be treated as an inspection of the lifting equipment, and

(b) where a report of the examination has been prepared under the relevant statutory provisions, the report shall be treated for the purposes of Regulation 119(4)(b) as the recording of the inspection.

Inspection of work equipment

119. (1) An employer shall ensure that, as regards work equipment to which Regulations 101 to 114 apply—

(a) where the safety of the work equipment depends on how it is installed or assembled, it is not used after installation or assembly in any position unless it has been inspected in that position,

(b) without prejudice to paragraphs (a) and (c), work equipment exposed to conditions causing deterioration which is liable to result in dangerous situations is inspected—

(i)   at suitable intervals, and

(ii) where exceptional circumstances have occurred that are liable to jeopardise the safety of the work equipment, as soon as practicable following these exceptional circumstances, and

(c) without prejudice to paragraph (a), a working platform—

(i)   used for construction work, and

(ii) from which an employee could fall 2 m or more,

is not used in any position unless it has been inspected in that position within the previous 7 days or, in the case of a mobile working platform, inspected on the site, within the previous 7 days.

(2) A person carrying out an inspection of work equipment to which paragraph (1)(c) applies shall—

(a) promptly prepare a report containing the particulars as set out in Schedule 5, and

(b) within 24 hours of completing the inspection, provide the report, or a copy thereof, to the person on whose behalf the inspection was carried out.

(3) An employer receiving a report under paragraph (2) shall keep the report or a copy of the report—

(a) at the site where the inspection was carried out until the construction work is completed, and

(b) thereafter, at an office of the employer.

(4) An employer shall ensure that—

(a) no work equipment under the employer's control is used in another place of work unless it is accompanied by evidence that the last inspection required to be carried out under this Regulation has been carried out, and

(b) the result of an inspection under this Regulation is recorded and kept available for inspection by an inspector for 5 years from the date of inspection.

PART 5

PHYSICAL AGENTS

CHAPTER 1 — CONTROL OF NOISE AT WORK

Interpretation

120. In this Chapter:

"daily noise exposure level" expressed as $(L_{EX\ 8h})$ (dB)(A) re: 20 uPa) means the time-weighted average of the noise exposure level for a nominal eight-hour working day as defined by international standard ISO (International Organization for Standardization) 1999: 1990, point 3.6, covering all noises present at work, including impulsive noise;

"exposure action values" mean the daily noise exposure level or peak sound pressure level which, if exceeded for any employee, requires specified action to be taken to reduce risk;

"exposure limit value" means the level of daily noise exposure or peak sound pressure which must not be exceeded for any employee;

"noise" means any audible sound;

"peak sound pressure" expressed as (p_{peak}) means the maximum value of the "C"-frequency weighted instantaneous noise pressure;

"weekly noise exposure level" expressed as $(L_{EX,\ 8h})$ means the time-weighted average of the daily noise exposure levels for a nominal week of five eight-hour working days as defined by international standard ISO 1999: 1990, point 3.6 (note 2).

Application

121. This Chapter, subject to Regulation 122, applies to activities in which employees are or are likely to be exposed to risks to their safety and health arising from exposure to noise during their work and, in particular, the risk to hearing.

Transitional periods

122. (1) In the case of employees on board seagoing vessels, Regulation 128 does not apply until 15 February 2011.

(2) Taking account of Regulation 3(1)(z) and (2), this Chapter does not apply to the music and entertainment sectors until 15 February 2008.

Exposure limit values and exposure action values

123. (1) For the purposes of this Chapter, the exposure limit values and exposure action values in respect of the daily noise exposure levels and peak sound pressure are as follows:

(a) exposure limit values—
$L_{EX,8h}$ = 87 dB(A) and p_{peak} = 140dB(C) in relation to 20 μPa;
(b) upper exposure action values—
$L_{EX,8h}$ = 85 dB(A) and p_{peak} = 137dB(C) in relation to 20 μPa;
(c) lower exposure action values—
$L_{EX,8h}$ = 80 dB(A) and p_{peak} = 135dB(C) in relation to 20 μPa.

(2) An employer, when applying the exposure limit values referred to in paragraph (1)(a) in determining an employee's effective exposure, shall take account of the attenuation provided by individual hearing protectors worn by the employee.

(3) The exposure action values referred to in paragraphs (1)(b) and (c) apply irrespective of the attenuating effect of any such hearing protectors as referred to in paragraph (2).

(4) For activities where the daily noise exposure varies markedly from one working day to the next, an employer, for the purposes of applying the exposure limit values and the exposure action values, may use the weekly noise exposure level in place of the daily noise exposure level to assess the levels of noise to which the employer's employees are exposed, provided that—

(a) the weekly noise exposure level as shown by adequate monitoring does not exceed the exposure limit value of 87db(A), and

(b) appropriate measures are taken in order to reduce the risk associated with these activities to a minimum.

**Determination and assessment of risks above a lower
exposure action value**

124. An employer shall—

(a) without prejudice to sections 19 and 20 of the Act, where employees are liable to be exposed to noise at work above a lower exposure action value, in consultation with the employer's employees or their representatives, or both, make a suitable and appropriate assessment of the risk arising from such exposure,

(b) in carrying out the risk assessment referred to in paragraph (a), if necessary, measure the levels of noise to which the employer's employees are exposed,

(c) be responsible for the assessment referred to in paragraphs (a) and (b) being planned and carried out competently at suitable intervals and for ensuring that any sampling is representative of the daily personal exposure of an employee to noise,

(d) ensure that the methods and apparatus used in the measurement of noise at work for the purposes of this Chapter are adapted to—

   (i) the prevailing conditions, particularly in the light of the characteristics of the noise to be measured,

   (ii) the length of exposure, ambient factors, and

   (iii) the characteristics of the measuring apparatus, and that it is possible to—

      (I) determine the parameters defined in Regulation 120, and

      (II) decide, whether in a given case, the values specified in Regulation 123 have been exceeded,

(e) give particular attention when carrying out a risk assessment under this Regulation to the following—

   (i) the level, type and duration of exposure, including any exposure to impulsive noise,

   (ii) the exposure limit values and the exposure action values specified in Regulation 123,

   (iii) the effects of exposure to noise on employees whose safety or health is at particular risk from such exposure,

   (iv) as far as technically possible, any effects on employees' safety and health resulting from interactions between noise and work-related ototoxic substances, and between noise and vibrations,

   (v) any indirect effects on employees' safety or health resulting from interactions between noise and warning signals or

        other sounds that need to be observed in order to reduce the
        risk of accidents,

(vi)   any information on noise emission provided by the manu-
        facturers of work equipment in accordance with section 16
        of the Act,

(vii) the availability of alternative equipment designed to reduce
        noise emission,

(viii) the extension of exposure to noise beyond normal working
        hours under the employer's responsibility,

(ix) appropriate information obtained from health surveillance
        including, where possible, published information, and

(x)   the availability of hearing protectors with adequate attenu-
        ation characteristics,

(f) without prejudice to section 19(3) of the Act, review a risk assess-
     ment undertaken for the purposes of this Chapter where the
     results of health surveillance undertaken in accordance with Reg-
     ulation 131 show it to be necessary,

(g) record in the safety statement drawn up pursuant to section 20 of
     the Act—

(i)   the findings of the risk assessment as soon as it is practica-
        ble after it is made, and

(ii) the steps which he or she has taken to comply with Regula-
        tions 125 to 130, and

(h) review the assessment and, if necessary, the measurement
     referred to in paragraph (b) at suitable intervals and, in particular,
     where either of the conditions specified in section 19(3) (a) and
     (b) of the Act are met.

Provisions aimed at avoiding or reducing exposure

125.   An employer shall—

(a) in compliance with the general principles of prevention set out in
     Schedule 3 to the Act, and in consultation with the employer's
     employees or representatives, or both, ensure, so far as is reason-
     ably practicable, that the risk arising from exposure of the
     employer's employees to noise is either eliminated at source or
     reduced to a minimum,

(b) in complying with paragraph (a), take into account, in particular—

(i)   other methods of work which eliminate or reduce exposure
        to noise,

(ii) the choice of appropriate work equipment, taking account
        of the work to be done, emitting the least possible noise,
        including the possibility of making available to employees
        work equipment in compliance with section 16 of the Act
        with the aim or effect of limiting exposure to noise,

(iii) the design and layout of places of work and workstations,

(iv) adequate information and training to instruct employees to use work equipment correctly and safely in order to reduce their exposure to noise to a minimum,

(v) noise reduction by technical means, such as—

    (I) reducing air-borne noise, for instance by use of shields, enclosures and sound absorbent coverings,

    (II) reducing structure-borne noise, for instance by damping or isolation,

(vi) appropriate maintenance programmes for work equipment, the place of work, workstations and systems of work, and

(vii) organisation of work to reduce noise by –

    (I) limiting the duration and intensity of the exposure, and

    (II) arranging appropriate work schedules with adequate rest periods,

(c) where, owing to the nature of the activity, rest facilities are provided, ensure that noise in those facilities is reduced to a level compatible with their purpose and the conditions of use, and

(d) adapt any measure taken in compliance with this Regulation and Regulations 126 and 127, to take account of any employee whose safety or health is at particular risk from exposure to noise.

Application of upper exposure action values

126. If a risk assessment referred to in Regulation 124 indicates that an upper exposure action value is exceeded, an employer shall establish and implement a programme of technical or organisational measures, or both, designed to reduce exposure to noise, taking into account, in particular, the measures referred to in Regulation 125.

Prevention of exposure above noise level of 85dB(A)

127. If a risk assessment indicates that there are workstations within the place of work where employees are likely to be exposed to noise above 85dB(A), an employer shall—

(a) display mandatory warning signs, in accordance with Chapter 1, Part 7, to convey information that—

    (i) the noise levels at those workstations are likely to exceed that upper exposure action value, and

    (ii) hearing protectors are available and must be worn, and

(b) ensure that the workstations are protected from unauthorised access by barriers or other suitable means that are technically feasible and justified by the risk of exposure.

Application of exposure limit value

128. Subject to Regulation 122, an employer shall ensure that—

(a) the employer's employees are not exposed to noise above the exposure limit value, or

(b) if, despite the measures taken to comply with this Chapter, exposure above the exposure limit value is detected—

(i) immediate action is taken to reduce exposure to noise to below the exposure limit value,

(ii) the reasons for that limit being exceeded are identified, and

(iii) the organisational and technical measures taken in accordance with Regulation 125 are amended to prevent the exposure limit value being exceeded again.

Personal protection

129. (1) An employer shall—

(a) in accordance with sections 8, 9, 10, 13 and 14 of the Act, and where the risks arising from exposure to noise cannot be prevented by other means, make available appropriate, properly fitting, individual hearing protectors which comply with the relevant statutory provisions,

(b) where noise exposure exceeds the lower exposure action values, make individual hearing protectors available,

(c) ensure that individual hearing protectors referred to in subparagraph (a) are selected following consultation with the employees concerned or their representatives, or both, so as to eliminate the risk to hearing or reduce the risk to a minimum, and

(d) ensure, so far as is reasonably practicable, that—

(i) hearing protectors are used in accordance with paragraph (2), and

(ii) the measures taken under this Regulation are effective.

(2) An employee whose exposure to noise equals or exceeds the upper exposure action values shall use individual hearing protectors.

Employee information, training and consultation

130. An employer shall—

(a) without prejudice to sections 9 and 10 of the Act, where the employer's employees are exposed to noise at work at or above the lower exposure action value, provide them or their representatives, or both, with suitable and sufficient information and training relating to risks resulting from exposure to noise,

    (b) ensure that, without prejudice to the generality of paragraph (a), the information and training provided under that paragraph includes—

        (i) the nature of such risks,

        (ii) the organisational and technical measures taken in order to comply with Regulation 125,

        (iii) the exposure limit values and the exposure action values specified in Regulation 123,

        (iv) the results of the assessment and measurements of the noise carried out in accordance with Regulation 124 and an explanation of their significance and the potential risks,

        (v) the correct use of hearing protectors,

        (vi) why and how to detect and report signs of hearing damage,

        (vii) the circumstances in which health surveillance is made available to employees and its purpose, in accordance with Regulation 131,

        (viii) safe working practices to minimise exposure to noise, and

    (c) ensure that the consultation of employees in relation to this Chapter is effected in accordance with section 26 of the Act and includes in particular consultation in regard to Regulations 124(a), 125(a) and 129(1)(c).

Health surveillance, records and effects

131. (1) Without prejudice to section 22 of the Act, an employer shall—

    (a) in the case of employees whose exposure exceeds an upper exposure action value, make available to them the services of a registered medical practitioner to carry out, or to have carried out on his or her responsibility, a hearing check, and

    (b) in the case of employees whose exposure exceeds a lower exposure action value, make available to them preventive audiometric testing.

  (2) The purpose of hearing checks and audiometric tests referred to in paragraph (1) shall be to provide early diagnosis of any hearing loss due to noise and to assist in the preservation of hearing.

  (3) An employer shall—

    (a) ensure that—

        (i) a health record in respect of each of the employer's employees who undergoes health surveillance in accordance with paragraph (1) is made and maintained, and

        (ii) the record or a copy of it is kept available in a suitable form so as to permit appropriate access at a later date, taking into account any confidentiality concerns,

    (b) on request, allow an employee access to his or her personal health record,

(c) provide the Authority with copies of such health records as the Authority may require, and

(d) if the employer ceases to trade, notify the Authority forthwith in writing and make available to the Authority all health records kept by the employer in accordance with this Chapter.

(4) Where, as a result of surveillance of the hearing function in accordance with this Regulation, an employee is found to have identifiable hearing damage, the employer shall ensure that a registered medical practitioner assesses whether such damage is likely to be the result of exposure to noise at work and, if so established—

(a) every relevant employee shall be informed by the registered medical practitioner of the result which relates to the employee personally; and

(b) the employer shall—

(i)   review the risk assessment carried out in accordance with Regulation 124,

(ii) review the measures provided to eliminate or reduce risks in accordance with Regulation 125,

(iii) take into account the advice of the registered medical practitioner or other suitably qualified person, or the Authority, in implementing any measures required to eliminate or reduce risk in accordance with Regulations 125 to 130, including the possibility of assigning the employee to alternative work where there is no risk of further exposure, and

(iv) arrange systematic health surveillance and provide for a review of the health status of any other employee who has been similarly exposed.

Exemptions

132. (1) Subject to paragraphs (2) to (4), the Authority, in exceptional situations, by a certificate in writing, may exempt any person or class of persons from Regulations 128 and 129 where, because of the nature of the work, the full and proper use of personal hearing protectors would be likely to cause greater risk to safety or health than not using such protectors.

(2) An exemption under paragraph (1) may be granted subject to conditions including a limit of time not exceeding 4 years.

(3) The Authority shall not grant an exemption under this Chapter unless—

(a) the Authority consults—

(i)   representatives of employers and employees, and

(ii) any other persons

as the Authority considers appropriate,

    (b) the risks resulting from the exemption concerned are reduced, so far as is reasonably practicable, to a minimum, and

    (c) appropriate health surveillance is available to the employees concerned.

(4) The Authority, by a certificate in writing, may revoke an exemption under paragraph (1) at any time as soon as the justifying circumstances no longer obtain.

CHAPTER 2 — CONTROL OF VIBRATION AT WORK

Interpretation

133. In this Chapter

"exposure action value" means the level of daily vibration exposure for any employee which, if exceeded, requires specified action to be taken to reduce risk;

"exposure limit value" means the level of daily vibration exposure for any employee which must not be exceeded, save as set out in Regulation 142(2);

"hand-arm vibration" means mechanical vibration that, when transmitted to the human hand-arm system, entails risks to the safety and health of employees, in particular vascular, bone or joint, neurological or muscular disorders;

"mechanical vibration" means vibration occurring in a piece of machinery or equipment, or in a vehicle as a result of its operation;

"whole-body vibration" means the mechanical vibration that, when transmitted to the whole body, entails risks to the safety and health of employees, in particular lower-back morbidity and trauma of the spine.

Transitional periods

134. (1) Subject to paragraph (2), Regulation 139 applies on and after 6 July 2010, but not until then, where work equipment is used which—

    (a) was first provided to employees before 6 July 2007 by an employer, and

    (b) does not permit compliance with the exposure limit values.

(2) Regulation 139 applies on and after 6 July 2014, but not until then, in respect of work equipment, which is used in the agriculture and forestry sectors only, and—

    (a) was first provided to employees before 6 July 2007 by an employer, and

    (b) does not permit compliance with the exposure limit values.

(3) In using work equipment described in paragraph (1) or (2), an employer shall take into account the latest technical advances and the organisational measures taken in accordance with Regulation 137.

Exposure limit values and action values

135. (1) For hand-arm vibration—

    (a) the daily exposure limit value standardised to an eight-hour reference period shall be 5 m/s^2,

    (b) the daily exposure action value standardised to an eight-hour reference period shall be 2.5 m/s^2, and

    (c) exposure shall be assessed or measured on the basis set out in Part A of Schedule 6.

(2) For whole-body vibration—

    (a) the daily exposure limit value standardised to an eight-hour reference period shall be 1.15 m/s^2,

    (b) the daily exposure action value standardised to an eight-hour reference period shall be 0.5 m/s^2, and

    (c) exposure shall be assessed or measured on the basis set out in Part B of Schedule 6.

Determination and assessment of risks

136. An employer shall

    (a) without prejudice to sections 19 and 20 of the Act, where employees are or are likely to be exposed to risks to their safety or health arising from exposure to mechanical vibration during their work, make a suitable and appropriate assessment of the risk arising from such exposure;

    (b) in carrying out the risk assessment referred to in paragraph (a), assess daily exposure to mechanical vibration by means of—

        (i) observation of specific working practices,

        (ii) reference to relevant information on the probable level of the vibration corresponding to the equipment or the types of equipment used in the particular working conditions, and

        (iii) if necessary, measurement of the magnitude of mechanical vibration to which the employer's employees are liable to be exposed, and carry out any such measurement on the basis set out in Schedule 6,

    (c) ensure that the assessment referred to in paragraphs (a) and (b) are planned and carried out by a competent person at suitable intervals,

    (d) in carrying out the risk assessment under this Regulation, give particular attention to—

(i) the level, type and duration of exposure, including any exposure to intermittent vibration or repeated shocks,

(ii) the exposure limit values and the exposure action values specified in Regulation 135,

(iii) the effects of exposure to vibration on employees whose safety or health is at particular risk from such exposure,

(iv) any indirect effects on employee safety or health resulting from interactions between mechanical vibration and the place of work or other work equipment,

(v) any information provided by the manufacturers of work equipment in compliance with section 16 of the Act,

(vi) the existence of replacement equipment designed to reduce exposure to mechanical vibration,

(vii) the extension of exposure to whole-body vibration beyond normal working hours under the employer's responsibility,

(viii) specific working conditions such as low temperatures, and

(ix) appropriate information obtained from health surveillance including, where possible, published information,

(e) record in the safety statement drawn up pursuant to section 20 of the Act—

(i) the findings of the risk assessment as soon as it is practicable after it is made, and

(ii) the steps which the employer has taken to comply with Regulations 137 to 141, and

(f) review the assessment and, if necessary, the measurement referred to in paragraph (b) at suitable intervals and, in particular, where either of the conditions specified in section 19(3)(a) and (b), of the Act are met.

Provisions aimed at avoiding or reducing exposure

137. An employer shall—

(a) having regard to the general principles of prevention in Schedule 3 to the Act, ensure, so far as is reasonably practicable, that risk from the exposure of the employer's employees to mechanical vibration is either eliminated at source or reduced to a minimum, and

(b) adapt any measure taken in compliance with this Chapter to take account of any employee who is at particular risk from mechanical vibration.

Application of exposure action values

138. If the risk assessment carried out under Regulation 136 indicates that an exposure action value is exceeded, an employer shall comply with the duty to reduce exposure to mechanical vibration and attendant risks to a minimum under Regulation 137 by establishing and implementing a programme of technical or organisational measures, or both, appropriate to the activity and consistent with the risk assessment, taking into account in particular—

(a) other methods of work which reduce exposure to mechanical vibration,

(b) the choice of work equipment of appropriate ergonomic design which, taking account of the work to be done, produces the least possible vibration,

(c) the provision of auxiliary equipment which reduces the risk of injuries caused by vibration, such as seats that effectively reduce whole-body vibration and handles which reduce the vibration transmitted to the hand-arm system,

(d) appropriate maintenance programmes for work equipment, the places of work, workstations and systems of work,

(e) the design and layout of places of work and workstations,

(f) adequate information and training to instruct employees to use work equipment correctly, safely and without risk to health in order to reduce their exposure to mechanical vibration to a minimum,

(g) limitation of the duration and intensity of exposure to mechanical vibration,

(h) appropriate work schedules with adequate rest periods, and

(i) provision of clothing to protect employees exposed to cold and damp.

Application of exposure limit value

139.   Subject to Regulations 134 and 142, an employer shall ensure that—

(a) the employer's employees are not exposed to mechanical vibration above the relevant exposure limit value, and

(b) if, despite the measures taken to comply with this Chapter, the exposure limit value is exceeded,

   (i)   take action to reduce exposure to mechanical vibration to below the exposure limit value,

   (ii)   identify the reason for that limit being exceeded, and

   (iii) amend the technical and organisational measures taken in accordance with Regulation 138 to prevent it being exceeded again.

Employee information and training

140.   Without prejudice to sections 9 and 10 of the Act, where employees are exposed to risk from mechanical vibration, an employer shall provide those employees or their representative, or both, with suitable and sufficient information, instruction and training, including—

(a) the technical and organisational measures taken in order to comply with this Chapter,

(b) the exposure limit values and the exposure action values,

(c) the results of the risk assessment and measurement of the mechanical vibration carried out in accordance with Regulation 136 and the potential injury arising from the work equipment in use,

(d) why and how to detect and report signs of injury,

(e) the circumstances in which health surveillance is made available to employees and its purpose, in accordance with Regulation 141, and

(f) safe working practices to minimise exposure to mechanical vibration.

Health surveillance, records and effects

141. (1) Without prejudice to section 22 of the Act, an employer shall ensure that appropriate health surveillance is made available to those employees for whom a risk assessment referred to in Regulation 136 reveals a risk to their health, including employees exposed to mechanical vibration in excess of an exposure action value.

(2) The purpose of health surveillance referred to in this Regulation is to prevent or diagnose rapidly any disorder linked with exposure to mechanical vibration, and shall be regarded as being appropriate, when—

(a) the exposure of an employee to mechanical vibration is such that an identifiable illness or adverse health effect may be related to the exposure,

(b) there is a reasonable likelihood that the illness or effect may occur under the particular conditions of his or her work, and

(c) there are valid low risk tested techniques available to the employee for detecting indications of the illness or the effect.

(3) An employer shall ensure that—

(a) the results of health surveillance carried out in compliance with section 22 of the Act are taken into account in the application of preventive measures at a particular place of work,

(b) a health record in respect of each of the employer's employees who undergoes health surveillance in accordance with paragraph (1) is made and maintained,

(c) the health record referred to in paragraph (b) or a copy of the record is kept available in a suitable form so as to permit appropriate access at a later date, taking into account any confidentiality concerns,

(d) on request, an employee is allowed access to his or her personal health record,

(e) the Authority is provided with copies of such health records as it may require, and

(f) if the employer ceases to trade, the Authority is notified forthwith in writing and all health records kept by the employer in accordance with this Regulation are made available to the Authority.

(4) A registered medical practitioner under whose responsibility an employee receives health surveillance under this Regulation shall—

    (a) keep an individual confidential medical record containing the results of the health surveillance and, where appropriate, medical examination carried out,

    (b) ensure that such record or a copy thereof is kept in a suitable form for an appropriate time from the date of the last entry made in it,

    (c) propose any protective or preventive measures necessary in respect of any individual employee,

    (d) give access to an employee, upon request by that employee, to his or her own health surveillance records, and

    (e) allow access to individual confidential medical records to a person who is designated under section 63(1) of the Act.

(5) Where, arising from health surveillance in accordance with this Regulation, an employee is found to have an identifiable illness or adverse health effect which, in the opinion of a registered medical practitioner, is the result of exposure at work to mechanical vibration, the registered medical practitioner shall inform —

    (a) the employee of the opinion and the reasons for that opinion, and

    (b) the employer of the opinion but not of the reasons.

(6) In informing an employee as set out in paragraph (5), the registered medical practitioner must include information and advice regarding the health surveillance which the employee should undergo following the end of the exposure.

(7) An employer shall, where as a result of health surveillance in accordance with this Regulation, an employee is found to have an identifiable illness or adverse health effect which, in the opinion of a registered medical practitioner, is the result of exposure at work to mechanical vibration—

    (a) review the risk assessment made under Regulation 136,

    (b) review the measures provided to eliminate or reduce the risk under Regulations 137 and 138,

    (c) take account of the advice of the registered medical practitioner or a relevant competent person, or an inspector, in implementing any measures required to eliminate or reduce risk in accordance with Regulations 137 and 138, including the possibility of assigning the affected employee to alternative work where there is no risk of further exposure,

    (d) arrange continued health surveillance and provide for a review of the health status of any employee who has been similarly exposed, and

    (e) take account of the recommendations of the registered medical practitioner or a relevant competent person regarding further medical examination.

(8) Where an undertaking ceases to trade, the employer shall ensure that any health records are made available to the Authority.

Exemptions

142. (1) Subject to paragraphs (3) and (4), the Authority, by a certificate in writing, may exempt any person or class of persons from Regulation 139 in duly justified circumstances in respect of whole-body vibration only in the case of sea and air transport, where the latest technical advances and the specific characteristics of the place of work do not permit compliance with the exposure limit value despite the technical and organisational measures taken.

(2) Subject to paragraphs (3) and (4), the Authority, by a certificate in writing, may exempt any person or class of persons from Regulation 139 where the exposure of an employee to mechanical vibration is usually below the exposure action value but varies markedly from time to time and may occasionally exceed the exposure limit value, provided that—

    (a) any exposure to mechanical vibration averaged over 40 hours in any one week is less than the exposure limit value, and

    (b) there is evidence to show that the risk from the actual pattern of exposure is less than the corresponding risk from constant exposure at the exposure limit value.

(3) The Authority shall not grant any exemptions under this Regulation unless—

    (a) the Authority consults the employers and the employees concerned or their representatives, or both,

    (b) it applies conditions to any such exemption, taking into account the special circumstances, to ensure that the resulting risks are reduced to a minimum, and

    (c) appropriate health surveillance is available to the employees concerned.

(4) Any exemption granted by the Authority under this Regulation shall be—

    (a) reviewed by the Authority at least once every 4 years, and

    (b) revoked by the Authority, by a certificate in writing, at any time as soon as the justifying circumstances no longer obtain.

PART 6

SENSITIVE RISK GROUPS

CHAPTER 1 — PROTECTION OF CHILDREN AND YOUNG PERSONS

Interpretation for Chapter 1

143.   In this Chapter:

"child" means a person resident in the State who is under 16 years of age;

"night work" means—

   (a) in the case of a child, any work between 8 p.m. on any one day and 8 a.m. on the following day, and
   (b) in the case of a young person, the hours mentioned in paragraph (b) of section 6(1) of the Protection of Young Persons (Employment) Act 1996 (No. 16 of 1996), as qualified by that section and sections 7 and 8 thereof;

"risk assessment" means the assessment of a risk referred to in Regulation 144;

"young person" means a person who has reached 16 years of age but is less than 18 years of age.

Risk assessment

144.   An employer shall—

   (a) carry out a risk assessment before employing a child or young person and whenever there is a major change in the place of work which could affect the safety or health of such child or young person,
   (b) without prejudice to the provisions of section 19 of the Act, assess any risk to the safety or health of a child or young person and any specific risk to their safety, health and development arising from—

      (i)   his or her lack of experience, absence of awareness of existing or potential risks or lack of maturity,
      (ii) any work activity likely to involve a risk of harmful exposure to the physical, biological and chemical agents specified in Part A of Schedule 7, and
      (iii) the processes and work specified in Part B of Schedule 7,

   and take the necessary preventive and protective measures,

   (c) take account of the following when carrying out a risk assessment:

     (i)   the fitting-out and the layout of the place of work and of the workstation,

     (ii) the nature, degree and exposure to any physical, chemical or biological agent at the place of work,

     (iii) the form, range and use of work equipment, in particular agents, machines, apparatus and devices, and the way in which they are handled,

     (iv) the arrangement of work processes and of work operations at the place of work and of the way in which these may be organised in combination for the purposes of carrying out work, and

     (v) the training, instruction and level of supervision provided to a child or young person at the place of work,

(d) in taking the protective and preventive measures in accordance with paragraph (a) and as regards planning for and implementing measures to monitor and protect the safety and health of a child or young person, take account of section 18 of the Act, and

(e) without prejudice to the provisions of section 9 of the Act, inform a child or young person of any risk identified in accordance with paragraph (a) and of the preventive and protective measures taken and, in the case of a child, inform the parent or guardian of such child of such risk and such preventive and protective measures.

Circumstances prohibiting employment of a child or young person

145. An employer shall not employ a child or young person at work where a risk assessment reveals that the work—

(a) is beyond the physical or psychological capacity of the child or young person concerned,

(b) involves harmful exposure to agents which are toxic, carcinogenic, cause heritable genetic damage, or harm to the unborn child or which in any other way chronically affects human health,

(c) involves harmful exposure to radiation,

(d) involves the risk of accidents which it may be assumed cannot be recognised or avoided by a child or young person owing to insufficient attention to safety or lack of experience or training, or

(e) which presents a risk to health from exposure to extreme heat or cold or to noise or vibration.

Health surveillance

146. An employer shall—

(a) where a risk assessment reveals a risk to safety or health or to the physical or mental development of a child or young person, make available health surveillance in accordance with section 22 of the Act,

(b) make available to a child or young person a free assessment of his or her health and capabilities before assignment to night work and at regular intervals thereafter, and

(c) inform a child or young person of the result of any health surveillance or health assessment carried out in accordance with paragraphs (a) or (b) and, in the case of a child, inform the parent or guardian of the child of the results of any health surveillance or health assessment.

CHAPTER 2 — PROTECTION OF PREGNANT, POST NATAL AND BREASTFEEDING EMPLOYEES

Interpretation for Chapter 2

147.   In this Chapter:

"agent, process or working condition" includes an agent, process or working condition, lists of which are shown in Part A of Schedule 8;
"employee" means a pregnant employee, an employee who is breastfeeding or a post natal employee;
"employee who is breastfeeding" means an employee who, having given birth not more than 26 weeks previously, is breastfeeding;
"post natal employee" means an employee who gave birth not more than 14 weeks preceding a material date;
"pregnant employee" means an employee who is pregnant.

Application of Chapter 2

148.   (1) This Chapter applies to an employee subject to her—

(a) notifying her employer of her condition as soon as is practicable after it occurs, and,

(b) at the time of the notification, giving to her employer or producing for her employer's inspection a medical or other appropriate certificate confirming her condition.

(2) Section 6(2) of the Act does not apply to the application of this Chapter.

Risk assessment

149.   Without prejudice to section 19 of the Act, an employer shall—

(a) assess any risk to the safety or health of employees and any possible effect on the pregnancy of, or breastfeeding by, employees, resulting from any activity at that employer's place of work likely to involve a risk of exposure to any agent, process or working condition as referred to in Part A of Schedule 8 and, for that purpose, determine the—

    (i)   nature,

    (ii) degree and

    (iii) duration

of any employee's exposure to any agent, process or working condition;

(b) take the preventive and protective measures necessary to ensure the safety and health of such employees and avoid any possible effect on such pregnancy or breastfeeding; and

(c) without prejudice to paragraph (a) and the relevant statutory provisions relating to chemical agents and to the occupational exposure limits laid down in any relevant approved code of practice—

    (i)   assess any risk to safety or health likely to arise from exposure of a pregnant employee to an agent or working condition listed in Part B of Schedule 8 resulting from any activity at that employer's place of work,

    (ii) assess any risk to safety or health likely to arise from exposure of an employee who is breastfeeding to an agent or working condition listed in Part C of Schedule 8 resulting from any activity at that employer's place of work, and

    (iii) ensure that any such employee is not required to perform duties for which the assessment reveals such risk.

Protective or preventive measures

150. An employer shall—

(a) where—

    (i)   the risk assessment carried out under Regulation 149 reveals a risk to an employee's safety or health, or any possible adverse effect on the pregnancy or breastfeeding of an employee, and

    (ii) it is not practicable to ensure the safety or health of such employee through protective or preventive measures,

adjust temporarily the working conditions or the working hours, or both, of the employee concerned so that exposure to such risk is avoided, and

(b) in cases in which the adjustment of working conditions or working hours, or both, referred to in paragraph (a)—

    (i)   is not technically or objectively feasible, or both, or

    (ii) cannot reasonably be required on duly substantiated grounds,

take the measures necessary to provide the employee concerned with other work which does not present a risk to the safety or health of, or any possible adverse effect on the pregnancy or breastfeeding by, the employee.

Night work

151. (1) In this Regulation "night work" means work in the period between the hours of 11 p.m. on any day and 6 a.m. on the next following day where—

(a) the employee works at least 3 hours in that period as a normal course, or

(b) at least 25 per cent of the employee's monthly working time is performed in that period.

(2) An employer shall—

(a) if a registered medical practitioner certifies that it is necessary for the safety or health of an employee that she should not be required to perform night work during pregnancy or for 14 weeks following childbirth not oblige her to perform night work during that period, and

(b) in a case to which subparagraph (a) relates—

(i)   transfer the employee to daytime work, or

(ii)   where such a transfer is not technically or objectively feasible on duly substantiated grounds, or both, grant the employee leave or extend the period of maternity leave.

Information

152. An employer shall, without prejudice to the provisions of section 9 of the Act, take appropriate steps to ensure that employees or their representative, or both, are provided with information on—

(a) the results of the assessment referred to in Regulation 149, and

(b) the measures to be taken concerning employees' safety and health pursuant to this Chapter.

CHAPTER 3 — NIGHT WORK AND SHIFT WORK

Interpretation for Chapter 3

153.   In this Chapter:

"1997 Act" means the Organisation of Working Time Act 1997 (No. 20 of 1997);

"night work" and "night worker" have the same meaning as they have in the 1997 Act;

"shift work" and "shift worker" have the same meaning as they have in the 1997 Act.

Application of Chapter 3

154. This Chapter applies in respect of—

    (a) an employee and employer to whom the 1997 Act applies, and

    (b) a self-employed person.

Night work risk assessment

155. For the purposes of section 16(2)(a) of the 1997 Act, an employer shall carry out, in compliance with section 19 of the Act, a risk assessment, taking account of—

    (a) the specific effects and hazards of night work, and

    (b) the risks to the safety and health of the employee concerned that attach to the work that a night worker is employed to do,

so as to determine whether that work involves special hazards or a heavy physical or mental strain.

Protective or preventive measures with respect to night workers and shift workers

156. An employer, taking account of the risk assessment under Regulation 155, shall—

    (a) take such steps as, having regard to the nature of the work concerned, are appropriate for the protection of the safety and health of a night worker or an employee who is a shift worker, and

    (b) in taking steps to comply with section 18 of the Act, have regard to the employer's duty under paragraph (a).

Health assessment and transfer to day work

157. (1) An employer,

    (a) before employing a person as a night worker, and

    (b) at regular intervals during the period that that person is employed as a night worker,

shall make available to that person, free of charge, an assessment by a registered medical practitioner, or a person under the practitioner's supervision, in relation to any adverse effects of that night work on the night worker's health.

(2) In discharging the duty under paragraph (1) the employer—

    (a) may take into account any entitlement to an assessment referred to in that paragraph that is provided by the State, and

    (b) shall facilitate the night worker's attendance at the assessment if so required.

(3) The person who performs an assessment referred to in paragraph (1) shall—

(a) endeavour to detect if the health of the employee concerned is being or will be adversely affected by the fact that the employee performs or will perform night work, and

(b) on the completion of the assessment, inform the employer and employee concerned—

    (i)   of the opinion of the person who performs the assessment as to whether the employee is fit or unfit to perform the night work concerned, and

    (ii)   if that opinion is that the employee is unfit to perform that night work by reason only of the particular conditions under which that work is performed, suggesting changes in those conditions that could be made so that the employee could be considered fit to perform that night work.

(4) Neither a registered medical practitioner nor a person acting under his or her supervision shall disclose—

(a) the clinical details of the assessment referred to in paragraph (1) to any person other than the employee concerned or a person designated under section 63 of the Act, or

(b) the opinion of the registered medical practitioner of such an assessment to any person other than the employee and employer concerned.

(5) If a night worker—

(a) becomes ill or otherwise exhibits symptoms of ill-health, and

(b) that illness is or those symptoms are recognised as being connected with the fact that the night worker performs night work,

the employer, whenever possible, shall assign duties to the employee that do not involve performing any night work and to which the employee is suited.

PART 7

SAFETY SIGNS AND FIRST-AID

CHAPTER 1 — SAFETY SIGNS AT PLACES OF WORK

Interpretation for Chapter 1

158. In this Chapter:

"acoustic signal" means a coded sound signal which is released and transmitted by a device designed for that purpose, without the use of a human or artificial voice;

"emergency escape or first-aid sign" means a sign giving information on emergency exits or first-aid or rescue facilities;

"hand signal" means a movement, position, or both, of the arm, hands, or both, in coded form, for guiding persons who are carrying out manoeuvers which constitute a hazard or danger for persons at work;

"illuminated sign" means a sign produced by a device made of transparent or translucent materials which are illuminated from the inside or the rear in such a way as to give the appearance of a luminous surface;

"information sign" means a sign providing information other than that referred to in prohibition, warning, mandatory or emergency escape or first-aid signs;

"mandatory sign" means a sign requiring specific behaviour;

"prohibition sign" means a sign prohibiting behaviour likely to incur or cause danger;

"safety colour" means a colour to which a specific meaning is assigned;

"safety or health signs" means signs referring to a specific object, activity or situation and providing information or instructions about safety, health, or both, at work by means of a signboard, a colour, an illuminated sign, an acoustic signal, a verbal communication or a hand signal;

"supplementary signboard" means a signboard used together with one of the signs covered by the definition of "signboard" and which gives supplementary information, including, where appropriate, information in writing;

"signboard" means a sign which provides specific information or instructions by a combination of a geometric shape, colours and a symbol or pictogram, without written words, which is rendered visible by lighting of sufficient intensity;

"supplementary signboard" means a signboard used together with one of the signs covered by the definition of "signboard" and which gives supplementary information, including, where appropriate, information in writing;

"symbol or pictogram" means a figure which describes a situation or requires specific behaviour and which is used on a signboard or illuminated surface;

"verbal communication" means a predetermined spoken message communicated by a human or artificial voice;

"warning sign" means a sign giving warning of a hazard or risk.

Application of Chapter 1

159. (1) Subject to paragraphs (2) and (3) of this Regulation and to Regulation 160(2), this Chapter applies to every place of work.

(2) This Chapter does not apply to signs used for the placing on the market of dangerous substances and preparations, products or equipment except to the extent that any other enactment relating to the use of such signs may refer to these Regulations.

(3) Subject to Regulation 160(1)(d), this Chapter does not apply to signs used for regulating road, rail, inland waterway, sea or air transport.

(4) This Chapter is without prejudice to sections 8 to 11, 13, 14, 18 to 23 and 25 to 31 of the Act.

Provision of safety signs

160. (1) An employer shall—

(a) provide safety or health signs, or both, at the place of work where hazards cannot be avoided or adequately reduced by techniques for collective protection or measures, methods or procedures used in the organisation of work,

(b) ensure that such signs are in place,

(c) have regard to the risk assessment made under section 19 of the Act and the safety statement prepared under section 20 of the Act when determining whether or not to provide a sign under paragraph (a),

(d) use the appropriate sign prescribed under any enactment regulating transport or movement of traffic involving road, rail, inland waterway, sea or air in relation to risk, where such forms of transport—

(i)   are present at the place of work, and

(ii) give rise to a risk to the safety or health of any employee, and

(e) ensure that a safety or health sign used at work complies with Schedule 9.

(2) Where a signboard is in place at the commencement of these Regulations, which, solely because it includes a word or words, is not a signboard as defined in Regulation 158, an employer may leave that signboard in place until 1 January 2011.

Information and instruction for employees

161. Without prejudice to sections 9 and 10 of the Act, an employer shall—

(a) provide information to the employer's employees or representative, or both, as regards measures to be taken concerning safety or health signs used at work, especially signs incorporating words and the general and specific behaviour to be adopted in relation to those signs, and

(b) give the employer's employees suitable instruction, in particular in the form of specific directions concerning the safety or health signs used at work, which must include the meaning of the signs.

Prohibition of unauthorised information on signs

162. An employer shall ensure that signs at work which are displayed for the purposes of this Chapter do not include information other than that authorised by this Chapter.

CHAPTER 2 — FIRST-AID

Interpretation for Chapter 2

163. In this Chapter:

"first-aid" means—

(a) in a case where a person requires treatment from a registered medical practitioner or a registered general nurse, treatment for the purpose of preserving life or minimising the consequences of injury or illness until the services of a practitioner or nurse are obtained, or

(b) in a case of a minor injury which would otherwise receive no treatment or which does not need treatment by a registered medical practitioner or registered general nurse, treatment of that minor injury;

"occupational first-aider" means a person trained and qualified in occupational first-aid.

Application of Chapter 2

164. (1) Subject to paragraph (2), this Chapter applies to every place of work.
(2) Regulation 166 does not apply to the following places of work:

(a) means of transport used outside the undertaking or a place of work inside a means of transport;

(b) a fishing boat;

(c) a field, wood or land forming part of an agricultural or forestry undertaking which is situated away from the undertaking's buildings.

Provisions for first-aid

165. (1) An employer shall—

(a) provide and maintain suitably marked and easily accessible first-aid equipment, as is adequate and appropriate in the circumstances for enabling first-aid to be given to persons at every place where working conditions require it, at a place of work under the employer's control,

(b) designate at each place of work under the employer's control the number of occupational first-aiders as is necessary to give first-aid at the place of work concerned,

(c) ensure that the number of occupational first-aiders, their training and the equipment available to them is adequate, taking account of the size or hazards, or both, of each such place of work, and

(d) ensure that—

    (i) details of arrangements made for the provision of first-aid, including the names of occupational first-aiders and the location of first-aid rooms, equipment and facilities for or at the place of work are included in the safety statement, and

    (ii) the names, addresses and telephone numbers of the local emergency services are clearly displayed at each place of work.

(2) Where an occupational first-aider provided under paragraph (1)(b) is absent in temporary and exceptional circumstances, it shall be sufficient compliance with that paragraph if the employer designates a person, or ensures that a person is designated, to take charge of an injured or ill person.

First-aid rooms

166. An employer shall provide—

(a) one or, as appropriate, more first-aid rooms at every place of work under the employer's control where the size of the undertaking, the type and scale of activity being carried out and the frequency of accidents so require, without prejudice to—

    (i) Regulation 165(1)(a), and

    (ii) existing requirements in the relevant statutory provisions as regards the provision of first-aid rooms, and

(b) ensure that every first-aid room provided under paragraph (a) is fitted with essential first-aid equipment and facilities and is easily accessible for stretchers.

PART 8

EXPLOSIVE ATMOSPHERES AT PLACES OF WORK

Interpretation for Part 8

167. In this Part:

"ADR" means—

(a) the European Agreement concerning the international carriage of dangerous goods by road,

(b) the protocol of signature to that agreement, done at Geneva on 30 September 1957,

    (c) the amending protocol to that agreement adopted at Geneva on 28 October 1993, and

    (d) Annexes A and B to the ADR referred to in Annexes A and B to Council Directive No. 94/55/EC of 21 November 1994 as amended;

"explosion protection document" shall be construed in accordance with Regulation 169;

"hazard" means the physico-chemical or chemical property of a substance which has the potential to give rise to fire, explosion, or other events which can result in harmful physical effects of a kind similar to those which can be caused by fire or explosion, affecting the safety of a person, and cognate words shall be construed accordingly;

"risk" means the likelihood of a person's safety being affected by harmful physical effects being caused to him or her from fire, explosion or other events arising from the hazardous properties of a substance in connection with work;

"substance" includes any natural or artificial substance whether in solid or liquid form or in the form of a gas or vapour;

"workplace" means any premises or part of premises used for or in connection with work, and includes—

    (a) any place within the premises to which a person has access while at work, and

    (b) any room, lobby, corridor, staircase, road or other place—

        (i) used as a means of access to or egress from that place of work, or

        (ii) where facilities are provided for use in connection with that place of work, other than a public road.

Application of Part 8

168. (1) Subject to paragraph (2), this Part applies to a workplace where employees are potentially at risk from an explosive atmosphere.

    (2) This Part does not apply to—

    (a) areas used directly for and during the medical treatment of patients,

    (b) the use of appliances burning gaseous fuels in accordance with Council Directive 90/396/EEC of 29 June 1990[3] on the approximation of the laws of the Member States relating to appliances burning gaseous fuels as amended by Council Directive 93/68/EEC of 22 July 1993[4],

    (c) the manufacture, handling, use, storage and transport of explosives or chemically unstable substances,

---

[3] O.J. No. L 196, 26.7.1990, p. 15
[4] O.J. No. L 220, 30.8.1993, p. 1

(d) mineral extractive industries as referred to in the relevant statutory provisions, and

(e) the use of means of transport by land, water and air, to which the relevant provisions of the international agreements, including ADR, and the European Community directives giving effect to those agreements apply, but means of transport intended for use in a potentially explosive atmosphere shall not be excluded.

Assessment of explosion risk and explosion protection document

169. (1) An employer shall—

(a) where an explosive atmosphere is or is likely to be present at or may, from time to time, arise in a workplace, make a suitable and appropriate assessment of the risk arising from such explosive atmosphere to the employees concerned having regard to all the circumstances,

(b) in carrying out the assessment referred to in paragraph (a), have regard to—

(i) the likelihood that explosive atmospheres will occur and their persistence,

(ii) the likelihood that ignition sources, including electrostatic discharges, will be present and become active and effective,

(iii) the installations, substances used, work processes and their possible interactions,

(iv) the scale of the anticipated effects,

(v) any places which are or can be connected via openings to places in which explosive atmospheres may occur, and

(vi) such additional safety information as the employer may need in order to complete the assessment;

(2) Having carried out an assessment under and in accordance with this Regulation, an employer shall—

(a) prepare an explosion protection document, as soon as practicable and before the commencement of work,

(b) revise that document as necessary if the workplace, work equipment or organisation of work undergoes significant changes, extensions or conversions,

(c) include that document, or make reference to it, in the employer's safety statement and

(d) make that document or any revision of it available to the employees concerned.

(3) The employer shall specify in the explosion protection document each of the following:

(a) that the explosion risks have been determined and assessed;

(b) that measures have been or will be taken pursuant to this Part and that such measures are adequate having regard to the risks;

    (c) the places which have been classified into zones in accordance with Regulation 170 and, in respect of such classification, where Schedule 10 applies;

    (d) that the workplace and work equipment, including warning devices, are designed, operated and maintained with due regard for safety and that, in accordance with Part 2, Chapter 1 and Part 7, Chapter 1, adequate arrangements have been made for the safe use of work equipment;

    (e) the purpose of any co-ordination required by Regulation 175 and the measures and procedures for implementing it.

(4) An employer, in drawing up the explosion protection document, may combine existing explosion risk assessments, documents or other equivalent reports which have been prepared by or on behalf of the employer under any other enactment.

Classification of places where explosive atmospheres may occur

170. (1) An employer shall—

    (a) classify places at the workplace where explosive atmospheres may occur into hazardous or non-hazardous places in accordance with Part A of Schedule 10,

    (b) having done so, classify those places classified as hazardous into zones in accordance with paragraph 2 of that Part, and

    (c) display in a prominent position in any place that is classified as hazardous in accordance with paragraph (b), a sign at or near each point of entry to the hazardous place and ensure that the sign complies with Part B of Schedule 10.

(2) Before a workplace containing a place that is classified as hazardous pursuant to paragraph (1) is used for the first time, an employer shall ensure that—

    (a) the overall explosion safety of both the workplace and that place it contains is verified by a competent person, and

    (b) any condition or conditions that are necessary, pursuant to this Part, for ensuring protection from explosion, is or are maintained.

(3) This Part applies to—

    (a) the places classified as hazardous under paragraph (1)(a), as required by the features of workplaces, workstations, the equipment or substances used or the danger caused by the activity related to the risks from explosive atmospheres, and

    (b) equipment in non-hazardous places which is required for, or helps to ensure, the safe operation of equipment located in hazardous places.

Prevention against explosion

171. An employer shall—

(a) for the purpose of preventing and providing protection against explosions, take technical and organisational measures that are appropriate to the nature of the operation and in order of priority ensure that those measures—

    (i) either

        (I) prevent the formation of explosive atmospheres, or

        (II) where the nature of the activity does not allow that, avoid the ignition of explosive atmospheres including by electrostatic discharges where persons at work or the working environment act as charge carrier or charge producer, and

    (ii) mitigate the detrimental effects of an explosion so as to ensure the health and safety of persons at work,

(b) where necessary, combine and supplement the measures referred to in paragraph (a) with measures against the propagation of explosion,

(c) review the foregoing measures regularly and whenever significant changes occur,

(d) take the necessary measures, in compliance with Regulation 169, to ensure that—

    (i) where explosive atmospheres may or are likely to arise in such quantities as to endanger the safety and health of persons at work, or of others, the working environment is such that work can be performed safely,

    (ii) in working environments where explosive atmospheres may arise in such quantities as to endanger the safety and health of employees—

        (I) there is appropriate supervision of employees, and

        (II) that supervision includes the appropriate technical measures,

    (iii) any escape or any release, or both, whether intentional or not, of flammable gases, vapours, mists or combustible dusts which may give rise to explosion hazards are suitably diverted or removed to a safe place or, if that is not practicable, safely contained or rendered safe by some other suitable method, and

    (iv) if an explosive atmosphere contains several types of flammable or combustible gases, vapours, mist or dusts, or any combination of them, protective measures are appropriate to the greatest potential risk.

Safety of plant, equipment and protective systems

172. (1) An employer shall ensure that—

   (a) plant, equipment, protective systems and any associated connecting devices are only brought into service if the explosion protection document indicates that they can be safely used in an explosive atmosphere,

   (b) necessary measures are taken to prevent confusion between connecting devices,

   (c) all necessary measures are taken to ensure that the workplace, work equipment and any associated connecting device made available to employees are—

      (i) designed,
      (ii) constructed,
      (iii) assembled,
      (iv) installed,
      (v) maintained, and
      (vi) operated,

     in such a way as—

        (I) to minimise the risks of an explosion, and
        (II) if an explosion does occur to control or minimise the propagation of the explosion within that workplace, work equipment, or both,

   (d) for a workplace referred to in paragraph (c), appropriate measures are taken to minimise the risks to employees from the physical effects of an explosion,

   (e) where the risk assessment shows it to be necessary—

      (i) it is possible, where power failure can give rise to the spread of additional risks, to maintain equipment and protective systems in a safe state of operation independently of the rest of the installation in the event of power failure,

      (ii) manual override by a competent employee is possible in order to shut down the equipment and protective systems incorporated within automatic processes which deviate from the intended operating conditions, provided that this does not compromise safety, and

      (iii) on operation of the emergency shutdown, accumulated energy is dissipated as quickly and as safely as possible or isolated so that it no longer constitutes a hazard,

   (f) if the explosion protection document drawn up pursuant to Regulation 169(2) does not state otherwise, equipment and protective systems for all places in which explosive atmospheres may occur is selected on the basis of the categories set out in the relevant statutory provisions intended for use in potentially explosive atmospheres, and

(g) in particular, the following categories of equipment are used in the zones indicated in Schedule 10, provided they are suitable for gases, vapours, mists or dusts, or any combination of them, as appropriate—

    (i)   in zone 0 or zone 20, category 1 equipment,

    (ii) in zone 1 or zone 21, category 1 or 2 equipment, and

    (iii) in zone 2 or zone 22, category 1, 2 or 3 equipment.

(2) Paragraph (1)(a) applies also to any equipment or protective systems to which the relevant statutory provisions relating to equipment and protective systems intended for use in potentially explosive atmospheres do not apply if their incorporation into an installation can in itself give rise to an ignition hazard.

Training, instructions, permits to work

173. An employer shall—

(a) provide persons at work in workplaces where explosive atmospheres may occur with sufficient and appropriate training with regard to explosion protection, and

(b) ensure that, where required by the explosion protection document—

    (i)   work in hazardous places is carried out in accordance with written instructions issued by the employer,

    (ii) a system of permits to work is applied for carrying out both hazardous activities and activities which may interact with other work to cause hazards, and

    (iii) permits to work are issued by a competent person responsible for this function, before the activity concerned commences.

Protection of employees from explosion

174. An employer shall—

(a) provide work clothing which does not give rise to electrostatic discharges for use in places classified as hazardous pursuant to Regulation 170(1)(b) to any employee who is obliged to carry out work or duties in such places and is appropriate for the carrying out of such work or duties in such places;

(b) where necessary, ensure that persons at work are given optical or acoustic warnings, or both, and are withdrawn before the explosion conditions are reached; and

(c) where required by the explosion protection document, provide and maintain escape facilities to ensure that, in the event of danger, persons at work can leave endangered places promptly and safely.

Coordination at workplaces

175.   Without prejudice to section 21 of the Act—

> (a) where employees are present in or at the same workplace to which this Part refers and they are employed by different employers, each employer shall ensure the safety of the employer's employees and for that purpose shall ensure that the matters that arise under the employer's control comply with this Part, and
>
> (b) where 2 or more employers share the same workplace in which an explosive atmosphere may occur, the employer responsible for the workplace shall co-ordinate the implementation of all the measures required by this Part to be taken to protect employees from any risk from the explosive atmosphere.

SCHEDULE 1

Regulations 43, 46, 52, 53, 55

REQUIREMENTS FOR WORK EQUIPMENT

PART A — EXEMPTION FROM CERTAIN PROVISIONS OF REGULATION 46

Class or description of hoist or hoistway	Requirements of Regulation 46 which do not apply	Condition
1. Pavement hoist for goods. Hoistways of pavement hoists, that is to say, hoists in the case of which the provision of a permanent enclosure at the top landing would obstruct a street or public place or yard or other open space where persons are required or liable to pass.	Paragraph (2)(a) in so far as it requires the hoistway to be protected by an enclosure and gate at or above the top landing. Paragraph (2)(b) in the case of the top landing.	The hoistway shall be securely covered and fastened at the top landing except when access is required for goods or materials. Measures shall be taken to minimise the risk of persons falling down the hoistway whilst the top landing is open.
2. Hoists used solely for lifting material directly into a machine.	Paragraph (2)(a) and (b).	Measures shall be taken to prevent hazards from falling objects or contact with moving parts.

(continued)

3. Hoists used for raising or lowering or tipping-standard gauge or broader gauge railway rolling stock.	Paragraph (2)(a), (b) and (h)(ii).	So far as is reasonably practicable, means shall be provided at such entrances to the enclosure to prevent any person from falling down the hoistway or being struck by any moving part of the hoist.
4. Drop-pit hoists used for raising or lowering wheels or bogies detached from standard-gauge or broader gauge railway rolling stock.	Paragraph (2)(a), (b) and (h)(ii) and (iii).	
5. Hoistways of hoists into or from which goods or materials are loaded or unloaded automatically and to the carrier to which there is no access for persons.	Paragraph (2)(a) in so far as it requires the fitting of gates at the openings in the enclosure where goods or materials are loaded or unloaded.	So far as is reasonably practicable, means shall be provided at such openings to the hoistway to prevent any person from falling down the hoistway or being struck by any moving part of the hoist.
6. Any hoist or lift used to raise a motor vehicle.	Paragraphs (2)(a), (b) and (c).	
7. Hoists and lifts, used as working platforms, not of a movable type, which do not pass through any floor and which are used in the butchering of animals.	Paragraphs (2)(a), (b) and (h)(iii).	

PART B — PERIOD OF THOROUGH EXAMINATION OF LIFTING
EQUIPMENT, LIFTING ACCESSORY EQUIPMENT OR OTHER
MISCELLANEOUS EQUIPMENT

Column 1	Column 2
Description of lifting equipment or lifting accessory or other miscellaneous equipment	**Period within which a thorough examination must occur**
Hoist or Lift	6 months
Tailboard goods lift	12 months
Suspended access equipment	6 months
Mast climbing work platform	6 months
Lifting accessories including chains, ropes, rings, hooks, shackles, clamps, swivels, spreader beams and spreader frames, vacuum lifting devices	6 months
Items provided for support of lifting equipment	12 months
Mobile elevating work platform	6 months
Crane	12 months
Tower crane climbing rig	6 months
Crane used in dock work, shipbuilding, ship-repairing	12 months
Fork lift truck including interchangeable accessories	12 months (6 if used to lift persons)
Telehandler including interchangeable accessories	12 months (6 if used to lift persons)
Vehicle lifting table	12 months
Hoisting equipment on fishing vessels	12 months
Winches used for lifting loads	12 months

(continued)

Other lifting machines (materials only) unless specified in Part D of this Schedule	12 months
Other lifting machines (personnel) unless specified in Part D of this Schedule	6 months
Equipment located in premises used primarily for generating, transforming switching or otherwise regulating electrical energy.	In compliance with a scheme of inspection and testing drawn up by a competent person
Patient hoist	6 months

PART C — CIRCUMSTANCES REQUIRING TESTING OF LIFTING
EQUIPMENT AS PART OF A THOROUGH EXAMINATION

Column 1 **Description of Equipment**	**Column 2** **Period within which or conditions under which testing is required**
All lifting equipment	After any substantial alteration or repair affecting its strength or stability
Fixed lifting equipment	Before first use
Tower crane	After each assembly and every 4 years
Mobile crane	Every 4 years
Winch	Every 4 years
Self erecting crane	After erection and before first use on site and after any change in configuration or support conditions
Pulley block, gin wheel, sheer legs used with loads weighing 1,000 kg or more	Before first use in a new position

PART D — EQUIPMENT THAT HAS A LIFTING FUNCTION, IS SUBJECT TO
REGULATION 30 AND IS NOT SUBJECT TO REGULATION 52

(a) Bottle jack
(b) Pallet truck
(c) Tractor hitch
(d) Height adjusting components of machine tools
(e) Fixed machinery for raising/lowering pallets
(f) Vehicle wheelchair hoist
(g) Lifting equipment designed to lift wheelie bins of volume less than 360 litres
(h) Escalators and conveyors
(i) Platform lifts for level changes of 1.2 m or less

PART E — INFORMATION TO BE CONTAINED IN REPORT
OF THOROUGH EXAMINATION

1. The name and address of the employer or owner for whom the thorough examination was made.
2. The address of the premises at which the thorough examination was made.
3. Particulars sufficient to identify the lifting equipment including, where known, its date of manufacture.
4. Date of this examination and date of the last thorough examination if known.
5. The safe working load of the lifting equipment or, where its safe working load depends on the configuration of the lifting equipment, its safe working load for the different configurations that have been determined.
6. The purpose of the examination including examination before putting into use for the first time, examination after installation or after assembly at a new site or in a new location, examination after repairs or alterations and periodic examination.
7. In relation to every thorough examination of lifting equipment—

   (a) identification of any part found to have a defect which is or could become a danger to persons and a description of the defect;
   (b) particulars of any repair, renewal or alteration required to remedy a defect found to be a danger to persons;
   (c) in the case of a defect which is not yet but could become a danger to persons—

      (i) the time by which it could become such danger;
      (ii) particulars of any repair, renewal or alteration required to modify it;

   (d) the latest date by which the next thorough examination must be carried out;
   (e) where the thorough examination included testing, particulars of any test;
   (f) identification of parts not accessible for examination.

8.   The name, address and qualifications of the individual making the report and, where appropriate, the name and address of the individual's employer.

9.   Where appropriate, the name and position of a person signing or authenticating the report on behalf of its author.

SCHEDULE 2

Regulation 62

PERSONAL PROTECTIVE EQUIPMENT

PART A — GUIDE LIST OF ACTIVITIES AND SECTORS OF ACTIVITY WHICH MAY REQUIRE PROVISION OF PERSONAL PROTECTIVE EQUIPMENT

1.   Head Protection (Skull Protection)

Protection helmets

Building work, particularly work on, underneath or in the vicinity of scaffolding and elevated places of work, erection and stripping of formwork, assembly and installation work, work on scaffolding and demolition work.

Work on steel bridges, steel building construction, masts, towers, steel hydraulic structures, blast furnaces, steel works and rolling mills, large containers, large pipelines, boiler plants and power stations.

Work in pits, trenches, shafts and tunnels.

Earth and rock works.

Work in underground workings, quarries, open diggings, coal stock removal.

Work with bolt-driving tools.

Blasting work.

Work in the vicinity of lifts, lifting gear, cranes and conveyors.

Work with blast furnaces, direct reduction plants, steelworks, rolling mills, metalworks, forging, drop forging and casting.

Work with industrial furnaces, containers, machinery, silos, bunkers and pipelines.

Shipbuilding work.

Railway shunting work.

Work in slaughterhouses.

2.   Foot Protection

Safety shoes with puncture-proof soles

Carcase work, foundation work and roadworks.

Carcase demolition work.

Scaffolding work.

Work with concrete and prefabricated parts involving formwork erection and stripping.

Work in contractors' yards and warehouses.

Roof work.

Safety shoes without pierce-proof soles

Work on steel bridges, steel building construction, masts, towers, lifts, steel hydraulic structures, blast furnaces, steelworks and rolling mills, large containers, large pipelines, cranes, boiler plants and power stations.

Furnace construction, heating and ventilation installation and metal assembly work.

Conversion and maintenance work.

Work with blast furnaces, direct reduction plants, steelworks, rolling mills, metalworks, forging, drop forging, hot pressing and drawing plants.

Work in quarries and open diggings, coal stock removal.

Working and processing of rock.

Working and processing in relation to flat glass products and container glassware manufacture.

Work with moulds in the ceramics industry.

Lining of kilns in the ceramics industry.

Moulding work in the ceramic ware and building materials industry.

Transport and storage work.

Work with frozen meat blocks and preserved foods packaging.

Shipbuilding work.

Railway shunting work.

Safety shoes with heels or wedges and pierce-proof soles

Roof work.

Protective shoes with insulated soles

Work with and on very hot or very cold materials.

Safety shoes which can easily be removed

Any work where there is a risk of penetration by molten substances.

Safety shoes fitted with toecaps

Any work where there is a risk of impact on or crushing of the foot caused by falling or projecting objects or collision of the foot with an obstacle.

3.   Eye or Face Protection

Protection goggles, face shields or screens

Welding, grinding and separating work.

Caulking and chiselling work.

Rock working and processing work.

Work with bolt-driving tools.
Work on stock removing machines for small chippings.
Drop forging.
The removal and breaking up of fragments.
Spraying of abrasive substances.
Work with acids and caustic solutions, disinfectants and corrosive products.
Work with liquid sprays.
Work with and in the vicinity of molten substances.
Work with radiant heat.
Work with lasers.

4.   Respiratory Protection

Respirators/breathing apparatus

Work in containers, restricted areas and gas-fired industrial furnaces where there may be gas or insufficient oxygen.
Work in the vicinity of the blast furnace charge.
Work in the vicinity of gas converters and blast furnace gas pipes.
Work in the vicinity of blast furnace taps where there may be heavy metal fumes.
Work on the lining of furnaces and ladles where there may be dust.
Spray painting where dedusting is inadequate.
Work in shafts, sewers and other underground areas connected with sewage.
Work in refrigeration plants where there is a danger that the refrigerant may escape.
Work in processes where harmful dust or fumes are likely to be present.

5.   Hearing Protection

Ear protectors

Work with metal presses.
Work with pneumatic drills.
Work with turbines.
The work of ground staff at airports.
Pile-driving work.
Wood and textile working.

6.   Body, Arm and Hand Protection

Protective clothing

Work with acids and caustic solutions, disinfectants and corrosive cleaning substances.
Work with or in the vicinity of hot materials and where the effects of heat are felt.
Work on flat glass products.
Shot blasting.
Work in deep-freeze rooms.

Fire-resistant protective clothing

Welding in restricted areas.

Pierce-proof aprons

Boning and cutting work.
Work with hand knives involving drawing the knife towards the body.

Leather aprons

Welding.
Forging.
Casting.

Gloves

Welding.
Handling of sharp-edged objects, other than machines where there is a danger of the glove being caught.
Unprotected work with acids and caustic solutions. Metal mesh gloves
Boning and cutting.
Regular cutting using a hand knife for production and slaughtering.
Changing the knives of cutting machines.

7.   Weatherproof Clothing

Work in the open air in rain and cold weather.

Waterproof clothing.

Work in wet processes.

8.   Reflective Clothing

Work where the employees must be clearly visible.

9.   Safety Harness

Work on scaffolding.
Assembly of prefabricated parts.
Work on masts.

10. Safety Ropes

Work in high crane cabs.
Work in high cabs of warehouse stacking and retrieval equipment.
Work in high section of drilling towers.
Work in shafts and sewers.

11. Skin Protection

Processing of coating materials.
Tanning.

PART B — GUIDE LIST OF ITEMS OF PERSONAL PROTECTIVE EQUIPMENT

1. Head Protection

    Protective helmets for use in industry, including mines, building sites, other industrial uses.
    Scalp protection (caps, bonnets, hairnets with or without eye shade).
    Protective headgear (bonnets, caps, sou'westers, etc. in fabric with proofing, etc.).

2. Hearing Protection

    Earplugs and similar devices.
    Full acoustic helmets.
    Earmuffs which can be fitted to industrial helmets.
    Ear defenders with receiver for Low Frequency (LF) induction loop.
    Ear protection with intercom equipment.

3. Eye and Face Protection

    Spectacles.
    Goggles.
    X-ray goggles, laser-beam goggles, ultra-violet, infra-red, visible radiation goggles.
    Face shields.
    Arc-welding masks and helmets (hand masks, headband masks, headband masks or masks which can be fitted to protective helmets).

4. Respiratory Protection

    Dust filters, gas filters and radioactive dust filters.
    Insulating appliances with an air supply.
    Respiratory devices including a removable welding mask.
    Diving equipment.
    Diving suits.

5. Hand and Arm Protection

    Gloves to provide protection:
        from machinery (piercing, cuts, vibrations, etc.).
        from chemicals.
        for electricians and from heat.
    Mittens.
    Finger stalls.
    Oversleeves.
    Wrist protection for heavy work.
    Fingerless gloves.
    Protective gloves.

6. Foot and Leg Protection

    Low shoes, ankle boots, calf-length boots, safety boots.
    Shoes which can be unlaced or unhooked rapidly.

Heat-resistant shoes, boots and overboots.
Thermal shoes, boots and overboots.
Vibration-resistant shoes, boots and overboots.
Anti-static shoes, boots and overboots.
Insulating shoes, boots and overboots.
Protective boots for chain saw operators.
Clogs.
Kneepads.
Removable instep protectors.
Gaiters.
Removable soles (heat-proof, pierce-proof or sweat-proof).
Removable spikes for ice, snow or slippery flooring.

7. Skin Protection

    Barrier creams/ointments.

8. Trunk and Abdomen Protection

    Protective waistcoats, jackets and aprons to provide protection from machinery, piercing, cutting, molten metal splashes, etc.
    Protective waistcoats, jackets and aprons to provide protection from chemicals.
    Headed waistcoats.
    Life jackets.
    Protective X-ray aprons.
    Body belts.

9. Whole Body Protection

    Equipment designed to prevent falls

    Fall-prevention equipment (full equipment with all necessary accessories).
    Braking equipment to absorb kinetic energy (full equipment with all necessary accessories).
    Body-holding devices (safety harness).

10. Protective clothing

    "Safety" working clothing (two-piece and overalls).
    Clothing to provide protection from machinery, piercing, cutting etc.
    Clothing to provide protection from chemicals.
    Clothing to provide protection from molten metal splashes and infra-red radiation.
    Heat resistant clothing.
    Thermal clothing.
    Clothing to provide protection from radioactive contamination.
    Dust-proof clothing.
    Gas-proof clothing.
    Fluorescent signalling, retro-reflecting clothing and accessories (arm-bands, gloves, etc.).
    Protective coverings.

SCHEDULE 3

Regulation 69

RISK FACTORS FOR MANUAL HANDLING OF LOADS

1.   Characteristics of the load

The manual handling of a load may present a risk particularly of back injury if it is:
   too heavy or too large,
   unwieldy or difficult to grasp,
   unstable or has contents likely to shift,
   positioned in a manner requiring it to be held or manipulated at a distance from the trunk, or with a bending or twisting of the trunk, or
   likely, because of its contours or consistency (or both), to result in injury to employees,
   particularly in the event of a collision.

2.   Physical effort required

A physical effort may present a risk particularly of back injury if it is:
   too strenuous,
   only achieved by a twisting movement of the trunk,
   likely to result in a sudden movement of the load, or
   made with the body in an unstable posture.

3.   Characteristics of the working environment

The characteristics of the working environment may increase a risk particularly of back injury if:
   there is not enough room, in particular vertically, to carry out the activity,
   the floor is uneven, thus presenting tripping hazards, or is slippery in relation to the employee's footwear,
   the place of work or the working environment prevents the handling of loads at a safe height or with good posture by the employee,
   there are variations in the level of the floor or the working surface, requiring the load to be manipulated on different levels,
   the floor or foot rest is unstable, or
   the temperature, humidity or ventilation is unsuitable.

4.   Requirements of the activity

The activity may present a risk particularly of back injury if it entails one or more of the following requirements:
   over-frequent or over prolonged physical effort involving in particular the spine,
   an insufficient bodily rest or recovery period,
   excessive lifting, lowering or carrying distances, or

a rate of work imposed by a process which cannot be altered by the employee.

5.   Individual Risk Factors

The employee may be at risk if he or she:
is physically unsuited to carry out the task in question,
is wearing unsuitable clothing, footwear or other personal effects, or
does not have adequate or appropriate knowledge or training.

SCHEDULE 4

Regulation 72

MINIMUM REQUIREMENTS FOR ALL DISPLAY SCREEN EQUIPMENT

1.   Equipment

(a) Display screen

(i)   The characters on the screen shall be well defined and clearly formed, of adequate size and with adequate spacing between the characters and lines.

(ii)   The image on the screen shall be stable, with no flickering or other forms of instability.

(iii) The brightness or the contrast (or both) between the characters and the background shall be easily adjustable by the employee and easily adjustable to ambient conditions.

(iv)   The screen shall be free of reflective glare and reflections liable to cause discomfort to a user.

(v)   The screen shall be able to swivel and tilt easily and freely to suit the needs of the user.

(vi)   It shall be possible to use either a separate base for the screen or an adjustable table.

(b) Keyboard

(i)   The keyboard shall have a matt surface to avoid reflective glare.

(ii)   The arrangement of the keyboard and the characteristics of the keys shall be such as to facilitate the use of the keyboard.

(iii) The symbols on the keys shall be adequately contrasted and legible from the design working position.

(iv)   The keyboard shall be tiltable and separate from the screen so as to allow the user to find a comfortable working position which avoids fatigue in the arms or hands.

(v)   The space in front of the keyboard shall be sufficient to provide support for the hands and arms of the user.

(c) Work desk or work surface

    (i)   The work desk or work surface shall have a sufficiently large, low-reflectance surface and allow a flexible arrangement of the screen, keyboard, documents and related equipment.

    (ii)   The document holder shall be stable and adjustable and shall be positioned so as to minimise the need for uncomfortable head and eye movement.

    (iii) There shall be adequate space for users to find a comfortable position.

(d) Work chair

    (i)   The work chair shall be stable and allow the user easy freedom of movement and a comfortable position.

    (ii)   The seat shall be adjustable in height.

    (iii) The seat back shall be adjustable in both height and tilt.

    (iv) A footrest shall be made available to any user who requires one.

2.   Environment

    (a) Space Requirements

    The workstation shall be dimensioned and designed so as to provide sufficient space for the user to change position and vary movements.

    (b) Lighting

        (i)   Lighting (including room lighting, spot lighting or work lamps) shall ensure satisfactory lighting conditions and an appropriate contrast between the screen and the background environment, taking into account the type of work and the user's vision requirements.

        (ii)   Possible disturbing glare and reflections on the screen or other equipment shall be prevented by co-ordinating the layout of workstations within the place of work with the positioning and technical characteristics of the artificial light sources.

    (c) Reflections and glare

        (i)   Workstations shall be so designed that sources of light, such as windows and other openings, transparent or translucent walls and brightly coloured fixtures or walls cause no direct glare and, as far as possible, no distracting reflections on the screen.

        (ii)   Windows shall be fitted with a suitable system of adjustable covering to attenuate the daylight which falls on the workstation.

3.   Interference

    Regulation 136 applies, in particular, where the mechanical vibration interferes with the proper handling of controls or reading of indicators.

4.   Indirect risks

    Regulation 136 applies, in particular, when the mechanical vibration interferes with the stability of structures or the security of joints.

5.   Individual protectors

    Personal protective equipment against hand-arm vibration may contribute to the programme of measures referred to in Regulation 138.

PART B — WHOLE-BODY VIBRATION

1.   Assessment of exposure

    (a) The assessment of the level of exposure to mechanical vibration is based on the calculation of the daily exposure A(8) expressed as equivalent continuous acceleration over an eight-hour period, calculated as the highest (rms) value, determined on three orthogonal axes ($1,4awx,1,4awy$, awz for a seated or standing employee), in accordance with Chapters 5, 6 and 7, Annex A and Annex B to ISO Standard 2631-1(1997).

    (b) The assessment of the level of exposure may be carried out on the basis of an estimate based on information provided by the manufacturers concerning the level of emission from the work equipment used and based on observation of specific work practices or on measurement.

    (c) In the case of maritime shipping, only vibrations exceeding a frequency of 1 Hz need to be considered.

2.   Measurement

    When measurement is carried out under Regulation 136, the methods used may include sampling, which must be representative of the personal exposure of an employee to the mechanical vibration in question with the methods and apparatus used adapted to the particular characteristics of the mechanical vibration to be measured, to ambient factors and to the characteristics of the measuring apparatus in accordance with ISO Standard 2631-1(1997).

3.   Interference

    Regulation 136 applies, in particular, where the mechanical vibration interferes with the proper handling of controls or reading of indicators.

4.   Indirect risks

    Regulation 136 applies, in particular, when the mechanical vibration interferes with the stability of structures or the security of joints.

5. Extension of exposure

    Regulation 136 applies where, owing to the nature of the activity, an employee benefits from the use of rest facilities supervised by the employer, on condition that exposure to whole-body vibration in those facilities is reduced to a level compatible with their purpose and conditions of use, except in cases of "force majeure".

SCHEDULE 7

Regulation 144

PROTECTION OF CHILDREN AND YOUNG PERSONS

PART A — GUIDE LIST OF AGENTS, PROCESSES AND WORK

Agents

1. Physical AGENTS

    (a) Ionising radiation;
    (b) Work in a high-pressure atmosphere such as in pressurised containers or diving.

2. Biological agents

    Biological agents of risk groups 3 and 4 within the meaning of Regulation 2(1) of the Safety, Health and Welfare at Work (Biological Agents) Regulations 1994 (S.I. No. 146 of 1994) as amended by the Safety, Health and Welfare at Work (Biological Agents)(Amendment) Regulations 1998 (S.I. No. 248 of 1998);

3. Chemical agents

    (a) Substances and preparations classified under the—

        (i) European Communities (Classification, Packaging, Labelling and Notification of Dangerous Substances) Regulations 2003 (S.I. No. 116 of 2003) as amended by the European Communities (Classification, Packaging, Labelling and Notification of Dangerous Substances) (Amendment) Regulations 2006 (S.I. No. 25 of 2006), and
        (ii) European Communities (Classification, Packaging and Labelling of Dangerous Preparations) Regulations 2004 (S.I. No. 62 of 2004) as amended by the European Communities (Classification, Packaging and Labelling of Dangerous Preparations) (Amendment) Regulations 2007 (S.I. No. 76 of 2007)

(referred to elsewhere in this Schedule as the "CPL Regulations") as toxic (T), very toxic (T+), corrosive (C) or explosive (E) and with one or more of the following risk phrases:

Risk of explosion by shock, friction, fire or other sources of ignition (R2)

Extreme risk of explosion by shock, friction, fire or other sources of ignition (R3)

Toxic by inhalation (R23)

Toxic in contact with skin (R24)

Toxic if swallowed (R25)

Very toxic by inhalation (R26)

Very toxic in contact with skin (R27)

Very toxic if swallowed (R28)

Causes burns (R34)

Causes severe burns (R35)

Danger of very serious irreversible effects (R39)

Danger of serious damage to health by prolonged exposure (R48);

(b) Substances and preparations classified under the CPL Regulations as carcinogenic, mutagenic or toxic to reproduction and with one or more of the following risk phrases:

Limited evidence of a carcinogenic effect (R40)

May cause cancer (R45)

May cause heritable genetic damage (R46)

May cause cancer by inhalation (R49)

May impair fertility (R60)

May cause harm to the unborn child (R61)

Possible risk of impaired fertility (R62)

Possible risk of harm to the unborn child (R63)

Possible risk of irreversible effects (R68);

(c) Substances and preparations classified under the CPL Regulations as harmful (Xn) and with one or more of the following risk phrases:

Danger of very serious irreversible effects (R39)

Danger of serious damage to health by prolonged exposure (R48);

(d) Substances and preparations classified under the CPL Regulations as irritant (Xi) and with one or more of the following risk phrases:

May cause sensitisation by inhalation (R42)

May cause sensitisation by skin contact (R43);

(e) Substances and preparations referred to in the Safety, Health and Welfare at Work (Carcinogens) Regulations 2001 (S.I. No. 78 of 2001);

(f) Lead and compounds thereof, in as much as the agents in question are absorbable by the human organism;

(g) Asbestos.

PART B — PROCESSES AND WORK

1. Processes at work referred to in the Safety, Health and Welfare at Work (Carcinogens) Regulations 2001 (S.I. No. 78 of 2001).

2. Manufacture and handling of devices, fireworks or other objects containing explosives.

3. Work with dangerous, fierce or poisonous animals.

4. Animal slaughtering on an industrial scale.

5. Work involving the handling of equipment for the production, storage or application of compressed, liquefied or dissolved gases.

6. Work with vats, tanks, reservoirs or carboys containing chemical agents referred to in item 3 of Part A of this Schedule.

7. Work involving a risk of structural collapse.

8. Work involving high-voltage electrical hazards.

9. Work the pace of which is determined by machinery and involving payment by results.

SCHEDULE 8

Regulations 147, 149

LISTS OF AGENTS,PROCESSES AND WORKING CONDITIONS RELATING TO PREGNANT,POSTNATAL AND BREASTFEEDING EMPLOYEES

PART A — PREGNANT, POST NATAL AND BREASTFEEDING EMPLOYEES

1. Agents

(a) Physical agents

Physical agents where these are regarded as agents causing foetal lesions or likely to disturb placental attachment (or both), and in particular—

(i)   shocks, vibration or movement,
(ii)   handling of loads entailing risks, particularly of a dorsolumbar nature,
(iii) noise,
(iv)   ionising radiation,

    (v)   non-ionising radiation,

    (vi) extremes of cold or heat,

    (vii) movements and postures, travelling, either inside or outside the place of work, mental or physical fatigue and other physical burdens connected with the activity of the employee.

(b) Biological Agents

Biological agents of risk groups 2, 3 and 4 within the meaning of relevant statutory provisions relating to biological agents, in so far as it is known that these agents or the therapeutic measures necessitated by such agents endanger the health of pregnant employees and the unborn child but excluding those referred to in Part B of this Schedule.

(c) Chemical Agents

The following chemical agents insofar as it is known that they endanger the health of pregnant employees and the unborn child but excluding those referred to in Part B of this Schedule—

    (i)   Substances and preparations classified under the

        (I)   European Communities (Classification, Packaging, Labelling and Notification of Dangerous Substances) Regulations 2003 (S.I. No. 116 of 2003) as amended by the European Communities (Classification, Packaging, Labelling and Notification of Dangerous Substances) (Amendment) Regulations 2006 (S.I. No. 25 of 2006), and

        (II) European Communities (Classification, Packaging and Labelling of Dangerous Preparations) Regulations 2004 (S.I. No. 62 of 2004) as amended by the European Communities (Classification, Packaging and Labelling of Dangerous Preparations) (Amendment) Regulations 2007 (S.I. No. 76 of 2007)

with one or more of the following risk phrases—

        Limited evidence of a carcinogenic effect (R40)
        May cause cancer (R45)
        May cause heritable genetic damage (R46)
        May cause cancer by inhalation (R49)
        May cause harm to the unborn child (R61)
        Possible risk of harm to the unborn child (R63)
        May cause harm to breastfed babies (R64)
        Possible risk of irreversible effects (R68),

    (ii) Substances and preparations referred to in Schedule 1 to the Safety, Health and Welfare at Work (Carcinogens) Regulations 2001 (S.I. No. 78 of 2001),

   (iii) Substances and preparations released by a process referred to in Schedule 1 to the Safety, Health and Welfare at Work (Carcinogens) Regulations 2001 (S.I. No. 78 of 2001),

   (iv) mercury and mercury derivatives,

   (v) antimitotic (cytotoxic) drugs,

   (vi) carbon monoxide,

   (vii) chemical agents of known and dangerous percutaneous absorption.

2.   Processes

Industrial processes listed in Schedule 1 to the Safety, Health and Welfare at Work (Carcinogens) Regulations 2001 (S.I. No. 78 of 2001).

3   Working Conditions

Underground mining work.

PART B — PREGNANT EMPLOYEES

1.   Agents

(a) Physical Agents
Work in hyperbaric atmosphere, such as in pressurised enclosures and underwater diving.

(b) Biological Agents
The following biological agents—
Toxoplasma
Rubella virus,

unless the pregnant employees are proved to be adequately protected against such agents by immunisation.

(c) Chemical Agents
Lead and lead derivatives insofar as these agents are capable of being absorbed by the human organism.

2.   Working Conditions

Underground mining work.

PART C —EMPLOYEES WHO ARE BREASTFEEDING

1.   Agents

Chemical Agents

Lead and lead derivatives insofar as these agents are capable of being absorbed by the human organism.

2.   Working Conditions

Underground mining work.

SCHEDULE 9

Regulation 160

SAFETY AND HEALTH SIGNS AT WORK

PART A — GENERAL REQUIREMENTS

1. Types of signs

   1.1. Permanent signs

      1.1.1. Permanent signboards shall be used for signs relating to prohibitions, warnings and mandatory requirements and the location and identification of emergency escape routes and first-aid facilities.

      Signboards or a safety colour (or both) shall be used to mark permanently the location and identification of fire-fighting equipment.

      1.1.2. Signboards on containers and pipes shall be placed as laid down in Part C of this Schedule.

      1.1.3. Places where there is a risk of colliding with obstacles or of falling shall be permanently marked with a safety colour or with signboards (or both).

      1.1.4. Traffic routes shall be permanently marked with a safety colour.

   1.2. Occasional signs

      1.2.1 Illuminated signs, acoustic signals or verbal communication (or both) shall be used where the occasion requires, taking into account the possibilities for interchanging and combining signs set out in Paragraph 2, to signal danger, to call persons to take a specific course of action and for the emergency evacuation of persons.

      1.2.2. Hand signals or verbal communication (or both) shall be used where the occasion requires, to guide persons carrying out hazardous or dangerous manoeuvres.

2. Interchanging and combining signs

   2.1. Any one of the following may be used if equally effective—

      -a safety colour or a signboard to mark places where there is an obstacle or a drop,
      -illuminated signs, acoustic signals or verbal communication,
      -hand signals or verbal communication.

   2.2. Some types of signs may be used together—

      -illuminated signs and acoustic signals,
      -illuminated signs and verbal communication,
      -hand signals and verbal communication.

3. The instructions in the table below apply to all signs incorporating a safety colour—

Colour	Meaning or Purpose	Instructions and Information
Red	*Prohibition sign*	*Dangerous behaviour*
	Danger alarm	Stop, shutdown, emergency cut-out devices Evacuate
	Fire-fighting equipment	Identification and location
Yellow or Amber	Warning sign	Be careful, take precautions Examine
Blue	Mandatory sign	Specific behaviour or action Wear personal protective equipment
Green	Emergency escape, first aid sign	Doors, exits, routes, equipment, facilities
	No danger	Return to normal

4. The effectiveness of a sign shall not be adversely affected by:

4.1. the presence of another emission source of the same type which interferes with visibility or audibility; therefore, in particular—

4.1.1. the placing of too many signs too close together shall be avoided,

4.1.2. two illuminated signs which are likely to be confused shall not to be used at the same time,

4.1.3. an illuminated sign shall not be used in the proximity of another similar illuminated source,

4.1.4. two acoustic signals shall not be used at the same time,

4.1.5. an acoustic signal shall not be used if there is too much ambient noise.

4.2. poor design, insufficient number, incorrect positioning, poor state of repair or incorrect functioning of the signs or signalling devices.

5. Depending on requirements, signs and signalling devices shall be cleaned, maintained, checked, repaired, and if necessary replaced on a regular basis to ensure that they retain their intrinsic or functional qualities (or both).

6. The number and positioning of signs or signalling devices to be installed will depend on the extent of the hazards or dangers or on the zone to be covered.

7. Signs requiring some form of power shall be provided with a guaranteed emergency supply in the event of a power cut, unless the hazard has thereby been eliminated.

8. The triggering of an illuminated sign or acoustic signal (or both) indicates when the required action should start and the sign or signal shall be activated for as long as the action requires.

   Illuminated signs and acoustic signals shall be reactivated immediately after use.

9. Illuminated signs and acoustic signals shall be checked to ensure that they function correctly and that they are effective before they are put into service and subsequently at sufficiently frequent intervals.

10. If the hearing or the sight of the persons concerned is impaired, including impairment caused by the wearing of personal protective equipment, measures shall be taken to supplement or replace the signs concerned.

11. Areas, rooms or enclosures used for storage of significant quantities of dangerous substances or preparations shall be indicated by a suitable warning sign taken from paragraph 3.2 of Part B, or marked as provided in paragraph 1 of Part C of this Schedule, unless the labelling of the individual packages or containers is adequate for this purpose.

PART B — SIGNBOARDS

1. Intrinsic features

   1.1 The shape and colours are set out in paragraph 3, in accordance with their specific object (signboards indicating a prohibition, a warning, a mandatory action, an escape route, an emergency or fire-fighting equipment).

   1.2. Pictograms shall be as simple as possible and shall contain only essential details.

   1.3. The pictograms used may be slightly different from or more detailed than those shown in paragraph 3, provided that they convey the same meaning and that no difference or adaptation obscures the meaning.

   1.4. Signboards shall be made of shock and weather-resistant material suitable for the surrounding environment.

   1.5. The dimensions and colorimetric and photometric features of signboards shall be such that they can be easily seen and understood.

2. Conditions of use

   2.1. Signboards shall be installed at a suitable height and in a position appropriate to the line of sight, taking account of any obstacles, either at the access point to an area in the case of a general hazard, or in the immediate vicinity of a specific hazard or object, and in a well-lit and easily accessible and visible location.

Without prejudice to the provisions of Part 2, Chapter 1, phosphorescent colours, reflective materials or artificial lighting shall be used where the level of natural light is poor.

2.2. The signboard shall be removed when the situation to which it refers ceases to exist.

3. Signboards to be used

3.1. Prohibitory signs—

Intrinsic features:

Round shape;
Black pictogram on white background, red edging and diagonal line (the red part to take up at least 35% of the area of the sign);
The script underneath each of the following pictograms is included here to show the meaning of the sign but is not to be included in the signboard.
That script or any other relevant script may be shown on a supplementary signboard.

Signs to be used

No Smoking	**Smoking and naked flames for bidden**	**No access for pedestrians**
Do not extinguish with water	**Not drinkable**	**No access for unauthorised persons**

No access for
industrial vehicles

Do not touch

3.2.   Warning signs—

Intrinsic features:

Triangular shape;
Black pictogram on a yellow background with black edging (the yellow part to take up at least 50% of the area of the sign);
The script underneath each of the following pictograms is included here to show the meaning of the sign but is not to be included in the signboard.
That script or any other relevant script may be shown on a supplementary signboard.

Signs to be used

Flammable material
or high temperature

Explosive material

Toxic material

Corrosive material

Radioactive material

Overhead load

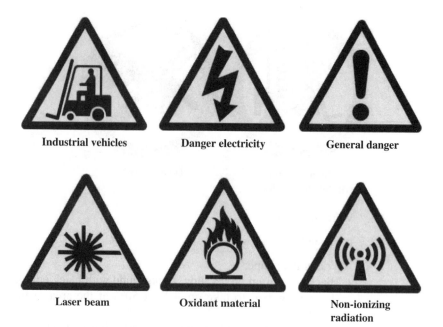

Note—"Flammable material or high temperature" sign in the absence of a specific sign for high temperature

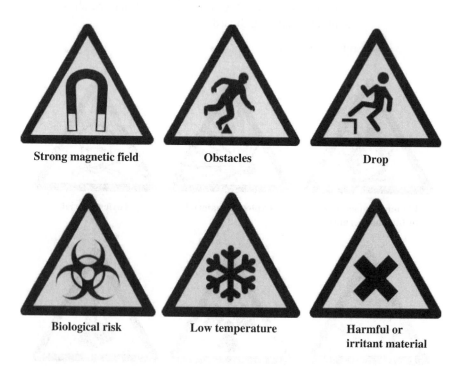

Note: The background to the "Harmful or irritant material" sign may excep-
tionally be amber if justified in order to differentiate it from a similar road

safety sign except that it, or other relevant script, may be shown on a supplementary sign.

    3.3.   Mandatory signs

        Intrinsic features:

        Round shape;

        White pictogram on a blue background (the blue part to take up at least 50% of the area of the sign);

        The script underneath each of the following pictograms is included here to show the meaning of the sign but is not to be included in the signboard.

        That script or any other relevant script may be shown on a supplementary signboard.

        Signs to be used

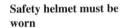

Eye protection must be worn

Safety helmet must be worn

Ear protection must be worn

Respiratory equipment must be worn

Safety boots must be worn

Safety gloves must be worn

Safety overalls must   **Face protection must**   **Safety harness must**
be worn   **be worn**   **be worn**

Pedestrians must use this   **General mandatory sign**
route   **(to beaccompanied**
                            where necessary by
                            another sign)

3.4.   Emergency escape or first-aid signs

Intrinsic features:

Rectangular or square shape;

White pictogram on a green background (the green part to take up at least 50% of the area of the sign.);

The script underneath each of the following pictograms is included here to show the meaning of the sign but is not to be included in the signboard.

That script or any other relevant script may be shown on a supplementary signboard.

Signs to be used

 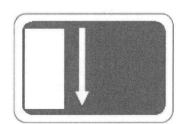

Emergency exit/escape route

**This way
(supplementary information sign)**

First-aid post   **Stretcher**   **Safety Shower**   **Eye wash**

Emergency telephone for first-aid or escape

3.5.   Fire-fighting signs

Intrinsic features:

Rectangular or square shape;

White pictogram on a red background (the red part to take up at least 50% of the area of the sign);

The script underneath each of the following pictograms is included here to show the meaning of the sign but is not to be included in the signboard.

That script or any other relevant script may be shown on a supplementary signboard.

Signs to be used

Fire Hose   **Ladder**   **Fire extinguisher**   **Emergency fire telephone**

This way
(supplementary information sign)

PART C — SIGNS ON CONTAINERS AND PIPES

1. Containers used at work for dangerous substances or preparations to which the relevant statutory provisions apply and containers used for the storage of such dangerous substances or preparations, together with the visible pipes containing or transporting dangerous substances and preparations, shall be labelled (pictogram or symbol against a coloured background) in accordance with those provisions.

This paragraph does not apply to containers used at work for brief periods nor to containers whose contents change frequently, provided that alternative adequate measures are taken, for information, training, or both, which guarantee the same level of protection.

The labels referred to in this paragraph may be—

(a) replaced by warning signs as provided for in Part B of this Schedule, using the same pictograms or symbols,

(b) supplemented by additional information, such as the name, formula, or both, of the dangerous substance or preparation and details of the hazard, and

(c) for the transporting of containers at the place of work, supplemented or replaced by signs applicable throughout the European Union for the transport of dangerous substances or preparations.

2. Signs shall be mounted as follows—

(a) on visible sides, and

(b) in unpliable, self-adhesive or painted form.

3. Where appropriate, the signs referred to in paragraph 1 of this Part shall have the intrinsic features defined in paragraph 1.4. of Part B and shall fulfil the conditions of use for signboards laid down in paragraph 2 of Part B.

4. Without prejudice to paragraphs 1, 2 and 3, the labels used on pipes shall be positioned visibly in the vicinity of the most dangerous points, such as valves and joints, and at reasonable intervals.

5. Areas, rooms or enclosures used for the storage of significant quantities of dangerous substances or preparations shall be indicated by a suitable warning sign taken from paragraph 3.2 of Part B, or marked as provided in paragraph 1 of this Part, unless the labelling of the individual packages or containers is adequate for this purpose, taking into account paragraph 1.5 of Part B, with regard to dimensions.

Stores of a number of dangerous substances or preparations may be indicated by the warning sign for general danger.

The signs or labels referred to above must be positioned, as appropriate, near the storage area or on the door leading into the storage room.

PART D — IDENTIFICATION AND LOCATION OF FIRE-FIGHTING EQUIP-
MENT USED EXCLUSIVELY FOR FIRE-FIGHTING PURPOSES

1. Fire-fighting equipment shall be identified by using a specific colour for the
   equipment and placing a location signboard, or by using a specific colour or
   both for the places where such equipment is kept, or their access points.

2. For the purposes of paragraph 1 the specific colour shall be red.

   The red area shall be sufficiently large to allow the equipment to be identified easily.

3. The signboards provided for in paragraph 3.5 of Part B shall be used to mark
   the locations of this equipment.

PART E — SIGNS USED FOR OBSTACLES AND DANGEROUS LOCATIONS
AND FOR MARKING TRAFFIC ROUTES

1. Signs for obstacles and dangerous locations

   1.1. Places where there is a risk of colliding with obstacles, of fall-
         ing or of objects falling shall be marked with alternating yellow
         and black, or red and white stripes in built up zones in the place
         of work to which employees have access during their work.

   1.2. The dimensions of the markings shall be commensurate with
         the scale of the obstacle or dangerous location in question.

   1.3. The yellow and black or red and white stripes shall be at an
         angle of approximately 45° and of more or less equal size.

   1.4. Example:

2. Marking of traffic routes

   2.1. Where the use and equipment of rooms so requires for the pro-
         tection of persons, traffic routes for vehicles shall be clearly
         identified by continuous stripes in a clearly visible colour, pref-
         erably white or yellow, taking into account the colour of the
         ground.

   2.2. The stripes shall be located so as to indicate the necessary safe
         distance between the vehicles and any object which may be
         nearby, and between pedestrians and vehicles.

2.3.   Permanent traffic routes in built-up areas outdoors shall, as far as is practicable, be similarly marked, unless they are provided with suitable barriers or pavements.

PART F — ILLUMINATED SIGNS

1.   Intrinsic features

1.1.   The light emitted by a sign shall produce a luminous contrast which is appropriate to its environment, in accordance with the intended conditions of use of the sign, but without producing glare or an excessive amount of light or poor visibility as a result of insufficient light.

1.2.   The luminous area emitting a sign may be of a single colour or contain a pictogram on a specified background.

1.3.   The single colour shall correspond to the table of colours and their meanings set out in paragraph 3 of Part A.

1.4.   When the sign contains a pictogram, it shall comply with all the relevant requirements of Part B.

2.   Specific rules governing use

2.1.   If a device can emit both continuous and intermittent signs, the intermittent sign shall be used to indicate a higher level of danger or a more urgent need for the requested or required intervention or action than is indicated by the continuous sign.

The duration of each flash and the frequency of the flashes of an intermittent illuminated sign shall be such as to ensure the proper perception of the message, and avoid any confusion either between different illuminated signs or with a continuous illuminated sign.

2.2.   If a flashing sign is used instead of or together with an acoustic signal, identical codes shall be used.

2.3.   Devices for emitting flashing signs in the event of grave danger shall be under special surveillance or be fitted with an auxiliary lamp.

PART G — ACOUSTIC SIGNS

1.   Intrinsic features

1.1. Acoustic signals shall:

(a) have a sound level which is considerably higher than the level of ambient noise, so that it is audible without being excessive or painful, and

(b) be easily recognisable, particularly in terms of pulse length and the interval between pulses or groups of pulses, and be clearly distinct from any other acoustic signal and ambient noises.

1.2. If a device can emit an acoustic signal at variable and constant frequencies, the variable frequency shall be used to indicate a higher level of danger or a more urgent need for the requested or imposed intervention or action in relation to the stable frequency.

2.   Code

The signal for evacuation shall be continuous.

PART H — VERBAL COMMUNICATION

1.   Intrinsic features

1.1.   Verbal communication between a speaker or emitter and one or more hearers shall take the form of (sometimes coded) short texts, phrases, groups of words or individual words.

1.2.   Spoken messages shall be short, simple and clear as possible and in a language understood by the persons involved; the verbal skills of the speaker and the hearing abilities of hearers shall be such as to ensure reliable verbal communication.

1.3.   Verbal communication may be direct (by means of the human voice) or indirect (by means of a human or artificial voice which is broadcast by whatever means is appropriate).

2.   Specific rules governing use

2.1.   The persons involved must have a good knowledge of the language used so thst they are able to pronounce and understand the spoken message correctly and consequently behave in a way which is appropriate to safety or health (or both).

2.2.   If verbal communication is used instead of or together with gestures, code words should be used such as:

- *'start'*	to indicate the start of a command
- *'stop'*	to interrupt or end a movement
- *'end'*	to stop the operation
- *'raise'*	to have a load raised
- *'lower'*	to have a load lowered
- *'forwards'*	to be coordinated with the corresponding hand signals
- *'backwards'*	to be coordinated with the corresponding hand signals
- *'right'*	to be coordinated with the corresponding hand signal
- *'left'*	to be coordinated with the corresponding hand signals
- *'danger'*	foran emergency stop
- *'quickly'*	to speed up a movement for safety reasons

PART I —HAND SIGNALS

1. Features:

    1.1. Hand signals shall be precise, simple, expansive, easy to make and to understand, and clearly distinct from other such signals.

    1.2. Where both arms are used at the same time, they shall be moved symmetrically and for giving one sign only.

    1.3. Without prejudice to other codes applicable at European Union level, used for the same manoeuvres in certain sectors, hand signals used shall be consistent with any relevant code of practice.

2. Specific rules governing use:

    2.1. The person giving the signs, hereinafter referred to as the "signaller", shall use arm or hand movements to give manoeuvring instructions to the person receiving the signs, hereinafter referred to as the "operator".

    2.2. The signaller shall be able to monitor all manoeuvres visually without being endangered thereby.

    2.3. The signaller's duties shall consist exclusively of directing manoeuvres and ensuring the safety of persons in the vicinity.

    2.4. If the conditions described in paragraph 2.2. are not fulfilled, one or more extra signallers shall be deployed.

    2.5. The operator shall interrupt the ongoing manoeuvre in order to request new instructions if unable to carry out the orders received with the necessary safety guarantees.

    2.6. Accessories:

    2.6.1. The operator shall be able to recognise the signaller without difficulty.

    2.6.2. The signaller shall wear one or more appropriate distinctive items, e.g. jacket, helmet, sleeves or armbands, or carry bats.

    2.6.3. The distinctive items shall be brightly coloured, preferably all of the same colour and for the exclusive use of signallers.

3. Coded signals to be used

    Preliminary remark

        The following set of coded signals are without prejudice to other codes applicable at European Community level, used for the same manoeuvres in certain sectors:

Meaning	Description	Illustration
A. General signals		
START Attention Start of command	Both arms are extended horizontally with the palms facing forward	
STOP Interruption End of movement	The right arm points upwards with the palm facing forwards	
END Of the operation	Both hands are clasped at chest height	
B. Vertical movements		
RAISE	The right arm points upwards with the palm facing forward and slowly makes a circle	
LOWER	The right arm points downwards with the palm facing inwards and slowly makes a circle	
VERTICAL DISTANCE	The hands indicate the relevant distance	
C. Horizontal Movements		
MOVE FORWARDS	Both arms are bent with the palms facing upwards and the forearms make slow movements towards the body	
MOVE BACKWARDS	Both arms are bent with the palms facing downwards and the forearms make slow movements away from the body	

RIGHT To the signaller's right	The right arm is extended more or less horizontally with the palm facing downwards and slowly makes small movements to the right	
LEFT To the signaller's left	The left arm is extended more or less horizontally with the palm facing downwards and slowly makes small movements to the left	
HORIZONTAL DISTANCE	The hands indicate the relevant distance	
D. Danger		
DANGER Emergency stop	Both arms point upwards with the palms facing forwards	
QUICK	All movements faster	
SLOW	All movements slower	

SCHEDULE 10

EXPLOSIVE ATMOSPHERES

Regulations 169 and 170

PART A — CLASSIFICATION OF PLACES WHERE EXPLOSIVE
ATMOSPHERES MAY OCCUR

1.   Places where explosive atmosphere may occur:

(a) A place in which an explosive atmosphere may occur in such quantities as to require special precautions to protect the health and safety of the workers concerned is deemed to be hazardous within the meaning of Part 8 of these Regulations.

(b) A place in which an explosive atmosphere is not expected to occur in such quantities as to require special precaution is deemed to be non-hazardous within the meaning of Part 8 of these Regulations.

Flammable or combustible substances are considered as materials, which may form an explosive atmosphere unless an investigation of their properties has shown that in mixtures with air they are incapable of independently propagating an explosion.

2.   Classification of hazardous places

Hazardous places are classified in terms of zones on the basis of the frequency and duration of the occurrence of an explosive atmosphere.

The extent of the measures to be taken in accordance with Part 8 is determined by this classification.

Zone 0:

A place in which an explosive atmosphere consisting of a mixture with air of flammable substances in the form of gas, vapour or mist is present continuously or for long periods or frequently.

Zone 1:

A place in which an explosive atmosphere consisting of a mixture with air of flammable substances in the form of gas, vapour or mist is likely to occur in normal operation occasionally.

Zone 2:

A place in which an explosive atmosphere consisting of a mixture with air of flammable substances in the form of gas, vapour or mist is not likely to occur in normal operation but, if it does occur, will persist for a short period only.

Zone 20:

A place in which an explosive atmosphere in the form of a cloud of combustible dust in air is present continuously or for long periods or frequently.

Zone 21:

A place in which an explosive atmosphere in the form of a cloud of combustible dust in air is likely to occur in normal operation occasionally.

Zone 22:

A place in which an explosive atmosphere in the form of a cloud of combustible dust in air is not likely to occur in normal operation but, if it does occur, will persist for a short period only.

Notes:

1.   Layers, deposits and heaps of combustible dust must be considered as any other source, which can form an explosive atmosphere.
2.   "Normal operation" means the situation when installations are used within their design parameters.

PART B — WARNING SIGN FOR PLACES WHERE EXPLOSIVE
ATMOSPHERES MAY OCCUR

Place where explosive atmospheres may occur

Distinctive features:

triangular shape,
black letter on a yellow background with black edging (the yellow part to
take up at least 50% of the area of the sign).

GIVEN under my hand

14th June 2007

TONY KILLEEN

Minister of State at the Department of Enterprise, Trade and Employment

EXPLANATORY NOTE

(This note is not part of the Instrument and does not purport to be a legal interpretation.)

1. These Regulations, inter alia, revoke and replace -

    (a) those provisions of the Safety, Health and Welfare at Work (General Application) Regulations 1993 (S.I. No. 44 of 1993) (other than Part X and the Twelfth Schedule relating to the notification of accidents and dangerous occurrences, which remain in place) that were not already revoked under the Safety, Health and Welfare at Work (General Application) (Amendment) (Revocation) Regulations 2005 (S.I. No. 392 of 2005) following their incorporation in the Safety, Health and Welfare at Work Act 2005 (No. 10 of 2005), and

    (b) the Safety, Health and Welfare at Work (General Application) (Amendment) Regulations 2001 (S.I. No. 188 of 2001).

2. The Regulations also revoke and replace an additional 20 full sets and 4 part provisions of—-

    (a) Factories (Report of Examination of Hoists and Lifts) Regulations 1956 (S.I. No. 182 of 1956),

    (b) Factories Act 1955 (Hoists and Lifts) (Exemption) Order 1957 (S.I. No. 80 of 1957),

    (c) Factories Act 1955 (Lifts) (Exemption) Order 1960 (S.I. No. 129 of 1960),

    (d) Regulations 22 to 35 and 37 and 38 and the Schedule to the Docks (Safety, Health and Welfare) Regulations 1960 (S.I. No. 279 of 1960),

    (e) Factories Act, 1955 (Hoistways) (Exemption) Order 1962 (S.I. No. 211 of 1962),

    (f) Quarries (Electricity) Regulations 1972 (S.I. No. 50 of 1972),

    (g) Mines (Electricity) Regulations 1972 (S.I. No. 51 of 1972),

    (h) Quarries (General) Regulations 1974 (S.I. No. 146 of 1974) to the extent of in Regulation 3, the definitions of "lifting appliance" and "safe working load", Regulations 40 and 41, in the First Schedule "FORM No. 3" and "FORM No. 5" and the Second Schedule,

    (i) Shipbuilding and Ship-Repairing (Safety, Health and Welfare) Regulations 1975 (S.I. No. 322 of 1975) to the extent of in Regulation 3(1), the definitions of "lifting equipment" and "lifting gear" and Regulations 32 to 48,

    (j) Factories Act 1955 (Hoistways) (Exemption) Order 1976 (S.I. No. 236 of 1976),

    (k) Factories Act 1955 (Hoists) (Exemption) Order 1977 (S.I. No. 13 of 1977),

    (l) Mines (Electricity) (Amendment) Regulations 1979 (S.I. No. 125 of 1979),

(m) Quarries (Electricity) (Amendment) Regulations 1979 (S.I. No. 126 of 1979),

(n) Safety in Industry Acts 1955 and 1980 (Hoists and Hoistways) (Exemption) Order 1985 (S.I. No. 100 of 1985),

(o) Safety, Health and Welfare at Work (Signs) Regulations 1995 (S.I. No. 132 of 1995),

(p) Safety, Health and Welfare at Work (Miscellaneous Welfare Provisions) Regulations 1995 (S.I. No. 358 of 1995),

(q) Safety, Health and Welfare at Work (Children and Young Persons) Regulations 1998 (S.I. No. 504 of 1998),

(r) Safety, Health and Welfare at Work (Night Work and Shift Work) Regulations 2000 (S.I. No. 11 of 2000),

(s) Safety, Health and Welfare at Work (Pregnant Employees etc.) Regulations 2000 (S.I. No. 218 of 2000),

(t) Regulations 80 to 123 of the Safety, Health and Welfare at Work (Construction) Regulations 2001 (S.I. No. 481 of 2001),

(u) Safety, Health and Welfare at Work (Explosive Atmospheres) Regulations 2003 (S.I. No. 258 of 2003),

(v) Safety, Health and Welfare at Work (Work at Height) Regulations 2006 (S.I. No. 318 of 2006),

(w) Safety, Health and Welfare at Work (Control of Vibration at Work) Regulations 2006 (S.I. No. 370 of 2006), and

(x) Safety, Health and Welfare at Work (Control of Noise at Work) Regulations 2006 (S.I. No. 371 of 2006), except Regulation 11(3) of those Regulations.

Regulation 11(3) of the Safety, Health and Welfare at Work (Control of Noise at Work) Regulations 2006 (S.I. No. 371 of 2006) is revoked on 14 February, 2008.

The above revocations are supplemented by the Safety, Health and Welfare at Work Act 2005 (Repeals)(Commencement) Order 2007 (S.I. No. 300 of 2007) which, in accordance with sections 1(2) and 4(2) of the Safety, Health and Welfare at Work Act 2005 (No. 10 of 2005) activates the repeal of sections 33 to 35 and 115 and 116 of the Factories Act 1955 (No. 10 of 1955) and sections28 and 29 of the Safety in Industry Act 1980 (No. 9 of 1980).

In replacing the above statutory provisions, these Regulations are presented in a more self-contained, easily accessible and user-friendly format, for example, through the restructuring of the layout of the Regulations and through reducing the overall number of Schedules by the incorporation of provisions formerly set out in Schedules in the main text of the current Regulations. However, the overall thrust and the vast majority of the substantive requirements and prohibitions of the Regulations being replaced are maintained in these Regulations.

3. The Regulations retranspose the following 14 EU Directives relating to occupational safety, health and welfare:

   (a) Council Directive 89/654/EEC of 30 November 1989 concerning the minimum safety and health requirements for the workplace [Chapter 1 of Part 2 refers];

   (b) Council Directive 89/655/EEC of 30 November 1989 concerning the minimum safety and health requirements for the use of work equipment by workers at work, as amended by Council Directive 95/63/EC of 5 December 1995, amending Directive 89/655/EEC [Chapter 2 of Part 2 and Schedule 1 refer];

   (c) Council Directive 89/656/EEC of 30 November 1989 on the minimum health and safety requirements for use by workers of personal protective equipment [Chapter 3 of Part 2 and Schedule 2 refer];

   (d) Council Directive 90/269/EEC of 29 May 1990 on the minimum health and safety requirements for the manual handling of loads where there is a risk particularly of back injury to workers [Chapter 4 of Part 2 and Schedule 3 refer];

   (e) Council Directive 90/270/EEC of 29 May 1990 on the minimum safety and health requirements for work with display screen equipment [Chapter 5 of Part 2 and Schedule 4 refer];

   (f) Directive 2001/45/EC of the European Parliament and of the Council of 27 June 2001 amending Council Directive 89/655/EEC relating to the use of work equipment when carrying out work at a height [Part 4 and Schedule 5 refer];

   (g) Directive 2003/10/EC of the European Parliament and of the Council of 6 February 2003 on the minimum health and safety requirements regarding the exposure of workers to the risks arising from physical agents (noise) [Chapter 1 of Part 5 refers];

   (h) Directive 2002/44/EC of the European Parliament and of the Council of 25 June 2002 on the minimum health and safety requirements regarding the exposure of workers to the risks arising from physical agents (vibration) [Chapter 2 of Part 5 and Schedule 6 refer];

   (i) the health and safety aspects of Council Directive 94/33/EC of 22 June 1994 on the protection of young people at work [Chapter 1 of Part 6 and Schedule 7 refer];

   (j) the occupational safety and health provisions of Council Directive 92/85/EEC of 19 October, 1992 on the introduction of measures to encourage improvements in the safety and health at work of pregnant workers and workers who have recently given birth or are breastfeeding [Chapter 2 of Part 6 and Schedule 8 refer];

   (k) in respect of night workers and shift workers, the safety and health protection provisions of Article 9 of Council Directive 93/104/EC of 23 November 1993 concerning certain aspects of the organisation of working time [Chapter 3 of Part 6 refers];

(l) Council Directive 92/58/EEC of 24 June 1992 on the minimum requirements for the provision of safety and/or health signs at work [Chapter 1 of Part 7 and Schedule 9 refer];

(m) Directive 1999/92/EC of the European Parliament and of the Council of 16 December 1999 on minimum requirements for improving the safety and health protection of workers potentially at risk from explosive atmospheres [Part 8 and Schedule 10 refer].

4. These Regulations also modernise legal requirements concerning the safe use of electricity in the workplace [Part 3 refers] and the provision of first-aid facilities at work [Chapter 2 of Part 7 refers].

5. Part 1 of the Regulations covers standard Interpretation and General provisions comprising citation and commencement, interpretation and revocations and savings.

6. Part 2 of the Regulations relates to the Workplace and the use of Work Equipment at work.

Chapter 1 of Part 2 of the Regulations sets out requirements relating to places of work as regards various matters including structural stability, ventilation, temperature, lighting, floors, walls, ceilings and roofs, windows and sky lights, doors and gates, emergency routes and exits fire detection and fire fighting, movement of pedestrians and vehicles danger areas, loading bays and ramps, room dimensions and air space, general welfare requirements, sanitary and washing facilities.

For the purposes of Chapter 1 of Part 2 of the Regulations "place of work" means a place of work intended to house work stations, excluding (a) means of transport used outside the undertaking or a place of work inside a means of transport, (b) construction sites, (c) extractive industries, (d) fishing boats and (e) fields, woods and land forming part of an agricultural or forestry undertaking but situated away from the undertaking's buildings.

Chapter 2 of Part 2 and Schedule 1 to the Regulations set out requirements relating to the use of Work Equipment at work as regards various matters including employers' duties regarding the use of work equipment by their employees, information and instruction, inspection of work equipment, maintenance control devices, guards and protection devices, connection to energy sources, contact with wheels or tracks of mobile work equipment, drive systems of mobile work equipment, combustion engines of mobile work equipment, fork-lift trucks, safety of self-propelled work equipment, traffic rules for mobile work equipment, work equipment for lifting loads, cranes, work equipment for lifting goods or persons, hoists and lifts, lifting accessories, signalling and operation of lifting equipment, periodic examination and testing of lifting equipment, reports by competent persons, records and registers of lifting equipment, safe working loads for excavators, telehandlers and loaders, requirements for scotch and guy derrick cranes and construction, testing, examination and safe working load of lifting accessories. In addition to retransposing Council

Directive 89/655/EEC and Council Directive 95/63/EC, Chapter 2 of Part 2 of the Regulations also modernises and replaces various provisions of the "relevant statutory provisions" relating to the use of work equipment at work by standardising requirements and removing anomalies or inconsistencies relating to the use of the same work equipment at different places of work.

Chapter 3 of Part 2 and Schedule 2 to the Regulations set out requirements relating to the provision and use of Personal Protective Equipment (PPE) as regards various matters including the provision and use of PPE, assessment of PPE, conditions of use and compatibility of PPE, personal use of PPE, maintenance and replacement of PPE and information, training and instruction.

Chapter 4 of Part 2 and Schedule 3 to the Regulations set out requirements relating to the Manual Handling of Loads as regards the duties of employers to take appropriate organisational measures or means to avoid the need for the manual handling of loads or, where the need for the manual handling of loads cannot be avoided, to take appropriate measures or use appropriate means to reduce the risk to employees involved in the manual handling of loads.

Chapter 5 of Part 2 and Schedule 4 to the Regulations set out requirements relating to the provision and use of Display Screen Equipment (DSE) as regards the duties of employers concerning the analysis of the workstation, planning of work, minimum requirements for DSE, information and training and provision of eye tests and corrective appliances.

7. Part 3 of the Regulations relating to Electricity sets out a range of requirements including suitability of electrical equipment and installations, adverse or hazardous environments, identification and marking, protection against electric shock, portable equipment, connections and cables, overcurrent protection, auxiliary equipment and battery supply, switching and isolation for work on equipment made dead, precautions for work on electrical equipment, working space, access and lighting, competent persons, testing and inspection, earth leakage protection for higher voltage, switch rooms, fencing of outdoor equipment and overhead lines and underground cables.

8. Part 4 and Schedule 5 to the Regulations relating to Work at Height set out a range of requirements as regards various matters including organisation, planning and risk assessment of work at height, checking of places of work at height, weather conditions, avoidance of risks from work at height, protection of places of work at height, selection of work equipment for work at height, condition of surfaces for supporting structures, stability of supporting structure, guard-rails, toe-boards, barriers etc., stability of working platforms, safety on working platforms, loading of working platform and supporting structures, additional requirements for scaffolding, collective safeguards for arresting falls, personal fall protection systems, work positioning systems, rope access or positioning

technique, fall arrest systems, work restraint systems, ladders, fragile surfaces, falling objects, danger areas and inspection of work equipment.

9.   Part 5 of the Regulations relates to exposure to Physical Agents at work.

Chapter 1 of Part 5 of the Regulations sets out requirements relating to the Control of Noise at Work including exposure limit values and exposure action values, determination and assessment of risks above a lower exposure action value, provisions aimed at avoiding or reducing exposure, application of upper exposure action values, prevention of exposure above noise level of 85dB(A), application of exposure limit value, personal protection, employee information, training and consultation, health surveillance, records and effects and exemptions.

Chapter 2 of Part 5 and Schedule 6 to the Regulations set out requirements relating to the Control of Vibration at Work including exposure limit values and action values, determination and assessment of risks, provisions aimed at avoiding or reducing exposure, application of exposure action values, application of exposure limit value, employee information and training, health surveillance, records and effects and exemptions.

10. Part 6 of the Regulations relates to Sensitive Risk Groups.

Chapter 1 of Part 6 and Schedule 7 to the Regulations set out requirements relating to the Protection of Children and Young Persons including risk assessment, circumstances prohibiting employment of a child or young person and health surveillance. The purpose of these provisions is to retranspose the health and safety aspects of Council Directive 94/33/EC on the protection of young people at work. The other requirements of this Directive have been implemented by the Protection of Young Persons (Employment) Act 1996.

Chapter 2 of Part 6 and Schedule 8 to the Regulations set out requirements relating to the Protection of Pregnant, Post Natal and Breastfeeding Employees including risk assessment, protective or preventive measures, night work and information. The purpose of these provisions is to transpose the occupational safety and health provisions of Council Directive 92/85/EEC of 19th October, 1992 on the introduction of measures to encourage improvements in the safety and health at work of pregnant workers and workers who have recently given birth or are breastfeeding.

Chapter 3 of Part 6 of the Regulations sets out requirements relating to Night Work and Shift Work including general duties of employers with respect to night workers and shift workers, night work risk assessment and health assessment and transfer to day work. The purpose of these provisions is to give effect, in respect of night workers and shift workers, to the safety and health protection provisions of Article 9 of Directive 93/104/EC of 23 November, 1993 concerning certain aspects of the organisation of working time. Inter alia, they require employers, who employ night workers, to carry out, for the purposes of the maximum hours of night working permitted under sections 16(2)(*a*) and 16(2)(*b*) of the

Organisation of Working Time Act 1997 (No. 20 of 1997) (i.e. the Act by which the main provisions of the Directive have been implemented in Ireland), an assessment of the safety and health risks attaching to the work of night workers whom they employ with a view to determining whether that work involves special hazards or a heavy physical or mental strain. They also require employers, whose night workers become ill or exhibit symptoms of ill-health as a result of performing night work, to reassign such workers to day work suited to them whenever possible.

11. Part 7 of the Regulations relates to Safety Signs and First Aid.

    Chapter 1 of Part 7 and Schedule 9 to the Regulations set out requirements relating to the provision of Safety Signs at Places of Work including provision of safety signs, information and instruction for employees, prohibition of unauthorised information on signs, signboards, illuminated signs, acoustic signs and hand signals. These provisions apply to all places of work and they relate to signs referring to a specific object, activity or situation which provide information or instructions about safety and health at work.

    Chapter 2 of Part 7 of the Regulations sets out requirements relating to First-aid at places of work including provision of first-aid equipment, occupational first-aiders and first-aid rooms.

12. Part 8 and Schedule 10 to the Regulations relate to Explosive Atmospheres at Places of Work and set out various requirements including in relation to assessment of explosion risk, classification of places where explosive atmospheres may occur, prevention against explosion, safety of plant, equipment and protective systems, training, instructions, permits to work, protection of employees from explosion and coordination at workplaces. These provisions of the Regulations transpose Directive 1999/92/EC of the European Parliament and of the Council of 16 December 1999 on minimum requirements for improving the safety and health protection of workers potentially at risk from explosive atmospheres. Directive 1999/92/EC defines "explosive atmosphere" as "a mixture with air, under atmospheric conditions, of flammable substances in the form of gases, vapours, mists or dusts in which, after ignition has occurred, combustion spreads to the entire unburned mixture".

    Employers are required to classify places at the workplace where explosive atmospheres may occur into hazardous or non-hazardous places. They must classify those places classified as hazardous into zones and apply the specified preventive measures. These measures include the selection of equipment and protective systems according to the categories set out in Part 8 and Schedule 10 to the Regulations. Such equipment and protective systems are defined in Directive 94/9/EC (which was transposed in Ireland through the European Communities (Equipment and Protective Systems Intended for Use in Potentially Explosive Atmospheres) Regulations 1999 (S.I. No. 83 of 1999)) as follows:

    (a) 'Equipment' means machines, apparatus, fixed or mobile devices, control components and instrumentation thereof and detection or prevention systems which, separately or jointly, are intended for the generation, transfer, storage, measurement, control and conversion of energy for the processing of material and which are capable of causing an explosion through their own potential sources of ignition.

    (b) 'Protective systems' means design units which are intended to halt incipient explosions immediately and/or to limit the effective range of explosion flames and explosion pressures. Protective systems may be integrated into equipment or separately placed on the market for use as autonomous systems.

13. Subject to the particular periods referred to in Regulations 9, 122 and 134, these Safety, Health and Welfare at Work (General Application) Regulations 2007 come into operation on 1 November 2007.

SAFETY, HEALTH AND WELFARE AT WORK ACT 2005 (APPEALS FORMS) RULES 2005

S.I. No. 548 of 2005

I, Michael McDowell, Minister for Justice, Equality and Law Reform, in exercise of the powers conferred on me by sections 66(7), 67(7) and 72(3) of the Safety, Health and Welfare at Work Act 2005 (No. 10 of 2005), and having consulted with the Minister for Enterprise, Trade and Employment, hereby make the following rules:

Citation

1. These Rules may be cited as the Safety Health and Welfare at Work Act 2005 (Appeals Forms) Rules 2005.

Interpretation

2. (1) In these Rules "Act of 2005" means the Safety, Health and Welfare at Work Act 2005 (No. 10 of 2005).

(2) In these Rules, any reference to the Schedule or a rule which is not otherwise identified is a reference to the Schedule or a rule of these Rules.

(3) In these Rules, any reference to a sub-rule which is not otherwise identified is a reference to a sub-rule of the provision in which the reference occurs.

Commencement

3. These Rules shall come into operation on 1 September 2005.

Appeals

4. (1) An appeal brought under —

(a) section 66(7) of the Act of 2005 against an improvement notice,
(b) section 67(7) of the Act of 2005 against a prohibition notice, or
(c) section 72(3) of the Act of 2005 against an information notice,

shall be brought, heard or determined at a sitting of the District Court for the district court district in which such notice was served.

(2) An appeal referred to in sub-rule (1) shall be preceded by the issue and service of a Notice of Appeal in the form set out in Part 1 of the Schedule, or a form to like effect, on each party directly affected by the appeal.

(3) The Notice of Appeal referred to in sub-rule (2) shall be served in accordance with the provisions of section 3 of the Act of 2005.

(4) When service has been effected, the appellant shall lodge with the district court clerk the original of the Notice of Appeal together with a statutory declaration as to service thereof.

Application to suspend operation of prohibition notice

5. Upon issuing a Notice of Appeal against a prohibition notice which said prohibition notice is declared to take effect immediately it is received by the person on whom it is served, or at any time thereafter, the appellant may apply, at any sitting of the District Court for the district court district in which the appeal is listed for hearing, under section 67(6) of the Act of 2005 to have the operation of the said prohibition notice suspended until the appeal is disposed of, provided that the appellant first gives 48 hours notice of the application (in the form set out in Part 2 of the Schedule, or a form to like effect) to each party directly affected by the appeal and lodges the original of Form 2, together with a statutory declaration as to service thereof, with the district court clerk and such form may, where appropriate, be served at the same time as, and together with, the Notice of Appeal.

Copy of notice appealed form to be lodged

6. The appellant shall lodge with the district court clerk or produce at the hearing of the appeal a copy of the notice against which the appeal has been brought.

SCHEDULE

PART 1

Form 1

Safety, Health and Welfare at Work Act 2005, sections *66(7) *67(7) & *72(3)

NOTICE OF APPEAL TO THE DISTRICT COURT

District

Court Area   District No.

of

....Appellant

....Respondent

....*(the Health and Safety
                                                         Authority)

....*(a person prescribed
                                                         under section 33 of the
                                                         above-mentioned Act)

TAKE NOTICE that the above-named appellant, of

....

WILL APPEAL at the sitting of the District Court to be held at
...............…….on the….…..day of…......…..20…..at…...…...…..a.m./p.m.

AGAINST the *improvement notice *prohibition notice *notice requiring
information served on the appellant by the above-named respondent,
of…….....................on the….…...day of….......20…....at…....…........in the
court district aforesaid under section *66(1) *67(1) *72(1) of the above-
mentioned Act,

*[AND WILL APPLY under section 67(9)(b) of the above-mentioned Act
for a direction suspending the application of the said prohibition notice
under section 67(8)]

ON THE FOLLOWING GROUNDS—

Dated this......day of.........20....,

Signed.........................

Appellant *Solicitor for Appellant.

To the above-named respondent.

To

of

*(the Health and Safety Authority)

*(a person prescribed under section 33 of the above-mentioned Act)

*Delete if inapplicable.

PART 2

Form 2

Safety, Health and Welfare at Work Act 2005, section 67(6)

**NOTICE OF APPLICATION TO HAVE OPERATION OF
PROHIBITION NOTICE SUSPENDED**

District   Court

Area   District No.

of

....Appellant

....Respondent

....*(the Health and Safety
                                                              Authority)

....*(a person prescribed
                                                              under section 33 of the
                                                              above-mentioned Act)

WHEREAS the above-named applicant, of.............., was on the.....day
of.............20....at............in the court district aforesaid served by the
above-named respondent, of...................with a prohibition notice under
section 67(1) of the above-mentioned Act,

AND WHEREAS the said prohibition notice is declared to take effect immediately it is received by the person on whom it is served,

AND WHEREAS the applicant has issued * (and served) * (and intends to
serve) * a notice of appeal against the said prohibition notice,

TAKE NOTICE that an application will be made by the applicant at the sitting
of the District Court to be held at....................on the.........day of..........
20.......at......a.m./p.m. under section 67(6) of the said Act to have the operation of the said prohibition notice suspended until the appeal is disposed of,
on the following grounds—

Dated this.........day of.....................20........,

                    Signed..

                                        *Appellant *Solicitor for Appellant.

To the above-named respondent.

To

Of

*(the Health and Safety Authority)

    *(a person prescribed under section 33 of the Act of 2005)

    *Delete if inapplicable

                      GIVEN under my Official Seal,
                      This 1st day of September 2005

                      Minister for Justice, Equality
                      and Law Reform

DISTRICT COURT RULES

AMENDMENT TO: ORDER 100

S.I. No. 209 of 2006: District Court (Safety, Health and Welfare at Work Act 2005) Rules 2006

The District Court Rules Committee, in exercise of the powers conferred on them by section 91 of the Courts of Justice Act 1924, section 72 of the Courts of Justice Act 1936, section 34 of the Courts (Supplemental Provisions) Act 1961 and section 24 of the Interpretation Act 2005, do hereby, with the concurrence of the Minister for Justice, Equality and Law Reform, make the following rules of court:-

1. These rules may be cited as the District Court (Safety, Health and Welfare at Work Act 2005) Rules 2006.

2. These rules shall come into operation on the 22nd day of May 2006 and shall be read together with all other District Court rules for the time being in force.

3. The District Court Rules 1997 (S.I. No. 93 of 1997) shall be amended by the insertion immediately following rule 4 of Order 100 of the following rule:

    "5.(1) In this rule-

    > *the "Act of 2005" means the Safety Health and Welfare at Work Act 2005 (No. 10 of 2005).*

    (2) Where an appeal has been brought in the manner prescribed under -

    > *(a) section 66(7) of the Act of 2005 against an improvement notice,*
    > *(b) section 67(7) of the Act of 2005 against a prohibition notice, or*
    > *(c) section 72(3) of the Act of 2005 against an information notice,*

    > *an order of the Court made on such application shall be in the Form 100.3, Schedule D and the applicant shall cause the said order to be served upon the respondent and upon any other person directly affected by the said order.*

    (3) Where an application has been brought in the manner prescribed under section 67(6) of the Act of 2005 for the suspension of a prohibition notice, an order of the Court made on such application directing that the operation of a prohibition notice be suspended shall be in the Form 100.4, Schedule D and the applicant shall cause the said order to be served upon the respondent and upon any other person directly affected by the said order."

4. The Forms in the Schedule hereto shall be added to the Forms in Schedule D to the District Court Rules 1997 (S.I. No. 93 of 1997), immediately following Form 100.2.

Given this 20th day of February 2006
Uinsin Mac Gruairc
John P Brophy
Mary C Devins
Thomas E O'Donnell
Fiona Twomey
Noel A Doherty
Elizabeth Hughes Secretary

I concur in the making of the foregoing rules
Dated this 24th day of April 2006

Michael McDowell
Minister for Justice, Equality and Law Reform

DISTRICT COURT RULES

S.I. No. 209 of 2006: District Court (Safety, Health and Welfare at Work Act 2005) Rules 2006 - Forms 100.3 & 100.4

SCHEDULE

SCHEDULE D

O. 100, r. 5(2)

Form 100.3

Safety, Health and Welfare at Work Act 2005, section *66(7)*67(7)*72(3)

ORDER ON HEARING AN APPEAL

District Court Area of District No.

Between

....…..…. Appellant

of ....

....…... Respondent

of ....*(the Health and Safety Authority) *(a person prescribed under section 33 of the above-mentioned Act of 2005)

UPON HEARING AN APPEAL brought before this Court by the above-named appellant, of .... against

*an improvement notice which was served on him under section 66(1)

*a prohibition notice which was served on him under section 67(1)

*an information notice which was served on him under section 72(1)

of the above-mentioned Act by the above-named respondent, of .... on the ..... day of .... 20... at .... in the court (area and) district aforesaid

THE COURT

BEING SATISFIED that notice of the said appeal has been duly served, and

HAVING HEARD THE EVIDENCE tendered by or on behalf of *the appellant, *the respondent, *the Authority, *a person prescribed under section 33 of the Act of 2005

AND BEING SATISFIED that it is reasonable to do so

HEREBY ORDERS

*that the said notice against which the appeal was brought be confirmed,

*that the said notice against which the appeal was brought be confirmed with the following variations:—

*(and on the application of the appellant the Court hereby suspends the operation of the *prohibition notice *information notice for the period of..................)

*that the said notice against which the appeal was brought be cancelled.

Dated this ...... day of .... 20.....

Signed ....

Judge of the District Court

*Delete if inapplicable.

SCHEDULE D

O. 100, r. 5(3)

Form 100.4

Safety, Health and Welfare at Work Act 2005, section 67(6)

ORDER DIRECTING THAT THE OPERATION OF A PROHIBITION NOTICE BE SUSPENDED

District Court Area of District No.

Between

.... Applicant

of..

.... Respondent

of...*(the Health and Safety Authority) *(a person prescribed under section 33 of the above-mentioned Act of 2005)

UPON HEARING AN APPLICATION made to this Court by the above-named applicant, of .... under section 67(6) of the above-mentioned Act to have the operation of a prohibition notice which was served on him on the ...... day of .... 20..... at .... in the court (area and) district aforesaid suspended until an appeal against that notice is disposed of

THE COURT

BEING SATISFIED that notice of the said appeal has been duly issued and served,

BEING SATISFIED that notice of the within application has been duly served, and

HAVING HEARD THE EVIDENCE tendered by or on behalf of *the applicant, *the respondent, *the Authority, *a person prescribed under section 33 of the Act of 2005

and thinking it proper to do so

HEREBY DIRECTS that the operation of the said prohibition notice be suspended until the said appeal is disposed of.

Dated this .... day of .... 20......

Signed ....

Judge of the District Court.

*Delete if inapplicable.

PART IV

NEW SAFETY STATEMENT GUIDELINES

(Health and Safety Authority, 2006)

CONTENTS

Who should Read these Guidelines?

These guidelines are designed to help an employer or self-employed person to manage safety and health at their place of work. When the guidelines refer to safety and health, they mean the safety, health and welfare of workers while at work.

Why is it Important to Carry out a Risk Assessment and Prepare a Safety Statement?

1 *Financial reasons*

There is considerable evidence, borne out by companies' practical experiences, that effective safety and health management in the workplace contributes to business success. Accidents and ill-health inflict significant costs, often hidden and underestimated.

2 *Legal reasons*

Carrying out a risk assessment, preparing a safety statement and implementing what you have written down are not only central to any safety and health management system, they are required by law.

Health and Safety Authority inspectors visiting workplaces will want to know how employers are managing safety and health. If they investigate an accident, they will scrutinise the risk assessment and safety statement, and the procedures and work practices in use. Make sure that these stand up to examination.

3 *Moral and ethical reasons*

The process of carrying out a risk assessment, preparing a safety statement and implementing what you have written down will help employers prevent injuries and illhealth at work. Employers are ethically bound to do all they can to ensure that your employees do not suffer illness, a serious accident or death.

How will these Guidelines Help Me?

They will help employers and those who have a duty to do so to carry out risk assessments and to prepare a safety statement.

Please note, however, that the guidelines may not meet the more stringent approach to identifying hazards and assessing risks that is required by some sector-specific laws, e.g. controlling major accident hazards in chemical companies, carrying dangerous goods by road, or classifying and labelling dangerous substances. Further information on these areas and more general workplace safety and health issues may be obtained from the Workplace Contact Unit at the Health and Safety Authority or from the Authority website at www.safework.ie.

MANAGING WORKPLACE SAFETY AND HEALTH

What does the Law say?

As an employer you are required to manage safety and health at work so as to prevent accidents and ill-health.

Controlling dangers at work is no different from tackling any other task. You need to recognise the problem, know enough about it, decide what to do and put the solutions into practice.

The law requires employers to:

• identify the hazards

• carry out a risk assessment

• prepare a written safety statement

This process has a practical purpose. It will help employers and other duty holders to manage employees' safety and health, and get the balance right between the size of any safety and health problems and what has to be done about them. This is because the system must be risk-based; the required safety measures must be proportionate to the real risks involved and must be adequate to eliminate, control or minimise the risk of injury. The system must involve consultation between you as an employer and your employees, who are required by law to cooperate with you in the safety-management process.

What is a Risk Assessment?

Section 19 of the Safety, Health and Welfare at Work Act, 2005 requires that employers and those who control workplaces to any extent must:

• identify the hazards in the workplaces under their control

• assess the risks presented by these hazards

In this context a *hazard* is something with the potential to cause harm (for example, chemical substances, machinery or methods of work), while measuring the *risk* depends on:

• the *likelihood* of that harm occurring in the workplace

• the *potential severity* of that harm (the degree of injury or ill health following an accident)

• the *number of people* who might be exposed to the hazard

Employers must write down these workplace risks and what to do about them. This is known as a risk assessment.

Assessing risk means you must examine carefully what, in the workplace, could cause harm to your employees, other employees and other people, including customers, visitors and members of the public. This allows you to weigh up whether you have taken enough precautions or whether you should do more to prevent harm.

Employers are required to implement any improvements considered necessary by the risk assessment. The aim is to make sure that no-one gets hurt or becomes ill.

It is important to remember that, in identifying hazards and assessing risks, employers should only consider those which are generated by work activities. There is no need to consider every minor hazard or risk which we accept as part of our lives. For example, you do not need to identify lifting 1kg of material as a workplace hazard; but lifting a 25kg box of 1kg packages off the floor would be a hazard.

The results of any risk assessments should be written into the safety statement.

What is a Safety Statement?

Section 20 of the Safety, Health and Welfare at Work Act, 2005 requires that an organisation produce a written programme to safeguard:

- the safety and health of employees while they work

- the safety and health of other people who might be at the workplace, including customers, visitors and members of the public

The safety statement represents a commitment to their safety and health. It should state how the employer will ensure:

- their safety and health

- the resources necessary to maintain and review safety and health laws and standards

- The safety statement should influence all work activities, including

- the selection of competent people, equipment and materials

- the way work is done

- how goods and services are designed and provided

Writing down the safety statement and putting in place the organisation and arrangements needed to implement and monitor it show to staff, and anyone else, that hazards have been identified and risks assessed, eliminated or controlled.

Why Carry out Risk Assessments and Prepare a Safety Statement?

Carrying out risk assessments, preparing and implementing a safety statement and keeping both up to date will not in themselves prevent accidents and ill health but they will play a crucial part in reducing their likelihood.

The aim is to make sure that no one gets hurt or becomes ill. Accidents and ill health can ruin lives, and can affect your business too if output is lost, machinery is damaged, insurance costs increase, or you have to go to court.

Employers, managers and supervisors should all ensure that workplace practices reflect the risk assessments and safety statement. Behaviour, the way in which everyone works, must reflect the safe working practices laid down in these documents. Supervisory checks and audits should be carried out to determine how well the aims set down are being achieved. Corrective action should be taken when required.

If a workplace is provided for use by others, the safety statement must also set out the safe work practices that are relevant to them.

When an inspector from the Health and Safety Authority inspects a workplace, he or she will place great emphasis on ensuring that a good safety and health management programme is in place.

If an accident happens, Authority inspectors and others will examine carefully the relevant risk assessments, safety statement, procedures and work practices. Make sure they stand up to the examination. If the inspector finds that one of these is inadequate, he or she can ask the employer to revise it. Employers can be prosecuted if they do not have a safety statement.

What should be Covered by a Safety Statement?

The areas that should be covered by the safety statement are specific and are set out in Section 20 of the Safety, Health and Welfare at Work Act, 2005. The statement should be based on the identification of the hazards and the risk assessments carried out under Section 19. It must:

- specify how the safety and health of all employees will be secured and managed

- specify the hazards identified and risks assessed

- give details of how the employer is going to manage his or her safety and health responsibilities, including (a) a commitment to comply with legal obligations, (b) the protective and preventive measures taken, (c) the resources provided for safety and health at the workplace, and (d) the arrangements used to fulfil these responsibilities

- include the plans and procedures to be used in the event of an emergency or serious danger

- specify the duties of employees including the co-operation required from them on safety and health matters

- include the names and job titles of people being appointing to be responsible for safety and health or for performing the tasks set out in the statement

- contain the arrangements made for appointing safety representatives, and for consulting with and the participation by employees on safety and health matters, including the names of the safety representatives and the members of the safety committee, if appointed

- be written in a form, manner and language that will be understood by all

- have regard to the relevant safety and health legislation

Who is Responsible for Preparing the Risk Assessments and Safety Statement?

All employers, those who control workplaces to any extent or provide workplaces for use by others and the self-employed are required to prepare risk assessments and a safety statement.

If three or fewer people are employed and a code of practice relating to safety statements, prepared by the Authority, exists for a sector or work activity, then compliance with that code is sufficient. However, a risk assessment must always be prepared for that place of work.

Consultation should take place with employees and others, as necessary, when preparing the statement to ensure that they understand and take ownership of the safety and health measures proposed. There is a duty on everyone at work to cooperate effectively in developing and promoting safety and health.

Who Needs to Read the Risk Assessments and the Safety Statement?

You must ensure that your safety statement, which includes the risk assessments, is brought to the attention of all employees and others at the workplace who may be exposed to any risks covered by the safety statement. The statement must be in a form and language that they all understand.

In particular, all new employees must be made aware of the safety statement when they start work.

Other people may be exposed to a specific risk dealt with in the safety statement and the statement should be brought to their attention. These people could include:

- outside contractors who do cleaning, maintenance or building work

- temporary workers

- delivery people who stack their goods in your premises and come in contact with activities there

- self-employed people who provide a service for the employer

Where specific tasks are carried out which pose a serious risk to safety and health, the relevant contents of the safety statement must be brought to the attention of those affected, setting out the hazards identified, the risk assessments and the safety and health measures that must be taken.

How Often do My Staff Need to Read the Safety Statement?

You should ensure that the relevant contents of the safety statement are brought to the attention of your employees and others affected at least annually, and whenever it is revised.

You have an ongoing responsibility to ensure that all relevant persons are aware of the safety statement and understand its terms.

A campaign to discharge this responsibility could include a combination of written and verbal communication, including:

- distributing the safety statement, specific risk assessments or relevant sections of it to all employees when first prepared and whenever significant changes are made
- making the safety statement and specific risk assessments available electronically on company intranet sites which can be easily interrogated
- verbal communication of the terms of the safety statement or particular risk assessments
- inclusion of the relevant parts of the safety statement and specific risk assessments in employees' handbooks or manuals
- through ongoing training

GETTING STARTED: SIX SIMPLE STEPS TO FOLLOW

A comprehensive safety statement, if properly implemented, is a practical tool for Reducing accidents and ill health at work. For small to medium-sized businesses the Preparation of a safety statement should be simple and straightforward.

There are six simple steps to be followed, one of which is the process of assessing risk. In developing a safety and health management programme for an organization, all steps Are important. These are set out in the following diagram and explained below:

STEP 1: DRAW UP A SAFETY AND HEALTH POLICY

Employers have ultimate responsibility for safety and health. The safety statement should begin with a declaration, signed at senior, responsible management level on the employer's behalf. The declaration, should give a commitment to ensuring that a workplace is as safe and healthy as reasonably practicable and that all relevant statutory requirements will be complied with.

This declaration should spell out the policy in relation to overall safety and health Performance, provide a framework for managing safety and health, and list relevant objectives.

Because the safety statement must be relevant at all times to the safety and health of employees and others in the workplace, the policy declaration should indicate:

> that the safety statement will be revised as changes occur and evaluated at set intervals;

> how the relevant contents of the statement are to be brought to the attention of employees and any other people in the workplace who might be affected by the statement.

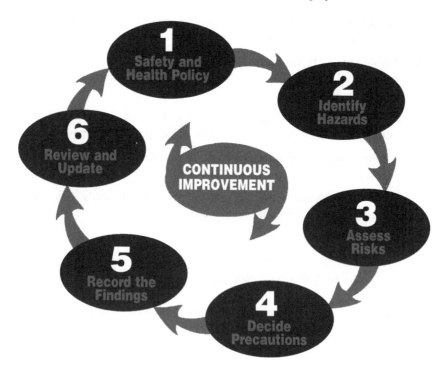

The safety and health policy should also take account of the general employer duties as set out in the 2005 Act and other legislation that applies to the workplace. Duty-holders must ensure, as far as is reasonably practicable, that they:

- manage and conduct work activities so as to ensure the safety and health of employees

- prevent improper conduct likely to put an employee's safety and health at risk

- provide a safe place of work which is adequately designed and maintained

- provide safe means of access and egress

- provide safe plant, equipment and machinery

- provide safe systems of work, e.g. operating procedures

- prevent risk to health from any article or substance (including plant, tools, machinery, chemical substances and equipment)

- provide appropriate information, instruction, training and supervision, taking account of the employee's capabilities, when an employee begins work or is transferred to new tasks, and when new technology is introduced

- provide suitable protective clothing and equipment where hazards cannot be eliminated

- prepare and revise emergency plans

- designate staff to take on emergency duties

- provide and maintain welfare facilities

- provide, where necessary, a competent person to advise and assist in securing the safety, health and welfare of employees. (A competent person, as defined in the 2005 Act, must have the necessary qualification as well as sufficient training, experience and knowledge appropriate to the nature of the work to be undertaken

If any of these issues are particularly relevant to the workplace being covered, employers may comment on them in the policy declarain. Otherwise do so in the main part of the safety statement.

The managing director or another senior manager who has overall responsibility for safety and health should sign the safety and health policy and communicate it to all staff.

Example of a Company's Policy Declaration

To all employees:

As your employer, we are required to comply with all safety and health legislation that applies to this company. With this in mind we have carried out risk assessments of all our key operations and processes in all the workplaces we control. We have discussed these risk assessments with all relevant employees and worked with the safety committee in preparing this safety statement

This statement sets out the safety and health measures we are implementing to protect everyone who works here

The Board of ABC Ltd has endorsed this statement and gave me the responsibility to implement it. I am committed to ensuring that the safety and health measures set out in our safety statement are met

John Kelly, Safety and Health Manager, will give advice and information on how to comply with this safety statement but everyone, especially if you are in a management or supervisory position, is responsible for ensuring compliance where they work

We expect all employees to co-operate with us so that we can achieve our target of avoiding accidents. Consultation on safety and health maters, between senior managers and all employees, will be carried out through the safety committee, which you have selected

You must play your part under the safety statement. Comply with all the safety and health rules for your area. Work safely and think of others as you do. know and understand the risk assessments for your area. Report safety and health problems to your supervisor. Know who your safety representative is and contact him or her with any safety and health enquiries you may have

Signed

Joan Mc Carthy
Managing Director

———————————
DATE

STEP 2: IDENTIFY THE HAZARDS

Here are the common definitions of the terms *hazard, risk, risk assessment* and *control* as they apply in the workplace.

HAZARD in general means anything that can cause harm but, for your purposes, this must be workplace-generated (e.g. dangerous chemicals, electricity, working at heights from ladders, poor housekeeping).

RISK is the likelihood, great or small that someone will be harmed by the hazard, together with the severity of harm suffered. Risk also depends on the number of people exposed to the hazard.

RISK ASSESSMENT is a careful examination of what, in the workplace, could cause harm to people, so that the employer can weigh up whether he or she has taken enough precautions or should do more to prevent harm.

CONTROLLING RISK means that the employer (as the law requires) does all that is reasonably practicable to ensure that a hazard will not injure anyone (e.g. by eliminating the hazard, enclosing it in a totally enclosed container, using general or local exhaust ventilation, implementing safe operating procedures, or providing personal protection, as a last resort).

The first step in safeguarding safety and health is to identify hazards from materials, equipment, chemicals and work activities. You are required to systematically examine your workplace and work activities to identify workplace-generated hazards.

If you control more than one work location, different types of work activity or changing work locations (as in road repairs or building work), you may need to prepare a safety statement that has separate sections dealing with the different locations or activities.

Employers will be familiar with the hazards associated with the type of work they are involved in. But to identify the main hazards and put risks in their true perspective, employers can also check:

• records of accidents. ill health and insurance claims

• any relevant legislation or standards covering the hazard (e.g. the Construction Regulations for construction-site hazards, the Chemical Agents Regulations and Code of Practice for chemical hazards and their control)

• manufacturers' instructions or datasheets

Some hazards are obvious, such as unguarded moving parts of machinery, dangerous fumes, electricity, working at heights, or moving heavy loads. Less obvious, but at the root of many accidents, are hazards presented by untidy workplaces and poor maintenance. In the case of some hazards, such as excessive noise, it may take months or even years before damage materialises.

Don't be overcomplicated. In most firms in the office, retail, commercial, service and light industrial sector, the hazards and hazardous work activities are few and simple. Checking them is common sense, but necessary. In small firms, employers understand their work and can identify hazards and assess risks themselves. For larger firms, a responsible experienced employee or safety officer should be used. Consult and involve as necessary all employees, including the safety representatives. But remember – the employer is responsible for seeing that the work is adequately done.

If you use external advisers to help prepare the safety statement, make sure they know the work activity and have the appropriate experience. If you do the work yourself, walk around the workplace and look afresh at what could reasonably be expected to cause harm. Ignore the trivial and concentrate on the significant hazards that could result in serious harm or affect several people. Ask employees and their representatives what they think. They may have noticed things that are not immediately obvious.

The following checklists provide a systematic, though not exhaustive, approach to identifying hazards:

Physical Hazards

Some common causes of accidents, with examples, are:

- manual handling (heavy, awkward or hard-to-reach loads, handling patients, treating farm animals)

- slipping/tripping hazards (poorly maintained or untidy floors, passageways or stairs)

- falling from a height (from mezzanine floors or scaffolding)

- being struck by material falling from above

- getting caught or cut by machinery, especially moving parts of machinery (blades or rollers, power take-off shafts on tractors and farm machinery)

- equipment (poorly maintained or whose guards have been disabled)

- falling objects

- being struck by internal transport (fork-lifts) or external transport (delivery trucks at loading bays)

- introduction of new machinery or work systems

- fire (from flammable or combustible materials, hay, waste material)

- ejection of material (from plastic moulding or woodworking machines)

- electricity (poor wiring or not being protected by residual current devices)

- special hazards of maintenance of equipment and the workplace itself (the roof, windows or gutters)

- injury by another person or an animal

- hot substances or surfaces

- hand tools (noise, eye injury, electrocution)

- poor housekeeping

- burial in trenches or by loose material such as grain or soil

- suffocation by drowning or from exposure to carbon monoxide (from portable generators)

- pressure systems (steam boilers)

You can find out the most common causes of accidents in your sector by consulting the Health and Safety Authority website or the most up-to-date Summary of Fatality, Injury and Illness Statistics published by the Authority – available at www.safework.ie.

Health Hazards

- negative stress (e.g. from poor work organization or control, repetitive strain,etc)

- noise (e.g. if people must raise their voices to be heard)

- harmful dusts (e.g. from grinding)

- unsuitable lighting levels

- some types of light (e.g. from over-exposure to ultra-violet light can cause skin cancer)

- vibration (e.g. from pneumatic rock or concrete breakers or drills)

- sources of radiation

- extremes of temperature

- injury through poor design of tasks or machinery

- radiation hazards including naturally occurring radon

Chemical Hazards

Chemical substances are used in nearly all organisations. They range from common everyday products such as glues and correction fluids to industrial solvents, dyes, pesticides or acids. In most cases the hazards are well documented and information is available on safety precautions to be taken. Regulations require certain chemicals to be labelled according to their hazards.

Manufacturers and suppliers are legally required to provide material safety data sheets, which give information on the safety and health risks of any chemical substances. They should be asked for this information. The code of practice for the Chemical Agents Regulations lists several hundred dangerous chemical agents. Check this list if chemicals Are used in your operations.

To identify chemical hazards and assess their risks, you need data on at least the Following:

- immediate problems,(e.g. acute toxic effects or catching fire)

- long-term effects of exposure on health (e.g. cancer-causing)

- likelihood of explosion

- likelihood of skin problems (e.g. skin irritation or sensitiser causing dermatitis)
- likelihood of chest problems (e.g. respiratory irritation or sensitization, asthma)

Biological Agent Hazards

These include viruses and bacteria that can cause infection and substances from plants or animals that can lead to other health problems. These hazards are likely to occur in places such as laboratories, hospitals,farms or abattoirs. They include:

- tuberculosis from contact with infectious cases

- brucellosis

- farmer's lung, caused by spores from mouldy hay

- hepatitis from unprotected handling of infected body fluids or waste

If you work in or are responsible for any of the above activities you should consult the Biological Agents Regulations for further information on identifying biological agent Hazards and methods of control.

Human-Factor Hazards

Apart from physical surroundings, human factors must also be taken into account when identifying hazards:

- People should be mentally and physically capable of doing their jobs safely.
- The workplace, the work system, the organization of work and the job should be designed so as to avoid causing sustained stress.
- Workers should not be subjected to bullying by or violence from other workers or members of the public.
- Some groups are particularly vulnerable:
- young workers, who have a higher accident rate
- pregnant women (see the General Application Regulations)
- people with disabilities
- new or inexperienced workers
- workers who have recently changed roles or jobs or started work in a new workplace
- older workers
- workers whose first language is not English

Step 3: Carry out a Risk Assessment

Risk means the likelihood, great or small, that someone will be harmed by a hazard, Together with the severity of the harm suffered. Risk also depends on the number of People who might be exposed to the hazard.

In assessing the risk, you should estimate:

- how likely it is that a hazard will cause harm

- how serious that harm is likely to be

- how often and how many workers are exposed

Then you can weigh up whether you have taken enough precautions or should do more To prevent harm. You can also decide if any corrective measures are especially urgent.

Who should Carry out the Risk Assessment?

It is the employer's duty, under section 19 of the 2005 Act, to carry out the risk assessment so you should try to do it yourself, while involving managers and employees as much as possible. Where the in-house expertise is not available, employ the services of an external competent person to help. Check that they are familiar with and have the ability to assess specific work activities. Involve as many employees as possible in order to encourage them to share ownership of the finished assessments.

Is there a Formula I can Use to Assess Risk?

There are various qualitative and quantitative methods for carrying out risk assessment. Choose one which best suits the organization. A generic format for carrying out risk assessments in tabular form is given in the Appendix.

What Factors Affect the Level of Risk?

Risk will depend on many, often related, circumstances:

- Who is exposed to the hazard?

- Is the hazard likely to cause injury to my workers or others?

- How serious would the injury be?

- Is the hazard well controlled?[1]

---

[1] If one uses dangerous chemicals, the hazards and the precautions will be listed on the label or the material safety data sheet. There may also be safety and health regulations, industry standards, and codes of practice or guidelines dealing with a particular hazard. For example, regulations require stop controls to be provided at each work station for machinery. Guidance on stop controls and emergency stop controls is available in the Use of Work Equipment Guide to the Safety Health and Welfare at Work (General Application) Regulations. Employers should use these to help assess the risks and to decide if existing precautions are adequate.

- Is the level of supervision adequate?

- How long are people exposed? What levels of exposure should not be exceeded? (These levels apply to chemicals, temperature, noise, heavy loads, radiation, etc.)

Who do I Need to Consider?

Apart from employees (e.g. operators, maintenance personnel, and office staff) think about people who may not be in the workplace all the time, for example:

- cleaners

- visitors

- contractors

- outside maintenance personnel

- customers

- others (such as students in a school)

- members of the public or people who share the workplace, if there is a chance they could be hurt by the work activities

Pay particular attention to staff with disabilities, visitors, inexperienced staff, workers who do not have English as a first language and lone workers.

If changes such as new plant, new working practices or new materials occur in the workplace, the employer must carry out a new risk assessment, implement any necessary improvements and update the safety statement accordingly. The risk assessments and any subsequent revisions must be brought to the attention of everyone affected by them.

How do I Assess Risk to Travelling or Mult-Site Workers?

The risk assessment and safety statement should relate to the place of work. Where Workers will be working away from their normal base, the risk assessment and safety statement should address the type of work to be performed in that place of work.

It may not be practical to have the full safety statement or risk assessment at particular workplaces or certain work activities (e.g. at roadworks or working on a roof). In these cases a simplified method statement or work procedure, which covers the risks at hand, is sufficient, provided that employees are familiar with their own safety statement.

The Authority has produced a Safe System of Work plan to help supervisors and workers in the construction industry to carry out simple risk assessments for many types of construction work.

STEP 4: DECIDE WHAT PRECAUTIONS ARE NEEDED

Employers may already have in place some safety measures. The risk assessments will tell whether these are adequate.

Employers must ensure they have done all that the law requires. Remember that all safety and health laws provide guidance on how to assess the risks and establish appropriate safeguards. For example, there are legal requirements on preventing access to dangerous parts of machinery. Then ensure that generally accepted industry standards are in place. But do not stop there—because the law also says that you must do what is reasonably practicable to keep the workplace safe. The real aim is to make all risks small by adding to existing precautions if necessary.

Improving safety and health need not cost a lot. For instance, placing a mirror on a dangerous blind corner to help prevent vehicle accidents, or putting some non-slip material on slippery steps, are inexpensive precautions considering the risks. Sometimes changing the way a job is done can reduce the risk of an accident.

Employers need to ask themselves:

• Can I get rid of the hazard altogether?

• Can I change the way the job is done so as to make it safer?

• If not, what safety precautions are necessary to control this risk?

How do I Control Risk?

Common sense tells us that life cannot be totally risk-free. However, employers are required to do all that is reasonably practicable to minimise the risk of injury. Employers will have done all that is reasonably practicable if they have:

• exercised care in putting in place necessary preventive measures

• have identified the hazards and risks relating to the place of work

• have put in place appropriate measures such that it would be grossly disproportionate to do more

Some common methods of controlling risk are:

• replacing a hazardous system of work with a less hazardous system, e.g. pre-assembling components on the ground to reduce the need to work at a height, or using mechanical aids to reduce or eliminate the need for manual handling

• replacing a substance with a less hazardous substance, e.g. replacing a flammable with a non-flammable substance

• designing the workplace to reduce risk,e.g. providing guardrails around roof-mounted equipment or designated walkways and crossing points through areas with moving vehicles.

• ensuring a clean and tidy workplace to prevent trips and slips

- extracting or containing the hazard at source, e.g. providing a fume cupboard with extraction

- adapting the work to the individual, e.g. providing adjustable height tables or chairs to reduce muscle injuries

- ventilating an area of the workplace where extraction at source is not possible

- isolating the process or the worker (e.g. switching off and isolating machines before carrying out repairs or alterations)

- safeguarding machinery, e.g. providing interlocked guards that switch off the machine if someone tries to gain entry to dangerous parts of it

- providing adequate training and supervision

- establishing emergency planning procedures, including first aid

- providing protective equipment, clothing or signs (they should be used only as a last resort after all other ways of eliminating the hazard have been fully explored)

- setting up adequate health-surveillance programmes including pre-placement or regular health check where appropriate

- analysing and investigating accidents (including ill-health) and dangerous occurrences

- using permit-to-work systems or safe working procedures

- putting in place adequate welfare facilities

- establishing other policies as appropriate, e.g. to eradicate bullying, etc

What if I Share a Workplace?

If you share a workplace, tell the other employers and self-employed people there about any risks they might face and what precautions they should take. Also, think about the risks to your workforce from those who share the work-place.

The need for the various risk-control methods will vary according to the needs of your Workplace.

Examples of Factors to be Considered in Specific Risk Assessments

Risk of a slip, trip or fall

Slips, trips and falls are the second most common type of accident in most places of work. The risk depends on:

- the premises being kept clean, tidy and uncluttered

- the flooring and stairs being kept in good repair and on the type of flooring used

- the control of other trip hazards
- the quality of lighting
- spillages of liquid being cleaned promptly

The extent of injury may vary from relatively minor to severe, depending on a variety of factors including the nature of the fall, whether at the level or from a height.

Risk of being stuck by a fork-lift truck

Vehicles in the workplace are a risk to other employees on foot. The risk is a combination of the chance that someone will be struck, together with the likely severity of the injury. This will depend on:

- whether pedestrians use walkways which keep them away from moving fork-trucks
- the number of pedestrians and fork-lift trucks using the same areas
- the training and instruction provided to both drivers and pedestrians
- the degree of supervision and enforcement of safe procedures (e.g. for separating pedestrians and forklifts)
- the mechanical condition of the fork-lift truck (e.g. brakes and flashing beacons)
- the wearing of high-visibility PPE

The extent of injury is likely to be severe and may result in death or disability.

Isocyanate paint risk assessment

Paints containing isocyanates are a hazard to health. The material safety data sheet and the label on the paint container give this information. Breathing in isocyanate fumes can cause asthma. The risk is a combination of the chance that someone's lungs will be damaged together with the extent of the likely damage. This will depend on:

- the amount of isocyanata in the air
- how often the job is done (all day every day or once or twice a year)
- the work method—how the paint is used (e.g. if it is sprayed the risk will be greater than if brushed on)
- the number of people that could be affected. (Does just one person work with the paint or do many? Could their work affect others?)
- What could go wrong (the errors that could lead to spillage and atmospheric emissions)
- the adequacy of precautions taken, such as exhaust ventilation and personal protective equipment. (Do they comply with the legal requirements? How do they compare with good practice and national or 'trade' guidance?)

The extent of the likely damage is severe. An employee could develop asthma, which might make him or her unemployable in that industry.

Permit-to-work systems

A permit-to-work system is a written system of the procedures which must be taken to Safeguard workers doing work such as repair, maintenance or cleaning work in Potentially dangerous areas. It involves mechanical, electrical or process isolation procedures or monitoring the atmosphere for the presence of dangerous fumes. It sets out in a systematic way the work to be done, the hazards involved and the precautions to be taken.

Situations where this is necessary include when machinery could be restarted with the worker still inside it, or working in confined spaces where there is a danger of chemical or physical contamination.

The employer should write down in the safety statement what work activities require a permit-to-work system. Employers may also need to consider the Confined Space Regulations and associated code of practice.

STEP 5 : RECORD THE FINDINGS

The safety statements is the place to record the significant findings of the risk assessments. This means writing down the more significant hazards and recording the most important conclusions. For example:

A safety statement where electrical installations may pose a risk may include: "Electrical Installations: insulation and earthing to be checked every six months and after any modifications."

A workplace where fumes from welding may pose a risk may state: "Local exhaust ventilation has been provided. Supervisor to ensure that it is always used and is checked every month."

Employers should inform employees about these findings. The employer should also State in the safety statement where the results of these checks are retained.

To make things simpler, the safety statement can refer to specific procedures contained in other documents. These documents might include:

• quality manuals

• operating instructions

• company rules

• manufactures' instructions

• company safety and health procedures

These may already list hazards and precautions. There is no need to repeat all that, and it is up to the employer whether to combine all the documents or keep them separately. But the employer must make sure employees are made aware of these risks and precautions.

The safety statement must also specify how you are going to orgainse and assign responsibilities to safeguard your employees safety and health on a day-to-day basis. The areas it must cover are:

- available resources

- safety and health competence

- responsibility and control

- co-operation by employees

- consultation

- participation of employees and representation

- planning and setting standards

- measuring safety and health performance

Resources

The safety statement must detail the resources provided by the employer in terms of time, people and finance, to ensure the safety and health of employees. For example, the employer should specify the budgets and the commitments to ensure safety and health training for all employees.

Safety and Health Competence

Under the 2005 Act other safety and health laws, employers required to have "competent persons" to do various tasks. These people need to have sufficient training, experience and knowledge appropriate to the work to be done.
   You need to:

- assess the skills needed to carry out all tasks safety

- provide the means to ensure that all employees, including managers, supervisors and temporary staff, are adequately instructed and trained in safety and health requirements

- ensure, in particular, that those who do especially dangerous work have the necessary qualifications, training, experience and other qualities to carry out the work safely

✱ It is recommended by the 2005 Act to have in—house safety and health experts. If this is not practicable, ensure that external advice and help is available.
   When carrying out restructuring or reorganization, the employer must ensure that those taking on new safety and heath responsibilities are competent.

Responsibility and Control

An organisation chart showing the safety and health management structure and the names and responsibilities of key personnel should be written down in the safety statement. As a minimum it must include the name of the person at senior management or director level with delegated responsibility for safety and health in the company. Make sure the board of directors or other management body in charge know they have safety and health responsibilities as well.

Responsibilities should be clearly identified.

- Identify people responsible so particular safety and health jobs, especially where special expertise is called for, e.g. for carrying out risk assessments, monitoring compliance with safety and health standards, driving forklift trucks, etc.

- Ensure that managers supervisors and team leaders understand their responsibilities and have the time and resources to carry them out.

- Lines of communication should also be down between the different levels of responsibility.

- Ensure that everyone knows what they must do and how they will be held accountable – set objectives.

- Lead by example. Demonstrate a commitment and provide clear direction. Let everyone know that safety and health is important.

Co-Operation, Required from Employees

All employeed have a duty to take care of their own safety while at work. They must co-operate in the use of personal protective equipment or clothing provided for their safety and health and in enabling the employer to comply with the law. They must attend any safety and health training provided by their employer.

The co-operation required must be clearly spelt out in the safety statement and must not be couched in vague generalities. Where disciplinary procedures for failure to comply with safety and health requirements are appropriate, these should be specified.

Since employees are required to report to either the employer, their manager or their supervisor any defects in plant, equipment, place or system of work that might endanger safety and health, the safety statement should indicate the system for doing so.

Consultation, Participation of Employees, and Representation

The law requires employees to put in place a safety consultation programme that facilitates participation by all employees in safety and health matters. Also the law allows employees to select a safety representative.

Participation by employees supports the risk control by encouraging their ownership of safety and health policies and procedures. It also gives them an understanding that the workplace and the people working in it benefit from good safety and health performance.

Pooling knowledge and experience through employee consultation, participation and representation means that safety and health becomes everybody's business. Under the 2005 Act, safety committees can be used for this consultation. Details on how these committees can operate are set out in the Act.

The safety statement must specify the arrangements to be used for consultation with and participation by employees on safety and health matters. These would include the procedures to facilitate effective co-operation and communication on safety and health matters between the employer and employees. Other consultation areas include:

• any issues which can substantially affect safety and health

• appointment of persons to deal with emergencies and any prevention measures

• carrying out risk assessments, preparing the safety statement

• provision of safety and health information to employees

• the planning and organisation of safety and health training

• introduction of new technologies which can affect safety and health

To demonstrate commitment to safety and health, the employer or a senior manager should be a member of the safety committee, if there is one. Involve the safety committee in:

• planning and reviewing safety and health performance

• writing safety and health procedures

• solving problems

It can also review the safety and health performance of contractors who work on the premises and ensure they fit into the safety and health regime.

The names and functions of the safety representatives and the safety committee members should be detailed in the statement.

Planning and Setting Standards

Planning is the key to ensuring that the safety and health efforts really work. It involves setting objectives, assessing your risks, implementing standards of performance and developing a safety culture. The employer should record the safety and health plans in the safety statement. The planning should provide for:

• identifying hazards and assessing risks, and deciding how they can be eliminated or controlled

• complying with the safety and health laws that apply to the business

• agreeing safety and health targets with directors, managers and supervisors

• board decisions which reflect the safety and health policies as set out in the safety statement

• a purchasing and supply policy which takes safety and health into account

• the design of tasks, processes, equipment, products and services, and safe systems of work

- procedures to deal with emergencies and serious and imminent danger

- co-operation with neighbours and/or subcontractors

- setting standards against which performance can be measured

- ensuring co-operation between mangers so that safety and health obligations are complied with

Measuring Safety and Health Performance

Just as in finance, production or sales, the employer needs to measure safety and health performance to find out if the effort is successful. Two key components of measuring performance are:

- Active monitoring (before things go wrong). The employer needs to carry our routine inspections and checks to see that standards are being maintained. Are the objectives and standards which were set being achieved? Are they effective?

- Reactive monitoring (after things go wrong): investigating injuries, cases of illness, bullying complaints, property damage and near misses—specifying in each case why performance was sub-standard.

The procedures for monitoring safety and health performance need to be set out in the safety statement.

Once the safety statement has been written, the employer should keep the written document for future reference or use. It may be needed if a Health and Safety Authority inspector questions the precautions used, or if there is an action for civil liability. It can also remind employers to keep an eye on particular matters, and it helps to show that they are doing what the law requires.

STEP 6: REVIEW THE PROGRAMME AND UPDATE AS NECESSARY

Keeping Safety Statements Up to Date

Implementing the safety statement should be an integral part of everyday operations. A copy of the statement or relevant extracts of it must be kept available for inspection at or near every workplace to which it relates.

The safety statement needs to be relevant at all times. It may be necessary to revise it whenever there are changes, or when risk assessments are carried out and improvements made that have an impact on safety and health. Such changes may include changes in work processes, organisational structure, equipment or substances used, technical knowledge, and legislation or standards.

Changes in the workforce may also have an impact; e.g. altering the number of workers on a particular process, replacing more experienced workers with trainees or as a result of experience gained through training.

Do not amend the safety statement for every trivial change, or for each new job, but if a new job introduces significant new hazards, you need to assess the risks assessments and implement the necessary prevention measures.

A Health and Safety Authority inspector may review the safety statement during an inspection of the workplace. If he or she finds that it is inadequate or does not cover risk assessments for processes currently going on during the inspection, he or she can direct that it be revised within 30 days.

Periodic Review of Safety Statements – Learning from Experience

The safety statement should be periodically reviewed. The review serves two purposes:

• a backward look to review how effective the safety and health management has been

• a forward look to ensure you have considered any proposed changes

Employers should always try to improve on the last performance. The monitoring programme covered above should help you to do this.

Employers are responsible for drawing up, reviewing and revising the safety statement. If they are not competent to do so, they must obtain assistance from a competent person. It may also be appropriate to call on outside experts (e.g. an engineer, scientist, occupational physician, ergonomist, occupational hygienist or other relevant safety and health adviser) to solve particular problems.

How Should the Safety Statement be Reviewed?

In reviewing the safety statement, employers should consider at least the following:

• Were the aims in the safety statement relevant and appropriate?

• Did it identify the significant hazards, assess their risks and set out the necessary preventive and protective safety measures?

• Were the safety and health measures, which were identified, implemented in practice? Was the planned progress achieved?

• Were new work practices or processes introduced since the last review and if so were they risk-assessed?

• Did you put in place the measures necessary to comply with the relevant statutory provisions (e.g. on safety and health management, safety consultation and training, etc)?

• Did you comply fully with safety and health performance standards (including legislation and approved codes of practice)?

• Are there areas where standards are absent or inadequate?

• Have you analysed your data to find out the immediate and underlying causes of any injuries, illness or incidents? Have you identified any trends and common features?

- What new safety and health measures were applied following any reportable accidents or other incidents, or following any enforcement measures relating to your workplace?

- Were adequate financial, physical, human and organisational resources committed to safety and health?

- What improvements in safety and health performance need to be made?

As part of the review, employers will find it helpful to refer to any records which have been kept, such as accident/incident reports, health-surveillance results, training records, inspection and audit reports, maintenance logs, or atmospheric monitoring figures. Employers must also consult safety representatives and others who may be affected by the review.

When should the Safety Statement be Reviewed?

It is recommended that employers review the safety statement at least annually. However, in deciding the frequency of the review, they should consider the nature of their operations and any changes that might affect workers' safety and health.

What should the Employer do after the Safety Statement has been Reviewed?

Employers should bring any changes made to the attention of the safety representatives, employees and any other persons who may be affected by the new measures set out in the safety statement. Inform them about the new findings and of any changes in the required safety and health precautions. Make sure all modifications or improvements required by the new risk assessments and safety statement review are implemented as soon as possible.

Further Information

The Health and Safety Authority has produced many publications that can be consulted for further information when carrying out risk assessments or preparing and implementing safety statements. They cover:

- specific workplace hazards (on manual handling, noise, stress, violence, bullying, chemicals, carcinogens, asbestos, petroleum and confined spaces)

- specific work sectors (construction, quarries, agriculture, forestry, chemical processing, LPG filling, offices, shops, transport of dangerous goods, security industry, hotels, catering and restaurants, retail and distribution)

- sector-specific safety statements for agriculture, shops, fishing vessels, offices and small businesses

- other work-related issues (on workplace safety and health management, obligatory safety signs, pregnancy and work, child safety on farms, safety and workplace vehicles, rider-operated lift trucks, occupational asthma, safety consultation and representation, scaffolding, cranes and roofwork

• construction sites—see the Safe System of Work Plan

All these publications are available on the Health and Safety Authority website at www.safework.ie or telephone 1890 289 389. Many are free of charge.

APPENDIX

The appendix includes three forms:

1   Guidance on Carrying Out Risk Assessments

2   Risk Assessment Examples

3   Risk Assessment Pro Forma

GUIDANCE ON CARRYING OUT RISK ASSESMENTS

Company name _____   Assessment undertaken by _____

Company address _____

Area/department/activity _____

Signed _____ Date _____

Assessment review date _____   Page _____ of _____

Hazards and risks:	Who might be harmed?	Is the risk adequately controlled or do you need to do more?	Responsible persons:
Look only for hazards, which you could reasonably expect to result in significant harm under the conditions in your workplace. Use the following examples as a guide:	There is no need to list individuals by name-just think about groups of people doing similar work or who may be affected, e.g.:	Have you already taken precautions against the risks from the hazards you listed? For example, have you provided:	You can list individuals by name and job title. It should be clear who is responsible for controlling the risks.
• Slipping/tripping hazards (e.g. poorly maintained floors or stairs) • Fire (e.g. from flammable materials) • Chemicals (e.g. battery acid) • Moving parts of machinery (e.g. blades)	• Office staff • Maintenance personnel • Contractors • People sharing your workplace • Operators • Cleaners • Member of the public	• adequate information, instruction and training? • adequate systems and procedures? **Do the precautions:** • meet the standards set by a legal requirement?	

	Pay particular attention to:	
• Work at height (e.g. from mezzanine floors) • Ejection of material (e.g. from plastic molding) • pressure systems (e.g. steam boilers) • Vehicles (e.g. fork-lift trucks) • Electricity (e.g. poor wiring) • Dust (e.g. from grinding) • Fume (e.g. welding) • Manual handling • Noise • Poor lighting • Low temperature.	• Staff with disabilities • Visitors • Inexperienced staff • Lone workers. *They may be more vulnerable.*	• comply with a recognized industry standard? • represent good practice? • reduce risk as far as reasonably practicable? If so, then the risks are adequately controlled, but you need to indicate the precautions you have in place. You may refer to procedures, manuals, company rules, etc., giving this information.

RISK ASSESSMENT EXAMPLES

(This list of hazards and controls is not intended to be exhaustive. While they may apply to certain situations in your workplace, the controls that you require to comply with the law can only be determined by your own risk assessment.)

Company name _____ Assessment undertaken by _____

Company address _____

Area/department/activity _____

Signed _____ Date _____

Assessment review date _____ Page _____ of _____

List hazards and risks here:	List groups of people who are especially as risk from the significant hazards	List required controls here or note where the information may be found:	Responsible persons: which you have identified:
Hazard: Faulty electrical equipment **Risk:** Shock likely to occur and severe injury could Result	• Employees • Cleaners • Contractors	• Report defective equipment • Ensure all leads checked monthly • Residual current device (RCD) provided and checked every 4 months	• Employees • Supervisor • Supervisor
Hazard: Manual handling of 25kg boxes of material **Risk:** Back injury likely to occur and be reportable	• Employees in packing department	• Push trucks provided and should be used • Employees trained in manual handling	• Supervisor • General Manager

Hazard: Working near edge of mezzanine floor over Offices **Risk:** Falls likely to occur and severe injury could result	• Employees in stores department	• Guard-rail in place at edge of mezzanine floor and kept in place at all times • Loading bay protected with gates, must be kept closed when not loading • Gate fitted with lift-up rail to enable gate to be opened and shut safely	• General Manager • Supervisor • Supervisor and operators
Hazard: Sheep dipping with organophosphates **Risk:** Exposure to slashes or spray could result in Poisoning	• Farmers, agricultural contractors and farm workers	• Wear suitable waterproof clothing and rubber boots. Use face visor when mixing concentrates. Check safety data.	• Farmer/Agricultural Contractor

RISK ASSESSMENT PROFORMA

Company name _____ Assessment undertaken by _____

Company address _____

Area/department/activity _____

Signed _____ Date _____

Assessment review date _____   Page _____ of _____

List hazards and risks here:	List groups of people who are especially at risk from the significant hazards which you have identified:	List required controls here or note where the information may be found:	Responsible persons:

DIGNITY IN THE WORKPLACE

(*Health and Safety Authority, 2001*)

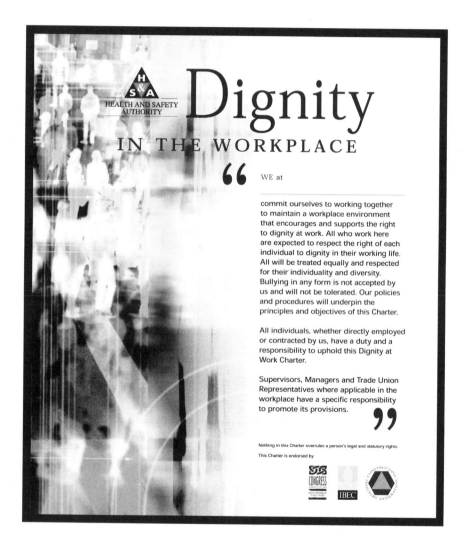

INDEX